THE

PRESIDENTS'

COOKBOOK

THE
PRESIDENTS'
COOKBOOK

Practical Recipes
from George Washington
to the Present

****

BY

POPPY CANNON

&

PATRICIA BROOKS

Funk & Wagnalls

✳✳✳

DEDICATION

✳✳✳

This book is for my all-time heroine and most treasured friend Eleanor Roosevelt, the first First Lady of the World. Years ago she veered my thoughts in this direction when she shared with me her mother-in-law's recipe for Kedgeree, talked to me of her own ways with scrambled eggs for Sunday nights at the White House, and why she served hot dogs to the Queen of England at Hyde Park.

Even though she admitted ruefully "I have always been considered a poor housekeeper," she liked to talk about food. Perhaps more than any other presidential wife, she appreciated the noble role of cooking in shaping and reflecting the history of our land.

POPPY CANNON

✶✶

CONTENTS

✶✶

✳✳

INTRODUCTION

✳✳

What am I doing here, I ask myself, when it is known that I consider intro-
ductions to cookbooks unnecessary, and that I myself am never found in any
kitchen unless it is occupied by an especially tasty-looking cook?

Yet here I am, pen in one hand, tasting spoon in the other, oven heated, and
every available pot at a rolling boil. Why? Because Poppy Cannon, who works
for me as food editor, came bursting into my office with, "How would you like
to try Bess Truman's Brownies?" "Swell," I answered, "But aren't they getting a
bit stale?" Sure, though, I was game. No one exposed as I have been over the
years to the exotic and imaginative experimentation of a dozen darling and insist-
ent food editors could be in any condition to write about it if he didn't have a
cast-iron stomach. Well, not cast-iron, maybe, but at least Teflon-coated.

Undaunted, cutting through my reserve like a French knife through a stalk of
celery, Poppy swept me into this culinary exploration of history like leftovers into
a *pot au Boeuf miroton.* So it was I found that *The Presidents' Cookbook* by Poppy
Cannon and Patricia Brooks is as much history as recipe collection. History of a
time when Washington was a good place to live in, the air shuttle hadn't been
invented, the personal touch prevailed, and cooks were First Ladies. I confess
there were many Presidents I never really warmed to. Since grammar school I
have learned to recite the experiences, exploits, and homely virtues of our Chief
Executives. After hearing a lot more about them than I really care to, with the

exception of a few favorites such as T. Jefferson and H. Truman, most had about as much appeal for me as tomato aspic.

Then came *The Presidents' Cookbook,* with anecdotes and recipes done to a turn. From the boisterous, bountiful table of Andrew Jackson down to the mess hall quartermaster cook of William Howard Taft. Quite seriously, I think you may well understand more about this part of our history from reading this book and trying these recipes than from all the textbooks you've explored to date. Poppy Cannon's enthusiasm for food, her understanding of it as a language in itself, spans the years to communicate to us what life was like, what the people were really like who lived in the big white house at 1600 Pennsylvania Avenue.

I know of no one better equipped to do this interpretation than the authors. It is only a slight exaggeration to say that I've known Poppy since her mudpie days. (As a matter of fact, even her mudpies had an artistic edge over those of the other little girls, probably from a pinch of sand at the proper moment.) More recently, I've watched her at work in her pine-panelled kitchen at Break-neck Hill, tasting, testing, and improving right up to the time of setting the dish before the guest, always trying for peak flavor with individual flair. Indeed, Poppy seems akin to Dolley Madison, who, you will find as you read, loved entertaining, loved having people about to feed, and was described by Washington Irving as a "fine, buxom dame who has a smile and a pleasant word for everybody."

Oh, where are the recipes of yesteryear: Gooseberry Fool, Billygoat Cookies, Mr. Jefferson's Persimmon Beer? They are in this cookbook, that's where.

And I, for one, thank you, ladies.

JOHN MACK CARTER
Editor, Ladies Home Journal
New York, N.Y.

THE

PRESIDENTS'

COOKBOOK

I

The Father
of
Us All

The etiquette attending the Presidency is taken pretty much for granted today. Of course, through the decades there have been subtle changes in style and custom, as each President put his stamp on the office. There have been a few dramatic swings from austerity to opulence, but in general the transition from Presidency to Presidency has been gradual. Each Presidential family has been able to adapt, adjust, amend, or eliminate within an established framework.

Each Presidential family but one. It is rarely realized what innovators the George Washingtons were—through necessity, not choice. One of the most pressing problems of our newly elected First President was etiquette. Previously, the country had been ruled by royal governors, appointed by the King of England. But now, the War of Independence behind us, we were on our own. Traditions had been broken; new ones had to be established.

How should the President be addressed? Should he be called His Highness or His Excellency? Should his wife be called Lady Washington or simply Mrs. Washington? How much pomp and ceremony should surround the office of the Presidency? How elaborate should the dinners and official entertaining be? These were questions of great moment when Washington took office in 1789. It was up to him to provide a "white paper" of etiquette.

He tackled the job almost immediately by calling his Cabinet together to discuss it. Vice-President John Adams, Alexander Hamilton, James Madison, John Jay, and Colonel Humphreys, Washington's Master of Ceremonies, appeared and were given questionnaires. These formed the basis of "a tenable system of etiquette," which decreed that the President would return no visits, invite to dinner only officials and "strangers of distinction," and limit visits of courtesy to Tuesday afternoons. There would be separate receptions for foreign ministers, heads of departments, and members of Congress. In addition, the President would see anyone with important business to discuss.

Specifically, the President would hold a levee, or reception, every Tuesday afternoon, from three to four o'clock, for foreign ambassadors and "strangers of distinction," and a Congressional dinner each Thursday evening. Friday was the evening chosen for Mrs. Washington's drawing-room receptions. There were also frequent state banquets. It was an uncomplicated schedule for a Head of State.

Simplicity and decorum were key words to Washington in planning the social regimen of his office. He felt the only ceremony necessary was that which would preserve the dignity of the Presidency. This disappointed the many would-be social arbiters in the new country who wanted to turn the President into a king-substitute, with all the ceremonial attendant on such a figure. Fortunately, Washington's own common sense prevailed. Because of his aristocratic Virginia background, he was able to move with grace and dignity into the leadership of the country. Difficult as the job of establishing social patterns must have been, it was undoubtedly easier for a man of Washington's breeding than it would have been for later frontier Presidents.

Mount Vernon hospitality was legend in an area where hospitality was the rule. After a visit, the Marquis de Chastellex commented on the graciousness: "Your apartment was your house. The servants of the house were yours; and while every inducement was held to bring you into the general society of the drawing room, or at the table, it rested with yourself to be served or not with everything in your own chamber."

Washington said: "My manner of living is plain, and I do not mean to be put out by it. A glass of wine and a bit of mutton are always welcome. Those who expect more will be disappointed." This, however, is an example of the "plain living" offered guests at a Presidential dinner:

> There was an elegant variety of roast beef, veal, turkey, ducks, fowls, hams, etc.; puddings, jellies, oranges, apples, nuts, almonds, figs, raisins, and a variety of wines and punch [one guest observed]. We took our leave at six, more than an hour after the candles were introduced. No lady but Mrs. Washington dined with us. We were waited on by four or five men servants dressed in livery.

The nation's first capital was New York. When Washington moved there after his inauguration, he acquired one of the handsomest houses in the city and furnished it so grandly with damask hangings and sofas, silk curtains, inlaid and carved mahogany furniture, pictures, and other costly adornments that it was soon nicknamed The Palace.

One wonders, in view of certain reports about Martha Washington at the time, if such a nickname was totally free of malice. Our first First Lady was accused of limiting her hospitality to members of her husband's Federalist party and being openly hostile to democrats. Albert Gallatin, a leading statesman of the time but an opponent of the Federalists, was barely tolerated. He rewarded her by commenting: "She is Mrs. President, not of the United States, but of a faction." Another observer, perhaps prejudiced, said: "Without the tact to conceal her prejudices, she was a grudging hostess to all but her own circle."

The President, on the other hand, held his once-a-week official dinners for "as many as my table will hold." The official entertainments, held to an appropriate minimum by the President, more than compensated in quality what they lacked in number. Most contemporaries agreed that "Washington's dinner parties were entertained in a very handsome style."

Much of the responsibility for the style belonged to the steward of the President's house, a West Indian tavernkeeper named Samuel Fraunces, popularly called Black Sam.* After the inauguration, President Washington called on Black Sam, who had performed many services for him during the Revolution, when Washington's troops were stationed in New York. The President requested Samuel to find a steward for the Presidential household. No one measured up to the responsibility, in his eyes at least, so he took the job himself. He appears to have been an all-round man. "Besides being an excellent cook," Washington wrote later, "he knew how to provide genteel dinners. He gave aid in dressing them, prepared the dessert, made the cakes and did everything that is done by the new steward and his wife together."

Devoted to Washington, Fraunces wanted the President's table to be "bountiful and elegant." At dinner parties he cut quite a figure in his silk knee breeches, white ruffled shirt, and carefully powdered black hair as he stood at the sideboard throughout the meal, watching to be sure the footmen attended all the guests properly.

Why Samuel Fraunces left the Presidential family service is a subject of some disagreement among historians. One story has it that his wife desperately needed his help in running their tavern. Another claims that the "bountiful and elegant" table applied to his own as well, and that the President, exasperated at his extravagance, fired him.

Whatever the circumstances, what *is* a matter of record is that the First Family suffered the same servant problems lesser Americans have suffered many times since. Cooks came and went. In the winter of 1789, this advertisement appeared in the papers:

* For some curious reason, certain historians have insisted that Fraunces, was not a Negro. There is every indication that he had some African ancestry.

A COOK

Is wanted for the family of the President of the United States. No one need apply who is not perfect in the business, and can bring indubitable testimonials of sobriety, honesty and attention to the duties of the station.

It took two months for a satisfactory cook to appear. In the meantime one of the kitchen maids, Mrs. Rachel Lewis, did the cooking—a not very satisfactory arrangement, it would seem, judging by a letter Washington wrote to his secretary at the time the government was being removed to Philadelphia. Suggesting that Mrs. Lewis be replaced, he wrote: ". . . the dirty figures of Mrs. Lewis and her daughter will not be a pleasant sight in view (as the kitchen always will be) of the principal entertaining rooms of our new habitation." A far cry from the dandyism of Samuel Fraunces!

Mrs. Lewis was replaced by a Frenchman named Lamuir, who lasted a month and was replaced by a Baltimore import named John Vicar. Vicar's one weakness was cake, a favorite food of the Washingtons. His inability to make it meant that all the cakes served at dinner parties and drawing rooms had to be bought, a fact that displeased Martha Washington greatly.

It was finally decided to bring Hercules (Uncle Harkles), the Mount Vernon cook, to Philadelphia. The city made a great impression on the black man from Virginia. Before long he became quite a celebrated figure in the capital. After he had prepared the dinner, he would walk jauntily down the streets in black silk breeches, waistcoat with a long watchchain dangling from a fob, and black cocked hat, swinging a gold-headed cane.

Pennsylvania law at the time allowed slaves their freedom after six months' residence. To avoid the possibility of losing a first-rate cook, Washington would send Hercules back to Mount Vernon just before the six months were up. Then, several months later, he would have him returned to the capital. This worked out very well for the Presidential household. (By this time Samuel Fraunces had returned to the fold at $300 a year, twice his original salary.) But in spite of all this prudence, the pull of city life became too strong for the sartorial giant, who was as huge as his name implied. At the end of the President's administration, as the family prepared to return to Virginia, Hercules disappeared and was never seen again. Washington searched for him many months without luck. (One finds it intriguing to think of a man the size of Hercules with his penchant for fashionable clothes simply fading into the background of what was then a not very large city.)

Whatever turmoil existed in the Presidential kitchen from time to time, the dining room and drawing room were studies in serenity. Or perhaps solemnity. Some of the guests found the full-dress levees particularly formal and frigid affairs. The President always stood in front of the fireplace in his large dining room, waiting to greet his guests. Dressed formally in black velvet breeches and coat, with silver knee- and shoe-buckles gleaming in the firelight, he wore yellow gloves and held his cocked hat under his arm. Bowing formally to each guest (he never shook hands, even with close friends), he greeted those he knew by name. He had the politician's asset of rarely forgetting the name of someone who had once been introduced to him. Fifteen minutes after the levee began, the door was closed, the gentlemen (levees were always stag) moved into a circle, and Washington moved from one to the next, exchanging a few pleasantries with each man. At the end of the circle, the President returned to the fireplace; the departing visitors came up to him, bowed, and withdrew.

The official Thursday dinner parties seem to have been equally gay, thus setting the tone for official entertainments for generations to come. William Maclay, Senator from Pennsylvania, described one of the dinners this way:

> The President and Mrs. Washington sat opposite each other in the middle of the table, the two secretaries, one at each end. It was a great dinner—all in the tastes of high life. I considered it as part of my duty as a Senator to submit to it, and am glad it is over. The President is a cold, formal man; but I must declare that he treated me with great attention. I was the first person with whom he drank a glass of wine. It was a great dinner, and the best of the kind I ever was at. The room, however, was disagreeably hot. First was the soup; fish roasted and boiled; meats, gammon [smoked ham], fowls, etc. This was the dinner. The middle of the table was garnished in the usual tasty way, with small images, flowers (artificial), etc. The dessert was, first apple-pies, puddings, etc., then iced creams, jellies, etc.; then water-melons, musk-melons, apples, peaches, nuts. It was the most solemn dinner ever I sat at. Not a health drank, scarce a word said until the cloth was taken away. Then the President, filling a glass of wine, with great formality drank to the health of every individual by name around the table. Everybody imitated him, changed glasses, and such a buzz of "health, Sir," and "health, Madam," and "thank you, Sir," and "thank you, Madam," never had I heard before. . . . The ladies sat a good while, and the bottle passed about, but there was a dead silence almost. Mrs. Washington at last withdrew with the ladies. I expected the men would now begin, but the same stillness remained. The President told of a New England clergyman who had lost a hat and wig in passing a river called the Brunks. He smiled, and everybody else laughed. He now and then said a sentence or two on some common subject, and what he said was not amiss. . . . The President kept a fork in his hand, when the cloth was taken away, and that for the purpose of picking nuts. He ate no nuts, but played with the fork, striking on the edge of the table with it. We did not sit long after the ladies retired. The President rose, went up stairs to drink coffee; the company followed.

Such perhaps is the penalty of official entertaining. The joke about the Brunks seems to have been as incomprehensible to some of the dinner guests as it is to us today, but one fact is clear, even from this point in time. Washington had many claims to fame, but a raconteur he was not. The necessity of making small talk with a number of basically incompatible guests has always been one of the burdens of public office. Some Presidents have been better adapted to it than the reticent Washington, as we shall see later.

Martha Washington's Friday evenings appear to have been far less formidable. The reason may lie in her guest list. Less official in nature, the drawing rooms consisted of closer friends and companions, people the First Lady liked and with whom she felt comfortable. Guests arrived about 7 P.M. Mrs. Washington, always beautifully groomed and dressed in satin or velvet, received them alone. The President, in a colored coat and waistcoat, wearing black breeches, but without hat or sword, mingled casually with the guests, exchanging pleasantries. Tea, coffee, and plum cake were usually served, and at nine o'clock Mrs. Washington withdrew, bringing the evening to an end.

The hours designated for entertaining in Washington's day seem somewhat strange to us today, indicating the subtle changes that have taken place through the years. For one thing, official dinners began at 4 P.M. When the Presidential family dined alone, or at private dinner parties, they dined at three, as had been their custom at Mount Vernon.

It was also customary with the Washingtons to be on time. The President was known to tell late guests: "Gentlemen . . . I have a cook who never asks whether the company has come, but whether the hour has come." And Martha Washington believed in punctuality as much as her husband did. At an evening party in 1790 she arose at nine, as was her habit, and prepared to leave. But this particular evening she had a parting word: "The General always retires at nine, and I usually precede him."

Table habits differed as well. It was the fashion of the day (and the Washingtons followed tradition) for a dinner to consist of three courses, with two tablecloths used for the service. The cloth was changed between the first and second courses, and the last course, consisting of fruit, nuts, and wines, was served on the bare table. The President's table was a long one, always covered with a handsome cloth, ornately beautiful silver, and a bevy of small dishes scattered about it.

Three courses does not sound too elaborate, but consider what each course consisted of—sometimes as many as twenty distinct dishes, all brought to the table at once (no wonder large staffs were needed!), with the hot dishes under covers. The *pièces de résistance* were usually five or six large platters, placed crosswise the length of the table (in many cases the table stretched to nearly the full length of the room). A tureen of soup at each end of the table began the dinner, the tureens being replaced by fish. Smaller platters and bowls with vegetables, sauces, and secondary dishes were arranged at right angles to the main platters. Symmetrical arrangement of the dishes taxed the ingenuity of a hostess, who tried to make the display as decorative as possible. At a large company dinner, it was almost a point of etiquette to have so many side dishes that the tablecloth could hardly be seen. There was rarely any adornment on the table other than food. Flowers were seldom used. Occasionally splendid pieces of silver would be displayed. The Washingtons (as well as the John Adamses and Jeffersons) possessed an elaborate *plateau de dessert,* which may be seen today at Mount Vernon. Such ornaments were rare at this time, however.

The following menu, from Martha Washington's cookbook, illustrates just how elaborate a three-course dinner might be.

FIRST COURSE

Small Chicken Patties	Soup Purée	Pork Cutlets
Red Cabbage Stewed	(replaced by salmon)	Sauce Robert
Boiled Chickens	Shoulder of Mutton in	Mashed Potatoes
Plain Butter	Epigram	Boiled Turkey
Shrimp Sauce	Ham	French Beans Fricasseed
Dressed Greens	Beef Tremblongue	Celery Sauce
	Soup Santea	Oyster Loaves
	(replaced by Stewed Carp)	
	Scotch Collops	

SECOND COURSE

Maids of Honor	2 Wild Ducks	Rhenish Cream
Asparagus *à la Pettit Poi*	Lambs Tails	Prawns
Sauce	(*au Béchamel*)	Sauce
2 Teal	Hare Roasted	Plovers
Crayfish	Sweetbreads	Sauce
Sauce	*à la Dauphin*	Chardoons
Fruit in Jelly	3 Partridges	Fricasseed Birds
		Custards

Notice how the second course combines meats, game, fish, and desserts and sweets. The variety of foods to choose from is reminiscent of a Chinese banquet, as is the custom of putting so many dishes on the table at once.

After the second course, the tablecloth was removed, fresh glasses and decanters of wine were placed on the table, with an assortment of fruits and nuts. The ladies retired and the men settled down to talking. In general, dinner parties were the exclusive property of the men, although occasionally the host's wife would be present (Martha Washington usually availed herself of this privilege), and sometimes other women as well.

Breakfast seems to have been the only meal in the Presidential house that was really relaxed. At least the report of Henry Wansey, an English manufacturer, who had breakfast with the President and his family on June 8, 1794, indicates this to be so:

> Mrs. Washington made tea and coffee for them; on the table were two small plates of sliced tongues and dry toast, bread and butter, but no broiled fish, as is generally the custom. Miss Eleanor Custis, her granddaughter, in her sixteenth year, sat next to her, and next, her grandson, George Washington Parke Custis, two years older. There were but few indications of form; one servant only attended who wore no livery.

The expenses involved in running the Presidential household were considerable, and at this time there was no such thing as an entertainment allowance for the President. The cost of his official entertainments came from his own pocket. (No wonder he was distressed at the lavish extras supplied by Fraunces, although in fairness to Fraunces it should be mentioned that the food bills of his successor, John Hyde, were far larger, a fact duly noted by Washington.) This may be the reason Washington supervised his household accounts so closely, even keeping a minute record of the daily use of all supplies. With a steward and fourteen other servants on his staff, Washington spent more than six hundred dollars a month on servants' wages and food. Food for the Presidential table cost $143 to $165 per week, exclusive of wines. There is little doubt that Washington's Presidential salary was used up during his term of office.

By contrast with the elaborate hospitality of the President's household, George Washington's own eating habits were relatively simple. One observer of the time said that he "took what came with philosophy"; certainly no one could accuse our first President of having been a gourmet. Custis, Martha Washington's grandson, described Washington's food preferences:

"He ate heartily, but was not particular in his diet, with the exception of fish, of which he was excessively fond. He partook sparingly of dessert, drank a home-made beverage, and from four to five glasses of Madeira wine."

Another observer, Ashbel Green, related that at state banquets Washington "generally dined on one single dish and that of a very simple kind. If offered something either in the first or second course which was very rich, his usual reply was 'That is too good for me.'"

A special passion of the President's was nuts. He would buy hazelnuts and shellbarks by the barrel. In 1792 he wrote his overseer at Mount Vernon to "tell houseman Frank I expect he will lay up a more plenteous store of the black common walnuts than he usually does." On another occasion, the Prince de Broglie reported that "at dessert he eats an enormous quantity of nuts."

Although a temperate man, Washington was very fond of good wine in moderation. References to wine dot the social history of the Washington administration. Wine was served on all occasions. Washington's special favorite was Madeira. Indicative of the interest in wines of both George and Martha Washington is an instruction in Martha's will: "It is my will and desire that all the wine in bottles in the vaults be equally divided between my granddaughters and grandson . . ." a treasured legacy.

It is easy for latter-day historians to misinterpret George Washington's formality and austerity. He was, to be sure, a reserved, reticent man, but it was more a reserve of manner than intent. While declining to shake hands even with close friends, he nevertheless welcomed all who came to see him and was generous in his hospitality. And he was a popular and much-loved President.

Food reflects the man. In Washington there is the interesting dichotomy of a man disinterested in the refinements of the table, yet anxious to offer as many refinements as possible to his guests, simple in his own tastes but generous toward others. One wonders, too, if a gourmet could have withstood the rigors and deprivations of Valley Force that long cold winter of 1777–1778. Washington's physiognomy suggests his self-discipline, his ability to fast if necessary, his austerity.

As food reflects the man, it also reflects the times. The food served at the President's table from 1789 to the end of Washington's second term, 1797, indicates the new nation's dependence on the land. Game, fowl, meats, plantation-grown fruits and vegetables, fish from local rivers or the Atlantic reveal the abundance of the land. Spliced throughout the menus are the remnants of Washington's English heritage—puddings, cream trifles, a taste for port and wine.

R E C I P E S

INDIAN HOE CAKES

Washington was an early riser, usually up by 5 or 6 A.M. He would occupy himself with a ride or a book until breakfast was served, usually between seven and eight o'clock. A favorite breakfast, Samuel Stearns noted, was "three small Indian hoe cakes, and as many dishes of tea." George Washington Parke Custis confirmed this: "Indian cakes, honey and tea formed this temperate repast." Washington was also inordinately fond of honey.

Hoe cakes, a favorite in the South during Colonial times, were originally baked right on a hoe in the open hearth. They were commonly served as accompaniment to vegetable soup. Soup was a typical breakfast dish of the time, as was meat.

Washington ate an unusually small breakfast for his day, considering that his next meal was dinner at three or four in the afternoon.

| *Water-ground white cornmeal* | *Melted lard or other shortening* |
| *Salt* | *Boiling water* |

Combine the cornmeal (1 cup) with ½ teaspoon salt. Add 1 tablespoon lard or shortening and enough boiling water to make a dough that is solid enough to hold a shape. Form the dough into 2 thin oblong cakes and place them in a hot, well-greased heavy pan (not a hoe today). Bake in a preheated moderately hot (375° F.) oven for about 25 minutes. Serve the cakes hot. *Serves 4 to 6.*

PEGGY STEWART TEA

England was once a nation of coffee-drinkers; in America tea was drunk, which only goes to prove how national tastes can change. In October 1774, a shipowner named Anthony Stewart sailed his ship, the *Peggy Stewart,* into Annapolis Harbor stocked with tea. Stewart was prepared to pay the stiff tariff on tea, but his fellow colonists decreed differently. Boston had held its famous tea party almost a year before. Annapolis decided it was time to resist the English tax too, and Stewart was forced to set fire to his ship. The few housewives who still had a supply of tea on hand were determined to preserve its flavor. A cookbook of Martha Washington's tells how:

To season tea, keep it in a canister (a) with rose leaves
                                or (b) with one drop of attar of roses added
                                        to a cloth and put in the canister with
                                        the tea.
Keep the canister tightly closed, and the tea will develop a delicious rose flavor.

NOTE: George Washington was fond of tea, and legend has it that he actually kept a cow in lower Manhattan during his administration's stay in New York to provide milk for his tea. Tea experts admire his perspicacity in preferring milk to cream. They claim that the true tea flavor emerges when milk is used but that cream distorts the tea's distinctive flavor.

RICE WAFFLES WITH FERRY FARM SAUCE

This delicious dish is an old Virginia classic. It is at its best when served with a sauce that was a specialty of Mary Washington, George's mother. There was no baking powder in the original, otherwise this recipe follows precisely the one used in the Washington family. Note the use of honey, a Washington favorite, in the sauce. Ferry Farm, across the Rappahannock River from Fredericksburg, was the home of Mary Washington for thirty-four years.

Flour	*Melted butter*
Baking powder	*Honey*
Salt	*Maple syrup*
Milk	*Cinnamon*
Eggs, separated	*Caraway seeds*
Hot cooked rice	

Sift together 1 cup flour, 1 teaspoon baking powder, ¼ teaspoon salt. Add 1 cup milk, 2 well-beaten egg yolks. Then add 1 cup hot cooked rice. Stir in 2 tablespoons melted butter. Last, fold in 2 stiffly beaten egg whites. Bake as you would regular waffles. *Makes 6 to 8 waffles.*

For the sauce: Heat together 1 cup strained honey, ½ cup pure maple syrup, 1 teaspoon powdered cinnamon, and a few caraway seeds if desired. Serve warm. *Makes 1½ cups.*

BUTTERED EGGS

A small brown leather-bound book lies in the archives of the Pennsylvania Historical Society. It is a treasure for social historians and cooks alike, for it is one of Martha Washington's recipe books. She did not personally compile the book, but its many recipes and household hints added greatly to her reputation as a hostess and homemaker. The book was actually written by Frances Parke Custis, the mother of Martha Washington's first husband, and given to Martha. Toward the end of Martha Custis Washington's life, she in turn presented the book to her beloved granddaughter, Nelly Custis. The book's inscription reads:

This book, written by Eleanor Parke Custis's great grandmother, Mrs. John Custis, was given to her, by her beloved Grandmother Martha Washington— formerly Mrs. Daniel Custis.

This recipe comes from that book:

Anchovies	*Pepper*
Lamb (or beef) gravy	*Butter*
Eggs	*Grated nutmeg*
Salt	

Crush two anchovies with a fork and add them to ½ cup of lamb (or beef) gravy. Beat 6 eggs slightly with a silver fork and add the gravy mixture to them, along with ¼ teaspoon salt and freshly ground black pepper. Melt 1 large tablespoon butter in a skillet, add the egg mixture, then scramble over slow heat. Turn onto a hot platter and grate nutmeg over the top. *Serves 3 to 4.*

GLOUCESTER SALT CODFISH

This New England favorite seems a strange choice to include with favorite foods of a Southern President. Yet when he could get it, salt codfish was the mainstay of Washington's Sunday dinner. He was, in fact, fond of all salt fish, but particularly cod.

Cut boneless salt codfish into 2-inch pieces. Cover them with warm water and let stand 15 minutes. Drain, dry on a towel, and sauté the pieces in butter in a hot frying pan until delicately browned. Add rich milk or thin cream, enough to cover the fish halfway. Bring the milk slowly to boiling point. Pour into a hot serving dish.

BAKED SHAD WITH ROE SAUCE

Considering the prices of shad and shad roe today, it comes as a shock to learn that in Washington's time shad were so plentiful they were downright unfashionable. Wealthy people ate shad secretly, for fear of losing status. Nevertheless, Washington loved shad, and even had his own fisherman (a slave named Jack) as well as several fishing stations along the Potomac to catch shad (and other fish, too, of course). So commonplace was the lowly shad that no recipe for it is to be found in any of Martha Washington's cookbooks. The Negro cooks at Mount Vernon, however, were undoubtedly so familiar with it that directions for preparation were unnecessary. Like boiling eggs, cooking shad was something everyone could do!

Shad	*White wine*
Salt and pepper	*Cayenne*
Butter	*Nutmeg*
Lemon wedges	*Flour*
Parsley	*Chicken stock*
Shad roe	*Beef extract*
Sherry	

Clean and split a 3-pound shad. (Better still, have it done for you. It's harder than it sounds.) Put it skin side down on a buttered plank, sprinkle it with salt and pepper, then brush with melted butter. Cook it in an oiled dripping pan or a shallow baking dish for 25 minutes in a hot (400° F.) oven or broil 2 inches from the heat. Spread with butter, garnish with lemon wedges and parsley, and serve with Roe Sauce. *Serves 6.*

To make Roe Sauce: Place ½ shad roe in a small, shallow baking pan. Sprinkle with salt, pepper, cayenne, and nutmeg to taste. Add 2 tablespoons butter, 2 tablespoons white wine. Cover with buttered paper and bake 30 minutes. Then remove the membranes. Meanwhile, brown 3 tablespoons butter, add 4 table-spoons flour, continue browning. Pour 1 cup chicken stock on gradually, stirring all the while. Bring to a boil, add ¼ teaspoon beef extract, the roe, and more salt to taste. Pour over the shad and serve. *Makes about 1½ cups.*

CHESAPEAKE SURPRISE

Mary Margaret McBride, for years First Lady of Radio, has a favorite story about Washington that she always prefaces by saying "It may be apocryphal." The great General was traveling to Cambridge, Massachusetts. Arriving late at the Pixlee Tavern in Bridgeport, Connecticut, on the way, he noticed that not a single seat was available. The waiters were so busy serving the guests they seemed not to notice him. To make matters even worse, the guests were eating one of the General's favorite foods, fried oysters.

In a loud voice, Washington is said to have commented: "Horses are very fond of oysters." Everybody immediately stopped eating to argue this point, and Washington suggested that it could be tested at that moment. His own horse was tethered outside; a dish of oysters could be taken to him. . . . The guests rushed outdoors en masse. And Washington sat down at one of the many vacated tables and enjoyed a leisurely meal . . . of oysters, of course.

This particular oyster recipe comes from Martha Washington's own cookbook, *Rules for Cooking,* with a notation in her own hand that the recipe was given to her by Elizabeth Monroe, wife of James Monroe.

> *French bread*   *Relish, pickles, ketchup or*
> *Melted butter*   *chili sauce*
> *Oysters*

Remove the top of a long or round loaf of French bread. Scoop out the middle. Brush with melted butter or vegetable oil and toast lightly in the oven or under the broiler. Fill to the brim with 2 dozen broiled or fried oysters (you could substitute fried clams or shrimp). Replace the top crust, which should also be buttered and toasted. Serve with relish, pickles, ketchup and/or chili sauce. *Serves 4.*

TO SOUSE A ROCK

Picturesque names were a commonplace in Colonial cookbooks and are today a source of delight to cooks. "To souse a rock" we discovered means to salt a fish.

Washington loved salt fish, so it is natural to find a recipe for salting it in the leaves of Martha's *Rules for Cooking.* This book is a compilation of recipes

Martha Washington evolved or collected from neighbors and friends. In those days, Virginia was just one big neighborhood, and recipes were freely exchanged from house to house. Mrs. Washington would send the *receipt* for her latest dish to Mrs. Thomas Jefferson, who would add it to her collection and send a copy along to Mrs. James Madison or Mrs. James Monroe. The name of the source would be duly noted in each lady's collection.

These instructions for "sousing a rock" are Mrs. Washington's own:

Cut a rock fish into pieces and put it down into a kettle with water only sufficient to cover; tie a small bunch of sage and put it in the bottom of the kettle to prevent it from mixing with the fish. Put in a large handful of salt, some whole white pepper, a tablespoon of allspice, a few cloves and mace. When the fish is nearly done, add a quart of vinegar, or to your taste. In packing away, put as much liquor as will cover it. Cast away the sage. The solution will not jell for three days.

MARTHA WASHINGTON'S CRAB SOUP

Certain favorite dishes of one Presidential family have come down through the years and have, through continued use, become favorites of many Presidential families. This is such a dish. Martha Washington served it to her seafood-loving husband. Later it became a favorite soup of Franklin Roosevelt. And a White House chef served it to President and Mrs. Dwight Eisenhower, who also admired it.

Fresh crabs	*Salt and pepper*
Butter	*Milk*
Flour	*Cream*
Hard-boiled eggs	*Sherry*
Lemon rind, grated	*Worcestershire sauce*

Boil enough crabs in salted water to make ½ pound (or use 1 cup canned or frozen) crabmeat. Combine 1 tablespoon butter, 1½ tablespoons flour, 3 hard-boiled eggs that have been mashed, rind of one lemon grated, and salt and pepper to taste. Bring 4 cups milk to boil in a saucepan. Then pour it slowly into the egg mixture. Add the crabmeat to the milk–egg mixture and cook gently five minutes. Add ½ cup heavy cream; remove from heat before it reaches a full boil. Add ½ cup sherry and a dash of Worcestershire sauce. Serve piping hot. *Six servings.*

STOVED POTATOES

Mutton looms large in any record of the Washingtons' food preferences. When Washington traveled to New York to assume the duties of the Presidency, Martha was four weeks late following him. She remained at Mount Vernon to supervise the packing, and arrived May 27, 1789. The next day the President gave a small informal dinner in her honor. It seemed a natural choice to include mutton in the menu.

One of the guests, Senator Paine Wingate of New Hampshire, later wrote that "The dinner was the least showy of any . . . given by the President. There was no clergyman and the President himself said grace upon taking his seat. He dined on leg of mutton, as it was his custom to eat only one dish. After dessert a single glass of wine was offered each guest." After dinner, Wingate reported, the President sat at the table about ten or fifteen minutes, then left his secretaries "to tarry with the convivial diners" while he joined Mrs. Washington and the ladies for coffee.

This recipe, a favorite with the First Family, comes from Martha Washington's favorite *Rules for Cooking.*

Potatoes	*Salt and pepper*
Mutton chops	*Onions*

Peel and cut the potatoes, trim muttom chops, and put them in layers in a large stewing pan, first a layer of potatoes, then a layer of mutton. Cover the mutton with salt, pepper, and onions. Then put another layer of potatoes, then mutton, until the pan is full. Bake in a low oven until tender. (Note for today's cook: lamb may be substituted for mutton with good results. Provide 1 chop, 1 potato and 1 small onion sliced for each person. Bake about 1 hour at 325° F.)

SCOTCH COLLOPS

At sixteen, Washington made a list of more than a hundred maxims of good conduct. Some were his own ideas; others he had read or learned. Many deal with etiquette, some with virtues, all with values. Number 6 reads: "Be not angry at table whatever happens and if you have reason to be so, show it not. Put on a cheerful countenance especially if there should be strangers present, for good humor makes one dish of meat a feast." This principle seems to have guided him throughout life. Perhaps it was a key to some aspects of Mount Vernon hospitality. This dish, featuring Washington's much-enjoyed mutton (or lamb) is more than a mere "one dish of meat"; it is a veritable one-dish feast.

Leg of lamb (or veal or beef)	*Dry bread cubes*
Vinegar	*Anchovies*
Strong stock	*Capers*
Water	*Oysters*
Salt and pepper	*Butter*
Thyme	*Lemon juice*
Sweet marjoram	*Triangles of bread*
Winter savory	*Lemon slices*
Onion	

The collops may be made from lamb, veal, or beef. If lamb, use a leg; if veal, a piece of the top of the leg, weighing 4 pounds; if beef, 3 pounds, top of the round. Have the butcher cut the meat into thin slices and pound it with the flat side of his knife. Marinate the meat in vinegar for several hours or overnight. Wipe it off, place it in an iron frying pan. Cover with 1 pint strong stock and ½ pint water. Season with salt and pepper to taste, 1 sprig thyme, marjoram, savory and 1 onion. Let simmer until meat is tender. Strain the gravy into another pan, add ½ cup dry bread cubes, 6 anchovies, 1 tablespoon capers, 1 dozen oysters, 2 tablespoons butter, and a dash of lemon juice. Let simmer until the consistency of gravy. Place the meat on a platter, pour the sauce over it, surround with bread triangles that have been browned in butter, decorate with lemon slices dotted with capers.

RED DEER OF BEEF

Roast beef was often included as one of the dishes at a Presidential dinner. One of our favorite anecdotes concerns the time, during the Revolutionary War, General Washington and his men were sitting down to a good roast beef dinner. As Chevalier de Pontigibaud, a French volunteer, told it: "One day we were at dinner at head-quarters; an Indian entered the room, walked around the table, and then stretching forth his long tattooed arm seized a large joint of hot roast beef in his thumb and fingers, took it to the door, and began to eat it. We were all much surprised, but General Washington gave orders that he was not to be interfered with, saying laughingly, that it was apparently the dinner hour of this Mutius Scaevola of the New World."

This recipe of Martha Washington's tastes as good today as it must have in the Presidential dining room. It is quite similar to the German sauerbraten.

Top of round of beef	*Bay leaf*
Salt	*Peppercorns*
Nutmeg	*Water*
Ginger	*Butter*
Claret	*Sugar*
Vinegar	*Flour*

Have your butcher lard the beef well; you need 3 pounds. Rub it over with 1 teaspoon salt, ½ teaspoon nutmeg, and ¼ teaspoon ginger. Place the meat in a bowl and cover with 1 pint claret and ½ cup vinegar. Add 1 bay leaf, ½ teaspoon peppercorns, and ½ cup water. Let the beef stand two days, turning it over twice a day. Before cooking, dry the meat off, melt 2 tablespoons butter in a Dutch oven and brown the meat quickly. Reduce the heat and add two cups of the liquid in which the meat has soaked. Cover and cook slowly until tender, turning frequently. Add ½ teaspoon sugar to the gravy, and thicken it with a little flour dissolved in water. For variation, you might try, as the original recipe suggests, instead of beef, "A Neat's tongue [ox] seasoned . . . and all soe Veale."

SMITHFIELD HAM

Mount Vernon was self-sufficient. Fruits and vegetables were home-grown. Enough flour was produced to ship to England (in Mount Vernon's own schooner). Even the ham served at the table came from home-nurtured pigs. After butchering, the meat was sugar-cured and smoked over a hickory fire in the old smokehouse (still standing today). After months of aging, the ham was boiled in a large kettle in the great open fireplace in the Mount Vernon kitchen. Sometimes the ham was boiled in home-pressed cider. Or sometimes, as indicated in this recipe of Martha Washington's, in water—a recipe listed as "The original Tidewater, Virginia, Receipt."

Ham	*Cracker crumbs*
Brown sugar	*Sherry*
Dry mustard	*Watercress*
Celery seed	*Curly parsley*

Soak the ham overnight, then boil it next morning, cooking very slowly. When cooked, remove from fire and allow it to cool in its own essence. When cold, remove the skin, gash the top with a knife. Sprinkle on top of the ham 2 cups brown sugar, a dash of dry mustard, some celery seed, a sprinkling of cracker crumbs ("cracker dust," Martha called it), and a wineglass of sherry. Put the ham in the oven, bake a few minutes; garnish with watercress and curly parsley and serve warm.

A present-day version dispenses with the need for a wash-boiler (used for cooking) and a great deal of watchful simmering. Scrub ham and soak overnight. Drain place in center of a large piece of heavy duty foil. Sprinkle with 2 cups dark brown sugar, ½ cup sherry, 2½ cups water. Wrap well. Bake 5 to 6 hours in very slow (250° to 275° F.) oven. When tender and bones protrude, remove and let cool in wrappings. Remove rind. Score fat with knife. Sprinkle over length with dry mustard (about 1 tablespoon). Sprinkle with 1 tablespoon celery seed and cover with about 1 cup brown sugar. Bake in a moderately hot (375° F.) oven about 5 minutes per pound or until ham is heated through and sugar melts into a fine crustiness. For extra flavor baste with a little more sherry or use bourbon.

BISKETT

Martha Washington's Biskett is not the Biscuit we know today. Bisketts were flat, thin cakes, rather hard, with no leavening agent. Some contained sugar, others did not. The Virginia beaten biscuit resembles the older biskett.

Flour	*Caraway or coriander seed*
Sugar	*Eggs*
Salt	*Rose water*
Aniseed	

Sift together 4 cups flour, 2 cups sugar, ¼ teaspoon salt. Add 1 tablespoon aniseed and 1 tablespoon caraway or coriander seeds. Beat well 8 egg yolks and 4 egg whites; mix with 4 tablespoons rose water and add to the dry mixture. Knead and beat with a rolling pin until blisters appear. Roll dough ⅛ inch thick, cut into rounds, and set on baking sheets dusted with sugar and flour. Bake in a moderate (350° F.) oven. *Makes about 4 dozen biscuits 1½ inches in diameter.*

FILBERT BISCUITS

George Washington liked nuts in any form, plain for nibbling or chopped up in pastries and desserts. A favorite way of serving them in Virginia was in biscuits such as these.

Barcelona filbert nuts (any old fil-	*Eggs*
bert will do)	*Powdered sugar*

Shell the nuts (the original recipe suggests doing this in a mortar), grind them very fine, mix egg whites with them. Then mix 3 pounds powdered sugar with the nuts and egg whites to a proper thickness. Drop them on a cooky sheet (the old way says to drop small pieces, "about half as big as a nutmeg," and bake them on two or three sheets of paper), bake until brown; and "let them be cold" before you remove them.

MOUNT VERNON CORNBREAD

Although the big meal of the day for the President was dinner, served at 3 P.M. or, when entertaining officially, at four o'clock, Washington liked to have a light supper at 9 P.M. before retiring. One of his favorite menus consisted of hot cornbread and cheese, fruit compote and nuts, sherry or port wine. Martha always included coffee as well—good and strong.

Washington's original cornbread recipe has been modified for today's cooking habits—baking powder has been added.

Cornmeal	*Salt*
Flour	*Milk*
Sugar	*Egg*
Baking powder	*Shortening*

Mix and sift all dry ingredients: ¾ cup cornmeal, 1 cup flour, ⅓ cup sugar, 3 teaspoons baking powder, ¾ teaspoon salt. Add 1 cup milk, 1 well-beaten egg, and 2 tablespoons melted shortening (butter, margarine, or oil). Bake the mixture in a shallow buttered baking pan 20 minutes in a hot (425° F.) oven. Serve piping hot with butter.

Martha Washington's Rules for Good Coffee

Our forefathers insisted on a good-quality coffee; Mocha and Java were most in demand. For drip coffee, Mrs. Washington used one heaping tablespoon of "specially selected coffee, pulverized as fine as cornmeal," to a cup of water. She then recommended a cotton filtering material, such as muslin, if the process is "true Colonial." Use a freshly rinsed and scalded pot, galloping hot water. Pour the bubbling water through the coffee in its muslin bag, letting the liquid filter. "To keep very hot, put pot in a pan of hot water." Furthermore, black coffee is served with sugar before breakfast and after dinner. "Your breakfast cup is served with hot milk."

FRIED APPLES AND BACON

In April 1755 General Braddock and the Colonial governors held a conference on taxation in the Carlyle House in Alexandria, Virginia (the Carlyle House was then Braddock's headquarters). This dish, a favorite of the General's, was served. Although on the opposite side during the Revolutionary War, Martha Washington did not mind borrowing the recipe, nor did *her* General mind eating it. In fact, it was served often at Mount Vernon.

Tart apples	*Sugar*
Bacon	

This delicious dish is easy to prepare. Peel tart apples and cut them into 1-inch cubes. Meanwhile fry the bacon in a heavy skillet. When done, drain bacon on paper towel and keep warm. Leave ¼ cup bacon fat in the skillet and fill it with apples. Sprinkle 2 or 3 teaspoons sugar on the apple cubes. Cover and cook slowly until tender. Remove cover and turn, keeping the apples shape. Let them brown lightly, then place on a steaming platter, surround with the bacon, and serve.

SAUCES FOR ROAST CHICKEN AND OTHER FOWL

Wild fowl and game were abundant in the forest near Mount Vernon. Washington had a hunter, Tom Davis, to keep the table well supplied with wild ducks, pheasants, and partridge. Even so, chicken was never displaced as a great family favorite. Prepared a variety of ways, it was often just roasted over wood coals in the huge open hearth. Various sauces were used as accompaniment. These are two from Martha Washington's cookbook.

A WINTER SAUCE

Mary Randolph brought this delicious but sketchy idea to Mount Vernon from Whitehall Mansion, a handsome Southern Colonial house in Maryland.

To one quart cranberries or cranberry sauce add one generous cup raisins. An interesting present-day application of the same thought: Place 1 quart cranberries in an ovenproof dish. Add 1 cup sugar, 1 cup raisins, 1 cup water. Cover. Bake at 300° F., 1 hour.

CHICKEN SAUCE

We would call this an Oyster Sauce for Chicken.

Oysters	*Salt and pepper*
Burgundy wine	*Lemon juice*
Mace	*Butter*
Onion	*Slice of bread*

Drain 2 dozen oysters (1 pint) well. Cook the oyster liquor, ½ cup Burgundy, ⅛ teaspoon mace, and 1 small shredded onion together until the onion is tender. Add salt and pepper to taste, the juice of ½ lemon, 2 tablespoons butter, 1 slice grated bread, and the oysters. Cook until the oysters are plump and crinkled, but do not boil. Pour over individual servings of roast or broiled chicken.

PHILADELPHIA PEPPER POT

Legend has it that this famous Pennsylvania specialty originated with Washington at Valley Forge. During that brutal winter of 1777–1778 the troops were cold, ragged, and half-starved. To boost morale, General Washington is supposed to have ordered a good meal one night, only to be informed by his cook that the only food available was tripe, a few scraps, and peppercorns—not very promising!

But the cook, an ingenious fellow, used his imagination and came up with a soup he called Philadelphia (after his home) Pepper Pot. Some Philadelphians like to credit this improvised dinner with the success of the Revolution. Other Philadelphians are spoilsports and claim the dish existed long before Valley Forge. It is quite possible that it had its origins in Africa by way of the West Indies. There fish, not tripe, was the basic ingredient. Transplanted to Philadelphia with West Indian cooks, it took on a local flavor.

Whichever version you prefer, you will find this an authentic Pepper Pot of the era:

Plain tripe	*Parsley*
Honeycomb tripe	*Onion stuck with whole clove*
Knuckle of veal (containing some	*White potatoes*
meat)	*Butter*
Water	*Flour*
Salt	*Veal kidney suet*
Pepper	*Ice water*
Soup herbs	*Flour dumplings*

To do it properly, the soup takes two days to make. Scrub the tripe (1 pound of each kind); wash in cold water. Put it in a deep kettle and cover with warm water. Bring to simmer, simmer 8 hours. Allow it to stand in its broth overnight. Wipe off the beal knuckle. Put it in a deep kettle and cover with 3 quarts cold water. Add 1 tablespoon salt and ¼ teaspoon black pepper. Bring to a simmer. Skim as necessary, cover and simmer for 3 hours, skimming occasionally. Then strain and return this broth to the soup kettle. Wash soup herbs and sprigs of chopped parsley and add to the soup pot along with a bay leaf. Add 1 large onion stuck with 1 whole clove to the pot. Cut bits of veal from the knuckle, cut tripe into 1-inch squares; add both to soup. Taste and add salt and pepper. Add two potatoes, cut into small cubes. Simmer. Meanwhile, make a smooth paste of 2 tablespoons each of butter and flour. Chop fine ¼ pound veal kidney suet; use twice the amount of flour. Stir salt into flour and suet; work them together as if making pie crust. Then fork in just enough ice water to hold crumbs together (about ¼ cupful). Shape this mixture with floured fingers to make 50 marble-size dumplings. Work butter-flour mixture into simmering soup gradually, stir until it thickens slightly. Drop in dumplings, a few at a time. Simmer 15 minutes, then serve. *Makes 2 quarts.*

GLAZED ONIONS

President Washington's favorite vegetable was the onion. He was fond of onions any way they were prepared, and even ate them cored and stuffed with mincemeat. New England abounds with inns where George Washington is reputed to have slept. But the Munroe Tavern in Lexington, Massachusetts (now a museum), has a more distinctive claim to Washingtonian fame. "George Washington ate glazed onions here" it could proudly proclaim, for he did just that in 1790. The Munroe Tavern has other claims, too. On the day of the Battle of Lexington, the British set it afire. Neighbors rushed to its rescue and saved it for posterity—and for George Washington and his glazed onions.

Onions *Honey*
Salt   *Butter*
Pepper

Cut 10 medium-sized onions in half crosswise, butter each one and arrange in a baking dish. Add ½ teaspoon salt, ¼ teaspoon pepper. Pour 1 teaspoon honey over each onion. Dot with butter (4 tablespoons in all). Bake uncovered in a hot (450° F.) oven for 45 minutes. (You may want to bake potatoes at the same time, as both require approximately the same baking time.) The glazed onions may be served plain, as you would boiled onions, or on strips of hot toast, garnished with parsley that has been dipped in vinegar.

ONIONS BRAZILIAN STYLE

A note in Martha Washington's *Rules for Cooking* says that this dish was served at Washington's farewell dinner to his officers, held in New York in 1783 at Fraunces' Tavern.

Onions   *Egg*
Mincemeat

Peel the number of onions needed and force out the cores (you may have to parboil them slightly). Fill the openings with mincemeat. Beat 1 egg and glaze the opening on each side, where the meat was inserted, so it will not drop out. Then fry the onions in butter or cooking oil.

HARTY CHOAK PIE

Translation: Artichoke pie. This old English recipe comes from an old recipe book in Martha Washington's family. The coffin used, lest you become alarmed, was a pastry-lined dish or pan shaped like a (you guessed it!) coffin. The *verges* mentioned is verjuice or green juice—any sour juice of green fruit used in place of vinegar. Grape juice was commonly used this way.

Artichokes	*Sugar*
Pastry	*Verges (green juice)*
Butter	*Cinnamon*
Marrow bones	*Ginger*

Take 12 harty choak [artichoke] bottoms, good and large and boil them. Discard the leaves and core, and place the bottoms on a coffin of pastry, with 1 pound butter and the marrow of 2 bones in big pieces, then close up the coffin, and bake it in the oven. Meanwhile, boil together ½ pound sugar, ½ pint verges, and a touch of cinnamon and ginger. When the pie is half-baked, put the liquor into it, replace it in the oven until it is fully baked.

TRY-AGAIN ARTICHOKES

The Harty Choak Pie listed above may divert you, but Martha Washington had included in her standard recipes a sauce for plain boiled artichokes that is just as appealing today as it was when she served it to guests. Artichokes were popular (and a good deal less costly) in Colonial times.

Artichokes	*Pepper*
Butter	*Sifted flour*
Grated nutmeg	*Lemon juice*

Trim the artichokes, boil them in salt water ¾ hour (if they are small, they require far less time, perhaps 15 minutes). Serve with the following sauce:

To make the sauce: Put 4 ounces, ¼ pound, butter into a pan with nutmeg and pepper to taste. Add 4 ounces sifted flour. Boil 20 minutes, then add 1½ pounds butter. Squeeze in the juice of ½ lemon and serve hot.

TRIFLE

Martha Washington's *Rules for Cooking* was by no means a complete recipe book, nor did it pretend to be. Rather, it contained "receipts" for her and her family's favorite dishes. Considering the disproportionate number of desserts listed, it is not hard to deduce that Martha had a considerable sweet tooth. A great favorite at Washington dinner parties was Trifle, a holdover from the Washington English heritage.

Sponge cake	*Heavy cream*
White wine	*Sugar*
Boiled custard (recipe below)	*Preserves*

Place slices of sponge cake at the bottom of a deep dish. Moisten the cake with white wine, used sparingly. Fill the dish to the top with rich boiled custard. Season ½ pint heavy cream with white wine and sugar to taste; whip to a froth. As the froth rises, skim it off and place it on top of the custard. Pile the whipped cream as high as possible and decorate it with preserves or canned fruit cut so thin it will not weigh the whipped cream down.

RICH BOILED CUSTARD

Milk	*Eggs*
Sugar	*Vanilla or other flavoring*
Salt	

Scald 1 quart milk, ½ cup sugar, and a good pinch of salt. Beat 6 eggs; add ½ cup cold milk, stir, and gradually add to the hot milk mixture. Cook in a double boiler until the custard coats a spoon. Add flavoring after the custard has cooled.

LETTUCE TART

This most unusual and interesting dish was served at Mount Vernon. Today it is hard for us to conceive of lettuce as a dessert. The sugar and spices may be omitted though Martha Washington would never approve. It is a tasty combination even without beef marrow.

Pastry	*Water*
Butter	*Large prunes*
Sugar	*Beef marrow*
Cinnamon	
Ginger	
Romaine lettuce	
Salt	

Line a deep pie dish with pastry. Dot all over it with bits of butter and spinkle with sugar, a little cinnamon and ginger. Cook 4 heads of Romaine lettuce in boiling salted water until tender. Drain thoroughly and spread in the pastry shell. On top of the lettuce arrange 1½ dozen large prunes that have been soaked, pitted, and cooked until tender. Dot with cubes of beef marrow, a little sugar and cinnamon. Cover with the upper pie crust, bake ¾ hour in the oven at the usual temperature for pies. (About 400° F.)

CATS' TONGUES *NEÉ* SPOON BISCUITS

At the time of the American Revolution and well into the nineteenth century, every American housewife probably had a little tongue pan. "What is it?" we ask today—indicative of the transitions in food fashions through our history. Originally the tongue pan was designed for *langues chat,* cat tongues, a popular dish in France. But the shape of the pan and several recipes from Colonial days suggest a concoction similar to our lady fingers. Martha Washington used her tongue pans for Spoon Biscuit, which she called "an excellent wafer."

Eggs   *Lemon juice*
Powdered sugar

Break 4 eggs; separate them. Add ¼ pound powdered sugar to the yolks, then add the juice of one lemon. Mix together well for 10 minutes (the old recipe calls for mixing with a spatula, but those were pre-eggbeater days—we suggest a rotary or electric beater). Whip the egg whites until stiff. Add half to the yolk mixture, mix it in well, then add the remaining whites. Stir very gently, then place them on paper, using a spoon to make each "tongue" about 3 inches long and the breadth of a finger. Glaze with powdered sugar; place the paper on a baking sheet and, as the sugar dissolves and they shine, put the biscuits into a preheated moderate (350° F.) oven. Keep the oven open 7 or 8 minutes, then close it, watching until the biscuits are "a proper color"—delicately browned. Remove the paper from the baking sheet. When cool, remove the biscuits from the paper with a thin-bladed knife or metal spatula. "Lay them by, in couples," says the original recipe, with the glazed sides face up, until needed.

THREE FRUIT DELIGHTS

President Washington was very fond of fruit. One observer noted that he "was a frequent buyer of fruit of all kinds and of melons." Certainly the lush orchards and fruit trees of his beautiful Virginia countryside were inviting. Nectarines, wild plums, seckle pears, prunes, lemons, limes, pineapples, myriad berries, as well as oranges, apples, and grapes, were all to be found during his day. (Of course Washington knew all about cherries.) While the third course of a Presidential dinner always consisted of a number of fruits served fresh, the Washingtons were also fond of fruit preserved, jellied, and made into appetizing desserts.

BLACKCAPS

Apples   *Cream*
Brown sugar   *Water*

Here is Martha Washington's recipe for baked apples verbatim:

Take a dozen good pippins, cut them in half and core. Place them in a tight mazarine dish with the skins on, the cut side down; put to them a little water, scrape on them some brown lump sugar. Put in a hot oven till the skins are burnt black, and your apples are tender. Serve them on plates with good cow cream.

CANDIED ORANGE PEEL

Oranges   *Water*
Sugar

Boil the rinds of 3 fairly large oranges in water. Boil 1½ hours, changing the water twice. Drain and dry slightly. Cut into strips, then boil in syrup made of 1½ cups sugar and ½ cup water. Stir constantly until syrup crystallizes. Turn out onto buttered tins; straighten the pieces with a fork. Cool.

ORANGE BUTTER

Orange/juice and rind   *Butter*
Powdered sugar   *Lemon juice*
Egg yolks, beaten

Add 1 cup orange juice to 1 cup powdered sugar and the grated rind of 1 orange. Add 3 beaten egg yolks, 2 tablespoons butter. Cook in double boiler until mixture is thick. Take from fire, add 1 tablespoon lemon juice. Delicious for filling tarts.

MARTHA WASHINGTON BONBONS

"Refreshments of all kinds" were served at the President's levees and at Mrs. Washington's drawing-rooms, according to the reports of George Washington Parke Custis. Coffee, tea, punch, lemonade, cakes, and sweetmeats were among the "goodies" frequently mentioned. It is likely that Martha Washington's celebrated candies were often on hand. These bonbons became so famous that later a commercial brand of candy was named after them.

Light brown sugar   *Butter*
White sugar   *Vanilla*
Cream or milk

Cook 2 cups light brown sugar, 1 cup white sugar, and ½ cup cream or milk in a covered pan to the soft-ball stage (234° F.). Pour the candy onto a buttered platter. Cool. When cool beat in 1 tablespoon butter and 1 teaspoon vanilla until creamy. Knead the candy on a marble slab (formica would do today—or any hard surface); divide it into as many portions as you want varieties. Mix one portion with chopped nuts, another with chopped citron, another with fruit flavoring or rum extract. After mixing each type, shape the bonbons. Leave some plain; dip others in melted chocolate, decorate with nut halves and/or candied cherries. Put each finished piece on wax paper and let it stand until firm ("Let it ripen," says the old cookbook).

FRESH CHEESE WITH ALMONDS

Cheese was a food much favored by George Washington. He liked plain sharp Cheddar served with fruit and nuts at the end of a dinner. Or he liked cheese with biscuits as a supper snack before bed. He was also partial to this cheese-and-nut dessert, prepared from his wife's recipe.

Almonds	*Salt*
Rose water	*Currants*
Cottage cheese	*Cream*
Sugar	

Blanch, chop, and pound ½ pound almonds with 2 tablespoons rose water until you have a smooth paste. Add 1 cup cottage cheese (Martha called it "fresh cheese"), ½ cup sugar, and ⅛ teaspoon salt and beat well. Add ½ cup currants soaked in rose water for an hour. Press into a mold and let stand for several hours. Turn out, surround with cream, sweetened and flavored with sugar to taste. A delicious dessert, today as then.

CUSTARD PIE WITH ALMONDS

In Martha Washington's recipe collection—which totaled more than five hundred of her favorite dishes—there is advice about making pie dough as sound today as when she lived. "Take heed to be not made too stiff, nor worke it overmuch, nor heat it with ye hand," she wrote. This is a recipe she used; it too has stood the test of time.

Cream	*Sugar*
Nutmeg	*Salt*
Cinnamon	*Almonds*
Bay leaf	*Rose water*
Eggs	*Pastry*
White wine	

Scald 2 cups cream with a piece broken from a whole nutmeg, a piece of stick cinnamon, and ¼ small bay leaf. Set aside to cool a little. Beat well the yolks of 4 eggs and 2 egg whites. Add 2 tablespoons white wine, 3 tablespoons sugar, and a pinch of salt, and continue beating. Combine this mixture with the cream. Pound ½ cup almonds well in a mortar (or use an electric blender) and mix with 2 tablespoons rose water. Have a pie dish ready, lined with pastry. Strew the crushed almonds in the bottom of the pie pan, add the custard mixture, and bake in a moderate (350° F.) oven until set about 1 hour.

RICH BLACKCAKE

In Martha Washington's day, there were of course no mixes and no short cuts in baking. It was a long, long labor of love to make a cake, with emphasis on the labor. Fruit extracts, ground spices, seedless raisins, gelatine, baking powder—such conveniences of modern cooking did not exist. Nor did that basic tool of cooking (or so we would think), an eggbeater! The actual baking was hard work, too. The oven had to be heated with a fire made from certain types of wood—red or white oak, spruce or gum, sassafras or hickory logs, depending on whether a slow, moderate, or hot oven was required. The fire had to be brushed out of the oven before the cakes or breads were to be inserted. Only experienced bakers could guess by feel about oven temperature. Yet, in spite of all these obstacles, Colonial dames made and served exquisite cakes. The recipe for this special cake may seem astonishing to us today. Yet it was much admired at Nellie Custis' wedding, when she married Lawrence Lewis, the son of Betty Washington and Colonel Fielding Lewis, proprietors of Kenmore.

Butter	*Mace*
Eggs	*Nutmeg*
Powdered sugar	*Wine*
Flour	*French brandy*
Fruit	

Cream 2 pounds of butter. Beat 20 egg whites until fairly stiff, then spoon them into the butter. Spoon in 2 pounds of powdered sugar the same way. Add 20 egg yolks beaten slightly, 2½ pounds flour, 5 pounds mixed candied fruits, ¼ ounce mace, 1 ounce nutmeg, ½ pint wine, and a little French brandy. Mix well. Bake slowly in warm (325° F.) oven for 2 hours or until done. Recipe can be halved.

A TANSY WITH SLICED ORANGES

Martha Washington colored this superb bread pudding with "bruised spinach and sorrel." It sounds picturesque, but for expediency we recommend substituting green vegetable coloring, and for Martha's "handful of tansy leaves" try a touch of aromatic bitters.

Breadcrumbs	*Rose water (or vanilla)*
Milk	*Almond extract*
Cream	*Aromatic bitters*
Sugar	*Green food coloring*
Salt	*Eggs*
Butter	*Orange juice and oranges*

Soak 1 cup fine breadcrumbs in 1 cup milk and 1 cup cream. Add ⅓ cup sugar, ⅛ teaspoon salt, 4 tablespoons melted butter, 3 tablespoons rose water (or 1 teaspoon vanilla), ½ teaspoon almond extract, and ½ teaspoon aromatic bitters. Color subtly with green coloring. Add 4 well-beaten eggs. Turn into a buttered baking dish. Bake in a moderate (350° F.) oven about 25 minutes, or until pudding sets. When removed from oven, sprinkle the pudding with orange juice and decorate with triangles of thinly sliced oranges. A festive dish.

MARTHA WASHINGTON'S GINGERBREAD
(OR FACSIMILE THEREOF)

Visitors to Kenmore, the beautiful mansion of George Washington's sister and family near Fredericksburg, Virginia, develop a sense of Colonial history from the lovely rooms, walks, and gardens. When they finish their tour, they are invited into the old kitchen for tea and gingerbread. The gingerbread is made from a recipe of Mary Washington's. She served it to the Marquis de La Fayette when he visited Fredericksburg in 1784. Legend has it that he was so impressed with the gingerbread *and* with Washington's mother in general that he explained "I have seen the only Roman matron of my day." Some historians assume this was a compliment. From the rest of his comments we rather doubt it.

By adding some of Martha Washington's flavorings to a gingerbread package mix, you will have a really unusual and delicious cake.

Instant coffee	*Gingerbread mix*
Powdered mace	*Orange juice*
Orange rind	

Add 1 teaspoon instant coffee, 1 teaspoon mace, and 1 teaspoon grated orange rind to a package of gingerbread mix. Follow the package directions for making the mix, adding the necessary eggs and liquid, but substitute ½ cup orange juice for the same amount of liquid. Bake according to the package instructions. At serving time (it is best served warm), cut into squares and serve with applesauce or whipped cream.

MAIDS OF HONOR

The history of these delicious tartlets supposedly goes back to 1480, when King Henry VIII of England found Anne Boleyn and her maids eating these cakes. He sampled, was charmed, and named them after her. Somewhere along the way the name was changed to Maids of Honor (considering Anne's fate perhaps it should be Maids of Dishonor—hardly appropriate for such delicacies). As such, the cakes were popular throughout Virginia. Martha Washington has her own interpretation:

Milk	*Ground almonds*
Rennet	*Grated lemon rind*
Egg yolks	*Cinnamon*
Whipped cream	*Brandy*
Sugar	*Nutmeg*
Currants	*Pastry*

Warm 1 pint milk slightly, add 1 teaspoon rennet; allow to stand until a curd forms. Drain through cheesecloth overnight. Next day press the curds lightly; turn into a bowl. Add 2 egg yolks, 4 tablespoons whipped cream, 2 ounces sugar, currants, ½ cup ground almonds, one teaspoon grated lemon rind, a pinch of cinnamon, a wineglass of brandy, grated nutmeg, and then mix well. Line tartlet tins with pastry and fill with the mixture. *Makes 6 small tartlets.*

MARTHA WASHINGTON FAMOUS GREAT CAKE

The day after Christmas 1776 General Washington won the Battle of Trenton. That same day he received a Mount Vernon fruit cake from his wife. Reading about this, at this point in time, we might naturally assume that fruit cake was the traditional Christmas cake in Colonial times. Not so. Fruit cake was *the* cake—*anytime.* Loaded with spices and "currans and raisins of ye sun," fruit cake was immensely popular all year round for any festive occasion, from state dinners to dinners *en famille.* But at this time, fruit cake was called Great Cake (its other name was a Victorian innovation). And a great cake it was, as this recipe from an old Mount Vernon manuscript (dated 1781) indicates:

Eggs	*Mace*
Butter	*Nutmeg*
Powdered sugar	*Wine*
Flour	*French brandy*
Fruit	

Take 40 eggs and divide the whites from the yolks, then beat them to a froth. Then work 4 pounds butter to a creamy state, and put the egg whites into it, a tablespoon at a time, until it is well worked. Then add 4 pounds (8 cups) sugar, finely powdered, to the butter mixture. Then add the egg yolks, 5 pounds flour, and 5 pounds fruit. Add ½ ounce (1 tablespoon) mace, one nutmeg, ½ pint of wine, and some French brandy. Two hours will bake it. (Martha Custis made this cake for her grandmother Martha. Next time you have 40 eggs on hand, you might try it. Speaking more practically, the recipe can be cut in half successfully or even quartered.

Note from P. C.: If 1 whole nutmeg seems a lot—and it is—read 1 tablespoon powdered nutmeg. "Some French brandy" can be translated into 1 cup.

MARTHA WASHINGTON'S WHITE FRUIT CAKE
(OR GREAT CAKE)

This adaptation of another of Martha Washington's Great cakes is better suited to the present-day household, which is not accustomed to the great volume of guests that visited the Washingtons. Considering the number of visitors they had, even the most enormous Great Cake probably did not last too long (though in theory it could keep for months). Several months after Washington's term of office had ended and he had returned to Mount Vernon, he wrote a friend that he and Martha were sitting down to dinner alone for the first time in twenty years.

Butter or margarine	*Nutmeg*
Extra-fine granulated sugar	*Diced candied fruit or peels*
Eggs	*Red table wine*
Sifted flour	*Brandy or brandy flavoring*
Mace	

Cream 1 cup butter or margarine until it has the consistency of mayonnaise. Add 1 cup sugar gradually, then 5 egg yolks. Cream until light and fluffy. Mix and sift 2½ cups flour, 1 teaspoon mace, ¼ teaspoon nutmeg. Combine the dry ingredients with 1 cup mixed diced candied fruits or peels. Blend them into the creamed mixture. Then add 2 tablespoons red table wine and 2 teaspoons brandy flavoring. Beat 5 egg whites until stiff and fold them in. (The batter is stiff, so the folding will take some time.) Turn into a greased and floured 9-inch tube cake pan. Bake in a 325° F. oven for 1 hour and 15 minutes, or until done. Cool on rack. Frost and decorate if desired, or serve plain. (Plain? with all that fruit, wine, and spices!)

SHREWSBURY CAKES

Martha Custis and George Washington were married on Twelfth Night 1759, so the Christmas season always had a double significance for them. They liked to spend the holiday together if possible. Even during the intense fighting of the Revolutionary War, Martha once traveled the icy winter roads with a special escort so she could spend the holiday with her husband in his winter army quarters. Mount Vernon, celebrated at all seasons for its hospitality, became even more festive at Christmastime. One of the seasonal specialties of the big Mount Vernon kitchen was Shrewsbury Cakes. This is Martha Washington's recipe for them:

Flour	*Butter*
Sugar	*Egg whites*
Salt	*Rose water*
Mace	*White wine*
Cinnamon	*Warm cream*
Cloves	

Sift together 4 cups flour, 1 cup sugar, ½ teaspoon salt, ½ teaspoon mace, 1 teaspoon cinnamon, and ½ teaspoon cloves. Work in ¾ pound butter with fingertips. Beat 2 egg whites slightly, and add ½ cup rose water to the egg whites, along with ½ cup white wine. Blend with the first mixture, adding just enough warm cream to form a soft dough. Roll out, cut into fancy shapes, and bake in a moderate (350° F.) oven. Although called cakes, they resemble more closely today's cookies.

JUMBLES

Sometimes referred to in the old cookbooks as "Jumballs," these rich cookies were a great Washington favorite during the Christmas season. This recipe comes from Martha Washington's *Rules for Cooking.*

Butter	*Rose water*
Sugar	*Cream*
Eggs	*Flour*
Caraway seeds	*Salt*

Cream ¾ cup butter well. Gradually add 1½ cups sugar and the well-beaten yolks of 6 eggs, the whites of 3 eggs, 1 tablespoon caraway seeds, 6 tablespoons rose water, 6 tablespoons cream, and enough flour sifted with ½ teaspoon salt to make a soft dough. Chill the dough. Then roll it out about ⅛ inch thick and cut it into circles. Place circles on a buttered cooky sheet, prick each with a fork, and bake in a moderate (350° F.) oven about 8 minutes. *Makes about 80, 1½ inches in diameter.*

WAVERLY JUMBLES

This variation on Jumbles was given to Martha Washington by James Monroe's wife Elizabeth. They are different but just as delicious.

Flour	*Brown sugar*
Nutmeg	*Eggs*
Butter	*Rose water*

Sift one pound of flour with ½ teaspoon nutmeg. Cream separately ½ pound butter. Add gradually ¾ pound (1½ cups) brown sugar, 2 eggs, and 2 tablespoons rose water. Mix with the dry ingredients. Roll out into long rectangle, then cut into strips. Form the strips into rings and bake in a moderate (350° F.) oven about 8 minutes. *Makes about 8 dozen.*

"A CHEAP DESSERT"

When Washington's army went into winter quarters at Valley Forge in 1777, it was a time of severe hardship for the struggling Colonists. Those not fighting tried to economize to help the Army. At this time Martha Washington, home in Mount Vernon, ordered "a cheap dessert" served. By today's standards, it is not very tasty, but it satisfied Martha's sweet tooth at the time because already it was served with syrup or honey.

Hominy	*Milk*
Cornmeal	*Butter*
Eggs	

Wash 1 pint small hominy very clean and boil it until tender. Add 1 pint cornmeal. Form it into a batter with eggs, milk, and a piece of butter, until the right consistency is reached. Then bake it like a batter cake on a griddle. Serve it with butter and molasses.

MARTHA WASHINGTON CAKE

Another variation of the preferred Great Cake, or fruit cake, this version uses sour cream and is lusciously spicy and fragrant. Martha Washington was the one in the family with the notorious sweet tooth, yet it was George, as every visitor to Mount Vernon has seen for himself, who required the false teeth. Legend has it that Washington's tooth problems stemmed from pewter poisoning from eating on pewter plates (a legend that will make pewter manufacturers turn gray). No matter. It is a fact, not legend, that Washington would have had no trouble eating this cake.

Butter	*Nutmeg, grated*
Sugar	*Mace*
Eggs	*Lemon rind, grated*
Sour cream	*Lemon juice*
Flour	*Citron*
Soda	*Currants*

Cream 1 cup butter with 4 cups sugar; add 6 well-beaten egg yolks. Stir in 2 cups sour cream. Sift 5½ cups flour with 1 teaspoon soda, 1 grated nutmeg and 1 teaspoon ground mace. Add gradually to the creamed mixture, beating thoroughly. Fold in 6 stiffly beaten egg whites, then add the grated rind of 2 lemons and the juice of 1 lemon. Slice 1½ pounds citron and cut it into little strips. Flour the citron and 1 pound currants and stir in last. Bake in a big deep cake pan for 2 hours in a moderate (325°–350° F.) oven. (The cake is enormous, but it will keep a long time. If you prefer a smaller one, the recipe can be halved.)

MARTHA'S CHERRY BREAD-AND-BUTTER PUDDING

A collection of Washington recipes would not be complete without one for cherry something-or-other. Many dishes, particularly cherry dishes, have been named in honor of our first President. This pays him tribute right enough, but it often confuses the social historian seeking foods Washington really did eat. Many of the George Washington pies, cakes, or cherry-this-and-thats became popular after his death (George Washington instant coffee?). That this recipe was *Martha's* favorite we do know as gospel, but—we cannot tell a lie—we cannot vouch for George. We do know this much: he did love cherries, as he did most fruits, so it is probably a safe guess that he enjoyed this dessert as much as his wife did.

Bread	*Lemon peel, grated*
Butter	*Eggs*
Cherry preserves	*Sugar*
Nutmeg, grated	

Cut slices of bread and butter very thick. Put a layer on the bottom of a baking dish. Then put a layer of cherry preserves on top of it. Add grated nutmeg and lemon peel. Continue making alternate layers until the dish is filled. Make a custard of 4 or 5 eggs, with sugar to taste. Boil it, then pour it boiling hot slowly over the bread mixture. Let stand until the bread has soaked it up, then bake in moderate (325°–350° F.) oven about 1 hour or until set and lightly browned. Most delicious served warm.

To make 6 servings you will need 12 slices of bread, about 6 tablespoons butter, ½ cup preserves, 2 teaspoons lemon peel, ½ teaspoon nutmeg. It is not necessary to cook custard beforehand. Simply combine 3 cups milk, 4 eggs, slightly beaten, ⅓ cup sugar. Pour over bread. Bake 1 hour at 325°–350° F.

"MISS BLYDEN"

As a young man, in 1751–1752, George Washington visited Barbados, his first and only trip outside of our continent. During the course of his stay, he sampled the British island's "Miss Blyden" and liked the drink so much he actually wrote home about it. This contemporary version is somewhat more to contemporary taste, using less sugar than Washington would have liked. It is a great cooler-offer in hot weather.

Sugar	*Prickly pear juice*
Rum	*or*
	Guava nectar

Dissolve ½ teaspoon sugar in a glass, add a jigger of West-Indian rum, one or two ice cubes, and fill up the glass with the juice of prickly pears, guava nectar, or (how exotic can you get?) guanabana juice from a tin if necessary. Stir and sip. And sip.

"GOOD JULEP"

In the eighteenth century in the Southern colonies, gentlemen indulged in considerable social drinking at their many social occasions. The climate and the more leisurely way of life created a tolerance for wines, brandies, and punches that did not exist in the more puritanical New England. Washington was considered a temperate man, yet he often had four or five glasses of wine with dinner, some homemade brew before dinner, and brandy or wine after dinner. This was, perhaps, par for the Virginia course. Punches (alcoholic of course) were served at galas and receptions. On many occasions Washington and his guests would assemble on the lovely shaded piazza of Mount Vernon sipping "wine imported twice a year with the rest of the household stuff from London" (as a report from the time stated it). At other times, the assembled friends might be served a home-brewed drink, possibly even the nonalcoholic "Good Juleps" Martha Washington wrote about in her *Rules for Cooking.*

Grape juice	*Sugar*
Orange juice	*Charged water*
Chopped mint	*Lemon or lime slices*

Mix ½ pint grape juice and ½ pint orange juice with ½ cup chopped fresh mint. Let stand on ice for one hour. Add a dash of sugar to taste. Add 1 pint charged water (club soda) and pour into glasses half-filled with ice. Pop a sprig of mint into each glass and serve at once. Garnish with slices of lemon or lime.

SACK POSSET

Whether or not Sir Walter Raleigh invented this drink, as has been claimed, it is truly a festive holiday potion. The Washingtons traditionally served it with Virginia ham served in beaten biscuits, pound cake, or gingerbread squares. Toasts were undoubtedly offered on the occasion. (One wonders if Washington ever heard the toast once proposed in his honor by his fellow countryman Benjamin Franklin. As Minister to France, Franklin was dining with the French and English ambassadors. The Englishman arose to offer a toast to "England—the Sun whose beams enlighten and fructify the remotest corners of the earth!" Undaunted, the Frenchman satisfied his national pride by toasting "France—the Moon whose mild, steady, cheering rays are the delight of all nations, consoling them in darkness and making their dreariness beautiful!" Franklin then arose and, with a wry smile at such rhetoric, responded: "To George Washington—the Joshua who commanded the Sun and Moon to stand still—and they obeyed him.")

Sugar	*Sherry*
Milk	*Grated nutmeg or powdered cloves*
Egg yolks	

Add ½ cup sugar to 2 quarts milk. Beat well, then heat just to the point of scalding. Add the hot milk and sugar to 4 beaten egg yolks, beating while adding. Stir in 4 cups medium sweet sherry. Serve warm in punch cups, small mugs, or champagne saucers, with grated nutmeg or powdered cloves sprinkled lightly over the top. *Serves 22 to 24.*

SYLLABUB

A relative of eggnog, syllabub is always made with wine instead of strong liquors. This Old English drink is part of the history of eighteenth-century Virginia, when it was traditionally served during the Christmas holidays. During Washington's terms of office, the only time he failed to hold his weekly Tuesday levee was the Tuesday before New Year's Day, 1790. New Year's that year fell on Friday, the day of Mrs. Washington's weekly reception. It was decided to combine the two and have only one reception that week, on New Year's Day, from 12 to 3 P.M. A Presidential tradition thus began—and receptions were held every New Year's Day (barring wartime) until Franklin Roosevelt's administration. It is likely that at the first, syllabub was served, along with the usual cookies and cakes; it was ever so with Colonial Virginians on New Year's. Syllabub's mildness made it a drink even the children could share on that festive occasion.

White wine	*Milk*
Grated lemon rind	*Light cream*
Lemon juice	*Egg whites*
Sugar	*Nutmeg*

Combine 2 cups white wine with 5 tablespoons grated lemon rind and ⅓ cup lemon juice. Stir in 1 cup sugar and let the mixture stand until the sugar is dissolved. Then combine 3 cups milk with 2 cups light cream. Add the wine mixture and beat with rotary beater until frothy (in the old days, supposedly, the mixture at this point was taken to the dairy, where the milk was squirted right from the cow into the bowl, giving the mixture an airiness and frothiness that is the essence of syllabub). Beat 4 egg whites until stiff, add ½ cup sugar gradually, beating all the while, until the egg whites stand in high peaks. Pour the wine mixture into a festive punch bowl, top with the mountains of egg whites and sprinkle with nutmeg.

II

Our First Family in the White House

When John Adams became President, the seat of government was still in Philadelphia, but when he left office four years later, in 1801, the Presidency had found its permanent home in Washington.

The Adams family had only a taste of life in Washington. But the records indicate that, at least as far as Abigail was concerned, the taste was sour. One can hardly blame Mrs. Adams for her lack of enthusiasm about the new Executive Mansion. The Adamses had spent the eight years of John's Vice-Presidency in the comfort of the beautiful mansion Richmond Hill in New York, then in a charming home in Philadelphia.

For three years and eight months of John Adams' Presidency, the family enjoyed the continuity of life in Philadelphia. They knew the city well; they enjoyed the busyness of Philadelphia life, the bustle and activity of a "civilized" community. Like their beloved Boston, Philadelphia had played a leading role in their country's Revolution, and the Adamses felt very much at home there.

But by the end of Adams' term of office, the new Capitol was ready. Although subject to some criticism, the plan to move the government to a new location and let the city grow up around governmental activities met general approval. Space was needed for the conduct of governmental business. And if Washington—Federal City—had little else to recommend it, space it had—in spades. This, of course, was one of the objections to the choice of site. Damp, depressing, on the banks of the Potomac away from the bustle and commerce of Philadelphia and New York, to many people (Abigail Adams among them) the choice of location was not auspicious.

Another factor must have loomed large when the move became imminent, as the Executive Mansion reached completion. John Adams had lost his bid for a second term, which meant that in only four months Thomas Jefferson would be moving into the Executive Mansion. No housewife could possibly be happy at the prospect of packing, moving, and unpacking an entire family's belongings for a four-month sojourn. In Abigail's day, there were no moving vans with crews assigned to come into the house, pack everything efficiently, and then reassemble it as the destination. Moving was a long, laborious task. The ride was bumpy, uneven, and seemingly took forever. To top it off, by the time everything arrived in Washington, many treasures—including more than half of Abigail's tea china—had been broken or stolen en route.

Like his predecessor, who left Mount Vernon ahead of his wife to take up the reins of government in New York, Adams traveled to Washington alone, while Abigail packed and supervised the move from Philadelphia. Arriving in the new capital on November 2, 1800, Adams immediately wrote his wife his prayer for the President's new house and its future inhabitants. Many generations later another President, Franklin Roosevelt, sharing Adams' sense of the historic significance of the move into the White House, resurrected Adams' letter and ordered its words inscribed in gold on the fireplace, just under the mantel in the state dining room:

> I pray Heaven to Bestow
> The Best of Blessings on
>   THIS HOUSE
> and on All that shall hereafter
> Inhabit it. May none but Honest   Nov. 2, 1800
> and Wise Men ever rule under This Roof!   JOHN ADAMS

When Abigail joined her husband, the President's residence was still incomplete. Not a single room was ready for occupancy. There were a few servants on hand to help, but no bells to summon them. There were fireplaces, but no wood ready to use. There was coal on hand, but no grates in which to put it. "Nor were there enough 'lusters,' or lamps," Abigail wrote, "so candles were stuck here and there for light . . . neither the chief staircase nor the outer steps were completed, so the family had to enter the house by temporary wooden stairs and platforms."

To add to the list of grievances, the house had no water supply and, naturally, no bathrooms. Spacious as the grounds were to seem in time, when the Adamses arrived, they were only rough and muddy. The vastness of the mansion made it seem like a huge, cold, empty barn. To heat it, Abigail had to chop wood and keep a fire going constantly in every room. Her efforts helped keep the chill off the house during Washington's cold, miserable winter. (Mrs. John F. Kennedy, in a television tour of the White House in 1962, described Mrs. Adams' fires as the only means she had for keeping the house hospitable. Mrs. Kennedy then commented wryly that "the British added to the flames by burning the White House on the night of August 24, 1814." White House history came full circle with the Kennedys when Mrs. Kennedy, for aesthetic rather than utilitarian reasons, ordered the home fires burning in all the reception rooms, in order to make the White House more inviting and hospitable-looking.)

Mrs. Adams, in addition to her hatchet work, had to clean the White House, and do her own cooking and the family washing. She dried clothes on a line strung across the still-unfinished East Room. Only a woman with Abigail Adams' resilience and indomitable will could have pitched in and worked as she did to get her house in order. Though discouraged about conditions in the "great castle," as she called it, she recognized its potential. "This house is built for ages to come" she said with pride.

Abigail Adams was an extraordinary woman. Many historians have referred to her as the most intellectually gifted of all the First Ladies. She had all the social graces as well, having been the first American woman ever presented at the British court. In addition she had the old New England virtues of industriousness and economy. Just as George Washington combined great personal reserve with generosity of spirit, so too was Abigail Adams a paradox of sorts, a mixture of graciousness and frugality.

Having seen the Washington hospitality at first hand, she was well aware of the out-of-pocket expenses of our first President's official entertaining. She attempted to keep official entertainments to a minimum in order to save as much as possible of her husband's $25,000 salary.

While the Presidency was still ensconced at Philadelphia, Abigail wrote her sister (on June 23, 1797): "Today will be the 5th great dinner I have had, about 36 Gentlemen today, as many more next week, and I shall have got through the whole of Congress, with their apendages. Then comes the 4th of July which is a still more tedious day, as we must have then not only all Congress, but all the Gentlemen of the city, the Governor and officers and companies, all of whom the late President [Washington] used to treat with cake, punch, and wine. What the House would not hold used to be placed at long tables in the yard. As we are here we cannot avoid the trouble or the expense. . . ."

Actually, as her husband did, Abigail loved the significance of Independence Day, and celebrated it with gusto. But when it came to entertaining hordes of politicians and strangers, her New England thrift dominated.

Of course it was imperative that there be some official celebration of the opening of the new Executive Mansion. The ladies of fashion were anxious to see the new home of the President. Pressure was mounting for a scheduled reception. But Mrs. Adams had to replace that broken tea service before she could receive properly. Finally plans were completed, and the big reception was scheduled for New Year's Day, 1801. This was the day the White House was formally opened to the public.

The preparations were elaborate. This was the Adamses' most lavish reception, and Abigail organized it beautifully. Tea, coffee, punch, and wine were served. There were also cakes and tarts, all baked in the new ovens on either side of the enormous kitchen fireplace. In addition, curds, creams, trifles, jellies, floating island, syllabub, sweetmeats, and assorted fruits graced the tables and were passed among the guests. Borrowing court etiquette from Europe, where she had been so well received, Abigail greeted her guests from a thronelike chair. Standing by her side was her husband, nicknamed by a local wag His Rotundity, well-decked out in velvet breeches and lace, his hair powdered in the current fashion.

Everything after the New Year's Day reception was anticlimactic. Because of the short time left in office, the Adamses did little formal entertaining. There were still, of course, the formal calls, which had begun the moment the family arrived in Washington. Despite the hazardous "roads," largely footpaths and cowpaths, the coaches and carriages of ladies from miles away arrived at the White House door. Distances of three and four miles were considerable in those days. Yet everyone was anxious to pay a call on the First Lady in her new home.

Many of the visitors carried or sent gifts of welcome. Meats, vegetables, milk, and yeast were received gladly. Martha Washington, Betty Lewis (George Washington's sister), and George Washington Parke Custis all sent a servant with a haunch of venison for the First Family. With it was included a letter congratulating the Adamses on their arrival in the new house and inviting them to visit Mount Vernon. It was not long before Abigail was spending most of her "spare" time returning calls—there were often as many as fifteen a day to be made.

The dining habits of the Presidential family were relatively simple, at least by Virginia standards. Menus were based largely on the couple's New England heritage, which differed considerably from the Southern heritage of Washington. The difference between our first two Presidents was by and large one of degree, not as dramatic, say, as between McKinley and Teddy Roosevelt, Wilson and Harding, or Eisenhower and Kennedy. The differences between Washington and Adams were largely differences of environment, indicating the cultural climate of Virginia versus that of Massachusetts.

Yield of the land had much to do with the regional differences. The lush soil of the Old Dominion produced luxury crops aplenty. Slaves working in the fields and in the kitchen made life for the well-to-do colonists easy and comfortable. The lavish hospitality offered visitors from plantation to plantation was made possible by the surplus of servants, busy baking cakes, hot breads, and beaten biscuits. The comfortable life of Virginia was patterned after English country living.

Life was considerably harder in Massachusetts, where the rocky land was not so easy to cultivate, where the women of the family helped and worked as hard as the men. A severe climate and shorter planting season resulted in a more restricted, no-nonsense diet, shorn of most luxuries. New England settlers borrowed much from the Indians and became skilled in the uses of basic crops—corn, apples, potatoes, pumpkins, cranberries, and other cold-climate crops. Survival was more difficult, life less polished.

The net result was a plainer cuisine. John Adams noted in his diary that his guests were served dinners that consisted of Indian pudding, molasses, and butter as a first course, with veal, bacon, neck of mutton, and vegetables as a second. Not exactly gourmet cooking at its most inspirational!

However, the Adamses' wide experience in Paris and London and later in social Philadelphia, and their exposure to the Southern cuisine of the Washingtons and others, gave them a taste and respect for a more varied diet. It may well have been Abigail's determined economy that limited their menus, for John noted in his diary several dinners worthy of comment. Adams described one at the home of Miers Fisher, a young Quaker lawyer: "This plain Friend, with his plain but pretty wife with her Thees and Thous, had provided us a costly entertainment: ducks, hams, chickens, beef, pig, tarts, creams, custards, jellies, fools trifles, floating islands, beer, porter, punch, wine."

Another time Adams saw fit to mention the quality of a meal at the home of Chief Justice Chew, describing it wryly: "About four o'clock we were called to dinner. Turtle and every other thing, flummery, jellies, sweetmeats of twenty sorts, trifles, whipped syllabubs, floating islands, fools, etc., with a dessert of fruits, raisins, almonds, pears, peaches. A most sinful feast again! Everything which could delight the eye or allure the taste . . . Parmesan cheese, punch, wine, porter, beer."

The ironic intent of "a most sinful feast" suggests that Adams was not averse to rich foods. One suspects that Abigail's eye on that $25,000 accounted for the more mundane menus at home. It must be said in her favor, however, that what the Adams table lacked in grace, it made up for in graciousness. Abigail was considered a charming and delightful hostess, which suggests perhaps that good conversation is at least half the battle in entertaining.

Years later, John Adams was to write, commenting somewhat critically on Thomas Jefferson's elaborate entertaining at the White House, that "I held levees once a week, that all my time might not be wasted by idle visits. Jefferson's whole eight years was a levee. I dined a large company once or twice a week. Jefferson dined a dozen every day." It was hard for someone brought up with the frugal outlook of New England to understand the hospitality of the South, a hospitality that reached a crescendo during Jefferson's administration.

The food and entertainment habits of our Presidents provide fascinating studies in contrasts. John Adams, with his New England Puritan tradition, wedged in his place in history between two Virginians, provides a vibrant illustration of such contrasts.

◇◇

R E C I P E S

CODFISH CAKES

Although a strong advocate of temperance, John Adams always drank a large tankard of hard cider first thing in the morning. (His liquid equivalent of "an apple a day"?) For breakfast he was exceedingly fond of codfish cakes, which seem to have been eaten by dwellers in the Land of the Cod almost any time of day. And the symbol of Massachusetts is still popular there today. This recipe for codfish cakes has been modernized somewhat, but is essentially the same as in Adams' day.

> *Box of dehydrated codfish (1.6 oz.)*   *Egg*
> *Potatoes*   *Fat for frying*

The dried codfish should be covered with cold water, soaked for 1 hour. Squeeze out as much water as possible. Then place fish and 3 medium potatoes that have been pared and quartered in a saucepan. Fill with cold water until the fish and potatoes are almost covered. Cook over moderate heat. When potatoes are tender drain thoroughly and mash smooth. Beat 1 egg thoroughly, then beat it into the potato-fish mixture. Drop by tablespoons into hot fat (375° F., or until fat browns a 1-inch cube of bread in 1 minute). Cook quickly. Drain on paper towels. John Adams might not approve, but this is delicious served for supper with tomato sauce. *Serves 4*

BAPTIST CAKES

These delicious things make a good hearty breakfast. In John Adams' day, they were as popular as today in certain parts of New England. Only the name changes from state to state. They were called Holy Pokes in Connecticut, Huffjuffs along the Maine coast. On Nantucket today they are called Fried Bread Dough, which of course is precisely what they are—bits of bread dough deep-fried. We like to call them Baptist Cakes. When dough is risen pull up small pieces of the dough. Drop piece by piece into a kettle or pot full of hot fat (bacon fat gives them an extra zing, although plain cooking oil is all right). Immediately the pieces rise to the top, browned on the underside. Quickly turn them over to brown the other side. Do not leave them in the fat more than 2 minutes. They cook very rapidly.

Drain on absorbent paper. Sprinkle with salt and eat warm. Or, even better, serve them with butter and maple syrup, as you would pancakes.

P.S. You can use frozen dough (thawed, of course) or ready-to-bake refrigerated biscuits.

CREAM OF CORN SOUP

Corn was one of the mainstays of the Pilgrims' diet. From friendly Indians the first settlers learned many new uses for this abundant crop. John Adams, like all Massachusetts inhabitants, was brought up on corn dishes. A great favorite was this corn soup.

Onions	*Milk*
Melted butter or margarine	*Cream-style corn (canned)*
Flour	

Cook ¼ cup minced onions in 3 tablespoons melted butter or margarine in a double boiler over low heat. Stir and cook until tender. Then add 3 tablespoons flour and stir until smooth. Slowly add 4 cups milk and continue stirring until smooth. Cook until thickened slightly. Then add 2 cups canned creamed corn. Cook about 5 minutes, but do not boil; serve hot. *Serves 6.*

GREEN TURTLE SOUP

Shortly before an elaborate dinner party for the diplomatic corps, Abigail Adams had a caller. A good friend, Captain Hay, had just returned from the West Indies. He had with him a small remembrance for Abigail, a token from his trip—a 114-pound turtle! Abigail later wrote: "Though it gave us a good deal of pain to receive so valuable a present, we could not refuse it without affronting him. And it certainly happened in a most fortunate time!" Lucky diplomatic corps!

Veal knuckle	*Bay leaf*
Carrots	*Thyme*
Onions	*Salt and pepper*
Tomatoes	*Turtle meat*
Celery	*Sherry*
Water	*Hard-boiled egg*
Marjoram	*Lemon slices*

Brown 4 pounds veal knuckle in a large kettle. Use just enough fat to keep the meat from burning. When deeply browned, add 2 carrots, 2 sliced onions, 3 cups tomatoes, and 2 stalks celery. Put in 3 quarts water, along with ¼ teaspoon marjoram, 1 bay leaf, ¼ teaspoon thyme, and salt and pepper to taste. Simmer slowly over a low fire for 3 or 4 hours. When nearly tender, cook the cut-up meat from 1 turtle in a separate pan with 1 cup sherry. Cook slowly for 15 minutes. Strain the veal broth and add it to the turtle. Add 1 hard-boiled egg, minced fine, and serve the soup hot, with slices of lemon floating on top. If you prefer a thicker soup, add a little flour blended with butter. *Serves 10 to 12,* a handful by Presidential standards.

NEW ENGLAND POACHED SALMON WITH EGG SAUCE

Visitors to the New York World's Fair in 1964 and 1965 at the Festival of Gas Restaurant were able to eat the same dinner Abigail and John Adams served at their Massachusetts home on the first Independence Day, July 4, 1776. Actually, Mrs. Adams had first served the meal in 1773. It was so memorable she decided the "American" quality of it made it perfect as an Independence Day dinner. It has since become a tradition in many New England homes. The menu consisted of Green Turtle Soup and New England Salmon with Egg Sauce, with Apple Pan Dowdy for dessert. As accompaniment to the salmon were the first new potatoes and early peas. Salmon begin to run along the Atlantic Coast in late June, so this was a most seasonal dinner.

Whole salmon	*Onions*
Peppercorns	*Clove*
Bay leaf	*Butter*
Lemon slices	*Flour*
Parsley	*Salt*
Milk	*Pepper*
Light cream	*Eggs*

To poach a salmon: Use a whole salmon or a 4-to-6 pound center-cut piece. Wrap the washed, cleaned piece in cheesecloth, leaving long ends extending, so it may be removed from the broth after cooking. Boil in 2 to 3 quarts salted water 3 or 4 peppercorns, a bay leaf, a couple of lemon slices. Boil 15 minutes, reduce heat and let liquid simmer, then add the salmon. Turn up the heat until liquid boils again, then simmer slowly until salmon is cooked. Allow 6 to 8 minutes per pound. When salmon flakes easily it is done. Do not overcook. When done, lift fish from the broth and remove cheesecloth. Place on a hot serving platter, skin carefully, and garnish with lemon wedges and parsley. Serve with Egg Sauce. *Serves 4 to 6.*

To make Egg Sauce: Heat 1 cup milk with 1 cup light cream, 2 small onions sliced thin, ½ bay leaf, and 1 whole clove until a film forms. Skim the surface.

Melt 3 tablespoons butter in a pan, stir in 3 tablespoons flour, stir till smooth; cook over low heat a few moments. Pour in scalded milk mixture and continue cooking over low heat until mixture bubbles. Remove from fire, season with 1 teaspoon salt and a dash white pepper, then strain into a saucepan. Add 2 hard-boiled eggs, coarsely chopped, and heat through. If sauce is too thick, add a little light cream. Serve separately in a sauceboat.

NEW ENGLAND CLAM CHOWDER

Chowder, a distortion of the French word *chaudière,* means any stewed concoction of fish or shellfish or both. Controversy still rages between New England and New York about the merits of clam chowder with or without tomatoes. (Down Easters in Maine once introduced a bill in the state legislature to outlaw forever the mixing of clams with tomatoes, which shows how heated the dispute can become.) Every New England state has its own favorite variation of the basic clam chowder, which MUST have clams and salt pork (or bacon). This particular one is favored by Massachusetts addicts, such as the Adams family.

Hard clams	*Potato*
Onion	*Milk*
Salt pork	*Pepper*
Flour	

Strain the juice from 1½ dozen hard clams through a dampened piece of cheesecloth. Set aside. Take out the clams and put them and 1 medium-sized onion through a meat grinder. Put 3 ounces of salt pork, chopped into 3 or 4 pieces, into a heavy kettle over a low heat. Remove the salt pork after it has heated a few minutes, and sauté the clams and onions in the remaining fat for about 5 minutes. Then sift in 2 tablespoons flour. Mix well with the onion and clams, and continue cooking. Add 1 diced potato and the clam juice. Cover and simmer until the potato is cooked—about 10 minutes. Meanwhile bring 3 pints milk to a boil and combine with the clam mixture. Season with pepper (and salt if necessary) and serve hot, accompanied by oyster crackers. *Serves 4.*

JOHNNY CAKE

No, Johnny Cake was not named after John Adams, tempting as it might be to believe so. The name is a corruption of *journey cake,* a hard compact biscuit that could easily be carried in the pocket on a long trip. In Adams' day, it was the custom to serve johnny cakes with clams and always to have them at a clambake. Even more popular at breakfast or as dessert at Sunday night supper, johnny cake was served with maple syrup or maple sugar. Rhode Island Johnny Cake is most famous and was always made with a special oyster-gray-colored cornmeal, even today stone-ground. In the times of John Adams johnny cake was jonny cake. You ate it and liked it. Everyone did.

Salt	*Scalded milk*
White cornmeal	*or*
	Boiling water

Add 1 teaspoon salt to ½ cup white cornmeal (use yellow if you prefer to be New England-authentic—white was favored in the South) and pour on 1 cup scalded milk or boiling water gradually. Spread the mixture ¼ inch deep in a shallow buttered oblong baking pan. If you prefer, you may drop by teaspoonfuls in small buttered muffin pans. Dot with butter if desired. Bake in moderate (350° F.) oven until crisp. Split and spread with butter. Serve hot, *for 4.*

OLD-FASHIONED WELSH APPLE BUTTER

Apples, the staple crop of our forefathers, lent themselves to many delicious dishes. New Englanders loved them in pies, tarts, and other desserts. Or in apple butter served with hot biscuits and breads. This Massachusetts favorite would have been a side dish on the Adams table.

Applesauce	*Cinnamon*
Brown sugar	*Vinegar*
Cloves	

Mix 7 cups of smooth apple sauce (Abigail Adams would have had to make her own. Today we have access to the supermarket. Changing times.) with 5 cups brown sugar, ½ teaspoon cloves, 1 teaspoon cinnamon, and 1 cup vinegar. Mix until smooth. Then bake in a moderate to slow (325°–350° F.) oven, stirring now and then to keep from sticking. When the mixture is thick and clear, remove and cool. *Makes 5 pints.*

MONKEY BISCUITS

Another old-timer delicious served with butter and jam or apple butter. It's a fine way to use up stale biscuits.

Butter	*Day-old biscuits*
Molasses	

Put 2 tablespoons butter and ½ cup molasses into a skillet. Heat slightly, then put in split day-old biscuits. Fry both sides. Serve hot.

SCOOTIN-LONG-THE-SHORE

New Englanders had an amusing way of naming rather plain cooking. Visitors to Massachusetts are always particularly mystified by the popular Scootin-long-the-shore—until they taste it. It is actually a type of New England boiled dinner, made with potatoes, onions, and salt pork. Fishermen invented it and prepared it on the beach as they "scooted along," tending their lines.

Potatoes
Onions
Salt pork or bacon fat

Slice raw potatoes very thin; add thinly sliced onions. Cook in a skillet in bacon fat until crusty. Serve, as they do on Martha's Vineyard where the dish originated, as an accompaniment to fried or boiled fish. Or, if you prefer, as a side dish with meat.

ELEVEN FISH ROASTED ON A PLANK

Eleven Fish was the name the Dutch settlers gave shad, because it arrived on the eleventh of March. The first shad was presented to the Governor. Times changed, subsequently, as shad became more and more common. Delicious as it was, it nevertheless became known as the "poor man's fish." This didn't keep the rich from enjoying it on the sly. Adams, like his predecessor, was a shad man. In Adams' day, the rule in New England was to cook the dark meat of the shad 5 minutes longer after the bones were removed (or cover the white meat with buttered paper so it would not overcook). The Dutch cooked their shad on a birch plank over the coals of a wood fire. New Englanders used a clean oak board.

Shad
Salt
Butter

The most important ingredient, next to the shad, is a good oak board about 3 inches thick and 2 feet square. Stand the board next to the fire until it is very hot, almost charred. Meanwhile split the shad down the back, clean, wash, wipe dry, and season with salt to taste. When the board is ready, fasten the fish to the board with a few small nails. The skin side should be next to the board. Put the board over the fire with the head down. When the juices begin to run, reverse it. It should be turned quickly to retain the juices. As soon as the shad is cooked, butter it and serve piping hot. It should be served on the board.

SUMMER AND WINTER SUCCOTASH

Corn and beans were the Massachusetts colonists' first vegetables. The Indians taught them to use corn (which they called "our life") in soup, bread, mush—in fact as their staff of life. When the Indians boiled corn whole, they called it M'sickquatash. The settlers combined it with beans and called it Succotash. Summer Succotash was made from tender ears of corn and young string beans. Dried corn and dried beans became Winter Succotash. Today we find it a dish for all seasons.

Lima beans	*Sugar*
Corn	*Water*
Butter	*Heavy cream*
Salt and pepper	

Cook 2 cups fresh lima beans or 2 packages frozen limas in boiling salted water until they are tender. (Frozen ones should be cooked according to package directions.) Mix the beans with 2 cups whole-kernel corn (if fresh, cut it off the cob; if canned, drain it; if frozen, use right from the package), 2 tablespoons butter, 1 teaspoon salt, a dash of pepper, 1 teaspoon sugar, and ½ cup water. Cook over low heat 10 to 15 minutes. Drain, then add ¼ cup heavy cream. Heat thoroughly, but do not boil. *Serves 4 to 6.*

PLYMOUTH SUCCOTASH

Even before John Adams' day, it was the custom in Plymouth, Massachusetts, to celebrate Forefathers' Day, December 21, the day the Pilgrims landed, with a special feast consisting of Succotash, hot johnny cake, and Indian pudding, all foods native to the New World. Plymouth succotash is a very special dish, still cherished for its history and associations. Different from regular succotash, it is really a stew that gets better and better as it gets older. It is in truth a leftover delight. This recipe dates back to the old days of Plymouth.

Navy or pea beans	*Bay leaves*
Onions	*Parsley*
Bouquet garni	*Thyme*
Salt	*Turnip*
Chicken	*Potatoes*
Corned beef rump	*Hulled corn*
Salt pork	

Soak 1½ lbs. navy or pea beans overnight (change water several times). Then place in a large pot, cover with cold water, add 3 medium onions peeled and quartered, and a bouquet garni made of 1 large bay leaf and 12 sprigs of fresh parsley tied together with thread. Salt lightly and bring the mixture to a boil. Turn down heat and simmer slowly until almost tender. Discard the bouquet garni. Keep the mixture in the pot warm.

Then clean and wash a 5-pound chicken and put a peeled onion inside. Wash a 4-pound piece of corned beef rump and a 1-pound piece of fat salt pork. Put all 3 in a pot, cover with cold water, bring to a boil. Then add 3 bay leaves, small bunch of fresh parsley, and 2 sprigs thyme, all tied together. Bring to a slow boil, then let simmer gently until all are tender. Remove each as it is cooked—chicken first, salt pork next, corned beef last. Save the broth for soup stock or sauces.

Meanwhile cut 1 small yellow turnip into small cubes and 5 medium potatoes into thin slices; cover with cold water and cook until tender. In another pan cook 3 quarts hulled corn (or 3 large cans hominy) in enough water to tenderize. Remove most of the fat from the first broth. Take 1½ gallons of broth; bring to a boil. Add the cooked beans (sieved) and mashed turnip-potato mixture. Cut the meat and chicken into serving pieces, add to the mixture, and heat well. Season to taste with salt and pepper. Serve hot, although it can be kept for days, the flavor getting better and better as the days pass. *Serves 20 generously.*

INDIAN PUDDING

References to Indian pudding occurred frequently in John Adams' letters. That it was served in the Adams home on the first Fourth of July indicates the honor the family accorded it. It was a standard and favorite dessert throughout New England, a real classic with the Adamses.

> *Milk*
> *Cornmeal*
> *Butter*
> *Molasses*
> *Salt*
> *Cinnamon*
> *Ginger*
> *Eggs*

Scald 1 quart milk. Put ½ cup cornmeal in the top of a double boiler and pour the scalded milk over it slowly, stirring constantly. Cook for 20 minutes over hot water. Mix together 2 tablespoons butter, ½ cup molasses, 1 teaspoon salt, 1 teaspoon cinnamon, ¼ teaspoon ground ginger, and 2 eggs. (Use dark molasses for the true Indian pudding flavor.) Add slowly to the cornmeal mixture. Put in a heavy buttered baking dish and set it in a pan of hot water in the oven. Bake at 350° F. for 1 hour. If you let it stand a full hour after baking it will be firmer. Serve with heavy cream, hard sauce, or vanilla ice cream. *Serves 6.*

NEW ENGLAND GINGERBREAD

John Adams once called molasses "an essential ingredient in American independence." He was referring to the Molasses Act of 1733, passed by the British Parliament. He might as well have been referring to its role in American cooking. Crisp ginger cookies, light gingerbread, the perennially popular Indian pudding, and strong New England rum all owed their existence to good, stout, dark molasses. Three cheers!

Butter	*Egg*
Molasses	*Flour*
Soda	*Ginger*
Sour milk	*Salt*

Add ⅓ cup butter to 1 cup molasses and heat over low fire until the butter melts. Add 1½ teaspoons soda and beat thoroughly. Next add ½ cup sour milk and 1 well-beaten egg to the mixture. Sift 2 cups flour with 2 teaspoons ginger and ½ teaspoon salt. Add the sifted ingredients to the molasses mixture. Beat well. Spread the mixture in a well-buttered shallow baking pan. Bake in a moderately slow (325° F.) oven 25 to 35 minutes. Serve warm with a spoonful of whipped cream on top of each piece.

APPLE PAN DOWDY

Apples, like molasses, were a standby in New England desserts. John Adams showed his preference for Apple Pan Dowdy by having it on Independence Day. And, indeed, what could be more American than Apple Pan Dowdy? Or the taste of John Adams himself?

Flour	*Sugar*
Salt	*Cinnamon*
Shortening	*Nutmeg*
Ice water	*Apples*
Melted butter	*Molasses*

To make the pastry: Sift 1½ cups flour with a dash of salt. Blend in ½ cup shortening until the mixture is mealy. Sprinkle a little ice water over the mixture, just enough to hold the dough together. Roll the pastry out, brush with ¼ cup melted butter, and cut pastry in half. Place the halves on top of each other and cut again. Repeat until you have 16 separate but equal pieces of pastry piled on top of each other, then chill them a full hour. Roll the pastry once again, cut in half, and line the bottom of a baking dish with one half. Save the other half for the top. Keep both on ice while making the filling.

To make the filling: Mix ½ cup sugar with ½ teaspoon cinnamon, ¼ teaspoon salt, and ¼ teaspoon nutmeg. Peel and core 10 large apples. Cut them into thin slices. Mix the apples with sugar-spice mixture and place in pastry-lined dish. Combine ½ cup molasses (or maple syrup) with 3 tablespoons melted butter and ¼ cup water. Pour this over the apples. Cover with the top pastry layer and seal. Place in a preheated hot (400° F.) oven for 10 minutes, then reduce heat to low (325° F.). After reducing the heat, "dowdy" the dish by cutting the crust into the apples with a sharp knife. Return dish to oven and bake a full hour. Serve hot with vanilla ice cream or with heavy cream or whipped cream. *Serves 6.*

APPLE TREATS

Although apples suggest New England, this recipe came from a cookbook written by Martha Jefferson. After Martha collected the recipes, her proud gourmet father had the book printed, and Abigail Adams brought it home to Quincy, Massachusetts, where she fixed apple treats for her husband and family. Loving apples as they did, it was naturally a hit. As there was no baking powder in the eighteenth century, the recipe has been amended a little—but only a little.

Egg	*Baking powder*
Brown sugar	*Salt*
Milk	*Melted butter*
Flour	*Apples*

Beat 1 egg slightly. Add it to ½ cup firmly packed brown sugar and ½ cup milk. Sift ½ cup flour with 2 teaspoons baking powder and 1 teaspoon salt. Add to the egg mixture and beat well. Add ¼ cup melted butter and 2 cups diced tart apples. Mix well and spread the mixture evenly in a well-buttered 9- by 7-inch pan. Bake in a fairly hot (375° F.) oven for 25 minutes or so, until done. Delicious served warm. *Serves 4 to 6.*

FLUMMERY

John Adams spoke lovingly of this old New England dessert whenever it was served him. Sometimes made with raspberries or strawberries, it is really at its best with blueberries. Like many a Yankee dish, it often travels incognito under various other names, two of the most curious being Blueberry Grunt or Blueberry Slump. But to President Adams it was Flummery, and that is good enough for us.

Blueberries
Sugar
Buttered bread

Place 4 cups washed blueberries in a pan, add 1 cup sugar, and cook for 10 minutes over a low fire. Butter 8 bread slices generously. Trim the crusts and line a baking dish with the bread. Cut the slices to make them fit well. Pour a little of the berry mixture over the bread, add a layer of bread, then more berries, alternating layers until finished. Make the last layer berries. Bake the "pudding" in a moderate (350° F.) oven for 20 minutes. Chill in the refrigerator until time to serve. Serve with whipped cream flavored with nutmeg. *Six servings.*

FLOATING ISLAND

President Adams feigned dismay at such rich and fancy dishes as Floating Island. In truth he loved rich desserts. Floating Island is simply a boiled custard with whipped cream or meringue on top. But if you want to be extra fancy, you can make it the way Thomas Jefferson's cook James did and call it, as Jefferson was wont to do, *Oeufs à la Neige,* Snow Eggs. James flavored his with rose or orange-flower water. We have used almond extract.

Eggs	*Milk*
Sugar	*Salt*
Vanilla	*Almond extract*
Light cream	

Beat 4 egg yolks with ½ cup sugar until well blended. Flavor with ½ teaspoon vanilla. Put aside. Heat 1 cup light cream with 1 cup milk in a saucepan. Beat 3 egg whites with a dash of salt until they stand in stiff peaks. Beat in ½ cup sugar, then 1 teaspoon almond extract. With a teaspoon scoop out egg-shaped sections of the meringue. Remove the milk-cream mixture from the fire and drop the meringue "eggs" into the hot milk, a few at a time. Put the pan on a low heat again. Poach the meringues 2 to 4 minutes, turning them once gently. Lift the meringues out of the milk and place on a tea towel or paper towel. Now add the hot cream–milk mixture to the custard in a slow steady stream, stirring all the while. Put in a double boiler and cook about 15 minutes over low heat, stirring constantly, until custard is thick enough to coat a wooden spoon. When finished, chill. When ready to serve, put custard in serving bowl and arrange Snow Eggs (or Floating Island) decoratively around the top. *Serves 6.*

HASTY PUDDING

Puddings were a favorite New England commodity in Adams' time. They were easy for a housewife to make for a large gathering, the ingredients usually were at hand, they were an unpretentious way to satisfy a hankering for sweets, and they were economical. All these reasons made them ideal to Abigail Adams, who served puddings frequently. Least pretentious of any, and eaten in all eighteenth-century homes, was Hasty Pudding, which is nothing more or less than boiled cornmeal mush served hot with maple sugar and butter. A magazine account of the period tells how to eat Hasty Pudding:

> The hasty-pudding being spread out equally on a plate, while hot, an *excavation* is made in the middle of it with a *spoon,* into which *excavation* a piece of butter as large as a nutmeg is put, and upon it a spoonful of brown sugar. . . . The butter, being soon heated by the heat of the pudding, mixes with the sugar and forms a sauce, which, *being confined in the excavation,* occupies the *middle of the plate.* Thus for the array—now for the battle! Dip each *spoonful* in the *sauce, before it is carried to the mouth,* care being had in taking it up to begin on the outside and near the brim of the plate, and to approach the center by gradual advances, in order not to demolish too soon the *excavation* which forms the reservoir of *sauce.*

Recipes for Cornmeal Mush are on the sides of all cornmeal packages. We prefer using yellow cornmeal, as its golden color is more appetizing when cooked. For a change, instead of maple sugar or brown sugar, try using maple syrup with it. It is a delicious breakfast dish on cold winter mornings.

In order to avoid lumps you may mix 1 cup cornmeal with 1 cup of water and stir into 3 cups rapidly boiling, salted water. Or use *all* cold water. Unorthodox but very easy. Simply cook and stir till thick. Cover and keep warm *over* hot water to develop mellow flavor.

PUMPKIN PIE

Sometime after Columbus discovered America, the lowly pumpkin (*pompion* the Indians called it) found its way to Europe via the Middle East. Europeans called it Turkish cucumber and didn't know quite what to do with it. It took the Pilgrims a while to find out themselves. First they tried mixing stewed pumpkin with cornmeal to make bread. Finally they stumbled on the idea of pie and insured their culinary reputation forever. Pumpkin pie was a great favorite in the days of John and Abigail Adams; its fame later spread from New England to the whole country. Fortunately today, with canned pumpkin, much of the work has been taken out of pumpkin-pie making.

Cooked pumpkin, canned or fresh	*Cinnamon*
Brown sugar	*Cloves*
Granulated sugar	*Eggs*
Flour	*Milk*
Ginger, Salt	*Unbaked pastry shell*

Mix 1½ cups cooked pumpkin with ½ cup brown sugar, firmly packed and ½ cup granulated sugar. Then sift 1 tablespoon flour, ¼ teaspoon ginger, ¼ teaspoon salt, 1 teaspoon cinnamon, and ¼ teaspoon cloves together. Combine 2 slightly beaten eggs with 1 cup milk. Mix pumpkin mixture with dry mixture and stir thoroughly. Add the egg–milk mixture, being sure all ingredients are well mixed. Pour the mixture into an 8-inch unbaked pie shell. Bake in a hot (425° F.) oven for 45 to 50 minutes, or until done. Serve warm or cold, topped with whipped cream.

GOOSEBERRY FOOL

This particular dish has been claimed as a Colonial Virginia invention, but it actually came from England—name and all—and its fame went far beyond Virginia's border. John Adams enjoyed it many times when he dined out, and there is no reason to believe that he might not have eaten it at home too. Popular dishes had a way of traveling quickly through the new states. Indicative of the changes in food preferences through the centuries, gooseberries are now long gone from the marketplace. Unless you have your own private gooseberry patch, you may want to substitute strawberries, raspberries, or blackberries— today's more popular berries—and call it a plain Berry Fool. Presumably once you have tasted it, you will be a fool for it every time.

Gooseberries (or other berries)	*Grated lemon rind*
Water	*Heavy cream*
Sugar	*Crumbled macaroons*

Combine 1 quart ripe berries with ¼ cup water in a pan, cooking over a low fire until the fruit is tender. Remove from fire and put through a sieve until you have a smooth purée. While still hot, stir 1 cup sugar and 1½ teaspoons grated lemon rind into purée and set mixture aside to cool. Whip 1½ cups heavy cream until it has shape, then fold it into the cool purée. Spoon the mixture into a serving bowl, sprinkle the top with macaroon crumbs, and chill thoroughly. (Or serve it as it was served in Adams' day, with a plate of cookies.) *Serves 6.*

NEW ENGLAND CIDER CUP

As soon as he got out of bed, President Adams indulged a practice he had followed all his adult life—he drank a large tankard of cider. Whether apple cider is as efficacious as a plain apple is a point that may be debated, but the fact remains that Adams lived to the ripe age of ninety-one. One might reasonably claim the cider couldn't have *hurt* him.

Sweet cider	*Lemon juice*
Sparkling water	*Lemon peel*
Sherry	*Sugar*
Cognac	

Add 1 quart sweet cider to 1 pint sparkling water, ⅓ cup sherry, ¼ cup cognac, 2 tablespoons lemon juice, and the peel of ½ lemon, cut into thin strips. Add sugar to taste. Then stir the mixture with ice until thoroughly chilled. To be fancy, as this drink deserves, you may abandon Adams' tankard and serve in punch cups or champagne glasses, dusted with a dash of nutmeg. A delightful party drink. *Makes 12 servings, 4 ounces each.*

III

A Gourmet in the White House

Thomas Jefferson distinguished himself in many areas of American life. The eighteenth-century equivalent of the Compleat, or Renaissance Man, he applied his incisive mind to many diverse activities. His brilliance and accomplishments in many fields make him, still, our most intellectual President. In fact, in 1963, President John F. Kennedy, on the occasion of a dinner for Nobel Prize winners at the White House, commented that there had never been such a gathering of brilliant minds in the White House, "with the possible exception of Thomas Jefferson dining alone."

Much has been written of Jefferson's importance in our nation's political life. Less is known of his contributions to our culinary heritage. Many of his innovations are today an accepted part of our national diet. Yet without his adventurous palate and active interest in a wide range of foods, American cuisine might have continued indefinitely along a humdrum English path. Of course later waves of immigration brought new dishes and flavors to our cuisine, but it was Jefferson who pioneered diversity in our diet.

During the 1785–1789 period, Jefferson served as Treaty Commissioner to France. In his four years in Paris he sampled widely French cuisine, making copious notes of dishes he liked so he could serve them back home. Today there are organized Gourmet Tours of Europe, but in the 1790s Jefferson made similar tours on his own. (His was perhaps the *original* cook's tour.) Everywhere he traveled he explored the delicacies of the region.

In Holland he sampled waffles for the first time and was so pleased he immediately bought a waffle iron, noting the cost at 1.3 florins. A particular tea in Amsterdam appealed to him; he bought some to take along. In Nancy it was chocolate that caught his fancy, and in southern France he made notes on the differences in oranges in various communities he visited. At Nice he discovered ortolans (small birds eaten in Europe) and paid 6 francs for a dozen. Notes made on a visit to Rozzano included details of butter- and Parmesan-cheese-making. He tasted a frozen delicacy and observed that "snow gives the most delicate flavor to creams, but ice is the most powerful congealer and lasts longer."

Like many a traveler returning home, Jefferson missed the dishes to which he had become accustomed. To his valet returning after him he sent a request for him to "bring a stock of macaroni, Parmesan cheese, figs of Marseilles, Brugnoles, raisins, almonds, mustard, *vinaigre* d'Estragon, other vinegar, oil and anchovies."

Jefferson's inauguration brought many changes to the Presidency. Even the inauguration was a portent of a new style to come. Jefferson walked to the ceremony from his boardinghouse, wearing his usual clothes, those of an ordinary citizen, and later walked home again. It was his intention to simplify the trappings of the Presidency, to remind the people that the President was, after all, simply one of them. He wanted the first Presidential inauguration in the new Federal City kept simple.

One of Jefferson's first official acts as President was to abolish the levees and drawing rooms. A fifty-seven-year-old widower, he had become accustomed to dining informally. He was to continue this in the White House. His daughter Mary was a retiring young woman, shy with strangers, but her sister Martha had been educated in Paris and was used to the official and diplomatic niceties. It was Martha, therefore, who attempted to spend as much time as she could with her father, acting as his official hostess whenever necessary. Unfortunately, with a family of twelve children, her time at the White House was limited.

It was Jefferson's wish to limit public ceremony to the traditional Fourth of July and New Year's Day receptions. He declined to celebrate his own birthday—April 13—with the usual Birthday Ball. The "only birthday which he wished to Commemorate" was the Declaration of Independence.

Other changes in custom were small, but significant for later generations. The President's Palace became the President's House. (It was not actually called the White House until much, much later, as we shall see.) Instead of bowing to those he met, Jefferson began the practice of shaking hands with them. He dressed in homespun, not out of affectation but to signify that he was a common citizen and—even more important—to stimulate the development of home industries in the new states. Further, he abolished preferential treatment for official dining, substituting what he called the "pell mell" system. People invited for dinner simply went into the dining room as they reached the door; rank was ignored. To eliminate the protocol of precedence at the table, Jefferson installed a circular table, so all might be equal. He considered this more democratic.

Even dinner invitations became less formal. Instead of *The President of the United States invites . . .* Jefferson wrote by hand *T. W. Jefferson requests the favor of ——'s company to dinner the day after tomorrow at half after three o'clock. . . .*

Of course such changes did not occur without repercussions. Hostesses in Washington were outraged that the levees and drawing rooms had been abolished. In fact, a group of ladies called on Jefferson to protest his decision. The Jefferson charm must have been considerable, for the ladies left completely won over to his position.

He had less luck with the British Minister and his wife, Mr. and Mrs. Merry. Never was a couple so misnamed—at least in reference to Jefferson, for they were to plague him as long as they remained in Washington. They were first affronted by his democratic manners when they came to call. The President greeted them in carpet slippers. Soon thereafter they were insulted again, or so they thought. Dinner was announced, and President Jefferson offered his arm to Mrs. James Madison, who served as his hostess when his daughter was not present. Secretary of State Madison proceeded to offer his arm to the lady nearest him. Other Cabinet members followed the leader and did the same. The Merrys were in a state of shock at such neglect. The "first come, first served" rule was an affront to their etiquette system. When a similar incident occurred at the Madisons' some time later, the Merrys became so incensed that they refused further invitations from both Jefferson and the Madisons, who seemed not to notice. Once, however, when Mrs. Merry made a particularly caustic remark about Dolley Madison, Jefferson was irritated enough to comment that if she kept it up, "She will have to eat her soup at home."

During his sojourn in France, Jefferson had acquired "the habit of mitigating business with dinner." He followed this custom ever after. Even during his years as President, he entertained informally at dinner each day, almost always inviting a small group, usually no more than fourteen, sometimes as few as four. The company was selected, according to one observer, "in reference to their tastes, habits, and suitability in all respects, which attempt had a wonderful effect in making his parties more agreeable than dinner parties usually are."

Jefferson valued the informality and conviviality of the dinner table as a background for political discussions. Many a relationship with a friendly foreign country was solidified over *veau l'estaufade*. In fact, when Jefferson was Secretary of State, the plans for the site of the new Capitol and its name were decided upon at one of his dinner parties.

There were two dining rooms in the White House, but Jefferson, preferring to dine intimately, ate most frequently in the smaller of the two, the Green Room. He complained that the White House itself was "big enough for two emperors and the grand llama" and if he had had his way (he had submitted a design anonymously before the building was constructed) it would have been a much smaller house.

Jefferson's Monticello hospitality was legend; his overseer claimed that guests arrived "in gangs" and "almost ate him out of house and home. I have killed a fine beef and it would all be eaten in a day or two. There was no tavern in all that country that had so much company." Even so, in his official entertaining, Jefferson always favored small dinners, where good conversation could flow through half the night. The guests did not leave soon after dinner, as they had at Washington's parties.

One of Jefferson's guests commented on the quality of the Presidential dinners: "Never before had such dinners been given in the President's house, nor such a variety of the finest and most costly wines. In his entertainments republican simplicity was united with epicurean delicacy; while the absence of splendor, ornament and profusion was more than compensated by the neatness, order and elegant sufficiency that pervaded the whole establishment. . . ."

Senator Plumer of New Hampshire wrote, December 25, 1802: "His way is to have about ten members of Congress at a time. We sat down to the table at 4 P.M. and rose at 6 and walked immediately into another room and drank coffee. We had a very good dinner with a profusion of fruits and sweetmeats. The wine was the best I ever drank, particularly the champagne, which was delicious."

It was Jefferson's custom to limit his invitations severely whenever he wished "to enjoy a free and unrestricted flow of conversation." When Alexander, Baron von Humboldt, a distinguished German scientist, visited Washington, he was invited to dinner *tete à tete*. The visitor commented on the dumbwaiters, small hand-operated elevators that brought all the dishes from the kitchen below to the dining room. In this way there were no interruptions by servants, no tales from the dinner table repeated by outsiders, spies or gossips. Jefferson often told visitors from abroad: "You need not speak so low. We are alone and our walls have no ears."

In answer to Humboldt's remark about the dumbwaiters, the President replied that when he had friends for dinner whose conversation he valued or with whom his talk was confidential, he used these "silent servants." The Baron said later: "Surely I was more gratified by this compliment than I would have been by the most costly and splendid banquet."

Congressmen, foreign ministers, and private citizens invited to the President's house for dinner left with much the same impression. They were elated by the cuisine, invigorated by the high level of conversation, and charmed by the attention of the President himself. Two of Jefferson's favorite dinner companions were James Madison and Albert Gallatin, Secretary of the Treasury and a financier of the first rank. Henry Adams wrote about this triumvirate: "Three more agreeable men than Jefferson, Madison and Gallatin were never collected round the dinner table of the White House; and their difference in age was enough to add zest to their friendship; for Jefferson was born in 1743, Madison in 1751 and Gallatin in 1761."

Jefferson invented another type of dumbwaiter to insure security and privacy at his dinners. Ever the gadgeteer, he developed revolving shelves in the wall between the dining room and the pantry. A touch of a hidden spring and the shelves would swing into the dining room loaded with hot delicacies, while the shelves stacked with empty dishes would swing away into the pantry. Visitors were impressed by his ingenuity and reassured by the privacy such ingenuity maintained.

You might think that by abolishing levees and drawing rooms, Jefferson was trying to simplify the obligations of the Presidency. On the contrary. He wanted to maintain a freer, more open type of Presidency than had existed before, one in which all the people could participate. People appeared at the White House before breakfast and were welcomed by the President. He even invited his butcher to dinner one evening. The man arrived with his son, saying that he had heard one of the other guests was ill, and since there would be an extra plate, he thought his son would enjoy coming along. With his usual aplomb, Jefferson introduced the butcher and son to the distinguished company and saw to it they were well provided for during the evening. It seems to have been Jefferson's intention to combine the hospitality of his native Virginia with his own innate republicanism and feelings toward his fellow citizens. Judging by records of his food bills, he certainly succeeded.

After adding up his first-year-in-office expenses, the President discovered that his income did not cover the cost of his dinner parties. He kept careful and detailed accounts of expenses. Costs for that first year came to $4504.84 for provisions, $2003.71 for groceries, $2787.28 for wines, and $2675.84 for servants. The President maintained a staff of fourteen, which was five more than the entire personnel of the State Department. Jefferson's wine bill for his eight years in office came to $10,855.90. Considering the average costs of his era, the President's out-of-pocket entertainment expenses were enormous.

It is a fascinating paradox that Jefferson should have had such fervent republican convictions and at the same time such epicurean tastes, such simplicity in dress and manner, and such style and polish in his dining habits. He eliminated the pomp and ceremony of official entertaining and offered superb food simply but elegantly served. He took great pride in the White House. To protect the splendid floor of the large dining room, he had a green canvas cover spread over it the day of a dinner party. After dinner the canvas was removed. This was done, he said, "to secure a very handsome floor from grease and the scouring which that necessitates."

President Jefferson was particularly addicted to intricate dishes and brought back from Paris a large repertoire of French specialties. His bouilli, daubes, ragoûts, gâteaux, soufflés, ices, sauces, and wine cookery, which had delighted dinner guests from Washington's administration onward, prompted a certain amount of criticism as well. Patrick Henry denounced him in a political speech as a man who had "abjured his native victuals" and turned his back on good, old-fashioned roast beef. Jefferson confessed a preference for French cooking "because the meats were more tender."

Actually, Jefferson was not dogmatic about food, but was willing to accept a dish on its merits, be it French, Italian, or Indian. His menus at the White House were often combinations of diverse cuisines. This caused a New England clergyman to complain that "fried eggs and fried beef were served at the same dinner with turkey, ducks, and rounds of beef."

So interested was Jefferson in what he called the technical art of cooking that he often accompanied his servant to market, in the hopes of finding some special delicacy he particularly liked. He was especially fond of fresh vegetables and kept a careful chart of the seasons when certain ones would be available in the local market. Several of his favorites were not commonly accepted by his fellow Americans until many generations, in fact over a century, later. His long list of thirty-seven vegetables included:

> Broccoli — purchasable from April 7 to April 20
> Mushrooms —   "   "   August 11 to October 19
> Endive —   "   "   September 27 to February 29

In addition, he kept a *Garden Book* that noted the time each vegetable was planted at Monticello, its full name and origin (the seeds were often imported or traded with neighbors or friends), and the date it was first served during the season. Here are a few of his notations for 1774:

May 14.   Cherries ripe.
May 16.   First dish of peas from earliest patch.
May 26.   A second patch of peas come to table.
June 4.   Windsor beans come to table.
June 5.   A third and fourth patch of peas come to table.
June 13.   A fifth patch of peas come in.
July 13.   Last dish of peas.
July 18.   Last lettuce from Gehee's.
July 23.   Cucumbers from our garden.
July 31.   Watermelons from our patch.
Aug. 3.   Indian corn comes to table.
          Black-eyed peas come to table.
Nov. 16.   The first frost sufficient to kill anything.

Jefferson did not limit his marketing to the Washington area. He had wagons traveling from Baltimore, Richmond, and Monticello to bring foods not available in Washington. In spite of the fact that staples were brought from out of town, his steward often spent $50 in a single day for meats and fresh greens at the local market.

A gourmet, never a gourmand, Jefferson ate lightly (his youthful figure proved that) but discriminatingly. He preferred vegetables to meats, and was particularly fond of olives, figs, mulberries, crabs, shad, oysters, partridge, venison, pineapple, and light wines. He was a connoisseur as well of delicate French pastries, soufflés, light cakes, and "concoctions." Late in life he wrote: "I have lived temperately, eating little animal food."

President Jefferson never drank strong liquors. His table drinks were cider and malt drinks. But his greatest field of expertise was wine. He spoke of wine "as a necessity of life." Toward the end of his life, when Congress was considering reducing the import tax on wine, he wrote: "I rejoice as a moralist at the prospect of a reduction of the duties on wine. . . . It is an error to view a tax on that liquor as merely a tax on the rich. It is a prohibition of its use to the middling class of our citizens, and a condemnation of them to the poison of whiskey, which is desolating their houses. No nation is drunken where wine is cheap; and none sober, where the dearness of wine substitutes ardent spirits as the common beverage."

While traveling through France and Germany in 1788 Jefferson did exhaustive research into the cultivation of grapes. He had tried to introduce the culture to Virginia before the Revolutionary War, and he was still interested. His account book of this time reveals that he purchased many vines to be sent to America. He also noted the estates yielding the best crops of grapes. One note—that "the vignerons of Rudesheim dung their vines about once in five years, putting a one-horse tumbrel load of dung on every 12 feet square"—indicates the depth of his interest.

Undoubtedly discussion of various wines was a favorite topic of Jefferson's conversation. It was natural that his friends relied on his knowledge and taste in ordering their own wines. In 1790 a note reveals that he ordered 65 dozen bottles for President Washington. In 1818 all but six lines of a letter of congratulation to James Monroe on his inauguration were devoted to a dissertation on the best wines then available for official functions.

During Jefferson's own terms of office, his house was as famous for its wine cellar as for its cuisine. The consumption, listed baldly, seems shocking to us today. In his usual fashion, Jefferson kept detailed notes on his supply. On March 20, 1804, he wrote: "There remain on hand 40 bottles of the 247 of champagne received from Fulwer Skipwith December 1st. The consumption then has been 207 bottles, which on 651 persons dined is a bottle to 3 and $1/7$th persons. Hence the annual stock may be calculated at 415 bottles a year, or say 500." It has been said that Jefferson, during his Presidency, was eaten out of house and home. One is tempted to add, drunk out of h-and-h as well. In the same year, 1804—an election year—his bill for champagne, Madeira, claret, and sauterne was almost $3000.

Even so, the quantities consumed in off years were staggering. Wines from Spain, Portugal, France, and Italy flowed by the barrel into the White House storage rooms. In 1801, for example, the President bought "five pipes of Brazil Madeira, a pipe of Pedro Ximenes Mountain (1269 gallons, 424 bottles of it sent to Monticello); a quarter cask of Tnet; a keg of Pacharette doux; 400 bottles of claret; 540 bottles of Sauterne."

Although the President's favorite wine was Madeira, his taste was astonishingly catholic. He bought the best brands of Spanish, Portuguese, French, German, Italian, and even Hungarian vineyards.

Wine was used extensively in the White House kitchen. In fact, Lemaire, Jefferson's *maître d'hôtel* during his Presidency, prepared a list of the quantities and varieties of wine to be used in specific dishes. It might well be America's first written record of wine cookery. Notations include:

Boef a la mode   — ½ pint white wine
Veal l'estaufade   — ½ pint white wine
Une fricassee de lupin — ½ pint red wine
Un Gateau au ri   — 1 pint sherry for the sauce
Les Beg'nais de pain — ½ pint Madeira

When Thomas Jefferson assumed the Presidency he had the monumental job of furnishing a still unfinished house. Even more important, from his viewpoint, was the organization of a White House staff. For reasons obscured by time, he decided not to bring some of his numerous slaves from Monticello to supervise the White House. Perhaps his experience in France had prejudiced him in favor of a French steward who would take charge of the entire house. In any case, just before his inauguration, Jefferson wrote a Frenchman in Philadelphia, asking his assistance:

> . . . I find great difficulty in composing my household. . . . You know the importance of a good maitre d'hotel in a large house and the impossibility of finding one among the natives of our country. I have imagined that such a person might be found, perhaps, among the French of Philadelphia, that no one would be more likely to know than yourself, and that no one would be a better judge of his qualifications. Honesty and skill in making the dessert are indispensable qualifications, that he should be good humored and of a steady, discreet disposition is also important. If there be such a one within the compass of your knowledge will you have the goodness to engage him to come to me immediately? . . . I have a good cook, but it is *pour l'office,* and to take charge of the family that I am distressed.

The anonymous "good cook" apparently gave notice (perhaps after seeing the still inadequate facilities in the White House), for soon Jefferson was appealing to the Chevalier d'Yrugo, Spanish Minister to the United States, to help him find a good French cook. He wrote: "I have understood that twenty dollars a month is what is given to the best French cook. However, the Chevalier d'Yrugo having been so kind as to undertake to get the one which he deemed the best in Philadelphia, I authorized him to go as high as twenty-eight dollars."

Through combined French and Spanish efforts, Jefferson managed to get together an exceedingly capable staff, headed by Joseph Rapin as *maître d'hôtel*, with one Julien as chef. Rapin had a short stay and was replaced by the efficient Etienne Lemaire, who was mentioned again and again in Jefferson's letters and notes. These French influences were apparent to all who came to dinner at the President's house.

Less apparent, though there, were the Southern influences. Jefferson had two of his slaves, Edy and Fanny, brought from Monticello to serve as apprentices to Julien, so that when the President retired they could continue the French tradition at Monticello. Annette, the Monticello cook, also came to Washington so the President could have the Southern breakfast he so much prized. She "knew just how he liked batter cakes, fried apples, and hot breads served with bacon and eggs at breakfast."

When Jefferson retired from the Presidency in 1809, the Republic was only twenty years old. Yet in those twenty years there had been numerous culinary changes and developments. Washington, influenced in his taste by his pre-Republic English—Virginia background, in a sense represented the past. John Adams, with his roots in Pilgrim New England, suggested the widely prevalent "plain solid cooking" view that dominated the new country at the time. But Jefferson, fascinated by the Continent, reaching out for new ideas, may intangibly have given direction to the future. As the country continued to grow, trends and countertrends developed in Presidential eating and entertaining habits.

Although certain of Jefferson's influences may have been intangible, many were not. Innumerable innovations of his—vanilla, waffles, macaroni, to cite only three—were well documented in his own notebooks and in the social histories of the period. Other gourmet Presidents were to follow Jefferson—men such as Chester Arthur and William Howard Taft—but none has yet replaced him as the greatest connoisseur of fine foods we have ever had in the Presidency.

◇◇

RECIPES

OLD-FASHIONED COFFEE CAKE

Jefferson was an early riser, up at daybreak, writing letters, waiting for the family and guests to assemble for a traditional 9 A.M. breakfast. A Monticello breakfast was an elaborate one. Daniel Webster remembered having hot breads and cold meats in addition to the standard bacon and eggs, fried apples, and batter cakes when he was a guest at Monticello. Certainly a wide variety of hot breads and cakes were served, such as this one. Be sure to serve it warm, *à la* Jefferson.

Milk   *Eggs*
Yeast cake   *Bread flour*
Water   *Salt*
Sugar   *Cinnamon*
Butter

Scald 2 cups milk, cool to lukewarm, then add 1 yeast cake dissolved in 1 cup water. Cream ½ cup sugar with ½ cup butter and add it to the yeast mixture. Beat 2 eggs and add them as well. Sift 7 cups flour with 1½ teaspoons salt and add to the mixture. Put the bowl in a warm place and let rise for 3 hours. Add more flour—enough to form a stiff dough. Then let the mixture rise again, until double its size. Roll out ¾-inch thick in a baking pan. Spread with melted butter, sprinkle ½ teaspoon cinnamon mixed with granulated sugar over the top. Bake in hot (375° F.) oven for 30 minutes or until done. Serve warm for breakfast. *Serves 6 to 8.*

DUTCH WAFFLES

Gleaning what pleased him from the various cuisines of Europe, Thomas Jefferson was much taken in Holland with the quality of the waffles. We are too, even at this late date. (Essentially this recipe is Jefferson's but has been updated.)

Eggs   *Salt*
Heavy cream   *Baking powder*
All-purpose flour

Separate 3 eggs and beat the yolks vigorously. Add 1 cup cream, beating all the time. Sift together 1 cup flour, ¼ teaspoon salt, and 4 teaspoons baking powder. Add to the egg–cream mixture and beat all together with an electric or rotary beater. Beat until smooth. In a small bowl beat the egg whites until stiff and dry, fold them into the batter, and put into the refrigerator 30 minutes or longer. Preheat waffle iron and bake waffles until lightly browned and crisp. Serve piping hot with butter, maple syrup, sour cream, or honey. *Makes 6 large waffles.*

CAPITOLADE OF CHICKEN

Breakfast at Monticello was essentially Southern, but occasionally it would include a French touch, such as braised partridges or this Capitolade of Chicken on toast. Basically this is a *de luxe* chicken hash. Today, in the era of a smaller breakfast, this could be served for brunch or Sunday night supper.

> *Melted butter*   *Cooked chicken*
> *Onion, chopped*   *Salt and pepper*
> *Shallots*   *Parsley*
> *Garlic*
> *Mushrooms*
> *Flour*
> *White wine*
> *Stock or leftover chicken gravy*

Melt 2 tablespoons butter in skillet. Cook 2 tablespoons chopped onion in the butter until yellowed. Stir in 1 tablespoon finely chopped shallots, 1 clove crushed garlic, and 1 cup sliced mushrooms. Cook over low heat for 5 minutes or until lightly browned. Stir in 1 tablespoon flour; keep stirring until smooth. Add ⅓ cup wine and 1 cup soup stock or leftover chicken gravy. Cook slowly until the sauce begins bubbling. Reduce the heat and simmer for 10 minutes. Dice 2 cups leftover chicken and stir into the sauce. Add salt and pepper to taste. Serve over toast with chopped parsley on top. *Serves 4 to 6.*

BATTER CAKES

Breakfast without batter cakes did not seem like breakfast to Thomas Jefferson. For that reason he brought his Monticello cook, Annette, to Washington during his terms of office. The French chef was superb at making most everything else, but only a plantation-bred cook like Annette could make batter cakes just right. (When Jefferson went to France earlier, he took along James Hastings, one of his Monticello slaves. Ostensibly the reason was to have James trained in French cuisine, so he could prepare French foods at home for Jefferson later, but part of the reason may have been so that Jefferson could continue to have certain of the Southern dishes he loved.)

> *Cornmeal*   *Milk*
> *Salt*   *Eggs*

Stir 4 level tablespoons cornmeal and ½ teaspoon salt into 2 cups milk and cook 5 minutes, stirring constantly. Cool. Then add 2 very well-beaten eggs. Drop by the tablespoon on a hot, well-greased griddle or skillet (375° F.) Bake on one side until the cake is popped with little holes. Turn only once. Do not stack, as the cakes are so tender they will stick together. Serve with maple syrup or honey. *Makes 24 2-inch batter cakes.*

SOUP À LA JULIENNE

Jefferson was particularly fond of soups. In the careful way that he noted down other recipes he made lengthy observations on the preparation of soup. One such notation reads: "Always observe to lay your meat in the bottom of the pan with a lump of butter. Cut the herbs and vegetables very fine and lay over the meat. Cover it close and set over a slow fire. This will draw the virtue out of the herbs and roots and give the soup a different flavor from what it would have from putting the water in at first. . . ."

Carrots, turnips, potatoes	*Sorrel*
Butter	*Spinach*
Beef broth or stock	*Celery, beets, peas*

Take ¾ cup each of carrots, turnips, and potatoes and cut them into short match stick strips. Melt 2 tablespoons butter in a skillet; add the cut vegetables and sauté gently until they begin to shrivel. Put them into a pot with 2½ quarts beef broth or stock (or water as a last resort). When the soup begins boiling, add ¼ cup sorrel and ½ cup scalded, drained, and chopped spinach. Add also 3 stalks celery and 2 beets, all cut up the same as the carrots. Allow soup to simmer gently for 1½ hours, never boiling. Add ½ cup fresh peas. Cook ½ hour longer. Serve with croutons. *Makes about 2 quarts.*

If sorrel is not available use ¾ cup spinach and add 1 tablespoon lemon juice or vinegar.

GUMBO

When President Jefferson signed the Louisiana Purchase in 1803, he did more than enlarge the territorial boundaries of the United States. He enlarged the gastronomical boundaries as well, for New Orleans and the whole southern Mississippi River area offered a range of cooking unknown to Colonial America. French and African influences, decades of trading with exotic ports, all produced spices, scents, and commodities unknown in the South and East. Garlic, hot Creole mustard, thyme, shallots, saffron, and rice served as a main course or dessert all were new sensations to many in the U.S. A great Louisiana favorite—a thick soup or stew of meat or fish, corn, tomatoes, and okra—was Gumbo. That it became a Jefferson favorite as well is evident from the recipe in one of his old cookbooks.

Meat of any kind, preferably	*Tomatoes*
veal or chicken	*Water*
Flour	*Salt and herbs*
Butter	*Green pepper*
Onion	*(optional)*
Okra	

Cut up 1 pound meat, chicken, or fish in small pieces and roll in flour. Fry the meat in 1 tablespoon butter in a large pot until brown. Add 1 large onion, cut up. Brown it; add 1 quart cut-up okra and 1 quart tomatoes cut into small pieces; fry them until browned. Cook the mixture for 15 minutes. Then add 2 quarts water, salt, pepper, and other herbs (garlic, thyme, basil) to taste. Cook over low heat 4 or 5 hours, stirring often. One green pepper, finely chopped, may be added during the cooking. The recipe notes that dried and powdered sassafras leaves may be used instead of okra, but should not be added until just before the soup is done. Today's cook could use 2 tablespoons filé. *Serves 6.*

POTATO SOUP

Jefferson was partial to many soups, including this one made for him at Monticello by his cook Annette. Jefferson once observed that "soup is better the second day in cool weather."

Potatoes	*Rice or tapioca*
Water	*Sorrel or tomatoes*
Salt	*Egg yolks*
Butter	

Peel 3 large potatoes and cut them into pieces. Put into a cooking pot and boil them in water until tender. Then force the potatoes through a sieve, add 3 cups water, and bring to a boil again. Add salt to taste, 2 tablespoons butter, ¼ cup rice (or 1 tablespoon tapioca). Cook over low heat for 25 minutes. Add 1 tablespoon sorrel, chopped fine (spinach is a good substitute). Continue cooking, stirring often. Beat 3 egg yolks until light, add them to the soup, then serve. (Before adding the eggs, remove the soup from direct heat.) *Serves 4.*

MEXICAN BLACK BEAN SOUP

This recipe of Martha Jefferson's traveled, as did so many good ones in Colonial Virginia, from plantation to plantation. It was a favorite at Monticello, but history also records that Martha Washington used it too.

Black beans	*Beef or veal*
Water	*Salt and pepper*

Wash a quart of black Mexican beans, add them to a pot with a gallon of cold water. Add 2 or 3 pounds stewing veal or beef or soup bones, and cook the mixture 2 or 3 hours, or until the beans have become soft (letting them soak overnight is recommended). Pour off the liquid and save; mash the beans through a sieve.

Season the purée with salt and pepper to taste. Add it to the soup liquid and simmer 15 minutes. Serve with small squares of bread that has been browned and toasted crisp in melted butter. *Makes about 2 quarts.*

PEA SOUP

Thomas Jefferson was a dedicated gardener who liked to grow vegetables almost as much as he enjoyed eating them. His garden book listed his predictions of the dates the first vegetables of the season would be ready for picking. He predicted with such accuracy that his judgment seemed almost infallible. There was, at the time, good-natured competition among neighbors as to whose garden would produce the first sweet peas of the season—the first "mess of peas," as the neighborhood called them. It was customary for the owner of the first crop to serve them to his neighbors at an annual dinner. The dinner took place so often at Monticello that one year Jefferson wrote his daughter not to tell a particular neighbor, James Driver, that the Jefferson peas had done it again. Evidently Mr. Driver so much wanted the honor of being first for once that good neighbor Jefferson let him enjoy giving the annual dinner. Fresh peas were Jefferson's favorite of all vegetables. He was particularly fond of this soup, made by Annette at Monticello.

Green peas	*Flour*
Water or stock (chicken, beef, or	*Butter*
veal)	*Egg yolks*
Sugar	
Sorrel or parsley	

Drop 1 cup fresh green peas into 2½ cups boiling salted water. Cook until peas are tender. Drain the peas, saving the water for the soup. Press peas through a sieve (or even in a blender!), add them to the water, along with ½ teaspoon sugar and ½ tablespoon chopped sorrel or parsley, 2 cups stock or water. Simmer 15 minutes. Thicken with 1 tablespoon flour mixed with 1 tablespoon butter. Add 2 well-beaten egg yolks to the soup, after removing it from the direct heat. Mix well and serve. *Makes 1 quart.*

TOMATO SOUP

Served regularly at Monticello every Monday, this recipe was passed along to an admiring Martha Washington by the mistress of Monticello, Martha Jefferson. Though she died at thirty-three, Mrs. Jefferson seems to have shared her father's interest in food and in "receipts."

Tomatoes	*Saltines*
Water	*Butter*
Soda	*Salt and pepper*
Milk	

Skin 1 quart (6 to 8) tomatoes and chop them fine. Boil in 2 cups water 15 minutes. Then add ¼ teaspoon soda and stir until the bubbling stops. Add 1 pint milk and 2 saltines, mashed to a powder. Cook mixture gently another 15 minutes, season with 1 tablespoon butter and salt and pepper to taste, then serve. *Makes about 2 quarts.*

OKRA SOUP

This is more or less a simple forerunner of Brunswick stew, which was later to become a favorite in Brunswick, Virginia, as well as other places in the South. The recipe is listed in Martha Jefferson Randolph's name at Monticello.

Okra	*Tomatoes*
Water	*Butter*
Lima beans	*Flour*
Fresh meat or chicken	

Add 1 quart chopped okra, young and crisp, to 2 cups cold water. Bring to boil and cook 1 hour. Add 1 cup lima beans (fresh or dried), 1 pound fresh meat or chicken cut in serving pieces. Simmer gently for 1 hour. Add 5 tomatoes, cut into small pieces. Add more water if needed. Let simmer slowly. When almost done, add 2 tablespoons butter rolled in 1 tablespoon flour. The soup should not be too thick. (Fresh corn, cut from the cob, may be added at the same time as the lima beans if desired. And a thicker version may be made by simmering longer, until the meat and vegetables are a porridgelike mass.) *Makes about 2 quarts.*

SORREL SOUP

The tradition of fine cooking became a Monticello inheritance. Jefferson's daughters passed his recipes along to their daughters. All six of his granddaughters copied the favorite dishes collected by their mothers, grandfather, Lemaire the steward, Julien the chef, Annette, or family friends. These handwritten cookbooks were neatly bound together with ribbon and carried by the girls to their new homes when they married. Their trousseaus contained few more treasured items. From a Monticello menu comes this recipe for Sorrel soup.

Fresh sorrel	*Light cream*
Butter	*Chicken broth*
Onion	*Salt and pepper*
Egg yolks	

Take 1 pound fresh sorrel leaves; wash and chop very fine. Melt ¼ cup butter in saucepan and sauté 1 chopped onion until limp but not brown. Stir in the sorrel leaves and cook gently until wilted—about 5 minutes. Meanwhile blend together 2 beaten egg yolks and 1 cup light cream. Heat 3 cups chicken broth. When it just begins to boil, add a little to the egg mixture, beating furiously. Pour back into the broth and heat, beating all the while, so that the mixture does not boil. Add the sorrel and onion mixture, with salt and pepper to taste. Soup may be served hot or may be refrigerated and served very cold. (For a smoother soup, blend in electric blender.) *Serves 4 to 6.*

JAMBALAYA

This New Orleans dish contained many of the ingredients Thomas Jefferson most enjoyed: crab, shrimp, rice, vegetables. The dish may have been African or Spanish in origin, but the cooks of the South turned it into a local specialty. This version is made with shrimp, but the beauty of Jambalaya is its great versatility—almost anything goes.

Shortening	*Parsley*
Ham or pork sausage	*Rice*
Green pepper	*Water*
Flour	*Salt*
Shrimp	*Thyme*
Onion	*Worcestershire sauce*
Tomatoes	*Red pepper*
Garlic	

Melt 1 tablespoon lard or shortening in a large frying pan; add 1 pound ham or pork sausage cut into ½-inch cubes. Add also ½ cup chopped green pepper. Cook for 5 minutes, stirring often. Next, stir in 1 tablespoon flour until smooth and cook 1 or 2 minutes longer. Add 3 cups cooked, cleaned shrimp, 1 large sliced onion, 3 cups skinned diced tomatoes, 1 clove minced garlic, 2 tablespoons chopped parsley. Cook until mixture starts to boil, then stir in 2 cups uncooked long-grain rice. Also add 4 cups water, 1¼ teaspoons salt, ½ teaspoon dried thyme, 2 tablespoons Worcestershire sauce, and ¼ teaspoon red pepper. Cover pan and cook gently for 30 minutes, or until rice is tender and all the liquid is absorbed. Sprinkle with chopped parsley and serve. *Serves 8.*

NOODLES *A LA* JEFFERSON

When Jefferson left France in 1789, his protégé and confidential secretary, William Short, remained as *chargé d'affaires* in Paris. Among the many diplomatic messages exchanged between Jefferson and Short were detailed instructions for *"de faire cuire un poulet en cassette,"* notes about other delicacies, and requests for special ingredients that Jefferson found wanting in America. Short even made a special trip to Naples to get his mentor a "macaroni mould," as Jefferson sorely missed this dish at home. Short described this macaroni machine: "It is of a smaller diameter than that used at the manufactories of macaroni, but of the same diameter with others that have been sent to gentlemen in other countries. I went to see them made. I observed that the macaroni most esteemed at Naples was smaller than that generally seen at Paris. This is the part of Italy most famous for the excellence of the article." Short did not realize it, but what he saw was not macaroni, but its cousin spaghetti. While today pasta is rarely made at home, except in certain Italian households, we thought it of interest to include Jefferson's recipe for the from-scratch preparation of what he called "Noodles à la Macaroni."

Eggs	*Salt*
Milk	*Flour*

Beat 6 eggs until light and foamy. Then add 1 cup milk and ½ teaspoon salt. Add enough flour (about 4 cups) to make a thick but rollable dough. Roll with rolling pin to ⅛-inch thickness. Cut into small pieces, roll between fingers into long strips. Cut them into proper macaroni length. Drop strips into boiling salted water; cook 15 minutes. They may also be served boiled in soup.

A modern version, using Jefferson's favorite Parmesan cheese, follows: Cook 1 package noodles according to directions. Drain well. Add 1 cup soft or melted butter and 2 cups freshly grated Parmesan cheese. Toss gently until mixed. Add freshly ground black pepper to taste. Serve hot. *Serves 4.*

MACARONI AND CHEESE PUDDING

A guest at the President's House on February 6, 1802, Mr. Manasseh Cutler, later commented that there was "a pie called macaroni, which appeared to be a rich crust filled with the strillions of onions, or shallots, which I took them to be, tasted very strong, and not agreeable. Mr. Lewis told me there were none in it; it was made of flour and butter, with a particularly strong liquor mixed with them." It was obvious that not all of Mr. Jefferson's guests shared his predilection for foreign foods and flavors. But macaroni and cheese have become such a part of

American life we almost think of them as indigenous—which only serves as further comment on "our changed and changing times."

Elbow Macaroni	*Milk*
Butter	*Salt and pepper*
Flour	*Cheddar cheese*

Cook 2½ cups macaroni according to package directions until tender and drain thoroughly. Meanwhile, melt ¼ cup butter in pan, stir in ¼ cup flour, little by little, then add 2¼ cups milk, and cook until the sauce bubbles. Add 1 teaspoon salt and a dash of black pepper. Arrange alternate layers of macaroni and 1¾ cups grated Cheddar cheese in a medium-size glass baking dish. When finished, pour hot sauce over the dish, sprinkle ¼ cup grated cheese over the sauce, and dot with bits of butter. Bake in a preheated hot (400° F.) oven for 35 minutes, or until top is golden brown. *Serves 4 to 6.*

A DRUNKEN LOAF

This dish combines two of the foods President Jefferson was fondest of— macaroni and Parmesan cheese. It makes a somewhat different dish for Sunday night supper. The wine, presumably, is what makes the loaf drunken.

Loaf of French bread	*Butter*
Red wine	*Heavy cream*
Macaroni	*Parmesan cheese*

Heat a loaf of French bread until nicely warmed. Pour 1 pint red wine over it, and wrap the loaf tightly in aluminum foil for ½ hour. Meanwhile, boil 1 pound macaroni in boiling salted water. When the macaroni is cooked, drain it and put it in a large pot or mixing bowl. Add 1 tablespoon butter, enough heavy cream to mix, and 6 ounces grated Parmesan cheese. Mix all together until it has a custardy consistency. Then unwrap loaf and ladle macaroni and cheese over the loaf. Brown the top under the broiler and serve piping hot. *Serves 6 to 8.*

JEFFERSON'S ICE CREAM MODERNIZED

As frequently as Jefferson served ice cream, you might be led to think it was easily made. On the contrary, the process was arduous. There were no extracts of flavorings, so the cream had to be seasoned by boiling a vanilla bean in the milk. There were no electrical gadgets to do the whirling and turning. The cream had to be turned by hand, a tedious job that took an hour of constant work—hard work by strong arms. Here, simplified, is Jefferson's recipe for today's cook.

Eggs	*Cream*
Sugar	*Vanilla*
Salt	

Beat 6 egg yolks until thick and lemony in color. Combine with 1 cup sugar and a dash of salt. Heat 1 quart cream and pour slowly over the egg–sugar mixture. Place the mixture in the top of a large double boiler and cook slowly about 10 minutes. When it thickens, remove and strain through a fine sieve into a bowl. After it cools, add 2 teaspoons vanilla. Freeze with 1 part salt to 3 parts ice surrounding. Place in a mold, pack the ice and salt around it, and chill for 2 or 3 hours. Stir frequently. Very rich. *Makes 6 to 8 servings.*

JEFFERSON'S BAKED ALASKA

Although the name came much later, it is likely that a dish similar to Baked Alaska was served in the White House in 1802. One guest commented on the dessert at a Presidential dinner consisting of "ice-cream very good, crust wholly dried, crumbled into thin flakes." Another guest at another White House dinner noted that the dessert was "ice-cream brought to the table in the form of small balls, enclosed in cases of warm pastry."

BACHELOR BUTTONS

Jefferson filled the deep windows of the White House with rare and exotic plants, the subjects of his botanical experiments. The sight of them gave him pleasure. He was also fond of handsome and well-made furniture and objects. One cabinet particularly pleased him. It was an unusual shape and was designed in such a way that when it was touched, the doors flew open revealing all the things he most welcomed when he was studying or reading late at night—such things as a candle, a decanter of wine, a goblet of water, a plate of light cakes. These Bachelor Buttons would have filled the bill exactly.

Butter	*Flour*
Sugar	*Baking powder*
Eggs	*Salt*
Vanilla	*Maraschino cherries*

Cream ⅔ cup butter with 1¾ cups sugar. Add 2 well-beaten eggs, 1 teaspoon vanilla and beat the mixture well. Sift 3 cups flour, 2 teaspoons baking powder, and ½ teaspoon salt. Add the sifted ingredients to the creamed mixture. Mix thoroughly. Drop by teaspoonfuls on a well-greased baking sheet, making sure they are spaced quite a distance apart. Place a maraschino cherry on top of each "button" and bake in a hot (450° F.) oven for 8 to 10 minutes, or until lightly browned. *Makes about 3 dozen.*

JEFFERSON'S FRENCH COFFEE RECIPE

It was President Jefferson's custom to serve both coffee and tea after elaborate dinners, "coffee as a settler and tea, usually green, to awaken and excite the senses after they had been lulled by wine." This particular coffee recipe comes from Petit, who was employed by Jefferson in Paris as his *valet de chambre* and who came back to America with his master. This recipe came too, and was used ever after at Monticello. This is the way Jefferson wrote it:

> On one measure of the coffee ground into meal pour three measures of boiling water, boil it, on hot ashes mixed with coal, til the meal disappears from the top, when it will be precipitated. Pour it three times through a flannel strainer, it will yield 2⅓ measures of clear coffee. An ounce of coffee meal makes 1½ cups of clear coffee in this way. The flannel must be rinsed out in hot or cold water for every making.

MONTICELLO CURAÇAO LIQUEUR

Jefferson's interest in spirits extended beyond an expertise in wines to an interest in distilling and bottling his own liqueurs and beer, as is evidenced by this old Monticello recipe.

Seville oranges	*Saffron*
Lemon	*Pure spirit (alcohol)*
Coriander seed	*Sugar*
Cinnamon	

Peel 6 Seville oranges and 1 large lemon. Put the peels in a large glass jar, add ¼ ounce coriander seed and ¼ ounce stick cinnamon and ½ teaspoon saffron (the recipe actually says "as much saffron as will lie on a shilling"). Pour over this 3 pints pure alcohol. Cork the jar carefully, put it in a dry, warm place for 6 weeks. After this time filter the mixture through a cheesecloth (flannel). Clarify 2 pounds loaf sugar in 3 pints water. When cold mix it with the bottled liqueur. Rebottle and cork it tightly.

JEFFERSON'S SPICED HOT TODDY

This recipe was later used by other Presidents. The Dwight Eisenhowers were fond of it.

Spice bag—nutmeg, allspice, cloves   *Sugar*
Brandy   *Baked apples*
Rum

Make spice bag of ½ teaspoon nutmeg, ½ teaspoon whole allspice, and 1 teaspoon whole cloves. Heat 2 quarts water and add the spice bag to it, along with 2½ quarts brandy, 1 cup rum, and 1 cup sugar. Simmer 15 minutes, then remove the spice bag. Pour the toddy into 4 sterile quart jars in the bottom of which are 2 baked apples. Let stand at least 2 hours. Reheat and serve hot. If more sugar is required, add it at the time of the reheating. *Makes 5 quarts, about 40 (½ cup) servings.*

JEFFERSON'S APPLE TODDY

This toddy of Thomas Jefferson's makes a delicious party punch. Could be a standby today as it was at Monticello. Tastes smooth but can be lethal.

Bake 18 pippin apples. Pour 1 gallon boiling water over them and let stand until cold. Then press the apples through a sieve to remove skins and seeds. Put the sieved apples in a large bowl and add to them 2 quarts sugar, 1 quart brandy, 1 quart rum, 1 quart sherry, 1 pint Madeira, ½ pint arrack (anise-flavored liqueur), ½ pint peach brandy, ½ pint Curaçao liqueur, and 1 grated nutmeg. Mix well and serve in punch cups. *Makes 2 gallons.*

SPICED CIDER

As American as apple pie, this homemade cider was a tradition at Monticello. It was kept in the old wine cellar. There was almost always some on hand for a thirsty guest or member of the family.

Sweet cider   *Stick cinnamon*
Sugar   *Whole cloves*
Salt   *Whole allspice*

Mix 1 quart sweet cider with ¼ cup sugar, a dash of salt, 8 short pieces of stick cinnamon, 12 whole cloves, and 8 whole allspice. Bring the mixture to a boil, cool, and let stand several hours. Strain all the spices out of the cider, reheat, and serve. Especially good with cookies or doughnuts.

MR. JEFFERSON'S PERSIMMON BEER

Jefferson was not prejudiced against native American food. The beauty of his table was that he combined his native dishes so well with foreign delicacies. Many of his recipes were as indigenous as the flag. His recipe for persimmon beer, for instance, was so highly praised by all who tasted it that it actually appeared in print. The first issue of the *American Farmer,* April 2, 1819, carried the full "receipt":

> Gather the persimmons perfectly ripe and free from any roughness, work them into large loaves, with bran enough to make them consistent, bake them so thoroughly that the cake may be brown and dry throughout, but not burnt, they are then fit to use; but if you keep them any time, it will be necessary to dry them frequently in an oven moderately warm. Of these loaves broken into a coarse powder, take 8 bushels, pour over them 40 gallons of cold water; and after two or three days draw it off; boil it as other beer, hop it; this makes a strong beer. By putting 30 gallons of water to the same powder, and letting it stand two or three days longer, you may have a very fine small beer.

✳✳

IV

Indomitable Dolley—and Mister Madison

✳✳

In considering the social side of James Madison's administration, it becomes immediately apparent that the dominant figure was Mrs. Madison. No President's wife before her was so thoroughly in charge of the nation's social life. Jefferson, a widower, had no First Lady. Abigail Adams, by temperament and timing, was not interested in the social scene. And Martha Washington, although a gracious hostess, limited her interest to a select few.

Dolley Madison was Madame Hospitality herself. In a sense she was our first real First Lady. And for years after leaving that role, she still managed to dominate Washington's social scene.

There were intimations of the type of First Lady Dolley Madison would be even before her husband became President. She served as hostess for President Jefferson on certain state occasions and proved herself a charming, gracious welcomer of his guests. Dinners at the Madisons were invariably festive affairs, with an abundance of good food and drink. Guests left feeling pleased with their host and hostess and the world in general.

Or most of them did. An exception was Mrs. Merry, the ill-tempered British Minister's wife, mentioned earlier. To her dinner at the Madisons was "more like a harvest home supper than the entertainment of a Secretary of State." When Dolley heard this comment, as Mrs. Merry intended she should (after all, it had been repeated often enough), she regarded it with equanimity. Her answer indicates the tactful, gracious person she was. "The profusion of my table," she said, "arises from the happy circumstance of abundance and prosperity in our country." A classic example of how to win points and friends at the same time!

Dolley Madison, raised in a strict Philadelphia Quaker household, wearing the quiet gray of the Friends, might not seem a likely candidate for anybody's Hostess of the Year vote. Yet somewhere along the way she blossomed into quite a fashion plate, wearing lavish and colorful velvet or satin gowns. And as First Lady, her feathered and glittering headdresses—or turbans, as everyone called them—were the talk of Washington.

The gay, even gaudy, clothes were merely superficial aspects of Dolley Madison. What really won so many people to her was her charm and good humor. Not really a beauty, if pictures of the time are proof, she radiated cheerfulness. Washington Irving described her as "a fine, portly, buxom dame who has a smile and a pleasant word for everybody." Irving was not as taken with Mr. Madison, of whom he said ". . . as to Jeemy Madison—ah, poor Jeemy!—he is but a withered little apple-john."

On the surface, the social scene during Madison's administration followed the pattern established by Jefferson. The cuisine was French as well as English–Virginian; the wines were the finest French vintages; the hospitality was as open and cordial as Jefferson's. But Dolley Madison was an innovator in her own right, with a style of her own. She did not share Jefferson's preference for intimate gatherings above all else, but enjoyed having masses of people about—for dinner, lawn parties, luncheons, teas, and dances. Although Jefferson, too, was gregarious, he favored small dinners devoted to much amiable conversation, while Dolley's idea of entertainment was in effect "the more the merrier."

Not that Dolley was averse to small dinner parties. She gave them often, skillfully combining groups of intimate friends with distinguished guests who happened to be in town. She chose her guests for their congeniality and made her parties, large or small, as informal and unceremonious as possible.

Like Jefferson politically, the Madisons shared his aversion to formality and pompousness. But they did not share his need for privacy when entertaining. When the Madisons entertained, at small or large functions, there were servants galore. Neighboring plantations lent their slaves at thirty-five cents an hour each for the evening, and there was a servant per guest.

Dolley Madison was close to forty when her husband became President, but immediately she launched into a social program so exhausting that it would make a teen-ager's head spin. One of her first official acts was to reinstate the levees that Jefferson had eliminated from his social schedule.

It took Dolley almost three months to prepare for her first "drawing room," but that first one set a pattern that was followed throughout the Madison administration. Dolley sent out no formal invitations to her drawing rooms. She didn't have to—her Wednesday evenings quickly became celebrated, and all Washington society focused on them. Ladies attended to show off their new clothes; politicians conducted informal business during the course of the evening; talented singers or musicians among the guests could always be assured of being asked to display their talents; young blades conducted their courtships. The prevailing mood, in short, was gaiety.

The White House Wednesday evening was so popular it was called simply *the* drawing room. Other hostesses may have had parties, but they were not in the same class. So popular was the White House with the young set that a rhyme made the rounds:

> Tom Tingey, Tom Turner, Tom Elwell, Tom Digges,
> All go to the palace to eat up the figs.

So celebrated were Dolley's drawing rooms that even Washington Irving, as far away as New York, decided he would have to visit one himself. After a tedious coach trip from New York, he arrived in the capital just in time to get dressed up, "in pease blossom and silk stocking," and make his way to the President's house. In spite of his fatigue and long journey, Irving almost immediately felt at home. Mrs. Madison welcomed him as an old friend.

It was the custom at the drawing rooms, levees—in fact all Madison parties—for the newly arrived guest to advance to the upper end of the room, and, in the words of an observer, "pay your obeisance to Mrs. Madison, curtsey to his highness and take a seat, or chat with acquaintances. After this formality you may conduct yourself as at any other party." A simple custom, to be sure, easily complied with, as is evident from the hordes who attended the Madison soirées. Dolley generally received her guests in the Oval Drawing Room. Yellow was the dominant color, with yellow damask everywhere. Dolley herself stood in front of a yellow sunburst fire screen make of fluted damask. In her elegant gown and bejeweled turban she must have been quite a sight.

The servant problems that nagged at the preceding Presidencies did not seem to affect Dolley Madison. For one thing, she supervised her own kitchen, eliminating the function of a steward for the first time since the Republic began. Then she promoted Jean Pierre Sioussat, the Frenchman who had been President Jefferson's doorman and earlier a servant at the home of British Minister Merry, to her all-round assistant. French John or John Suse, as he was called, regulated the frenetic social and domestic schedule of the Madisons with quiet efficiency.

When the President and his wife had a dinner party, provisions were lavish. Mrs. Seaton, wife of the owner of the *National Intelligence,* commented on one occasion:

The dinner was certainly very fine, but still I was rather surprised, as it did not surpass some I have eaten in Carolina. There were many French dishes and exquisite wines, I presume, by the praise bestowed upon them; but I have been so little accustomed to drink that I could not discern the difference between sherry and rare old Burgundy Madeira. Comment on the quality of the wine seems to form the chief topic after the removal of the cloth and during the dessert, at which, by the way, no pastry is countenanced. Ice creams, macaroons, preserves and various cakes are placed on the table, which are removed for almonds, raisins, pecan-nuts, apples, pears, etc. Candles were introduced before the ladies left the table, and the gentlemen continued half an hour longer to drink a social glass. Meantime Mrs. Madison insisted on my playing on her elegant grand piano a waltz for Miss Smith and Miss Magruder to dance, the figure of which she instructed them in. By this time, the gentlemen came in, and we adjourned to the tea room. . . .

At dinner Dolley presided. James preferred to sit in a chair at the middle of the table, as it "relieved him from the trouble of serving guests, drinking wine, etc." On matters domestic and social, there is little doubt that "Jeemy" deferred to his wife. Opposite Dolley sat one of her husband's Cabinet members, often the Secretary of State.

Dolley, following the customary form of her day, was expected to do the serving and even the carving. This seemed natural at the time, as one social arbiter wrote, for the Lady of the House was presumed "to understand carving perfectly well, and to know where the best bit lay."

After dinner and the second dessert of fruit and nuts, there were parlor games, songs, music, and even dancing at the White House. Dolley's wit and naturalness made every occasion festive.

And there were occasions aplenty. It was Dolley Madison who introduced the Easter Egg Rolling on the White House lawn, which was to become a tradition with almost all succeeding Presidents' families. Even a routine visit by a Congressman or diplomat to the President prompted Dolley to offer some refreshments to make an occasion of it. And she gave "dove parties" for the Cabinet wives, to be sure they were having fun while their husbands consulted with the President.

New Year's Day was always particularly gay at the President's House. But the levee of January 1, 1814, seems to have been even more of an event than usual. In spite of the fact that the country was involved in war with the British, Washington social life continued at its usual high speed. The big public reception was going on full swing.

Mrs. Seaton, the Boswell of the Madison administration, noted the grandeur of Dolley's gown, pink satin trimmed with ermine. Her turban was of white satin with enormous ostrich plumes. The gathering seemed gay and unconcerned. Only in the face of the President did Mrs. Seaton observe anxiety and apprehension about the events taking place outside Washington. His pale face, a greater reserve than usual, and a distracted manner indicated to her his worries about the war.

Still, it was a fantastic occasion. The French Minister treated the company to a spectacle they would long remember. Mrs. Seaton's notes fairly burst with excitement. After eating her ice cream and drinking a glass of Madeira (she had evidently grown accustomed to wine after her years in Washington), she was about to leave. Suddenly she saw through a front window what she first thought was "a rolling ball or burnished gold carried with swiftness through the air by two gilt wings. Our anxiety increased the nearer it approached, until it actually stopped before the door; and from it alighted, weighted with gold lace, the French Minister, M. Serurier, and suite. We now perceived that what we thought were wings were nothing more than gorgeous footmen with *chapeaux bras,* gilt-braided skirts and splendid swords. Nothing ever was witnessed in Washington so brilliant and dazzling. You may well imagine how the natives stared and rubbed their eyes to be convinced 'twas no fairy dream."

The legendary Madison entertaining gave rise to the story that even when the British were descending on Washington, about to set it afire during the War of 1812, Dolley was in the midst of plans for a dinner party. An English writer, Gleig, said that the British troops arrived at the Executive Mansion and "found a bountiful dinner spread for forty guests. This they concluded was for the American officers who were expected to return victorious from the field of Bladenburg." One assumes that if the report is true, the British consumed the meal before plundering and burning the White House.

While this is an intriguing story, there is nothing on the record that substantiates it. The White House was burned August 24, 1814, and Dolley's letter of August 23 to her sister indicates that she had dozens of things on her mind—but not a dinner party.

What perhaps gave currency to the feasting-while-the-capital-burns story was a book published in 1865 called *A Colored Man's Reminiscences of James Madison.* The author was Paul Jenings, a slave of Madison's, and in the book he corroborated Gleig's report of the dinner. Jenings was there at the time and wrote: "I set the table myself." Still, he wrote many years after the incident had supposedly occurred, and memory in an old man plays tricks.

While most of the country mourned the devastation of the Executive Mansion, there were a few critics who felt that perhaps now the Madisons would abandon their extravagant entertainments. Wrote one such critic: "The destruction of the President's House cannot be a great loss in one point of view, as we hope it will put an end to drawing rooms and levees; the resort of the idle and the encouragers of spies and traitors."

This negativist reckoned without the indomitable Dolley. Even though the Madisons had to seek refuge in smaller quarters—the Taylor house, generally called the Octagon House—the entertainment went on—and on, until the end of Madison's second term of office in 1817.

The Madisons present a paradox. Considering the length of time they were on the national scene, there is little known about their private persons. Madison, a thorough, sensible, conscientious public servant, always seemed to be in Jefferson's shadow politically and in his wife's shadow socially. But at least his record of service and accomplishment speaks for him to later generations.

But poor Dolley Madison! For all the ecstacizing over her by social commentators of the time, so little remains known. She was described as "the brilliant, sunny-hearted, witty little Quakeress from Philadelphia," yet almost no examples of her brilliance or her wit survive; few *bons mots* or anecdotes demonstrate the charming personality she was credited with having. And though her diversions were lavish and raved over, few records were kept of the meals she served or the foods she particularly liked herself.

James Madison, small and slender, was undoubtedly a sparing eater. But what foods pleased him most? Dolley, described variously as plump, buxom, and round, undoubtedly liked food. But of her special favorite dishes little is known. Some few choice recipes and preferences were recorded, but they were relatively few, considering the frequency of her entertaining.

It is an interesting enigma. In spite of it (or perhaps because of it), the legend of Dolley Madison continues. Each First Lady since her day has been inundated with stories about the gay, hospitable Dolley. There is no denying that she set a style that various other First Ladies through the decades have tried to emulate, not always with the same success.

◇◇

RECIPES

DOLLEY MADISON'S BOUILLON

One of Dolley's most charming and appreciated innovations was her habit of serving bouillon at afternoon receptions "when the weather was cold and dreary." It was, in the words of an observer, "a comforting practice." Perhaps it was such small, but thoughtful, gestures as this that gave such luster to her reputation for hospitality.

Beef	*Carrots*
Veal knuckle	*Red pepper*
Bouquet garni	*Onions*
Water	*Salt*
Turnips	*Sherry*

Put 4 pounds juicy beef, 1 knuckle of veal, and a bouquet garni of herbs tied in a cheesecloth into a large kettle, along with 6 quarts water. Add 2 small turnips, 2 small carrots, 1 small pod of red pepper, 2 small whole onions, salt to taste, and simmer all together for about 6 hours. When finished, strain through a fine sieve. Allow the soup to stand overnight to congeal. Skim off all the grease. Put the soup back into a kettle to heat. Just before serving, add sherry to taste. (Made with stock instead of water it is even better, though Dolley's recipe says simply water.)

CHICKEN AND OKRA SOUP

From Martha Washington's *Rules for Cooking* comes the notation that this delicious soup was one culled from Dolley Madison.

Bacon	*Tomatoes*
Chicken	*Salt*
Lard	*Green pepper*
Okra	

Brown bacon slices and cut-up chicken in a spoonful of lard in a large skillet. When the chicken is browned add okra (about ¼ peck) and tomatoes. Turn the heat to low and pour boiling water over the meat and vegetables. Simmer slowly, adding water from time to time. Salt and a green pepper may be added shortly before the soup is ready for serving, allowing enough time to cook the green pepper.

PICKLED EGGS

On a visit to the Quaker Meeting House in Sandy Spring, Maryland, Dolley Madison was given this unusual recipe by a friend who was a Friend in deed.

Salt	*Cloves*
Mace	*Vinegar*
Pepper	*Eggs*

Boil salt, mace, pepper, and cloves in vinegar. Boil some eggs separately. When the eggs are hard-boiled, remove the shells. Chill. When the eggs are cold, put them in an earthenware jar and pour the vinegar mixture over them. Cover them tightly and keep for several days before using, allowing time for the vinegar–spice mixture to permeate the eggs. (Use a wooden spoon for stirring the vinegar mixture.)

CRAB OMELET

Crab was a favorite of the Washingtons. Martha borrowed this recipe from Dolley Madison, who served it at the Madisons' Virginia home, Montpelier. Like the Washingtons, Jefferson, and the James Monroes, the Madisons spent many happy years on their Virginia plantation, indulging in gentleman farming.

Crabs	*Thyme*
Eggs	*Butter*
Salt	*Eggplant (optional)*
Pepper	*Tomatoes (optional)*
Parsley	

Boil 6 large crabs and pick. Beat 12 eggs for 15 minutes, until light and frothy. Season the eggs with salt, pepper to taste, parsley, and a pinch of thyme. Mix with the crab and sauté in butter. Eggplant chopped very fine and quartered tomatoes may be added to the pan in season.

CROQUETTES

After the Madisons retired from Washington in 1817, they returned to Montpelier. Theirs was hardly a sedentary retirement, however, for guests descended on them constantly. The Madison hospitality continued in as great abundance as when Madison had been in public life. In fact, their generosity almost caused their financial ruin. This dish, for the economy-minded, is fine for leftovers, though it is doubtful if Dolley ever had much left over for it. Hers was usually made from scratch.

Meat	*Eggs*
Ham	*Onion*
Breadcrumbs	*Mace or nutmeg*

Chop any meat, cooked or uncooked, very fine (we suggest putting it through the meat grinder). Add half as much ham as meat, chop it equally as fine. Mix them together, adding 1 cup breadcrumbs. Mix well, and add 2 beaten eggs, chopped onion, and a pinch of mace or nutmeg. Mix all together, form into balls, and fry.

Variation: Chop any kind of fine fish. Add leftover mashed potatoes, 1 hardboiled egg, and pepper and salt to taste. Roll into egg-size balls, brush with the yolk of an egg, and fry until crispy brown.

CORN OYSTERS

Dolley Madison was not a native Virginian, but she shared her adopted state's fondness for freshly baked breads, rolls, and muffins, serving them frequently at Montpelier. This recipe was passed along, as were so many, to Mount Vernon.

Corn	*Eggs*
Milk	*Salt and pepper*
Flour	*Lard*

Shred 1 quart corn coarsely. Add 2 cups milk, 1 cup flour, and mix all together with 2 well-beaten eggs. Season to taste with salt and pepper. Heat lard or cooking oil to the boiling point, then drop the batter into the hot oil in small spoonfuls. Serve hot as a luncheon accompaniment. *Serves 6 to 8.*

PUFF POPS

From a Pennsylvania Quaker upbringing to the lavish hospitality of a Virginia plantation to the elegance of France, Dolley Madison ran the gamut of culinary experience. As the bride of Madison, Dolley aquired many recipes in her new Virginia home, recipes such as this old English version of the popover.

Egg	*Salt*
Milk	*Butter*
Flour	

Beat 1 egg thoroughly, add 1 cup milk, then slowly add 1 cup flour sifted with ½ teaspoon salt. Stir until well blended (2 minutes with a rotary beater or 1 minute with an electric beater). Do not overheat. The batter should have the consistency of heavy cream. Melt 1 tablespoon butter; use it to grease custard cups or muffin tin. Fill the pans ⅓ full with the batter. Bake in a good hot (450° F.) oven for about 20 minutes, then reduce heat to moderate (350° F.) and bake 15 to 20 minutes longer. Remove immediately from the tins and serve fast while hot and puffed. *Makes 8 to 12 popovers.*

ORANGE AND CRANBERRY RELISH

During Madison's Presidency, the White House food bills were high, sometimes as much as fifty dollars a day. That fifty dollars seems even higher when one learns that a whole turkey cost as little as seventy-five cents. We have no record of the cost of this relish, used as accompaniment for those inexpensive White House turkeys.

Oranges	*Sugar*
Cranberries	

Put 3 small unpeeled but thin-skinned oranges through the coarse blade of a meat grinder. Do the same with 1 cup uncooked cranberries. Combine. Add sugar to taste, keeping the flavor on the tart side. Put the mixture in a covered bowl in the refrigerator and chill overnight. A delicious accessory for any fowl.

CRANBERRY CHUTNEY

This recipe shows the versatility of the cranberry, for whose cultivation we should be eternally grateful to our Founding Fathers.

Tart apples	*Lemon juice*
Cranberries	*Sugar*
Green peppers	*Ginger*
Raisins	*Cayenne*
Vinegar	*Allspice*

Pare, core, and chop 1 dozen tart apples. Chop 2 cups cranberries. Mix the two together, adding 3 chopped green peppers and 1 cup raisins. Stir in 2 cups vinegar and lemon juice to the equivalent of 4 lemons. Mix well. Add 2 cups sugar, 1 tablespoon ginger, ¼ teaspoon cayenne, and ½ teaspoon allspice. Be sure all ingredients are well mixed. Cook them in a saucepan over low heat. Cook until mixture is thickened. Stir often to prevent burning. Pour the mixture into clean, hot, sterile jars and seal.

VIRGINIA POTATOES

Recipes traveled from hand to hand in the early days of our Republic. The women's magazines with their many recipes were a thing of the future. This particular "receipt" was sent to the Madisons by Sarah Mason from Gunston Hall on the Potomac.

Ham	*Salt and pepper*
Onion	*Mustard*
Cold boiled potatoes	

Sauté small slices of ham, leaving the fat on; add ½ onion, sliced. When both are lightly cooked, remove from the pan. Cut into small pieces leftover boiled potatoes. Season with salt and pepper to taste, with a dash of dry mustard. Put potatoes into the skillet and fry in the remaining ham fat. When delicately browned, return ham and onion to the skillet, stir constantly, and heat all ingredients thoroughly. Serve hot.

FAIRY BUTTER

Dolley Madison was much praised for her ingenuity in entertaining. Special arrangements and embellishments seemed natural to her. While she did not invent Fairy Butter, it was the kind of extra touch she loved so much. It was known to other Virginia cooks of the period too.

Hard-boiled eggs	*Powdered sugar*
Orange-flower water	*Butter*

After boiling 2 eggs until they are hard-boiled, shell them and beat the yolks in a mortar until they are fine-grained. Add 1 tablespoon orange-flower water and 1 tablespoon powdered sugar. Beat all together until you have a fine paste. Mix it with equal parts butter ("fresh out of the churn," the old recipe says), and force the mixture through a strainer with small holes onto a fancy plate or small dish. It makes a pretty accompaniment to a dinner party.

DOLLEY MADISON'S LAYER CAKE

Lucia B. Cutts, niece of Mrs. Madison, wrote that her aunt "delighted in company and her table fairly groaned with the abundance of dishes." This recipe for layer cake was a Madison specialty, frequently served to guests.

Egg whites	*Cornstarch*
Butter	*Flour*
Sugar	*Vanilla*
Milk	

Beat the whites of 8 eggs until stiff and in peaks. Put aside. Cream 1 cup butter with 2½ cups sugar. Add 1 cup milk slowly, mixing well. Add ¾ cup cornstarch and 3 cups sifted flour to the butter–egg mixture. Mix well and add 2½ teaspoons vanilla. Fold in the egg whites carefully. Bake in 4 layer pans, well-greased. Bake in a medium (350° F.) oven 30 to 35 minutes, or until the cake springs back when touched lightly. Cool on racks and frost with Dolley Madison's Caramel.

CARAMEL

Brown sugar	*Butter*
Light cream	*Vanilla*

Mix well 3 cups brown sugar, 1 cup cream, and 2 tablespoons butter. Put mixture in the top of a double boiler and cook gently for 20 minutes. Just before removing from the stove, after the caramel has thickened, add 1 teaspoon vanilla, stir constantly. Remove and cool. Fill the layers of the cake and put icing on top as well.

SEED CAKE

Seed cake, more than any other food, became synonymous with Dolley Madison during her White House years. In 1809, when the new British Minister came to confer with President Madison, Dolley sent a Negro servant in with a tray full of seed cake and glasses of punch to lighten the conference. It was her custom to offer refreshments to all who came to call, whether on business or pleasure, a fact that surprised and pleased the visiting Briton.

Butter	*Caraway seed*
Flour	*Grated nutmeg*
Sugar	*Eggs*
Ground mace	*Brandy*

Beat 1 pound butter to the creamy stage. Dredge in 1 pound sifted flour. Add ¾ pound sifted sugar, along with mace, caraway seed, and nutmeg to taste. Mix all together well, then beat thoroughly. Beat 6 eggs with a wire whisk, stir 1 wine glass of brandy into them, and add to the creamed mixture. Beat for 10 minutes. Pour cake batter into a greased cake pan and bake in a moderate (325° F.) oven for 1½ to 2 hours. (Cake can be made with currants instead of caraway seeds and is equally good.)

DOLLEY MADISON'S SOFT GINGERBREAD

This gingerbread has a long and lovely history. Dolley Madison referred to it as "the Jefferson gingerbread" and was reputedly very fond of it. She in turn passed it along to Martha Washington, who meticulously recorded it for posterity. Preserved in White House files, the recipe has been used by many another First Lady, right up to our day. Chef François Rysavy wrote of serving it to the Dwight D. Eisenhowers. And no wonder—it is a recipe that deserves preservation, with its marvelous light and moist pungency. (WARNING: make it in the winter with the windows closed. If the delicious scent wafts into the neighborhood, you'll have a line forming outside your kitchen door.)

Molasses	*Flour*
Beef drippings (or lard)	*Ground ginger*
Baking soda	*Ground cinnamon*
Hot water	*Powdered sugar*

Mix 1 cup molasses (Dolley's "receipt" specifies New Orleans molasses) with ⅔ cup fresh beef drippings. Add 1¼ teaspoons baking soda dissolved in ¼ cup hot water. Sift your dry ingredients: 2¼ cups flour, 4 teaspoons ginger, and 1 tablespoon cinnamon. Next pour ¾ cup hot water which has almost reached the boiling point into the molasses mixture alternately with the flour mixture. Beat thoroughly with a rotary or electric beater. The dough should be soft enough to pour. Bake in a shallow, well-greased baking dish in a preheated medium (350° F.) oven 25 to 30 minutes, or until a toothpick inserted in the center of the cake comes out clean. Delicious served warm, sprinkled with powdered sugar.

GINGER POUND CAKE

Like most other Americans of her period, Mrs. Madison was a great believer in gingerbread and served it often, in one form or another. Here is another recipe:

Flour	*Molasses*
Sugar	*Sour cream*
Butter	*Ginger*
Eggs	*Soda*

Sift 2 pounds flour and add it to 1 pound sugar creamed with 1 pound butter. Beat 10 eggs slightly and add them to the dough, along with 1 pint molasses and ½ pint sour cream. Add 1 large cup chopped preserved ginger and 1 teaspoon soda dissolved in warm water. Mix and beat altogether. Bake in a well-greased and floured deep pan in a medium-slow (325° F.) oven for 1 hour, or until done.

CINNAMON (WOODBURY) CAKE

That prolific letter-writer, Mrs. Seaton, described many of the Madison activities, such as a typical "tea" in Washington society: "It is customary to breakfast at nine, dine at four, and drink tea at eight. I am more surprised at the method of taking tea here than any other meal. In private families, if you step in of an evening, they give you tea and crackers, or cold bread; and if by invitation, unless the party is very splendid, you have a few sweet-cakes, macaroons from the confectioner's. This is the extent. Once I saw a ceremony of preserves at tea; but the deficiency is made up by the style of dinner." A Madison tea would often include Cinnamon Cake.

Butter	*Baking powder*
Sugar	*Cinnamon*
Flour	*Milk*

Cream 2 tablespoons butter with 1 cup sugar. Add 2 cups sifted flour mixed with 1 teaspoon baking powder and 2 tablespoons cinnamon. Add milk and beat together thoroughly. Bake in a large pan at 350° F. 20 to 30 minutes, or until done.

CINNAMON CAKES

A variation on the same theme, these are more like tea cookies and can be made in a variety of different shapes.

Eggs	*Cinnamon*
Rose water	*Flour*
Sugar	

Beat 6 eggs with a wire whisk; add 3 tablespoons rose water while beating. Add the eggs to 1 pound sifted sugar, 1 teaspoon cinnamon, and enough flour to make a paste. Roll the dough thin and cut it into whatever shapes you choose. Place the cutouts on brown paper on a baking sheet and bake them in a moderate (350° F.) oven. When lightly browned, remove from the oven and the paper. Keep them stored in an air-tight container. *Makes 60 large cookies.*

DOLLEY MADISON CAKE

There has been a dispute among historians as to how Dolley Madison really spelled her name. Her own records indicate that *Dolley* it was, not *Dolly*. There is no disputing that this recipe, passed along in Dolley Payne Todd Madison's family, is a delicious one that even today's families will enjoy. Tastes change in subtle ways from generation to generation, but a good cake goes on forever.

Butter	*Brandy*
Sugar	*Rose water*
Flour	*Ground nutmeg*
Eggs	*Raisins*
Baking soda	*Citron*

Cream 1 pound butter with 1 pound sugar. Add 1 pound sifted flour. Beat 6 eggs lightly and add them as well. Dissolve ½ teaspoon baking soda in a little hot water; add it to the dough, along with 1 gill (¼ pint) each brandy and rose water. Mix thoroughly, then add one whole nutmeg, ground, 1 pound raisins, and ½ pound citron, chopped fine. Bake in slow (275°–300° F.) oven until cake shrinks from the sides of the pan or a toothpick comes out clean, approximately 40 minutes.

APRICOT ICE CREAM

It is a fanciful myth that Dolley Madison introduced ice cream to America. (We have already learned who did.) But it is no myth that she enjoyed this dessert herself and took pride in serving it to her many White House guests. Dolley's celebrated inventiveness came into play often when she served ice cream. Not content with plain vanilla, she served fancy flavors, created in the White House kitchen and, inevitably, served them with a flair in unusual molds and settings. This particular recipe may seem a bit archaic, but it offers a glimpse of the complexities of cooking *anything* in the "good old days," before frozen, canned, and processed foods.

Fresh apricots	*Light cream*
Sugar	

Pare very thin 12 ripe apricots. Stone them, scald with boiling water, and put them in a mortar and beat them fine. Add 6 ounces sugar and 1 pint scalding hot heavy cream to the apricots. Put the mixture through a sieve, then set it in a tin with a close cover. Put the tin in a tub of ice broken into small pieces, along with 4 handfuls salt mixed with the ice. When the cream gets thick around the edges of the tin, stir it well, then set it back in the tub until it becomes thicker. When it freezes well, take the cream out of the tin and place it in a mold with a lid, insert it in another tub prepared the same way, with the ice on top and underneath it. Let it stand 4 hours. Turn it out of the mold when you are ready to serve it. "Dip the mould into cold spring water," says the recipe; remove the lid, and turn it onto a serving plate. Other fruit may be used the same way. *Makes 6 servings.*

PINK PEPPERMINT ICE CREAM

As Mrs. Seaton wrote in the *National Intelligencer* in 1812, "Pastry and puddings are going out of date, and wines and ice creams coming in." This breathless pronouncement, harbinger of the type of social forecast that would come later in the heyday of ladies' magazines, had a direct connection with the White House. There was no question that the precedent established by Jefferson continued, with innovations by Dolley Madison. Ice cream was very much "in" among the elite. As has happened throughout our social history, the Presidential family set the pattern, and the nation rushed to follow it.

> *Peppermint-stick candy*   *Sugar*
> *Cream, light and heavy*

Crush 1 pound red peppermint-stick candy and soak it in 1 quart light cream. Allow it to remain standing until dissolved. Then add 1 quart heavy cream whipped. Sweeten with sugar to taste. Freeze in an ice tub with salt packed into the ice. Or simply set in freezer. *Makes 3 quarts.*

CRANBERRY SHERBET

At the second inauguration of President Madison one observer commented: "Mrs. Madison always entertained brilliantly, but last night there was a sparkle in her eye that set astir an air of expectancy in her guests. . . . When finally the brilliant assemblage, America's best, entered the dining room, they beheld in the center, high on a silver platter, a large shining dome of pine ice cream!" Also popular at the White House were sherbets, sometimes made with cream mixed with almonds, pistachios, chocolate, tea or coffee and sugar, then iced, or sometimes made with various fruit juices sweetened and frozen. This particular one was a favorite as a dessert or a relish with chicken or turkey.

Cranberry jelly	*Orange juice*
Lemon juice and rind	*Egg whites or whipped cream*

Beat together 1½ cups cranberry jelly with the juice and grated rind of 1 lemon and the juice of 1 orange. Freeze to a mushy state in the refrigerator. Then fold in 2 egg whites, beaten stiff so they stand in peaks, or ½ pint whipped cream. Gently pour into a mold and finish freezing. *Makes 1 quart.*

HEN'S NEST

The first inaugural ball to be held in the new capital was held in 1809 when James Madison became President, and surely no First Lady ever enjoyed one more than Dolley. Refreshments were, as ever after during the Madison regime, lavish and unusual. A frequently served unusual and beautiful dessert at the Madisons, inauguration or no, was an old Virginia dish known descriptively as Hen's Nest. This is a rather tricky recipe, taking practice and patience. A fine conversation piece!

Eggs	*Lemon rind*
Blancmange pudding	*Jelly, currant or grape*

Take 5 small eggs, make a small hole at one end and empty the shells. Carefully fill each shell with blancmange. Put the shells in the refrigerator. After they have become cold, gently remove the shells, leaving the stiff blancmange in the shape of eggs. Pare the rind from 6 lemons in very thin strips to resemble straw; preserve them with sugar. Fill a small deep dish with jelly. Put the "straw" lemon rind on top to make a nest and place the blancmange "eggs" in it. *Serves 5.*

A YARD OF FLANNEL

Punch was frequently served at the White House during the Madisons' stay. Often it was served in an elegant French punch bowl with the Three Graces encircling the pedestal, a piece that must have delighted Dolley with her eye for grandeur. Not so grand, but much more delicious than it sounds, is this old Virginia recipe which was used by the Madisons as well as their famous neighbors—though it is doubtful if it ever saw the inside of that French punch bowl.

Ale	*Grated nutmeg or ginger*
Eggs	*Rum or brandy*
Sugar	

Warm some ale over a low flame. Beat 3 or 4 eggs with 4 ounces moist sugar and 1 teaspoon nutmeg or ginger. Slowly add 1 quart rum or brandy. As the ale approaches the boiling stage, pour it into one pitcher, and pour the rum, eggs, and sugar mixture into a second pitcher. Pour the contents of the one pitcher into the other, then back and forth until the mixture is as smooth as cream. You don't exactly measure it by the yard, and it certainly doesn't taste like flannel. Nevertheless, a Yard of Flannel it is.

✶✶

V

The Monroe (Social) Doctrine

✶✶

In school we learn about James Madison and James Monroe in sequence and tend always to think of them that way, in tandem, as adjuncts to the Jefferson period. Aside from the double James and double *M*s of their names, the two men were not much alike. True, they were both deeply influenced by Jefferson and Jeffersonian ideals, but they reacted from totally different personalities.

If the two Presidents were unlike in most things, their wives were unlike in everything. Where Dolley Madison was open and spontaneous in her hospitality, Elizabeth Monroe was aloof and reserved, hospitable only when she chose to be. As a result, the contrast in the social aspects of the two administrations was enormous.

The Monroe social regime in Washington was a dramatic pendulum-swing away from the preceding two administrations. James Monroe was influenced by Jefferson politically, but not one whit socially. Where Jefferson and Madison favored an open White House policy, receiving official visitors at whim, the Monroes let it be known immediately that such visitors were not welcome unless specifically invited well in advance.

We have already noted quick turnabouts in procedure that have occurred in our history from one Presidency to the next. But the transition from James Madison's "rule" to that of James Monroe was the sharpest yet encountered, even more abrupt than from Washington to Adams or Adams to Jefferson.

In a sense it all began with the burning of the White House. The Madisons were never able to return to it. The rebuilding was not finished until the fall of 1817, months after Monroe had been inaugurated. The reconstruction had been started in 1815, but the work was tremendous: the only parts left intact were the exterior walls and interior brickwork. These were badly damaged, however, because a heavy rainstorm came while the walls were still hot from the fire, thus causing deep cracks.

Inasmuch as all the furniture used in the Presidential house since Washington's day had been destroyed in the 1814 burning, the job of replacement fell to the Monroes. The manner in which they did it established a tone that affected their entire time in office.

Having served many years in France and in negotiations with France, Monroe was a devout Francophile in his affections, his taste, and his manners. As a result the furniture and accessories chosen for the White House were French or French in feeling, suggesting pomp, elegance, majesty. The sense of luxury was imposing.

The State Dining Room was an example. Lighted with gilded and carved lamps and sconces, it was filled with impressive accessories. Most dominant was the thirteen-foot-long carved bronze centerpiece for the state dining table. This ornate *surtout-de-table* consisted of seven main parts, with mythological figures and numerous detachable pedestals, garlands, vases, piques, and candle-holders. It was a dazzling sight and would continue to impress visitors in each succeeding generation. It came from France, by Monroe's order, at a cost of six thousand francs. With it came matching candelabra, epergnes, and flower vases, all equally ornate. In addition, the Monroes selected a gilded porcelain table service and dessert service, and, as an extra touch, even gold-plated spoons.

It is small wonder that such a formal setting would have its effect on the diners at an official dinner party. Monroe's intention was to create an atmosphere of ceremony. As a Minister in France he had been received with a similar formality. It was his view that a Chief of State should receive guests in a situation that suggested the importance of his office.

While foreign ministers and other visiting dignitaries might be accustomed to such formality, it came as a shock to local inhabitants. One can imagine the effect of such austerity on a Congressman from the hills of Vermont.

To make matters even more strained, Mrs. Monroe declined to make the customary first calls and even refused to return calls, arguing that it was the function of the First Lady to be called upon, but unceremonious and not in keeping with her position to return calls like any normal citizen.

While Washington matrons were outraged at Elizabeth Monroe's audacity and "airs," many a First Lady since has praised her for her courage in eliminating a tedious and time-consuming job. Her break with tradition was a clean one: to this day First Ladies do not return calls. (One recalls with sympathy the agony of Abigail Adams, rushing around returning calls while trying to put a new, unfinished house in some kind of order.)

Elizabeth Monroe had the courage of her convictions, but she suffered for it. Washington society snubbed her during half of her eight years as mistress of the White House. In December 1819, Mrs. Seaton, that indefatigable reporter of the Washington social scene, noted that "The drawing-room of the President was opened last night to a beggarly row of empty chairs. Only five females attended, three of whom were foreigners."

The fact that the Monroes insisted on their invitations being formal did not mean they were niggardly in their hospitality. When they did invite guests for dinner, it was a superb dinner, with all the accouterments absolutely perfect—formal, yes, but nonetheless perfect. The style was French, a preference the Monroes had developed during their years in Paris. Both cuisine and service were French, although the food was "a little Americanized," according to James Fenimore Cooper, who was invited to dinner frequently.

The dinner hour for official entertaining was changed by the Monroes from the traditional American four o'clock to six. From all reports, the dinners were formidable affairs. Author Cooper commented on the serious manner of the guests, the ordinary quality of the conversation, and the feeling that the average dinner had "rather a cold than a formal air." In spite of the restrictive atmosphere, Cooper noticed how certain uninhibited souls helped themselves to any dish within arm's distance—even with a bevy of liveried waiters on hand to serve at request. Such uncouth manners on the part of their fellow countrymen must have offended the cultivated Monroes.

By the fall of 1819 the many Presidential dinners and receptions were almost completely masculine. The Washington ladies were staying away in droves. Mrs. Monroe's sister was the only female she could count on for sure to be present at her Tuesday-evening receptions.

Elizabeth Monroe seemed to have a gift for alienating friends and influencing people—negatively. But little by little the wounds began to heal, and by the time of Monroe's second term, ladies were beginning to return to the First Lady's drawing rooms. Eventually the receptions became so popular that extra help was needed. One could not boycott the President's wife forever, if only because the President's house was such a charming place to spend an evening. Great hickory-wood fires in the fireplaces, Negro servants in livery passing around good wine and delicious little cakes from silver trays, and an atmosphere of elegance and refinement all contributed to making the White House the fashionable place to go.

Mrs. Smith Thompson, wife of Monroe's Secretary of the Navy, was obviously one of those awed by the splendor of the Monroe style. After one dinner party, she commented: "We had the most stylish dinner I have been at."

Perhaps because he was a writer who appreciated good talk, Cooper was more critical. In describing a particular dinner, he wrote: "The whole entertainment might have passed for a better sort of European dinner party, at which the guests were too numerous for general or very agreeable discourse, and some of them too new to be entirely at their ease. Mrs. Monroe arose at the end of the dessert, and withdrew, attended by two or three of the most gallant of the company. No sooner was his wife's back turned than the President reseated himself, inviting his guests to imitate the action. After allowing his guests sufficient time to renew, in a few glasses, the recollections of similar enjoyment of their own, he arose, giving the hint to his company that it was time to rejoin the ladies. In the drawing room coffee was served, and everyone left the house before nine."

It would have been difficult for any woman to follow Dolley Madison as hostess of the President's house. For a reticent, somewhat regal personality such as Elizabeth Monroe it was impossible. Her contemporaries may have judged her rather harshly, but perhaps this was inevitable, because they were, after all, judging her in relation to her predecessor. From this distance, we can see that she had to set her own style, even though she was cursed for it. The flamboyance of Dolley was not for Elizabeth. Hers was the aristocratic, subdued, reserved approach.

Pale, pallid, "genteel" as the Monroe social regime may seem to us today, it had its own particular influence on the official life of the White House for generations. The appointments arranged and purchased by the Monroes have been used down through our history, sometimes by Presidents whose rough cut ways would have made the sensitive Monroes shudder with disdain. Considering the lack of enthusiasm with which Elizabeth Monroe was received in her day as First Lady, it is ironic that the "Monroe look" in the Executive Mansion still exists today. As a tribute to the taste of our fifth First Family, it still looks handsome and elegant indeed.

◇◇

R E C I P E S

SPOON BREAD

New York-bred, married to a Virginian, Elizabeth Monroe's long stays in Paris and London helped her develop a cultivated palate. On the Monroe family plantation in Virginia, Oak Hill, she served many old Southern recipes, dishes her husband had known from boyhood. One of the most famous, spoon bread, dates back to early Indian days, and still has the consistency of Indian porridge or pudding.

Butter or lard	*Boiling water*
Cornmeal	*Milk*
Salt	*Eggs*

Preheat oven to 425° F. Put 5 tablespoons butter or lard in a medium-size glass or pottery baking dish, then place in oven and allow to melt while you prepare the batter. Mix 1 cup cornmeal with 1 teaspoon salt, adding 2 cups boiling hot water, stirring as you pour to avoid lumpiness. Allow to cool several minutes, then stir in 1 cup cold milk. Add 4 eggs, one at a time, beating the batter after each egg is added. Remove casserole from oven, stir the melted butter into the batter. Mix well. Pour batter into baking dish and return to oven. Bake 25 to 30 minutes. Delicious served hot, right from the casserole, with plenty of additional butter popped into it. *Serves 4.*

TOMATOES AND EGGS

Although Washington and Monroe had their political disagreements, this never interfered with their wives' recipe exchanges. This Monroe favorite was passed along to Martha Washington and recorded in her "receipt" book.

Tomatoes	*Toast*
Salt and pepper	*Parsley*
Eggs	*Grated cheese*
Butter	

Place 1 thick slice of fresh tomato in each of 6 well-buttered muffin tins. Season with salt and pepper. Break an egg on top of each tomato. Once again season with salt and pepper. Place a small dab of butter on top of each egg. Bake in a medium (325°–350° F.) oven until the eggs are set. Scoop each tomato egg out of the tin and serve it on a round of buttered toast. Garnish with parsley. For an extra touch, sprinkle grated cheese over the top of the egg while it is still hot. A good brunch dish. *Serves 6.*

CAPON FLANDERS STYLE

James Monroe, like his former teacher and mentor, Thomas Jefferson, was fond of Continental cuisines, but he was equally fond of the foods of his Virginia childhood. In this dish the capon, raised at home, was combined with a Flemish preparation method, a happy combination.

Capon (or chicken)	*Sugar*
White wine, preferably Sauterne	*Mace*
Boiling water	*Carrots*
Salt	*Parsley*

Cut a 6- or 7-pound capon or chicken into serving pieces. Wash the pieces and put them in a large pot with 2½ cups Sauterne, plus enough boiling water to cover. Add 1 tablespoon salt, 2 tablespoons sugar, and ⅛ teaspoon mace. Cover, bring to a boil, and allow to simmer slowly over low fire until amost tender—2 to 2½ hours. Add 6 carrots, cut into long strips. Cook until carrots are tender, then remove capon and carrots to a hot platter. Keep warm while making gravy from the stock, adding ½ cup Sauterne to flavor. Pour the gravy over the capon and carrots and serve, garnished with parsley. *Serves 6.*

CHICKEN FRIED WITH RICE

This recipe is rich with history. Used frequently by Elizabeth Monroe at the Monroe plantation, Oak Hill, it was borrowed by Martha Washington. Martha served it often too, and actually served it to General La Fayette during a visit of his to Mount Vernon.

Chickens	*Eggs*
Butter	*Salt and pepper*
Rice	*Nutmeg*
Water	

Cut into serving pieces 2 or 3 small chickens. Partially fry them in a skillet with butter. Set aside. Meanwhile boil 2 cups rice in 1 quart water until the grains are cooked but not mushy. Stir 1 tablespoon butter into the rice while it is hot. After slight cooling beat 5 eggs into the rice, adding salt and pepper to taste and a dash of nutmeg. Place the chickens in a deep casserole and cover with the rice. Brown in a medium (350° F.) oven about 20 to 25 minutes. *Serves 6 to 9.*

CHICKEN PUDDING

Chicken was as much a favorite in the early nineteenth century as it is today. This particular recipe was taken from the family cookbook of President Monroe.

Chicken	*Salt and pepper*
Onion	*Flour*
Parsley	*Thyme*
Celery	*Butter*

FOR BATTER
TOPPING:

Eggs	*Flour*
Milk	*Salt*
Melted butter	

Cut a 4-to-4½-pound chicken into serving pieces. Place the back, neck, and giblets in a pot, cover with water, and add 1 onion halved, a few sprigs of parsley,

1 stalk celery in chunks, 1 teaspoon salt, ¼ teaspoon pepper, and ½ teaspoon dried thyme. Cook over low heat for 45 minutes. Strain the broth and set it aside. Put ½ cup flour, 1 teaspoon salt, and ¼ teaspoon pepper into a paper bag. Put pieces of the chicken into the bag and shake them around until evenly coated with the flour mixture. Heat ⅓ cup butter in a skillet with a tight-fitting cover. Then add the chicken and sauté it until evenly browned on all sides. Add the reserved broth, bring to a boil, cover the skillet tightly, and simmer for an hour or more, until chicken is tender when tested. Remove the chicken to an 8-inch square baking dish. Again reserve the broth.

To make the batter: Beat 3 eggs well; slowly add 1 cup milk and 2 tablespoons melted butter. Sift 1¼ cups flour with ½ teaspoon salt and stir it into the butter–egg mixture slowly, keeping it smooth. Pour the mixture over the chicken in the baking dish, making sure the chicken is covered evenly. Bake in a preheated hot (450° F.) oven for 15 minutes, then reduce oven temperature to 350° F. and continue the baking for 20 to 25 minutes. Top puffs up like Yorkshire Pudding. If you like, make a gravy of the reserved broth. Add a flour-and-water paste to it and cook until thickened. Pour over the chicken pudding as soon as it is done, or serve it separately if you prefer. *Serves 4 to 6.*

SAUTÉED EGGPLANT

So many of Martha Washington's recipes seem to have had Elizabeth Monroe as a source. This is one more example of a "receipt" that wound its way over the Virginia hills from Oak Hill to Mount Vernon.

Eggplant	*Egg yolks*
Water	*Breadcrumbs*
Salt	*Lard and butter*
Pepper	

Slice an eggplant about 1 inch thick, but do not peel it. Let it soak 1 to 2 hours in enough water to cover. Sprinkle liberally with salt while it soaks. When soaked, remove the eggplant, dry, and season with pepper. Beat 2 to 3 egg yolks (depending on size of egg plant) well. Dip the eggplant slices into the yolks, then into another dish full of grated breadcrumbs (about 1 cup). Then sauté eggplant in a preheated skillet in a mixture of butter and lard. Turn and cook until eggplant slices are nicely browned.

EGG BREAD

Hot breads and biscuits were a way of life in James Monroe's Virginia. His wife may not have grown up in this tradition in her native New York, but she quickly adapted to it after her marriage. Both this recipe and the one for Colonial Biscuits are from her Oak Hill collection.

White cornmeal	*Scalding water*
Lard or butter	*Eggs*
Salt	*Milk*

Sift two times 1 pint white cornmeal. Add to it 1 tablespoon lard (or butter), a dash of salt, and then scald the mixture with boiling water. Stir well. Beat well 2 eggs and add them to the cornmeal mixture. If too thick, thin with a little scalding milk. Bake in a hot (375°– 400° F.) oven until done, about 15 minutes.

COLONIAL BISCUITS

Flour	*Lard*
Salt	*Egg*

Sift 1 pint flour, add a pinch of salt and 1 tablespoon lard. Mix well, then add milk until you have a fairly stiff dough. Roll quite thin on a floured board and cut with a biscuit cutter. Stick each biscuit with a fork, then bake a short time in a hot (400° F.) oven. *Makes 12 small biscuits.*

WILLIAMSBURG BUNS

The scent of hot breads coming from the big open kitchen was as much a part of life at Oak Hill as the thicketed beauty of the Virginia country surrounding the plantation. Such recipes as this were a trademark of country life. They were popular served with tea.

Milk	*Eggs*
Melted butter	*Flour*
Sugar	*Nutmeg and mace (optional)*
Salt	*Sherry (optional)*
Yeast cakes	

Scald 1 cup milk. Add to it ½ cup melted butter, ½ cup sugar, and 2 teaspoons salt. Cool to lukewarm. Then add 2 yeast cakes dissolved in ¼ cup warm water. Beat 3 eggs thoroughly and add them to the liquids. Beat in 4½ cups flour, mixing well. If desired for extra flavor, beat in as well 1 teaspoon each of nutmeg and mace and 1 wine glass of sherry. Allow the dough to rise until doubled. Turn it out and knead lightly. Fill muffin pans ⅔ full and let dough rise again until light, approximately 20 minutes. Brush the tops with melted butter and bake in a moderate (350° F.) oven 20 minutes, or until lightly browned. *Makes about 36 small buns.*

MASSIE STACK CAKE

It was not unusual in the Monroe household, super-elegant as it was, to fall back on certain pioneer dishes that had found favor with James Monroe's family. Such a dish as Massie Stack Cake was an old Virginia favorite made before sugar became plentiful, when molasses was used to satisfy the hankering for something sweet. It was the custom for wedding guests to arrive at the big bridal dinner with a thin layer for the bride's cake. Each bride took pride in the height of her stack cake, for it indicated the number of friends present at the affair. (It is rumored that high cake plates came into fashion so that even less popular brides could have the appearance of a high stack cake. A likely—and likable—story!)

Shortening	*Salt*
Sugar	*Soda*
Molasses	*Milk*
Eggs	*Applesauce*
Flour	

Cream ¾ cup shortening, adding 1 cup sugar a little at a time. Blend well. Add 1 cup molasses; mix thoroughly, then add 3 eggs, one at a time, beating after each one is added. Sift 4 cups flour with 1 teaspoon salt, and ½ teaspoon soda, and add to the molasses mixture alternately with 1 cup milk. Beat the mixture until it is smooth, then pour it ⅜ inch deep in six greased and floured 9-inch pans. Bake in a warm (375° F.) oven about 18 to 20 minutes. When the layers have cooled, stack them, coating each with a generous amount of applesauce. You may put applesauce on the top layer too, or frost it with any flavor frosting desired.

WILLIAMSBURG SALLY LUNN

This standby of Colonial Virginia was a Monroe mainstay, as it was in most households of the time. Its English origins are obscure, but it was long considered a bun. By the time it crossed the Atlantic it had become a bread, baked always in a special Sally Lunn or Turk's-head mold.

Yeast cake	*Sugar*
Milk	*Eggs*
Butter	*Flour*

Soak 1 yeast cake in 1 cup warm milk. Cream ½ cup butter with ⅓ cup sugar, then add 3 well-beaten eggs. Mix all together well. Sift 1 quart flour, then add it alternately with the yeasty milk to the creamed mixture. Let the dough rise in a warm place, then beat it well. Butter 1 Sally Lunn mold or 2 smaller molds and pour the dough in. Allow it to rise again. Bake in a moderate (350° F.) oven until done, about 50 minutes.

CRY BABIES

Another expressively titled dish, this is, as its name suggests, a pioneer recipe. Like others of the type, it was a favorite as well of discerning eaters such as the Monroes. Virginia cooking of their time was a lively blend of old English recipes kept reasonably authentic, English recipes livened up a bit with African influences by the plantation Negro cooks, and the inventive improvisation of pioneer enterprise. This recipe falls into the last category, though it is remarkable for its delicate texture and taste.

Sugar	*Salt*
Black molasses	*Boiling water*
Vegetable shortening (or lard)	*Baking soda*
Egg	*Flour*
Powdered ginger	

Mix together ½ cup sugar, ½ cup black molasses, and ½ cup vegetable shortening. Add 1 slightly beaten egg, 1½ teaspoons powdered ginger, ¼ teaspoon salt, ⅜ cup boiling water, and 1½ teaspoons baking soda. Mix all together thoroughly. Then stir in 2 cups flour, just enough to make a stiffish batter. Drop by the teaspoon onto a greased cooky sheet at least 2 inches apart—this allows room for the "babies" to spread. Bake in a moderately hot (375° F.) oven about 15 minutes, or until the touch of your finger leaves no mark. *Makes 3 dozen.*

APPLE CHARLOTTE

One should really call this Apple Elizabeth, since it was Mrs. Monroe who recorded this rich dessert and then passed it along to Martha Washington, to be added to the huge Washington recipe collection.

Chocolate	*Apples*
Sugar	*Powdered sugar*
Milk	*Cinnamon*
Eggs	

Boil 1 pound chocolate and 6 ounces sugar in 1 quart milk. When the chocolate comes to a boil, take it from the fire. Add 6 egg yolks and 2 egg whites, all well beaten. Add to the chocolate mixture very slowly, little by little. Place a thick layer of peeled apple slices, sprinkled with sugar and cinnamon to sweeten, on the bottom of a deep-dished baking pan. Pour the chocolate mixture carefully over the apples. Place the dish in a large saucepan of boiling water (or heat in the oven at medium temperature—350° F.) and cook until the cream is firm. Sift powdered sugar over the top. Glaze under the broiler ("Glaze with a red-hot shovel," the Monroe recipe reads).

LITTLE FINE CAKES

The little tea cakes served at receptions and drawing rooms by Mrs. Monroe were a constant during her eight-year tenure in the White House. This particular recipe goes back to 1758.

Butter	*Coriander seed*
Sugar	*Currants*
Flour	*Eggs*
Mace	

Cream 1 cup butter, add 1 cup sugar, and mix well. Sift 2 cups flour with 1 teaspoon mace and ½ teaspoon coriander seed. Add the sifted ingredients to the creamed mixture. Then add 1 cup currants. Separate and beat thoroughly 3 egg yolks and 2 egg whites. Add yolks to the dough, beating all together thoroughly. Then fold in whites. Pour the mixture into greased and floured muffin tins and bake in a medium (350° F.) oven until lightly browned. Frost with a simple white icing or serve plain. *Makes about 3 dozen cakes.*

CHESS CAKES

In spite of their name, these delicate tarts were not served at solitary chess matches, but at crowded and busy parties, such as the receptions given by President and Mrs. Monroe. No matter how formal the occasion, the food at the Monroes was always mouth-wateringly delicious; even the most biased reporters of the day conceded that. In some handwritten books they were called Cheese cakes, even though no cheese is involved.

Pastry shells	*Egg yolks*
Butter	*Salt*
Sugar	*White wine*

Prepare pie dough as for a double crusted pie. Roll it, and shape it into 12 individual tart shapes. Then cream 1 cup butter with 1 cup sugar. Beat 6 egg yolks until light-lemon color. Add to the butter–sugar mixture and mix well. Add a dash of salt and stir in ⅓ cup white wine. Beat thoroughly. Place the tart-shaped pastry shells in muffin tins. Fill them with the butter–egg–sugar mixture about ¾ full. Bake in a moderately hot (375° F.) oven for 25 to 30 minutes, or until light gold in color. Remove and chill. Serve cold. (Can be kept several days in the refrigerator or weeks in freezer.) *Makes 12 to 15.*

TIPSY PUDDING OR TIPSY BREAD

By whatever name you choose to call this, it is a splendid way to use up stale bread and turn it into a company dish. Such "economies" were commonplace in Colonial Virginia, even in such stately homes as the Monroes'.

Stale rolls or sponge cake	*Eggs*
Raspberry or strawberry jam	*Salt*
Sherry	*Scalded milk*
Sugar	*Vanilla*
Blanched almonds	

Cut the crusts off stale rolls or French bread and cut the bread into thin round slices. Spread them generously with raspberry or strawberry jam. Pile the slices on top of one another in a glass dish. Pour sherry, sweetened slightly with sugar, over the bread until the bread has absorbed all it can. Around the sides and all over the top insert long thick slivers of blanched almonds. Then pour custard all around the bread. Chill until ready to serve (may be made a day ahead). Serve as is or topped with whipped cream.

To make custard: Beat 3 eggs lightly with a fork, adding ¼ cup sugar and ⅛ teaspoon salt. Add 2 cups scalded milk slowly, stirring constantly. Cook the mixture in the top of a double boiler over boiling hot water until it coats a spoon. Strain, chill, and flavor with ½ teaspoon vanilla. *Serves 4.*

OLD-FASHIONED SPONGE CAKE

A mainstay when it came to official or informal entertaining, this fine-textured cake seemed ageless even during the Monroe administration. It was unlikely that a servant would appear with cake and punch in the middle of a conference at the White House, *à la* the days of the Madisons, for when President Monroe invited diplomats to his official home to discuss business, the session was invariably brusque, businesslike, and of short duration. Nevertheless, at parties a tray with sponge cake on it was a familiar sight.

Eggs	*Baking powder*
Sugar	*Lemon juice*
Salt	*Lemon rind*
Flour	

Beat together 10 egg yolks and 2 cups fine sugar, blending until the mixture is pale, frothy, and very light. Add a touch of salt. Beat separately 10 egg whites until very stiff and in peaks. Measure 2 cups flour, 1 level tablespoon baking powder, and a pinch of salt, *then* sift and add to the egg yolks, folding in carefully. Do not beat; merely cut down through the batter in a folding motion. (According to this recipe, "beating the eggs makes the cake light, but beating the batter makes the cake tough.") Fold the egg whites gently into the batter; flavor with 2 tablespoons lemon juice and the grated rind of 1 lemon, and turn carefully into a large, ungreased angel-food cake pan. Bake at once in a moderate (350° F.) oven for approximately 45 minutes, or until a toothpick comes out clean. Turn the cake upside down on a cake rack. Let cool for an hour or more, then loosen the edges and carefully turn the cake onto a cake plate. When serving, sprinkle powdered or plain fine sugar over the top, or frost with a lemon frosting. A really superb cake, by the standards of any age.

CHATHAM ARTILLERY PUNCH

When President Monroe visited Savannah, Georgia, in 1819 to see the first steamship begin its maiden journey across the Atlantic Ocean, he was served a specialty of the city, Chatham Artillery Punch. There is no record of his having carried the recipe back to Washington with him, but there can be little doubt he enjoyed the drink all the same—as we think you will, too. With its myriad ingredients, it is indeed nectar for a visiting President.

Catawba wine or other white wine	*Strong tea*
Rum	*Brown sugar*
Gin	*Oranges*
Brandy	*Lemons*
Bénédictine	*Maraschino cherries*
Rye whiskey	*Champagne*

In a barrel, mix the following ingredients together at least 3 to 4 days before the time you plan to serve the punch: 1½ gallons Catawba or mellow white wine, ½ gallon rum, 1 quart gin, 1 quart brandy, ½ pint Bénédictine, 1½ quarts rye whiskey, 1½ gallons strong tea, 2½ pounds brown sugar, the juice of 1½ dozen oranges (about 9 cups juice), and 1½ dozen lemons (about 3½ cups juice), and the contents of one bottle Maraschino cherries. Cover tightly. Just before serving, add 1 case (12 bottles!) iced champagne. A very special occasion punch! *Makes 10 gallons, about 320 servings for 150 guests.*

MINT JULEP, NONALCOHOLIC VARIETY

At Oak Hill President Monroe had a favorite recipe for a mint julep without the julep—that is, the punch. Nonalcoholic, it is a cooling summer drink.

Orange juice	*Sugar*
Grape juice	*Soda water*
Lemon or lime juice	*Mint*

Mix together ½ pint orange juice, ½ pint grape juice, and the juice of 6 lemons or limes. Allow it to stand on ice a full hour. Add a little sugar to taste, but not so much that it becomes too sweet. Just before serving, add 1 pint soda water and pour into glasses that have been chilled and are half-full of ice. Put a sprig of fresh mint into each glass and serve immediately.

VI

The Adams Family: Second Time Around

When John Quincy Adams assumed the Presidency in 1825, it was in many ways a hollow honor. The close election had been thrown to the House of Representatives, and Adams had been voted in by a tiny majority, thus defeating the far more popular war hero Andrew Jackson.

The four years of Adams' Presidency were not particularly happy ones. Jackson's forces were preparing for what they hoped would be a victorious comeback for their hero in 1828. There were accusations and whispered innuendos that Adams had "bought" the Presidency by bribing Henry Clay for his support in the House. Washington was somewhat uneasy with the play between opposing forces.

It was a pity that the election clouded the social scene, for under happier circumstances, Louisa Adams would have made quite a remarkable First Lady. Born in London of an American father from Maryland and an English mother, she had been extraordinarily well educated for her day—or any day. Gifted in French, English, and Greek literature, she had a connoisseur's love of music, wrote poetry, and enjoyed intellectual discussion on the highest plane. She had served with her husband in many European courts and felt comfortable with the most sophisticated Europeans. Yet she had important links with her own country, for her uncle had been a signer of the Declaration of Independence and one-time governor of Maryland. She was a distinguished addition to one of the most distinguished American families, the Adamses.

In fact, from 1818 on, Louisa and John Quincy Adams had lived in the capital, and Louisa assumed a prominent place in Washington society. One would have expected that such a place would serve her in good stead as First Lady. Of course it did, to some extent, but the rumors under which her husband took office took some of the joy out of her entertainment efforts from then on, and the White House was not the cynosure it might have been.

There were parties, receptions, and drawing rooms as usual, but John Quincy Adams' formal, somewhat stilted personality had a dampening effect on the superficial gaiety in which Washington society usually abounds.

Adams was himself aware of his inability to make small talk. In his diary he once noted:

> I went out this evening in search of conversation, an art of which I never had an adequate idea. Long as I have lived in the world, I never have thought of conversation as a school in which something was to be learned. I never knew how to make, to control, or to change it. I am by nature a silent animal, and my dear mother's constant lesson in childhood, that children in company should be seen and not heard, confirmed me irrevocably in what I now deem a bad habit. Conversation is an art of the highest importance, and a school in which, for the business of life, more may perhaps be learnt than from books. It is, indeed, and must be, desultory and superficial; and, as a school, consists more in making others talk than in talking. Therein has been, and ever will be, my deficiency—the talent of starting the game.

This self-appraisal must have been accurate; at least it was borne out in reports of visitors to the White House. Guests seated near the President at dinner had, according to one observer, "a hard time of it." Adams smiled amiably enough, but seemed unable to initiate any table talk. He was at his best in political discussions with his peers, for he had inherited his interest in political affairs from his father. But John Quincy's real forte was literary discussion. Conversations about books, plays, and art sparkle through the pages of his diary. His greatest—and unfulfilled—ambition was to produce a work of literary importance that would have significance through the ages.

If the guests at the Adamses' found difficulties in talking with their host, he in turn bridled at this aspect of the Presidency. In his diary entry for February 28, 1829, he observed: "This evening was the sixth drawing room. Very much crowded; 16 Senators, perhaps 60 Members of the House of Representatives and multitudes of strangers. . . . The heat was oppressive and these parties are becoming more and more insupportable to me." He did not have a long way to go. This was virtually the end of his Presidency. It had taken its toll.

The Adamses' parties at the White House were far more elaborate affairs than those of the first Adamses. John Quincy seems to have inherited his share of the

Adamses' New England frugality. Earlier in his career he made occasional notes in his diary about his expenses while living abroad; and he carefully kept a "monthly expense book," noting, at one time, with Yankee canniness: "The firewood is, luckily, included as part of my rent. On all these articles of consumption the cook and steward first make their profits on the purchase, and next make free pillage of the articles themselves. The steward takes the same liberty with my wines. In dismissing my cook I shall attempt to escape from a part of these depredations. To avoid a great part of them is impossible. It is, I believe, the law of nature between master and servant that the servant shall spoil or plunder the master."

Louisa Adams, having a Southern background and having lived abroad so long, was more accustomed to the necessary expenses involved in entertaining. Consequently, when the Adamses entertained at all, it was—as one observer put it—"usually lavish."

E. Cooley in his *Etiquette at Washington City*, published in 1829, described an Adams levee:

> Gentlemen and ladies both attend, arrive about eight and leave around ten. . . . The company is treated with coffee, tea and a variety of cakes, jellies, ice-cream, and white and red wine, mixed and unmixed, and sometimes other cordials and liquors, and frequently with West Indian fruit; all of which are carried about the rooms amongst the guests, upon large trays by servants dressed in livery; each one takes from it what he pleases, when a opportunity offers, which, at some of the fullest levees, may not happen very often; not because there is any scarcity of refreshment, but the difficulty the waiters find in making their way through the crowd with their trays. . . . After some part of the company have retired, so as to give more room for the waiters to move freely about the rooms with refreshments, everyone is furnished bountifully; which shows that the articles were not wanting so much as an opportunity of presenting them freely to the guests.

In his *Reminiscences,* Benjamin Perley Poor, a journalist of the period, noted that during John Quincy Adams' administration the Washington parties were "ceremonious and exclusive." He elaborated:

> A "minuet de la cour" and stately "quadrille," varied by the "basket dance," and on exceptional occasions, the exhilarating "cheat" formed the staple for saltatorial performance, until the hour of eleven brought the concluding country dance when a final squad of roysterers bobbed "up the middle and down again" to the airs of "Sir Roger de Coverly" or "Money Musk." The music was furnished by colored performers on the violin, except on great occasions when some of the Marine Band played an accompaniment on flutes and clarinets. The refreshments were iced lemonade, ice-cream, Port wine, negus, and small cakes, served in a room adjoining the dancing hall, or brought in by colored domestics, or by the cavalier in his own proper person, who oftimes appeared upon the

dancing floor, elbowing his way to the lady of his adoration, in the one hand bearing well-filled glasses, and in the other a plate heaped up with cakes.

Another observer, Mrs. Basil Hall, an Englishwoman who visited America in 1827–1828, reported on a Presidential open house somewhat more critically:

There was a queerish enough kind of medley of persons, though, on the whole, not so many odd looking persons as I expected to see. The President is a short, elderly man with an expression of much care and anxiety. Mrs. Adams I could scarcely see, the crowd around her was so great. A suite of four or five rooms was thrown open and refreshments, smelling strongly of gin, were handed around. Ice, too, there was, but the greater part of the eatables was devoured by the most ordinary of the company, who pounced upon the trays like those not much accustomed to such fare.

Mrs. Hall was later invited to dinner, and couldn't resist her two cents' worth of comment on this as well: "Mrs. Adams is a very ladylike person. The dinner was very showy, but no American ever understands doing those things really well, and there were strange inconsistencies and altogether a clumsiness very unlike the elegance of Mr. Vaughn's entertainments." Mr Vaughn—need we note—was the British Ambassador to Washington.

Louisa Adams made it a rule that all were welcome at her drawing rooms, whether friend of political foe. She was a charming hostess in spite of the fact that her health was sporadically poor, and greeted all her guests graciously. Although she, like her husband, cherished good conversation about meaningful subjects, she was far more adroit than he at sparring with mundane topics.

She would stand in the circle of Cabinet ladies; new arrivals to the reception would come up to her for her curtsey and an exchange of greetings before passing on to see others, chat with cronies, listen to the musicians playing gay airs, or have some of the generous portions of cakes and wine. Only in the last part of the last Adams year in the Executive Mansion did Louisa abandon her position in the Cabinet wives' circle. Then she passed freely from group to group, extending cordial welcomes to all.

So much was being spent on wines and liquors at the receptions that finally President Adams insisted that there be cards of admission issued, to control to some extent the number of people who surged through the White House. It may have been his New England thriftiness that prompted such action, or it may have been irritation at the criticism leveled against him by his enemies for almost any reason at all.

Louisa had furnished the East Room—the room in which her mother-in-law had once hung her laundry—in the French manner. She turned the vast chamber into a comfortably modest salon with a number of pieces of French furniture. Instead of praising her prudence in managing this with a relatively small expenditure, her husband's political enemies ranted at the extravagance. When the

President bought a billiard table for the Executive Mansion there were outcries that he was turning the nation's First House into a gambling den. Such a charge against the mild, temperate John Quincy Adams seems ridiculous today, but in the heat of the 1820s it caused a real furor.

Basically, President Adams' schedule was as simple as he could keep it. He arose early, between 5 and 6 A.M., and had a one-to-two-hour swim in the Potomac before breakfast. Breakfast was usually served at nine. From then on until five it was official business time. Dinner was served from five to six-thirty. The evenings not devoted to official entertaining Adams spent writing in his diary or reading state papers requiring his attention. He usually retired between eleven and midnight.

In spite of Adams' self-deprecation (his diary is studded with references such as "I said two or three silly things to Sir James Mackintosh, and was altogether stiff and dull beyond my usual measure"), he was a lively dinner companion in small groups of his peers. Even political enemy Martin Van Buren commented: "In a small and agreeable party, he was one of the most entertaining table companions of his day. . . . I . . . always derived [on such occasions] unqualified delight from his society and valuable information from his conversation."

Small talk was one thing, good conversation another, and President Adams prized the latter as much as he was impatient with the former. This was evident long before he assumed the Presidency, as the following account of a dinner with the Duke of Waterloo in London will show.

Then Minister to England, Adams wrote: "The dinner was of turtle and venison, and otherwise luxurious as usual. At the dessert the loving cups of champagne punch and the basins of rosewater went round. . . . Every toast, excepting the first, was drunk standing, with what they call three times three—hip! hip! hip! and nine huzzas—for the Lord Mayor observed that it was impossible to do anything in the City without noise. With all this, the dinner was inexpressibly dull. The company was obviously not well assorted."

Ironically, Adams' Presidential dinners were to suffer from the same sickness, although there were some festive times at the White House in his day. The wedding of his son John in the Blue Room was such an occasion. It was such a gay celebration that John Quincy Adams even joined in a Virginia reel, unusual as it was for him to unbend in public.

It is a matter of some curiosity that Adams, with all his exposure to diverse European cuisines, showed so little interest in food. His culinary education had certainly been extensive. By the time he was twelve he had been abroad four times, and by the age of seventeen he had journeyed over most of the Continent. He was married to a cultivated woman who had grown up abroad, well accustomed to the assorted dining patterns of other countries. He had even gone so far as to bring back a French chef, Michael Anthony Guista, from his Amsterdam tour.

Yet throughout the Adams diary food references are sparse. Adams never failed to mention with whom he dined and how often, but the contents of the meals obviously concerned him so little they were not worthy of comment. The reference to turtle and venison at the dinner with the Duke of Waterloo was atypical. He did describe a dinner in England on June 2, 1816, with Lord Holland at Holland House, which suggests some awareness and expertise in food: "Eighteen sat down to table. The dinner was elegant, the wines choice, the dessert excellent, and might have seemed to me better but that Madame Bourke, an accomplished epicure, had forewarned me that Lord Holland had the best confectioner in London. The tone of society was easy and agreeable."

During Adams' sojourn in Washington while Thomas Jefferson was President, personal relations between the two men were cordial, and the Adamses were frequent dinner guests at the Executive Mansion. Yet Adams did not comment on the quality of the Jeffersonian cuisine, or even make fleeting references to it, as he had noted Lord Holland's dinner. Instead, Adams seemed almost critical of Jefferson's epicurean ways.

One of President Jefferson's dinners did nevertheless deserve special comment in Adams' diary. November 3, 1807, John Quincy Adams joined a number of members of Congress at the Executive Mansion and later wrote:

"There was, as usual, a dissertation upon wines; not very edifying. Mr. Jefferson said that the Epicurean philosophy came nearest to the truth, in his opinion, of any ancient system of philosophy, but that it had been misunderstood and misrepresented. . . . Mr. Jefferson said that he had always been extremely fond of agriculture, and knew nothing about it, but the person who united with other sciences the greatest agricultural knowledge of any man he knew was Mr. Madison. He was the best farmer in the world. On the whole, it was one of the most agreeable dinners I have had at Mr. Jefferson's."

It might have been the discussion of agriculture that piqued Mr. Adams' interest so much at this particular dinner. Certainly this was a topic in which he was deeply interested. In fact, while President, he put into practice some of his theories about agricultural development, planting rows of trees, shrubs, assorted vegetable gardens, and herbs.

Adams was especially fond of fruit. The White House orchards flourished and eventually the apricot, plum, apple, and pear trees blossomed and bore fruit. Other seedlings grew—oaks, locusts, beeches, twenty rows of shellbarks, pignuts, and black walnuts. Adams' diary notations were exuberant: "May 26, 1828—This has been a harassing day; but I perceived a tamarind heaving up the earth in the center of tumbler No. 2; and I planted in tumbler No. 1 three whole Hautboy strawberries."

Although one sees only oblique references to it, it is likely that John Quincy Adams was a connoisseur of wines. Actually a temperate man, he served wine and knew quality when he tasted it. As a boy of fifteen he had inspected the celebrated wine cellars of Bremen and even sampled some 160-year-old Rhenish wine. He had had many opportunities to educate his palate to good wine, and evidence suggests that he probably did.

For instance, his disinterest in the evaluation of wines at President Jefferson's dinner may have stemmed from boredom with a subject in which he was well versed. On another occasion, November 2, 1822, he noted in his diary: "We had company to dinner—we were twenty at table. The dinner was pleasant, with the exception of one incident: in a desultory conversation upon wines, Mr. Tazewell asserted and perseveringly insisted, that Tokay was a species of Rhenish wine. After insisting to the contrary for some time in perfect good humor and civility, as he still persisted, in the warmth of the collision I said, 'Why, you never drank a drop of Tokay in your life.' I set this down as a token of self-disapprobation for having said it. Tazewell made no reply but looked hurt. The conversation turned upon other topics. . . ."

In later years, after John Quincy Adams had left the Presidency and become a member of Congress, he became so preoccupied with his work that he seemed even less interested in food, good or otherwise. He would stuff a few pieces of bread into his pockets when he left his home in the morning, nibble on them throughout the day, and return home late in the evening, having had no other nourishment at all.

The Presidency of John Quincy Adams is a classic example of the way in which political realities influence social amenities. Both Adams and his wife Louisa were beautifully equipped for their responsibilities. But the circumstances of his ascent to the office, the closeness of the election, and the bitterness of opposing factions conspired to make the Adams Presidency tense and trying. The four years were ended none too soon for John Quincy Adams. But if the political climate had been more auspicious, he might have been able to relax and enjoy his duties as the nation's host, and the public might have been able to remember him as the warm, lively, intelligent man his family knew him to be.

◊◊

R E C I P E S

GREEN CORN PUDDING

Gardening, farming, horseback riding, and swimming were the simple pleasures John Quincy Adams pursued throughout his life. Exposed as he was to the many epicurean dishes of Europe, he retained a fondness for the plainer foods of his Massachusetts upbringing. One could not grow up in New England in his day and not like corn. It was served in myriad ways, including as a special breakfast pudding.

| *Fresh corn on the cob* | *Milk* |
| *Eggs* | *Sugar* |

Take 1 dozen fresh ears of corn. Cut the corn off the cob. Beat 5 eggs until light and foamy. Add 1 quart milk, with a dash of sugar to taste, and stir in the corn. Mix all together well. Pour the mixture into a well-buttered glass baking dish (be sure the sides as well as the bottom are buttered) and bake for 2 hours in a low oven (about 300° F.). When firm, remove from oven. Serve for dessert with any sweet sauce, or as a main dish for breakfast with daubs of butter on it. *Serves 6 to 8.*

RICH JOHNNY CAKES BAKED IN A BUTTERED IRON SKILLET

There were subtle changes in dining habits between the days of old John Adams and those of his son John Quincy. Even the old pioneer standbys were glamorized by cooks constantly seeking improvements and innovations, as this later recipe for good old Johnny Cakes indicates.

Water-ground white cornmeal	*Cold milk*
Salt	*Eggs*
Boiling water	*Butter*

Mix 2 cups cornmeal with 1 teaspoon salt. Pour enough boiling water on it to make a thick paste. Allow to cool slightly, then thin with just enough milk that has been vigorously beaten with 2 eggs to give the batter a smooth, free pancakey consistency. Stir in 2 tablespoons melted and cooled butter and mix well. Pour the batter into a sizzling hot, well-greased large skillet. Pour in all the batter at once and bake in a moderate (350° F.) oven until the big cake is brown on top. Bubbles will form, similar to those that form on pancakes cooked on top of the stove. When done, turn the big Johnny cake upside down on a hot, round platter. Dot generously with butter, cut in wedges, and serve immediately. Delicious with maple syrup, too. *Serves 6.*

SUCCOTASH SOUP

Succotash was as much a part of John Quincy Adams' growing up as the corn from which it was made. Later Massachusetts generations disdained the traditional Pilgrim specialty, calling it "supper trash," but in Adams' day it was plain succotash and plain delicious. This variation is tasty and filling.

Green corn cut from cob or kernel   *Pickled (we would say salt)*
  corn   *pork*
Lima beans, fresh or frozen

If the pork is very salty, let it soak in cold water an hour or so before you are ready to cook it. To 1 quart green corn cut off the cob, add 1 quart fresh lima beans. Put 2 pounds salt pork in a large pot, cover with 3 quarts water, and boil until it is half-cooked about 1 hour before adding the vegetables. Then add the corn and beans; boil until they are tender and the water has boiled down to half. Remove the meat at serving time. Put it in a separate plate, slice and serve along with the soup. Makes about 2 quarts.

CREAM OF CORN SOUP

As John Quincy Adams himself was a curious mixture of the simple and the sophisticated, so were his food preferences. One day he could say "Five or six small crackers and a glass of water give me a sumptuous dinner." Shortly thereafter he could describe "an elegant supper." Exposure to the finest European dining, as well as the New England fare he grew up on, undoubtedly gave him a broad and deep appreciation of variety in diet. This soup was part of his heritage, and savored as such.

Melted butter   *Milk*
Minced onion   *Cream-style corn*
Flour

Melt 3 tablespoons butter in the top of a double boiler over very low heat. Add ¼ cup minced onion and cook until tender. Stir in 3 tablespoons flour, keeping it smooth. Slowly add 4 cups milk, stirring continuously to keep smooth. Cook until mixture is thickened slightly. Add 2 cups corn. Cook just below boiling for 5 minutes, and serve hot. *Makes 6 servings.*

SPICED SHAD

Fondness for shad ran in the Adams family. This unusual recipe is especially tasty. The original recipe calls for 3 teaspoons cayenne pepper. We restrain ourselves to about ½ teaspoon. You decide!

Shad	*Cayenne*
Salt	*Vinegar*
Whole allspice	

Split 1 large shad open and rub it well with 2 tablespoons salt. Allow to stand for 2 or 3 hours. When ready to cook, fill a large kettle with boiling water (enough water to cover the fish), and 1 teaspoon salt for every quart of water used. Cook shad 20 minutes. Remove from the water and drain. Crack the grains of 2 tablespoons whole allspice and sprinkle over the shad, along with 3 teaspoons cayenne. Completely cover the fish with cold vinegar. Serve immediately or keep several days in the refrigerator.

ROAST RACK OF VENISON

While venison is even more of a treat today than in John Quincy Adams' day, there is evidence that he enjoyed it when it was well prepared. For the best flavor, venison should be served rare. Actually, it is as versatile as beef, and lends itself to as many treatments.

Rack of venison	*Cayenne*
Garlic	*Butter or salt pork*
Pepper or paprika	

Place a 6-to-8-pound rack of venison in a roasting pan. Rub it with 1 cut clove garlic. Sprinkle with ½ teaspoon paprika or ¼ teaspoon pepper and a dash of cayenne. Rub the meat over with butter or cover it with a piece of salt pork. If butter is used, be sure to baste the meat frequently during the roasting. Roast uncovered in a preheated moderate (325° F.) oven, allowing 16 to 18 minutes per pound. Serve with mushrooms and wild rice and/or with Cumberland Sauce.

To make Cumberland Sauce:

Currant jelly	*Vinegar*
Egg yolk	*Salt and pepper*
Dry mustard	*Raisins (optional)*
Sugar	

Put 1 glass currant jelly in the top of a double boiler. Cook over hot water until jelly is soft. Then beat in 1 egg yolk, ¾ teaspoon dry mustard, 2 tablespoons sugar, 2 tablespoons vinegar, and salt and pepper to taste. Cook until sauce is thickened—stirring continuously—about 15 minutes. Add ¼ cup raisins if desired.

SPICY CRANBERRY RELISH

Christmas was always a particularly joyful season in the Adams family, as with most families in old New England. Accompanying the traditional Christmas dinner it was natural, in the Massachusetts area where they were grown, to serve cranberries in one form or another.

Jellied cranberry sauce	*Powdered cloves*
Lemon juice	*Raisins*
Cinnamon	

(This can be made with canned jellied cranberry sauce, but it is better if made from scratch.) Crush 2 cups cranberry sauce with a fork to break it up a bit. Add the juice of 1 lemon, ½ teaspoon cinnamon, ¼ teaspoon powdered cloves, and ½ cup raisins, plumped. Mix well. Chill 2 or 3 hours at least. Serve cold with turkey.

BEEFSTEAK AND KIDNEY PIE

In a poem he wrote describing one of his typical days, President Adams concluded with these lines:

> At home I find the table spread,
>   And dinner's fragrant steams invite,
> But first the twofold stairs I tread,
>   My atmospheric tale to write.
> Then, seated round the social board,
>   We feast, til absent friends are toasted,
> Though sometimes *my* delays afford
>   The beef or mutton *over-roasted*.

It is not likely that he found this a problem during his stay in England, when served the favorite English beefsteak and kidney pie. In this dish, the beef *must* be well cooked.

Pastry	*Onion*
Veal kidneys	*Water*
Salt	*Bay leaf*
Dry red wine	*Parsley*
Round of beef	*Celery tops*
Flour	*Dried marjoram*
Shortening	*Mushrooms*

Prepare the pastry for a 1-crust pie. Chill it in the refrigerator while you make the filling. Trim fat and membranes from 4 small veal kidneys, sprinkle them with salt and cover with 1 cup dry red wine. Set aside. Next, cut 1½ pounds round steak into thin strips. Sprinkle them with flour, pounding it into the meat thoroughly. Heat 4 tablespoons shortening and sauté 1 chopped onion in it for a few moments, then add beef and cook over high heat, stirring often, until nicely browned. Separate the kidney clusters, remove them from the wine (but save the wine), and flour them lightly. Add them to the beef–onion mixture and stir until browned. Add ½ cup water, along with 1 bay leaf, 5 sprigs chopped parsley, 5 sprigs chopped celery tops, and ½ teaspoon marjoram. Reduce heat to low, cover pan, and cook until all meat is tender, about 1 hour. When ready, stir in ¼ pound sliced mushrooms and the wine marinade. Pour mixture into a 2-quart baking dish that can be brought to the table. Cover the top with thinly rolled pastry, slashed to allow steam to escape. Seal the edges well, and bake in a preheated hot (450° F.) oven for ½ hour, or until the crust is nicely browned. *Serves 6 to 8.*

NEW ENGLAND GREENS

Two greens that have declined in fame but not in flavor since John Quincy Adams' day are ostrich ferns and fiddlehead ferns. Before the family garden gave birth, the women and children would go into the woods a-greening. Other edible ferns to be found in many woods are the cinnamon fern and bracken, or turkey-foot fern.

FIDDLEHEAD FERNS À LA PIONEERS

This type of fern came originally from France. Today the best varieties are grown in Maine. In taste, the fiddlehead most resembles a blend of asparagus, broccoli, and artichoke. It can be boiled and served on toast, creamed, or cold in salad with French or vinaigrette dressing.

> *Fiddlehead ferns*   *Salt pork*
> *Water*

Boil a large "mess" of the ferns in a pot of boiling water "in which salt pork has been cooking." Boil very quickly; do not overcook. Serve hot with melted butter. A touch of garlic may be added to the butter.

BUTTERED OSTRICH FERNS NEW ENGLAND STYLE

If you plan to gather your own ostrich ferns, look for them on wet, marshy land or on land that overflows with water each spring. The fern clumps usually have from 10 to 20 heads and produce fronds for 3 or 4 weeks. Pick them while the brown sheath is on them.

> *Ostrich ferns*   *Salt*
> *Water*

Clean off the brown sheath. Soak the ferns 1 hour in cold water, then rinse under cold running water. Put the greens into rapidly boiling water, lower heat, add salt, and cook until just tender. Drain and serve piping hot with melted butter. They are also good cooled, with sliced hard-boiled eggs added, along with quartered tomatoes and a French or vinaigrette dressing.

BOSTON BAKED BEANS

The ritual of baking Boston baked beans is older than John Quincy Adams and was as complicated in his day as it is today. If residents of Boston are snobs about anything, it is about the proper technique for baking beans. First off, you have to use pea beans. Then you need a bean pot of heavy stoneware. The salt pork must be properly streaked with lean. But the real trick, according to local experts, is the water. You must add hot water from time to time as the beans cook, but add it slowly, not all at once or in haste. Flooding the beans is a worse offense in Boston than asking where Patrick Henry made his famous midnight ride.

> *Pea beans*   *Hot water*
> *Baking soda*   *AND a proper bean pot!*
> *Salt pork*
> *Onion*
> *Brown sugar*
> *Dark molasses*
> *Dry mustard*
> *Salt and pepper*

Soak 2 pounds pea beans overnight in enough water to cover. Next morning cook the beans 10 minutes, with 1 teaspoon baking soda. Run cold water through the beans in a strainer. Cut 1 pound salt pork into 1-inch squares and cut the rind in half. Put half the pork in the bottom of the bean pot, along with 1 large onion. Add the beans, then the rest of the pork. Mix ½ cup brown sugar with ⅔ cup molasses, 2 teaspoons dry mustard, 4 teaspoons salt, ½ teaspoon pepper, and 2 cups hot water. Pour the mixture over the beans. Bake in a slow (300° F.) oven about 6 hours. Add hot water, no more than 1 cup at a time, whenever the beans look dry. Serve right from the sizzling crock. As accompaniment, serve Boston brown bread, coleslaw, and relish. *Serves 10 to 12.*

GREEN CORN SOUFFLÉ

It was only natural that the light soufflé principle of France would be wedded to the fondness for corn that was American, thereby creating a dish fit for a king—or a President, namely John Quincy Adams.

Fresh young corn	*Salt and pepper*
Cream	*Corn juice*
Butter	*Eggs*

Remove the corn from 8 ears and boil 5 minutes. Add ½ cup cream, 3 tablespoons butter, and salt and pepper. Place the mixture in a skillet and stir well. Mix 1 cup corn juice (the water it was cooked in) with 4 beaten egg yolks. Add to corn mixture. Beat 4 egg whites until stiff. Add ⅓ of the beaten whites to the corn mixture. Pour into a baking dish. Spread the remaining egg white over the top. Bake at 375° F. about 25 minutes or until puffed and golden brown. *Serves 8.*

MATRIMONY CAKE (A PIE!)

This old English dish, familiar to the early Adamses as well as their descendants, was a tried-and-true recipe in the "olden days" cookbooks. It's an appetizing version of apple pie.

Pie crust	*Sugar*
Tart apples	*Lemon*
Currants (or raisins)	*Ground nutmeg*
Walnuts	

Make the pastry according to your standard recipe and line a pie tin with it. Then slice 4 large tart applies in thin rings. Place the rings in the bottom of the pastry shell, overlapping one another. Fill the centers with currants (or raisins) mixed with chopped walnuts. Sprinkle sugar generously over the apples. Place 3 slices lemon in the middle of the pie. Dust the pie with ground nutmeg. Cover with thin pastry and seal edges. Bake the pie in hot (400° F.) oven until browned. *Serves 6 to 8.*

BLACK WALNUT CAKE

It was part of President Adams' pleasure in planting so many nut trees on the White House grounds to watch them grow. He loved taking daily walks to measure the seedlings sprouting, looking forward to the day when they would be full-grown trees. Fruit and nuts were of great interest to him. It is likely that you will find this Black Walnut Cake equally interesting.

Butter	*Baking powder*
Brown sugar	*Milk*
Corn syrup	*Vanilla*
Eggs	*Black walnuts*
Flour	

Cream ½ cup butter, then beat in ½ cup brown sugar and ¾ cup white corn syrup. Add 4 whole eggs one by one, beating after each addition. Sift 2½ cups flour with 3 teaspoons baking powder. Add the sifted ingredients to the butter mixture alternately with ½ cup milk. Add 2 teaspoons vanilla. Mix well all together. Spread the batter in a shallow greased baking pan. Sprinkle ¼ cup black walnuts and ¼ cup brown sugar over the top. Bake in a moderately hot (375° F.) oven about 20 minutes. Cool on a rack for 10 minutes before cutting.

THE GOLDEN ALLIGATOR SPRING HOUSE CAKE

A prize example of Americana was on display at a recent antiques show in New York. It was a six-foot-long carved gilded wooden alligator that once graced the roof of President John Quincy Adams' spring house in Quincy, Massachusetts. The old-fashioned spring house was the nineteenth-century substitute for modern refrigeration. Where the sedate Adams family's golden alligator came from we know not, but we do feel grateful to it for lending its name to this unusual cake-pudding, which is something of a cross between syllabub and an icebox pudding. The origins of the dish go back to pre-Colonial England. (An Italian version is known as Zuppa Inglese—English Soup.)

Sponge cake	*Almond flavoring (extract)*
Madeira or sherry	*Sugar*
Whipping cream	*Red food coloring (optional)*

Take a homemade or store-bought sponge cake with 2 layers (you may substitute packaged shortcake layers). Cut each layer horizontally to make 4 layers in all. Press 1 layer into an 8-inch bowl. Sprinkle with 4 tablespoons Madeira or sherry. Whip 1 cup heavy cream and flavor with ½ teaspoon almond extract, 2 tablespoons sugar, and 1 or 2 drops red food coloring (just enough to color the cream pale pink). Spread ⅓ of the cream over the cake layer in the bowl. Add a second layer, pressing it firmly but gently to shape it to the bowl. Sprinkle the second layer with 4 tablespoons wine, spread with more cream. Add the third layer. Repeat. The top layer should be cake alone. Chill several hours or overnight in your spring house (refrigerator). At serving time, unmold on a chilled cake plate, garnish with bits of bright-colored jelly or candied fruits. Slice into small wedges. *Serves 10 to 12.*

DROP GINGER COOKIES

Ginger and molasses, mainstays of the New England kitchen, form as happy a marriage in our day as they did in the days of John Quincy Adams. But in his day, cookies such as these were still called "little cakes" and were frequently served at drawing rooms and official levees with punch or wine.

Flour	*Shortening*
Salt	*Egg*
Baking soda	*Vinegar*
Ground ginger	*Milk*
Cinnamon	*Molasses*
Sugar	

Sift together 1½ cups flour, ½ teaspoon salt, 1 teaspoon baking soda, ½ teaspoon each ground ginger and cinnamon. Set aside for a moment while you cream ½ cup sugar with ⅓ cup shortening. Add 1 egg and beat the mixture vigorously. Set aside. Mix together 1 teaspoon vinegar and ⅓ cup milk. Then add ¼ cup molasses and mix thoroughly. Add to the creamed egg–shortening mixture alternately with the sifted ingredients, beating until smooth after each addition. (Begin the adding with the sifted ingredients and end with them.) Drop the batter by level teaspoonfuls on a greased baking sheet. Leave 2 inches space between each cookie. Bake in a medium hot (350°–375° F.) oven for 10 minutes, or until done. *Makes 4 dozen.*

PLUMS IN WINE JELLY

President Adams was extremely fond of fresh fruit. In fact, his grandson Henry Adams later wrote that as a child he saved the choicest fruit from the garden for Grandfather Adams, and "ate only the less perfect. Naturally he ate more by way of compensation, but the act showed that he bore no grudge." Nor is it likely that John Quincy would bear a grudge against us for modernizing this old favorite.

Canned plums (purple, red, or greengage)	*Red or white wine*
	Unflavored gelatin

Drain 1 large can (1 pound 13 ounces size) plums. Save the syrup. Pit the plums and put them in a kitchen bowl. If you use purple or red plums, use a moderately sweet red wine. But if you choose greengage plums, your wine should be white and light, perhaps a Chablis or Lake Niagara. Measure your plum syrup separately. Along with the wine they should measure 1 pint. Pour the wine over the plums. Sprinkle 2 envelopes unflavored gelatin over ½ cup cold water, to soften the gelatin. Heat the plum syrup and slowly stir in the gelatin until it dissolves. Combine with the plums and wine and pour into a mold. Refrigerate until firm. When ready to serve, turn out of the mold onto a fancy serving dish. *Serves 4 to 6.*

NEW ENGLAND HARD BUTTERED CIDER RUM

While President Adams was a temperate man, he was by no means a teetotaler. One visitor to the Executive Mansion remembered the occasion when Adams received a group of mail contractors. Henry Clay, then Secretary of State, introduced them. "Cakes and wine were served," and the President "drank success to them all through highways and byways." While knowledgeable about wines, John Quincy Adams was no slouch in discussions of cider either.

Hard cider	*Sweet butter*
Light brown or maple sugar	*Rum*
Salt	*Cinnamon*

Heat 2 quarts hard cider "till you see beads over the surface but never let it actually come to a big boil." Remove from the heat, add ½ cup light brown sugar (or maple sugar), a speck of salt, and ¼ cup sweet butter. Stir well until all ingredients are dissolved. Keep the mixture piping hot. When serving, place 1 jigger of good rum into each heated mug. Fill the mugs with the hot cider mixture; sprinkle cinnamon over the top of each. For an extra touch, serve a cinnamon stick as a stirrer in each mug. Serve steaming. *Serves 8.*

VII

"Old Hickory" or "King Andrew"?

****

When Andrew Jackson was inaugurated seventh President of the United States on March 4, 1829, it was like the homecoming of a hero. His loyal supporters, who had felt cheated four years earlier, now converged on Washington like locusts, eager to celebrate what they considered the long-delayed victory of their champion.

Much has been written about our first Frontier President. His inauguration sparked a celebration that did everything but set fire to the White House. Twenty thousand fervent fans poured into the building, and little thought was given to the delicate French furniture, elegant draperies, and fine china. The refreshments—ice cream, punch, cakes, and ices—were gobbled up as fast as they appeared on the long serving tables. Class distinctions disappeared for the day: those in formal dress gobbled every bit as fast as woodsmen in coonskin caps.

Margaret Bayard Smith, still chronicling the changing age in which she lived, was caught up in the surge and observed sadly: ". . . a rabble, a mob, of boys, negroes, women, children, scrabbling, fighting, romping, what a pity, what a pity!" This might have been the understatement of 1829, but Mrs. Smith continued: ". . . the people forcing their way into the saloons, mingling with the foreigners and citizens surrounding the President. . . . China and glass to the amount of several thousand dollars were broken in the struggle to get at the ices and cakes, though punch and other drinkables had been carried out in tubs and buckets to the people; but had it been in hogsheads it would have been insufficient besides unsatisfactory to the mob, who claimed equality in all things."

Another chronicler of the day's events wrote:

A profusion of refreshments had been provided. Orange-punch by barrels full was inside, but as the waiters opened the door to bring it out, a rush would be made, the glasses broken, the pails of liquor upset, and the most painful confusion prevailed. To such a degree was this carried, that wine and ice-cream could not be brought out to the ladies, and tubs of punch were taken from the lower story into the garden to lead off the crowds from the rooms.

Jackson had wanted to share his inaugural celebration with his devoted following—but at a distance. The plan was to have the masses on the White House lawn, eating, drinking, and being merry while inside, diplomatic representatives, prominent citizens, and other invited guests would celebrate "more genteely" with the President and his associates. The best laid plans of Presidents, as well as other men, often—— In this instance, the plans went hopelessly awry almost immediately. Returning from the inauguration ceremonies, President Jackson rode his horse, surrounded by swarms of cheering crowds. They followed him to the grounds of his new residence. They followed him right up to the door of the house. Soon they were pushing, shoving, and kicking their way inside.

The policemen seemed to have disapppared. Pioneer women in their high boots jumped up on the damask chairs to get a glimpse of "Old Hickory." Muddy-booted farmers couldn't find spittoons, so used the nearest rug. Fist fights ensued as the jostling and shoving got worse and worse. The new President was pushed and shoved back to the wall by well-wishers until his only thought was escape. Lured to the lawn by the shout of lemonade and ice cream, the people finally gave him breathing space and a chance to escape by a back door to the peace and safety of a nearby hotel.

Actually, the inauguration was but a harbinger of the happy holocaust to come. Our memories of Jackson's terms of office center on such phrases as *The Era of the Common Man, Old Hickory,* and *Hero of the Battle of New Orleans.* We think of him in terms of fringed buckskins, muddy boots on expensive rugs, the jubilation of the frontiersmen at having "one of their own" in the Executive Mansion for the first time since the Republic was founded.

Jackson was indeed the first President of "humble" origins, but one aspect of his Presidency has become obscured, even in social histories. These "'umble origins" did not prevent him from enjoying the fruits of privilege. He may not have had the education, experience, and sophistication to have initiated the customs and traditions established by his more aristocratic predecessors, but he very quickly learned to enjoy them.

For example, the French chef Michael Anthony Guista, whom John Quincy

Adams had brought from Amsterdam in 1814 and left reluctantly behind in the White House when his Presidency was ended, served the new President as he had the old with soufflés, *crème brûleé,* and other *specialités.*

While the outlying areas might be calling him Old Hickory, a term that has come down in history, Washington had another nickname for him. Observing the enormous expenditures for White House acquisitions, the huge sums spent on the finest furniture, china, silver, and cut glass, local wags dubbed the President "King Andrew." During his two terms of office, $45,000 was spent on accouterments for the Presidential home.

It is one of those ironies of history that the man who preceded Jackson and the man who followed him in the Presidency were both flailed for their supposed expensive taste. Yet, Jackson, because of his reputation as a man of the people, escaped criticism for expenses far exceeding anything spent by either John Quincy Adams or Martin Van Buren. Which only goes to show that a popular President can get away with almost anything.

Adams had spent $50 for a billiard table, $5 for cues, $6 for billiard balls, and $23.50 for chessmen, and the furor that arose shook the walls of the mansion. A hostile opposition accused him of corrupting the youth of the country, of running a heinous gaming establishment, and of using the White House as a trysting place for debauched desperados to have their orgies. (A less likely candidate for an orgy than John Quincy Adams would be hard to imagine. But such is the fate of a controversial President. . . . Adams subsequently paid for the billiard table from his own pocket. It happened to be a form of recreation he enjoyed, playing frequently with his children.)

By contrast, the popular Jackson had the White House completely modernized. For the first time, spring water was piped into the house. The austere, threadbare interior became a veritable palace. Decorations for the new East Room cost almost $10,000. "Three very splendid gilt chandeliers, each for eighteen candles, the style of which is entirely new" were $2000. An ornate Brussels carpet, blue satin damask upholstery, bronzed and gilded tables "with Italian black and gold slab," heavy chandeliers, and gigantic mirrors all contributed to the palatial effect. A dinner and dessert set of *sterling silver plate* from France was priced at $4308.82. Every known type of wine and champagne glass was ordered, as well as decanters by the dozen. A blue-and-gold dessert service decorated with the American eagle was made to order for Jackson.

Paradoxically, although Jackson was hailed as King Andrew for his extravagances, his detractors called the Executive Mansion "the White House" for the first time, to signify that Jackson was not worthy of an Executive Mansion. Always before, the Presidential home had been referred to by a more formal title. But when the man of the people came into power, the Presidential residence deserved to be called simply the White House. Soon the name ceased to be opprobrium and became the descriptive term it is today.

In spite of (perhaps because of?) the Spartan life he had once lived as a soldier, Jackson enjoyed haute cuisine, or the facsimile of it served in the White House. Visitors who had come to dinner through a number of administrations noticed that, while the service and subtleties of dining were not quite up to that of some of his predecessors, Jackson was not sparing in the food he offered guests.

An hour before dinner was served, wine and "whets" were offered guests in the Red Room. Jackson had brought up several of his best slaves from the Hermitage, the beautiful home he had acquired for his beloved wife Rachel in Tennessee, to assist Guista in preparing meals as lavish as could be dreamed up. Even ordinary dinners were gala events, with the finest wines flowing freely, Negro waiters solicitously helping the guests to turkey, fish, canvasback duck, and partridges, and a general air of festivity. Coffee and brandies were always served later in the parlors.

One impressed guest wrote home after a Presidential dinner describing the chicken that was served. It was cold and "interlaid with slices of tongue and garnished with salled."

At first Jackson's receptions were enormous. But the crush was so great, the crowds so unmanageable that he decided to limit the affairs to invitational receptions. As many as a thousand people would be invited. A lavish supper would be served in the State Dining Room, on tables laden, and almost literally groaning, with delicacies of all kinds. Jackson reportedly spent more than his salary on his official entertaining; the descriptions of some of his parties substantiate this.

Jessie Benton, daughter of the Missouri Senator and later wife of explorer John Charles Frémont, recalled many childhood visits to the White House during Jackson's administration. "The great wood-fires in every room, the immense number of wax lights softly burning, the stands of camelias. . . . After going all through this silent waiting fairyland, we were taken to the State Dining Room, where was the gorgeous supper table shaped like a horseshoe, and covered with every good and glittering thing French skill could devise, and at either end was a monster salmon in waves of meat jelly."

Despite the abundance of fancy foods and the splendor of Presidential entertaining, it is probable that Andrew Jackson did not really have his heart in his responsibilities as the Nation's Host. His wife had died suddenly December 22, 1828, only a few months before he would have led her triumphantly to his inauguration as President of the United States.

All the years of vilification and slander might have been erased if Rachel Donelson Robards Jackson had lived to be First Lady. Jackson's story has been told before: how he married his wife before her divorce was final, although both he and she believed it to be final. In those wild and woolly days of political campaigning, this fact was used, misused, abused continuously against Jackson, even though he and Rachel went through a second marriage ceremony when the first proved invalid. Even so, Jackson's enemies would not leave the story alone.

Rachel Jackson was not exactly the physical embodiment of a storybook heroine: short, dumpy, addicted to a corncob pipe. But she was a warm, loving, moral, good-hearted woman who, though childless, raised and supported nieces and nephews by the score and was much loved by all who knew her, including her husband, Andrew, who fought two duels for her. Her honor and its defense were always on his mind. When she died, more than ten thousand people attended the outdoor funeral. Jackson said, when he had to depart for Washington, "My heart is nearly broke. I try to summon up my usual fortitude, but in vain."

Aware of his obligations as the President of all the people, Jackson knew he was expected to entertain his admirers. To help him and ease the burden, he asked Mrs. Emily Donelson to come to the Capitol. Emily was Rachel's niece. As a child she had been adopted by the Jacksons. As a young army wife, Emily—Mrs. Major André Jackson Donelson—was a country bumpkin when she first appeared in Washington. But the auburn-haired Emily had Southern charm, a quick intelligence, and in no time at all she developed into a capable and popular White House hostess. Major André became Jackson's secretary, and the family's closeness sustained Jackson in his time of grief.

It is possible that much of the reason for the lavishness of the Jackson hospitality was a post-mortem vindication of Rachel, a subconscious desire to show his critics and enemies how grandly he could do things, how elegant the White House could be—and would also have been with Rachel there. When one considers the nature of the attacks on Rachel—in the 1824 Presidential campaign, a Washington newspaper warned the voters "to think and ponder well before they place their tickets in the box, how they can justify it to themselves and posterity to place such a woman as Mrs. Jackson at the head of the female society of the United States"—it is easy to understand why this might have been a factor at work in Jackson's entertainment pattern.

Of course one cannot discount a natural, spontaneous Southern hospitality either. Jackson was a warm, responsive man. He had been denied the Presidency once, after a very close race, and now that he had won the prize it was fitting that he and his supporters enjoy the fruits of it.

Yet the other side of the Jackson coin was a fondness for simplicity, rusticity, and homeliness. A friend of Emily Donelson's described the domestic side of life at the Executive Mansion:

There was light from the chandeliers, and a blazing fire in the grate; four or five ladies sewing around it; Mrs. Donelson . . . Mrs. Edward Livingston, etc. Five or six children were playing about regardless of documents or work-baskets. At the farther end of the room sat the President in his arm-chair, wearing a long loose coat and smoking a long reed pipe, with a bowl of red clay; combining the dignity of the patriarch, monarch and Indian chief. Just behind was Edward Livingston, the Secretary of State, reading him a dispatch from the French Minister for Foreign Affairs. The ladies glance admiringly now and then at the President, who listens, waving his pipe towards the children when they become too boisterous.

A grandniece of Jackson's wrote of a memorable Christmas at the White House. Two small Jacksons, grandnephews, and five Donelsons, Rachel's nephew's children, hung up their stockings in "Uncle's Room." One of the boys, with great glee, tied one of the President's stockings to the fireplace tongs, saying "Now, let's see how Santa Claus will treat you, Mr. Uncle Jackson, President of the United States!"

Later in the day, there was a party in the East Room. Washington children were sent notes: "The children of President Jackson's family request you to join them on Christmas Day, at four o'clock, in a frolic in the East Room." When the company gathered, they played "Puss in the Corner," "Blind Man's Buff," and other merry games. Martin Van Buren, Dolley Madison, and her grandniece all joined in the games.

"To the music of 'The President's March,' the happy little guests were ushered into the supper-room, where a feast was served. . . . Amid the many dainties which loaded the beautiful table was a pyramid of snowballs, surmounted by a gilt game-cock, with head erect and outspread wings. The snowballs were made of non-combustible, starch-coated cotton, were distributed among the children, who were allowed to have a royal game of snowballs in the East Room after supper. At the close of the evening the happy children marched around the room, kissing their hands as they passed the President, and saying 'Good-night, General.' Mrs. Madison, who stood by the side of the genial host enjoying the gay scene, exclaimed, 'What a beautiful sight it is! It reminds me of the fairy procession in the *Midsummer Night's Dream.*'"

Jackson was by no means just the hero-from-the-hills that his political admirers made him out to be. His popular image as a rough-cut frontiersman was not totally accurate. Certainly his culinary exposure was far greater than that of the average frontiersman of his day. Born in the Carolinas, where food preparation even then was a cultivated art, he had traveled widely in the South. Exposure to the spicy, aromatic seasonings of New Orleans deepened his palate's appreciation for "different" foods.

Even in backwoods Tennessee food was important, so important that the mountaineers sang songs about it. Even today you can hear the old tunes in East Tennessee, such as "Slop the Hogs," "Possom Pie," "Jimmy Crack Corn," and "Chicken in the Bread Tray." One county was so renowned for its chitterlings that a tune was composed in its honor—"When It's Chitlin' Time in Cheatham County."

At first the pioneers who settled in Tennessee survived on a rather austere basic diet. But little by little, as the rich fields and farms began to yield crops of great magnitude, prosperity came to the country. With it came the slave-holding customs of Virginia and the Carolinas. As soon as the first Negro slaves appeared, the hardy pioneer diet began to undergo subtle changes. The rich, spicy, tangy flavors of Africa began to blend with the rough foods of the hill folk.

Jackson, in building his handsome Tennessee mansion, the Hermitage, seemed to draw on the various elements in the South of his day. With its six fluted Grecian columns across the front, the elegant balcony, and two exquisite door-ways, it suggested grandeur of the South. The food served in his new home was a combination of the hearty backwoods Tennessee fare and the subtler delicacies of the Old South, as exemplified by Virginia and the Carolinas.

When Jackson ascended to the Presidency, he added one more culinary ingre-dient to his repertoire: the imagination of French cuisine as demonstrated by Quincy Adams' legacy, Guista.

In leaving the White House, Jackson wrote Mrs. Blair at Blair House, to thank her for many kindnesses. He told her he was leaving her "a heifer used by me since my second election. . . . She will bring you in mind my fondness for good milk. . . ."

Many foods appealed to the Jacksonian palate besides good fresh milk. He was fond of meat jelly, or "savory jelly" as it was known then, a popular favorite of his day. Many a White House menu of his era listed a meat jelly as part of the dinner. Venison, wild turkey, duck, goose, and partridge were all devoured with considera-ble pleasure by President Jackson. Chicken in almost any form, including hash for breakfast, waffles, corn prepared a variety of ways, all were eaten with gusto by Jackson. He was also very fond of cheese. And therein lies a tale. . . .

One might say that Jackson's administration went out not with a whimper but with a bang, and all because of a 1400-pound cheese. The eight years had gone full circle. What had started in 1829 with a wild melee ended with an even wilder one. In the seventh year of Jackson's administration he was presented with a gigantic cheese, produced by a New York dairyman who had been supplying the President with smaller cheeses throughout his terms of office. This cheese, though, outdid all the others. It was four feet in diameter and three feet thick. President Jackson ordered it taken to the White House cellar for aging and ripening.

Just before leaving office, Jackson decided to share the cheese with his devoted public. He announced that all were invited to come to his last reception, on Washington's Birthday, 1837, to partake of the now-ripened cheese—"an evil-smelling horror," someone dubbed it.

One would have thought that the inauguration debacle might have been a lesson to Jackson, but his sense of hospitality must have outweighed his ordinary sense. Ten thousand cheese-lovers marched on the White House, coming from as far away as Baltimore and Annapolis. Shops and offices declared a holiday, as everyone turned toward the White House. Whole families boarded the train in Alexandria heading for Washington and the final show of King Andrew.

The result was chaos.

One report of the time said: "The cheese was served up in the *salle-à-manger*, and the whole atmosphere of every room and throughout the city, was filled with the odor. We have met it at every turn—the halls of the Capitol have been perfumed with it, from the members who partook of it having carried away great masses in their coat-pockets. The scene in the dining room soon became as disagreeable as possible."

Another observer, N. P. Willis, wrote: "I joined the crowd on the 22nd of February to pay my respects to the President and *see the cheese* . . . in the center of the vestibule stood the 'fragrant gift,' surrounded with a dense crowd, who without crackers, or even 'malt to their cheese' had, in two hours, eaten, purveyed away *1400 pounds!*"

It was impossible to escape the smell of the cheese, even blocks away in the city. People carried chunks away in pieces of newspaper, and the odor wafted through the Washington air. In the White House itself, the crowds were so thick that men had to leave their hats on while munching at the cheese—there simply was not room enough to remove their hats. One witness said: "The company reminded one of Noah's Ark—all sorts of animals, clean and unclean."

When the last guests finally left, all that remained was the empty wooden stand on which the cheese had been displayed. Oh, there were a few other reminders of the day: cheese ground into the carpets, smeared on the damask walls, on the satin furniture and the silken draperies. The scent of the cheese in the East Room was to last another month.

When Martin Van Buren took the oath of office several weeks later and entered his new Executive Mansion, he took one sniff and decided such goings-on were not for him.

It was the end of an era.

◇◇◇

RECIPES

CHICKEN HASH

One of Andrew Jackson's favorite breakfasts consisted of chicken hash, hot corn cakes or waffles, blackberry jam, and hot coffee—a good hearty meal for an active man.

Cooked chicken	*Butter*
Heavy cream or gravy	*Parsley*
Salt and pepper	*Pimiento*
Tarragon	

Chop leftover or cooked chicken into smallish—but not too smallish—cubes. Moisten with gravy or heavy cream. Season to taste with salt and pepper and a dash of tarragon. Heat a shallow flameproof baking dish with a little butter in it. Turn the chicken mixture into the pan, sprinkle with chopped parsley and cook until thoroughly heated but not dry. When hot, put little pimiento dots on it for decoration, and serve.

HOT CORN CAKES

This breakfast favorite of Andrew Jackson's was usually made right over the hot coals in an old iron frying pan with legs called a "spider." Today we make corncake in a nice hot oven. Ah, progress!

Butter	*Flour*
Sugar	*Baking powder*
Milk	*Salt*
White cornmeal	*Egg whites*

Cream ¼ cup butter and slowly beat in ½ cup sugar. Add 1⅓ cups milk alternately with dry ingredients sifted together: 1¼ cups cornmeal, 1¼ cups flour, 4 teaspoons baking powder, and 1 teaspoon salt. Beat all thoroughly. Add 3 egg whites beaten until stiff. Bake the batter in a buttered cake pan for about ½ hour. Bake in hot (425° F.) oven. Serve with blackberry jam, *à la* Jackson, or syrup, or just plain butter.

"OLD HICKORY" NUT SOUP

When the throngs appeared at the White House on Jackson's inaugural day, the women showed their allegiance to him by wearing necklaces of hickory nuts, strung together with string. The famed old warrior of the War of 1812 might be King Andrew to his enemies, but he remained Old Hickory forever to his legions of followers. This particular home-grown soup was a local favorite with the Cherokee Indians of Jackson's native North Carolina.

Hickory nuts	*Sugar*
Hot water	

Crack 1 gallon hickory nuts, remove the hulls, crush together into a mass. Pour 1 quart hot water over the nuts, allow to stand for 10 minutes. Strain, add 4 tablespoons sugar, and serve hot.

BARBECUED WILD GOOSE

Even today North Carolina abounds with wild geese. In the days when Andrew Jackson was growing up there, wild geese were almost as common as canvasback duck in Maryland. We do not guarantee that Jackson liked his wild goose marinated in wine, but like goose he did.

Red wine	*Wild goose*
Water	*Potato*
Vinegar	*Apple*
Salt	*Salt and pepper*
Tabasco sauce	*A-1 sauce*
Onion	*Melted butter*
Celery tops	*Watercress*
Bay leaf	

Make a marinade of 2 cups red wine, 2 cups water, 1 cup vinegar, 1 teaspoon salt, several dashes of Tabasco sauce, 1 large onion, thinly sliced, 1 handful celery tops, and 1 bay leaf. Heat all ingredients together, cool, then pour over the goose. Let it stand in a cool place overnight or 24 hours. When ready to cook, stuff the goose with 1 potato, either Irish or sweet, peeled. Add 1 onion and 1 apple, peeled or not, as you wish. Sprinkle the bird both inside and outside with salt and pepper before putting the potato, apple, and onion inside. This dissipates any gamy taste the bird may have. Truss the goose and barbecue it slowly on a spit or in a medium (350° F.) oven for 2 to 3 hours. Baste frequently with barbecue sauce. Make the sauce by mixing a full 4½-ounce bottle A-1 sauce with ½ pound hot melted butter. *To serve:* Slice the goose thin, garnish with watercress. Make a gravy by adding hot water to the goose drippings. A green vegetable makes a very complementary side dish. Pokeweed is particularly recommended—and is true to the Jackson tradition.

FRIED HAM AND HAM GRAVY

Old-fashioned ham gravy can be rich, thick and brown, or, in another part of the country, thin, red and peppery. Neither variety can be found in cookbooks, and both cry out for hot baking-powder biscuits. This recipe is vintage Jackson, as tasty today as in his time.

Ham	*Milk*
Flour	

Fry slices of raw ham in its own fat at a temperature of 300° F. Remove the ham from the skillet when lightly browned. Allow the remaining fat to reach

400° F. Sift 3 or 4 tablespoons flour into the skillet to form a bubbly paste. Stir continuously while it browns. When enough flour has been added to absorb the fat, stir in gradually approximately 2 cups milk—just enough to make a gravy the consistency of heavy cream. When thick, allow the gravy to simmer a few minutes at 200° F. Serve in a gravy boat as accompaniment to the ham. (And don't forget those hot biscuits! They're part of the Southern ritual.)

BRAISED WILD DUCK

The fact that wild duck and other game is more of a luxury in this mechanized, processed age than it was when Jackson was alive doesn't mean that he enjoyed it any less. Its very plentifulness was a source of joy to Jackson, who loved game so much he served it as often as possible at the White House. This particular recipe is especially good with mallards, but equally so with the canvasbacks President Jackson favored even more.

Wild duck	*Celery stalks with leaves*
Dried apricots	*Dried thyme*
Dry breadcrumbs	*Onion*
Melted butter	*Flour*
Salt and pepper	*Orange marmalade*
Green pepper (optional)	

Dress the duck (or ducks). Stuff with apricot dressing. (To make the dressing, combine 1 cup dried apricots with 1 cup cold water. Bring to a boil, let simmer 5 minutes, then drain the fruit, saving the water. Cut the apricots into strips and mix with 4 cups dry breadcrumbs, ¼ cup melted butter, ½ teaspoon salt, ⅛ teaspoon pepper, and ½ cup chopped green pepper or celery. Moisten the dressing lightly with the apricot water. This makes enough dressing for a 4-pound duck.) Place the duck in a roasting pan and add boiling water ½ inch deep. Put 3 stalks celery with leaves on, ½ teaspoon thyme, and ½ sliced onion into the pan; cover it and cook the duck for 1 hour in a slow (325° F.) oven. Add water if necessary. After 1 hour, remove the cover and cook an extra ½ hour. Thicken the drippings with flour and add 1 tablespoon orange marmalade to flavor the gravy. Serve hot with the duck.

FISH IN ASPIC

You don't need "a monster salmon in waves of meat jelly" to impress your guests, as Jackson did. Any kind of fish in aspic makes an elegant impression. And it is not nearly as complicated as your guests will think it was.

Fish	*Lemon juice*
Celery with leaves on	*Lemon rind*
Onion	*Peppercorns*
Parsley	*Paprika*
Dried herbs (tarragon, basil)	*Fish stock*
Gelatin	*Dry white wine (optional)*
Capers	*Chopped chives, tarragon & parsley*
Sour cream	

Bring to a boil the following: 5 cups water, 1 small sliced onion, 3 or 4 stalks celery with leaves on, 1 inch lemon rind, 3 tablespoons lemon juice, 5 sprigs parsley, 3 peppercorns, ½ teaspoon paprika, 1 teaspoon salt, ½ teaspoon mixed dried tarragon and basil. Drop a 2½ pound fish into the stock when it comes to a boil. Simmer until tender. Do not let it come to a boil again. Cooking time for most fish is about 5 minutes. Remove fish from stock when done. Strain the stock and save 3½ cups. Set aside. Soak 2 tablespoons gelatin in ¼ cup cold fish stock. Dissolve it then in the hot fish stock. Add 2 tablespoons capers (more if you prefer) and 1 tablespoon caper juice. Season the stock with salt and paprika, a little dry white wine or lemon juice. Chill until it starts to get thick. Skin and bone the fish, meanwhile. Keep it in large pieces or flakes. Prepare a mold, wet it, place a layer of the gelatin-aspic on the bottom. Cover it with a layer of fish. Repeat until the ingredients are used, making sure the aspic is the top layer as well as bottom. Chill until very firm. Serve cold with sour cream topping. 1 or 2 tablespoons chopped chives, parsley and tarragon added to the sour cream make it extra special. Decorate the serving platter with watercress or parsley sprigs. For a flourish, surround the aspic with sliced deviled eggs, black olives, tomato wedges and radishes. Ideal for a summer dinner, Sunday lunch or special fancy luncheon-for-the-ladies. *Serves 8.*

FISH À LA DAUB

Andrew Jackson displayed a fondness for fish, so plentiful in the mountain streams of his beloved Tennessee, and for the aspic or jellied treatment with fish. Records of his Presidential galas reveal variations of this throughout the White House menus.

Perch (or other fish)   Savory jelly

Boil gently as many large white perch as are needed for the company. Do not remove the heads, tails, or skin. When cold, place them in a dish and cover with savory jelly. Chill. At serving time, loosen the mold with warm water, and turn out on a serving platter. Decorate with lemon wedges and sprigs of parsley. (Rockfish is happily presented in the same fashion.)

HOPPING JOHN

Southerners of Andrew Jackson's day were as adept as New Englanders at naming food. The results were often as amusing—and as mysterious to later-day cuisine etymologists—as those of their New England counterparts. In the days of President Jackson, many superstitions were connected with foods. Tennessee lore is full of advice of the time. For instance, a man should never plant peppers when angry with his wife. Only a poor crop can possibly result. In the case of Hopping John, it would be courting bad luck to start the New Year without having a dish of it on January first.

Water	*Onion*
Black-eyed peas	*Bay leaf*
Ham hock	*Salt and pepper*
Celery	*Uncooked rice*

Place 2 to 3 cups water in a kettle, along with 1 cup black-eyed peas, 1 medium ham hock, 2 stalks chopped celery, and 1 diced onion. Add 1 bay leaf, ½ teaspoon salt, and ¼ teaspoon pepper. Simmer gently until peas are tender. Cook 1 cup rice, then add it to the peas. Cut all the ham off the ham hock, mince it, and put it back into the pot with the peas and vegetables. Simmer all together for a few minutes. Serve hot. *Serves 8.*

LEATHER BRITCHES

Covered wagons bumped along Daniel Boone's Wilderness Trail into Tennessee in the years following the American Revolution. The women in those pioneer caravans soon learned how to keep and preserve food, so that they would have it in reserve for leaner days ahead. This frontier dish of Andrew Jackson's Tennessee was also called Shucky Beans. (We don't really suggest you go to all this bother, but we thought these directions deserved inclusion as a reminder of the work involved in living during the "good old days.")

Green beans	*Bacon*
Hot water	

Wash fresh green beans in water. Then dip them into boiling water. With a needle and waxed thread, thread the beans as close together as is possible. Hang in a cool place in the house until the beans are thoroughly dried. Store in clean bags. The beans will keep for months. When ready to cook, just soak them overnight in water. Discard the water when cooking. Cook in boiling water with bacon or salt pork in it. Cook until just tender.

CORN IN CANE JUICE

This recipe also belongs in our Old Curiosity Corner, a further proof of changing times. "What's juice for the goose makes the gander wonder."

Ears of fresh corn	*Salt*
Sorghum juice	*Butter*

Husk ears of fresh corn, carefully removing all silk. Wash and dry the ears. Drop them into boiling "sorghum juice at syrup-making time." Leave for 15 minutes, then dip out the corn. Eat it with salt and butter.

SOUTHERN SUCCOTASH

While related to New England succotash, this dish shows how local products influence the cooking patterns of specific regions. Okra and tomatoes, commonplaces of the South, formed part of this simple and delicious dish, thus giving it a distinctive "Southern" quality. While both Quincy Adams and Andrew Jackson enjoyed their succotash, the differences in it reflect their different, though related, heritages.

Tomatoes	*Corn*
Onion	*Okra*
Clove	*Butter beans*
Salt	*Bacon drippings*
Sugar	*Butter*
Pepper	*Grated nutmeg*

Place 1 pint canned tomatoes into a saucepan. Add ½ minced onion, 1 whole clove, 1 teaspoon salt, 1 teaspoon sugar, ½ teaspoon pepper. Cook for 15 minutes, stirring often. Add 1 pint canned corn, 1 pint canned okra, and 1 pint canned butter beans. Simmer 10 minutes, then add 1 tablespoon bacon drippings and 1 tablespoon butter. Serve hot, as your main dish at lunch or Sunday supper. Sprinkle grated nutmeg over the top in serving.

Variation: Put the vegetables in a greased casserole, cover with ½ cup grated cheddar or Parmesan cheese or with buttered breadcrumbs, and bake in a hot (375° F.) oven for 10 or 15 minutes, or until the cheese melts or breadcrumbs brown. *Serves 6 to 8.*

POKEWEED

Pokeweed grows wild in most regions of America, and is particularly luxuriant in the South. The trick is in the picking. It should be picked while young, for then the flavor is at its most delicate. As it grows, it shoots up very rapidly and becomes stringy and coarse. Nowadays, we have an edge on Andrew Jackson. We can enjoy pokeweed year-round, as it freezes beautifully.

Pokeweed	*Salt*
Water	*Egg*

Cook the pokeweed exactly as you do spinach, in minimum salted water, for a very short time, until just wilted. To serve, break 1 raw egg over the pokeweed and toss it lightly. Or, if you prefer, slice a hard-boiled egg over it and serve. Equally good served with a dab of sour cream seasoned with dill weed.

POKE STALK PICKLE

In Jackson's day, the pioneer woman had to rely on all the resourcefulness she possessed. Food was often scarce at certain seasons, so much planning was necessary for the winter months. Canning and preserving were a part of every family's life. Many foods were utilized. While the family ate the pokeweed, the mother was busy canning and pickling the poke stalk. Here is how she did it:

Poke stalks	*Vinegar*
Water	*Mustard seed*
Salt	*Sugar*

Use tender stalks, no higher than 6 inches. Cut them into 3-inch lengths. Trim off the leaves (and cook like spinach). Cook the stalks in clear water briefly, about 5 minutes. Discard the water. Cover with fresh water and salt and boil about 5 minutes. Discard the water again. Pack the stalks vertically in jars. Cover with a mixture of 1 pint vinegar, ½ teaspoon mustard seed, and 2 tablespoons sugar. Heat to the boiling point and pour over the stalks. Seal.

ANDREW JACKSON'S BLACKBERRY JAM CAKE

Christmas was a cheery time at the Jacksons, as it was throughout the South. A great favorite of the holiday season in both Tennessee and Kentucky was inevitably jam cake, made with dewberry or blackberry jam. If Andrew Jackson had his way, it was always a blackberry jam cake in his household, for he had an inveterate fondness for blackberries in any shape or form.

Butter	*Salt*
Sugar	*Allspice*
Eggs	*Ground cinnamon*
Flour	*Sour milk*
Baking powder	*Thick blackberry jam (raspberry or*
Soda	*strawberry may be substituted)*

Cream ¾ cup butter (or margarine) with 1 cup sugar. Add 3 unbeaten eggs and beat thoroughly. Sift together 3 times 3 cups flour, 2 teaspoons baking powder, 1 teaspoon soda, ¼ teaspoon salt, 1 teaspoon each ground allspice and cinnamon. Add the sifted ingredients to the butter–egg mixture, alternately with ½ cup sour milk. Fold in 1 cup jam. Mix carefully. Pour into 2 greased layer-cake pans. Bake in medium (350° F.) oven for 45 minutes, or until a golden brown. Frost with any favorite white icing.

BEATEN SWEET CAKES

Jackson carried on the tradition, established by his predecessors, of having a New Year's Day open house for all who wanted to come and greet the President. At this time, as in earlier administrations, wine and cakes were passed around. It was customary in Jackson's day to refer to cookies as "little cakes." You will find these "cakes" delicious for teatime.

Butter	*Flour*
Sugar	*Pecans (or other nuts)*
Eggs	

Cream 2 cups butter (or magarine) with 2 cups sugar. Add 2 slightly beaten eggs and beat vigorously. Then add 4 cups sifted flour. Mix well. Put the dough on a breadboard and beat it with a rolling pin, as you would biscuit dough. Work in 1 cup chopped pecans or other nuts. Roll out the dough, cut into shapes, and bake. Use a moderate (350° F.) oven and bake 12 to 15 minutes. *Makes 5 dozen.*

BENNE CAKES

Many visitors to the White House commented on Jackson's hospitable custom of serving little tea cakes and other delicacies. Such "cakes" as these, made from benne (sesame) seeds, were a mainstay of the Carolina kitchens during Jackson's boyhood. The Africans who brought benne seeds to this country considered them good luck. They were used widely in candies, desserts, and cookies.

Butter	*Salt*
Sugar	*Nutmeg*
Orange rind	*Honey*
Egg	*Benne (sesame) seeds*
Milk	
Flour	
Baking powder	

Cream ¾ cup butter until soft, then add ½ cup sugar, a little at a time, until light and fluffy. Stir in the grated rind of 1 orange. Beat 1 egg slightly with ½ cup milk. Set aside a moment. Sift 3 cups flour with 2 teaspoons baking powder, ½ teaspoon salt, and ½ teaspoon nutmeg. Alternately add the flour mixture and the egg–milk mixture to the sugar and butter. Put a little flour on your hands, pinch off pieces of the dough, and roll into little balls about the size of a walnut. Bake on an ungreased cooky sheet in a preheated medium (350° F.) oven for about 10 minutes, or until delicately browned. Cool on a rack. *Makes 5 dozen.*

To glaze: Cook ¾ cup honey, 2 tablespoons butter, and 3 tablespoons benne seeds in a pan until a few test drops separate into hard threads in cold water (about 200° F. on a candy thermometer). Cool until the foam settles. Then dip the top of each cooky in the glaze. Work quickly as the glaze hardens fast. If it becomes unworkable, reheat the glaze over hot water. Stir to keep the seeds from rising to the top. Cookies should be eaten while fresh. (They're so good they won't last long.)

CHARLESTON BENNE WAFERS

These famed wafers are as much a part of Charleston today as they were in Andrew Jackson's time.

Brown sugar	*Vanilla*
Butter	*Benne (sesame) seeds*
Flour	
Egg	
Salt	

Cream 1 cup light brown sugar with 1½ tablespoons butter until light and smooth. Slowly add 2 tablespoons sifted flour, 1 beaten egg, ¼ teaspoon salt, and 1 teaspoon vanilla. Mix well. Add ½ cup untoasted benne (sesame) seeds. Mix again and drop by teaspoonfuls onto a greased baking sheet. Flatten with a knife dipped in cold water. Bake in a preheated moderate (350° F.) oven approximately 5 minutes, or until lightly browned. Delicious at teatime. *Makes 1 dozen.*

LADY CAKE

Surrounding Jackson's beautiful Hermitage, near Nashville, are his favorite magnolia trees. When he was transplanted to Washington for eight years, President Jackson transplanted his love for those Southern magnolias with him, and actually planted similar ones close by the White House. They still bloom today, outside the window of the Lincoln room. Other reminders of his Southern heritage accompanied Jackson to the capital as well. Slaves from the Hermitage came to the White House, and with them came some of the fine Southern recipes the Jacksons had prized in Tennessee. This one for Lady Cake goes back generations. Popular in Andrew Jackson's boyhood home in the Carolinas, it is every bit as delicious now as he found it then.

Egg whites	*Flour*
Butter	*Sugar*
Soda	*Milk*
Cream of tartar	*Peach or almond flavoring*

Allow 4 egg whites to stand at room temperature for several hours before using. Sift 2 cups flour, add ½ teaspoon soda and 1 teaspoon cream of tartar and sift all together 3 times. Cream ½ cup butter, then add 1½ cups sugar and a scant (⅞) cup milk. Blend well. Slowly add the flour mixture, then a dash of flavoring. Fold in 4 stiffly beaten egg whites. Pour the mixture into 3 well-greased 9-inch layer-cake pans. Bake in a medium-warm (325° F.) oven 15 minutes, then increase the heat to 350° F. and bake 10 or 15 minutes longer.

OLD HICKORY NUT CAKE

It seems neatly appropriate that Old Hickory was partial to hickory nuts. But then, he lived in a time when nut trees grew in great abundance, and imaginative cooks constantly found new ways to incorporate them into recipes.

Butter	*Cinnamon*
Sugar	*Nutmeg*
Eggs	*Seedless raisins*
Lemon juice	*Hickory nuts*
Flour	*Bourbon whiskey*
Baking soda	*Salt*

Cream ½ cup butter with 1 cup sugar until smooth. Beat 3 egg yolks hard and add them to the butter–sugar mixture. Then add 1 teaspoon lemon juice. Sift 2 cups flour with 1 teaspoon baking soda, 1 teaspoon each cinnamon and nutmeg. Add 1 cup raisins to the flour mixture, and 2 cups coarsely chopped nuts. Add the dry mixture to the batter alternately with 3 tablespoons bourbon. Beat 3 egg whites with ½ teaspoon salt until peaked. Fold into the batter carefully. Pour the mixture into 2 greased loaf pans. Bake in a very slow oven (250° F.) for 2 to 2½ hours, or until cake pulls away from the sides of the pan.

ANDREW JACKSON'S FLOATING ISLAND

This recipe comes straight from the kitchen of the Hermitage. Floating Island was a favorite dessert in much of the South, but it varied from locale to locale. Like many another plantation of the period, the Hermitage was celebrated for its open-handed hospitality. Rachel Jackson, generous and friendly to all who knew her, was a warm, responsive hostess. One helping of this old-time favorite pudding at the Hermitage would inevitably provoke another.

Sponge cake	*Almond or vanilla flavoring*
Blanched almonds	*Whipped cream*
Sherry	*Currant jelly*
Plain boiled custard	

Cover the bottom of a large bowl with sponge cake, either whole or broken into pieces. Sprinkle 1 cup chopped blanched almonds over the cake. Then sprinkle 1 tablespoon sherry over all. Take 1 quart Boiled Custard, flavored with almond or vanilla flavoring, and pour it over the top of the bowl. Then top with a generous amount of whipped cream and dab bits of currant jelly on the whipped cream. Serve directly from the bowl. *Serves 8 to 10.*

FRIED APPLE PIES

The homey foods of the Tennessee hills had special appeal for Andrew Jackson. Such a one was this old-fashioned recipe for fried pies.

Flour	*Cold water*
Salt	*Apples*
Shortening	

Mix together 2 cups flour and 1 teaspoon salt. With the help of 2 knives or a pastry blender, work ½ cup shortening into the dry ingredients. When the mixture becomes coarse like cornmeal, slowly add ½ cup cold water or enough to make the dough soft enough to roll. Roll it into rounds 5 inches in diameter. Put a spoonful of sweetened sliced apples on each round. Moisten the edges with cold water, fold over, press the edges together with fingers. Fry in 375° F. deep fat. Drain on paper towels. Serve warm or cool. *Makes 6 individual pies.*

BLACKBERRY SHRUB

Early settlers in the South soon discovered the advantages of the wild blackberry in both food and drink. No one was fonder of it than Andrew Jackson. This old-time drink was a special favorite.

Blackberry juice	*Grape juice*
Sugar syrup	*Lemon juice*

Strain the juice from canned blackberries, pressing through as much pulp as possible. Measure 1 quart. If you use fresh berries, prepare the juice by cooking the berries with just enough water to keep them from burning; strain. Sweeten to taste with sugar syrup. Add 1 cup grape juice, then juice of 2 lemons, and chill. Fill glasses ⅓ full. Fill them with soda water or crushed ice. (Fresh or frozen raspberries or loganberries may be substituted if necessary, although nothing quite matches the flavorful blackberry.) *Makes 1½ quarts.*

DANIEL WEBSTER'S PUNCH

This festive punch was a Washington favorite for many years. Named in honor of the great statesman, it was a nonpartisan drink, enjoyed by politicians of all parties. Jackson was no exception.

Lemons	*Bananas*
Sugar	*Oranges*
Green tea	*Pineapple*
Brandy	*Cherries*
Claret	*Strawberries*
Champagne	

Mix together the juice of 2 dozen lemons (about 4½ cups), strained; 2 pounds sugar, ½ pint green tea, strained; 1 quart brandy; and 3 quarts claret or dry red wine. Bottle tightly and let stand overnight. Then add champagne to taste, (2 to 3 bottles) along with slices of bananas and oranges, chunks of pineapple, whole strawberries and cherries, and other fruit if desired. Serve in chilled punch bowl with ice. *Makes about 2 gallons—about 64 servings (½ cup each).*

FROZEN EGGNOG

You don't need to be a native of Tennessee to find this drink appealing. Even such immigrants as Andrew Jackson admitted its attributes.

Egg yolks   *Whipped cream*
Milk   *Rum*
Sugar   *Whiskey*
Vanilla

Beat 4 egg yolks until thick and lemony. Heat 2 cups milk with 1 cup sugar until scalding hot. Stir until sugar is dissolved. Stir slowly and carefully into the beaten egg yolks. Add 1 teaspoon vanilla and allow to cool. Put into refrigerator when slightly cooled. Begin freezing, but as soon as the mixture is slightly thickened add 2 cups whipped cream, i.e., 1 cup cream, whipped. Put in freezing compartment of refrigerator and leave until solid. Just before serving, stir in 2 tablespoons rum and ¼ cup whiskey. A marvelous dessert. *Makes 6 servings.*

VIII

The Brief Reign of Martin the First

****

Although Martin Van Buren was Jackson's political heir and chosen successor, there were dramatic changes in the social regimen from one administration to the next.

Canny, shrewd, reflective, Van Buren had by nature a style totally different from Jackson's. The impulsive, open-handed, spontaneous hospitality of Jackson's eight years in the White House was not for him. Van Buren had a clear firsthand view of the chaos resulting from his predecessor's easygoing hospitality. As a result, although he assumed the Presidency early in 1837, the doors of the Executive Mansion were not opened to the public until New Year's Day, 1838. And to the disappointment of the Jackson-spoiled public, food and drink were nowhere in evidence.

The sight of all the cheese-smeared rugs and curtains offended the fastidious Van Buren beyond measure. One of his first acts as President was to get rid of much of the furniture left over from Jackson's administration, replacing the gaudy but ruined pieces with more "genteel" furnishings of his own choice. Twenty-seven thousand dollars was requisitioned from Congress to pay for housecleaning and the replacement of broken china, glassware, upholstery, and carpeting. Van Buren was determined that the new furnishings would not be demolished during *his* term of office and decreed that there would be no food served at public receptions. In fact, eating and drinking in the Mansion would be taboo, except at table. Hard cider, the mainstay of all public functions at the White House, was out, to the chagrin of the public and Congress alike.

Further to protect the furnishings of his temporary home, President Van Buren decided to limit public receptions to New Year's Day and the Fourth of July. To have abolished those traditional days might have meant mutiny in Washington social circles. As it was, there were plenty of grumbles about the scarcity of White House entertainment.

Part of Van Buren's decision to curtail official Presidential entertaining may have been politically inspired. He had the bad luck to be faced with a nation-wide financial panic almost immediately after assuming office. An economic crisis of major proportions engulfed the country as banks, factories, railroads all collapsed. The poor rioted for bread. Shadows of poverty loomed everywhere.

It was hardly an auspicious time for flamboyant Presidential entertaining, even if the President had been so inclined. To fulfill his obligations to Washington's diplomatic representatives and his close supporters, President Van Buren gave small, discreet dinners. Though intimate, the dinners were usually fairly elaborate, and Van Buren limited the guest list to the cream of Washington's diplomatic and political society.

Van Buren's chef had been brought over from London at the end of his master's term there as Minister. Much praised for his Continental style, the chef prepared dinners widely acclaimed for their excellence. Mrs. Frémont commented on dinner at Van Buren's: ". . . his dinners were as good and delicate as possible; but his was a formal household."

During Van Buren's many years in Washington before becoming President, he had acquired a reputation as a *bon vivant* and epicure. His table was always exquisitely prepared; food, wine, and service were impeccable; and the accouterments were refined and elegant. It was natural, therefore, for Washington to expect elaborate and constant social activities at the White House.

The simplicity of that first official New Year's reception and those that followed disappointed all the local fashionables. The lack of refreshments of any kind made the receptions rather formal, awkward affairs. One wag referred to the receptions as "the shabby court of Martin the First." Another visitor criticized the simplicity of the furnishings, compared to the showy display of Jackson, by saying: "We have seen the private dwellings of many merchants in Boston, New York, Philadelphia and Baltimore, the fitting up of which must have cost a much larger sum."

In a sense, President Van Buren was damned if he did, damned if he didn't. He was criticised for eliminating much official entertaining. At the same time, he was savagely attacked for the splendor of his quiet little dinners. Van Buren had taken a fancy to Monroe's mirrored plateau and had paid $75 to have it gilded. Using the matching Monroe candelabra and fruit epergnes, he added flatware of gold plate, as well as the finest-quality cut glass wine glasses, goblets, and water bottles. His table was often commented on as a work of art in keeping with the meal served on it.

But the very elegance of his table contributed to Van Buren's political downfall. In the spring of 1840, before the election, a Whig Representative from Pennsylvania, Charles Ogle, rose to speak in the House of Representatives and launched into a three-day tirade against Van Buren, the high point of which was an attack on the President's gold spoons.

Using the spoons as a symbol of Van Buren's supposed luxurious living, Ogle piously began by saying that the food at the White House "was hardly fit to eat," adding that he himself preferred "fried meat and gravy or hog and hominy." He continued describing dinner at the White House: "The tables were spread with utmost profusion and luxury; and champagne flowed most bounteously."

Ogle's diatribe went on for page after page: "How delightful it must be to a real genuine Loco Foco [certain political supporters of Van Buren's were known as Loco Focos] to eat his *pâté de foie gras, dinde desosse* and *salade à la volaille* from a silver plate with a golden knife and fork. And how exquisite to sip with a golden spoon his *soupe à la Reine* from a silver tureen. . . . What will honest Loco Focos say to Mr. Van Buren for spending the People's cash on *foreign Fanny Kemble green finger cups,* in which to wash his pretty, tapering, soft, white, lily fingers, after dining on *fricandeau de veau* and *omelette soufflé?*"

A friend asked Van Buren if Ogle was accurate in describing the dinnerware at the White House, especially the gold spoons. "He ought to know," Van Buren replied. "He has often had them in his mouth." Ogle had been a frequent and appreciative guest at the cozy White House dinners—before the expediency of the 1840 election forced him into the enemy camp.

Ogle's sardonic denunciation of the President was thorough. Hardly an element of his person or personality escaped assault. His humble beginnings as the son of a Dutch tavernkeeper among the "cabbage gardens at Kinderhook," his aristocratic pretentions, his sons all came under attack. Ogle then described the Whig candidate for President, William Henry Harrison, saying that he, "though not rich, has always had money sufficient to pay for hemming his own dish rags and grinding his own knives, and that he would scorn to charge the people of the United States with foreign cut wine coolers, liquor stands, and golden chains to hang golden labels around the necks of barrel-shaped flute decanters with cone stoppers. . . ."

Van Buren lost his bid for re-election at least partly through this issue. Ironically, his "extravagances" were actually the purchases of James Monroe, rejuvenated by Van Buren after Jackson had relegated them to closets to make room for *his* extravagances. Such is the fate of a President lacking in popular appeal!

After retiring from the Presidency, Van Buren continued to live much the same sort of life he had lived before being President. Having the means to live well, he enjoyed the comforts of a leisurely, mildly luxurious life.

During part of his term of office, his daughter-in-law, Angelica Singleton Van Buren, wife of his eldest son Abraham, served as his official hostess. Van Buren, a widower for nineteen years, appreciated the assistance of the charming Angelica. She did her best to lessen the formal atmosphere of the Executive Mansion, though as a young mother she did not always find the assignment an easy one: "My first state dinner is over; oh, such a long one, our first dinner in the state dining room. I was the only lady at the table. . . . I tried to be cheerful as possible, though I felt miserable all the time, as my baby was crying, and I received message after message to come to the nursery."

The daughter of a wealthy planter from South Carolina, Angelica Van Buren brought a Southern grace to the White House. She was related to Dolley Madison and had much of Dolley's charm and graciousness. While Angelica introduced an element of the South to Van Buren's Northern domain, contributing her favorite Carolina recipes to the White House kitchen, the President's tastes were already impressively catholic.

Although brought up with a natural Dutch frugality, Van Buren combined a taste for simple, hearty Dutch fare with a much more sophisticated taste than most of the natives of Kinderhook, New York, his birthplace. Exposure to London's high society, the cuisine of France, and a New York which even in the early nineteenth century prided itself on its cosmopolitan flair all contributed to Van Buren's *savoir faire*. New York society was quite *avant garde*. No entertainment in the city was complete without dancing and wine.

Fashionable New Yorkers began the custom of giving elaborate luncheons and calling them by the French name for a substantial breakfast. As one society leader wrote, "A *dejeuner à la fourchette* is something of a novelty in this country, and the last imitation of European refinement . . . in taste, elegance, and good management it goes beyond most things of the kind in Europe. . . . The company assembles at about one o'clock, and remains until four. Breakfast is served at two o'clock, and consists of coffee and chocolate, light dishes of meat, ice-cream and confectionery, with lemonade and French and German wines. . . . A band . . . plays at the head of the stairs during the whole time of the entertainment, and after the young folk have partaken of their breakfast-dinner, cotillions and waltzes are danced until the hour of reluctant departure. . . ."

Being accustomed to this milieu and to the similar elegance of Albany during his years there, Van Buren's social graces were, by the time of his Presidency, rather highly developed. He had moved a long way from his semi-impoverished childhood.

But he still, even in late years, enjoyed a glass of good, strong Dutch beer. Van Buren was not an intemperate man, but drank as much as most of his contemporaries—which is to say considerably more than most of *our* contemporaries on a day-to-day basis. The President always had wine with dinner, a fairly generous glass.

Earlier in his career, Van Buren wrote a friend who occasionally did errands for him: "I want about fifteen or twenty gallons of table wine—say prime Sicily, Madeira, or some other pleasant, but light and low wine to drink with dinner. I wish you would get Mr. Duer . . . to select it for me, and buy and send it up. Get me also a box of good raisins and a basket of good figs, and send them with the wine." Shades of General Washington!

Sometime later he bought sixty-three gallons of wine from Domenick Lynch, who seems to have been the source for all choice wines of the time. One guest at a Van Buren dinner described it: "Champagne without ice was sparingly supplied in long slender glasses, but there was no lack of sound claret, and with the dessert several bottles of Old Madeira were generally produced by the host who succinctly gave the age and history of each."

Martin Van Buren's term of office ended early in 1841. Politically he may have had regrets at his short term. But socially he was free once again to be the genial host and *bon vivant* he had reveled in being earlier in life. Some years later, New Year's visitors to Kinderhook reported the comfortable amiability of Van Buren's open house.

It was the custom for New York's Dutch to pay respects the first day of each new year. It was a ceremony of obligation. All the day, Van Buren played host to his neighbors. On a sideboard in the dining room rows of bottles, decanters of brandy and Schiedam, and other potent beverages were at the ready. The traditional punch bowl rested on a mahogany table in the great hall, filled with lemonade, but sparkling red in color—thanks to a generous dash of Burgundy. Surrounding the bowl were dishes of raisins, figs, and the familiar cookies of Van Buren's boyhood. Servants served the visiting men and women of the town, but Van Buren himself waited on the children.

Generally, though, as Van Buren aged, his appetite decreased, and his diet became a simplified version of the diet of his childhood. He still maintained a well-stocked cellar for visitors who took the trouble to call. But his own dining needs were modest, and he accompanied his meals with a single small wine glass of Madeira.

One visitor, John Bigelow, commented on Van Buren's avoidance of sweets, although they were offered in profusion to Bigelow and the other guests. The former President replied that he never ate pastries or puddings, preferring instead a little fruit. So saying, he ate an apple.

The simple life agreed with him. Although in his sixties, he mounted his horse with the agility of a youth and rode each morning before breakfast. It must at times have seemed a long ride from Ogle's *fricandeau de veau* to a crisp New York State apple. But stoical Martin Van Buren was a man who took pleasure in the variety of life's offerings.

◇◇

R E C I P E S

OLYKOEKS (RAISED DOUGHNUTS)

Oily cakes or olykoeks or doughnuts, call them what you will; the Dutch introduced them to the New World, which has been making variations ever since. Martin Van Buren's friend and compatriot Washington Irving described doughnuts in his *History of New York* as a "dish of balls of sweetened dough fried in hog's fat, and called dough nuts or oly koeks." To both Irving and Van Buren, doughnuts spelled *home*.

Milk	*Cinnamon or nutmeg*
Active dry yeast	*Eggs*
Flour	*Butter*
Brown sugar	*Fat for deep-fat frying*
Salt	

Scald 1 cup milk, allowing it to cool to lukewarm. Meanwhile sprinkle 1 package active dry yeast over ¼ cup lukewarm water to dissolve the yeast. Sift 6 cups all-purpose flour, 1 cup firmly packed brown sugar, and 1 teaspoon salt with 1 teaspoon cinnamon or nutmeg. Combine the milk and yeast in a large bowl. Stir the flour mixture in with your hands, then add 2 well-beaten eggs. Cover the dough, which is heavy at this point, and let it rise in a warm place until double its size. Punch down the dough and work in 1 cup soft butter, using your hands to blend the dough until smooth. Roll dough ½ inch thick on a lightly floured board and cut it with a doughnut cutter. Put the doughnuts on a tray or baking sheet lined with wax paper, cover again, and allow to rise until light and puffy. Preheat fat in a skillet to 375° F. on a deep-fat thermometer. Fry the doughnuts until nicely browned on both sides. Remove doughnuts from the fat, drain on absorbent toweling, and sprinkle with powdered sugar or granulated sugar and a pinch of cinnamon. *Makes approximately 40 doughnuts.*

RICE WAFFLES

From his South Carolina daughter-in-law Martin Van Buren learned the Southern custom of eating waffles for breakfast or supper with hash and a rich gravy. South Carolinians were fond of rice, so it was only fitting they amended their waffle recipes to include it.

Flour	*Eggs*
Salt	*Melted butter*
Soda	*Rice*
Buttermilk	

Mix and sift together 1¼ cups flour, ½ teaspoon salt, and 1 teaspoon baking soda. Add 1½ cups buttermilk gradually, then beat in 2 egg yolks and 4 tablespoons melted butter. Continue beating. Stir in 1½ more cups buttermilk, add 1 cup soft-cooked rice, and fold in 2 stiffly beaten egg whites. Bake in preheated waffle iron, then serve hot with butter. *Makes about 10 waffles.*

ROAST SUCKLING PIG WITH SAGE AND ONION DRESSING

When Van Buren was appointed Minister to England by Andrew Jackson, he developed a fondness for many English customs and dishes, particularly those of the Christmas season. With his friend Washington Irving he explored old castles and abbeys, drank wassail before the Yule log in charming old taverns, watched mummers and Morris dancers, and ate heartily of the English favorite, "boar's head crowned with holly and rosemary." Boar's head became a Van Buren favorite at Christmastime. Roast suckling pig, a delicious substitute, is as much a tradition today in many homes.

Suckling pig	*Small lady apple*
Salt	*Whole cranberries*
Hot water	*Watercress*
Melted butter or margarine	

Have your butcher clean thoroughly a 10-pound pig. Rinse the inside and pat dry. Fill loosely with sage and onion dressing (below). Tie the legs in place, hold the mouth firm with a small piece of wood, and put the pig in a kneeling position in the roasting pan. Sprinkle with salt. Cover the ears and tail with foil or heavy paper that has been greased. Pour 1 cup hot water into the bottom of the roaster. Cook approximately 4 hours in a slow (325° F.) oven. Baste often with ¼ cup melted butter to keep the skin from cracking. When meat is almost tender, remove the foil and allow ears to brown. When ready to serve, remove wood block and put a small firm apple in the pig's mouth. To be even more festive, put a cranberry necklace around his neck. Transfer pig to warm platter, still in kneeling position, and served surrounded by watercress. *Serves 10.*

SAGE AND ONION DRESSING

Bread	*Sage*
Water	*Salt and pepper*
Onion	

Crumble 2 loaves bread (about 18 ounces each) into mixing bowl. Add 3 cups water. Meanwhile, sauté 1 large minced onion in butter until golden. Add 1 tablespoon sage, 1½ teaspoons salt, and ⅛ teaspoon pepper. Mix well and add to the bread, tossing lightly. Stuff pig with this. Makes enough for a 10-to-12-pound suckling pig.

PICKLED OYSTERS

Van Buren, like Dutchmen of his day, was extremely fond of oysters. Dutch farmhouses of his period were equipped with large cellars, where fresh oysters and clams were bedded down in large quantities in special bins. The bins were filled with clean sand mixed with Indian meal. They were then watered often to keep the shellfish fat and fresh. Van Buren liked oysters prepared almost any way. He was particularly fond of them served raw, accompanied by wine. He once served them in this fashion to Aaron Burr, after his self-exile in Europe, and General Winfield Scott. Fearful that Scott would be offended at meeting the notorious Burr, Van Buren approached the meeting with apprehension. It is not recorded whether the oysters saved the day or not, but in any case, Burr and Scott chatted amiably and comfortably over oysters and wine. Oysters pickled as in the following recipe were a favorite Dutch appetizer in Van Buren's day.

Raw oysters	*Whole cloves*
Bay leaves	*Mace*
Red-pepper pod	*Whole allspice*
Salt	*Cider vinegar*
Peppercorns	*Lemon*

Cook 1 gallon shucked raw oysters in their own liquor until the edges begin to curl. Drain them, but save the liquor. Rinse the oysters in cold water and pat them dry. Put them aside. Add 2 bay leaves, 1 red-pepper pod, 2 teaspoons salt, 1 teaspoon whole peppercorns, and 1 teaspoon each whole cloves, mace, and allspice to the oyster liquor. Measure the liquor and add the same amount of cider vinegar. Bring the mixture to a boil, then add 1 sliced lemon. Pour the mixture over the oysters. Pack in hot sterilized jars. Seal. *Makes 4 quarts.*

FRIED GREEN TOMATOES

During Van Buren's Presidency, the "poisonous" tomato was just coming into use in the kitchen. As recently as 1830, Robert Gibbon Johnson ate a tomato in the Salem county courthouse to prove that the long-feared "love apple" really could be eaten with impunity. Several years later Van Buren and others were also demonstrating this fact.

Tomatoes	*Butter or margarine*
Salt and pepper	*Milk*
Flour	

Use firm, partially ripened tomatoes cut into thick slices. Season each slice with salt and pepper and sprinkle with flour. Sauté in hot butter, corn oil, or margarine until light brown on each side. Remove the tomatoes and set aside. Make a gravy of 1 cup milk, 1 tablespoon flour, and 1 teaspoon butter; mix and cook over low heat. Pour over the tomatoes and serve hot, preferably on toast.

BRANDIED MINCEMEAT PIE À LA SUNNYSIDE

One of Martin Van Buren's closest friends was the writer Washington Irving. They exchanged frequent visits and shared many common interests. Both enjoyed good conversation and good food, such as this mincemeat pie, which was a specialty of Irving's cook, Mrs. Robert McLinden.

Neck meat of beef	*Citron*
Suet	*Cinnamon*
Sugar	*Allspice*
Currants	*Mace*
Tart apples	*Salt*
Muscat raisins	*Boiled cider*
Orange peel	*Brandy*

Combine 2 pounds ground neck meat of beef with 1 pound suet, finely ground. Add 2 pounds sugar, 1 pound currants, 2 pounds muscat raisins, ½ pound chopped orange peel, ½ pound chopped citron, 1 teaspoon cinnamon, 1 teaspoon allspice, 1 teaspoon mace, 1 tablespoon salt, and 1 quart boiled cider. Put mixture into a large pot or kettle, cover, and simmer for 2 hours, stirring from time to time. Add more cider if necessary to keep mixture from drying out. Just before removing from fire, add brandy to taste. Pack into hot sterilized jars. Seal and store in a cool place. Allow mincemeat to mellow 1 month or longer before using. *Makes approximately 5 quarts.*

To make pie: Line a regular pastry pan with your usual pastry. Use enough mincemeat to fill the pan, then cover with additional pastry, rolled thin. Seal, slash the top in several places. Bake in hot (450° F.) oven 30 minutes. Serve warm, plain or with whipped cream or ice cream.

DUTCH KOEKJES

Exotic as it sounds, *koekjes* is merely Dutch for cookies, the sweet cakes our

Dutch settlers ate with their wine. Originally the *koekjes* were baked in molds, which imprinted a design on them, sometimes an eagle, sometimes the name of a famous person such as Washington. Martin Van Buren as a young man would return home from his business in Albany to visit his family. The entire Van Buren clan would gather around the well-scoured old white-pine table to visit with and hang on to every word of their illustrious Martin. As they talked, they plied him with his favorite *oli-koekjes,* which he devoured eagerly, a happy reminder of home.

Eggs	*Salt*
Sugar	*Nutmeg*
Heavy cream	*Baking powder*
Flour	*Caraway seed*

Beat 2 eggs until light and foamy. Beat in 1 cup sugar, little by little, and 1 cup heavy cream. Sift together 3 cups all-purpose flour, ½ teaspoon salt, 1 teaspoon nutmeg, and 1 tablespoon baking powder. Stir slowly into the egg mixture. Add 1½ tablespoons caraway seed. Keep in refrigerator several hours, until dough is stiff and easy to handle. Roll dough ¼ inch thick on a lightly floured board. Cut into a variety of shapes with small cooky cutters. Sprinkle sugar over the tops. Bake on a greased cooky sheet in a preheated (350° F.) oven for approximately 10 minutes. *Makes about 8 dozen.*

NOGA

As a small child, Martin Van Buren would find in his wooden shoe on St. Nicolas Day some *noga,* an old-time Dutch sweet that St. Nick delighted in hiding in the shoes.

Butter	*Blanched toasted almonds*
Sugar	

Melt 1 tablespoon butter in a large heavy skillet. Add 3 cups sugar and mix well. Cook over a medium fire until sugar has melted, stirring frequently. When sugar has become light golden brown, remove from fire and stir in 2 cups chopped almonds, blanched and toasted. Pour the mixture into 2 greased 9-by-9-by-2-inch pans. Lightly mark into squares. Cool thoroughly. *Makes 1½ pounds.*

HARTFORD ELECTION CAKE

Originally known simply as Election Cake when first mentioned in an 1800 cook book, this delicious fruity cake was eventually called Hartford Election Cake.

It had little connection with Connecticut, but was enjoyed throughout the States. It reached its greatest popularity during the 1830s, when Jackson and Van Buren were the Presidents.

Butter	*Large raisins*
Sugar	*Pecans*
Whole nutmeg, grated	*Eggs*
Baking soda	*Sherry*
Milk	
Cream of tartar	
Flour	
Currants	

Cream ½ pound butter with 2 cups sugar. Add 1 grated nutmeg. Put 1 teaspoon baking soda into 1 cup milk and stir until dissolved. Stir 2 teaspoons cream of tartar into 1 cup flour. Coat ½ pound currants with 1 cup flour. Coat 1 pound seeded raisins with 1 cup flour. Use 1 cup flour to cover the 1 pound pecans. Add the milk and soda to the creamed mixture, beating well. Beat 6 egg yolks and add them. Slowly add the floured currants, raisins, and nuts. Add ⅓ tumbler (i.e., ⅓ cup) sherry (or whiskey), then add flour-and-cream-of-tartar mix. At the last add 6 well-beaten egg whites, folding them in carefully. Grease a large, deep cake pan and line it with waxed paper. Turn batter into the pan. Bake in a slow (275° F.) oven 1½ hours, or until baked thoroughly. If it begins to brown too quickly, put a heavy piece of brown paper over the top while baking.

DUTCH APPLE CAKE

Fond as President Van Buren was of apples in any form, it seems only fitting to include this recipe for an old favorite, Dutch Apple Cake. This is a simplified version that is quick, easy to make, and delicious.

Butter	*Flour*
Sugar	*Baking powder*
Egg	*Tart apples*
Milk	

Mix together ¼ cup butter, ½ cup sugar, and 1 egg. Add ½ cup milk, 1½ cups sifted flour, and 2 teaspoons baking powder. Peel and slice several tart apples. Spread the dough into a round greased baking dish. Place the apples in rows on top. Sprinkle with cinnamon and sugar. Bake in a moderate (350° F.) oven about 35 minutes.

CHEDDAR BISCUITS

Being Dutch, it was natural for Martin Van Buren to be a cheese fancier. Even so, the memory of the Jackson cheese fiasco loomed large in his mind. Consequently, when an admiring constituent presented President Van Buren with a 700-pound cheese, he had it sold and the money donated to charity. There would be no more cheese-ground rugs at the White House if he had anything to say about the matter! Had the admirer presented him with these Cheddar biscuits, he might have been more indulgent and less charitable.

> *Flour*   *Butter*
> *Salt*   *Grated Cheddar cheese*

Sift 1 cup all-purpose flour with ¼ teaspoon salt. Cut in ⅓ cup butter with two knives or a pastry blender. Then add 1 cup grated Cheddar cheese. Mix lightly with your hands until the dough holds together. Roll ½ inch thick on a lightly floured board. Cut the dough with a small biscuit cutter. Prick the tops lightly with a fork. Preheat oven to 350° F. Place the biscuits on an ungreased cooky sheet. Bake for 12 to 15 minutes or until the biscuits are a rich Cheddar color but not browned. Cool. These biscuits, oddly enough, are at their best served cold, as an accompaniment to a tossed green salad or as cocktail appetizers. They keep well if stored. *Makes 22 to 24 biscuits.*

CHARLESTON BENNE WAFERS

From his charming daughter-in-law Martin Van Buren learned to appreciate the rich cuisine of her native South Carolina. Although his inherited sweet tooth subsided in his later years, Van Buren found the light benne wafers of Charleston as satisfying as his mother's *koekjes*.

> *Butter*   *Salt*
> *Brown sugar*   *Vanilla*
> *Egg*   *Benne (sesame) seed*
> *Flour*

Cream 1½ tablespoons butter with 1 cup light brown sugar until light and smooth. Add 1 egg, beaten. Then add 2 tablespoons flour and ¼ teaspoon salt. Add 1 teaspoon vanilla and ½ cup parched benne seeds. Mix well. Drop from teaspoon onto a greased baking sheet. Flatten with a knife dipped in cold water. Bake in a moderate (350° F.) oven about 6 minutes. *Makes approximately 1 dozen.*

CHARLOTTE RUSSE

Although this elegant dessert reached its peak of popularity during the 1880s, records show that it was served in the White House as early as the 1830s—at a banquet during Van Buren's administration. It is faintly ironic that it was also a great favorite of Chester Arthur's, another President who met political defeat because of calumnies about his dandyism and extravagant ways.

Sponge cake or ladyfingers	*Milk*
Wine	*Lemon juice or vanilla*
Water	*Eggs*
Sugar	*Powdered sugar*

Make or buy a sponge cake in the shape of a rounded mold, or use ladyfingers; line a deep glass dish with this. Mix together ½ pint wine with ½ pint water, sweeten to taste with sugar, and pour over the cake. Let stand until the cake has absorbed as much of the wine as it can. Then make a custard: Heat 3½ pints milk, sweetened and flavored with lemon or vanilla to taste. Just before the milk boils, stir in gradually 6 well-beaten egg yolks. As soon as the mixture begins bubbling a bit at the edges, remove from the heat. Let cool to lukewarm, then pour into the dish around the cake. Beat 6 egg whites until stiff and dry, sweeten with powdered sugar, flavor with lemon juice, and pile the whites on top of the cake. Serve immediately if you like, or chill 2 or 3 hours until firm. *Serves 6 to 8.*

WASSAIL BOWL

The Dutch celebrated Christmas to the fullest. Martin Van Buren was no exception. One of the customs he found most congenial in England was the Wassail bowl. With his friend and constant companion Washington Irving he partook freely of this convivial English Christmas cheer. (This recipe dates back to His Majesty's Royal Kitchen, vintage 1633.)

Ale	*Blanched almonds*
Eggs	*Cinnamon*
Roasted apples	*Cloves*
Sugar	*Ginger*

Bring 3 pints of ale to a boil; reduce heat and add to the ale 6 well-beaten eggs. Add several roasted or baked apples, sugar to taste, a few (½ cup) chopped blanched almonds, and a sprinkling of cinnamon, cloves, and ginger. Simmer slowly until all are somewhat mixed. Serve hot in heated mugs or cups. Sprinkle more cinnamon on top of each mug at serving time.

HERB TEA

Van Buren's fellow Dutchmen were even greater tea drinkers than the British. Late afternoon "high tea" would consist of a table filled with *olykoeks,* spice and honey cakes, and assorted pastries filled with tidbits of seafood or game. Like the Russians, also great tea drinkers, the Dutch had a distinctive way of drinking their tea. Instead of putting sugar in their teacups, they followed the custom of holding a lump of sugar between their teeth as they sucked the hot tea, thus melting the sugar gradually (which also put limitations on the conversation). Frequent experimenters, the New York Dutch mixed their China tea with various herb combinations, including exotic and expensive saffron.

Fennel, peppermint, sage, sassafras,   *Boiling water*
*   or tansy*

Pick the herb of your choice. Allow ½ tablespoon of the herb to each cup of boiling water used. Place herb in a teapot that has just been warmed with hot water (and emptied). Pour boiling water into the pot. Cover and allow to steep about 15 minutes.

IX

Tippecanoe and a Log Cabin, too

William Henry Harrison's most ardent supporters for the Presidency would probably have been in for quite a shock if their man had lived for even a year of his four-year term of office.

As it was, Harrison's Presidency lasted a single month, too short a time to provide a real clue as to what might have been, culinarily speaking. Whig partisans supported Harrison as a rugged, hard-fisted, hard-fighting, hard-drinking man of the people. A former Indian fighter and general, Harrison rallied support with the slogan *Tippecanoe and Tyler too*. For those who came in late, Tippecanoe was the scene of a Harrison Indian victory, Tyler his Vice-Presidential running mate.

It all began when a newspaper, the Baltimore *Republican* sneered at Harrison's poverty by writing "Give him a barrel of hard cider, and settle a pension of two thousand a year on him, and my word for it he will sit the remainder of his days in his log cabin. . . ." Never have words boomeranged so thoroughly. There was an immediate response of sympathy for Harrison, a bona fide war hero who had fallen on more or less hard times. Before long, log cabins were being fabricated at Harrison rallies all over the country. Hard cider was freely distributed to the party faithful.

The sympathy and identification created by the log cabin symbol helped carry Harrison to the White House. An enormous appeal was made to the mob, as all comers at Whig rallies were invited to drink themselves into a stupor, free of charge. Harrison was depicted as a frontier hero in buckskin. Pictures showed him building a crude stockade, leading a charge, fighting the Indians or guiding a plow. Always his opponent was pictured riding by in a gilded coach.

What the common frontier man who cast his vote for Harrison did not know (and probably never learned) was that his hero was far less a humble man of the people than his opponent, Van Buren. Lack of instant communication enabled the Whigs to keep one of the best secrets of American political (and social) history. Rough-cut, rustic old "Tippecanoe" was in fact the son of Benjamin Harrison, a very prominent and aristocratic member of the Virginia House of Burgesses, the Continental Congress of 1774–1777, a signer of the Declaration of Independence, and a Governor of Virginia.

William, before his days of glory, received a classical education at Hampden-Sidney College, Virginia, and actually began a medical course at the College of Physicians and Surgeons in Philadelphia, before leaving for the army in 1791. Then other vistas beckoned.

Even so, Harrison was far from the common man the Whigs painted him. His log cabin was a perfectly substantial home that had a portion that originally, before his time, *had* been a log cabin. Truth is often stretched in an election year. The 1840 election campaign ranks as one of the most elastic in our history.

It is likely that the hard-cider image would have been altered had Harrison lived. His Virginia upbringing, with its emphasis on comfortable food and living, could hardly have been erased by his years in Indiana and Ohio. His regime might well have been marked by grace and style.

One thing is certain, little as is known about President Harrison's gastronomical interests: he did enjoy food and took pleasure in selecting tidbits for his family table. One of his first expressed wishes regarding the social side of his Presidency was to do his own marketing for the White House table. And market he did, in spite of the fact that his enfeebled sixty-eight-year-old frame had not weathered the rigorous campaign well.

Harrison's log cabin may have been spurious, but his fondness for cider was genuine enough. In fact, he decreed that wine should be outlawed from his table and cider served at mealtime instead. Of course, the difficulties of getting good wine out in Indiana at that time may have influenced his decision. Once again in the social atmosphere of Washington, as Chief of State, Harrison might have reverted to wine-drinking.

What he might have done intrigues the social historian, but offers only idle speculation. Pneumonia, fatigue, and declining age combined to weaken the old hero. A month after his inauguration William Henry Harrison was dead.

◇◇

RECIPES

PAN-BROILED LAMB CHOPS À LA HARRISON

President Harrison, despite his age and frail condition, was one of the great walkers among our Presidents. He arose early and trotted off to market, for doing his own shopping was one of his great domestic pleasures. Usually he went off without an overcoat, in spite of the chilliness of the mornings, and thoroughly enjoyed selecting chops and steaks for his breakfast. Then back he would go to the White House, well satisfied that his choice of meat would be prepared by the cook to his satisfaction.

Lamb chops   *Mint or parsley*
Salt and pepper

Trim the edges of the lamb chops to eliminate the strong flavor of the outer skin. Then sear the chops in a hot, greaseless skillet. As the chops cook, reduce the heat and allow them to simmer. Pour the fat off as it builds up. Halfway through the cooking, season the chops with salt and pepper. Do not overcook; lamb is at its most delicious if slightly underdone and pinkish. Serve on a platter trimmed with fresh mint or parsley. President Harrison liked his chops at the breakfast table. Times have changed, and we find this a better luncheon or dinner dish.

ELECTIONEERING BURGOO

The custom of plying potential voters with food and drink was practiced by politicians from Washington's day onward. But it reached its zenith (or nadir, depending on your point of view) in the campaign of 1840, when Harrison lieutenants wined and dined the populace throughout the West. First step was to erect a log cabin, then invite all eligible males to a feast of cornbread, cheese, and hard cider. Little by little the feasts became more elaborate, culminating in a spread at Wheeling, West Virginia, in which 30,000 hungry voters were served 360 hams, 20 calves, 25 sheep, 1500 pounds of beef, 1000 pounds of cheese, 8000 pounds of bread, and 4500 pies. Burgoo, as Harrison learned, was the perfect election dish, as it was easily expandable to the size of the crowd. Perfected in Kentucky, this piquant stew became standard fare throughout the Western territory. And no wonder—anything on hand could go into the pot! Purists insist that squirrel is essential, but we are not purists to that extent.

Veal shoulder	*Butter beans*
Lean beef (shin bones are good)	*Red pepper*
Bacon fat	*Pepper*
Chickens	*Bay leaf*
Salt	*Brown sugar*
Onions	*Corn*
Cloves	*Tomatoes*
Garlic	*Okra*
Celery	*Flour*
Potatoes	*Butter*
Carrots	*Parsley*
Green peppers	

Brown 1 pound veal shoulder and 2 pounds beef shin bones in 3 or 4 tablespoons bacon fat or corn oil in a large pot or kettle. When brown on both sides, add 2 medium chickens that have been cut into quarters. Brown lightly and add 4 quarts water and 1 tablespoon salt. Cover kettle and cook over low heat until meat is tender. Remove from heat, cool, and cut all meat off the bones. Cut the meat and chicken into serving pieces and return them, *sans* bones, to the broth in the kettle. Lightly sauté 4 cups chopped onions in 2 tablespoons bacon fat until limp. Then add to the kettle, along with 1 chopped garlic clove, 1 bunch diced celery, 2 cups diced raw potatoes (peeled), 6 diced carrots, and 3 medium green peppers. Also add 1 pint fresh or 1 package frozen butter beans, ¼ teaspoon crushed red pepper, ½ teaspoon freshly ground pepper, 1 bay leaf, and ¼ cup dark brown sugar. Stick 1 small onion with 4 cloves and add it. Cook over a very low fire for approximately 2½ hours. Stir occasionally. When tender and gooey, add 2 packages frozen corn (or kernels from 6 ears fresh corn) 3 medium-sized tomatoes and 1 package frozen okra or 2 cups raw fresh okra sliced thin. Mix with the cooked mass and cook an additional 20 minutes. Combine 1 cup flour with ½ cup butter. Mix until well blended, then slowly stir into the burgoo. Continue cooking and stirring until the burgoo becomes slightly thickened. Taste and add more salt, pepper, and red pepper if desired. Just before serving, sprinkle with 1 cup chopped parsley. This is a great dish for an outdoor affair, picnic, church supper, or such. To be authentic, you should serve burgoo outdoors, preferably under a spreading elm or chestnut tree, preceded by a round or two of juleps and accompanied by delicious salt-rising bread. *Serves 20.*

MULLED CIDER

During Harrison's campaign for the Presidency, the hard cider flowed so freely at Whig rallies that Harrison became known as the Hard Cider Candidate. Using spirits to influence voters was no new touch in American politics. It began with

George Washington when he was running for the Legislature in 1758. His agent treated the prospective voters to 160 gallons of cider, rum, beer, wine, averaging about a quart and a half per voter. A generous amount, it would seem to us, but Washington was not pleased. After the election, he wrote his agent that "My only fear is that you spent with too sparing a hand." No such criticism could be leveled against the Whigs in 1840. In fact, a reporter later declared that hard cider won Harrison the election.

Whole cloves	*Freshly grated nutmeg*
Hard cider	*Applejack*
Sugar	

Add 1 teaspoon whole cloves (heads removed) to 3 quarts hard cider. Mix with a scant ½ cup sugar and ⅓ teaspoon freshly grated nutmeg. Boil all together for 5 minutes. Strain and serve immediately in heated mugs. This is a delicious drink for all ages, but if you want something harder for adults, add ½ to ¾ cup applejack.

MULLED CIDER VARIATION

Cider	*Sugar*
Egg	*Nutmeg*

Heat 1 pint cider. Beat 1 egg well and gradually pour cider over egg. Pour the mixture quickly from one bowl or pan to another several times. Add sugar and nutmeg to taste. Serve immediately.

GENERAL HARRISON EGGNOG

Taken from Harrison's own recipe, this eggnog does him honor. It seems logical that Harrison, who grew up on the syllabub of Virginia, should be partial to its close relative, eggnog.

Eggs	*Bourbon*
Heavy cream	*Granulated sugar*
Sweet milk	*Nutmeg*

Fold 4 well-whipped eggs into 1 pint heavy cream and 1½ quarts milk. (Be sure the milk and cream are cold.) Add ½ pint (more if desired) bourbon. Heat a little sugar in small amount of boiling water to make a sugar syrup. Sweeten to taste the egg mixture with the sugar syrup. Pour into a punch bowl and sprinkle nutmeg over the top. *Serves 12.*

X

Tippecanoe

and a

Tigress, too

The Tyler Presidency is an illustration of the feminine influence on a social system. Socially speaking, there were two Tyler administrations. The first began with the death of William Henry Harrison. At this time John Tyler, as Vice-President, assumed the reins of the Presidency.

At his side was his wife, Letitia Christian Tyler. Both Tylers were unceremonious, hospitable Virginians, who brought their Virginia way of life to the Executive Mansion. In contrast to the formality of Van Buren's official entertaining, the Tylers extended a warm, spontaneous welcome to all who came to call. In the words of one social arbiter, "The dinners and receptions, if less ceremonious than those of the previous administration, were characterized by a warmth and graciousness that are inherent in the sons and daughters of the Old Dominion."

The following year Letitia Tyler died. But the informal note struck at the beginning of Tyler's term of office remained. Charles Dickens visited Washington and was much feted. President Tyler received the famous man of letters, assisted in the reception by his daughter and daughter-in-law. Dickens called the official reception "extremely dignified, informal and well managed." He was surprised that a gathering of 3000 people created no disorder, confusion, or trouble. (We had come a long way from Jackson's day.)

John Tyler lived in Washington as he had in Virginia. He even brought to the White House the same slaves who had cared for his family in Williamsburg.

Gossips whispered that he rode in a second-hand carriage. At state functions, the colored waiters wore livery that was admitted to be secondhand. The unpretentious Tyler liked to invite his guests into the dining room and have them help themselves from a sideboard that was generously supplied with mint juleps.

For two years Tyler lived simply and comfortably at the White House. His daughter, Letitia Semple, one of his seven children, described their life in the Presidential house: "We breakfasted at eight-thirty and dined at three o'clock, except on state occasions, of course, and had tea served after our daily cares and duties, because my father's time was rarely his own. . . . 'Now, sing, Letty,' he would say when we found ourselves far from the mad crowd, enjoying the quiet of some country road. And then I would sing his favorite songs, the old Scotch ballads we both loved so well."

Such moments of peace and solitude were to Tyler a welcome respite from the tensions of political life. But these were coming to an abrupt end. For before long John Tyler was to marry again, this time to a high-spirited young girl with a highly developed sense of superiority and grandeur. Tyler's last eight months in office were to be far different from the rest of his term. There was to be an about-face, as pomp and ceremony became the fashion.

No one foresaw, in that winter of 1843, that the newly arrived beauty on the Washington social scene, Julia Gardiner, would within a short time be the arbiter of the city's taste and style. The daughter of a former New York state senator, David Gardiner, she came to the nation's capital fresh from triumphs in the most select circles of London, Paris, Rome, and New York.

By all accounts, Julia Gardiner was our country's most beautiful First Lady—at least until Jacqueline Kennedy came along. Like Mrs. Kennedy, her pedigree was assured. The Gardiners of Gardiner's Island, a seven-mile-long island at the tip of Long Island, rich, fertile, wealthy land that was a law unto itself, were proud of their family connections and continuous success in the world.

Most of the men who met Julia seem to have fallen under her spell. The President of the United States was no exception. Within months after their first meeting, he asked her to marry him. The age differential—he was fifty-three, she twenty-three—did not suit the gay, fun-loving Julia. No more was said of the matter.

Then, in the early spring of 1844, a freak accident aboard a Presidential cruise changed the course of both their lives. The President had invited a group of distinguished guests for a day's outing aboard the warship *Princeton*. One of the ship's guns exploded, killing David Gardiner and four other men. After a state funeral in the East Room of the White House, President Tyler spent many an hour with Gardiner's grief-stricken daughter. Their rapport grew, the age differential seemed less important to a more mature Julia, and within three months Julia Gardiner became the second Mrs. John Tyler.

The wedding took Washington by surprise (although many second-guessers recalled clues that *should* have intimated something of the sort was in the wind). The ceremony was performed very privately in the Church of the Ascension in New York; the marriage was kept a secret until the bridal couple returned to the White House. Their wedding night was spent in Philadelphia at Hartwell's Hotel. The wedding supper seems to have been a memorable one, "most elegantly prepared," according to a chronicler of the time.

As soon as the word was out, the newspapers began feeding elaborate details of the wedding feast to avid readers, fascinated by the story of the gorgeous New York belle and the aging Southern President. The *New-York Herald* headlined the wedding TREATY OF IMMEDIATE ANNEXATION RATIFIED WITHOUT THE CONSENT OF THE SENATE. The wedding supper was described in detail: "Cold woodcock, pigeons, chicken salad, oysters prepared in various ways, but no wines, this being strictly forbidden by the bridegroom and assented to by the bride. The supper was soon despatched, the President and his lady both eating heartily."

Breakfast appears to have been even more elaborate. Omelets, spring chicken, pigeons and woodcock, ham and eggs, salmon, beefsteaks, kidneys, boiled eggs, and young duck. Again, the *Herald* gave a keyhole view: "The President was in high glee, laughing heartily all breakfast time, and cracked jokes incontinently, diving all the time into the best part of a young duck."

There were a few souls who did not join in the laughing. John Quincy Adams in Washington heard the news of the wedding and wrote dourly in his diary that the bridal couple were the "laughing-stock of Washington." And down in Virginia, Tyler's seven sons and daughters maintained a tactful silence. Some of them were older than the bride.

Once the President and his new wife reached the capital, however, there were many on hand to help them celebrate. "A most magnificent Bride's Cake, and sparkling Champagne awaited the welcoming guests, and the distinctions of party and of opinion were all forgotten, kind feelings and generous impulses seemed to gladden the hearts of all."

When Tyler's first wife became ill, he had asked his daughter-in-law, Mrs. Robert Tyler, to act as his official hostess. A Philadelphia belle known for her wit and good humor, she had performed her function well—and with obvious pleasure. Now, with a new First Lady quickly ensconced, she had to relinquish this choice position. Change became immediately apparent.

With only eight months left of Tyler's term of office, Julia decided to make the most of it. Accustomed to the flourishes of high society in Europe, she set about duplicating some of the pageantry she had witnessed there. She received her guests at official entertainments in, as one observer put it, "almost regal splendor." Seated in a large armchair that simulated a throne and placed on a "slightly raised platform in front of the windows opening to the circular piazza looking on the river," she greeted each guest in a queenly manner. Surrounded by twelve "maids of honor," Julia was every inch a queen, from the crown of three enormous curled feathers which always adorned her head to the purple velvet gown with its long train. Arriving guests were announced at the door before entering, as though they were entering Windsor Castle.

Jessie Benton Frémont, who commented on the nuances of several administrations, noted that Martha Washington had dressed "with an elegant plainness," while Julia Tyler dressed with sumptuous elegance. "Other Presidents' wives have taken their state more easily," Mrs. Frémont commented wryly, but even she could not help being captivated by the imperious charm of Julia, who made no secret of her enjoyment of her new position of power and authority.

Not everyone was so tolerant of Julia's grand ways. Tyler's political enemies used Julia's pretentious ways as ammunition for attacking him publicly. When Julia saw that the Russian Minister had the finest horses in the capital, she managed to find four that were handsomer. Everywhere she went she went in her splendid coach and four, a fact noted satirically by Tyler's enemies. One Washington newspaper satirized the "lovely lady Presidentess . . . attended on reception days by twelve maids of honor, six on either side, dressed all alike . . ." while "her serene loveliness received upon the raised platform, with a headdress formed of bugles and resembling a crown. . . ."

The May–December aspect of the Tyler marriage lent itself to ridicule by his opponents. Like many another older man with a beautiful young wife, Tyler indulged Julia as he might a favorite, but spoiled, young daughter. He doted on her every whim. She introduced dancing to the White House. At her insistence, the Presidential band played "Hail To The Chief" the moment the President, with Julia on his arm, entered the ballroom.

In a mere eight months Julia Tyler made an impact on the White House that was felt for generations. When one realizes how she dazzled the country in such a brief time, one wonders how heady the next four years might have been. But Tyler's party was split, he withdrew his candidacy for a second term, and James Polk was elected the eleventh President of the United States.

Julia was determined to leave the White House in a blaze of glory. She decided to have a grand ball and sent out two thousand invitations. The date was set for February 1845, shortly before Polk was to be inaugurated. Tyler's power, because he was soon to leave the White House and had no real faction behind him, was all but gone.

Nevertheless, the ball was a gala occasion. Enormous bouquets of flowers filled the room. Side tables were loaded with every imaginable delicacy. The atmosphere radiated luxury and extravagance. All political feuds were forgotten as Senators and Representatives rushed up to pay their respects to the beautiful First Lady. The evening was a huge success, much talked of in Washington for years to come. Tyler himself, acknowledging the lame duck aspect of his Presidency, surveyed the enormous gathering and joked "They cannot now say I am a President without a party."

Footnote to the Tyler regime: Years later, after her husband's death, Julia visited Washington. As was her custom, she paid a call at the White House; on this particular occasion the occupant was Andrew Johnson. Discussing the Presidential portraits in the Executive Mansion, she asked why there were no portraits of the Presidents' wives. With Southern gallantry, Johnson said that if she sent her portrait, he would promise to have it hung. She quickly obliged, sending a portrait painted when she was twenty-eight and looked her regal best. She was the first First Lady to be "hung" in the White House, preceding even Martha Washington. The ambitious Julia must have derived some small pleasure from this fact.

For all John Tyler's casual ways, he was not a man to disdain luxury. It is mildly ironic that his running mate, William Henry Harrison, was so strongly identified with hard cider, while Tyler was the champagne type. He adored good champagne and the delicacies that accompanied it. Being informal in manner did not indicate any disinterest in good food. On the contrary, the comfortable, even luxurious cuisine of his native Virginia was part of his way of life.

Tyler particularly enjoyed the abundance of the Christmas season. In fact, he made Christmas *the* season for social Washington. All through the holidays, most Washington houses kept well-filled punch bowls, ready for all well-wishers who might drop in. A great favorite with Tyler and others in the capital was Daniel Webster Punch, an exuberant concoction often made of brandy, champagne, Medford rum, arrack menschino, strong green tea, lemon juice, and sugar, with endless variations.

There were many parties given during the holiday season for Washington officialdom. Always the tables were laden with substantial and varied foods. Roast ham, a saddle of venison or some other heavy roast, roast wild ducks, or other poultry all were in evidence. Enormous supplies of home-baked cakes and puddings were on hand. Puddings were a great Tyler favorite. Punch, Madeira, and the ubiquitous champagne were ready. Such galas, where the young were attracted to the dance floor and their elders to the punch bowl, usually began around eight o'clock and ended at eleven with a mad scramble for hats and cloaks.

In many ways, Tyler's tastes followed those of his illustrious predecessor from Virginia, Thomas Jefferson. Like Jefferson, Tyler favored informality blended with fine cuisine.

But Jefferson never met a tempestuous enchantress like Julia Gardiner. One wonders what effect she would have had on *him*.

◇◇
R E C I P E S

GARDINER'S ISLAND CAVIAR

A curious footnote to culinary history is the fact that in the nineteenth century, "Russian" caviar was a locally produced product of the Eastern tip of Long Island, the Gardiner's Island area. Sturgeon were caught in the waters there. Many had roe, which the local fishermen considered worthless. But a city slicker from the New York fish market went out to teach the fishermen how to cure the roe for caviar. He taught them to remove the membrane carefully, then wash the roe and drain it in a specially designed sieve. It was then mixed with rock salt in specific proportions, packed in small barrels, and sent to New York. From there it went on its way to Russia, where it was just as carefully repacked in small tins with Russian labels, shipped back to America, and sold at highly inflated prices as genuine Russian caviar. This makes a delicious canapé.

Cucumber	*Onion juice*
French or Italian dressing	*Lemon juice*
Toast	*Hard-boiled eggs*
Butter	*Capers*
Onions	
Caviar (Russian or not, Gardiner's	
* Island or not)*	

Dip cucumber slices into homemade French or Italian dressing. Drain on paper toweling. Then toast white bread, butter, and make into rounds. Slice small onions into rings. Put a ring on each toast round, then put the cucumber slice in the middle of the ring. Mix black caviar with a dash of onion juice and lemon juice and pile it on the cucumber slice. Garnish with riced hard-boiled eggs, capers, or nothing at all, as you desire.

TURTLE SOUP À LA TYLER

In his diary, former President John Quincy Adams noted that at a Fourth of July dinner he attended at the White House during Tyler's administration, turtle soup was served. It was made "from a turtle weighing three hundred pounds, a present from Key West" from a Tyler admirer.

Green turtle meat	*Lemon*
Water	*Onions*
Dried or fresh thyme	*Oil or bacon drippings*
Cloves	*Flour*
Cayenne	*Tomatoes*
Salt	*Parsley*
Pepper	*Garlic*
Bay leaf	*Sherry*
Allspice	*Hard-boiled eggs*

Cut up 1 pound turtle meat. Put it in a saucepan with 6 cups water, ⅓ teaspoon thyme, 2 cloves, a few grains cayenne, ½ teaspoon salt, ¼ teaspoon pepper, 1 bay leaf, ¼ teaspoon allspice, skin of ½ lemon, and juice of ½ lemon. Bring to a boil. Meanwhile, sauté 2 medium chopped onions in 2 tablespoons oil or bacon fat for 2 minutes. Add 1 tablespoon flour, stirring as you do, and 1½ cups fresh peeled tomatoes (or contents of a #1 can). Cook for 10 minutes, then add to the turtle mixture. Add 1 tablespoon chopped parsley and 2 cloves minced garlic. Simmer until the turtle meat is tender. Add 1 tablespoon sherry to each serving. Garnish, if you like, with lemon slices and 2 hard-boiled eggs chopped. *Makes 8 cupfuls.*

TORUP STEW

In the days when Julia Tyler was growing up off the Eastern shore of Long Island, on Gardiner's Island, a popular local specialty was "torup," the huge turtles that lived in local ponds. Local inhabitants thought that torup cooked in a stew tasted like chicken. Whether you agree or not, you will, we think, find turtle stew a real delicacy.

Hard-boiled eggs	*Madeira or sherry*
Butter	*Scalded cream*
Terrapin stock	*Salt*
Terrapin meat	*Cayenne*

Take the yolks of 5 hard-boiled eggs and put them through a sieve or ricer. Then work them into a paste with 2 tablespoons butter. Set aside. Combine 1 cup terrapin stock with 2 cups terrapin meat. Simmer for 5 minutes, then slowly add the egg-yolk mixture, stirring gently. Cook slowly for another 5 minutes. Remove the pan from the heat and add ½ cup Madeira or sherry, 1 cup scalded cream and a pinch of salt and cayenne. Serve piping hot with hot bread, cornbread, or corn sticks. *Serves 4.*

GARDINER'S BAY OYSTER STEW

The prevalence of oysters during the Tyler nuptial celebrations would indicate that both John and Julia were fond of this shellfish, as indeed they were. Growing up as she had in an oyster haven, Julia may even have had the edge on John in this respect. Oyster suppers were a commonplace on the Eastern shore of Long Island. An old saying described the typical Oyster Supper:

> Oyster stew and oyster fry;
> oysters raw and oyster pie.

The favorite accompaniment for such a supper would be potatoes, hardtack, and pickles, finished off with cake or pie. Hardy food for rugged islanders. This typical oyster stew is a classic of the locale.

Oysters	*Freshly ground pepper*
Milk	*Paprika*
Butter	

Heat the oysters in their own liquid until the edges curl. Heat separately milk to which chunks of butter have been added. Combine the hot buttery milk with the heated oysters. Season to taste with freshly ground pepper and/or paprika. Serve immediately, with oyster crackers.

CLAM PIE

Gardiner's Island has had its place in American history for several reasons. One of its favorite daughters married a President of course. And earlier, the British fleet, en route to Washington in the War of 1812, sojourned briefly on the island. After feasting sumptuously and enjoying the Gardiners' enthusiastic hospitality, the British then went on to burn the White House. We do not know for sure whether it was the famous Gardiner's Island clam pie or the New England cider and West Indian rum that the sailors imbibed that incited their passions to such a feverish state. We do know, however, that this clam pie will arouse *your* enthusiasm—not for burning the White House, but for more clam pie.

Pie crust	*Flour*
Potatoes	*Cream*
Onion	*Garlic*
Parsley	*Hard and soft clams, chopped*
Butter	

First, prepare a rich double crust for the pie. Keep it in the refrigerator until the filling is ready. Peel and cut up potatoes into fine pieces. Add ½ onion and 1 teaspoon parsley, and cook in a saucepan with a little water, until tender. Drain the water off, add 1 tablespoon butter, a light dusting of flour, a little cream, 1 garlic clove, minced, and chopped clams. Soft and hard clams together make the best pie. If no soft clams are available, use the juice of "skimmers" for a sweet flavor. Mix all the ingredients together, then fill the pie shell with the mixture. Add the top crust. Bake in a hot (425°–450° F.) oven until the crust is lightly browned. *Serves 4 if you use about 2 cups of chopped clams.*

CLAMBAKE

Clam-digging has been an American coastal sport since the earliest days of our history. Back in 1616 Captain John Smith extolled the virtues of digging when he wrote friends in England: "You shall scarce find any bay or cove of sand where you may not take many clampes, or lobsters, or both, at your pleasure." In the days of Julia Gardiner Tyler, clam-digging on Long Island was as common as today's outdoor barbeque. (Alas, today it seems to be a rare and dying diversion. For one thing, seaweed is no longer a commonplace along the shore. And a clambake without seaweed would be like a barbeque without charcoal. Then too, a really big clambake—and whoever had any other kind?—meant a lot of work for at least two men and a team of horses.) If you feel ambitious and want to stage a really marvelous production, here are a few hints. You will need:

Large flat stones	*Sweet potatoes*
Dry wood	*Bluefish*
Wet seaweed	*Fresh sweet corn*
Round hard clams	*Canvas*
Young chickens	*Butter and salt*
Small lobsters	

You will need some strong helpers to dig a large pit near the shore. Cover the bottom of the pit with large flat stones and heap huge quantities of wood over the stones. Light the fire well in advance so the stones will get good and hot. Then spread wet seaweed over the stones. Add the clams, chickens, lobsters, sweet potatoes, bluefish, fresh corn in its husk (remove the silk first), and any other delicacy of this sort that appeals to you (white potatoes are good, too). Place all the edibles carefully on the seaweed, cover with more seaweed. Then spread a large canvas over all and steam for several hours. The results are so delicious that only a little salt and butter are needed, for the corn and potatoes.

BARBEQUE QUAIL

Tyler was fond, as many Virginians of his day were, of game. This slightly modernized old Virginia recipe for preparing quail must have delighted him. Chestnuts, used in the stuffing, were as commonplace in his time as quail were.

Quail	*Green pepper*
Red wine	*White pepper*
Water	*Butter*
Cider or wine vinegar	*Breadcrumbs*
Onion	*Chestnuts*
Celery	*Apple*
Salt and pepper	*Chicken stock*
Parsley	*A-1 Sauce*
Thyme	

Prepare 12 quail and put them in a large bowl. Cover with a marinade made of 2 cups red wine, 2 cups water, 1 cup cider or wine vinegar, 1 thinly sliced onion, 4 thinly sliced stalks celery, 1 teaspoon salt, and ¼ teaspoon pepper. Keep the birds in the marinade overnight or 24 hours in a cool place, either the refrigerator, cool porch, or basement. (Do not use a tin, aluminum, or steel bowl for the marinating.) Just before cooking the birds, make a stuffing: Chop 1 whole head celery with 1 onion, 1 cup parsley, 1 teaspoon thyme, 1 large green pepper, 1 teaspoon white pepper; and sauté them all in 3 tablespoons butter until the onions and celery are tender. Then add ¾ cup breadcrumbs and 1 pound boiled chopped chestnuts. Stuff the birds. Cut 1 peeled apple into walnut-size pieces and use each piece as a plug to close the cavity. Truss the birds for baking and place them in a roasting pan. Cover with chicken stock and roast uncovered ¾ hour in a medium (350° F.) oven. Remove from the liquid. Place the quail on skewers and barbeque slowly, basting frequently with a sauce made of 1 bottle A-1 sauce mixed with ½ pound melted butter. When ready to serve, the quail may be served warm with bread sauce and chestnut purée or cold with pickled peaches, raw tomatoes, carrot sticks, and Bibb lettuce. *Serves 6.*

SOUTHERN FRIED QUAIL

In later years, Aunt Julia's wicker basket was a well-known accessory to all the Tyler relatives. Whenever the family went traveling, Julia was accompanied by her wicker basket full of fine foods. A favorite of all the relatives was her deep-fried quail, prepared in much the same way as Southern fried chicken. In fact, many associated Southern fried quail with Julia's excursions.

Quail	*Milk*
Flour	*Bread- or cracker crumbs*
Salt and pepper	*Butter or lard*
Egg	*Chicken stock or water*

Clean and cut in half a 4-to-6-ounce dressed quail per person. Mix flour with salt and pepper and dust the quail with it. Beat 1 egg lightly and add ¼ cup milk. Beat again, then dip the quail into the egg–milk mixture, then roll it in bread-crumbs crunched fine or cracker crumbs. Melt ¼ to ½ cup butter in a frying pan or electric skillet. When hot, brown the quail in it, then pour in ¼ cup boiling chicken stock or water. Cover the skillet and put it in a slow (300° F.) oven (or set the electric skillet at 300° F.). Cook until the quail is tender, usually about 20 to 30 minutes in the oven. To make a gravy, simply thicken the drippings and add chicken stock, cream, salt, and paprika.

TYLER PUDDING-PIE

Of all our Presidents, John Tyler had the most children—seven by his first wife, seven by his second, for a grand total of fourteen. No wonder pudding was a popular dessert at the Tyler table. This modified pudding-in-piecrust was a particular favorite with the family.

Butter	*Heavy cream*
Eggs	*Fresh coconut, grated*
Granulated sugar	*Unbaked puff pastry*

Cream ½ cup butter with 6 cups sugar. Then add 6 well-beaten eggs, along with 1 cup heavy cream and 1 grated coconut. Mix well, and then pour into 4 pie pans lined with puff pastry. Bake in a hot (450° F.) oven for 10 minutes, until pastry sets. Then reduce the heat to 350° F. and cook another 25 to 30 minutes, or until the pudding-pie is firm. *Makes 16 servings.*

A GRATEFUL PUDDING

The May–December marriage of John Tyler and Julia Gardiner seems to have been a happy one. In later years Julia told her friends that she and her husband had a mystical bond between them, enabling them to know what the other was thinking at any given time. One would hesitate to claim that a shared fondness for pudding intensified that bond in any way, but it *is* true that their food preferences were similar. New York and Virginia shared a wider and more sophisticated cuisine than the country in general at that time. The Gardiner and Tyler households in particular displayed a fondness for pudding. A special favorite was this

Grateful pudding, an old English pudding similar to bread pudding but with considerable flour and raisins and currants added.

White bread	*Raisins*
Flour	*Currants*
Eggs	*Sugar*
Milk or cream	*Ginger, ground*

Grate a 1 pound loaf of white bread and add to it 1 pound flour. Beat 8 egg yolks and 4 egg whites until light and mix with them 1 pint cream (much better than milk, if available). Stir in the bread–flour mixture. Mix well. Add 1 pound seedless raisins, 1 pound currants, ½ pound sugar, and a dash of ground ginger. Mix thoroughly, pour into a greased baking dish, and bake in a moderate (350° F.) oven. Cook until it sets, about ½ hour. *Serves 8.*

THE EMERALD BROOCH SWEET

This pudding received its name at a time when Gardiner's Island was a kingdom close to, but completely separated from, the United States. Charles I had granted the islanders their own charter, their own laws, their own courts, and even their own say over life and death. Because of the difficulties in sending prisoners to the assizes on the mainland, the ruler of the island (the head of the Gardiner clan) was granted the power of decapitation, a right rarely used (never in the past 300 years) but never revoked.

The only thing the islanders lacked was their own currency. To obtain pots and pans and other manufactured goods, the islanders bartered their famous cider, their apples, peaches, and pears. A tinker would arrive by boat from Connecticut and display his wares. In addition to utensils, he usually carried a line of glittering treasures, known today as junk jewelry. These he would display on the kitchen floor to the wonder and dazzlement of all. One day, after the tinker's visit, Mrs. Gardiner entered the kitchen and found Lucinda, her cook, in tears. Lucinda had fallen in love with a brooch of emerald glass, but being a slave, she had no money or possessions to trade for it. Mrs. Gardiner sent one of her children to call the tinker back. After a bit of bargaining, the brooch was secured. That night, with the brooch flashing in the firelight as she prepared the meal, Lucinda created a new glorified version of a pudding that had formerly been known as Grateful Pudding. The new creation was dubbed Emerald Brooch Sweet.

Milk or cream	*Salt*
Dry breadcrumbs	*Nutmeg (or vanilla or almond ex-*
Cornmeal	* tract)*
Butter	*Cloves*
Peach jam	*Sugar, Eggs*

Scald 1 quart milk or equal parts milk and cream. Stir 1½ cups dry bread-crumbs into the hot milk, along with ½ cup cornmeal and 4 tablespoons butter. Cool. Then stir in 1 cup peach jam, 4 slightly beaten egg yolks, ¼ teaspoon salt, ½ teaspoon freshly grated nutmeg, and ¼ teaspoon cloves. (Or 1 teaspoon vanilla instead of the nutmeg and cloves.) Pour into a greased baking dish and bake in slow (325° F.) oven for 1 hour. Remove from oven, and while pudding is still warm spread with a thin layer of jam and top with a meringue made from 4 egg whites and 4 tablespoons superfine sugar. Bake 5 minutes at 425° F. or set briefly under the broiler until the peaks are delicately browned. Serve warm from the baking dish. No sauce is needed. *Serves 6.*

TRANSPARENT PUDDING

Julia Tyler once said "Everyone adores me," and it was probably inconceivable to the lovely looking woman that someone might not. (It was probably inconceivable to the infatuated John as well.) While most of us today might worry a bit about the calories in this rich, delicious dessert, it is unlikely that the self-assured Julia ever gave calories a second thought. Certainly she ate—and enjoyed—a goodly share of pudding in her lifetime.

> *Dried apricots, dates, figs or peaches,*   *Butter*
>   *candied orange peel or ginger*   *Egg yolks*
> *Sugar*

Cover the bottom of a shallow buttered baking dish with dried pitted fruits, stewed till tender, then drained. Sliced candied orange peel or crystallized ginger may be used as is. Cream ½ pound sugar with ½ pound butter. Beat 8 egg yolks thoroughly, then add them to the butter and sugar. Pour over the dried fruit and bake in a slow (300°–325° F.) oven for ½ hour. When cool, turn out of the baking dish so the fruit is on the top. Refrigerate. Frost or garnish it if you desire—or serve as is. It looks particularly attractive garnished with Maraschino cherries. *Serves 6 to 8.*

CHAMPAGNE PUNCH

It is possible that Tyler's fondness for champagne saved his life. When the Presidential party cruised down the Potomac in the new warship *Princeton,* the 500 guests went below to the dining saloon for a champagne party. It was a gay affair, but some of the guests tired of the wine and toasts and decided to return to the deck. Someone came down to ask the President to come up and see the last shot fired from the *Princeton's* huge gun. Tyler, enjoying his conversation with

Julia and his favorite champagne, declined, saying he had better things to do. A few moments later the gun was fired, exploded, and wrought death and injury on those up on deck who had abandoned the champagne.

Lemon juice	*Brandy*
Powdered sugar	*Curaçao*
Soda water	*Champagne*
Block of ice	

Mix together the juice of 12 lemons (about 3 cups) with enough powdered sugar to sweeten, and 1 quart soda water. Place in a large punch bowl in which you have already placed a large block of ice. Stir well. Then add ½ pint brandy, ½ pint Curaçao, and 2 quarts champagne. Stir well. Top with fresh strawberries or other fruits that are in season. Serve in chilled champagne glasses or glass punch cups. *Makes about 1 gallon—about 32 servings.*

GARDINER'S ISLAND BORAGE PUNCH

The cider of Gardiner's Island was justly valued for drinking as well as for bartering. In East Hampton, where Tyler's summer White House was located during the "Gardiner period" of his administration, a special punch was served, like that of the Island, in a great glass bowl with the famous Pelletreau ladle, made by a colleague of Paul Revere. In addition to the special cider of the Island, an essential ingredient to this punch was borage. Its blue flowers and gray-green leaves gave a misty look and an old-fashioned flavor to this cooling drink. The punch was really a version of the English wine cup. Even today, in the brick-walled garden at Gardiner's Island and in East Hampton, borage still grows. Borage punch is still served—and with the same Pelletreau ladle.

Sweet cider	*Lemon juice and rind*
Sparkling water	*Sugar*
Sherry or Madeira	*Nutmeg*
Cognac	*Fresh borage or cucumber peel*

Pour into a large punch bowl 1 quart sweet cider, 1 quart sparkling water, (or dry champagne if you prefer), ½ cup sherry or Maderia, ¼ cup cognac, the juice of ½ lemon, and the grated rind of ¼ lemon. Add superfine sugar to taste, freshly grated nutmeg, and 3 sprays borage, both leaves and flowers. Additional borage may be frozen into a chunk of ice. It will escape into the punch as the ice melts. If borage is not available, use long, thin shavings of cucumber peel. Allow punch to stand 1 or 2 hours in the refrigerator (ice house or spring house in Tyler's day). The punch may be strengthened by additional cognac. At serving time add a large chunk of clear ice and 1 quart chilled sparkling water. *Makes 16 4-ounce servings.*

BORAGE WINE CUP (VARIATION)

Substitute Rhine wine or any other dry white wine for the sweet cider. Garnish with thin slices of lemon as well as the borage or cucumber.

✳✳

XI

Slow Polk in the White House

✳✳

James Knox Polk had many claims to fame, important political ones, but socially he introduced a new note to Presidential life: prudery. His was a harbinger of administrations to come.

There had been formal Presidencies before—those of the Adamses, Monroe, and Van Buren. But formality was not prudery. The Polks were the first real puritans in the White House.

The pendulum often swings rather abruptly from one administration to another. But from the opulence and ostentation of the latter-day Julia Tyler style to the severity and austerity of the Polks the pendulum didn't merely swing— it leaped.

Several years ago leading historians ranked Polk as one of our strongest, most dynamic Presidents, but no gourmet could make that statement. We do not dispute Polk's claim to greatness as a forceful President, a leader of vision and perspicacity. But a connoisseur of fine food—never!

James Polk himself would have been the last to make such a claim. In fact, he would have argued it if some ill-advised publicist of his day had ever tried to suggest such a thing. (None did.) Polk wore his plainness and simplicity as a badge of honor. (After the criticism of the Tylers for their lavish displays, perhaps it was.)

Polk was born in North Carolina, but his family went over the mountains into Tennessee while he was still a young boy. His taste in food followed the path of frontier families before him. Simple, hearty country fare was what pleased James Polk most.

Social Washington had its first inkling of the Polk pattern on his inauguration day. He had been a dark-horse candidate. Little was known of his personal habits before he became President. But it did not take Washington long to get the picture. The inaugural ball was dull and lackluster.

Sarah Polk was not what she seemed. The new First Lady looked like a Spanish beauty with a taste for fun and laughter. But her own brand of puritanism made her husband seem like a veritable Falstaff. James disapproved highly of "time unprofitably spent" in games and diversions, but his wife went even further and banned all food and drink from White House receptions. Her anxiety was not based on concern for the building's carpets, but for the country's soul.

Dancing, card-playing and other amusements were taboo during the Polk administration. As a result, official functions sank to a low level of tedium. Critics of Julia Tyler were now eating their words—plain, without sauce Bérnaise. Fancy cooking joined the list of Polk taboos.

Of course gaiety could not be completely outlawed from the capital. No President has ever wielded *that* much power. But one needn't look for it at the Executive Mansion. Instead one turned to certain embassies, private homes of affluent citizens, and to the famous house across Lafayette Park where Dolley Madison, now in her young eighties and still going strong, held court.

Many observers felt that the only time the official White House parties came to life was when Dolley Madison made her entrance on the arm of the President. Card-playing, snuff-taking, gay, ebullient, Dolley still had the knack of livening up any party she happened to attend.

Sarah Polk plunged into her official duties with indomitable spirit. Twice a week she held informal receptions. Each Tuesday and Friday evening guests yawned their way through a round of greetings, small talk, and forced conversation.

The President's levees were equally lively. Guests promenaded up and down the East Room, very much as if they were at sea on an endless voyage, forced to make conversation with ill-assorted fellow passengers.

One malcontent reported the quality of a Polk levee thus: "Such introducing, such scraping, such curtseying, such jabbering of foreign compliments and violent efforts of some of our people to do the polite in uncouth tongues—such a wild clamor of conversation rages—the band, too, has become insane and the room is oppressively warm, when the President enters leading a lady—probably Mrs. Madison—and followed by Mrs. Polk and all the great people of Washington."

Official dinners were as formal and simple as the Polks' Presbyterianism could make them. Informal dinners were even more so. Whatever brush James Polk might have had in his career with Virginia cooking had not even made a dent. His diet was the unadorned frontier diet of the South, without the ameliorating extras of genteel Southern cuisine.

It was a sad fact that, until Polk's term of office, President after President had impoverished himself to maintain a level of hospitality deemed fitting for the leader of the United States. The Polk view was that offering such embellishments was beneath the dignity of the Presidency. People calling on the President of the United States should be grateful for being allowed the privilege of conversation with him, without extra adornments of food and drink. Let conversation suffice. Alas, well-meaning as they were, the Polks were no Jeffersons in their conversational talents—this made for some long dry evenings.

As a result of the curtailment of food and drink, the Polks were able to leave Washington with a considerable portion of the President's salary intact. (Only a cynic would suggest that puritanism has its own rewards.) In fact, they left with enough cash in hand to purchase a rather splendid house in Nashville, Tennessee, which was, according to a local chronicler, "duly enlarged, ornamented, and put in the most complete and elegant order."

In spite of grumblings of discontent among Washington socialites, the Polks were popular with the nation at large. The nation's press sang the praises of the austere Presidential family, and the country was quick to follow suit. Their simple origins and friendly, unpretentious ways appealed to their fellow countrymen. Sarah Polk was esteemed the paragon her devoted husband had long claimed she was. Efficient housekeeper, straightforward pioneer-type woman, she was widely admired as the model woman.

When Polk's term of office ended, he and his wife decided to return to Nashville via New Orleans. The trip became a triumphal progress. "All along the route," it was reported, "the ex-President and his wife were feted and feasted, and they planned to top this off with a grand tour of Europe."

But they failed to account for Southern hospitality at its best and most abundant. Lavish meal was piled on lavish meal, until poor Polk's upset digestive tract cried out—in vain—for the plain food it was accustomed to. The climax came in New Orleans. Every imaginable elegant French dish was served to the frustrated Polks. Fish of every variety, a wide assortment of light wines, fanciful desserts rich and tempting, all were placed eagerly before the retiring President and his wife. In despair, Polk said, "As soon as an opportunity offered I asked a servant in a low tone if he could give me a piece of cornbread and boiled ham."

Ironically, food, which meant so little to Polk, was the cause of his demise. As one writer of the time put it, Polk, a Southerner, lacking the usual Southerner's zest for fine food, "died of an overdose of Southern hospitality, heaped upon a digestive system too tired to respond." Once installed in his impressive new home in Nashville, Polk sickened, failed to regain his strength, and died. Four hard-working—ferociously hard-working—years as President, during which much was accomplished for the country, followed by three months of excessive feting and overindulgence, and James Polk was dead at fifty-three.

Is there some moral in the fact that the fun-loving, long-playing Dolley Madison survived him by twenty-seven days?

◇◇

R E C I P E S

BEAR STEAK

In James Polk's day, even as now, Tennessee abounded in game. Local cooks were skilled in ways of preparing game, rabbit, doves, wild ducks, and geese. All these have become more numerous again since the coming of the gigantic TVA lakes. Once again there are white-tailed deer, black bear, and the fierce European wild boar. All of these appeared on the table of the Polk home at Columbia, Tennessee.

Butter   *Salt and pepper*
Bear steak

Put a mound of butter (2 tablespoons) in a hot skillet. When the butter is just melted, add the steak, cut about 1 inch thick. Sear and brown on one side, then turn and brown the other side equally. Add salt and pepper to taste, cook a minute or two longer, add butter to the top, and serve piping hot. There is no more trick to cooking bear steak than any other steak, except to be sure it is cooked through. Otherwise the flavor may be too strong and gamy for most people's taste.

FRIED COUNTRY HAM, RED GRAVY

A dish fit for a President—at least a President named James Polk. It was plain ham that Polk craved when he was being inundated with Creole specialties and delicate French succulents in New Orleans. So ham it is.

Ham fat   *Water*
Ham steaks

Heat a skillet until it is sizzling hot, then grease it lightly with a piece of ham fat. Add ham steaks and sear them on both sides. Slowly add 1 cup water to the skillet, cover, and lower the heat, allowing the ham to simmer until tender. Serve with the gravy poured over the ham. (In Kentucky, certain cooks use 1 cup coffee instead of water to make the ham gravy, but we favor the water.)

CORN PONE

Like President Polk, we believe in the affinity between fried ham and corn pone. This dish antedates Polk, but was a favorite mainstay with him, as with other Tennessee settlers. It originally came from the Indians, who baked it in ashes. The settlers kept it out of the fire and called it corn pone. When they baked corn cakes in hot ashes, they differentiated and called them ashcakes—subtle distinctions in a non-subtle age.

White cornmeal	*Shortening*
Baking soda	*Boiling water*
Salt	*Buttermilk*

Sift 2 cups cornmeal with ¼ teaspoon baking soda and 1 teaspoon salt. Work 4 tablespoons shortening (or lard) into the dry ingredients. Blend well. Add ¾ cup boiling water and continue blending. Slowly add ½ cup buttermilk until a soft dough is formed. The buttermilk should be added very slowly, making sure the dough retains enough consistency to be molded into small flat cakes. Grease a skillet, heat it, then place the cakes in it and bake them in a preheated medium-hot (350° F.) oven for ½ hour or 40 minutes, until lightly browned and done. *Makes approximately 12.*

LAPLANDS

Somewhat like popovers, laplands were a great Southern specialty in the early and middle nineteenth century. The Polks were fond of them. In that era every plantation had its "batter bread express," small Negro boys, who lived on the grounds, so fleet-footed they could rush the batter breads, soufflélike spoon breads, and corn puddings from the remote kitchens to the Master's table before the delicacies could fall. Well-baked laplands, however, should not fall, whether carried to the table by express or not.

Eggs	*Cream or milk and butter*
Flour	*Salt*

Blend together 3 egg yolks with 1 cup all-purpose flour and 1 cup cream. (If you prefer, you may use 1 cup milk and 1 tablespoon melted butter instead of the cream.) Blend in electric blender or with an eggbeater, 1 minute in electric blender, 2 or 3 with a beater. Add ¼ to ½ teaspoon salt, to your taste. Fold in 3 stiffly beaten egg whites. Grease small muffin tins well, flour, then pour batter in, allowing room for puffing up. Bake in medium-hot (375° F.) oven until the laplands become nicely puffed up and golden brown in color (usually about 40 minutes). Serve hot with butter and jam or honey. Deliciously delicate as an accompaniment to tea or with soup and salad at lunch or Sunday-night supper. *Makes 24 small laplands.*

TOMATO OMELETTE

Simple, hearty fare was what James Polk favored most. A dish such as this omelette was especially pleasing to his palate.

Eggs	*Tomatoes*
Flour	*Salt and pepper*
Milk	

Beat 6 eggs until light and foamy. Stir in 2 tablespoons flour that has been moistened with enough milk to blend it. Peel and cut into small cubes 4 ripe tomatoes. Salt and pepper them to taste. Add to the egg mixture. Heat a skillet with butter, then pour in the egg mixture. Cook as you would any omelette, turning it after one side is lightly browned. *Serves 4 to 6.*

LYE OR BIG HOMINY

This oddity was actually a standard way to prepare hominy in James Polk's day. Note that we said *a* standard way, not *the* standard way, inasmuch as there were as many variations of hominy as of johnnycake, another favorite of the time. We thought this recipe should be included in the Old Curiosity Corner—if for no other reason than to illustrate how simplified cooking has become for the American homemaker.

Sweet flat corn	*Boiling water*
Concentrated lye	

Use sweet, flat corn. Most early varieties of sweet corn have flat kernels. Make a solution of 2 ounces of concentrated lye in 1 gallon boiling water. Drop the corn into the mixture and boil furiously for 30 minutes. Drain the corn and drop immediately into a pan of cold water. If possible, run cold water over the corn for 3 or 4 *hours* to remove all tinges of the lye. (Now comes the part we enjoy most.) Put the corn in a barrel churn and churn for 10 minutes, to be sure the black eyes and hulls are removed. Next, place the corn in an enamel kettle or deep pan, cover with fresh boiling water and cook until tender. Wash once again and remove any eyes or hulls that were too tenacious the first time. (Are you still with us?) Serve hot with butter.

Note: You can now buy big hominy in cans. Looks like soft white popcorn. Just heat, add butter and pepper.

SCRATCH BACKS

In frontier days, foods were given picturesque names. Polk's Tennessee was particularly noted for its quaint nomenclature, as in this recipe for a variation of corn pone or cornbread. In Polk's rough-and-ready times, when the country was expanding faster than it ever had, this was frequently served as an accompaniment to the main meal. Simple Polk-type fare it was, too.

Cornmeal   Boiling water
Salt

Sift together 2 cups cornmeal with 2 teaspoons salt. Pour a little boiling water over the mixture, beating vigorously as you pour. Add just enough water to moisten, making sure the batter holds its shape when dropped from a spoon. Heat a greased cooky sheet in a very hot (400° F.) oven. Drop the batter on the greased sheet with a small spoon. Bake in the hot oven until cakes are a delicate brown. Serve hot with ham or other main dish. *Makes 36 cakes.*

JAMES K. POLK'S CHRISTMAS FRUIT CAKE

Although James Polk's family soon moved to Tennessee, our eleventh President was born in Mecklenburg County, North Carolina, near Charlotte, where a monument commemorates the fact. The home of Marshall Polk, James' brother, still stands on Providence Road in Charlotte. No monument commemorates *that* fact, but this recipe, handed down in Marshall's family, constitutes a monument of sorts. It was a great favorite of James.

Blanched almonds	*Ground allspice, mace, and nutmeg*
Orange juice	*Citron*
Butter	*Raisins*
Sugar	*Currants*
Eggs	*Candied pineapple*
Flour	*Dates*
Ground cloves	*Fruit juice*
Ground cinnamon	

Blanch and chop ½ pound almonds, mix them with juice of 3 large oranges. Cream 1 pound butter with 2 cups sugar. Add 12 eggs and beat well. Set aside while sifting dry ingredients. Sift 4 cups flour, 1 teaspoon cloves, 1 tablespoon cinnamon, 1 teaspoon each nutmeg, allspice, and mace. Add to the creamed mixture. Mix the dough thoroughly, then add 1 pound citron, 3 pounds raisins, 1 pound each currants and candied pineapple, and 2 pounds dates, dredging the fruit with flour before adding. When dough is stiff, add orange-juice-and-almond mixture. Little by little, add 1 pint of any kind of fruit juice. This recipe makes an enormous cake. It is possible to bake it in one large tube pan or 2 or 3 small tube pans. Cut brown wrapping paper double and line the bottom and sides of the tube with it. Grease the pan and paper, then pour in the batter. Allow 2 inches at the top for rising. Preheat the oven to 150° F. Bake at that temperature for approximately 6 hours. When a straw comes out clean, cake is finished. Let cake cool in pan. (It is better if you put a small pan of water to one side in the oven, to maintain moisture in the oven while cake is baking at such a low temperature.)

XII

Old Rough and Ready— but not for Long

✳✳

The most controversial thing about our twelfth President, Zachary Taylor, appears to have been his wife. Actually, Taylor's term of office was too brief for much real controversy to appear. Lasting a little more than one year, Taylor's administration was free of any major political or social contributions or controversies.

But poor Margaret Mackall Smith Taylor came in for more than her share of criticism. Not because of what she did but because of what she did not do.

What she did not do was monumental—at least in the eyes of social Washington. She did not fulfill her obligations as First Lady of the Land. Her reasons for reneging on her responsibility were admirable ones, but not to the social busybodies of the capital.

When Old Zach Taylor—"Old Rough and Ready" as the country knew him through his myriad battles with Indians—was elected President, he was sixty-four years old. His wife, boon companion of all his encampments, battles, and barricades, was sixty-two. Having reared six children, followed her husband uncomplainingly from frontier post to frontier post for thirty-eight years, and put up with all the inconveniences of army life at its most primitive, Margaret Taylor was ready for a rest.

She had not wanted her husband to run for President. Once he was elected, she relegated all the official hostessing to her daughter, pretty young Betty Bliss, wife of Major W. S. Bliss.

Rumors immediately besieged Washington that something must be wrong with President Taylor's wife. She must be a disgrace, probably a poor-white he had married early in his career on the march, a wretched woman he didn't dare show in public for fear of ridicule.

It was inconceivable to gregarious social-climbing Washington hostesses that any woman would not *want* the power and social distinction that accrued to the wife of the President. Whispers flew around the capital that Mrs. Taylor was kept locked from public view in an upstairs room of the White House, where she sat puffing a corncob pipe, living the same rustic life she had lived "on the trail."

In truth, Margaret Taylor came from a respected Maryland family. It was quite a step for her to marry a young soldier and take off for a frontier life. Well-born and well-bred, she found frontier life rugged and strange. But in the tradition of the times, she coped. In coping, she lost her health and vigor. By the time her husband was elected President, Margaret Taylor was a tired, semi-invalided old lady who wanted nothing better than the chance to rest.

Although officially her bright-eyed daughter carried on, Margaret did a small amount of unofficial entertaining for close family friends who visited the White House. One commented:

I always found the most pleasant part of my visit to the White House to be passed in Mrs. Taylor's bright, pretty room where the invalid, full of interest in the passing show in which she had not the strength to take her part, talked most agreeably and kindly to the many friends admitted to her presence. She always appeared at the family dinner, to which a few friends were unceremoniously bidden, of which many charming ones were given during General Taylor's Administration, and ably bore her share in the conversation at the table.

Other friends attested to her intelligence and ability to make conversation. As for the enigmatic corncob pipe, which has passed into White House legend, we have one footnote to offer. The son of a Doctor Robert Brooke Wood, regimental surgeon under General Taylor in several of his posts, testified that the General did not smoke himself because tobacco smoke made Mrs. Taylor "actively ill." It is just possible that Rachel Jackson's corncob pipe (which was real enough) became telescoped into Margaret Taylor's as well. History and legend blend in curious ways.

In any case, White House entertaining was handled by Taylor's daughter, and handled very deftly. For a twenty-two-year-old girl, reared on the frontier, married to an army major, to possess the poise and grace that Betty Taylor Bliss seems to have had speaks very well for her upbringing—another bow to the accomplishments of Maryland-born Margaret.

A society journal described Betty's qualities. In addition to good taste in clothes, a pleasing personality, and quiet charm, "she had that *je ne sais quoi,* that knowledge of how to be just cordial enough, and not too cordial. Never has the White House had a gentler, sweeter mistress!"

In addition to her ability to meet and greet with just enough cordiality, Betty Bliss had other attributes of a good hostess. She was a first-rate housekeeper, bought new carpeting and furniture for the White House, and managed to run the establishment in an orderly fashion in her brief year or so.

Entertaining during Taylor's term of office pretty much followed the pattern of Polk's. Dancing remained abolished, the President did not drink, and the general atmosphere was one of formality. Yet Betty Bliss managed, when she presided at the official state dinners, weekly morning receptions, and large public functions, to convey an air of graciousness and welcome.

For one thing, Betty gave frequent little afternoon teas for Cabinet wives, capital socialites, and other ladies of note. The teas were much praised for their elegance. Statuesque Negro waiters passed trays piled high with homemade cakes and cookies. Even gentlemen attended at times, and managed to balance plates heaped with goodies on one knee and a teacup and saucer on the other.

Then too, there was one difference between Polk's administration and Taylor's on the social front: Taylor had discovered New Orleans early in his life (before it could kill him). The food served at the Taylor table far surpassed that at the Polks'. Like Jefferson, General Taylor was not particularly careful about his mode of dress (they didn't call him "Rough and Ready" for nothing). Wrinkled, crumpled, and in frequent disarray, Taylor was no paragon of fashion. Yet, like his fellow Virginian, he was much concerned with what he ate.

Born in Virginia but transplanted early to Kentucky, Taylor spent much of his life "on the road," traveling from one army barracks to another, living throughout the countryside. He served in the Northwest Territory, in the Florida Everglades area, and finally was stationed in Louisiana. He became so attached to Louisiana that he bought a plantation at Baton Rouge and spent many happy times there between tours of duty.

His familiarity with Louisiana gave him firsthand knowledge of Creole cooking, and he became enamored of its variety and richness. Not that he had any claims to being the gourmet Jefferson was. Taylor would accept plain fare without complaint, but he did insist that it be decently cooked and well served.

The old soldier did not have much chance to demonstrate to the nation how extensively he cared about diverse cuisines. On July 4, 1850, just a little over a year after he took the oath of office, he became ill. Five days later he was dead. His death was caused by a number of cumulative things.

He had accepted an invitation to sit on the platform at the capital's big Independence Day celebration.

Perley, in his *Reminiscences,* described the day this way:

> The old hero sat in the sun at the Washington Monument during a long spreadeagle address by Senator Foote, with a tedious supplementary harangue by George Washington Custis—exposed to heat nearly three hours. He had drunk freely of ice-water, and on his return to the White House had found a

basket of cherries which he partook heartily, drinking at the same time several goblets of iced milk. After dinner, he still further feasted on cherries and iced milk against the protest of Dr. Witherspoon, who was his guest. When the time arrived to go to the Winthrop party, he felt ill and soon was seized with a violent attack of cholera morbus. This was on Thursday. On Sunday he is reported to have said to his physicians: "In two days I shall be a dead man." His gift of prophecy was accurate.

Like his predecessor, Polk, General Taylor was reported to be a total abstainer. Prohibitionists liked to emphasize this fact—until it was pointed out that ice-water and iced milk contributed to his death. Of course age, the toll of a rugged, overactive life, and general fatigue all played their parts. But you may be sure the facts that seemed of greatest pertinence to antiprohibitionists were the ice-water and iced milk. One wonders why the antivegetarians remained silent. Surely the cherries played their role too.

For all of that, we owe Zachary Taylor a debt of gratitude for broadening the base of American cooking in his day. Not content to fall into the pattern of official Washington in serving the standard Southern-New England-French fare, he introduced some of the Creole dishes he loved. The White House might have lacked a First Lady's influence during Taylor's short term, but it felt the firm guiding hand of a First Man.

◊◊◊

RECIPES

CALAS-TOUS-CHAUDS

These delicious little cakes are great favorites in New Orleans with morning coffee, as indeed they were in the days of Zachary Taylor. Well acquainted with the Creole delicacies, he brought them back to Washington with him.

Yeast cake	*Sugar*
Water	*Salt*
Cooked rice	*Flour*
Eggs	

Dissolve 1 yeast cake in ½ cup lukewarm water. When dissolved, stir into 2 cups cooked rice. Let rise overnight. Next morning, beat 2 eggs until light and lemony, add 4 tablespoons sugar and 1½ teaspoons salt. Combine with the rice mixture and blend in 4 cups flour. Let dough rise 1 hour. Drop by tablespoons into deep fat that has been heated to a medium-hot temperature (360° F.). Fry until browned lightly. Drain and serve piping hot, either with cane syrup or sprinkled with powdered sugar. Excellent either way. *Makes 50 fritters.*

OPELOUSAS OYSTER GUMBO

Zachary Taylor was one of the first Presidents to become well acquainted with Creole specialties. But many generations later, Herbert Hoover came to Opelousas, Louisiana, to have oyster gumbo at Dadees, an ordinary-looking place known to gourmet-huntsmen all over the United States. This recipe dates back to the days when Louisiana was still a territory. It bids you add your oysters half an hour before serving. Modernists like to cook oysters only a few minutes, but in Louisiana they still insist the old way allows the flavors to blend better and penetrate deeper. Often cookbook recipes suggest adding the filé powder (a combination of dried sassafras leaves, garlic, and thyme) *after* the gumbo has been removed from the heat, for if the liquid should boil after the filé has been added, the dish becomes "ropy." Real connoisseurs, however, prefer to sprinkle the filé powder into the tureen at the table, or over each portion as it is served. This sprinkling is an added refinement that marks you as belonging to the select group "who really know Louisiana cooking." Purists insist the best oysters come from Morgan City or Bayou Cook, Louisiana, but if you don't live in Louisiana you "pays your money and takes your chance."

Butter	*Chicken (optional)*
Flour	*Salt*
Onion	*Pepper*
Garlic	*Cayenne (optional)*
Bell pepper	*Oyster liquid*
Parsley, thyme, bay leaf	*Oysters*
Boiling water	*Filé powder*
Raw shrimps	*Cooked rice*

Melt 1 tablespoon butter in a heavy black iron skillet, allowing it to brown a bit. Remove from the heat, stir in 1 tablespoon flour. Add 1 clove garlic, crushed, 1 sweet bell pepper (green or red), chopped, 2 sprigs parsley, ¼ teaspoon thyme, 1 small bay leaf, 3 cups boiling water in which the shrimp were cooked. Cook all this together slowly for ½ hour, stirring often. Earlier, of course, the 2 dozen shrimp should have been shelled and cooked in 3 cups boiling water, seasoned with 1 teaspoon salt, ¼ teaspoon pepper, ⅛ teaspoon Cayenne pepper (optional). Cook 7 to 10 minutes or until the shrimp turn red.

Add the cooked shrimp and 1 quart oyster liquid to the herb mixture in the iron skillet. Bring mixture to a fast boil. Then add 2 dozen oysters and simmer 10 minutes to ½ hour, depending on whether you prefer your oysters lightly cooked or well cooked. When ready to serve, bring mixture to the table in a tureen or heated casserole. Sprinkle with 1 tablespoon filé powder and stir it in carefully to prevent lumping. Pass cooked rice at the table, so each person may add 1 or 2 tablespoons to his gumbo. Served with crusty bread and tossed salad, this gumbo makes a delicious lunch or supper. *Serves 6 to 8.*

OYSTERS ROASTED

It would be hard, if not impossible, to spend much time in Louisiana and not eat a lot of oysters. Taylor found it true in his day, even as we do in ours. A favorite way of fixing them is in the recipe that follows.

Oysters   Wood fire

Clean the oyster shells carefully. Place the oysters in pans and place them in the oven, or in rows on top of the stove. If you are lucky enough to be able to cook over a wood fire, they can be roasted on a hearthstone. As soon as the heat forces the shells open, remove the oysters (with their liquid) to a hot serving dish. Serve immediately and allow each person to dress his oyster as he chooses—with lemon juice, Worcestershire sauce, or as is.

FRIED OYSTERS

Another simple but delicious way to prepare good fresh oysters:

Oysters	*Egg yolks*
Cracker crumbs	*Heavy cream*
Salt	*Butter or lard*
Cayenne	

Choose the largest oysters obtainable for frying. Remove them from their liquor and clean off any shell particles. Dry the oysters. Crush some cracker crumbs and mix with salt and a dash of cayenne. Set aside. Beat egg yolks with heavy cream, allowing ½ tablespoon cream for each yolk used. Dip the oysters, one at a time, first in the egg mixture, then the cracker crumbs. Then fry them in a generous amount of hot butter or butter and lard mixed, until they are light brown on both sides. Serve piping hot.

STEWED OYSTERS

Here is still another simple way of serving oysters, as Taylor had them:

Oysters	*Cream*
Salt	*Cracker crumbs*
Cayenne	*Butter*
Mace	

Rinse oysters. Put them in a large stewing pan. Season with salt and cayenne and a dash of mace. As soon as they begin to boil (the only water used is the water which adhered from the washing), pour in ½ pint cream. Stir in ½ ounce butter mixed with a bit of grated cracker crumbs. Let the oysters come to a boil once. Serve hot.

BROWN OYSTER STEW

This is one of the most famous dishes containing the delicious benne seeds. It is as easy to prepare today as in Taylor's time.

Bacon	*Roasted benne (sesame) seeds*
Onions	*Oysters*
Flour	*Rice or hominy*
Oyster liquor	

First, fry some bacon in a skillet, then remove and drain. Next, pan-fry sliced onions, and when golden remove and drain. Brown a little flour in the bacon drippings. Stir in enough oyster liquor to make a smooth sauce. Add crushed or pounded roasted benne seeds, along with the oysters, measuring about 1 tablespoon seeds to 1 cup oysters. Add the bacon and onions and serve on a bed of rice or hominy.

GASPERGOU

New Orleans since the nineteenth century has been the paradise of American gourmets. Not only is its sophisticated cuisine—a blend of African, American Indian, Portuguese, Spanish, and French—truly superb, but it is in the heartland of an area rich in fine foods. Its waters abound in unusual and delicious fish and seafood. Its wild marshes and woods are dense with game. Of all the fish prized in Louisiana, few excel *gaspergou,* a freshwater specimen similar to redfish.

Gaspergou	*Parsley*
Garlic	

Make three slits in the sides of the *gaspergou,* in the fleshy portion. Mix chopped garlic and parsley together and press them into these pockets of the fish. Bake as you would any other fish. Serve hot with lemon slices or a butter sauce.

CHICKEN PIE À LA CREOLE
(PÂTÉ DE POULET À LA CREOLE)

When Zachary Taylor sought the Presidency, his wife was bitterly opposed. She was even more unhappy when he was elected, calling it a plot "to deprive her of his society." Knowing her happiness in her home in Baton Rouge, where all the comforts of good food and living were available to her, one wonders if Margaret Taylor was dreading the thought of leaving Creole cooking behind her, for the more staid menus of Washington. Such fears would have been in vain, for the Taylors were able to transport some of their Creole creations with them, thus broadening the horizon of many a sophisticated Washingtonian. Such an example is this Creole version of plain old chicken pie.

Brioche pastry	*Fat and lean salt pork*
Saffron	*Salt*
Chicken curry	

Make some brioche pastry. Sweeten and salt slightly and tint pale yellow with saffron. Make a chicken curry from a regular curry recipe, boiling the sauce down as much as possible. Make a compact forcemeat mixture of fat and lean salt pork, well salted and peppered and cooked for a moment lightly in fat. Spread the brioche pastry in the shape of a tart, with a hollow in the middle. Place a layer of the salt pork mixture on the bottom, then a layer of the chicken curry, another layer of the forcemeat. Close the top of the tart by bringing the pastry up over it. Bake in a medium-hot (375° F.) oven about 1 hour.

COON-AND-SQUIRREL DEEP DISH PIE

Oysters and exotic fishes were not Louisiana's only claim to fame. The woods were full of squirrels, raccoons, rabbits, quail. And Creole cooks were never at a loss for new ways to prepare game. President Taylor, drawing on years of resourcefulness as a hunter in the wilderness, had a few tricks of his own. This old recipe is an example. Originally one would have used 6 squirrels and 1 coon, but a good substitute would be 4 pounds fresh pork meat and 1 large fricassee chicken.

Squirrels and coons (or fresh pork	*Bay leaf*
and chicken)	*Butter or lard*
Water	*Carrots*
Vinegar	*Parsnips*
Celery	*Mushrooms*
Cloves	*Pepper*
Cinnamon	*Nutmeg*
Sugar	*Dry vermouth*
Salt	*Pie crust*
Onions	

Marinate the meat in 4 cups water, ½ cup vinegar, 4 cups chopped celery, 6 whole cloves, 2 teaspoons cinnamon, 1 tablespoon sugar, 1 teaspoon salt, 3 medium quartered onions, 1 bay leaf. The marinade should cover the meat. Allow to stand at least 24 hours in refrigerator or other cool place. When ready to cook, remove meat from marinade and brown lightly in a hot skillet in which you have melted 1 tablespoon butter or lard. Place the browned meat in a kettle, add enough water to cover and 8 carrots in ½-inch chunks, 6 peeled parsnips in large chunks, 12 stalks chopped celery, 6 medium sliced onions, 2 cups small whole mushrooms, 1 teaspoon salt, ¼ teaspoon pepper, ⅓ teaspoon nutmeg, and 2 cups dry vermouth. Cook slowly until meat is tender, approximately 4 hours. Remove bones after meat is thoroughly cooked. Place stew in deep baking dish or casserole. Cover with standard pie crust. Bake until lightly browned in fairly hot (375° F.) oven about 30 minutes. Serve hot from baking dish with green side vegetable and currant or grape jelly. *Serves 12.*

OKRA AND TOMATOES

Heading the list of favored vegetables in Louisiana—and in the Taylor household—was okra. An African import, okra soon took on its own local coloration. New Orleans would not be the same without it. Often it was prepared with onions, bacon, and tomatoes, as in this recipe.

Bacon drippings	*Curry powder*
Onion	*Brown sugar*
Okra	*Worcestershire sauce*
Tomatoes	*Green pepper (optional)*
Paprika	*Garlic (optional)*
Salt	

Heat 2 tablespoons bacon fat in a heavy skillet. Add ½ cup chopped onion and sauté lightly for 4 or 5 minutes. Then add 1 pound sliced okra. Sauté 5 minutes before adding 3 cups fresh or canned tomatoes, ½ teaspoon paprika, and 1¼ teaspoons salt. Stir in ¼ teaspoon curry powder, 2 teaspoons brown sugar, and a dash of Worcestershire sauce. Simmer 10 minutes, then add 1 large chopped green pepper and 1 clove minced garlic. Simmer all ingredients together with a cover on the skillet. When okra is tender, serve immediately. *Serves 4 to 5.*

MARYLAND BEATEN BISCUITS

Beaten biscuits seem to be a peculiarly American invention. Several states claim to have had the honor of first creating them, but Maryland and Virginia would seem to be the real homes of these unique biscuits. Margaret Taylor of Maryland no doubt introduced the famous biscuits to her husband, who enjoyed them as much as you will. The trick is in the beating. The biscuits were probably invented because of the shortage of various types of shortening. The basic ingredients are flour, lard, and a strong right hand. The lightness of the biscuits depends on the number of strokes taken in the beating. In some parts of the country the beating was timed to the singing of hymns. One old cookbook advises beating through seven verses of "Abide with Me." A recent innovation of Ann Seranne's is to put the dough through a meat grinder six or seven times. It works.

> *Flour*   *Salt*
> *Butter*   *Lukewarm milk*

Blend 1 pound flour with 1 ounce butter or lard. Add just a pinch of salt and enough milk to make a very stiff dough. Knead the dough. Pound it with a rolling pin. Break the dough in pieces, pound, and knead again. (At this point we advise putting it through the meat grinder.) If you insist on being a purist, repeat the pounding; kneading, breaking operation *for 2 or 3 hours*—that's what the old books say. Or beat it ferociously with a wooden spoon for 800 strokes. It's one way to get rid of aggressions. When smooth and light, roll the dough out and cut into small biscuit shapes. Bake in a 350° F. oven about 20 minutes. May be served hot or at room temperature. Especially good sliced, with butter and country ham inside. A Southern picnic usually includes beaten biscuits and ham. *Makes about 48 biscuits.*

EGG BISCUITS

One food in good supply almost everywhere the Taylors were stationed during their long army life was eggs. They used them a variety of ways, as in these egg biscuits.

> *Egg yolk*   *Flour*
> *Sugar*   *Baking powder*
> *Milk*   *Shortening*

Blend 1 egg yolk with 1 tablespoon sugar and ½ cup milk. Set aside. Sift together 1½ cups flour and 2½ teaspoons baking powder. Cut in 4 tablespoons shortening. Little by little add the egg–milk mixture. Mix well. Place dough on a floured board and roll to ¼-inch thickness. Cut with a biscuit cutter. Cover half the biscuits with melted butter. Place another biscuit over each buttered one. Bake in a medium (350° F.) oven 10 to 12 minutes, or until brown. *Serves 4.*

KENTUCKY TEA CAKES

The White House in Taylor's day was at its best at tea-party time. With the liveried colored waiters passing platter after platter of "little cakes" to the assembled guests, it took on a glamour that was sadly lacking at more formal functions. Betty Bliss, the President's daughter, delighted in serving homemade delicacies such as these tea cakes from the state in which her father spent his boyhood.

Butter	*Wine*
Sugar	*Lemon*
Eggs	*Flour*

Cream together ½ cup butter and 1½ cups sugar. Add 3 eggs that have been beaten until light and frothy. Mix well. Add 4 tablespoons wine and ½ lemon (both juice and rind). Add just enough flour to roll the dough evenly. Cut the dough in rounds and bake in a 400° F. oven until lightly browned. *Makes 30 cakes.*

MARYLAND BLACK PEPPER COOKIES

Margaret Mackall Smith Taylor could have told you that these regional specialties are far better than their name implies. A rich spicy cooky, it was an ideal accompaniment to her daughter's White House teas.

Eggs	*Ground cloves*
Brown sugar	*Black pepper*
Flour	*Baking soda*
Salt	*Baking powder*
Cinnamon	*Raisins and nuts*

First beat 2 egg whites, then beat 2 egg yolks, then combine them and beat together. Add 1 cup brown sugar and beat again. Sift 1 cup flour with ¼ teaspoon salt, 1 teaspoon cinnamon, ½ teaspoon cloves, ¼ teaspoon black pepper, ¼ teaspoon baking soda, and ¼ teaspoon baking powder. Add the sifted ingredients to the eggs. Then stir in 1 cup mixed raisins and nuts (preferably walnuts). If dough is not stiff, add more flour. Blend well. Drop by tablespoons onto a greased baking sheet. Bake in moderately hot (375° F.) oven for 5 to 7 minutes. *Makes 5 dozen small cookies.*

BROWNED-BUTTER AND BOURBON SAUCE

Although Zachary Taylor was a teetotaler, it is not likely that he complained about this delicious sauce served often in his day in Kentucky. It is especially good as a topping for gingerbread, cinnamon bread, or plum pudding.

Butter	*Bourbon whiskey*
Brown sugar	*Heavy cream*
Salt	

Brown 2 tablespoons butter in a heavy iron skillet. Add 1 cup brown sugar and ⅛ teaspoon salt, mixing well. Heat the mixture until smooth. Set aside until it has cooled slightly. Add 2 tablespoons bourbon and 1 cup heavy cream, whipped just before serving.

CHERRY SAUCE

Including a cherry recipe is perhaps a sad reminder of Zachary Taylor's fate. And yet it is only fitting to include one, as he was extremely fond of this fruit—a fact we have learned all too well. This sauce makes an excellent accompaniment for vanilla ice cream or as a topping for a white cake.

Canned cherries	*Lemon juice*
Sugar	*Cornstarch*
Corn syrup	*Cold water*
Cinnamon	

Drain 2 cups canned cherries and set aside. Save the cherry syrup. Add it to ¼ cup sugar, ¼ cup corn syrup, 1 stick cinnamon about 2 inches long, and 1 tablespoon lemon juice. Simmer all for 10 minutes, then remove the cinnamon stick. Mix together 2 teaspoons cornstarch with 1 tablespoon cold water until smooth. Add to the hot cherry sauce. Cover and allow to cook until it boils, stirring often. Add the cherries at the last moment. Can be served either hot or cold. *Makes 2 cups.*

PECAN PIE

One of the great contributions to American dessert cookery, pecan pie had been a Southern favorite for generations before the rest of us caught on to its greatness.

Certainly the Zachary Taylors, as born and bred Southerners, were in on the secret.

Eggs	*Vanilla*
Brown sugar	*Pastry*
Butter	*Pecans*
Salt	

Beat 3 eggs lightly, as if for a custard. Slowly add 2 cups brown sugar and ¼ cup melted butter. Flavor with a dash of salt and 1 teaspoon vanilla. Pour the mixture into an 8-inch pie tin lined with a standard pastry and sprinkled with ½ cup chopped pecans. Cover the nuts with the egg–sugar–butter mixture. Then sprinkle another layer of pecans over the top (½ cup pecan halves, not chopped up). Bake in a 350° F. oven 30 to 40 minutes, or until the pie is almost set. Then reduce the heat to 225° F. and bake 15 minutes longer, or until the pie is completely set. This pie is remarkably easy to make, yet looks impressively difficult. Good for gala parties.

✳✳✳

XIII

The Puritan Tradition Continues

✳✳✳

One social historian has called Millard Fillmore's term of office a "regime of conveniences." This may be the most anyone can say of the uninspired, uninspiring years 1850 to 1853.

Fillmore was the first of our Presidents to have a real bathtub with "centrally heated" running water. His wife, a former teacher, installed the first library in the White House. It seems inconceivable to us today, but in the mid-nineteenth century there were citizens who were actually shocked at the expense and highfalutin' notion of having a room designed exclusively for the display and reading of books.

Even more disturbing to many people of that era was the innovation of an iron cookstove in the Chief Executive's home. One writer commented at the time: "The fireplace of a kitchen is a matter of great importance and I have never been so circumstanced as to witness the operations of many of the newly-invented steam kitchens and cooking apparatuses which the last twenty years have produced. . . . To say the truth, the inventions of cast iron stoves seem to me to have had every other object in view but the promoting of good cooking, and I am sure that meat cannot be roasted unless it is before a good fire."

The public were not the only ones who disapproved the addition of a stove to the White House kitchens. Fillmore's Negro chef was horrified at the idea of cooking on such a "thing." His disgruntled comment was recorded for posterity:

"Fo' de Lawd's sake, Mistah Fillmo, who cu'd cook on sich a contraptshun as dat?"

But Fillmore, with the perseverance that had carried him from humble beginnings as an apprentice clothier to the Presidency, was determined to modernize and "tidy up" the Executive Mansion. His cook, accustomed to preparing state dinners for thirty-six guests in the traditional open fireplace, where a morass of hooks, cranes, pots, skillets, pans, and other utensils hung, could not master the new "contraptshun." There it stood in the basement kitchen—large, cold and menacing, a "small hotel size" stove, daring the staff to conquer it.

It took the President himself to master the stove. He was forced to pay a visit to the Patent Office to learn how to manipulate the stove's drafts and pulleys. Once this hurdle was overcome, the stove became standard equipment in the White House kitchen. Like all conveniences, after it became a habit, the staff wondered how they had ever managed without it.

We would like to be able to say that Fillmore's single-minded efforts on behalf of the Executive Mansion's new stove were merely indicative of his zest for fine food, his appreciation of a gourmet repast, his adventurous eating habits.

Alas, what we would like to say and what we *can* say are totally different things. Study, hard work, and temperance were the ruling factors in Fillmore's life. He had had little time for frivolity or luxuries, in dress or food, during his youth. By the time he was President, his life patterns were established. Plain food, prepared in a simple, farm style, was part of the pattern.

Born of English stock in upper New York State, Fillmore had a Spartan boyhood. Self-taught to a large extent, he began at nineteen the slow process of studying law. His climb up the political ladder was slow, thorough, and completely honorable. His wife, Abigail Powers Fillmore, was his "help-meet" in every sense. Two years his senior, a former schoolteacher (*his,* in fact), Abigail was as serious and single-minded about Millard's career as he was himself.

Temperate in all things, with the same "no-nonsense" view of life as the Polks, the Fillmores followed much the same social pattern. Dancing and gala partying were *verboten,* but the usual dinner parties and official entertaining continued as usual.

Abigail Fillmore, unlike her immediate predecessor, Margaret Taylor, was no recluse during her husband's Presidency. She was, however, not in the best of health. Long before, she had injured an ankle in a fall. As a result, the long hours of a White House reception line were hours of acute pain for her. But with a stoic sense of duty, she steeled herself for the receptions as best she could. Before each one, she stayed in bed several hours immediately beforehand, resting her weakened ankle, so it could bear the pressure of the long reception line.

The Fillmore receptions were frequent. Each Tuesday morning Abigail had to endure the line. Each Friday evening when Congress convened, the Fillmores held a "drawing room." Thursday was the evening of the large dinner party held in the State Dining Room. And on Saturday in the private dining room, Abigail presided over a small dinner. The Fillmores did not stint on entertaining. They regarded it as a duty, one of the requirements of their position. Parties given from a sense of duty differ in spontaneity from those given, *à la* Dolley Madison, from a sense of pleasure. *C'est la vie.*

No one could accuse Millard Fillmore or his wife of reneging on their Presidential duties. Nor could they be accused of making those duties seem fun.

◇◇

RECIPES

SHAKER FLANK STEAK

Meat, potatoes, and vegetables were the ingredients of life for the Fillmores. Fixed appetizingly in this fashion, they are delicious fare for all of us.

Flank steak	*Onions*
Flour	*Carrot*
Butter or margarine	*Celery*
Salt and pepper	*Lemon juice*
Potatoes, diced	*Ketchup*

Score both sides of a 2-pound flank steak diagonally. Dust with 1 tablespoon flour. Brown the steak in a skillet in 1½ tablespoons butter or margarine. Sprinkle with ¾ teaspoon salt and ¼ teaspoon pepper. Add 2 large peeled raw potatoes diced in fairly large cubes. Add 2 small onions, chopped, and 1 carrot chopped in medium chunks, as well as 1 stalk chopped celery. Pour over all the juice of ½ lemon and ⅓ cup ketchup. Cover skillet and simmer slowly for an hour or longer, until steak is tender. Serve with the vegetable sauce over the steak. *Serves 4.*

CORNMEAL AND CHEESE LOAF

The cheeses so prized by the Dutch of New York state were also savored by other New Yorkers of Fillmore's day. Fixed as in this particular dish, along with that basic American food, cornmeal, the cheese added an extra touch to simple fare.

Milk	*Salt*
Cornmeal (yellow)	*Flour*
Boiling water	*Butter or margarine*
Cheddar cheese	

Heat 1 cup milk with 1 cup cornmeal in a large saucepan. Add 2 cups boiling water, stirring constantly, and cook for 8 to 10 minutes over a low fire. When thickened, remove from heat and add ½ pound Cheddar cheese in cubes and 1 teaspoon salt. Stir until cheese melts and is well mixed with other ingredients. Pour the mixture into a loaf pan or square glass cake pan and refrigerate until firm. Cut into thin slices, dust lightly with flour, and fry in heated butter, margarine, or bacon drippings until crisp and lightly browned on both sides. Serve with bacon, fried ham, or sausages as a breakfast or supper dish. *Serves 4 to 6.*

CORN PUDDING

This American classic has been a favorite dish of simple eaters such as the Fillmores as well as of White House gourmets. Easy to prepare, particularly in this age of frozen vegetables, it is a marvelous way of dressing up a vegetable dish.

Frozen or fresh corn	*White pepper*
Eggs	*Light cream*
Flour, Salt	*Butter*

Thaw 1 package frozen corn or cut 2 cups fresh corn off the cob. Set aside. Meanwhile, beat well 3 eggs. Stir in corn, ¼ cup flour, 1 teaspoon salt, and ½ teaspoon white pepper. Mix well. Add 2 cups light cream and 2 tablespoons melted butter or margarine. Be sure all ingredients are well blended, then pour into a buttered glass baking pan (1- or 1½-quart size). Place the pan in a pan of hot water and bake in a preheated 325° F. oven until the custard is firm, about 1 hour. *Serves 6 to 8.*

OLD-FASHIONED SOUP

To thrifty, hard-working Millard Fillmore, it was natural that a good hearty soup would often serve as a full meal. But the type of soup we mean is not the delicately seasoned soup that interested Thomas Jefferson. Soup to a New York farm family such as Fillmore's was more of a stew of meat, potatoes, and vegetables; when ready to serve, the solids were removed from the soup kettle to a platter. The soup was served, consumed, then the soup bowls filled with the meat and vegetables from the platter. No sense in wasting time or dishes, reasoned the farm wife of the day.

Hock or shin of beef	*Onions*
Water (or beef stock)	*Carrots*
Sage	*Parsnips*
Summer savory	*Flour*
Potatoes	*Salt and pepper*

Put a hock of beef or some other inexpensive cut into a large kettle. Add water or stock to cover, along with ½ teaspoon sage and ½ teaspoon summer savory. Peel 2 or 3 large potatoes, cut in half, and add to the soup. Peel 3 medium onions and add them whole, along with 3 carrots cut in half and 2 quartered parsnips. Simmer soup for several hours, until meat is tender. Add a small amount of flour to thicken the soup slightly. Add salt and pepper to taste. When ready to serve, remove the meat and vegetables to a platter, to be served later. Cut the meat into manageable chunks. Serve the soup as a first course, followed by the other "victuals." Hearty, robust mid-century fare. (Choose your century.) *Serves 6.*

YANKEE TOMATO RELISH

The days of canning and preserving are, in this age of processed foods, slowly fading into the past. But in President Fillmore's time, canning was the only way of keeping seasonal fruits and vegetables on hand for the long winter months ahead. A great favorite of his age were relishes of one kind or another. This tomato relish was always a popular one, served year-round.

Fresh tomatoes	*Sugar*
Onion	*Cider vinegar*
Celery	*Mustard seed*
Green pepper	

Peel and chop fresh tomatoes. Measure 2 cupfuls, taking care to squeeze most of the juice out of the cup before measuring. Put the tomatoes in a bowl and mix well with ½ cup finely chopped onions, 1 cup chopped celery, ¼ cup finely chopped green pepper, 6 tablespoons sugar, ½ cup cider vinegar, and 1 tablespoon mustard seed. Pour the mixture into a sterilized jar; cover. Let stand at least 1 full day before using to allow the ingredients time to blend together properly. *Makes 1 quart.* (Recipe can be expanded for larger canning program.)

RESURRECTION PIE

How fitting a title for this dish of the strait-laced Millard Fillmores! The recipe came originally from the North Country of England, home of Fillmore's family. It resembles the hot pots of Lancashire, which called for equal parts of liver, steak, and rabbit. Made by the English settlers in New York State, beef or pork liver and cuts similar to round steak were used instead. This "pie" has no crust, but pie it was called in Fillmore's day, so pie it shall be. The other part of the title is equally ambiguous, suggesting perhaps that the dish is so good it merits being served Resurrection Day. *Or* could the name be satiric?

Liver	*Bacon*
Round steak	*Salt and pepper*
Onions	*Water or consommé*
Potatoes	

Cut the meat—1 pound beef or pork liver and 1 pound round steak—into slices ½ inch thick. Slice 2 onions and 6 medium potatoes ¼ inch thick. Arrange in layers in a well-greased casserole, beginning with a layer of meat sprinkled with 3 slices of lean bacon cut into bits, then a layer of onions and potatoes mixed, then meat and bacon again. Season with ½ teaspoon salt and ¼ teaspoon pepper. Cover with cold water or consommé. Make a topping of onions and potatoes. Dot with butter. Cover tightly with a lid or aluminum foil and bake 1½ hours in a moderate (350° F.) oven. *Modern adaptation:* Remove the lid and allow the dish to brown delicately for the last 15 minutes of cooking. Serve sprinkled with chopped parsley. A good accompaniment is a dish of sliced tomatoes and leaf spinach, served with a tart vinegar dressing. *Serves 6.*

PLUM PUDDING

A good solid English plum pudding was very much in the Fillmore tradition, particularly at the Christmas season. This particular recipe has been used in the White House for decades.

Raisins	*Cloves*
Currants	*Nutmeg*
Citron	*Salt*
Almonds	*Ginger*
Flour	*Baking powder*
Sugar	*Cinnamon*
Breadcrumbs	*Eggs*
Beef suet	*Lemon juice and rind*
Milk	*Sherry*

Mix together 1 pound raisins, 1 pound currants, ¼ pound thinly sliced citron, and 1 cup chopped almonds. Dredge with 1 cup flour. Add to the fruit ½ pound breadcrumbs, 1 pound finely chopped beef suet, and 2 cups milk. Sift 1 cup flour, ½ cup sugar with ½ teaspoon cloves, 1 teaspoon grated nutmeg, ¼ teaspoon salt, 1 tablespoon ginger, 2 teaspoons baking powder, and 1 teaspoon cinnamon. Add to the fruit mixture and mix well. Add 8 eggs that have been beaten until light and frothy. Add the rind and juice of 1 lemon and 1 wineglass sherry. Mix thoroughly. Pour into well-greased molds and steam for 3 to 4 hours. *Serves 24.*

EVE'S PUDDING

Puddings and pies were the solid foods that pleased the Fillmores most. This recipe for Eve's Pudding was in vogue, it comes from *America Cooks,* a compendium of folkloric American recipes. Basically an apple bread pudding, it makes a fine, filling dessert.

Eggs	*Sugar*
Apples	*Salt*
Breadcrumbs (*soft*)	*Nutmeg*
Currants	

If you want a good pudding, mind what you are taught.
Take of eggs six in number, when bought for a groat;
The fruit with which Eve her husband did cozen,
Well pared and well chopped, at least half a dozen;
Six ounces of bread; let Moll eat the crust,
And crumble the rest, as fine as the dust;
Six ounces of currants, from which the stems you must sort,
Lest you break out your teeth and spoil all the sport.
Six ounces of sugar won't make it too sweet,
Some salt and some nutmeg will make it complete;
Three hours let it boil, without any flutter.
But Adam won't like it without wine and butter.

XIV

Shadows in the Executive Mansion

There has never been as melancholic an administration as that of Franklin Pierce. Socially, his four years in office were shrouded in gloom and depression. Politically, his administration has vanished into obscurity.

The social depression had just cause. On January 6, 1853, just two months before Pierce was to assume the Presidency, his only son was killed, practically in front of his distraught parents' eyes. The family was traveling together on a train, when, in a freak accident, the car in which the Pierces were riding was wrenched from the roadbed. Franklin Pierce and his wife Jane were scarcely injured, but they saw their eleven-year-old son Benjamin, a bright and able boy, crushed under the wreckage.

It would have taken two stronger characters than Franklin and Jane Pierce to rise above such a tragedy. The Pierces were not, unfortunately, resilient folk. For one thing, this was the third of three tragedies in their domestic lives. Their two other sons had died in infancy. In an age and moral atmosphere of guilt and retribution, it was only natural for a woman such as Jane Appleton Pierce to believe that some higher vengeance was being wrought upon her and her husband.

Her fear of divine retribution came to her naturally, brought up as she had been in a stern New England household, the daughter of the president of Bowdoin College. Then too, her husband's continuous flirtation with alcohol was a source of considerable distress to the temperate, staid Jane Appleton Pierce.

Franklin Pierce was like the boy in everybody's high school graduating class who is voted "most likely to succeed" and twenty years later has sunk into middle-aged mediocrity. Handsome, superficially brilliant, popular, with great charm and personality, Pierce never rose to the expectations many had for him. His intelligence was basically a shallow one. And his addiction to alcohol kept him from the firm judgment that might have been expected of him.

The son of General Benjamin Pierce, a Revolutionary War veteran, Franklin was brought up in a household whose doors were always open to friends and visitors. The large Pierce house was usually bursting its walls with guests. In fact, General Pierce had to take out a liquor license on occasion, to accommodate the needs of his many visitors.

In this atmosphere of hospitality and constant drinking, young Franklin learned at a precocious age to enjoy both. Although he relished the light-headed times and gaiety that alcohol produced, he never learned to hold his own with liquor. Later in his life, he insisted that his craving for and intolerance of alcohol were inherited from his mother's side of the family.

But his infatuation with whiskey and the hearty company who drank it was almost lifelong. As a young Congressman in his early days in Washington, his associations were mostly with a rather fast (for his time) crowd. The less he could tolerate of alcohol, the more determined he was to master it. This led to challenges, competitions, and lengthy drinking sprees.

Later, when he fought in the Mexican War, Pierce did manage to control his yearning for alcohol. But the war did not end his battles. After he assumed the Presidency, with the loss of his most cherished son so fresh in mind, he turned again to the comforts and exhilaration of whiskey. It was an escape from his depression and from the burdens of an office he lacked confidence in mastering. Shortly after Pierce's inauguration, he traveled through New England. One member of his entourage wrote later: "I deeply, deeply deplore his habits. He drinks deep—— A great mistake was made in putting him in at all." And throughout the correspondence of Pierce's wife are veiled references to this "weakness," as she put it, of her husband's.

Much later, in 1863, when Jane Pierce died, and when Pierce's longtime friend Nathaniel Hawthorne died the following year, Pierce caved in completely. Much of his adult life had been a struggle against his weakness. At this point, Pierce gave up the struggle. There was no staunch, upright wife to reproach him. Pierce became a real alcoholic.

Actually, Pierce's final commitment to alcohol was short-lived. Two years later he turned to religion, summoned up the strength to withdraw from drink irrevocably, and took the pledge of teetotalism. It was a brief victory in his lifelong battle. In 1869 he died of cirrhosis of the liver, a sad testimonial to his years of struggle.

During the Pierce Presidency the struggle was evident. Publicly all was temperate at the President's house. Following the pattern of the earlier Puritans, the Pierces served no alcoholic beverages at their receptions. State dinners were held once a week while Congress was in session; thirty-six guests were invited. No wine was served. Privately Pierce was not so Puritanical.

Considering the home atmosphere at the time, one cannot help but be a bit sympathetic to the genial, gregarious President. His was an age in which grief was worn like a badge of honor, and Jane Pierce displayed hers endlessly. The country sympathized with the stricken mother and did not criticise her excessive display of mourning. But when one considers that she spent her four years at the White House writing notes to her dead son, one can be a little more tolerant of her husband's turn toward the bottle.

It was nearly two years after the Pierces arrived at the White House to live that Mrs. Pierce made her first appearance at a reception. It was on New Year's day, always a popular occasion in Washington. In fact, the New Year's reception was considered the most important public affair of the year. All Washington citizens (and important visitors) were invited to wander through the White House, shaking the President's hand, greeting familiar Senators and local celebrities.

Mrs. Pierce's entrance on the social scene did not signal any gala social activities in the capital. There were no refreshments served at the White House reception that day (or subsequently), no punch bowls in sight, no eggnog served. Even so, after the cloud of depression that had accompanied the Pierces to Washington, the city was cheered up considerably simply by Mrs. Pierce's appearance at a public function.

From then on Jane Pierce tried to rally and dutifully took her place at the formal weekly state dinners. The Monroe gold plate was used and bouquets were placed at each lady's place. Mrs. Pierce tried to perform her duties, but probably cast more gloom than light on the events she attended—being, as one guest put it, "the very picture of melancholy."

Mrs. Cassius Clay, wife of a Kentucky Senator and frequent visitor at the White House, "considered the Pierce State Dinners too stiff and formal." She described the ubiquitous bouquets at each lady's place: "They were stiff and formal things, as big around as a breakfast plate. . . . At every plate, at every State Dinner, lay one of these memorable rigid bouquets." (One can almost see them now, preserved in amber.)

Because Mrs. Pierce had no heart for managing the White House, the care and upkeep were assigned to others. Actually, even if the tragic death of young Bennie Pierce had not taken place, it is likely that the Pierce term of office would not have been marked with much more gaiety. Jane Pierce did not like Washington. She distrusted all its associations with her husband's youthful escapades. Nor was her heart, in mourning or not, ever fully in tune with the spirit of lavish entertainment.

A New Hampshire hotel proprietor, William H. Snow, and his wife were hired and brought to Washington by Pierce to act as caretakers, housekeepers, purveyors. Snow acted as steward and managed the servants. In general he took care of the comfort of the First Family—at least the couple's physical needs. It was Snow's job to hire the caterer for state dinners and receptions and to oversee the White House accounts.

By all reports, Snow must have done an admirable job, for Pierce was said to have saved $50,000 of his salary during his term of office. In fact, some unkind souls accused him of parsimony. But after all, the White House was scarcely a hub of social activity during his term of office. The informal family dinners were quiet affairs, with no more than half a dozen persons present.

In spite of the flamboyance of Pierce's upbringing, the lavish and openhanded hospitality of his father's house, Pierce himself was said to be "quiet in his tastes." Preferences for the solid, traditional fare of his native New Hampshire were strong in him.

The good, hearty, often quite inventive dishes of midcentury New Hampshire found favor with this native son. His palate was not aroused by Continental cuisine, but rather by the solid abundant specialties of upper New England.

On the whole, though, it was not food that offered Franklin Pierce his greatest challenges and satisfactions. *This* President could not live by bread alone.

RECIPES

WHITE MOUNTAIN ROLLS

New Hampshire has made important contributions to American cuisine. Long before Franklin Pierce's day, New Hampshire colonists had discovered squash and invented numerous delicious ways of preparing it. By the mid-nineteenth century, New Hampshire cooks had earned a considerable reputation for their breads, fried pies, and muffins. These White Mountain rolls were always a state specialty.

Yeast cake	*Salt*
Lukewarm water	*Shortening*
Flour	*Egg white*
Sugar	*Scalded milk*

Dissolve 1 yeast cake in ¼ cup lukewarm water. Set aside. Sift together 4 cups flour, 4 tablespoons sugar, and 1 teaspoon salt. Melt ¼ cup shortening and add it to 1 cup scalded milk. Allow to cool to room temperature, then add the yeast mixture. Mix well. Slowly stir in the sifted ingredients. Beat until stiff 1 egg white, then fold it into the liquid mixture. Set aside while dough rises. Keep it in a warmish place so that the dough rises very light. Cut it down and turn it out on a board to shape into long rolls. Place the rolls on a greased pan and allow them to rise at least 1 hour, or until light. Bake in a hot (400° F.) oven for 20 to 25 minutes. *Makes 1 dozen long rolls.*

FRIED CLAMS OR FANNIE DADDIES

New Hampshire residents were as inventive about names for their foods as their fellow New Englanders in Massachusetts. Fannie Daddies, as Franklin Pierce could have told you, are simply a delicious way of serving clams.

Eggs	*Lemon juice*
Milk	*Salt*
Flour	*Clams*
Melted butter	

Separate 2 eggs. Beat the yolks until they are thick and lemony in color. Then add ½ cup milk, 1 cup flour, 1 tablespoon melted butter, 1 tablespoon lemon juice, and ½ teaspoon salt. Beat 2 egg whites until very stiff. Fold them into the yolk mixture carefully. Add 1 pint clams, the fresher the better. Put the mixture into the refrigerator until thoroughly chilled (at least 2 hours; overnight if possible). When ready to cook, heat butter or lard in a kettle. Fry the clams in the deep hot fat. First they will sink to the bottom of the fat, then rise to the top. They will be big and wonderful—a real treat. *Serves 4.*

DANIEL WEBSTER'S CHOWDER

Daniel Webster may never have achieved the Presidency (although he tried hard enough), but he has a claim to fame few Presidents have had. He probably had more dishes named for him than most Presidents ever did. Certainly Franklin Pierce was never honored by his fellow New Hampshirites as Webster was. From the Dartmouth College archives comes this testament to the esteem that Webster enjoyed in Pierce's native state, in Pierce's own day.

Cod	*Water*
Salt pork	*Boiling milk*
Potatoes	*Hard crackers*
Salt and pepper	*Onion (optional)*

Clean 5 or 6 pounds of codfish. Leave the skin on and cut the fish into slices 1½ pounds thick. Do not remove the head. Cut ½ pound clear fat salt pork into thin slices. Cut 6 potatoes into thin slices. Heat a large kettle with a few slices of the salt pork in it. When warm, remove the pork, leaving the grease. Add a layer of codfish to the bottom of the kettle; cover with a layer of potatoes. Add 1 tablespoon salt, ½ teaspoon pepper, then a layer of salt pork. Add another layer of fish, and the rest of the potatoes. Fill the pot with water—enough to cover the ingredients. Put the kettle over medium-hot heat and boil slowly for 25 minutes. When done, add 1 pint boiling milk and 5 hard crackers, split and dipped in cold water. Cook another 10 minutes. (Onion may be added at the beginning, sliced and layered like the potatoes, if desired). Serve steaming hot. Tastes especially good on a crisp cold New Hampshire winter's day. *Serves 6 to 8.*

NEW HAMPSHIRE BOILED DINNER

This is really a New England boiled dinner, but because New Hampshire was the first state to begin producing potatoes on a large scale, we think it deserves the tribute of its own boiled dinner. As Pierce or any other native son would claim, a New England boiled dinner without New Hampshire potatoes in it was sadly lacking.

Brisket of beef	*White turnips*
Salt pork	*White potatoes (New Hampshire*
Onions	*ones, of course)*
Carrots	*Cabbage*
Parsnips	

Place 5 to 6 pounds well-cured brisket of (corned) beef in a large pot. Cover it with water and simmer, covered, for 1½ to 2 hours. Add ½ pound salt pork. Simmer an additional 2 hours. Skim the top at the end of 2 hours, and add 8 onions, 8 cleaned carrots, 8 peeled parsnips, and 8 peeled small white turnips. Continue cooking 30 minutes in the covered pot. Then add 8 peeled potatoes. Core and quarter 1 medium cabbage and add. Cook until potatoes are tender. (Potatoes may be halved if especially large.) Serve, with the meat in the middle of a large platter surrounded by the vegetables, garnished with parsley sprigs. (Any leftover meat is delicious made into corned beef hash—with more New Hampshire potatoes, of course.) *Serves 8.*

DANIEL WEBSTER'S BOILED POTATOES

Tit for tat. As a frequent visitor to Pierce's New Hampshire, Daniel Webster, after having a New Hampshire specialty named for him, did the potato state the honor of immortalizing (for his day anyway) the lowly spud.

White potatoes   Cold water

Cook peeled potatoes in cold, salted water. When they are done, pour off the water, "shake up the potatoes a little," put them back into the still-hot pot to "dry" for 2 or 3 minutes. Then serve.

NEW HAMPSHIRE FRIED PIES

This regional specialty was as much a favorite with the Pierce family as the state's ubiquitous maple syrup. Although every housewife had her version of this dish, this recipe is a particularly venerable one.

Dried apples	*Flour*
Sugar	*Salt*
Nutmeg	*Baking powder*
Butter	*Eggs*

Allow 1 quart dried apples to soak in cold water overnight or for 5 to 6 hours. Drain, put into a saucepan, and cook, with just enough water to keep from burning, into a thick applesauce. Add 1 cup sugar and 1 teaspoon nutmeg. Set aside. Make a pie crust of ½ cup butter or other shortening, 2½ to 3 cups flour, 1 teaspoon salt, and 1 teaspoon baking powder. Dough should be firm and have body. Roll it out and cut it into pieces each as wide as a butter plate. Beat 2 eggs into the applesauce and place 4 tablespoons applesauce in the center of each crust portion. Fold the dough over (like a turnover) and press the edges firmly. Bring deep fat to heat in a deep kettle. Drop the pies into the boiling fat (360° F.) and cook 4 to 5 minutes, turning so the whole pie is well browned. Best served hot, but may be reheated. *Makes 16 pies.*

SPARKIN' PIE

The marriage of Franklin and Jane Pierce, melancholic as it may seem to us today, was actually a satisfactory one. It bore a strong resemblance to the marriage of Pierce's friend Nathaniel Hawthorne. Melancholia may have been in the New England air, although New England courtships had their share of gaiety and promise. Witness this particular recipe. It was supposed to be made by a young lady who wanted to impress her beau. If it turned out well, he would propose, they would marry and, presumably, live happily—though in the Pierces' case, despondently—ever after.

Eggs	*Nutmeg*
Applesauce	*Salt*
Sugar	*Milk*
Cinnamon	*Unbaked pie shell*

Beat 3 eggs, then add 1½ cups strained applesauce and ½ cup sugar. Mix ½ teaspoon cinnamon with ½ teaspoon nutmeg and add to the applesauce mixture, along with ⅓ teaspoon salt and 1½ cups milk. Mix all together well. Pour into an unbaked 9 inch pie shell. Bake in a hot (450° F.) oven 8 to 10 minutes. Reduce the heat to 350° F. and continue cooking 30 minutes, or until the mixture is firm. May be served warm or cold. (We like it hot.) Delicious with a slice of Cheddar cheese or a dab of sour cream or whipped cream on top (Mark Twain was reputedly as fond of this pie as we are.) *Serves 6 to 8.*

MARLBOROUGH PIE

This variation of Sparkin' Pie deserves inclusion; it too was a New Hampshire favorite in Pierce's day.

Apples	*Sugar*
Eggs	*Lemons*
Heavy cream	*Pastry shells*

You may use commercial applesauce, but if you have the time to make your own it will make a better pie. Pare and cook tart green apples, making a good sour applesauce. Beat 6 eggs and add them to 2 cups applesauce, along with 1 pint heavy cream and 2 cups sugar. Add the juice and rind of 2 large lemons. Mix well. Pile the mixture in prebaked pie shells. Bake in a slow (325° F.) oven until the mixture is firm. You may put a meringue on top if you prefer; allow it to brown lightly under the broiler. *Serves 8 to 12.*

APPLE PAN DOWDY—MIDCENTURY STYLE

Apples were as popular in Pierce's day as in that of his fellow New Englander John Adams. Like Adams, Pierce was acquainted with many versions of the delicious pan dowdy. This one undoubtedly caught his fancy as much as it does ours. (It is also extra-special when made with rhubarb or blueberries.)

Egg	*Milk*
Sugar	*Tart apples*
Butter	*Brown sugar or molasses*
Flour	*Nutmeg*
Salt	*Cinnamon*
Baking powder	

First, make a cottage-pudding batter by creaming 1 well-beaten egg with ½ cup sugar and ¼ cup butter. Add 1½ cups sifted flour, ½ teaspoon salt, and 2 teaspoons baking powder alternately with ½ cup milk. Mix all well. Set aside. Preheat oven to 350° F. Grease a 1½-quart baking dish. Fill it with 3 cups peeled, sliced tart apples. Sprinkle a mixture of ½ cup brown sugar or molasses, ¼ teaspoon each of nutmeg, cinnamon, and salt over the apples. Bake until the apples are soft. Then pour the cottage-pudding batter over the apples and continue baking until the top is lightly browned and crusty. Serve directly from the dish if you wish, or turn it out with the apple-side up. Delicious with plain or whipped cream on top, or hard sauce or even ice cream. *Serves 6.*

NEW HAMPSHIRE SEED COOKIES

It is fascinating to anyone interested in the history of food to see how recipes traveled from one part of the country to another. In the earliest days of the American colonies, the benne (sesame) seed was "native" to South Carolina, brought there from Africa. Little by little, its fame grew, and the use of benne seeds became common throughout the Southern colonies. As we have noted earlier, it was a favorite plant of Thomas Jefferson. By the mid-nineteenth century, word of its value had spread north, and its use in New England kitchens was taken for granted. Like many another New Hampshire boy before and since, Franklin Pierce no doubt snitched many a seed cooky from his mother's kitchen. Freshly baked cookies and small boys are a natural twosome.

Butter or margarine	*Baking powder*
Brown sugar	*Sesame seeds*
Eggs	*Vanilla*
Flour	

Cream together ¾ cup butter and 1½ cups tightly packed brown sugar. Add 2 eggs and beat well. Sift together 1¼ cups flour, ¼ teaspoon baking powder, and ½ cup toasted sesame seeds. Stir into the egg–butter mixture carefully and mix well. Add 1 teaspoon vanilla and mix again. Drop by the teaspoon onto a greased cooky sheet. Leave space for the cookies to spread. Bake in a medium (325° F.) oven for 10 to 15 minutes. *Makes approximately 7 dozen.*

CROCK COOKIES

At the Pierce family home, there was always a crock full of cookies and other delectables on hand for the hordes of "dropper-inners" who constantly came to call. These old-fashioned sour-cream cookies belong in a cooky crock, handy for easy reaching.

Sour cream	Salt
Sugar	Nutmeg
Egg	Ginger
Soda	Flour

Mix 1 cup sour cream with 1 cup sugar and 1 beaten egg. Add 1 teaspoon baking soda, 1 teaspoon salt, ½ teaspoon nutmeg and 1 teaspoon ginger. Mix well. Add just enough flour to roll the dough, but not enough to make it stiff. The dough should be soft and loose. Cut the cookies into shapes and place on a greased cooky sheet. Brush the top of each cooky with cold milk and sprinkle with a little sugar. Bake in medium (350° F.) oven until lightly brown. *Makes 48 cookies.*

HOT RUM PUNCH

Perhaps it seems an unfair reminder of Franklin Pierce's problem to include a recipe for a drink made of hard liquor. Yet, as this was a partiality of Pierce's, and as this book is dedicated to Presidential partialities, we feel we must avoid pulling our punches, even our rum punches.

| Lemon or lime juice | Maple syrup |
| Rum | Grenadine |

Mix 1 cup lemon juice with 1¾ cups rum. Add ½ cup pure maple syrup and 2 teaspoons grenadine. Pour into a pan and heat until the punch reaches the boiling point, but remove before it actually boils. Serve hot in mugs decorated with cinnamon sticks. *Makes 4 drinks.*

★★★★★★★★★★★★★★★★★★★★★★★★★★★★★★★★★★★★★★★

XV

Bachelor's
Parties

★★★

For a brief moment before the storm of war—the four years before the Civil War—gaiety returned in full force to the White House, after four administrations of deprivation. Not that all the tenants in that time span had been grim themselves. But the atmosphere they created around them—the ban on most social activities such as dancing, and eating and drinking at receptions—was not conducive to the frivolity and festive air of preceding administrations.

James Buchanan was not himself a gay or abandoned man. Far from it. But he had in his niece, Harriet Lane, a great asset. A lovely blonde with violet eyes, a tall, slim figure, and the grace and social attributes of a princess, Harriet Lane very quickly became the cynosure of Washington.

There is a tendency, in assessing various Presidential administrations, to weigh one against the one or two just before and just following. The long view is seldom stressed by social historians. One reads again and again that "Never has there been a First Lady as charming and gracious as Mrs. X." But usually, the writer is comparing Mrs. X with Mrs. Y—who did not quite measure up—rather than with all the other First Ladies since the Republic began.

In comparison and contrast with the four simple ladies who preceded her, Harriet Lane seems to glow like a jewel. Perhaps it is irreverent to suggest that the glow might fade a bit if Dolley Madison or even Julia Tyler were allowed into the picture.

Certainly Harriet was beautifully prepared for her hostess duties. She was the youngest of four children of Buchanan's sister. When the sister and her husband died, Buchanan assumed the guardianship. It is to Buchanan's credit—and also a testament to his own *savoir vivre*—that Harriet was brought up in full possession of all the social graces and the ability to dispose gracefully of any social discomforts that might threaten to arise. When Buchanan was Ambassador to the Court of St. James, Harriet accompanied him and was able to cope with London society so successfully that she became a great favorite of Queen Victoria.

When her uncle became President, Harriet naturally assumed the role of official White House hostess. She was widely (though not universally) admired for her tact, poise, and social grace. The country responded happily to a First Lady who epitomized what a First Lady should be—beautiful, elegant, and correct. Harriet liked lace berthas, so women throughout America affected them. A revenue cutter was named for her, and at least one popular song was dedicated to her.

There were a few malcontents, however, who found Miss Lane's notions of etiquette a bit too stiff, too formal. Some of the charges against the Buchanan–Lane entertaining stir echoes of the criticism against the Monroe administration.

Buchanan, like Monroe, had had wide exposure to European manners and had developed a certain partiality for French cuisine. He liked the formal elegance of European society. Jefferson Davis supposedly compared Buchanan's administration to an "elegant republican court." The words and intent were highly complimentary, although the effect on later readers is chilling.

The President did not stint when entertaining. For elaborate dinners and receptions he called on the services of Gautier, a French caterer. Gautier had a reputation for the beauty and finesse of his service and preparations as well as the superb quality of his cooking. Gourmets exclaimed over the partridge, terrapin, oysters, lobster, and wild turkey served under his supervision.

Yet in spite of the enthusiasm for the food, some of the Presidential guests objected to the formal presentation before the party went into the dining room. President Buchanan was always correct in his entertaining style. He managed to keep the conversation going, telling anecdotes and making small talk, but basically he was not a warm, outgoing man. Harriet too, in spite of the warmth of her beauty, was not basically a bubbly, warm personality. Correct, gracious, yes—but she never exuded the Dolley Madison-type hospitality that made guests feel truly welcome. It is little wonder that guests often felt the nutty flavor of the fine Madeira and the excellence of the soufflés were not quite enough.

Even so, President Buchanan did not spare himself or his pocketbook in doing his official duties. The $25,000 Presidential salary was not enough to compensate for the elaborate entertaining necessary for a President of the United States in the mid-nineteenth century. Frequently, Buchanan was forced to pay the bills for his lavish dinners and receptions out of his own pocket. In spite of his innate formality, he did not mind this, for he rather enjoyed entertaining and wanted to do it well.

The biggest social event of Buchanan's four years was surely the visit of England's Prince of Wales to Washington. For decades afterward social commentators were still rehashing it breathlessly. Even now one senses the impact the visit had at the time.

This was the first visit to the former American colonies of an heir-apparent to the British throne. It was an emotional experience for all involved. It occurred, actually, very naturally. Buchanan learned that the young Prince was planning a visit to Canada and wrote Queen Victoria inviting him to visit the United States as well.

Albert Edward, Prince of Wales, was later to become King Edward VII, but at this time he was just nineteen, handsome and dashing. Washington socialites were beside themselves awaiting his arrival. Even President Buchanan was anxious to impress the young Prince. He sacrificed his bedroom to royalty and moved to a cot near his office, in order to offer his visitor the maximum comfort and make the finest impression. The Prince, of course, never knew he had dispossessed the master of the house.

Two lavish dinner parties were held for the Crown Prince. The chief claim to fame of one of them seems to have been that it was the occasion on which the popular song "Listen to the Mockingbird," was introduced to America. Its author, Alice Hawthorne, with a press-agent canniness uncommon in her day, used the occasion to dedicate the song to the lovely Harriet Lane.

While the entertainments for the Prince of Wales were unsurpassed by any other entertaining of Buchanan's day, they were almost equaled by his own inaugural ball in 1857. It was certainly a harbinger of the four years to come.

Buchanan felt a bit cautious, on assuming the Presidency, about overturning the social regimen of the four preceding administrations too abruptly, so he sidestepped very adroitly. Instead of rescinding the ban on dancing in the White House, he had a special structure built to house the inaugural ball. To the delight of socially starved Washington society, guests whirled, turned, and danced most of the night March 4, 1857.

In addition, they were treated to a preview of the culinary delights they might expect during the upcoming four years. The inaugural feast was Lucullan. The five thousand revelers were served eight rounds of beef, seventy-five hams, sixty saddles of mutton, four saddles of venison, four hundred gallons of oysters, five hundred quarts of chicken salad, one hundred twenty-five tongues, five hundred quarts of jellies, twelve hundred quarts of ice cream in assorted flavors, and pâtés of infinite variety. Three thousand dollars had been spent on the wines. And the high point of the evening was a pyramid of a cake, four feet high and cleverly ornamented with a flag bearing the insignia of every state in the Union—all thirty-one—and the territories.

Olympian as all this was, it was still but a hint of the gargantuan banquets of the administration to come. One might think that such quantities of food would be enough for several armies, but the food actually ran out before the guests had completely given up. Pierce's parsimony had left a hungry Washington behind him.

Those critics who may have objected to Buchanan's adherence to a formal etiquette had no complaint about the bounty of his service. His dinners were generally "pronounced superb in manner and style."

The Presidential routine was simpler than his entertaining patterns. He normally rose early, had an early breakfast, read the newspaper, and was busily at work at his desk by eight o'clock. At five in the afternoon, a brisk hour's walk gave him a good appetite for the elaborate dinner that usually followed. Dinner was served rather punctually at six. Buchanan followed the established pattern of dining almost always at the White House, rarely attending outside receptions or parties, never accepting outside dinner invitations. It was easier to refuse all invitations than to discriminate by accepting a select few.

One day a week, some of the Cabinet members and their wives were invited to have dinner at the White House *en famille*—or as *en famille* as Buchanan's formality permitted.

New Year's day became, under Buchanan, a more festive—if still formal—reception day than it had been for almost sixteen years. At his last New Year's reception in 1861, five thousand people put on their finery and paraded through the Presidential establishment. It was a fitting finale to a bright, hospitable four years.

◇◇◇

R E C I P E S

TERRAPIN À LA GAUTIER

When Preseident Buchanan entertained officially, the odds were good that terrapin would be on the menu, particularly if French chef-caterer Gautier was in charge. Gautier had a special way with terrapin. The beastie itself has been a favorite with many Presidents, as well as lesser mortals along the Potomac shores. This recipe belongs to the period. It is very rich, very elegant.

Terrapin	*Butter*
Cream	*Sherry or Madeira*

Boil a terrapin in the shell. After allowing it to cool, remove the shell. Remove also the bladder and other organs and cut the meat into good-sized chunks. Place

2 cups of the meat in a chafing dish over steady heat. Add 1 scant cup rich cream, ½ pound butter, and 2 wine glasses of Madeira or sherry (Madeira is richer and is preferred), making this a very elegant dish indeed. *Makes 8 to 10 servings.*

BOILED LOBSTER

Many Presidents since Buchanan's day have served Lobster at the White House, but it is doubtful if any enjoyed it any more than our fifteenth President. Whether "fancied up" with elaborate sauces by Gautier or boiled simply as in this recipe, lobster had a place of honor on Buchanan's menus.

Boiling water	*Live lobsters*
Rock salt	

Fill a large kettle ¾ full with water. When the water is boiling vigorously, add ⅓ cup rock salt for each quart water. Drop live lobsters into the boiling water, one at a time, allowing the water to come to a boil again each time. The lobsters should be completely covered by water. Cover and boil rapidly 20 to 30 minutes, depending on the size of the lobster. When done, lay each lobster on its claws to drain. To serve, split the lobster and serve it hot with melted butter or cold with mayonnaise. The meat may be removed and arranged on a platter, or the whole gorgeous creature may be served as is, with tools available for the guests to do their own picking and poking.

CALF'S HEAD DRESSED AS TERRAPIN

In lieu of terrapin, there was always calf's head masquerading as terrapin. An ample substitute, in the opinion of James Buchanan. This antique recipe may seem wildly impractical to today's cook, but we include it to give insight into culinary tastes and practices of yore.

Calf's head	*Salt*
Onions	*Marjoram*
Butter	*Water*
Flour	*Hard-boiled eggs*
Cayenne	*Forcemeat balls*
Black pepper	

Have the butcher split open and thoroughly clean the head of a calf. Place it, along with 6 or 8 small onions, in a large kettle. Cover with water and cook until tender. Remove the head and cut it into pieces, as you would terrapin. Melt ¼ pound butter or margarine in a skillet, then slowly blend in 1 teaspoon flour, stirring until the flour browns. Add 3 finely chopped onions, a dash of cayenne and black pepper, ½ teaspoon salt, ¼ teaspoon marjoram, and 3 tablespoons of the water in which the head was cooked. As the gravy thickens, add the meat and 6 or 8 finely chopped hard-boiled eggs. Mix thoroughly until meat and eggs are thoroughly heated. Remove to serving platter; garnish with forcemeat balls made of cooked turkey or veal and a little of the calf's brains, rolled into balls, deep-fried, and drained. *Serves 12.*

PANNHAS (SCRAPPLE)

This Pennsylvania Dutch specialty, whether you call it Pannhas, Ponhaws or, more familiarly, scrapple, was a great favorite in Buchanan's Pennsylvanian days, even as now.

Hog's head	*Powdered sage*
Salt and pepper	*Yellow cornmeal*

Have the butcher separate 1 hog's head, removing eyes and brains and scraping the head thoroughly. Place the cleaned head in a large pot and cover with 5 quarts cold water. Simmer slowly for approximately 3 hours, or until meat is so tender it falls off the bones. Skim the fat off the top. Remove meat, chop quite fine, and return to the liquid. Season with salt and pepper to taste and 1 teaspoon powdered sage. Slowly sift in yellow cornmeal (approximately 3 cups), stirring as you do, until the mixture thickens—it should be about as thick as soft cornmeal mush. Cook slowly over low heat for approximately 1 hour, then pour into buttered oblong pans and store until ready to use. Cut into thin slices, like hard cornmeal mush, and fry until brown and very crispy. *Makes 6 pounds.*

SAUERBRATEN

Although not of German stock, President Buchanan enjoyed the specialties prepared by the Pennsylvania Dutch inhabitants of his native state. Dishes such as sauerbraten had as much appeal in his day as they do with us today.

Chuck beef	*Cloves*
Salt and pepper	*Carrots*
Vinegar	*Onions*
Bay leaves	*Sugar*
Peppercorns	*Gingersnaps*

Wipe with a damp cloth 2 pounds chuck beef. Sprinkle it thoroughly with salt and pepper. Place in an earthen dish and add ½ pint vinegar and enough water to cover the meat. Add also 2 bay leaves, 6 peppercorns, and 2 whole cloves. Cover the bowl with a lid or plate, pressing down on the meat if possible. Keep tightly covered and place in a cool place for 4 to 5 days. Then drain the meat and put it in a Dutch oven, browning it carefully on all sides. Add ½ bunch of carrots, cleaned and cut into long strips, 3 medium-size sliced onions, and ½ cup spiced vinegar. Cover the oven tightly and cook for approximately 3 hours over low heat. When the meat is tender, add 1½ teaspoons sugar and 6 crumbled gingersnaps. Cook an additional 10 minutes. Serve the meat hot, with the spicy sauce over it. Delicious. *Serves 4.*

CHICKEN SALAD

This recipe illustrates the evolution of chicken salad through American history. Buchanan's version, as you'll see, differs considerably from many of today's quickie variations.

Chickens	*Oil*
Salt	*Vinegar*
Celery	*Mustard*
Eggs	*Salt and pepper*

Boil 2 medium-sized chickens in water, along with 1 teaspoon salt. When tender, allow to cool, then cut the meat into ¼-inch squares. Set aside. Cut 2 heads celery into small pieces and keep chilled in cold water until ready to use. Cook 8 eggs twenty minutes. Cool, remove the yolks ("yelks," the recipe says) and mash them fine with ½ pint oil (corn or a blend of olive and peanut oil). Add ¼ pint (4 ounces) vinegar, dry mustard, and salt and pepper to taste. Mix well with the egg yolks. Drain the celery, dry it lightly, and add to the chicken. Toss lightly, then combine with the egg-yolk mixture, taking care to mix well but lightly. *Serves 12.*

DUCK UN KRAUT

Game was plentiful in Pennsylvania in Buchanan's day, and the Pennsylvania Dutch had a way with it. Particularly appealing is the way they prepared duck, as in this old recipe.

Duck	*Sauerkraut*
Salt	*Water*
Pepper	*Sugar*

Carefully clean and wash 1 good-size duck. Rub with salt and pepper. Place in a roasting pan and stuff with sauerkraut. Add 1 cup water and 3 tablespoons sugar to the roasting pan and cover. Bake in a moderate (350° F.) oven until a golden brown, approximately 20 minutes per pound. Prick the skin frequently to allow the fat to escape. The skin should be crisp and shiny brown. Serve accompanied by fluffy mashed potatoes. Figure 1 pound per person in serving.

PENNSYLVANIA DUTCH SUCCOTASH

Fond as Buchanan was of the elegance of French cuisine, he was also steeped in the heritage of his native Pennsylvania. One could not live in Pennsylvania at this time and not be familiar with or partial to the famous succotash of the region. More a vegetable stew than a real succotash, it is delicious even today to non-Pennsylvanians.

Green peppers	*Salt and pepper*
Bacon fat	*Milk*
Corn	*Tomatoes*
Lima beans	*Brown sugar*

Lightly brown 2 sliced green peppers in a little bacon fat. Add 2 cups each cooked corn and cooked Lima beans. Stir. Season with salt and pepper. Add ½ cup milk and cook over a low heat. When liquid has cooked dry, add 1 cup canned tomatoes and 1 tablespoon brown sugar. Stir well. Continue cooking over low heat until mixture is thoroughly heated. Serve hot. *Makes 6 portions.*

PENNSYLVANIA RED CABBAGE

Even non-Pennsylvanians have a hard time resisting this delicious accompaniment to roast pork, goose, suckling pig, duck, or game. Partial as James Buchanan was to game and poultry, this was a natural for him.

Apples	*Salt and pepper*
Bacon drippings	*Bay leaf*
Onion	*Sugar*
Red wine vinegar	*Red cabbage*
Water	*Flour*

Peel, core, and slice into thin circles 2 apples. Then heat 2 tablespoons bacon drippings or other shortening in a heavy iron skillet or saucepan. Add 1 finely chopped onion. Sauté gently 3 to 5 minutes. Add apple slices, sauté a minute or two longer, and then stir in ½ cup wine vinegar, 1 cup water, 1 teaspoon salt, dash of pepper, 1 bay leaf, and 2 tablespoons sugar. Stir well and bring to a boil. Remove from the fire. Then shred 1 medium head cabbage and add it to the apple mixture. Cover tightly, return the pan to the stove, cook gently over very low heat for 30 to 45 minutes, stirring now and then. When ready to serve, add 1 tablespoon flour and stir until mixture thickens slightly. Serve hot. *Serves 4.*

JEFF DAVIS PIE

Jefferson Davis was an admirer of Buchanan's. He liked the restrained elegance of Buchanan's Presidential style. Buchanan, in turn, found much to admire in Davis, though he opposed Davis on the issue of slavery. But political issues did not affect the enjoyment of this famous dessert of the period. Nor should regional feelings prevent your enjoying it today.

Eggs	*Melted butter or margarine*
Light cream	*Pie crust*
Brown sugar	*Sugar*
Flour	

Separate 4 eggs and beat the yolks well. Blend in carefully 1 cup light cream. Set aside, while combining 2 cups brown sugar with 2 tablespoons flour. Gradually add to the egg mixture and cream it well. Slowly stir in ½ cup melted butter or margarine. Pour into a 9-inch baked pastry shell. Bake in low (250° F.) oven for 15 or 20 minutes. Remove from oven and cover with a meringue made of 4 stiffly beaten egg whites with ⅓ cup sugar gradually beaten in. Return pie to oven and bake at 350° F. for 15 minutes, or until the meringue is delicately browned. *Makes one 9-inch pie.*

CONFEDERATE PUDDING

Pennsylvania-born-and-bred Buchanan was no Confederate (even though he often straddled the fence politically), but he did enjoy some of the rich and elegant desserts for which the South was justly famous. This recipe is delicious, an improvisational version of the classic bread pudding.

Bread	*Sugar*
Butter	*Sweet cream*
Jelly or jam	*Cornstarch*
Milk	*Nutmeg*
Eggs	

Slice homemade-type bread extra thin. Butter 12 slices well and cover with jelly or jam of your choice. Butter a glass baking dish and fill it with the bread.

Pour over the bread 1 pint milk, mixed well with 2 beaten eggs. Allow to stand until the milk–egg mixture has soaked the bread thoroughly. Bake in a medium-low (325° F.) oven until the pudding is firm. Serve lukewarm with Confederate Pudding Sauce. *Serves 6.*

CONFEDERATE SAUCE

Mix 2 cups sugar with 1 cup sweet light cream. Add 1 beaten egg and 1 tablespoon soft butter. Add 1 teaspoon cornstarch and a dash of nutmeg. Mix all ingredients well and cook over low heat until the mixture has the consistency of thick syrup. Remove from the heat, add another dash of nutmeg, and serve hot over the pudding.

MOSS ROSE CAKE

This midcentury favorite couldn't help pleasing President Buchanan, who liked the subtle flavoring of almond in many dishes.

Sugar	*Almond flavoring*
Eggs	*Cake flour*
Milk	

Beat together 2 cups sugar with 4 eggs for 12 minutes. Heat 1 cup milk to the boiling point, then add ½ teaspoon almond flavoring and set aside. Stir 2 cups sifted cake flour into the egg–sugar mixture. Slowly add the warm scalded milk. Beat vigorously for 3 minutes, or until all ingredients are well mixed. Grease and flour two layer-cake pans. Pour mixture into the pans evenly. Bake in a moderate (375° F.) oven 20 to 25 minutes. Delicious as is with vanilla ice cream, or with a coconut-orange frosting.

PEACH CHARLOTTE

By the time of Buchanan's administration, American cooks were becoming slightly more adventurous. Desserts were richer, especially among city folks who prided themselves on their awareness of dishes with a foreign flair.

Sponge cake or ladyfingers	*Sugar*
Ripe peaches or canned brandied peach halves	*Heavy cream*
	Brandy (optional)

Line the bottom and sides of a glass serving dish with slices of fresh sponge cake or ladyfingers. Pare ripe peaches, cut them in half (or use brandied canned peach halves), sprinkle them with sugar, and fill up the dish. Whip 1 pint heavy sweet cream. Pile the cream on top of the peaches. Serve chilled. (Also delicious served with brandy sauce poured over the peaches. This should be done at the table.)

CHARLOTTE RUSSE

This famous dessert really reached its peak of popularity during the administration of Chester Arthur, but even back in Van Buren's day it was a favorite dessert among the knowledgeable who prided themselves on their gastronomic prowess. Certainly it was a great favorite at Buchanan's table, official or private. This particular recipe is vintage 1855, right in Buchanan's heyday.

Sponge cake	*Milk*
Wine	*Lemon or vanilla flavoring*
Water	*Eggs*
Sugar	

Place a day-old 2 to 2½-pounds sponge cake in the middle of a deep glass dish. Mix together ½ pint wine, ½ pint water, and enough sugar to sweeten. Pour over the cake slowly, letting cake absorb as much of the wine mixture as possible. Then make a custard: Cook over low heat 3½ pints milk sweetened with a little sugar and a dash of lemon or vanilla flavoring. Just before the milk boils, stir in gradually 6 well-beaten egg yolks. When the milk–egg mixture begins to bubble at the edges, remove from the heat. Cool to lukewarm, then pour around the cake in the dish. Beat 6 egg whites to a stiff-dry froth, sweeten with powdered sugar, and flavor with a dash of lemon juice. Pile the egg whites on top of the cake and serve immediately.

APEES

It is widely believed in Pennsylvania that these delicious cookies were named after Ann Page, a famous nineteenth-century cook of Philadelphia. True or not, it is certain that they were much enjoyed by Pennsylvanians such as James Buchanan, as well as non-Pennsylvanians who ventured into the state.

Flour	*Grated nutmeg*
Butter	*Milk*
Sugar	

Blend ¾ cup flour with ½ pound butter, cutting the butter into the flour carefully as you would with pie dough. Gradually add ½ pound sugar and 1 teaspoon nutmeg. Mix well, and stir in a little milk gradually, using only enough to make a firm dough. (Commercial sour cream may be used instead of milk.) Knead the dough, roll it into sheets, and cut into designs with a cooky cutter. Butter a cooky sheet, place the cookies on them far enough apart to prevent touching. Bake in a medium (350° F.) oven until very lightly browned. *Makes 48.*

MUSCADINE PIE

So fond of grapes was President Buchanan that he actually cultivated them at the White House. His one undying claim to fame (culinarily speaking) may well be his grape arbor, which he cared for fastidiously. After tasting this favorite Buchanan pie, you will understand why.

Muscadine grapes	*Salt*
Sugar	*Cinnamon*
Lemon juice	*Unbaked pie crust*
Flour	*Butter*

Wash 1 quart of muscadine grapes. Press them gently one at a time with your fingers to remove the pulp. Simmer the pulp with 1 cup sugar over low heat for about 15 minutes. Then cool slightly and mash through a sieve to remove the seeds. Set aside, while boiling the grape hulls in a small quantity of water until tender, about half an hour. Drain and add the hulls to the pulp. Combine 1½ tablespoons lemon juice, 2 tablespoons flour, and ⅛ teaspoon salt. Mix to a smooth paste and add to the pulp and hulls. Add ¼ teaspoon ground cinnamon. Mix well and pour into an uncooked pie shell. Carefully place strips of unbaked pastry over the top in a lattice arrangement. Bake in a hot (400° F.) oven 15 minutes, then lower heat to 325° F. and continue baking until the crust browns. Remove from oven, brush the top with melted butter, and sprinkle generously with sugar. Serve warm as is or topped with whipped cream. *Serves 6 to 8.*

XVI

The Tragic Time

Harriet Lane would have been a success hard for anyone to follow. For Mary Todd Lincoln, the new President's wife, the task was well-nigh impossible.

Short, rather dumpy, plain, from the Midwestern prairies, Mary was not very prepossessing. Social Washington took one look and assumed that the new First Lady would have a lot to learn.

Social Washington was wrong, but poor Mary Lincoln spent her entire four years in the capital trying to prove it. But the harder she tried, the more the city resisted.

In the first place, Mary was not a typical Illinois frontier wife. She came from a respected Kentucky family, proud of its distinguished lineage. In normal times she might have been a joyful mistress of the White House, for she was well qualified to entertain graciously with all the Southern hospitality with which she had been raised. She had taste and even a certain amount of style.

But 1861 was hardly a normal time. Storm clouds of impending war hung over Washington. Because of its geographic location, Washington had long been dominated socially by Southerners. Virginia and Maryland hospitality were an accepted way of life in the nation's capital. But with Lincoln's election, many of the city's "first families," sympathetic to the Southern cause, decided to close their houses and retire to the South to cast their lot with the secessionists. Those who stayed remained aloof from the "court of the black Republican queen."

It was an uphill fight for the First Lady. She had to prove that she had the taste and style *expected* of a First Lady. Defensive about her position, she often went to extravagant lengths to establish her "gentility" to skeptics. She spent huge sums on clothes to impress social Washington (what remained of it) that she was not just a dowdy pioneer woman.

For a short time Mary's efforts met with success. But with the death of the Lincolns' son, Willie, in 1862, a jinx seemed to descend on the White House. From then on, everything Mary did was misinterpreted, misunderstood, and—often—misguided. In a critical public's eyes, she could do no right.

While Southerners disparaged her, Northerners viewed her as a renegade. Rumors ran rampant that she was actually a Confederate spy, sending information South with impunity. The talk became so vicious that the President himself felt it necessary to appear before a Congressional investigating committee "to give them his solemn personal assurance that his wife was loyal to the Union cause."

Mary herself said, after learning that one of her brothers, who had decided to fight for the Confederacy, had been killed: "Of course it is but natural that I should feel for one so nearly related to me, but not to the extent that you suppose. He made his choice long ago. He decided against my husband, and through him against me." And later she spoke out even more strongly: "Why should I sympathize with the rebels? They would hang my husband tomorrow if it was in their power, and perhaps gibbet me with him. How then can I sympathize with a people at war with me and mine?"

Hints of treason were just one of Mary's many crosses during the Lincoln years in Washington. The death of her son was followed by a semi-breakdown of her spirits. When she saw her husband shot in front of her eyes in 1865, her grip on sanity loosened even more, giving way completely sometime later. Of all our First Ladies, surely the least enviable, most pathetic, and star-crossed was Mary Lincoln.

One must at least give her *A* for effort. In the face of constant criticism, she bravely tried to carry on the official functions of the White House. In fact, as a prelude to their Presidential entertaining, the Lincolns gave a levee February 7, 1861, in their Springfield home. A guest described it: "It was a grand outpouring of citizens and strangers, together with members of the legislature. . . . Mr. Lincoln threw open his house for a general reception for all the people who felt disposed to give him and his lady a parting call. The levee lasted from seven to twelve o'clock in the evening, and the house thronged by thousands up to a late hour. Mr. Lincoln received the guests as they entered and were made known."

Once settled in the White House, Mrs. Lincoln launched a program to renovate the establishment. Allotted $20,000, she visited New York and ordered a wide variety of elegant accouterments for the Presidential parlors. Handsome vases and mantel decorations for the Blue and Green rooms were purchased, and a 700-piece set of Bohemian cut glass soon decked the dining table.

When she held her first levee, in December 1861, she was prepared to meet a reserved community looking her best, and with the White House looking *its* best. She had few illusions about the reception she might receive, but confided to White House secretary W. O. Stoddard that she was prepared to do her duty "while her smiling guests pull her in pieces."

The pieces at least were handsomely clothed. She had splurged on a figured silk brocade dress, decked her head in a wreath of flowers, and decked the White House in new crimson satin upholstery, newly varnished furniture, and new wallpapers and carpeting. The evening was not the ordeal Mary Lincoln expected, and she began plans for regular receptions, small dinners, and official functions.

On February 5, 1862, Mrs. Lincoln gave her first elaborate soirée. An earlier dinner "quite *en famille*" for Prince Napoleon of France had been well spoken of as "elegant and *recherche*." Normally a prominent restaurateur catered such a dinner, but Mrs. Lincoln wanted everything prepared right at the White House on this occasion. A news report of the time spoke glowingly of the results: "To her exquisite taste alone is to be attributed the beautiful arrangements for the occasion and the surpassing geniality of the dinner party. Mrs. Lincoln has upon the occasion shown her practical good sense to be equal to her graceful courtesy and charming manners" (probably the first and last time she was ever praised for "practical good sense").

Such kind words must have warmed Mary's insecure heart. She approached her soirée with more self-confidence. At first she planned to have 550 guests, but the list was soon expanded to 800. The New York *Herald* praised her for trying to limit the function, so as "to weed the Presidential Mansion of the long-haired, white-coated, tobacco-chewing and expectorant abolitionist politicians." As she was responsible for "the Presidential spoons," the *Herald* continued, "it is not safe to trust an ice-cream thus manipulated in the itching fingers of these sweet-smelling patriots."

Certain abolitionists were, in spite of the *Herald*'s admonitions, invited. One of them, Ben Wade, refused with these words: "Are the President and Mrs. Lincoln aware that there is a Civil War? If they are not, Mr. and Mrs. Wade are, and for that reason decline to participate in feasting and dancing."

Other guests-to-be were not so critical and arrived in droves. The White House was handsomely prepared for them, the music was excellent, and the banquet was a veritable Roman feast, prepared by Maillard, the famous New York caterer.

While some newspapers of the day attacked Mrs. Lincoln for entertaining at all ("Don't you know there's a war on?" was the gist of the complaints), claiming she just wanted to "show those Southerners who had closed their homes and refused all social engagements that she was as good as they," the New York *Herald* supported and praised her. The paper described that evening's supper as "one of the finest displays of gastronomic art ever seen in this country."

Leslie's Weekly featured the event in a leading article, beautifully illustrated, and commented: "There has been a social innovation at the White House, and the experiment has been a brilliant success." Until that evening, there had been "a false deference to the false notion of democratic equality."

The magazine article continued, stating that until Mrs. Lincoln's party, White House entertainments (always excepting state dinners for foreign Ministers and Cabinet members) were thrown open "to everyone, high, low, gentle or ungentle, washed or unwashed," which resulted in a "horrible jam," endurable only "by people of sharp elbows and destitute of corns, who don't object to a faint odor of whisky."

Mrs. Lincoln's innovation was to invite "respectable people in private life," limiting her invitations to "distinguished, beautiful, brilliant" people who represented "intellect, attainment, position, elegance." The writer continued, for page after snobbish page, to chronicle the arrivals of the guests, "ladies in swishing, crinkling crinoline," and to detail Mrs. Lincoln's entire presentation.

The presentation was certainly dramatic enough. At eleven-thirty, the guests were led to the State Dining Room, ready for the sumptuous feast that awaited them. But lo, a servant had locked the door and misplaced the key. What might have been a moment of embarrassment became one of amusement, as one of the guests joked "I am in favor of a forward movement!" and another chimed in with "An advance to the front is only retarded by the imbecility of commanders," parodying a recent speech in Congress. General McClellan, the object of the Congressional criticism, joined the other guests in the general laughter.

The lost key was soon found, and the guests surged in, immediately aware that the delay was worthwhile, for the table was elegant indeed. It stretched almost the entire length of the room, and small tables were arranged along the walls.

The decorations on the table were almost beyond belief, setting a style that would not be matched until Grant's administration. High point was a replica of a United States steam frigate with forty guns and all sails set, the American flag flying at the main. In addition, the goddess of Liberty arose above an elaborate shrine within which was a lifelike water fountain. A replica of the Hermitage and a Chinese pagoda, with double cornucopias next to it, resting on a shell, and supported by nougat Parisienne mermaids were just a few of the many-splendored things that ornamented the tables.

A discreet reminder of the war was present in a helmet that sported spun-sugar plumes. In addition there was a beehive, swarming with lifelike bees and filled with Charlotte Russe. A sugared-cake of Fort Pickens was surrounded by delicious candied quail. The tables were piled high with stewed and scalloped oysters, boned and truffle-stuffed turkey, *pâté de foie gras,* aspic of tongue, canvasback duck, partridge, filet of beef, ham, vension, terrapin, chicken salad, pheasant, sandwiches, jellies, cakes, *biscuit glace,* bonbons, ices, fruits. James Buchanan's beautiful ten-gallon punch bowl brimmed over with champagne punch.

The Marine Band played joyfully on, guests promenaded after supper, and few thought of leaving until three o'clock in the morning. To those present, it was an evening they would never forget. For Mary Lincoln it was a night of triumph.

But her triumph did not sustain her long. While the *Herald* considered the affair the event of a decade, others compared it to the ball the Duchess of Richmond gave at Brussels the evening before the Battle of Waterloo.

In spite of the fact that the Lincolns had allowed no dancing at the soirée, a Philadelphian circulated a scurrilous poem entitled "The Queen Must Dance." And the *American Temperance Journal* ranted and raved about the affair, with the table "spread with all that can intoxicate and cheer."

Presidential entertaining nevertheless continued. Just before one official dinner, Willie Lincoln became ill. Mary had to alternate visits upstairs to his sickroom with half-hearted attempts to keep her guests merry and accommodated. Whatever she did seemed destined to displease a critical public. Instead of praising her courage in going through with a scheduled event, she was abused for entertaining while her son lay dying upstairs. (No account was taken of the fact that she did not at the time know that Willie was dying.) After Willie's death, malicious gossips decreed that it "was a judgment of God upon the Lincolns for sponsoring frivolities." And when Mary retired in her grief for her son, critics called her sorrow "excessive," a poor example to a nation at war, and not to be compared with the "genuine" grief of mothers who lost their sons on the battlefields. It was not exactly an era of tact and taste.

W. O. Stoddard was appointed by Mrs. Lincoln to screen all the vicious letters she received daily, with the admonition "Don't let a thing come to me that you have not read first yourself and that you are not sure I would wish to see. I do not wish to open a letter nor even a parcel of any kind, until after you have examined it. Never!" He felt that she would have had a different reputation if she had made an effort to let newspaper correspondents know of her daily hospital visits to wounded soldiers, her gifts of wine, delicacies, liquors, fruit, and other foods to the wounded, and her other frequent acts of generosity. Unfortunately, she was not an apt pupil in the school of image-building.

In spite of grief, fatigue, illness, and despair, the Presidential entertaining continued throughout the war, though never again on the magnificent scale of that one grand evening in 1862. That is, not until Lincoln's second inauguration. The inaugural ball, March 6, 1865, had all the appearance of a triumphant gala, though the country was still deeply wrenched by the War.

The supper served that evening was itemized by a *New York Times* correspondent:

Oyster stews, terrapin stews, oysters pickled; beef—roast beef, *filet de boeuf,* beef *à la mode,* beef *à l'anglaise;* veal—leg of veal, fricandeau, veal Malakoff; poultry—roast turkey, boned turkey, roast chicken; grouse, quail, venison *pâtés, pâté* of duck *en gelee, pâté de foie gras;* smoked hams, tongue *en gelee,* tongue plain; salads—chicken, lobster' ornamental pyramids—nougat, orange, caramel with fancy cream candy, coconut, macaroon, chocolate; tree cakes—cakes and tarts, almond, sponge; belle alliance, dame blanche, macaroon tart, tarte *à la Nelson*—tarte *à la Orleans,* tarte *à la Portugaise,* tarte *à la Vienne,* pound cake, sponge cake, lady cake, fancy small cakes; jellies and creams—calf's foot and wine jelly, Charlotte *Russe,* Charlotte *à la* vanille; *blanc mange, crême Nepolitaine, crême à la* Nelson, *crême, crême* Chateaubriand, *crême à la* Smyrna, *crême à la* Nesselrode, *bombe à la vanille,* ice cream vanilla, lemon white coffee, chocolate, burnt almond, maraschino, fruit ices, strawberry, orange, lemon; dessert—grapes, almonds, raisins, etc., coffee and chocolate.

A staggering list of viands. One shudders at the lacerations the twentieth-century press would give a President serving such a spread in wartime, inauguration or not. The *Times* writer commented further that "Mr. Lincoln was evidently trying to throw off care for the time, but with rather ill success and looked very old, yet he seemed pleased and gratified, as he was greeted by the people. He wore a plain black suit and white gloves."

And so, after a long way round, we come to President Lincoln. Just as so much about his life has been shrouded in latter-day myth and legend, making it difficult to assess the truth about the man, so, too, have his food habits and tastes been the subject of controversy.

If the only records extant were the menus of his state balls and banquets, one would, justifiably, conclude that Abraham Lincoln must have been a gourmet to end gourmets, a connoisseur of exquisite sensitivity, a *bon vivant* supreme.

Nothing could be further from the truth.

On the other hand, certain observers of the time (and later observers of those observers) dogmatically asserted that Lincoln was "almost entirely indifferent to food except that he liked apples and hot coffee." Helen Duprey Bullock, Historian of the National Trust for Historic Preservation, has written: "Authorities agree that Lincoln was indifferent to food, not particularly knowing or caring what was placed before him, whether it was cold or hot, and even whether he ate it or not. If not reminded of meal times he forgot them."

Still another writer asserted that Lincoln "was one of the most abstemious of men; the pleasures of the table had few charms for him. His breakfast was an egg and a cup of coffee; at luncheon he rarely took more than a biscuit and a glass of milk, a plate of fruit in its season; at dinner he ate sparingly of two courses."

Contradictory evidence comes from Colonel William H. Crook, the President's bodyguard. He wrote: "Mr. Lincoln was a hearty eater. He never lost his taste for the things a growing farmer's boy would like. He was particularly fond of bacon. Plentiful and wholesome food was one of the means by which he kept up his strength which was taxed almost beyond endurance in those days [1862]."

It seems to us that the food truth about Lincoln must lie somewhere between these extreme points of view. In the pattern of so many of our strongest Presidents (always, of course, excepting Jefferson), Lincoln relied on food to feed the furnace. He ate well when served a tasty meal, but was usually so preoccupied with problems of politics and power that he gave little thought to food unless faced with it. Then he could enjoy a delicious meal as well as the next one.

One aspect of Abraham Lincoln's characteristically gentle nature was apparent in his approach to food. His stepmother, Mrs. Thomas Lincoln, commented that "Abe was a moderate eater—he sat down and ate what was set before him, making no complaint. He seemed careless about this." Leonard Swett, a fellow lawyer who often accompanied Lincoln on his circuit-court trips, which meant riding hundreds of miles, stopping at primitive accommodations, and eating generally poor food, noted that "I never, in the ten years of circuit life I knew him, heard him complain of a hard bed or a bad meal of victuals."

Noah Brooks, an old Illinois friend, testified that he "was never attentive to the demands of attractions of the table. When Mrs. Lincoln, whom he always addressed by the old-fashioned title of 'Mother' was absent from the home, he would appear to forget that food and drink were needful for his existence, unless he were persistently followed up by some of the servants, or were finally reminded of his needs by actual pangs of hunger. On one such occasion he asked me to come in and take breakfast with him. He was evidently eating without noting what he ate, and when I remarked that he was different from most western men in his preference for milk at breakfast, he said, as if he had not before noticed what he was drinking, 'Well, I do prefer coffee in the morning, but they don't seem to have sent me in any.'" He was not about to complain.

One time, however, he did make his demands known. There is the charming tale of Lincoln and the tea, or was it coffee? It seems that a waiter handed him a cup of Something. After tasting it, Lincoln said, "If this is coffee, then please bring me some tea. But if this is tea, please bring me some coffee."

Temperamentally, as has been noted *ad infinitum,* Mr. and Mrs. Lincoln were totally unlike, "with sharply contrasting personalities." This was strikingly apparent when it came to food and food history. Although both came originally from Kentucky, they reflected two completely different Kentucky traditions. Mary had been raised in the lush bluegrass region of the state, where gracious, comfortable living and rich, elaborate cooking were legendary. Abe grew up on the frontier, where he ate very plain food, partly for economic reasons, partly because of the frontier tradition. Corn dodgers, cakes made of coarse cornmeal, were a staple. Wild game provided the protein a growing boy needed. During the days of his young manhood, when he boarded at the Rutledge Tavern in New Salem, his diet consisted largely of cornbread, mush, bacon, eggs, and milk. Several friends of that period recalled later that if Abe was partial to any one food it was honey, a great delicacy for him at the time.

Considering the difference in the Todd and Lincoln backgrounds, it is perhaps surprising that the couple got along as well as they did. Isaac N. Arnold noted that Mary Todd Lincoln was a superlative cook: "Her table was famed for the excellence of its rare Kentucky dishes, and in season was loaded with venison, wild turkeys, prairie chicken, quails and other game, which in those days was abundant."

Such an elegant spread presupposed elegant manners, and it was perhaps a bit disconcerting to the cultivated Mary that her husband, concentrating on conversing with his guests, would reach for the butter with his own knife rather than the butter knife. The Lincoln childhood cabin, the Rutledge Tavern, and the assorted makeshift inns on the judicial circuit in Illinois were not celebrated for their separate butter knives.

William H. Herndon, Lincoln's last law partner and bitter critic of Mary Lincoln, disputed Mary's culinary reputation, insisting that she "kept or set a poor table" for daily meals, then splurged a bit when guests were invited to dinner. Though Herndon's view of Mary must always be read with appropriate salt grains, it is possible that Mary Lincoln tired, after a while, of serving delicious and special dishes to a husband who never commented on them. For if Lincoln was slow to complain about food, he was equally slow to praise it—a condition scarcely conducive to culinary incentive.

During the couple's Springfield years, Mary was widely known as a generous and gracious hostess (if one overlooks Herndon's carping), and the Lincoln dinner parties and evening affairs were spoken of as abundantly generous and hospitable. Frances Affonsa, a Portuguese washerwoman, eventually became the Lincoln's full-time cook. The Lincolns were well pleased with her and her cooking.

When Frances was asked how she got along with Mrs. Lincoln—for even in those days, Mary's reputation for shrewishness was widespread—she replied: "If I please Miss' Lincum, she like me, she treat me very well, and she very hard to please, but I please her."

During Lincoln's Presidency, however, things did not run as smoothly domestically as they had at Springfield. The President allocated all social responsibilities to his wife, and, as noted earlier, she found the going rough. Wartime Washington was not sleepier, peacetime Springfield.

Colonel Crook commented on the domestic side of the White House: "The cook was an old time Negro woman. A good deal of domestic supervision was necessary with the mistress of the house. For State dinners the regular staff was entirely inadequate; a French caterer was called in, who furnished everything, including waiters."

Of all Mary Lincoln's tactical errors in her handling of White House social affairs, none was so serious as her firing of the steward. This was an example of efficiency being its own worst enemy. Mrs. Lincoln thought she alone was best qualified to handle details of the Executive Mansion's management. She needed to be completely in command. The immediate result was difficulty with the servants, who were confused and demoralized by her manic moods. She was alternately generous and niggardly, rational and kindly, then abruptly harsh and demanding.

But the long-range results of the steward's dismissal were far more serious. With no steward around to keep a check on the linen and silver, many valuables disappeared. After the President's death, Mrs. Lincoln remained secluded upstairs for five weeks. During all that time there was no caretaker, no single person to be responsible for the many White House treasures. As a result, the building was so badly plundered it looked like the sack of Rome. Anarchy ruled.

Family meals at the Lincolns' were routine. Early in the morning the President liked a "good hot cup of coffee." But often he would forget about breakfast until 9 or 10 A.M. John Hay, one of Lincoln's private secretaries, occasionally ate with the President. He noted that the frugal repast might consist of "an egg, a piece of toast, coffee, etc." On occasion breakfast was a single egg.

For lunch, Hay reported, Lincoln "took a little lunch—a biscuit, a glass of milk in winter, some fruit or grapes in summer. . . . He ate less than anyone I know." Lunch was usually eaten irregularly. One staff member commented: "I met a servant carrying a simple meal upon a tray upstairs. There the food might be eaten soon or perhaps two hours later."

One day Dr. Henry Whitney Bellows of the Sanitary Commission said to Lincoln: "Mr. President, I am here at almost every hour of the day or night, and I never saw you at the table; do you eat?"

"I try to," Lincoln replied. "I manage to browse about pretty much as I can get it."

One of the controversies concerning President Lincoln evolved around liquor. It was not a question of whether or not he drank to excess, but whether he indulged at all. Certain sources, in an attempt to bestow sainthood on their hero, maintained that no alcohol ever touched Blessed Abraham's lips. Campaign biographies in 1860 emphasized the fact that "in private life Mr. Lincoln is a strictly moral and temperate man. . . . He never drank intoxicating liquors of any sort, not even a glass of wine."

By contrast, the Southern press during the Civil War had its own particular axe to grind, and ground it *ad nauseum*. The Southerners "universally believed that Lincoln had been drunk ever since his inauguration and only goes out at night to escape suspicion."

The truth, as usual, lies somewhere between the extremes. Even though Lincoln in his early career had been co-owner of a tavern in New Salem, he was not, in a sense, a drinking man. In 1872, Ward Hill Lamon, whom Lincoln once called "entirely reliable and trustworthy—my particular friend," wrote that Lincoln "was neither what might be called a 'drinking' man, a total abstainer nor a prohibitionist."

Tolerance, which marked so much of Lincoln's character, was in evidence in his attitude toward drinking. Socializing as he did with so many rough-cut prairie politicians, he knew how to get along with them. As Lamon wrote, Lincoln would "take whiskey with a little sugar in it to avoid the appearance of discountenancing his friends. If he could have avoided it without giving offence he would have gladly done so."

Other friends recalled that Lincoln did on occasion have a glass of wine and, according to Leonard Swett, "he used to drink a glass of champagne with his dinner, but I believe that was prescribed for him." Certainly there are records in abundance of wine served at White House affairs.

Honest Abe probably summed it all up better and more directly than any of his virtuous apologists when he said: "I am entitled to little credit for not drinking because I hate the stuff. It is unpleasant and always leaves me flabby, undone."

A "drinking man" might not have been able to cope during those tragic, trying years between 1861 and 1865. They demanded all the straight-thinking, hard-driving determination of a Lincoln.

◇◇◇

RECIPES

NOB CREEK KENTUCKY CORN CAKES

Being a tall man, President Lincoln often joked that his appetite was equally tall. This was more of a joke than anything else except when it came to corn cakes. He could, it was said, "eat corn cakes twice as fast as anyone could make them." Even in the White House, Lincoln's favorite breakfast and Sunday-supper dish was corn cakes, especially when fixed as he had enjoyed them in childhood in Kentucky. Of course they had to be eaten, at least by the President, with great quantities of sorghum syrup poured over them.

Cornmeal	*Egg*
Soda	*Buttermilk*
Salt	

Sift 2 cups cornmeal with 1 teaspoon soda and 1 teaspoon salt. Add 1 egg and 3 cups buttermilk to the mixture and stir well, making sure mixture is well blended. The batter should be thin enough to bake with a lacy edge. Bake on a hot griddle, dropping on by small spoonfuls. If you are making these for a large family, bake all cakes at one time. As each is finished, stack or place flat on warm cooky sheets and cover with foil. Keep warm in a low (250° F.) oven or, at the last minute, heat for 5 minutes in a hot (400° F.) oven. Serve immediately. They are delicious with butter and maple syrup. *Makes 36 thin 2-inch cakes.*

THE WIDOW JOHNSTON'S HASTY PUDDING

A year after Nancy Hanks' death, Lincoln's father married Sarah Bush Johnston, a widow with three children of her own. A kindly, warm-hearted woman, she
made the desolate Lincoln cabin as cheery and orderly as possible. Although the
table she set was necessarily plain and spare, she was a good cook of simple foods.
Her hasty pudding, much loved by young Abe, was not so hastily cooked as to be
indigestible, which is more than could be said for many a hasty pudding of that
era. A recipe of the time decried the habit of certain careless cooks who made hasty
pudding "just as wanted and bringing it to the table with about fifteen minutes
cooking. In this way the meal is not thoroughly cooked and therefore was said to
disagree with many persons. A cast-iron pot with feet lessens the tendency to burn
and is therefore the best vessel to use." (This applied to fireplace cooking.) The
Widow Johnston's mush, or hasty pudding, was smooth, delicate, and without
lumps. Her trick, probably, was to stir the cornmeal into cold water before adding
it to hot water.

Hot water	*Salt*
Yellow or white cornmeal	*Cold water*

Boil 3 cups water in a saucepan. Mix 1 cup packaged yellow or white cornmeal
and 1 teaspoon salt with 1 cup cold water. Mix well. Slowly pour the mixture into
the boiling water, stirring all the while. Cook until thickened, stirring often.
When thick, cover and continue cooking over very low heat (or in a double
boiler) for another 10 minutes. *Serves 6.*

(We recommend doubling the quantity needed and pouring the leftover mush
into a long glass baking dish to be stored in the refrigerator for another day.
The then-solid mush may be cut into thin slices, fried in bacon drippings, and
eaten crisp and hot with butter and syrup. Double-duty dish.)

RAIL SPLITTERS

Named for our sixteenth President, these corn muffins are delicious served hot
with gobs of butter on top.

Egg	*Buttermilk*
Sugar	*Soda*
Salt	*Water*
Yellow cornmeal	*Flour*
Melted shortening	*Baking powder*

Beat 1 egg well and add to it 3 tablespoons sugar, 1 teaspoon salt, and 1 cup
yellow cornmeal. Mix well and slowly add 4 tablespoons melted shortening that

has been allowed to cool somewhat. Mix again and add 1 cup fresh buttermilk. Beat all together. Dissolve ½ teaspoon baking soda in 1 teaspoon cold water and add to the other mixture. Sift in 1 cup flour, previously sifted with 4 teaspoons baking powder. Beat vigorously. Grease well iron cornbread-stick pans and heat them to the sizzling point (use cup cake tins if you don't have stick pans). Pour batter in immediately. Bake in a preheated medium-hot (375° F.) oven for approximately 15 minutes or until lightly browned. Serve piping hot. *Makes 24.*

NANCY HANKS' STEAMED POTATOES

When the Lincoln family moved from Kentucky to Indiana and lived near Little Pigeon Creek in the Buckhorn Valley, there were many times they had literally nothing but potatoes to eat. In *The Prairie Years* Carl Sandburg described one of those lean occasions:

> Once at the table when there was only potatoes, the father spoke a blessing to the Lord for potatoes. The boy [Abe] answered, "These are mighty poor blessings."

Poor they were, but Nancy Hanks Lincoln always tried to make the potatoes as tasty as possible by steaming them in a baker, as was the custom then.

Potatoes	*Pepper*
Salt	*Butter*
Water	*Buttermilk*

Use good medium-sized potatoes, not too young. (If too young, they will taste soapy instead of mealy.) Scrub the potatoes well, allowing two per person. These are delicious steamed in a Dutch oven over the embers at a cookout, but also good prepared in a Dutch oven on top of the stove. Pile the potatoes into the Dutch oven, along with 1 cup well-salted water. Put the lid on upside down. Inside the lid place several pieces of glowing charcoal. Put the Dutch oven (or large kettle) on very low heat on top of the stove or in the oven. Allow to steam slowly for about 1 hour or until potatoes are tender. Do not lift the lid unless absolutely necessary. *To serve:* bring the Dutch oven to the table. Serve the potatoes in their jackets, along with salt, pepper, and butter. To be authentically Lincolnesque, you should serve a mug of fresh buttermilk with the potatoes.

DELMONICO POTATOES

In 1861 President Lincoln visited the uptown Delmonico's in New York. It was quite a ride uptown—way up to 14th Street and Fifth Avenue. The President's visit took place shortly before the Civil War began. Evidently the problem-pressured President found the new handsome restaurant a pleasant respite from his worries. After dinner he called the owner, Lorenzo Delmonico, over to his table, and said: "In my city of Washington there are many mansions, but alas, we have no cooks like yours." Such culinary perspicacity was unusual for Lincoln, proof that he must have found special enjoyment in his dinner.

Potatoes	*Salt and pepper*
Butter	*Grated cheese*
Flour	*Buttered breadcrumbs*
Cream	

Wash, peel, and dice 6 medium potatoes. Boil them in lightly salted water until just done, but not overdone. Drain and place in a buttered baking dish. Melt 4 tablespoons butter in a saucepan, blend in 4 tablespoons flour, and add 1¾ cups cream. Stir continuously until thickened. Season lightly with salt and pepper to taste. Pour over the potatoes, mixing lightly. Cover the mixture with ¾ cup grated cheese, dot with buttered breadcrumbs, and bake in a hot (400° F.) oven until the cheese becomes golden brown, approximately 20 minutes. *Serves 4.*

TRUFFLE RAGOÛT

When the Thomas Lincoln family moved to Illinois, Chicago was a small prairie village. The pioneers relied heavily on wild game and the fruit of the land for their food. Such "fruit" as mushrooms, puffballs, and truffles were common-place, easily found throughout the fields and countryside. Edible fungi were a basic resource of the settlers, in spite of the fear of and lack of knowledge of which were or were not edible varieties. Truffles, the "black diamonds" of today, were abundant around the ancient oak trees of the territory.

Truffles	*Salt and pepper*
Olive oil	*Egg yolk*
White wine	

Scrub the truffles with a brush until thoroughly cleaned, then soak in olive oil for several hours. When ready to cook, slice the truffles ¼ inch thick and place in a saucepan with equal parts dry white wine and olive oil. Add salt and pepper to taste and cook over a low fire until tender. When ready, mix 1 egg yolk with the truffle brew and add to a mixed vegetable ragoût that has been cooking at the same time. Be sure to underseason the ragoût so that the truffle flavor will dominate. Stir gently and serve.

MUSHROOM FRITTERS

Mushrooms	*Paprika*
Flour	*Eggs*
Salt	*Milk*
Baking powder	*Butter*

Lightly cook 1 cup mushrooms in a minimum amount of water. Drain and mince. Set aside. Mix 1 cup sifted flour with ¾ teaspoon salt, 1 teaspoon baking powder, and ⅛ teaspoon paprika. Slowly add 2 egg yolks and 2 tablespoons milk. Beat well, and then add the mushrooms and 1 tablespoon melted butter. Fold in 2 egg whites that have been beaten stiff. Mix very carefully and drop by the spoonful in a pan of hot (350° F.) fat. Cook until the fritters are golden brown, about 3 minutes. *Serves 6.*

CANDIED MINT LEAVES

This Kentucky favorite makes delicious nibbling and may be eaten like potato chips. Another interesting way is to add a few of the leaves to a salad. They provide an unusual tang and texture.

Fresh mint leaves	*Powdered sugar*
Egg white	

Take the mint leaves fresh from the garden and wash them carefully. Dry on a towel, keeping the leaves as unbroken as possible. Dip them in unbeaten egg white and press them into a layer of powdered sugar spread out on a breadboard or in a wide flat bowl. Shake off the excess sugar and place the leaves on wax paper on a cooky sheet and set into the refrigerator to harden.

SWEET PICKLED BEETS

Another food Lincoln knew and "tolerated" was this vegetable, always so delicious when pickled young.

Young beets	*Vinegar*
Boiling water	*Cloves*
Sugar	

Peel small young beets (older, bigger ones may be used, if the season is against you) and place them in boiling water in a porcelain or enamel saucepan. If you use the larger beets, cut them lengthwise after they have been cooked tender and cooled. Set aside. Boil equal parts of sugar and vinegar, along with ½ teaspoon ground cloves tied in a cheesecloth bag for every gallon of liquid used. Pour liquid over the beets, and place the mixture and liquid into pans. Refrigerate until ready to use—or cover with sterilized tops.

BROILED BEEFSTEAK

Although Lincoln was at times absent-minded about the food served him at the table, he was single-minded on the subject when he himself did the marketing, as he did on occasion. Like another former Kentucky-resident President, William Henry Harrison, Lincoln enjoyed stalking his prey (in both cases beefsteak) in the market place. Lincoln's neighbors often saw him buying his steak—ten cents bought a large enough steak for a meal. To save a few pennies more, he carried the brown-paper meat package home with him instead of having it delivered. Like other Midwestern men of his day, he enjoyed a good hearty beefsteak now and then.

| *T-bone steak* | *Butter* |
| *Salt and pepper* | *English mustard* |

Allow about ¾ pound meat and bone per person. Trim off some of the excess fat, then rinse and wipe the steak dry. Heat the oven, and place the steak on a hot greased rack over a broiling pan (to catch the drippings) about 3 inches from the flame. When the steak becomes very brown on top, turn gently with 2 spoons (to avoid piercing the meat) and broil 10 minutes longer for rare meat, longer still if you prefer it well done. When ready to serve, place the steak on a hot platter, season with salt and pepper on both sides, dot with butter and, if you like the juices, skim off the fat and pour the juice over the meat. Serve hot, accompanied by English mustard.

STEAMED OYSTERS

As shad was a commonplace in early American life, by the mid-nineteenth century it was oysters that seemed ubiquitous. During the Lincolns' years in Springfield, they often gave elaborate oyster parties, at which oysters were prepared and offered in every imaginable fashion. The menu at such a party would consist of oysters, more oysters, nothing but oysters. But such oysters! At that time, the oysters were six or eight inches in size and were served broiled, boiled, curried, fricasseed, panned, deviled, scalloped, stewed, pickled; in pies, fritters, omelets—you name it. One of the most popular ways was made famous by Harvey's Restaurant in Washington: steamed. As President, Lincoln frequently made the expedition to Harvey's for the justly celebrated steamed oysters, thus setting a precedent that several later Presidents—Grant, Garfield, Arthur, T. R., Taft, and Harding—followed.

Oysters   *Salt and pepper*
Butter

Carefully wash, drain and shuck 1 quart of oysters, place them in a shallow baking dish or small cake pan. Put the pan into a steamer over boiling water. Steam the oysters until they become plump, with the edges curled. Do not overcook. Transfer the oysters to a heated serving dish. Dot with butter; season with salt and pepper. Serve immediately. *Serves 4.*

STEAMED OYSTERS IN THE SHELL

Wash and scrub the oyster shells, and place them in an airtight container or casserole, with the upper shells facing downward (this prevents the liquor running out when the shells open). Place the casserole or pan over a kettle of boiling water in order to get the steam. Boil rapidly until the shells open, about 15 minutes. Do not overcook. Serve immediately.

THANKSGIVING DAY

We take Thanksgiving so for granted it is hard to realize that it was not proclaimed a national holiday until 1863. Of course, it had begun as a Pilgrim custom, a means of giving thanks for the harvest. Governor Bradford sent out four of his men to shoot some wild fowl so all the colonists "might have a more special manner to rejoice together." Then in 1789 George Washington proclaimed the first official Thanksgiving Day. But it was not declared a national holiday, and the custom withered in many states. But then an indomitable woman, Mrs. Sarah Josepha Hale, editor of the widely read nineteenth-century *Godey's Lady's Book,* began a lifetime crusade to make Thanksgiving Day a national holiday. She had celebrated the day in her childhood home in New Hampshire and felt the day should be celebrated all over America. "Our Thanksgiving Day should be hallowed and exalted," Mrs. Hale editorialized year after year, "and made the day of generous deeds and innocent enjoyments." Each fall she wrote letters to the then President of the United States and each Congressman, urging the proclamation of a national Thanksgiving Day.

For twenty years Mrs. Hale wrote her letters. Finally, in 1863, in the midst of a divisive civil war, a President heeded her pleas. Perhaps the bitterness of the war influenced President Lincoln to urge the nation to reflect on its early beginnings.

In any case, he took time from the war to "invite my fellow citizens in every part of the United States, and also those who are at sea or who are sojourning in foreign lands, to set apart and observe the last Thursday of November next as a day of thanksgiving and praise to our Beneficent Father." Sarah Hale, then seventy-five years old, was deeply gratified.

And so Thanksgiving Day it was, and has continued to be through the years. In recent years, the date was changed, but the holiday is the same as ever, a time of gratitude and abundance.

THANKSGIVING PUMPKIN PIE

In Lincoln's day, as now, Thanksgiving meant stuffed, roasted turkey with cranberry sauce, a covey of other vegetables and relishes, with pumpkin pie as the grand finale.

Pumpkin	*Salt*
Eggs	*Ginger*
Milk	*Cinnamon*
Butter	*Nutmeg*
Sugar	*Plain pie crust*

Strain 1½ cups cooked pumpkin (canned, frozen or fresh) and mix with 3 slightly beaten egg yolks. Add 1½ cups scalded milk in which 2 tablespoons butter have been melted. Mix well, then add 1 cup sugar, ½ teaspoon salt, ½ teaspoon ginger, 1 teaspoon cinnamon, and ¼ teaspoon nutmeg. Mix thoroughly, then add 3 stiffly beaten egg whites, folding them in carefully. Pour the mixture into an unbaked pie shell. Bake in a preheated hot (450° F.) oven 10 minutes. Then reduce the heat to moderate (350° F.) and bake an additional 20 to 25 minutes, or until the pie is firm. When a knife can be inserted in the filling and come out clean, the pie is ready to remove from the oven. *Makes one 9-inch pie.*

CHRISTMAS PUMPKIN PIE

In the fall of 1863, President Lincoln and his family were bequeathed a live turkey for their Christmas dinner. Young Tad Lincoln named the bird "Jack" and made him a household pet. The day before Christmas, Tad burst into a Presidential conference and sobbed to his father, "He's a good turkey, and I don't want him killed." The indulgent father-President immediately issued a written reprieve. Jack's life was spared, making Tad Lincoln's Christmas a happy one.

This variation on the old-fashioned pumpkin pie was a favorite in the White House for generations.

Eggs	*Mace*
Pumpkin	*Cinnamon*
Brown sugar	*Brandy*
Nutmeg	*Milk*

Beat separately 10 egg yolks and 10 egg whites. Add the yolks to 4 cups cooked, strained pumpkin. Add 2 cups dark-brown sugar, ½ teaspoon nutmeg, 1 teaspoon mace, and 1 tablespoon cinnamon. Mix well, then add 2 tablespoons brandy. Fold the stiffly beaten egg whites into the mixture and beat in the electric mixer. Slowly add 1¼ quarts whole milk to the mixture as you beat it. Pour into 2 unbaked pie shells. Bake 20 minutes in hot (425° F.) oven. Then reduce heat to 325° F. for 30 minutes. Makes two 9-inch pies.

RUTLEDGE TAVERN SQUASH PIE

Although Abe Lincoln was at one time a partner in a New Salem tavern, there is little evidence that he ate there. He was more inclined to take his meals at the Rutledge Tavern, where the daughter of the family, Ann, served him. This pie was a mainstay of the tavern—and the times. The original recipe was generous enough for four pies. We have amended it to one, for the present-day household is no tavern.

Unbaked pie shell	*Brown sugar*
Eggs	*Butter*
Milk	*Cinnamon*
Squash	*Nutmeg*
Salt	*Ginger*

Line one 9-inch pie pan with pie crust. Brush the crust lightly with 1 slightly beaten egg white to keep the filling from soaking into the crust. Then beat 2 eggs and 1 egg yolk slightly and mix them with 2 cups milk and 2 cups cooked mashed squash. Add ½ teaspoon salt, ¼ cup brown sugar, 1 tablespoon melted butter, 1 teaspoon cinnamon, ¼ teaspoon nutmeg, and ¼ teaspoon ginger. Mix together thoroughly and pour into the pie pastry. Bake 10 minutes in a very hot (450° F.) oven, then reduce the heat to 300° F. Bake until firm (until a toothpick comes out of the center clean), about 40 to 50 minutes.

PEACH PIE

Although indifferent to many foods, Lincoln did have one culinary obsession: he was inordinately fond of all kinds of fruit. In 1841 he wrote a friend, Miss Mary Speed of Louisville, Kentucky: "I am literally subsisting on savoury remembrances—that is, being unable to eat, I am living upon the remembrance of the delicious dishes of peaches and cream we used to have at your house." Peaches and cream or peach pie, it was all the same to Lincoln, so long as it contained fresh fruit.

Unbaked pastry shell	*Lemon juice*
Sugar	*Butter*
Fresh peaches	*Cream or melted butter*

Line a 9-inch pie pan with pastry. Sprinkle it lightly with ⅓ cup sugar, then line the pan with 2 cups peeled, sliced peaches. Pour 1 teaspoon lemon juice evenly over the peaches and dot with 2 teaspoons butter. Sprinkle ⅓ cup sugar over the top and cover with pastry. Cut gashes in the top to permit the steam to escape. Brush the pastry top with cream or melted butter. Bake in a preheated hot (425° F.) oven 10 minutes. Reduce oven temperature to 350° F. and bake an additional 35 to 40 minutes. Serve warm or chilled with whipped cream or vanilla ice cream on top.

NEW SALEM FRUIT PIES

As a lanky young lawyer, Abe Lincoln satisfied his sweet tooth with home-baked fruit pies. One of his biographers, the famed newspaperwoman Ida Tarbell, told how the ladies of New Salem, remembering his youthful fondness for their fruit pies, would bake and ship fruit pies to the by-then President Lincoln. The wrapping-shipping process was a chore, more trouble in a way than the baking. Special pie baskets were enclosed in homemade wooden boxes. Apple pies were the easiest to ship (there was no quick-service railway express in those days), but in season the ladies did not hesitate to ship the President sour-cherry or blackberry pie. For home consumption the pies were baked with lattice tops. But for protection in shipping, two crusts were generally used. The steam gashes were often fancifully made in the shape of a star or the letter *L* (for Lincoln, of course) or *B* for Blackberry or *C* for Cherry, or whatever. It was a labor of love the New Salem ladies performed—one much appreciated by the war-weary President, who must have thought often and nostalgically of the "good old days" when he was a young man in New Salem.

BLACKBERRY PIE

Sugar	*Blackberries*
Flour	*Unbaked pie shell*
Salt	

Mix together 1 cup sugar, 2½ tablespoons flour, and ¼ teaspoon salt. Add 1 quart well-washed blackberries. Mix well and pour into a pie plate lined with unbaked pastry shell. Cover the top with another crust and make gashes to let the steam escape. Bake in a hot (450° F.) oven 10 minutes, then reduce temperature to 350° F. and continue baking another 25 to 30 minutes. *Makes 1 nine-inch pie shell.*

To make sour-cherry pie: Substitute 1 quart sour red cherries for the blackberries (having washed and pitted them) and proceed as above.

GOOSEBERRY COBBLER

Elderberries, gooseberries—all the old-time berries and fruits found favor with President Lincoln. Such berries often grew wild in his home state of Illinois. The original recipe for this old-fashioned cobbler called for a dripping pan or 9-by-18-inch pudding dish, rather large for today's family. The recipe served 12, but can easily be adapted to 6 servings.

Flour	*Milk or water*
Lard or salad oil	*Sugar*
Salt	*Gooseberries*
Baking powder	

Combine 4 cups flour with 4 tablespoons melted lard or salad oil, ½ teaspoon salt, and 4 teaspoons baking powder. Mix as you would a biscuit dough, stirring in little by little about 1 cup milk or water. (Add only enough liquid to make a dough that can be rolled quite thin.) Roll the dough and line a pudding dish with it (or a 9-by-18-inch pan). Mix 2 tablespoons sugar with 3 tablespoons flour and sprinkle it over the crust. Then spread 6 cups washed gooseberries in the dish. Sprinkle with ¾ cup sugar (more if berries are too sour). Wet the edges of the crust with a little flour and water mixed. Place an upper crust on top, pressing the edges together. Make 2 openings by means of 2 inch-long incisions at right angles. Bake in a hot (425° F.) oven about 30 minutes. *To serve:* cut into squares and serve either warm or cold with rich milk or cream or whipped cream, vanilla sauce, foamy sauce, or vanilla ice cream.

LINCOLN'S FRUIT COOKIES

Psychologists might argue that Lincoln's excessive fondness for fruits was a result of his "deprived" childhood, with its fairly steady diet of potatoes and corn cakes and mush.

Sugar	*Nutmeg*
Butter	*Flour*
Egg	*Currants or raisins*
Baking powder	*Milk*

Combine 1½ cups sugar with 1 cup soft butter. Cream well, then add 1 slightly beaten egg. Add 2 teaspoons baking powder, 1 teaspoon grated nutmeg and just enough flour to make the dough rollable. Add 3 tablespoons English currants or chopped seedless raisins. Roll the dough smooth, cut with a large round cooky cutter, moisten the top of each cooky with milk, and sprinkle sugar over. Bake on well-greased cooky sheets in a hot (375° F.) oven. Cool on brown paper. *Makes 36 cookies.*

SPICED CRABAPPLES

Another Lincoln favorite, these apples were not a dessert, but a welcome accompaniment to a regular dinner or supper.

Crabapples	*Sugar*
Vinegar	*Cloves, mace, cinnamon*

Peel and cut in half 9 pounds crabapples. Place in a large kettle with 1 pint vinegar, 4 pounds sugar, 1 teaspoon whole cloves, 3 or 4 sticks of cinnamon, and a dash of mace. Boil about ½ hour, removing before the apples become too soft. Put in sterilized jars and seal or, if you plan to use shortly, chill in the refrigerator. *Makes 8 quarts.*

CONFEDERATE APPLE PIE WITHOUT APPLES

The Civil War created havoc with the traditionally rich Southern cooking. Although those in Washington were not noticeably deprived (note some of the White House menus for the period), and considering Lincoln's own Spartan tastes *he* certainly couldn't have cared less for himself, countrymen in the South were suffering from severe shortages of familiar foods. Witness the following recipes taken from *The Confederate Recipe Book,* subtitled "A Compilation of Over One Hundred Recipes Adapted to the Times."

Crackers	*Sugar*
Water or milk	*Butter*
Tartaric acid	*Nutmeg*

Making apple pie without apples isn't easy. But this is how it was done: Soak a large bowl of crackers in water or milk until all the crackers are soft and formless.

Add 1 teaspoon tartaric acid, sweeten to taste with sugar, dot with butter, and sprinkle a little nutmeg over the top. Pie crust, in case flour was scarce, could be made of boiled potatoes, salt, butter, and water.

FRIED OYSTERS WITHOUT OYSTERS

Lincoln had the oysters; the South had this recipe, which we include for its insights into a troubled time.

Green corn   *Butter*
Egg   *Salt and pepper*
Flour

Grate young green corn into a bowl, enough for 1 pint. Add 1 well-beaten egg, a "small teacup" of flour, 2 or 3 tablespoons butter, and season with salt and pepper. Mix all together. Drop by the spoonful into hot grease or oil. "A tablespoon of the batter will make the size of an oyster." Fry until light brown. Drain and butter. Then pretend.

REPUBLICAN PUDDING

One wonders why the Confederates even included such a recipe in the book: "Take one cup of soft boiled rice, a pint of milk, a cup of sugar, and a piece of butter the size of an egg. Serve with sauce."

KENTUCKY SORGHUM CAKE

In Lincolniana there are frequent comments about sorghum. Nancy Hanks used it in cooking. Later the Lincolns received many gifts of sorghum at the White House. We investigated and discovered that while references are made to sorghum molasses, sorghum is not molasses at all! Nor is sorghum syrup really cane syrup! Sorghum comes from a plant that resembles sugar cane, but is smaller and thinner. The stocks are usually no "thicker than your thumb" and grow in climates too cool for regular sugar cane. Often cane is grown in the southern part of states such as Alabama and Georgia, while sorghum is grown in the north. Kentucky, Tennessee, Indiana, and southern Illinois are all sorghum territory. In these areas one hundred years ago, sorghum boils were as social as sugar rituals in Vermont. In late autumn, around the time of Halloween, farmers for miles around would gather, bringing their sorghum to be ground like cane at some central mill. The crushed sorghum was placed in vats or large kettles and cooked many hours—

often all night long, "sweet scenting the autumn darkness and done with the dawn."

Lincoln was not the only President with a yen for sorghum. Another border-state President, Harry Truman, had sorghum sent to him from Missouri during his sojourn at the White House.

Butter	*Nutmeg and cinnamon*
Sugar	*Soda*
Egg	*Baking powder*
Sorghum syrup	*Sour milk*
Flour	

Cream together ½ cup butter and 1 cup sugar, slowly adding 1 slightly beaten egg and 1 cup sorghum syrup. Beat well. Then add to the mixture alternately 2 cups sifted flour mixed with ¼ teaspoon each of nutmeg and cinnamon, 1 teaspoon each soda and baking powder, and 1 cup sour milk. When all are added, beat well again. Bake in a greased and floured loaf cake pan in a slow (325° F.) oven about 1 hour or until done. Cake may be frosted with any favorite icing.

YOUNG ABE'S GINGERBREAD MEN

In *The Prairie Years* Carl Sandburg tells the story of Lincoln and his sad gingerbread experience. During one of the Lincoln–Douglas debates, someone asked why Lincoln seemed to have so little female companionship. Did he find no pleasure in the company of women?

"When we lived in Indiana," the future President began, "once in a while my mother used to get some sorghum and ginger and make some gingerbread. It wasn't often, and it was our biggest treat. One day I smelled gingerbread and came into the house to get my share while it was hot. My mother had baked me three gingerbread men. I took them out under a hickory tree to eat them. There was a family, near us, poorer than we were, and their boy came along as I sat down. 'Abe,' he said, 'gimme a man?' I gave him one. He crammed it into his mouth in two bites and looked at me while I was biting the legs off of my first one. 'Abe,' he said, 'gimme that other'n?' I wanted it myself but I gave it to him. 'You seem to like gingerbread.' 'Abe,' he said, 'I don't s'pose anybody on earth likes gingerbread better'n I do—and gets less'n I do.'"

Our gingerbread men are the same in spirit as Abe's, though we have used molasses instead of sorghum, inasmuch as sorghum is unavailable in many parts of the country. The old recipes are not the same, to the nostalgic regret of old-timers who may remember them. Aside from the somewhat different flavor that sorghum imparts to the gingerbread men (it wasn't as sweet as today's molasses), the old-fashioned soda was slightly different from today's. Never mind; gingerbread men are gingerbread men, and ever since the New York Dutch introduced them as a Christmas favorite they have remained so for generations of American children.

Butter or margarine	*Cloves*
Sugar	*Eggs*
Molasses	*Vinegar*
Cinnamon	*Flour*
Ginger	*Baking soda*
Nutmeg	

Cream 1 cup butter with 1 cup sugar. Add ½ cup dark molasses, along with 1 teaspoon each of ground cinnamon, ginger, nutmeg, and cloves. Mix well and pour into a saucepan. Bring to a boil, stirring constantly. As mixture reaches the boil, remove from heat and cool to lukewarm. Then add 2 well-beaten eggs and 1 teaspoon vinegar. Mix well and add 5 cups flour sifted with 1 teaspoon baking soda. Mix again until mixture forms a smooth dough. Chill for several hours or overnight in the refrigerator. When ready to bake, roll out on floured board and cut with a gingerbread-man cutter. Put pieces of raisins on the cookies before baking—to form eyes, nose, buttons. Bake the cookies on ungreased cooky sheets in a preheated medium (350° F.) oven approximately 10 minutes. You may prefer to do all your decorating after the cookies are cooled. At that time, you may decorate with a thin frosting, making trimmings with a pastry tube. *Makes about 50 gingerbread men.*

HOT WATER SORGHUM GINGERBREAD

If you can find the sorghum, this is a real "oldie" worth trying. It may make you a convert to sorghum, as it did Lincoln.

Shortening	*Flour*
Boiling water	*Baking soda*
Sorghum	*Salt*
Egg	*Cinnamon, ginger, and cloves*

Melt ⅓ cup shortening in ⅔ cup boiling water. Then add 1 cup sorghum and 1 well-beaten egg. Sift together 2¾ cups flour, 2 teaspoons baking soda, 1 teaspoon salt, 1½ teaspoons ground ginger, 1 teaspoon cinnamon, and ¼ teaspoon cloves. Add to the sorghum mixture and mix thoroughly. Pour into a well-greased square baking pan and bake for about 30 minutes in a medium (350° F.) oven. Delicious when eaten warm. *Serves 8.*

GUNJERS (GUNYERS)

This molasses gingery cooky dates back way before Lincoln, back to earlier pioneer days. But it was "his kind of eatin'" all the same.

Butter	*Flour*
Sugar	*Allspice*
Molasses	*Cinnamon*
Baking soda	*Cloves and ginger*

Cream ⅔ cup butter at room temperature with 1 cup sugar. Slowly add 1 cup molasses and mix well. Dissolve 1 tablespoon baking soda in ½ cup warm water and set aside. Sift 6 cups flour with 2 teaspoons each allspice and cinnamon and 1 teaspoon each ground cloves and ginger. Add the soda–water mixture to the butter mixture alternately with the sifted dry ingredients. Mix well and refrigerate several hours or overnight. Roll very thin on a floured board and cut with cooky cutters into plain or fancy shapes. Bake in a preheated moderate (300° F.) oven until lightly browned, about 6 minutes. *Makes about 12 dozen.*

GINGER POUND CAKE

Another ginger treat for ginger lovers everywhere!

Butter	*Ginger*
Sugar	*Cinnamon*
Eggs	*Baking soda*
Molasses	*Orange rind*
Flour	

Cream ¾ pound butter with ¾ pound sugar. Add 6 lightly beaten eggs and 1 pint molasses. Slowly stir in 1½ pounds sifted flour mixed with 3 tablespoons ginger and 2 tablespoons cinnamon. Dissolve 1 tablespoon baking soda in a small amount of warm water and add it to the mixture. Add the grated rind of 3 medium oranges. Beat vigorously by hand or at top speed with an electric beater. Pour the mixture into a greased cake pan (preferably a heavy one). Bake in a moderate (350° F.) oven about 45 minutes or until done.

MOLASSES PECAN PIE

Speaking of molasses, the recipe book of a famous Washington baker of the last century records the fact that President Lincoln was one of the steadiest customers for the specialty of the house—this unusually rich and delicious pecan pie. The molasses in it must have had something to do with its superior flavor.

Eggs	*Vanilla extract*
Butter	*Pecans*
Unsulphured molasses	*Flour*
White corn syrup	*Unbaked pie crust*
Salt	

Beat 3 eggs until light and frothy. Add them to 2 tablespoons melted butter. Mix well, and then add ¾ cup unsulphured molasses, ¾ cup white corn syrup, ⅛ teaspoon salt and 1 teaspoon pure vanilla extract. Mix well. Mix 1 cup chopped pecans with 1 tablespoon flour and add to the egg–butter mixture. Mix thoroughly and pour into an 8-inch pie pan lined with an unbaked pie crust. Bake 40 minutes in a preheated moderate (375° F.) oven, until the filling sets and becomes firm. *Serves 6.*

MARY TODD'S COURTING CAKE

Several of Lincoln's biographers mentioned the burnt sugar cake Mary Todd prepared for him when he came courting. Many recipes purport to be Mary's own. This one, we are pleased to say, actually can be traced down through the Todd family to Mary Hosford, a granddaughter of one of Mary's cousins, who included it in her *Missouri Traveler Cookbook*. Grandfather Carr was proud of being Mary Todd's cousin and told many a sad story about her much-maligned life. In a lifetime of controversy, only Mary's burnt sugar cake appears to have escaped criticism. Everyone who tasted it agreed, as we think you will, about its excellence.

Sugar	*Baking powder*
Caramelized sugar syrup	*Cake flour*
Egg whites	*Salt*
Butter	*Vanilla*

One begins by "burning" the sugar. Melt ½ cup sugar in a heavy iron skillet. Heat slowly, stirring continuously with a wooden spoon, until the sugar becomes a very dark brown. Then add ½ cup hot water and stir until sugar dissolves. This is the caramelized sugar syrup you will use in the cake. Now beat 3 egg whites until very stiff, adding to them a little at a time ½ cup white sugar. Set aside. In another bowl, cream ½ cup butter with ½ cup white sugar. Add 2 teaspoons baking powder to 1½ cups cake flour, along with a dash of salt. Sift together and then add to the butter–sugar mixture, alternating with the caramelized sugar syrup—first a little flour, then a little syrup, until all have been used. Fold in the stiffly beaten egg whites. Flavor with 1 teaspoon vanilla and bake in 2 greased and floured 8-inch cake pans. Bake about 45 minutes in a preheated moderate (350° F.) oven.

FROSTING FOR MARY TODD'S COURTING CAKE

Melted butter	*Powdered sugar*
Dark brown sugar	*Black walnuts (optional)*
Milk	

Melt ½ cup butter in a heavy saucepan. Add 1 cup dark brown sugar and cook over low heat for 2 or 3 minutes, stirring constantly. Remove from the heat, add ⅓ cup milk and bring to a boil again. Cool to lukewarm and stir in gradually 2 cups powdered sugar. Beat vigorously until mixture is smooth. This makes enough frosting to cover the top and sides of an 8-inch layer cake. If you like, even though it isn't strictly authentic, sprinkle black walnuts over the frosting. Delicious even if not Toddian.

MARY TODD'S VANILLA ALMOND CAKE

There are reports attributable to President Lincoln that this cake of his wife's was the best he ever ate. This was high praise indeed, considering that his sister-in-law, Mrs. Ninian Wirt Edwards, commented that "he ate mechanically—I have seen him sit down at the table and never unless recalled to his senses would he think of food." This delicious cake was the invention of Monsieur Giron, a Lexington caterer, who created it in honor of the visit to that city in 1825 of his famous fellow Frenchman, Lafayette. The Todd family acquired the recipe and cherished it ever after. The baking powder must have been added at a later date.

Sugar	*Milk*
Butter	*Blanched almonds*
Flour	*Egg whites*
Baking powder	*Vanilla (or almond extract)*

Cream together 2 cups sugar with 1 cup butter. Sift 3 cups flour and 3 teaspoons baking powder three times and add to the butter–sugar mixture alternately with 1 cup milk. Chop 1 cup blanched almonds until very fine and add them to the mixture. Beat vigorously, then fold in 6 stiffly beaten egg whites carefully. Add 1 teaspoon vanilla (almond extract if you prefer) and pour the mixture into a greased and floured angel-cake pan. Bake in a preheated moderate (350° F.) oven for approximately 1 hour, or until a toothpick comes out clean when inserted into the cake's center. Turn the cake out on a wire rack and allow to cool before frosting it. This makes a very large cake. If you prefer, you can bake it in 2 9-inch layer-cake pans. The cake may be made without the almonds and is a splendid plain white cake, very light and good.

MARY TODD'S CANDIED FRUIT FROSTING

Egg whites   *Salt*
Sugar   *Candied pineapple*
Water   *Crystallized cherries*
Vanilla (or almond extract)

Beat 2 egg whites until very stiff. Set aside for a moment. Beat together 2 cups sugar and 1 cup water until the syrup spins a thread about five inches long. Then slowly fold into the egg whites, a spoonful at a time, very slowly, beating well with an electric beater as you add. Beat at top speed (very hard if you use a hand beater) until all the syrup is used and the mixture forms peaks when dropped from a spoon. When stiff, slowly add 1 teaspoon vanilla or ½ teaspoon vanilla and ½ teaspoon almond extract. Fold into the mixture ½ cup diced candied pineapple and ½ cup crystallized cherries cut in half. Spread between the layers and over the top and sides of the vanilla almond cake. If desired, the candied fruit may be eliminated. The frosting is delicious without them.

Variation: Instead of candied fruit, use the frosting plain as the filling for the cake. After frosting the top and sides, sprinkle freshly grated coconut over the top of the cake. In ante-bellum days, this version was known as a Merry Christmas Cake, no doubt because of the snow-top.

SANGAMON COUNTY SOUR CREAM COOKIES

These delicious cookies were as familiar to Abraham Lincoln as the countryside of his childhood.

Eggs   *Flour*
Sugar   *Baking soda*
Sour cream

Beat 2 eggs well and add them to 1 cup sugar and ¾ cup sour cream. Mix well. Then add 2 cups sifted flour and ½ teaspoon baking soda. Beat together and drop by spoonfuls 1 inch apart onto a greased cooky sheet. Bake in a hot (375° F.) oven for 8 to 10 minutes. *Makes approximately 50 cookies.*

VARIATION: SPICED SOUR CREAM COOKIES

Make the same cooky dough, but add ¼ teaspoon nutmeg and/or ¼ teaspoon cinnamon or cloves. Mix well and bake as above. For an extra touch, cookies may be frosted with a simple thin white sugar frosting. It adds a festive look, but is not necessary to the taste of these yummy cookies.

MRS. LINCOLN'S CHAMPAGNE PUNCH

With her Bluegrass background, it was natural that Mary Lincoln would be inclined toward the serving of champagne and champagne punch on festive occasions. Several letters record her orders to a New York wine merchant for "a basket of Champagne . . . the choicest quality you have in the store." She was no connoisseur, but she always believed in serving the best. By serving champagne in the White House, she drew the fire of temperance groups. After her most celebrated soirée, the *American Temperance Journal* righteously stated: "With regard to the President, we had at his election, and have to this day, good reason to suppose that he was and is in principle and practice a decided temperance man. We never endorsed for his better half, but . . . we supposed that all was right in the family." One can almost visualize the upturned nose, the superior smile and slight sniff of the writer penning those words. Time to turn to Mary's own very superior champagne punch.

> *Champagne*   *Curaçao*
> *Sauterne*   *Fresh fruit*
> *Soda water*

Chill 3 quarts champagne, 2 quarts sauterne, 3 quart bottles of soda water, and 1 gill (4 ounces) Curaçao. At serving time, place a large chunk of ice in a large punch bowl. Mix the various liquors in another large bowl and pour into the punch bowl. Add fresh strawberries, washed and hulled, raspberries, slices of peaches, or whatever fruit is in season. Just a few pieces or slices adorning the top of the punch make a decorative (and tasty) embellishment. Serve at once. *Makes about 64 4-ounce servings.*

XVII

The Climate of Calumny

Andrew Johnson was not our country's weakest President, but he was surely the unluckiest. In addition to the constant vilification, calumny, and innuendos about his character, integrity, and qualifications for the Presidency, it was widely whispered that he was an alcoholic.

History plays cruel tricks. Franklin Pierce, who really was an alcoholic, mercifully passed quietly (and quickly) into obscurity. But Johnson, who drank only as much as the next man (true, in his time, the next man drank rather deeply), was viciously accused of being constantly inebriated while President.

Like many falsehoods, the belief that Johnson was a habitual drunk grew from a tiny kernel of truth. It started on the day of Lincoln's second inauguration in 1865. Suffering from a chronic gastrointestinal infection that had plagued him for five months, Vice-President-elect Andrew Johnson wasn't sure he could make the ceremony. Faint with cramps and diarrhea, he turned to his doctor for advice. The doctor recommended the classic treatment of the time: a tumblerful of whiskey. Grasping at any hope of relief, Johnson gulped the whiskey down and hurried to the Senate to be sworn into office.

That tumblerful of liquor had greater repercussions than poor Andrew Johnson could possibly have foreseen. During his inaugural speech, he slurred his words, rambled incoherently from topic to topic in a stump-oratory fashion, and babbled on and on about his humble beginnings—to the disgust and embarrassment of his sophisticated Capitol audience, who had the strong impression that the new Vice-President was intoxicated.

In point of fact, he was—just that once. The effect of that one glass of raw, potent whiskey on Johnson's severely weakened constitution was catastrophic. That one day's failing was to haunt him the rest of his life. No one present at the inaugural ceremonies knew what had led to Johnson's behavior. They only knew what they saw and delighted in believing the worst. His political enemies latched on to the incident as a pretext for forcing Johnson to resign as Vice-President. They were later to enlarge the incident into a full-scale attack on his character.

But there were a few people even in his own time who defended him. Several days after the inauguration, President Lincoln himself told an associate: "I have known Andy Johnson for many years; he made a bad slip the other day, but you need not be scared, Andy ain't a drunkard."

After Lincoln's death, when Johnson assumed the Presidency, a few others came to his defense. One of his Cabinet members later wrote: "For six weeks after Johnson became President, he occupied a room adjoining mine. . . . The President was there every morning before nine o'clock and he rarely left it before five. There was no liquor in his room. It was open to everybody. For nearly four years I had daily intercourse with him, frequently at night, and I never saw him under the influence of liquor. I have no hesitation in saying that whatever may have been his faults, intemperance was not among them."

Even a lifetime enemy, Parson Brownlow, said: "I have never failed to publicly denounce Andrew Johnson, but I never charged him with being a drunkard; in fact nobody in Tennessee ever regarded him as addicted to the excessive use of whiskey."

Such testimonials were not enough to combat the relentless whispering campaign against "that drunkard in the White House." And even today the label *alcoholic* clings tenaciously to poor Johnson's ghost.

Andrew Johnson had a rough enough time of it as President, without being called a drunkard. His battles with Congress over Reconstruction policies, the opposition of the Radical Northern Republicans, led by men of great power and prestige, and the cruel canards used against him in the impeachment proceedings would have been enough to send a less stoic man "over the hill."

But stout-hearted, stalwart Andrew Johnson, from the hills of Tennessee, had the courage to ride out the storm of his inherited administration. The impeachment attempt failed—by a single vote—and Johnson returned to Tennessee with his family. Undaunted, he later ran for Senator and won election, but died shortly thereafter, in 1875.

The tempestuousness of Johnson's four years in the White House were on the political seas alone. Socially it was smooth sailing. Although the President's wife was a semi-invalid, she contributed her share to the smooth-running household.

When the Johnsons first moved into the White House, Washington society did not know what to expect. Martha Patterson, Johnson's daughter, announced to one and all that "We are plain people from the mountains of Tennessee. I trust too much will not be expected of us." Although her remark was undoubtedly made in candor (a family characteristic), it had a unique psychological effect. Expecting next to nothing from such "plain people," official Washington was soon abuzz with the graciousness and efficiency with which the Presidential family entertained.

The credit, for the most part, went to Martha, who moved her family in as well, in order to act as official hostess for her father. The First Lady was really too ill to take part in company affairs. But from her bedroom overlooking the mall and the Potomac she kept a lively interest in all that was happening. She amused the grandchildren who popped in, chatted with friends, cheered up her husband on his return from a grueling battle with Congress, and advised her eldest daughter on household problems.

Not that Martha needed much advice. She was a born housekeeper, and soon gave the Presidential establishment a New Look. It needed a lot more than that. While Mary Lincoln had languished upstairs, the public rooms had been vandalized mercilessly by souvenir hunters and passers-by. Tobacco juice stained the rugs, upholstery, and draperies. Snips had been cut out of lace curtains as "relics"; bugs and filth were everywhere. Congress gave grudgingly and inadequately funds to clean and refurnish the White House.

A lesser housekeeper would never have been able to cope with the limited budget available. But frugal Martha, brought up by a tidy, efficient housekeeping mother, managed miracles. New wallpaper adorned the Red, Green, and Blue parlors. Linen slipcovers hid the decrepit furniture. When large receptions were held, Martha had the carpets covered with muslin to protect what remained.

Martha's efficiency went still further. She initiated the establishment of a spotless, immaculately run dairy to keep the White House supplied with the fresh milk and quality butter the Johnson family loved. Two Jersey cows were purchased, and the White House grounds became their paradise, to the delight of all capital inhabitants. One is tempted to take with a grain of salt the breathless report of an admiring journalist of the time who credited Martha with rising at dawn each morning. She would, in his words, quickly "don a calico dress and spotless apron, then descend to skim the milk and attend the dairy before breakfast." It all sounds a bit like contemporary image-building. But considering Martha Johnson Patterson's record, it just might have been true.

The "plain people from the mountains of Tennessee" continued to enjoy in the White House the pleasures that meant something to them back home. They had popcorn parties, in which the President joined heartily. They also roasted apples and chestnuts and enjoyed the conviviality of family get-togethers. Togetherness for them meant a party in itself. Every family meal was a party, for there were twelve of them under one roof, including five grandchildren.

While the President preferred the country cooking of his native Tennessee, he liked it properly prepared. Evidence of the thoroughness and efficiency of his wife and daughter as housekeepers may be seen today, if you visit the Johnson homestead in Greeneville, Tennessee. An attractive ante-bellum brick house, one of its most interesting aspects is its kitchen. The house is virtually intact as the Johnsons left it, and the kitchen is a tribute to the housekeeping skills of the Johnson women. For that period, the kitchen is excellently equipped, with all the utensils and tools necessary for preparing a good hearty meal. Even the sturdy wooden mallet remains, which Mrs. Johnson used to beat her dough the thousand strokes then considered necessary for beaten biscuits. The kitchen would hardly tempt a cook of today, but it does attest to the Johnsonian sense of order.

In spite of all the to-do over their plainness, Johnson and his hostess-daughter managed to entertain creditably. In addition to the usual assortment of dignitaries who ambled through the official receptions and state dinners, President Johnson entertained Queen Emma of the Sandwich Islands (Hawaii) when she visited Washington on a world tour. The President's naturalness and genuine interest in people made him a good host, genial and comfortable.

State dinners during the Johnson administration were held on Tuesday at seven o'clock. Dinner was usually finished by nine, and the guests were then encouraged to retire to the Blue Room for an hour of conversation.

In spite of the brouhaha Johnson found himself in politically, he won high marks for his social abilities. One newspaper of the time said: "The levees of President Johnson are especially brilliant, and frequenters of Washington society declare that under no former occupant of the White House has such good order and system reigned, as under the present." Shades of administrations past! (One is tempted to comment on the short memories of journalists.) It is just possible that the commentator was not without malice, and that the praise of Johnson was an oblique slap at the mismanagement and chaos of Mary Lincoln's days in Washington.

It was later said that Johnson was one of the few Presidents to leave the White House without being close to bankruptcy. While he entertained well and bountifully, his repasts in no way resembled the opulence of the Grant administration that followed.

Johnson, for all his simple, homey ways, had occasion to sample some of the high living that existed in his day. On a visit to New York August 29, 1866, he was feted by civic dignitaries with a modest repast at Delmonico's. The menu for the occasion, luckily, has been preserved:

Potages

Amontillado   Consommé Châtelaine   Bisque aux quenelles

Hors-d'oeuvre

Timbales de gibier à la Vénitienne

Poissons

Hechheimerberg	Saumon Livionienne	Paupiettes de kingfish, Villeroi

Relevés

Champagne	Selle d'agneau aux concombres	Filet de boeuf à la Pocahontas

Entrées

	Suprême de volaille Dauphine
	Ballotines de pigeons Lucullus
Chat. Margaux '48	Filets de canetons Tyrolienne
	Cotelettes à la Maréchale
	Ris de veau Montgomery
	Boudins à la Richelieu
	Sorbet à la Dunderberg

Rots

Clos-Vougeot	Becassines Bardées	Ortolans farcies

Entremets de Legumes

Petits pois à l'Anglaise	Tomates farcies
Aubergines frites	Artchauts Barigoule

Entremets Sucres

Tokai Imperial	Peches à la New York
Abricots Siciliens	
Macedoine de fruits	Moscovites aux oranges
Bavarois aux fraises	Galée Californienne
Crême aux amandes	Meringues Chantilly
Beauséjour au Malaga	Mille feuilles Pompadour
Gâteau soleil	Biscuits glaces aux pistache

Madere Faquart   *Fruits et Desserts*

Pièces Montées

Monument de Washington	Fontaine des Aigles
Temple de la Liberté	Trophée National
Casque Romain	Colonne de l'Union
Char de la Paix	Rontonde Egyptienne
Casolette Sultane	Corne d'Abondance

In case your French bogged down midway through, let us remind you that the dinner wound up with Madeira and *pièces Montées,* among them replicas of the Washington monument, a fountain of eagles, a temple of Liberty, an Egyptian obelisk, a column of the Union, and a horn of plenty.

The illiterate tailor's apprentice, whose wife taught him to read and write, had come a long, long way. From the Tennessee hills to Delmonico's—from log cabin to the White House—it was perhaps more possible in 1865 than a hundred years later.

◊◊

R E C I P E S

HOPPING JOHN

Like another Andrew who had lived in the White House—Jackson—Johnson was born in North Carolina and later moved to Tennessee. Perhaps the two Andrews had more than their first name and birth state in common: they shared a fondness for the Carolina specialty called Hopping John. With black-eyed peas and rice as the base, the recipe for this Southern mainstay varied from kitchen to kitchen. We don't insist, as both Andrews would have, that you serve it New Year's Day for good luck, but it does make a delicious family supper.

Black-eyed peas	*Red pepper (hot)*
Salt pork or bacon	*Water*
Onion	*Salt and pepper*
Rice	*Butter*

Soak 1½ cups dried black-eyed peas overnight. Bring them to a boil slowly in a heavy saucepan. Add 2 or 3 strips bacon, cut in pieces, or ¼ pound chopped salt pork, and 1 sliced onion. Boil gently for 1½ hours. Then add 1 cup uncooked rice, 2 slices hot red pepper (add more if you want the flavor hot-hot), and simmer another 30 minutes. Add additional water if necessary. Season with salt and pepper to taste. Serve hot with butter and strips of broiled bacon decorating the top. *Serves* 60.

PILAU, PERLOO, PILAF, OR WHAT-YOU-WILL

Whatever you choose to call it, *pilau, pilaf, perloo,* or *perlowe,* this mixture of rice cooked with chicken, shrimp, or other ingredients has been a Southern favorite ever since the introduction of rice to the region. The word probably stems from Turkey, Persia, or points East, but it was known as early as 1612 in England. Several variations follow, all equally familiar to pilau-partial President Johnson.

CHICKEN PILAU

The Carolinians of Andrew Johnson's day called this "French pilau."

Chicken	*Raisins*
Bacon	*Almonds*
Butter	*Curry powder (or saffron)*
Salt and pepper	*Rice*
Onions	

Place 1 large fryer in a large heavy skillet with 2 or 3 slices of chopped bacon or ¼ cup butter. Brown lightly. Then cover with boiling water and season heavily with salt and pepper. Cover and cook slowly until the chicken is tender. At that point, add 2 medium onions, chopped, ½ cup raisins, ½ cup slivered almonds, and 1 tablespoon curry powder (less if the curry is authentically hot Indian curry powder). Add 2 cups rice. If the water has cooked away, add 4 cups more (or 2 cups water, 2 cups chicken stock or consommé). Cover and continue cooking until rice is done fairly dry. Pilau is better on the dry side. *Serves 4.*

NOTE: Shrimp or pork may be used instead of chicken.

OKRA PILAU

Somehow or another slaves carried okra seeds with them from their homeland and invented or remembered this variation of pilau.

Okra	*Onion*
Bacon fat	*Rice*
Green pepper	*Tomatoes, canned*

Sauté 2 cups thin sliced okra in bacon fat until lightly browned and quite dry. Add chopped green pepper and chopped onion and sauté them as well. If more fat is needed, add an extra piece of bacon while the onions and peppers are browning. Then add rinsed rice—the same amount as okra—and double the quantity of cold water. (Example: 2 cups rice to 4 cups water.) Simmer, covered, until rice is tender. The secret is to have the rice turn out dry, not mushy. Near the end of the cooking, add 2 cups drained canned tomatoes and mix well with all other ingredients. Serve with strips of crisp bacon on top. *Serves 6.*

CHICKEN BOG

This Carolina and Georgia favorite is as popular today as in Andy Johnson's time. In the country, it is usually prepared for a large gathering, with the huge kettles full of rice and chicken perking away at daybreak. A one-dish meal, it adds up to something extra-special with the addition of a crisp tossed salad, a green vegetable, and hot rolls or bread.

Stewing hen	*Salt and pepper*
Rice	*Butter*

Cut a large fat hen into frying-sized pieces, but do not fry it. Instead, put in a large pot with enough water to cover (use stock if you prefer, or half and half). Add 3½ cups rice and salt and pepper to taste. Simmer until it comes to a boil. Then add ½ cup butter or margarine. Cook over low heat 30 to 40 minutes, until the rice is thoroughly done. You may stir now and then with a fork. Serve piping hot. *Serves 8.*

RED RICE

In spite of exposure to some of the fanciest foods of his day, Andy Johnson preferred the simple farm food of his early life, such plain "vittles" as this rice dish.

Bacon	*Tomatoes, canned*
Onions	*Tomato paste*
Garlic	*Rice*

Fry lightly 6 strips bacon until lightly crisped. Set aside. Use the bacon fat to sauté 2 sliced onions and 1 clove minced garlic. Slowly add 1 large can of tomatoes, with the juice. Stir well, then add 1 can tomato paste. Simmer 5 to 8 minutes over low heat, then sprinkle in 1 cup rice and the 6 slices cooked bacon. Cover skillet and steam until the rice is tender. (If the rice is not fully covered by the tomato liquid when you first begin steaming it, add just enough boiling water to cover.) You may want to use this dish as accompaniment for a meat or chicken dish at a company dinner. In Johnson's day, red rice was a meal in itself for humble folk. *Serves 6.*

ROASTED CANVASBACK DUCK

Legend has it that President Johnson once refused an invitation to a dinner of canvasback duck with the leader of his political party in order to fulfill a previously made engagement. The engagement? Dinner of bacon and cabbage with his washerwoman. A cynic might draw many conclusions, but the truth is that Johnson truly loved canvasback duck. The story, if true, says much about his fortitude and character. (Or is it merely a comment on the then-leader of his party?)

Breadcrumbs, soft	*Canvasback ducks*
Celery	*Salt and pepper*
Onions	*Bacon*
Raisins	*Worcestershire sauce*
Pecans	*Ketchup*
Salt	*Honey*
Scalded milk	*Chili sauce*
Eggs	*Parsley or watercress*

Prepare a pecan stuffing: Mix together 4 cups soft breadcrumbs, 1 cup each chopped celery, onions, raisins, and pecan meats. Add ½ teaspoon salt and toss well. Scald ½ cup milk and add it to 2 well-beaten eggs. Stir into the dry mixture and mix thoroughly. Dress 3 canvasback ducks (about 2½ pounds each), and rub a mixture of salt and pepper inside. Fill lightly with the pecan stuffing. Lace the birds with thread or skewer them tight. Place breast-down in an open roasting pan. Place 3 strips raw bacon on each duck. Roast in a moderate (350° F.) oven, allowing 20 minutes per pound. About 25 minutes before the ducks are ready to serve, turn them over, pour the fat from the pan, and baste with a sauce made of: ¼ cup Worcestershire sauce, 1 cup ketchup, ¼ cup honey, and ½ cup chili sauce, mixed well. Ducks should get a nice gloss. Garnish with parsley or watercress and serve hot. Serve sauce with ducks. *Serves 5 to 6.*

WILD TURKEY WITH CHESTNUT DRESSING

Fond as he was of canvasback duck, Andrew Johnson was also very partial to wild turkey. It was no feat to catch a wild one in his day; the hills and forests of Johnson's Tennessee were full of them. We consider it cricket today to use the usual domestic supermarket type bird. But if you *are* fortunate enough to have a wild one, you'll find the taste considerably different.

Turkey	*Salt and pepper*
Chestnuts	*Marjoram or savory (optional)*
Breadcrumbs	*Bacon*
Butter	

(If you do have a wild turkey, do not freeze it before using. Freezing destroys the flavor of a wild bird.) Clean and prepare bird as usual. To stuff: boil shelled chestnuts until mealy, then mash fine. Mix equal portions fine breadcrumbs and chestnuts with enough butter to moisten lightly and salt and pepper to taste. You may also add a pinch of marjoram or savory. Mix lightly but well. Stuff the turkey. Lard the bird with salted butter or margarine and put aluminum foil over it, covering well. Half an hour before serving, when bird is tender, remove foil and let the turkey brown. You may put several strips of bacon over the top before starting to brown the bird. Serve hot with sweet potatoes or wild rice.

PLANKED POTOMAC SHAD WITH SAUCE PIQUANTE

After the Civil War, the Harvey brothers came to culinary fame. It was at their restaurant in Washington that members of the Canvas-back Club ate their fill of that delicious duck. When the ducks were in short supply, the Canvas-backers, including Andrew Johnson, found pleasure in the way the Harveys treated the local river shad. The Harveys didn't invent planking—the Indians beat them to that—but they added a sauce that makes shad even more delicious than usual.

Shad	*Brown gravy*
Butter	*Onion*
Salt	*Green pepper*
Thyme	*Capers*
Nutmeg	*Cayenne*
Pepper	*Lemon juice*

Oil a good wooden plank somewhat larger than the whole shad. Place the plank in a cold oven and then bring the temperature up to 400° F. You may stuff the shad, but when served with a piquant sauce it does not need stuffing. Put the fish on the board and reduce oven heat to 375° F. Bake the shad, allowing 10 to 15 minutes per pound. Baste frequently with salted butter mixed with thyme and a dash of nutmeg and pepper. When ready to serve, pour hot sauce piquante over the fish. Serve hot. (You may, if you prefer, serve the sauce separately.)

To make the sauce: a short cut that makes very good sauce is to use canned brown gravy. Heat 1 can (approx. 10½ ounces), blending it with 1 tablespoon chopped onion, 1 tablespoon chopped green pepper, 1 tablespoon drained capers or chopped sour pickles, a pinch of cayenne, and 1 tablespoon lemon juice. Serve hot.

PINE BARK STEW

This Carolina favorite was a Johnson standby. The rivers of Tennessee were full of the fresh fish the Southern President liked so well.

Bacon	*Worcestershire sauce*
Onions	*Water*
Flat fish	*Ketchup*
Butter	

Chop 1 pound bacon into small pieces; brown in a skillet with 3 chopped onions. Set aside. Put a layer of flat fish (you will need 2 dozen in all) on the bottom of a deep pot. Then put a layer of the browned bacon and onions on top of the fish. Dot with butter. Repeat the layers until all the fish (and ½ pound butter) are used. Over the top pour 1 teaspoon Worcestershire sauce, 1 cup water, and 1 small bottle ketchup. Cover and cook until fish are tender, testing from time to time. A simple but delicious supper served with rice, salad, and homemade bread. *Serves 12.*

PAN FISH TENNESSEE STYLE

Pan fish, by Andrew Johnson's definition, could be any of the tasty fresh fish caught in the leaping waters of his adopted state—rainbow trout, walleyes, drumfish, mountain bass, crappy.

Fish	*Lard*
Cornmeal or oatmeal	*Lemon*

An old White House cookbook suggests rolling the fresh fish in meal (oat or corn). Then, after melting a little lard in a heavy skillet, place the fish, cleaned but with heads left on, in the pan, all facing the same way. Brown over a medium fire. When ready to turn, put a large plate over the pan, drain off the lard, then invert the pan, and presto, the fish land unbroken on the plate. Return the lard to the pan, heat it again, then slip the fish back. When the second side browns, try the plate trick again, slipping the fish onto a warm platter. Leave the heads of the fish on for appearance' sake, garnish with lemon slices, and serve hot and crisp. Delicious with hot biscuits and salad.

CATFISH

As common as cotton throughout the South, any youngster can catch a batch of catfish at the old water hole. Andrew Johnson, like most any Southern boy, probably never counted all he caught in his lifetime. The simpler they are prepared, the tastier they are.

Catfish	*Egg*
Salt	*Breadcrumbs*
Cayenne	*Lard*
Flour	

You cut each fish in two pieces, down the back and stomach. Remove the upper part of the backbone. Wash and drain well. Season with salt and cayenne (sparingly applied). Dredge flour over them or dip them in a beaten egg and then into fine breadcrumbs. Fry them in hot lard in a heavy skillet. They are also delicious dipped into beaten egg, *sans* crumbs or flour, and fried. Remove from the pan when the fish are browned crisp.

✓ CATFISH STEW (MODERNIZED)

This dish is best reserved for a cookout or camping trip.

Catfish	*Sugar*
Bacon	*Salt and pepper*
Tomato soup	*Onion*

Clean and bone an 8-to-10-pound catfish. Set aside. Fry ½ pound bacon in the bottom of a large iron kettle. Add the catfish, 1 can tomato soup, a dash of sugar, salt and pepper to taste, and 1 cup chopped onion. (The catfish can be cut into chunks, taking care to keep the chunks fairly good size.) Cover with 1 can water. Simmer over low heat for 20 to 30 minutes. If there is danger of the stew drying up, keep adding water, a little at a time. Serve when the fish is tender to the fork. *Serves 12.*

GUINEA SQUASH

Known long before the Civil War as guinea squash, eggplant is thought to be one of the vegetables brought to America by slaves from the Guinea coast of Africa. It was popular throughout the South, whether as guinea squash or mad apple, as it was also called to distinguish it from its cousin, the tomato or love apple. You might like to try it in a way familiar in Andrew Johnson's day.

Eggplant	*Pepper*
Breadcrumbs	*Nutmeg*
Salt	*Butter*

Boil a large eggplant until the skin becomes loose and easily removable. Cut its meat into pieces about the size of oysters. Set aside. Arrange a buttered baking dish with a layer of fine breadcrumbs, a sprinkling of salt, pepper, and nutmeg, and dot with butter. Add a layer of eggplant. Repeat the procedure until the baking dish is full, finishing off with a layer of breadcrumbs topped with butter. Pour a little water into the baking dish with care. Bake in a medium (350° F.) oven until tender and brown on top. Serve hot, as accompaniment to a meat, fish, or poultry dish, or as the mainstay of a Sunday-night supper, with salad and hot rolls. *Serves 4 to 6.*

SWEET POTATOES: AS YOU LIKE THEM

It is a tribute to Southern culinary skills that the lowly sweet potato, familiar to every sharecropper in Dixie, should be the object of such diversity. In the imaginative hands of Southern cooks, the sweet potato has been turned into delicious side courses accompanying roast ham, tasty puddings and pies, and bread dough. As a poor Southern boy who helped his widowed mother support the family, Andrew Johnson was no stranger to the resourcefulness of this humble vegetable. A few examples of this Johnsonian favorite follow.

SWEET POTATO PONE

Sweet potato	*Milk*
Butter	*Powdered ginger*
Sugar	*Orange peel*

Grate sweet potatoes until you have 4 cups. Mix well with ¾ pound butter and ¾ pound sugar. Slowly add ½ pint milk, 1 tablespoon powdered ginger, and the grated rind of 1 large orange. Mix together well and spread in a shallow pan. Bake in a slow (300° F.) oven about 1 hour. As a variation, you may dribble a little molasses over the top before baking. Serve hot as accompaniment to baked ham or fried chicken. *Serves 8.*

APPLE-STUFFED SWEET POTATOES, PIONEER STYLE

Sweet potatoes or yams	*Milk*
Apples	*Salt and pepper*
Cream	*Egg*
Butter	

If you can use yams for this recipe, it would be better; they generally are rounder in shape than the sweets. Scrub them well—using 6 medium-size ones—and bake in a medium (325° F.) oven 45 minutes. Remove them from the oven, cool, cut in half, and scoop the insides out, shaping the remaining skin round like a cup. Mash the insides with 3 boiled, chopped tart apples, 2½ teaspoons cream, 1½ tablespoons butter, and enough milk to mix well (just a dash). Sprinkle with salt and pepper and stuff the 6 potato skins with the mixture. Beat 1 egg yolk with 2 tablespoons butter and spread on top of the potatoes. Brown in a hot oven or under broiler.

SWEET POTATO PIE

Pastry	*Eggs*
Mashed sweet potatoes or yams	*Milk*
Brown sugar	*Butter*
Salt	*Pecans*
Cinnamon	

Prepare pastry your usual way. Line an 8-inch pie dish, and keep it chilled in the refrigerator while you prepare the filling. Mix 1½ cups mashed sweet potatoes (or yams, for a richer pie) with ½ cup tightly packed brown sugar, ½ teaspoon salt, and ¼ teaspoon cinnamon. Set aside while you beat together 2 eggs with ¾ cup milk and 1 tablespoon melted butter. Stir this slowly into the sweet-potato mixture. Mix well and pour into the pie shell. For extra effect, arrange pecan halves around the edge of the pie, next to the outer crust. Bake in a preheated hot (400° F.) oven about 45 minutes, or until a knife comes out dry when inserted into the center of the pie. Serve warm or cool, as is or with whipped cream on top. From such humble beginnings, you have a mighty fancy dessert!

ELIZA JOHNSON'S SWEET POTATO PUDDING

Besides teaching her husband to read and write and encouraging him in his political career, Eliza Johnson proved herself a capable homemaker and a splendid cook. She knew how to make do in the hard days before her Andy became President. For a make-do recipe, this is a delicious dessert.

Butter	*Cloves*
Sweet potatoes	*Nutmeats*
Sugar	*Cane syrup or molasses*
Raisins	*Eggs*
Allspice and cinnamon	

To be authentic, you must bake this pudding slowly in a heavy iron skillet. First, melt ½ cup butter. Set aside. Mix 4 cups grated raw sweet potatoes with ½ cup sugar, 1 cup raisins, 1 teaspoon each cinnamon and allspice, ½ teaspoon cloves, ½ cup chopped nuts, and 1 cup cane syrup or molasses. Add 3 eggs and mix all together well. Pour into the hot skillet with the butter in it, and stir until all the mixture is heated. Put the skillet into a moderate (325° F.) oven. When a crust forms around the edge and the top, turn the pudding under, allowing crust to form again. Repeat this after a while. Pudding takes about 30 to 40 minutes to bake. The iron skillet is an important ingredient in making this pudding authentic, as it causes the pudding to be dark in color, similar to a plum pudding. Traditionally, the pudding is served with Damson preserves accompanying it. Otherwise plain cream is used. No Southerner worth his salt (or sweet potato) would top the pudding with whipped cream. But as Northern outsiders, we find it equally delicious all three ways. *Serves 8.*

LEMON SORBET À LA BÉNÉDICTINE

A far cry from the simplicity of Eliza Johnson's sweet potato puddings and pies was the elegant sorbets served at the White House when the Johnsons entertained. Light, elegant, refreshing, the sorbet is a perfect punctuation mark to a rich and elaborate dinner. This version of a lemon ice was traditionally made with an Italian meringue, adapted in America to the old-fashioned boiled frosting. Making it was an endless (but never thankless) task. Fortunately, one of the joys of modernity is the fact that a truly special recipe such as this can now be made in a vastly simplified (but still authentically delectable) version. The trick involves freezing the lemon with crushed ice in an electric blender. Further modernization involves using a frozen lemonade concentrate. (For interesting variations, frozen concentrated limeade or orange juice or even bottled cranberry juice could be used.)

Unflavored gelatin	*Crushed ice*
Hot water	*Egg whites*
Frozen concentrated lemonade	*Sugar*

Put 1 envelope plain unflavored gelatin into an electric blender. Add ¼ cup hot water and blend at high speed for 40 seconds. Add 1 can (6 oz.) frozen concentrated lemonade mix that has partially thawed, 2 heaping cups finely crushed ice, 2 egg whites, and 4 to 5 tablespoons sugar. Cover and blend at high speed for 1 minute, or until the sorbet has the consistency of fine snow. Serve immediately in chilled glasses, or, if you prefer, place in trays or molds and keep in the freezer until needed. At serving time, a bottle of Bénédictine may be passed around, and guests may spoon as much or as little into their sorbet as desired. *Serves 6.*

ELDERBERRY BLOSSOM TEA

Admired in his home state for his stubborn integrity and honesty, Andrew Johnson did not think it proper to accept gifts of any real value during his term as

President. He made one exception, because of a gift he found irresistible: a silver, brass, and porcelain facsimile of a railroad locomotive and tender. The boiler received tea or coffee and discharged it through a spigot. The miniature steam whistle signaled when the beverage was ready to be served. The tender carried sugar, glasses, and a container for cognac. In addition, there were racks for cigars and a music box that played eight popular tunes. Who *could* have resisted such a treasure?

It is likely that the Johnsons experimented with this nineteenth-century wonder when making their favorite mountain tea, the refreshing and medicinal elderberry blossom tea. In Johnson's Tennessee, elderberry blossoms were gathered in the Roan Mountains in the northeast section of the state. They were widely valued for their delicate flavor as well as their medical properties. It was the common view that the blossoms acted as blood purifier and protector against colds.

Brewed in hot water like any other tea, elderberry blossom tea was generally served with a touch of honey or sugar added.

XVIII

Taking the White House for Grant(ed)

The inauguration of General Ulysses Simpson Grant in 1869 did more than usher into the Presidency an honored war hero. It launched an era of opulence the like of which the United States had not seen before and has seldom seen since.

There is irony in the fact that U. S. Grant, the simplest of men, should have had an administration renowned for its gaudy, lavish display of all the material vanities of the age. One might, without intending to pass too severe a judgment on the Grants, say that the epoch of the *nouveau riche* was upon us.

Grant, the unpretentious son of an impecunious Ohio farmer, and his plain, homely wife Julia were uncomplicated folk, vaulted by destiny into the highest position in the land. Their very simplicity, friendliness and faith in people caused them to be used rather heartlessly by various types of scoundrels. Politically, Grant suffered from his naïveté in appraising his subordinates and appointees. Socially, the Grants were used by every social climber in Washington.

And by 1869, the capital was aflood with such climbers. The new postwar wealth in the North brought forth a new breed of American. Seemingly with money to burn, he could afford the most ostentatious of parties, could court all the social lions in sight, and was constantly on the make to consolidate his newfound wealth and power.

The new President and his wife, being inexperienced, were catapulted from the humdrum routine of years of dreary army existence into a world they had never known. It is little wonder they embraced it and all who traveled in it with open, trusting arms.

A contemporary commentator noted that at one of President Grant's traditional New Year's Day receptions (1873) the guests present were a diverse crew:

> Nice people, questionable people and people who were not nice at all; every state, every age, every social class, both sexes and all human colors were represented. There were wealthy bankers, and a poor, blind, black beggar led by a boy; men in broadcloth and in homespun; men with beards and men without beards. Members of the press and of the lobby; contractors and claim agents; office holders and office seekers; there were ladies from Paris in elegant attire and ladies from the interior in calico; ladies whose cheeks were tinged with rouge and others whose faces were weather-bronzed by outdoor work; ladies as lovely as Eve, and others as naughty as Mary Magdalene; ladies in diamonds, and others in dollar jewelry; chambermaids elbowed countesses, and all enjoyed themselves.

American democracy at work (or play)!

When Ulysses Grant became President, he was only forty-seven years old. A devoted family man, he brought with him to the White House his wife and three sons—Fred, Ulysses, Jr., and Jesse—and a lovely daughter Nellie, as well as his cantankerous father-in-law, Colonel Frederick Dent. A man of simple tastes, President Grant perhaps thought his years in the White House would be a mere continuation of the previous years. On a slightly enlarged scale to be sure, but essentially the same.

If so, the President reckoned without the social instincts of his Southern-born wife. Julia Dent Grant was a good-hearted, motherly woman with great love of her family and a friendliness to strangers and friends alike. But from this distance, one also recognizes in her certain similarities to Mary Lincoln.

Both women shared a Southern–Midwestern heritage. Both came of slave-holding families. On being catapulted into the highest feminine position in the country, both seemed concerned that others might not deem them worthy of the role. Julia, as Mary before her, was determined to show Eastern society that she too was able to set a proper table, throw a dazzlingly triumphant party, and dress with splendor and style. Perhaps because the times were different, with the country at peace and growing signs of prosperity everywhere (except the South), and also because of certain personality differences, Julia's efforts met with success, where poor Mary Lincoln's were doomed to failure. Comparisons are never exact; Julia Grant did not have the tragic history that Mary coped with—or the personality disturbances that clouded much of Mrs. Lincoln's later life.

As soon as the Grants moved into the White House, the new President brought with him as cook a quartermaster from his army days. Julia refrained from comment at first, but it soon became obvious that the "chef" considered the White House dining room simply an enlarged mess hall, with quantity the chief ingredient to be considered. To him turkey represented the *sine que non* of any dinner. He planned turkey for a formal dinner, and varied the menu for a state dinner by having a bigger turkey.

Finally, Julia's patience reached the bursting point. The time had come to talk turkey. "Don't you think," she asked him at last," that we might have a change of menu? Something a little more fancy perhaps?" "Madam," was the cook's reply, in slightly injured tones, "we are living at the absolute pinnacle now."

It wasn't long before Julia found a replacement. She hired an Italian steward, named Melah, who had catered for some of the nation's most fashionable hotels. From the moment Melah entered the White House the cuisine changed radically. Turkey fled. In its place Melah offered a twenty-five-course dinner, often consisting of partridge, filet of beef, and myriad other elaborate concoctions of the era. Melah's special talent was for opulent banquets. He persuaded Mrs. Grant to try to limit such affairs to thirty-six guests, the maximum limit for really first-rate food and service.

Culinarily speaking, Julia Grant was a creampuff in Melah's hands. She literally turned the planning and execution of official entertainments over to his capable management. Melah preferred large and formal dinners to be served at a horseshoe-shaped table. And so they were. Melah was a wine connoisseur; consequently, the wines accompanying White House dinners were exemplary.

There were a few occasions during the Grants' eight years in the White House that must have tried the volatile Melah's nerves. One was the splendid dinner prepared for King Kalakaua of the Sandwich Islands (later known as Hawaii) on December 22, 1874. For all of Melah's intricate and expensive preparations, the King would eat only such dishes as his chief cupbearer deemed fit to serve him. Throughout the dinner, the cupbearer and two other personal attendants stood beside the King's chair, ever watchful. The King's fear of poisoning must have nettled the sensitive Melah.

President Grant's second inauguration was another trial for Melah. The first inaugural ball had been ruined by the treacherously cold weather. Alas, the second, in spite of Melah's fancy preparations, was to suffer the same fate. The weather March 4, 1873, was icy cold, with a bitter wind tearing the flags and decorations off the buildings. The building in which the Ball was held lacked heat. The ladies were forced to wear their coats to dance in, thus wasting thousands of dollars of finery purchased just for the inaugural event. In spite of vigorous efforts to keep warm by dancing, the inaugural guests were so chilled that they ignored Melah's elaborately prepared supper (ice-cold by then), his ornate ice-cream concoctions (frozen stiff by then), his carefully selected champagne and punch, and instead concentrated on gulping down as much hot coffee and hot chocolate as they could consume. Once the supply was exhausted, the guests fled a-trembling, long before midnight.

Such mishaps were relatively minor, compared to the general imperial level of White House entertainments. Like her predecessor Mary Lincoln, Julia Grant seemed to have little regard for economy. Foreign princes were entertained as lavishly as if they were in the court of an Eastern Maharajah. Prince Arthur of Great Britain, third son of Queen Victoria, was feted with a dinner that was reputed to have cost $2000. The average cost seems to have been between $700 to $1500, whopping big figures for that time. These sums did not include beverages. Considering Melah's decisiveness about serving only the finest wines, the costs snowballed easily. One wine bill listed $1800 for the champagne alone. There were generally six wines served during the course of the average official dinner.

Perhaps President Grant, who did not like to deny his beloved Julia anything that gave her pleasure, occasionally felt the need to economize. Such a moment might have occurred around New Year's, 1873, when a Presidential directive stated that the policemen and attendants at the New Year's reception, who customarily were invited to have something to eat and drink, were to have refreshments as usual—with one exception. Coffee was to be substituted for liquor.

Such moments of frugality were few. To visualize the grandeur of Presidential entertaining, one has only to read the menu for the President's own birthday dinner.

Clams

Haute Sauterne

Potages

Consommé Impératrice   Bisque de Crabes

Amontillado

Hors-D'Oeuvres Variés

Bouchées à la Regence

Poisson

Truites de rivière Hollandaise vert pré

Pommes de terre à la Parisienne

Concombres

Johannisberger

Relevé

Filet de Boeuf à la Bernardi

Ernest Jeroy

Entrées

Ailes de Poulets à la Périgord

Petits Pois au Beurre

Caisses de ris de Veau à l'Italienne

Haricots verts   Asperges, sauce Crème

Sorbet Fantaisie

Roti

Squabs   Salade de Laitue

Nuits

Entremets Sucres

Croute aux Mille Fruits   Cornets à la Chantilly

Gelée à la Prunelle

Pièces Montées

Glace Varietées

Fruits   Petits Fours   Café

Actually, by Melahian standards, such a dinner was rather sparse. On certain occasions there were thirty courses, requiring two or three hours of eating time. However long the guests might linger over their twenty-five or thirty courses, their post-prandial conversation in the Red Room or the Blue Room, to which they retired, must hold world records for brevity. After fifteen or twenty minutes had been ticked off on the large gilt clock on the mantle, President Grant would signal that the evening was at an end.

At private, quiet family dinners, Melah's fine Italian hand was barely discernible. Here the simple tastes of the old soldier held sway. The president adhered to a military punctuality at mealtime. As a holdover from the disciplines of army life, President Grant arose at seven each morning, read his newspapers, and waited until the rest of the household arose to have breakfast sharply at eight-thirty. Official duties began at 10 A.M. and ended fairly punctually at three. Dinner *en famille* was served at five sharp, and woe to any of the children who dashed in late. (The President was more tolerant of non-family members, and once waited an hour and a half at a state dinner for a tardy Senator to appear.)

The Grants made themselves very much at home in the White House and gave it a cosiness—despite the pomposity of the formal dinners—rarely seen in that mansion. Mealtimes with the family were especially happy occasions. Julia Grant, accustomed to unexpected guests appearing just as the family was about to begin dinner, had a standing order for six extra places to be set at all times—just in case.

But when the Grants were truly alone, the President loved to frolic with his children, and the dinner hour often became play time (to the dismay, no doubt, of any proper Victorian who might have observed it). It was the President's habit to roll his bread into tiny balls and shoot the balls as ammunition at Nellie and Jesse. This teasing became such a standard part of the family meal that much later it was noted "eyebrows went up when he was observed doing it also at Lady Thornton's table." Habit dies hard!

In spite of the Presidential exposure to concoctions he had never known existed in his youthful days in Ohio and Illinois, Grant retained a fondness for plain cooking. His paunch to the contrary, the President was not a heavy eater.

The one large meal that President Grant indulged in was breakfast. Leaner, more Spartan days, when breakfast consisted of cucumbers and coffee, may have been responsible for his insistence on a hearty morning meal. A favorite breakfast consisted of broiled Spanish mackerel, steak, bacon and fried apples, flannel cakes or buckwheat cakes, and a cup of strong black coffee—plain fare but bounteous.

At other meals, the President showed partiality for roast beef, wheat (or wheaten) bread, and boiled hominy. His fondness for simple rice pudding was almost a mania.

At the risk of being *déclassé,* President Grant insisted his meat had to be well-cooked. Early experience working in his father's tannery may have been responsible for his lifelong aversion to rare meat. His phobia about blood was so acute that he liked his steaks burned "practically to charcoal." For a military man, Grant appears to have been extraordinarily sensitive. At one point during the Civil War, he slept outside in the dampness rather than sleep in the hospital quarters where the sights and sounds of painful surgery would have been unbearable to him.

Socially, Ulysses Grant proved to be very much his own man as President. He refused to be tied down by rules of etiquette that had hampered other Presidents. For one thing, he returned calls when it suited him. And he frequently dined outside the White House as the spirit moved him. Even after eight years he found many of the social conventions depressing to him. Late in his second term, after dancing as a duty with one of the ladies present, he confided to a friend how onerous such "duties" were. "I'd rather storm a fort!" he blustered.

Julia, on the other hand, adapted very easily to the duties expected of a First Lady. Plump, cross-eyed, and plain as she was, she seems to have won much of Washington with her friendly, hospitable manner and her genuineness. Used and abused by snobs as they may have been, the Grants were no snobs themselves. They made visitors feel that the Executive Mansion was open to all.

It literally was. Mrs. Grant held an afternoon reception each week, between the hours of 2 and 5 P.M. The public was invited en masse, the only rule being that guests leave their calling cards at the door. The Presidential levees, also open to the public, were held frequently in the evenings between eight and ten. To be certain that the public knew it was invited, there would usually be an announcement in the newspaper.

The age of the society reporter was coming. With the opulence of the entertainments, both in Washington and New York, newspaper columnists had a field day. One reads the old newspapers for details of the various extravaganzas and is struck by the repetition of such classic phrases as "the most brilliant affair of the season," "our most popular Presidential couple," "the most gala party." It all sounds resoundingly familiar.

From all reports, though, one could not quarrel with the comments on Nellie Grant's wedding. There probably never has been anything like it in the White House—before or since.

President Grant did not approve his daughter's choice (his intuitions about the young man's instability much later proved to be right, but that's another story), but Nellie had her heart set on marrying the man she had met on a steamer returning from abroad. His name—Algernon Charles Frederick Sartoris—was romantic enough itself to appeal to a young girl like Nellie. In addition, he was English, charming, the nephew of the famous Fanny Kemble, and far more worldly than the President's only daughter.

Naturally the President wanted the best for Nellie, and it did not require much persuading to convince him that a wedding befitting a President's daughter must be a fairly sumptuous affair. The result makes *sumptuous* seem an understatement. There had not been a wedding in the White House in thirty years. Considering the burden of preparations that fell to the staff, there were probably a few disgruntled souls who hoped the next wedding would be at least another thirty years away.

The White house was a veritable fairyland for the occasion. Julia had a habit of turning the dining rooms into virtual greenhouses for the official dinners, but she outdid even her own elaborate floral arrangements for her daughter's wedding. Chandeliers were festooned with cords of fresh roses. Potted plants and flowers engulfed every inch of free space.

After the ceremony on May 21, 1874, the Grants and the newly married Sartorises led the way into the State Dining Room, followed by a distinguished assembly of guests, members of the diplomatic corps in their magnificent uniforms and orders, the President's Cabinet officers, Justices of the Supreme Court, important representatives of the army and navy, and other prominent personalities of the day.

The wedding breakfast probably provided more copy for the budding corps of society journalists than any other event of that event-studded era. High points of the occasion seem to have been the soft-shelled crabs on toast, chicken croquettes with fresh peas, aspic of beef tongue, woodcock and snipe on toast, decorated broiled spring chicken, and fresh strawberries with cream for dessert, as well as Charlotte Russe, Nesselrode pudding, and blancmange.

In addition, of course, there was the wedding cake, imaginatively embellished with doves, roses, and wedding bells. "From the pyramid of the pearly-white, flower-crowned bridal cake extended a decoration of natural flowers," one reporter described Melah's masterpiece. Of course there were myriad small fancy cakes, ices, ice cream, punch, coffee, and chocolate as well. Sweets were not exactly overlooked.

Each guest carried away, as a memento of the historic occasion, a small box tied with a white ribbon, with a small piece of the wedding cake inside. An additional memento was the white satin menu, listing the many courses, which each guest received.

Such mementos cost the Grants dearly, a fact they seemed unaware of in their eight-year-long euphoric state. Only later, after severe business failures in private life, did the ex-President realize the price he had paid for the elaborate partying of his eight years in office. Forced to write his memoirs as he lay dying of cancer in order to provide some security for his family, Ulysses Grant may have wondered if his lavish, open-handed entertaining, much of it for friends who later played him false, was worthwhile. Basically pragmatic, he probably did not indulge himself in too much idle speculation about the past.

As for the good-natured, outgoing Julia, one suspects she loved every minute of the eight years and would willingly have tried for an additional four. But the country at the time was not geared for third terms or for taking Grants for granted.

◇◇

R E C I P E S

BROILED MACKEREL, SPANISH OR OTHERWISE

Midwestern-born Ulysses Grant discovered at some time in his life the joys of having fish for breakfast—something every Southerner or Englishman could have told him. Whether or not you succumb to this delightful custom, we think you will find the following treatment worthy of consideration sometime during the day.

Fresh mackerel	*Lemon*
Melted butter or olive oil	*Parsley*
Paprika	

Split and bone a mackerel and put it skin side down in a shallow greased baking pan. Brush it lightly with melted butter, margarine, or olive oil. Sprinkle paprika over it. Then put it under the broiler for 15 or 20 minutes, or until tender. If it seems dry, baste occasionally with the pan drippings. Do not turn it over. Serve hot, garnished with lemon wedges and parsley. For an extra fillip, try serving it with anchovy butter.

To make anchovy butter:

Butter	*Onion juice*
Anchovy paste	*Cayenne*
Lemon juice	

Cream ¼ cup butter until soft. Then beat in 1 teaspoon anchovy paste, along with ¼ teaspoon lemon juice, ⅛ teaspoon onion juice, and a dash of cayenne. When well mixed, spread it on top of very hot broiled mackerel—or any broiled fish. It is also delicious spread on steak.

FRIED APPLES WITH BACON

As long as breakfast was hearty, it pleased President Grant. But usually, whether he had steak, broiled fish, or a good healthy slab of country bacon, he had a side dish of fried apples, a perennial favorite of his, year in, year out. The apples are especially good accessories for bacon.

Apples	*Lemon juice*
Flour	*Butter (optional)*
Sugar (powdered)	*Bacon*
Egg yolks	*Cinnamon*

Peel, core, and slice 8 medium-large firm, tart apples. Make a batter of ½ cup flour, ½ cup powdered sugar, and 3 beaten egg yolks. Squeeze the juice of ½ lemon and add it to the batter. Dip the apple slices, which should be about ½ inch thick to keep their shape in cooking, and then dust them lightly with flour. Fry the apple rings in a skillet in hot melted butter until browned lightly. (If you prefer, you may fry the bacon first, set aside, and then fry the apples in the bacon drippings.) In a separate skillet fry 1 pound bacon. When serving, pile the bacon in the center of a large platter and surround the bacon slices with apple rings sprinkled with cinnamon. *Serves 8.*

PRESIDENTIAL BUCKWHEAT CAKES

No wonder General Grant liked these buckwheats. The batter is so light it makes a heap o' cakes and keeps several days, if covered well and kept in the refrigerator.

Flour (all-purpose)	*Sugar or molasses*
Salt	*Buckwheat flour*
Baking powder	*Buttermilk or sour milk*
Baking soda	*Melted shortening*

Sift ½ cup regular flour ahead of time. Then sift it again with ½ teaspoon salt, ½ teaspoon baking powder, 1 teaspoon baking soda, and 2 teaspoons sugar. (Molasses may be substituted for the sugar—if so, add the molasses to the milk instead of to the dry ingredients.) Mix the sifted ingredients together thoroughly.

Then add 1½ cups buckwheat flour. Set aside. Mix 3¼ cups buttermilk or sour milk with 2 tablespoons melted butter or other shortening. Slowly add the dry ingredients and beat the batter just enough to blend it well. Do not overbeat. Drop the batter by spoonfuls onto a very hot, slightly greased griddle or skillet. Batter should be thin enough to spread easily but not runny. If too thick, add a bit more milk; if too thin add flour. Serve the buckwheat cakes piping hot with maple syrup or, if you prefer the Southern way, with molasses. *Makes approximately 36 3-inch cakes.*

POTOMAC PANCAKES WITH VIRGINIA HAM

Fond as he was of apples in any form, it is no wonder these apple pancakes appealed to President Grant.

Apples	*Sour milk*
Eggs	*Vanilla*
Sugar	*Flour*
Butter	*Virginia ham*

Peel, slice, and dice 4 large apples. Boil then until mushy, then strain and mash. Combine 3 beaten egg yolks, 1 tablespoon sugar, 1 tablespoon butter, ½ cup sour milk, 1 teaspoon vanilla, and 1 cup sifted flour. Mix thoroughly. Add the apples to the batter, and drop onto a hot griddle, frying them in the shape of pancakes. Serve each apple pancake on top of a piece of fried ham. *Makes 36 3-inch pancakes.*

VARIATION: RASPBERRY PANCAKES

Make the same dough as in the apple pancake. Instead of apples, use 1 pint fresh, cut-up raspberries. Frozen berries may be substituted, but nothing is quite like the delicate flavor of the fresh raspberries. Raspberry pancakes make a delicious dessert, served with a few whole berries on top and dusted with powdered sugar.

ALGONQUIN HOMINY GRITS SOUFFLÉ

A favorite side dish at the Grant family table was hominy, mainstay of many another American home of the period. Made from finely ground white corn kernels, hominy grits were a contribution to basic American cuisine by the Algonquin Indians. Grits have multiple functions. In some homes they were (and still are) served as cereal at breakfast time. Grits have also been a solid starchy substitute for rice or potatoes at the dinner table. This particular recipe shows how grits make a surprisingly original main dish for lunch or Sunday-night supper. Present-day quick-cooking grits require less cooking. Follow package instructions.

Hominy grits	*Cheddar or other mild cheese*
Milk	*Butter*
Water	*Salt and pepper*
Eggs	

Stir ½ cup hominy grits into 1 scalded cup milk and 1 cup water. Stir until thickened. Then cook the mixture in a double boiler over a low heat for almost 1 hour, stirring now and then. When quite thick, beat in 3 egg yolks, ½ cup grated cheese, 2 tablespoons butter, and salt and pepper to taste. When the cheese has melted, remove mixture from the fire and allow to cool. Meanwhile, beat until stiff 3 egg whites mixed with ¼ teaspoon salt. Fold the stiff whites into the cooled hominy. Pour into a greased casserole and bake in a low-medium (300° F.) oven for almost 1 hour—or until a knife inserted in the middle comes out clean. The soufflé is a light meal in itself, served with a tossed green salad. It may also be served as accompaniment to a fish main dish. You may wish to embellish the soufflé with a mushroom sauce. *Serves 4.*

HOMEMADE WHOLE-WHEAT BREAD

This familiar in Grant's household is equally pleasing today. A great favorite in the Midwest, it knows no state boundaries.

Scalded milk	*Compressed yeast cakes*
Black molasses	*Whole-wheat flour*
Lard or shortening	*White flour*
Salt	

Scald 2 cups milk and allow to cool slightly. Add to 3 tablespoons black molasses, 3 tablespoons lard, and 1½ teaspoons salt. Mix well in a large mixing bowl. When lukewarm, crumble 1½ cakes compressed yeast into the bowl. Then add 3 cups whole-wheat flour, beating as you add. More slowly, add 2 more cups whole-wheat flour and 1 cup white flour. Mix thoroughly. Cover the bowl and place it in a warm place to rise until double its size (it may take 4 to 5 hours). Grease 2 bread pans. Cut dough down and pour it into the pans. Let it rise again about 2 hours. Then bake for 20 minutes in a hot (375° F.) oven. Reduce heat to 325° F. and continue baking 45 minutes longer. *Makes 2 good-size loaves.*

JULIA'S VEAL ROLLS

When the newly married Grants were entertaining for the first time—having four or five of Ulysses' fellow officers to dinner—Julia was terrified. She had come from a slave-holding Missouri family and had been brought up with no knowledge at all of cooking. Her husband reassured her, telling her that he could "run up a savory mess himself, if need be. He had roasted apples at West Point and had even been known to cook a fowl." Julia survived the ordeal of that first company dinner and went on to become a respectable cook, as this recipe will testify. It was one of her favorites, later given to the Galena Presbyterian Church.

Leg of veal	*Salt and pepper*
Grated bread	*Eggs*
Butter	*Cloves*
Onion	

Here it is, in Julia Grant's own words:

Slice as large pieces as you can get from a leg of veal; make a stuffing of grated bread, butter, a little onion, minced, salt, pepper, and spread over the slices. Beat an egg and put over the stuffing; roll each slice tightly and tie with a thread; stick a few cloves in them, grate bread thickly over them after they are put in the skillet, with butter and onions chopped fine; when done lay them in a dish. Make their gravy and pour over them. Take the threads off and garnish with eggs, boil[ed] hard, and serve. To be cut in slices.

BROILED STEAK WITH MELAH'S WINE SAUCE

As we have observed, beef was President Grant's favorite meat—but only if well-done. This must have been a trial to Melah, who perhaps overcame it by serving the meat with varieties of sauces. This sauce is a particularly good companion to steak—rare, medium, or "practically charcoal."

Onions	*Flour*
Butter	*Salt*
Dry red wine	*Pepper*
Stock	*Paprika*
Mushrooms	*Steak*

Sauté over a medium fire ½ cup sliced onions in 2 tablespoons butter. When lightly browned, add ½ cup dry red wine and 1 cup stock, and simmer covered for 20 minutes. Meanwhile, sauté ½ pound sliced mushrooms in 2 tablespoons butter in another skillet. When browned, add ½ cup stock, cover, and cook slowly for 10 minutes. When the onion mixture has cooked sufficiently, dip out a spoonful of the liquid and blend it with 2 teaspoons flour, then add the blended flour to the entire onion mixture. Let the mixture come to a boil and remove from the heat. Add the simmering mushrooms, season with salt and pepper to taste, and a good sprinkling of paprika. Serve hot over a broiled steak. *Makes about 1½ cups.*

SOFT-SHELLED CRABS À LA NELLIE GRANT

President Grant was vehement on the subject of fowl, saying "I never could eat anything that goes on two legs." But he felt no such compunctions about seafood, which he enjoyed almost as much as beef. Soft-shelled crabs, always a favorite with Washington society, were given a place of honor on Nellie Grant's wedding-breakfast menu.

Soft-shelled crabs	*Bread or cracker crumbs*
Flour	*Fat*
Egg	*Salt and pepper*

Allow about 2 or 3 crabs per person. Preparing them will be easier if you have the fish market clean them for you. The procedure then becomes amazingly simple. Just sprinkle each crab lightly with flour, dip it in an egg beaten to a light froth, and then pop it into a bowl of finely crunched cracker crumbs (or breadcrumbs). Fry a few crabs at a time in a preheated deep frying pan. The fat in the pan should be so hot that a small cube of bread browns in less than 1 minute. The crabs should take about 5 minutes to become golden brown and crisp. Drain them on absorbent paper toweling. Then sprinkle with salt and pepper. Delicious served as is, with tartar sauce on the side.

BAKED BLUEFISH WITH WINE SAUCE

Mary Margaret McBride noted that Cape May was a favorite vacation haunt of a number of our Presidents, from Pierce and Buchanan to Lincoln, Grant, and Harrison. They liked the fresh salt air and the equally fresh bluefish, sea bass, oysters, and crabs for which the Cape was renowned. Prepared with a wine-and-butter sauce, the bluefish was particularly worth the trip.

Bluefish	*Salt and pepper*
Butter	*Parsley*
Onion	*Flour*
Dry white wine or sherry	*Paprika*

Split and bone about 4 pounds bluefish. Place on a cooky sheet covered with foil or an ovenproof platter and bake 15 to 20 minutes in a hot (400° F.) oven.

Meanwhile prepare a sauce by melting butter in a skillet and slowly sautéeing 1 small finely minced onion until golden. Add 1 cup wine and cook slowly. Salt, pepper, and 1 tablespoon parsley may be added. Then slowly add a little flour mixed with butter to thicken slightly. Add a dash of paprika for color, stir well, and add to the fish, spreading it all over the fish. Continue cooking the fish for a few minutes, until done. Then serve on a platter covered with sauce and with parsley sprinkled lightly over the top. *Serves 4.*

BAKED ALASKA

Both Thomas Jefferson and Dolley Madison introduced pioneer versions of this delicacy, but Baked Alaska as we know it appears to have been the invention of the famed Delmonico's Restaurant in New York. The date was 1876, nine years after the Alaska Territory had been purchased from the Czar of Russia for $7,200,000. Rarely has a historical event been so dramatically immortalized. Even today, when the event for which Baked Alaska was named has been forgotten, the trick of producing a frozen dessert from a warm oven remains a spectacular *coup de cuisine* and superb climax to a party dinner.

Light golden sponge cake   *Meringue*
Ice cream—very hard-frozen—
   usually strawberry

Place the sponge cake on a piece of brown paper on a wooden board. If the cake is round, you should mold your ice cream (2 quarts) in a round bowl before freezing it hard. The choice of ice cream depends on the occasion. Strawberry is standard, but for home parties it is fun to vary it. Cherry-vanilla or strawberry-pistachio, or any flavor or combinations you prefer. Just before serving, put the ice cream on top of the cake, leaving a one-inch edge all around the outside of the cake. Cover the ice cream and cake with a thick layer of meringue (prepared ahead of time). Be sure to bring the meringue right down flush to the board, sealing the edges well for insulation. Slip the cake on the board in a 500° F. oven for 3 to 5 minutes (just time enough for the meringue's peaks to brown). Place the desert on a serving plate, board and all, and bring immediately to the table. Stand back and wait for the oohs-and-ahs, then serve quickly. The ice cream should be just the right consistency for eating. *Serves 2.*

RICE PUDDING MELAH

No dessert at Delmonico's, no matter how special, ever pleased President Grant as much as simple rice pudding. The Grants' Italian steward Melah regarded this homy concoction a challenge to his ingenuity and tried to vary it from time to time. No matter how he embellished it, Grant liked it and had it as often as possible when the family dined alone. When the inventive Melah experimented with rice pudding, however, it was good enough to be served at official functions—and actually was.

Rice	*Sugar*
Milk	*Almonds*
Butter	*Cinnamon and nutmeg*
Eggs	

Measure ¾ cup long-grain rice into a saucepan. Add 1½ quarts milk and simmer very slowly until the rice is soft. Add 3 tablespoons butter, remove from heat, and cool. Meanwhile, beat 5 eggs well and stir them into the rice mixture. Add ½ cup sugar and mix carefully. Pour the mixture into a large greased baking pan and add ½ cup slivered almonds, mixing them gently into the pan. Bake in a medium-warm (325° F.) oven until the custard sets. Remove from the oven, sprinkle a mixture of cinnamon and nutmeg over the top and serve. Delicious either warm with cream or chilled. *Serves 8.*

DOLLY VARDEN CAKE

This two-color cake, popular during Grant's Presidency, was named after the heroine of Charles Dickens' novel *Barnaby Rudge.* In 1875 Dolly's name was given to a shirtwaist dress and a special type of fancy hat, as well as to this cake. Dickens was as popular as his Dolly with Americans of the time, and made lecture tours of the United States, reading from his novels. What Dickens thought of the United States of that time was less than flattering, but his audiences couldn't have cared less. They were hopelessly enamored of the characters in his novels, especially Dolly. It may take you as long to prepare this elaborate cake as to read *Barnaby Rudge,* but you may remember it longer.

Butter or margarine	*Maraschino cherries*
Sugar	*Cardamon*
Flour	*Nutmeg*
Baking powder	*Allspice*
Milk	*Walnuts*
Eggs	*Vanilla*
Citron	*Grated coconut*
Currants	

To make light layers: Cream ½ cup butter or margarine with 1 cup sugar. Add 2 cups sifted flour and 1 teaspoon baking powder alternately with ½ cup milk. Fold 4 stiffly beaten egg whites into the batter. Bake in 2 layer pans in a 350° F. oven until golden brown, about 30 minutes.

To make dark layers: Cream ½ cup butter with 1 cup sugar and 4 well-beaten egg yolks. Add 2 cups sifted flour and 1 teaspoon baking powder alternately to the batter with ½ cup milk. Beat constantly while adding the ingredients. Add 1 cup each of citron, currants, Maraschino cherries, 1 tablespoon ground cardamon, 1 teaspoon nutmeg, ¼ teaspoon allspice, and ¾ cup chopped walnuts. Mix well. Bake in 2 well-greased layer pans in a 350° F. oven about 30 minutes.

To make the Dolly Varden boiled frosting: Dissolve 4 cups sugar in 2 cups water. Stir well until dissolved. Boil the mixture until the syrup reaches a temperature of 236° F. or so, forming a thin thread from the spoon. Then pour the syrup into 4 egg whites that have previously been whipped into a light froth. Beat constantly until mixture begins to thicken. Add 1½ teaspoons vanilla.

After the cake layers have been allowed to cool, put them together, alternating light and dark layers, with frosting between each layer and on the top and sides. Sprinkle the top with grated coconut and decorate with a few maraschino cherries.

ROMAN PUNCH

This refreshing drink was usually served at the Lucullan Grant banquets right after the roast course. Considering that the courses at such banquets numbered between twenty-five and thirty, lasting up to three hours, it is no wonder a local wag dubbed this sorbet "the life-saving station." It wasn't just the quantities of food that were suffocating. The florid ostentation of the decor—done in the "Greek style," with gilded wallpaper, ebony and gold furniture, elaborate chandeliers encased in floral decorations so lavish and excessive they would have made any hay-fever sufferer stagger from the room—was enough to have been the inspiration for Veblen's theory of conspicuous consumption. Never has consumption been quite so conspicuous in the White House! Never was a "life-saving" sorbet more welcome!

Lemons	*Whiskey or champagne*
Oranges	*Egg whites*
Water	*Sugar*

Grate the rinds of 4 lemons and 6 oranges. Squeeze the juice and add it to 1 gallon water and 1 quart whiskey (or 1 bottle champagne), along with the grated rinds. Beat 8 egg whites to a froth and add. Freeze until ready to serve. Makes a delicious, refreshing finale for a dinner party.

COLONEL DENT'S MINT JULEPS

President Grant's father-in-law, Colonel Frederick Dent, Southern and pro-slavery, delighted in antagonizing his son-in-law with his opinionated views on current politics. He lived the role of Southern gentleman to the hilt (on his son-in-law's income), and felt most at home arguing his position with a mint julep in hand. It was a useful prop—but more than that, Grant had to concede it tasted rather good too. Even Charles Dickens, that hard-to-please tourist, found the julep "never to be thought of afterwards, in summer, by those who would preserve contented minds."

Crushed ice	*Sugar syrup*
Bourbon	*Fresh mint*

Chill mugs or goblets in the refrigerator as long as possible. At serving time, fill each glass with finely crushed ice almost up to the top. Add bourbon, enough to cover the ice, stirring until the glass gets frosted over on the outside. Stir in sugar syrup (1 lump per glass dissolved in a small amount of water) according to taste. Four or 5 sprigs of fresh mint protruding from the top of the glass provide the finishing touch.

✳✳

XIX

*Temperate
Times in an
Era of
Opulence*

✳✳

Surely one of the most dramatic episodes in American Presidential history occurred at the close of the Grant administration. Rutherford B. Hayes, the Republican candidate chosen to succeed Grant, had lost the popular vote in the election of
1876 to Samuel Tilden. But many of the returns were contested, so the decision
was turned over to an Election Commission which announced the results in favor
of Hayes—by one vote.

As Hayes and his wife boarded the train for Washington and the inaugural
ceremonies, they were not at all sure of the final outcome. They half-feared they
would arrive in Washington and find that Tilden was the President-to-be after all.
Only three days before Hayes' scheduled inauguration was he declared officially
the next President.

March 4, the officially designated inauguration day, fell on a Sunday in 1877,
which meant it had to be postponed until Monday. Grant was fearful that, with all
the controversy over the election still raging, it would be unsafe for even a single
day to leave the country without a duly inaugurated President. So he planned a
surprise.

The Grants had scheduled a farewell dinner for the night of March 3. Guests of
honor were Rutherford Hayes and his wife. A distinguished group of thirty-six
(Melah's favorite number) were on hand to welcome the President-elect. Just
before leading the way into the dining room, Grant took Hayes aside, along with

Chief Justice Waite and Secretary of State Hamilton Fish, and led them quietly to the Red Room. There, in less than four minutes, the oath of office was administered, and the men returned to the party. Thirty-six people sat down to a typical lavish Grantian dinner, many of them completely unaware that history had just been made, almost before their eyes. On Monday, Hayes repeated the ceremony again, with a considerably larger audience on hand, at the Capitol.

But that Saturday night the Hayes had a preview of what life in the White House was like. In a dining room garlanded with ropes of roses from ceiling to table, with a blossoming pink azalea ten feet high standing guard behind Mrs. Hayes' chair, a twenty-course dinner—sparse by the Grants' usual standards—was served. One wonders if the abstemious Mr. & Mrs. Hayes managed tight-lipped smiles at the six wine glasses at each plate.

The menu was about par for the era:

Consommé Impériale	Bisque de Crevisse	Sherry
Woodcock Patties	Salmon	White wine
	Roman Punch	
Filet of Beef	Crawfish Pudding	Red wine
Breast of Pheasant	Goose Livers	
Artichokes	Turkey	
Canvasback Duck	Warm Sweet Dish	
	Champagne	

For dessert there were the usual arrangements of exotic fruits, sweetmeats, ices, and ice creams, along with coffee.

Although the temperate Hayes may not have approved the copious servings of wine, they undoubtedly thought the rest of the dinner very grand indeed, for before long their own official entertainments were following the same opulent path. One reception alone cost $3000, and it was only one of a long procession of gala affairs.

There were a few changes from the casual, come-one, come-all atmosphere of the Grants' administration, however. The Hayes had not been entrenched in the White House long before they issued an edict banning alcohol, including wine, at state dinners. It was widely believed that the ban was the result of an embarrassing incident that occurred during the first spring of the Hayes' occupancy of the Executive Mansion. Two Russian Grand Dukes, Alexis and Constantin, were feted at an official dinner. The President and Mrs. Hayes followed diplomatic custom and allowed wine to be served at the dinner. Rumors were rampant that a drunken exchange at this affair prompted the subsequent ban.

It is likelier that the President may have used the incident as an excuse for doing what he had planned to do all along. When Washington society heard the news, there were waves of shock, and before long the blame for the ban came to rest on Mrs. Hayes' shoulders. Local wits dubbed her "Lemonade Lucy" and shuddered at the new Age of Prudery that had descended on the capital.

In truth, it was the President himself who opposed the serving of wine. As a young man he had been active in the temperance movement and had actually started his career of public speaking by pleading the cause of the Sons of Temperance.

Besides the ban on alcoholic beverages, the Hayes outlawed dances, balls, lawn parties, and card parties at the White House. Queen Victoria in England may very well have been the model for the high-minded moral tone set by Rutherford and Lucy Webb Hayes. In the words of one commentator, "virtue was at last fashionable." Lucy was widely praised by those of her countrymen (and women) who had been dismayed at the scandals and corruption rampant in the preceding administration. The First Lady was admired for her solid family virtues.

Lucy Hayes appears to have been quite a remarkable woman. She was the first First Lady to have graduated from college (no mean accomplishment in those pre-suffragette days), and she impressed the nation as a splendid motherly example of a model wife, mother, and woman. Even her critics grudgingly admired her. So strong a personality did Lucy have that many people felt she was the dominant figure in the Hayes household.

Years later a guest, lunching at Harvey's restaurant in Washington, was trying to pinpoint a certain date by naming the President of that time. He turned to the aged waiter for help.

"I disremember de President's name, suh. He come after General Grant, an' a right smart while befo' General Garfield was shot."

"Do you mean President Hayes?" the diner asked.

"Yes-suh. That's it! General Hayes. The gem-man whose wife run the White House!"

In spite of the grumbles of criticism among official Washington about the "ice-water regime" of the Hayes, Lucy became, by the end of her husband's four-year term, a much-loved First Lady. Three prominent poets of the age—Longfellow, Whittier, and Oliver Wendell Holmes—praised her in verse. Thomas Pendel, White House doorkeeper for several administrations, raptured that her cheerfulness and goodness permeated the entire house. The WCTU was so delighted with Lucy Hayes that its members presented her portrait to the White House, along with an impressive silk banner inscribed with her name and a quotation from the Bible: "She hath done what she could."

Her husband managed, despite being occasionally overshadowed by Lucy's shining and apparent goodness, to overcome the handicap in some quarters of being considered henpecked. His staunch, upright character and well-known honesty won him wide respect.

Respect for the man did not prevent local humorists from poking fun at his rules. After the President had scored a noteworthy political victory, one wag commented "Buttermilk will flow like water at the White House tonight."

Washington's favorite joke on Teetotaler Hayes had the capital in a state of controlled mirth for months. It seems that the Hayes' banquets followed the tradition of the Grants', being long, many-course affairs. Like the custom established by Melah, a sorbet was served midway. According to Perley, a noted journalist of the day, the White House waiters were kept busy replenishing this portion of the meal. "Glances telegraphed to one another that . . . concealed within the oranges was a delicious frozen punch, a large ingredient of which was strong old St. Croix rum." This Roman punch was served near the middle of every state dinner. Those who were in on the secret referred to this as the "life-saving station," thus putting a phrase from the days of the Grants to a totally different use.

In his diary, Rutherford Hayes had the last laugh on his critics: "The joke of the Roman punch oranges was not on us but on the drinking people. My orders were to flavor them rather strongly with the same flavor that is found in Jamaica rum. This took. There was not a drop of spirits in them."

Arid seems to have been a well-chosen word for the Hayes' official entertainments. The receptions were particularly sedate. At 10 P.M. sharp the Marine Band played "Home Sweet Home"; those present took the hint and dispersed immediately. The state dinners were almost as lengthy and elaborate as the Grants'. They differed in one respect, as one bored guest noted: "The water flowed like champagne."

Both President and Mrs. Hayes were at their best socially in small gatherings. They loved the White House and found it a comfortable home for themselves and their five children. When Congress passed a law outlawing egg-rolling on the Capitol grounds, the Presidential family opened the White House grounds every Easter Monday to the egg-rollers, beginning a tradition that has continued to this day. The children of Washington had enjoyed this sport for years (it all began with Dolley Madison), but when the Hayes invited them to use the White House lawn, the event assumed national importance.

Each Thanksgiving the President and his wife invited all the secretaries and clerks who worked at the White House to gather there for dinner to "consume the flock of turkeys which always cram the pantry shelves."

In his personal taste, the President enjoyed everything in moderation. He always had one cup of coffee at breakfast time, one cup of tea for lunch. In a day when extravagance was a way of life, when Boss Tweed's daughter paid $4000 for her wedding dress, the Hayes' regime must indeed have seemed "reasonably economical," as one reporter put it.

The social high point of Hayes' four-year term, when he threw his usual moderation to the winds, was the celebration of his and Lucy's silver wedding anniversary. Hayes planned the celebration to duplicate the original wedding. The Marine Band played the "Wedding March," Hayes and his wife stood before Bishop McCabe, who had married them twenty-five years before, and Lucy, radiant as always, wore, with no visible strain, her original white-flowered satin wedding dress. After the rerun of the ceremony, Hayes toasted his wife (nonalcoholically of course), saying: "I have existed thirty years—and lived twenty-five." This was probably an appropriate climax for what a later writer described as "that sentimental orgy of the seventies, the silver wedding."

To cope with the domestic side of life in the White House, the Hayes had brought with them from Ohio their regular cook, Winnie Monroe, described by Colonel Crook as "a fat old woman who was black as a crow." Winnie evidently responded with enthusiasm to the exciting life in Washington. In fact, it was such a "glorious period" for her, that she was not too happy returning to Ohio with the Hayes family at the end of four years. Before long Winnie had returned to the capital (like Washington's Hercules decades before).

As she explained it to one of her friends who had remained in White House service: "Law, chile, I can't stay in no Ohio—not after I been first colored lady in the land."

Winnie's culinary powers must have been impressive, for one guest said of the White House table that it "groaned with delicacies which called forth admiration."

Admiration and *respect* might well be the key words that sum up the feeling that Rutherford and Lucy Hayes inspired in their fellow citizens—not a bad accolade at that.

◇◇

R E C I P E S

DELICATE CORNMEAL BATTERCAKES

Long a favorite breakfast dish in the White House in the days of Lucy Hayes and since, these light, ethereal cakes are like little bits of heaven lighting on your plate. The composition is deceptively simple. (Of all the recipes of the Presidents, this is my own most treasured. P. C.)

Cornmeal	*Sweet milk*
Salt	*Eggs*

Sift together 4 tablespoons cornmeal with ¼ teaspoon salt. Add to 2 cups milk in a saucepan and cook over gentle heat for 5 minutes, stirring constantly. Let the mixture cool, then add 2 well-beaten eggs. Mix well and drop by the spoonful on a hot well-greased griddle or skillet. The surface for frying should be *very* hot—about 375° F. Bake on one side until each cake is full of bubbles. Turn gently just once. These cakes are so delicate they should not be stacked. Serve with butter and maple syrup or honey. *Makes about 24 2-inch cakes.*

ROASTED EGGS

Of the five Hayes children, two were in college during their father's administration and one, Webb, had just graduated from Cornell and served as his father's private secretary. But the youngest members of the family, Fanny and Scott, aged six and nine, probably had as much fun as any children in Washington rolling eggs Easter Monday on the White House lawn. Roasting eggs was another pastime guaranteed to amuse the children.

Wet paper   Hot ashes
Eggs

Roll each egg in four layers of wet paper. (Heavy brown paper or newspaper works best.) Put the wrapped eggs in the hot ashes of a restive fire and cover well with ashes. Let the eggs remain there until the outer layer of paper is well scorched. Remove from the ashes and allow to cool until they can be handled. Then remove the paper. Eat hot as is with salt and pepper. (Roasted eggs make a great breakfast diversion on a camping trip. Children love to make them.)

ANGEL CAKE

Considering the character of gentle, sweet-tempered Lucy Hayes, it seems fitting that Angel Cake should be one of her favorite desserts. The origins of Angel Cake, sometimes called angel-food cake, are mysterious, all the more so since they seem to derive from the mysterious East. The story goes, according to a cookbook published in 1883, that a family who lived along the Atlantic Coast moved to a quiet place along the Hudson River and opened a boardinghouse. A friend presented one of the ladies of the family, who was remarkably skilled as a cake-baker, a valuable "receipt" that had come to her from a friend in India. Sometime later, the family left their picturesque boardinghouse along the Hudson and returned to their original coastal home. There, the cake-baker of the family opened a bakery of sorts, specializing in various cakes, including the mysterious cake from the East. This special cake was produced under unusual circumstances: only one was baked at a time, behind closed doors and in the greatest secrecy. But like most secrets of the kitchen, it eventually was found out, improved upon, and perfected. We offer it in its highly perfected state—without secrets and hidden doors.

Cake flour	*Cream of tartar*
Egg whites	*Sugar*
Salt	*Almond extract*

Sift 1 cup cake flour 3 times and set it aside. Measure 1½ cups egg whites (about 12 large eggs) into a large mixing bowl and add ¼ teaspoon salt. Beat frantically with either rotary or electric beater until whites are foamy. Sprinkle 1 teaspoon cream of tartar over the egg whites and beat eggs again until they stand in peaks. Sprinkle 1½ cups sugar into the egg whites, 2 or 3 tablespoons at a time, then fold gently in to be sure it is mixed. (Use as few strokes as possible, but be sure it is thoroughly mixed.) Next, stir in 1 teaspoon almond extract. Sift about ¼ cup of the flour over the egg-white mixture and fold it gently in with a rubber or plastic spatula. Continue sifting and folding the flour in until it is all used. The trick is to be sure the mixture is well mixed, but not overmixed. Pour the mixture into an ungreased 10-inch tube pan. Bake it in a preheated hot (375° F.) oven for 35 to 40 minutes, or until cake springs quickly back when gently pressed. Cake reacts best at serving time if it is pulled apart with two forks. Cutting it with a knife mashes it down and flattens the marvelous lightness of the texture.

JOHNNY APPLESEED PUDDING

Both Rutherford and Lucy Webb Hayes had their roots in Ohio, land of Johnny Appleseed. Simple recipes from "back home" frequently found their way to the White House table. After all, Winnie Monroe, the Hayes' cook, was another Ohioan, so it was natural for home-grown recipes to be repeated in Washington. This particular pudding is an old American favorite, in all parts of the country where apples are harvested each autumn, be it Ohio, New York, or New England.

Tart apples	*Nutmeg*
Sugar	*Salt*
Cinnamon	*Biscuit dough*

Peel, slice, and core 3 firm but not mealy large tart apples. Put them in a deep saucepan with just a little water—just enough to keep the apples from burning. Stir in ¾ cup white or light brown sugar, ½ teaspoon cinnamon, ½ teaspoon nutmeg, and ¼ teaspoon salt. Roll out some biscuit dough (in this day and age, using a mix is perfectly respectable—and much faster), enough to cover the top of the saucepan. Spread it over the apples, seal tightly, and cook over moderate heat for 15 minutes. Turn out and serve with cream or whipped cream. *Serves 4 to 6.*

TILDEN CAKE

It may seem like rubbing salt in old wounds to include a Tilden Cake with Hayes' recipes. But actually, the cake was so popular during Hayes' administration it seems natural for it to be considered an adjunct of his period. Samuel J. Tilden was, after all, prominent enough at the time to win the popular vote in the 1876 election. We think his cake good enough, too, to win your vote.

Butter	*Baking powder*
Sugar	*Salt*
Eggs	*Milk*
Flour	*Lemon extract*
Cornstarch	

Cream 1 cup butter with 2 cups sugar and slowly, one at a time, add 4 eggs. Beat well after each egg is added. Set aside. Sift 3 cups flour, ½ cup cornstarch, 2 teaspoons baking powder, and ½ teaspoon salt together. Then add to the butter–egg mixture alternately with 1 cup milk. Mix well and add 2 teaspoons lemon extract. Pour into two 9-inch cake pans and bake in a preheated medium (350° F.) oven for 30 to 35 minutes.

LUCY'S CAKES

As the mother of five healthy, active children, Lucy Hayes had the age-old problem of keeping the cooky crock filled. Considering that four of her five children were boys, her problem was quadruply acute. But formidable planner and efficient homemaker that she was, Lucy solved the problem with cookies such as these—a hint to mothers of today.

Butter	*Salt*
Brown sugar	*Baking soda*
Eggs	*Cinnamon*
Flour	*Nuts*
Baking powder	*Raisins*

Cream ¾ cup butter and 1½ cups brown sugar together. Add 3 well-beaten eggs and mix thoroughly. Mix and sift 2 cups flour, 2 teaspoons baking powder, ¼ teaspoon salt, and ½ teaspoon soda. Add 1 teaspoon cinnamon, ½ cup chopped nuts (preferably walnuts), and 1 cup raisins. Add to the butter–egg mixture and mix well. Drop by spoonfuls on a well-greased baking sheet. Bake in a 450° F. oven for 8 to 10 minutes. Cool on brown paper. *Makes about 60 2-inch cakes.*

LIME AND ORANGE SHERBET IN ORANGE BASKETS

Lucy Hayes' major purchase for the White House was an elaborate state dinner service of almost 1000 pieces. The original designs were watercolors illustrating the flora and fauna of the U.S. These designs were then reproduced on porcelain. The elegant set of Limoges faïence that resulted became Lucy's main legacy to future White House families. One can well imagine the pride she felt at an official banquet when "her" dinner service was in use. How lovely those controversial orange baskets filled with rum (or rum flavoring) must have looked. You may not have such historic plates to serve your sorbets on, but we think you'll find the orange basket (or shell) idea a clever and different way to brighten up your own entertaining.

Gelatin	*Oranges*
Sugar	*Limes*
Water	*Egg whites*

Soak ½ package gelatin in a little water to soften. Add 2 pounds sugar to 2 quarts boiling water. Stir vigorously and add the gelatin. Allow to cool. Cut 6 oranges in half, scoop out the insides with a sharp knife, taking pains to clean them out completely. Squeeze the juice from the orange pulp. Add the orange juice, along with the juice from 5 limes, to the gelatin mixture. Beat 4 egg whites to a froth and add them to the gelatin gradually. Put in the freezer. At serving time, serve in the orange halves.

LEMONADE LUCY'S ROMAN PUNCH

General Grant had his own version of this well-known sorbet, which we have presented earlier. But we think it only proper, in view of the controversy it aroused, to include the Hayes version. We offer you your choice of the *real* Hayes version or the version that official Washington thought it was enjoying *in spite* of Hayes.

| *Lemon sherbet* | *Scooped-out oranges* |
| *Jamaica rum—or rum flavoring* | |

If you prefer the alcoholic version, mix 1 quart lemon sherbet with 1 cup rum. Spoon it into chilled punch glasses or serve it as the President did in scooped-out orange bowls. Serve immediately.

For the non-alcoholic punch, mix the lemon sherbet with a generous amount of rum flavoring (1 tablespoon). Serve immediately. *Serves 6 to 8.*

XX

Intellectual Intellude

Lucy Hayes may have been a college graduate, but the home atmosphere of the Hayes couldn't hold a candle to the intellectual intensity of the Garfields.

Our twentieth President, James Garfield, was a self-made man who elevated himself through study and hard work to the professorship of ancient languages and literature at an Ohio college. So serious and purposeful was the Garfield family life that mealtime was devoted to the education of his seven children. Across the potatoes and stew he instructed them by the Socratic method.

Garfield's sobriety seems to have given purpose to his wife's life as well. One catches a glimpse of their relationship in a letter Lucretia Garfield wrote her husband ten years before he was elected President:

> I am glad to tell you that out of all the toil and disappointments of the summer just ended, I have risen up to a victory; that silence of thought since you have been away has won for my spirit a triumph. "There is no healthy thought without labor, and thought makes the labor happy." Perhaps this is the way I have been able to climb higher. It came to me one morning when I was making bread. I said to myself: "Here I am compelled by an inevitable necessity to make our bread this summer. Why not consider it a pleasant occupation, and make it so by trying to see what perfect bread I can make?" It seemed like an inspiration, and the whole of life grew brighter.

Throughout their correspondence, one sees poor Crete, as she was called, struggling constantly to live up to the aspirations set for her by her serious-minded husband. A mixture of Pollyanna and Victorian righteousness form the image we have of her. Yet one wonders, as one compares the Garfield homilies and family scenes with the public man who was so ignominiously accused of corrupt political practices, collusion with party bosses, and the routine scandals of a scandalous age, could there also have been a touch of Victorian hypocrisy to mar the carefully cultivated image?

From this point in time, it is impossible to tell. Perhaps even more sadly, it is almost impossible to care. Poor Garfield, President for only three and a half months before he was shot, was a poor third choice for the office anyway, a compromise candidate when the Grant and Blaine factions were stalemated.

As President, Garfield continued the sincere, friendly atmosphere created by the Hayes family, but with far less extravagance. He considered his house, White House or not, a "place for plain living and high thinking."

The Century Magazine described the Garfield habits and tastes thus:

> His home life was that of the plain New England farmer element from which he sprang, broadened and beautified by culture, but taking little note of the fancies of fashion. He liked substantial furniture, good engravings, a big cane-seated chair, an open fire, a simple meal, a wide brimmed felt hat and easy-fitting clothes. His table was bountifully supplied with plain well-cooked food, but he made his meals such feasts of reason that his guests scarcely noticed what they ate.

After years of emphasis on fashion, fads, and fancies in food, suddenly the new President popularized the word *nutrition*. Guests at his table found an abundance of "wholesome, nutritious food," as well as coffee, tea, and a bountiful supply of milk.

The abundance was more than evident at President's Garfield's inaugural supper, held in the annex of the new National Museum building. (There was something curiously appropriate about scholarly Garfield being inaugurated in a museum.)

More than 1500 pounds of turkey was served at the gargantuan feast. With it, for statistical purposes, were served 100 gallons of oysters, 50 hams, 200 gallons of chicken salad (an inaugural specialty, it would seem), 700 loaves of bread (not baked this time by Lucretia), 2000 biscuits, 350 pounds of butter, fifty gallons of jelly, 15,000 cakes, 150 gallons of ice cream, 50 gallons of water ices, 250 gallons of coffee, along with other unspecified delicacies. Guests were served 500 at a time. The only statistic missing is the total number of guests present. One wonders how many hordes were present to consume such army-sized rations.

Lucretia Garfield approached her role as First Lady with the strong desire to make "the labor happy," as happy as bread-making at least. Washington society warmed to her "lady-like, sweet-voiced, unruffled, well-informed" personality. There was genuine distress in the capital when the First Lady became ill with typhoid fever and was forced to abandon her official duties.

Although the atmosphere at the Garfield table was rather rarefied, the general atmosphere in the White House during Garfield's brief term was considerably more relaxed than it had been—at least in certain respects.

For one thing, President Garfield, like his learned predecessor John Quincy Adams, enjoyed billiards. Adams' long-banished billiard table returned to a place of honor. Times had changed considerably since John Quincy's day. There was no vilification of the new President for indulging in the game. America had grown increasingly sophisticated in the intervening sixty years.

Garfield's other vices were equally mild ones. On occasion he would drink a glass of champagne or Rhine wine, and he particularly liked beer. Once again the social patterns of the White House were swinging round. No one was aghast when the President indulged himself in an occasional cigar.

James Garfield seems to have been a well-liked man, for all his moralizing. When he died, September 19, 1881, a shocked nation grieved deeply.

◇◇

R E C I P E S

SODA BREAD

This old-time favorite was well received in Garfield's day, and most assuredly had a high place on the family table.

Flour	*Raisins*
Salt	*Egg*
Baking powder	*Buttermilk*
Baking soda	*Anise seed or caraway seed*
Butter	*(optional)*
Sugar	*Milk or cream*

Sift together 2 cups flour, ½ teaspoon salt, 1 teaspoon baking powder, and 1 teaspoon baking soda. Mix well. Mix 3 tablespoons each butter and sugar. Soak 1 cup raisins in boiling water. Drain well and add them to the butter–sugar mixture. Add 1 beaten egg and slowly stir in the flour mixture alternately with ⅔ cup buttermilk. Add 1 tablespoon caraway seed. Mix well and turn the dough onto a floured board. Knead until smooth and then shape into a ball. Butter a 1½-quart casserole and put the dough in it. Make 5 gashes around the outer edge of the dough. Brush the top of the dough with a little milk or cream. Bake in a hot (375° F.) oven for approximately 45 minutes. Delicious at breakfast or teatime. *Makes 1 loaf.*

INSPIRATION BREAD

Lucretia Garfield may have derived her inspiration from any number of tasty breads of her day, but we like to believe it came from this truly unique salt-rising bread.

Scalded milk	*Water*
Salt	*Flour*
Sugar	*Lard*
Cornmeal	

Scald 1 cup milk and allow to cool. When lukewarm, add 1½ teaspoons salt and 1¼ tablespoons sugar. Mix together well and add ¼ cup cornmeal, preferably white. Pour the mixture into a jar or crock and cover. Place the jar in a bowl of very hot water. Keep jar in a warm place until the dough ferments, usually about 6 hours. When gases escape from the jar, pour in 1 cup lukewarm water, 1¼ tablespoons sugar, 2 cups flour, and 2 tablespoons lard. Beat vigorously, *à la* Mrs. Garfield. Place the jar back in the bowl of very hot water. Allow to rise until batter is light and bubbly. Warm a large mixing bowl in the oven and pour the batter into it, slowly adding enough extra flour to make the batter into a good stiff dough. Turn onto a floured breadboard and knead about 12 or 15 minutes. Grease 2 bread pans and place the dough in them. With a pastry brush, lightly "dust" the tops with milk and cover with a clean, slightly damp cloth. Place dough in a warm place and let it rise until it is 2½ times its original size. Preheat oven to 375° F. and bake bread for 10 minutes; reduce heat to 350° F. and bake an additional 20 to 25 minutes.

EXTRA-FLUFFY MASHED POTATOES

Good substantial fare was the criterion set at the Garfields' table. Plain food it had to be, but well prepared, a criterion of many other Presidential families as well. These extra-light mashed potatoes fill the bill exactly.

Potatoes	*Butter*
Scalded milk	*Salt and pepper*

Boil 6 peeled medium-size potatoes in enough salted water to cover them. To expedite the cooking, halve the potatoes before putting them into the pot. Drain the potatoes well when tender, and set them back on the stove again for just a minute to be sure they are thoroughly dried (this adds to their lightness after mashing). Add about ¾ cup scalded milk, little by little, to the potatoes in the mashing process. Beat vigorously, with an electric beater if you have one. Slowly add 6 tablespoons butter and salt and pepper to taste. Serve with butter welled in the center of the high potato mound. *Serves 4 to 6.*

⟍ PARSNIPS À *LA* GARFIELD

Parsnips served as cakes are an old Midwestern tradition, familiar to Ohioans of Garfield's day. We think you will find this a delicious way to serve this old-fashioned, somewhat dated vegetable.

Parsnips	*Egg*
Onion	*Flour or breadcrumbs*
Butter	

Peel and slice very thin 4 average-size parsnips. Cook in boiling salted water until tender. Add a dash of minced onion (½ teaspoon). When tender, drain the parsnips and mash, adding 2 tablespoons butter. Add 1 beaten egg, 2 tablespoons flour (or ¼ cup soft breadcrumbs) and mix well. Drop by the spoonful in hot fat and brown lightly on both sides, or form into small cakes before dropping into the hot fat. Serve as an accompaniment to baked ham or pork chops. *Serves 4.*

GARFIELD PIE

This delicious pie was a favorite of President Garfield's, which shows that he had excellent taste in his food for thought.

Sour apples (or canned apple slices or apple-pie filling)	
Egg yolks	*Sugar*
Butter	*Flour*
Lemon juice and rind	*Unbaked pie shell*

Combine 2 cups stewed tart apples with 2 egg yolks. Add 1 tablespoon butter, the juice of ½ lemon, and the grated rind of 1 whole lemon. Sprinkle with sugar to taste. Then sprinkle with 1 tablespoon flour. Place the mixture in an unbaked 9-inch pie shell and bake in a moderately hot (375° F.) oven for about 20 minutes. (Although this was favored by President Garfield as a one-crust pie, it is also tasty with a lattice top.)

GARFIELD HERBAL TEA

This drink, a favorite of Garfield's, is something of a curiosity today. But if you are a health-food addict, you may find it as much to your liking as our twentieth President did.

Catnip	*Hot water*
Pennyroyal	

Fill your teapot with hot water. Let it stand until the pot is good and warm. Empty it. Put ½ teaspoon herbs per cup of water into the pot. Pour in boiling water. Cover and let stand for 10 to 20 minutes, then serve.

SPICE TEA

Many of our Presidents, including the vigorous Teddy Roosevelt and John F. Kennedy, were as partial to tea as Garfield was. (Who says tea is a lady's drink?) A special favorite is this easily brewed spice tea.

Water   *Mint leaves*
Sugar   *Orange juice*
Black tea   *Lemon juice*
Allspice

Boil together 1 cup water and 1 cup sugar for 5 minutes. Then add 2 teaspoons black tea, ½ teaspoon allspice, and 2 fresh mint leaves (dried will do, if fresh mint is not available). Cover the pan and allow the mixture to steep at least 10 minutes. Strain and add to the liquid 2 quarts boiling water, ¾ cup orange juice, and 6 to 8 tablespoons lemon juice. Bring the mixture to a boil and serve. *Serves 12.*

✳✴✳✴✳✴✳✴✳✴✳✴✳✴✳✴✳✴✳✴✳✴✳✴✳✴✳✴✳✴✳✴✳✴✳✴✳✴✳

XXI

The Elegant Era of "His Accidency"

✳✴✳✴✳✴✳✴✳✴✳✴✳✴✳✴✳✴✳✴✳✴✳✴✳✴✳✴✳✴✳✴✳✴✳✴✳✴✳

If gourmetship were the chief ingredient in Presidential greatness, our twenty-first President would score near the top. Few Presidents have ever equaled Chester Alan Arthur in social and culinary style. Only one, the master of all—Thomas Jefferson—surpassed him.

Politically, Arthur proved that there is actually some truth in the tired cliché that "the office makes the man." His political career, up to the moment fate declared him President, was hardly auspicious. In the thick of the unruly patronage system that dominated New York City politics of the 1870s, Arthur was chosen as Garfield's running mate merely as a sop to appease warring factions of the Republican party. No one was more surprised than Arthur himself at suddenly finding himself President.

Yet, as President, he performed honestly and efficiently. If not an inspired leader, he was at least an honorable one who functioned as President of all the people, not merely the captain of one special-interest group. Considering the rough and ruthless aspects of American politics of that period, this was no small feat in itself. It required courage. Arthur proved to have this in abundance.

On the night Arthur took the oath of office, right after Garfield's death, his close friend Elihu Root commented:

Surely no more lonely and pathetic figure was ever seen assuming the powers of government. He had no people behind him, for Garfield, not he, was the People's Choice; he had no party behind him, for the dominant faction of his party hated his name, were enraged by his advancement and distrusted his motives. He had not even his own faction behind him, for he already knew that discharge of his duties would not accord with the ardent desires of their partisanship, and that disappointment and estrangement lay before him there.

Before long, Arthur's former patron, Roscoe Conkling, New York's party boss, was sarcastically referring to the new President as His Accidency, as he had formerly called Rutherford Hayes His Fradulency because of his close election and vote recounts. Undaunted, Arthur performed as President in a way that was true to himself and to the obligations of his high office.

Socially, too, President Arthur soon showed that he was his own man. In an age that was abuzz with Presidential doings, he managed very deftly to separate the public and private aspects of the Presidency. His only son was away at school during Arthur's Presidency; his ten-year-old daughter Nellie lived with him at the White House, but Arthur forbade photographs taken of her. She was tutored by a French governess, who shielded her from the spotlight.

A year before Chester Arthur became President, his beloved wife, Ellen, had died. Consequently, all during his term of office, society gossips and newspaper columnists attempted to link him romantically with any and every woman who bade him "Good evening." When word got around that the President ordered fresh flowers every day, tongues began to wag and speculation arose over which of the eligible Washington ladies might be the recipient of the daily floral bouquet. There were many red faces when it became known that the President bought the flowers to place in front of his dead wife's portrait, because he had "always given them to her when she was alive."

One word, perhaps, sums up Chester Arthur better than all others: *fastidious.* In his clothes, his food, his sense of decor and style, he cared, he had a sense of the rightness of a thing.

This was obvious in his refusal to move into the White House before long-overdue repairs and renovations were made. In a hassle with Congress over the appropriation of funds, Arthur in exasperation said: "I will not live in a house looking this way. If Congress does not make an appropriation, I will go ahead and have it done and pay for it out of my own pocket. I will not live in a house like this."

The President got his way, and was not forced to pay for the changes himself. A lucky thing, too, for the repairs were considerable. Arthur called in a famous New York decorator, Louis Comfort Tiffany, to undertake innovations in the decor, to refurnish what Arthur called the "badly kept barracks."

Twenty-four wagonloads of tarnished and tattered White House furniture were carted away and auctioned. Ancient bric-a-brac and dreary settees disappeared. Even, according to one source, "the trap that caught the rat that ate the suit of clothes of President Lincoln" was dumped.

Meanwhile, plastering, painting, and redecorating were going on apace, all supervised by the new President, who dropped in each evening to see the work in progress and give instructions for any changes. No detail was too small to be uninteresting to the President. Two new bathrooms and an elevator were installed. The Blue Room became a Robin's-Egg Blue Room.

But the room that occupied most of the President's attention was the private dining room. The elegance of the room was, for the period, almost overwhelming. Heavy gold paper covered the walls. The draperies were of pomegranate plush and the wall lights of crimson glass. On December 7, 1881, Arthur took up residence in the White House and celebrated his arrival with a cosy, intimate dinner in this, his favorite of all rooms. An open, glowing fire welcomed him.

We have no record of that first small dinner of President Arthur's, other than the knowledge that it was prepared by the French chef Arthur brought with him to Washington. The chef had worked for New York gourmets and was well acquainted with the elaborate dinners of the *haute monde* of the day.

Washington soon became aware of the kind of "original" the new President was. He disdained the services of a bodyguard, but employed his own valet, Aleck Powell. Considering his wardrobe, one realizes why. His clothes were usually ordered from New York, sometimes as many as twenty-five outfits at a time. For his inauguration as Vice-President, Arthur wore "light trousers, a blue Prince Albert coat, colored necktie and light gloves." There was always a boutonnière in his lapel.

In appearance, Arthur had real presence. He was fifty-one when he became President and still cut quite a dashing figure. Brown-haired, with side-whiskers, dark-eyed, over six feet tall, somewhat on the heavy side, he had an innate dignity, augmented by his impeccable taste in clothes. Someone noted that no President since Washington had dressed so well.

This was written at the time:

In General Arthur we have a new type of man in the White House. There have been Presidents of all kinds. We have had stately Virginia gentlemen of the old school, and self-made men from the West. We have had soldiers of several varieties, rural statesmen and frontiersmen, but the "city man," the metropolitan gentleman, the member of clubs—the type that is represented by the well-bred and well-dressed New Yorker—the quiet man who wears a scarf and a pin in it and prefers a sack coat to the long-tailed frock coat that pervades politics, and a Derby hat to the slouch that seems to be regarded in various quarters of this Union as something no statesman should be without—this is a novel species of President.

As one reads about Arthur, one sees more and more similarities between him and another early President from New York, Martin Van Buren. Like his predecessor, Arthur had had simple country origins, in his case farm life in Vermont. Although better educated and more intellectual than Van Buren, Arthur found himself also involved in the hurly-burly of New York politics. But there was a dignity, a formality and style about the two men that linked their Presidencies. They even made the same kind of enemies. When someone in the press called Arthur "the dude President" it brought back echoes of Van Buren's "gold spoons."

Arthur very quickly replaced the free-and-easy manners of the sixties and seventies with a more old fashioned, formal etiquette. There was no more back-slapping at the White House or the casual use of first names.

Other social rules were changed. The laborious three-hour dinners of the previous administrations were shortened—from twenty-nine to a mere fourteen. Conspicuous consumption was not good enough—it had to be correct. Colonel Crook observed that Arthur "wanted the best of everything and wanted it served in the best manner . . . he was always well-groomed, almost faultless in his dress." And, one is tempted to add, in his taste in general—for his day.

To assist in his official entertaining, President Arthur called on his younger sister, Mary, wife of the Reverend John E. McElroy of Albany. Mary proved to be a popular asset, warm and charming, even at the most formal event. Her afternoon receptions, held between two and four o'clock were enlivened by her introduction of tea, tiny sandwiches, cakes, candies, tea, coffee, and punch. Her guests were delighted at this generous addition to the usual formality of a reception.

The official dinners at the White House became models of the finest cuisine of the day. The excesses of the Grants, the food-for-food's-sake philosophy of so many of the recent Presidencies, gave way in Arthur's time to a real style of dining. Dinners were elaborate, yes, in the spirit of the age, but elaborate with taste. Mrs. James Blaine, wife of one of Arthur's most bitter critics, who tried so often and so desperately for the Presidency himself, wrote of one of the Presidential dinners: "The dinner was extremely elegant, hardly a trace of the old White House taint being perceptible anywhere, the flowers, the damask, the silver, the attendants, all showing the latest style and an abandon in expense and taste." But then, malice got the best of her, as she added, "But this is all there is of it." The implication was strong that Arthur's taste was superficial, that he was a shallow man.

Yet there is evidence to the contrary. His favorite diversion while President—and the real reason he was interested in having the decor of his private dining room perfect—was to invite two or three personal friends in to dinner and a long evening, *à la* Jefferson, of conversation.

In fact that first winter as President, 1881–1882, the President dined out frequently—at private, unpublicized parties with congenial friends. He hated to bring a pleasant evening to a close, referring to himself as a "night bird." Since etiquette required that all guests must remain until the President left, one friend wrote: "It becomes an interesting problem to end a dinner before 12 o'clock."

Chester Arthur was a sociable man of considerable charm. The charm appears to have been lost on one woman, however, who described him as "a tall gentleman, very grand and dignified, quite like a gigantic icicle." Mrs. Blaine, too full of sour grapes to enjoy Arthur's company, found him frivolous: "All his ambition seeming to center on the social aspect of the situation. Flowers and wine and food, and slow pacing with a lady on his arm, and a quotation from Thackeray or Dickens, or an old Joe Miller told with an uninterfered-with particularity, for who would interrupt or refuse to laugh at a President's joke, made up his book of life, whose leaves are certainly not for the healing of the nation."

Others disagreed. John S. Wise considered Arthur "a very prince of hospitality and nothing could betray him into discourtesy." He was a good host at both the small chatty parties he enjoyed most and at large formal dinners. One guest commented on his "handsome presence" and called him "courteous, witty, tactful and possessing infinite *savoir faire.* He was the living refutation of the taunt which Europeans sometimes level at us, to the effect that eminence in American politics is not attainable by one who is a gentleman at heart."

Arthur had graduated from Union College in Schnectady, New York, at eighteen, and at twenty was the principal of an academy in Vermont. All his life he cherished serious conversation, liberally sprinkled with classical and literary allusions. Though something of a dilettante, he prided himself on his aesthetic judgments.

For their day, his aesthetic values were the model of restrained elegance. By our day's standards, they may seem overblown, but remember the florid age in which Arthur lived. The Lucy Hayes portrait is a case in point. When Arthur first noticed it in the White House, he decided the frame would have to go. It was a carved oak monstrosity almost ten feet high, with pilaster sides, oak branches in high relief, the American flag, lilies to symbolize purity, acorns for power and strength, laurel for victory, and English hawthorne and water lilies for the sheer joy of decorative effect. Arthur substituted a relatively simpler gilt frame, shorn of the gingerbread.

Arthur managed better than most Presidents to isolate his private life from his public. When personal friends came to the White House of an evening, it was the President's custom to serve them a rather elaborate midnight supper, a conceit he much preferred to a heavy evening dinner. Colonel Crook commented on the fact that the White House was "so staid and so orderly during the day" and so "gay and even convivial at night. The President loved late hours." The staff, understandably, did not—not when it meant washing dishes at 3 A.M.

The President averaged one formal dinner party a week, usually on a Wednesday evening. While he cut the courses down, he expanded the guest list from

Grant's 34 or 36 to 50 or 54 guests. No longer could guests expect dinner supplied by a caterer at $2 a plate, embellished with cheap wines. Arthur continued the Grant custom of serving six wines with dinner, but they were six wines of quality. Perley wrote: "A gastronomic artist served the delicacies of the season, cooked the latest Parisian style, while the wines were of the rarest vintages. Never had epicures so enjoyed themselves at Washington, and they rejoiced when they contrasted this dispensation with the barbaric reports of former years, when 'hog and hominy' was the principal dish and tangle-fast whiskey punch was the fashionable table beverage."

Chauncey Depew, one of the country's most experienced gourmets, claimed that President Arthur, "in all the arts and conventionalities of what is known as 'the best society' could have taken equal rank . . . with the Prince of Wales, who afterwards became King Edward VII." The English writer Matthew Arnold met the President and found him possessed of "pleasant, easy manners."

The President's daily schedule stressed moderation. He usually arose about nine-thirty, had a light Continental breakfast of coffee and a roll as he dressed, and then went to his office. He was capable of long shifts of hard work, but often broke the work schedule for a very light lunch about noon. Lunch consisted of oatmeal, fish, and fruit—no meat or heavy side dishes—and then he was back at his desk until four. Then he rode horseback with his daughter or took a ride in his carriage (a rather spectacular landau of naval design) drawn by his "splendid pair of mahogany bays."

Dinner was at six. He dined lightly, but with style. His favorite meal was a mutton chop with a glass of ale, or a slice of rare roast beef with hot baked potatoes and fruits. Accompanying this was a glass of claret. Arthur was discerning in his wine taste, but drank in moderation. When told that a prominent government official had been seen in a drunken state, the President commented, "No gentleman ever sees another gentleman drunk."

If Arthur lacked moderation and restraint in any area of life it was in his addiction to flowers. Late in his term of office, he had improvements made in the greenhouses, but until then he used so many flowers and plants at his receptions and dinners that additional ones sometimes had to be ordered from New York. His favorite creation was a templelike floral fantasy, which he delighted in calling the "Swinging Garden of Babylon." It was built up from a mirror base, with cascading roses, honeysuckle, carnations, and other more exotic plants. When he introduced this centerpiece at a state dinner in the winter of 1884, he even carried the floral motif one step further, by having bouquets of roses for each lady and boutonnières of rosebuds for the men. The rose room of the greenhouse must have been severely taxed that evening—in spite of its hundred varieties. Arthur's floral bill for one state dinner came to $1500.

One guest called President Arthur "an expert in significant detail," who used many sophisticated touches in his entertaining. These touches may have endeared him to Mark Twain, who wrote: "I am but one in 55 million; still, in the opinion of this one-fifty-fifth millionth of the country's population, it would be hard to better President Arthur's administration. But don't decide til you hear from the rest."

Some of the rest, however, were beginning to be influenced by tales of Arthur's extravagances which his enemies circulated. He enjoyed giving musical evenings at the White House. Leading concert performers were invited. One of the most elegant evenings at the Executive Mansion occurred the night the President gave a dinner party for Christine Nilsson, the Swedish soprano. On another occasion, Madame Adelina Patti and her company performed for the President, his Cabinet members, and other guests. Of course embellishing such evenings were always the jungles of floral arrangements.

Little by little, stories of Arthur's evenings grew. It was insinuated that all the dinners, the fancy French dishes, the excessive floral favors, were being paid for by the public funds. These whispered calumnies, when squared with the public image of the immaculately dressed President riding through the city in his splendiferous carriage with his lap robe of Labrador otter, with his monogram embroidered in silk, seemed believable to the credulous public.

Although Arthur was scrupulous about paying for all his expenses for entertaining from his own funds, he was also too reticent to bother answering the charges against him. He felt it beneath his dignity. While he would have liked a second term as President, he felt it too undignified to "beg" for the nomination. With his vociferous enemies at large in the convention, he did not get it. Later, Representative Joseph Gurney Cannon of Illinois said: "Arthur was defeated by his trousers"—the 1880s version of Van Buren's spoons again!

When Arthur retired from the Presidency in the early spring of 1885, he returned to New York, to the life he had enjoyed before. Unfortunately, there was not to be much left of it. In February 1886 it was recognized that he had Bright's disease. By the end of the year he was dead.

Even as he lay dying, however, he inspired sermonizing. A commentator noted that "Arthur's illness is largely due to his life in the White House. He lived too high, exercised too little, and kept too late hours. He did not breakfast much before ten o'clock, and his [formal] dinners did not begin until nine or ten in the evening. He often sat at the table until after midnight, where, though he was not a glutton, he consumed fine wines and terrapin and other rich food. . . . President Arthur rode horseback for a time, but in spite of his doctor's advice, he discontinued this, and grew heavier and heavier from lack of exercise."

One wonders if Arthur read this. If so, he kept his usual dignified silence and did not deign to reply. At that stage of the game, it was hardly worth the effort.

◇◇◇

RECIPES

RHODE ISLAND EELS

President Arthur was fond of seafood of all kinds. As a "Down Easter" himself, he was particularly keen on this dish, which was more popular in his time than today. The eels are caught in the bay, cut into pieces, dipped in batter and fried like clams. They may be served with coleslaw.

Eels	*Egg*
Cornmeal	*Lard or salad oil*

Cut the eels into pieces. Dip them into a batter made of cornmeal and egg. The batter should be moist, so add just a little meal at a time. Preheat a deep skillet with lard or oil in it until very hot. Drop eel pieces in, one at a time, brown quickly, and turn. Remove and drain on absorbent paper. Serve hot.

COLD SALMON MOUSSE

President Arthur was a sportsman of sorts. He went fox hunting with his son and was knowledgeable about horses and horse breeding, but his real obsession was fishing. He went to the Thousand Islands and particularly enjoyed salmon fishing—and salmon eating, of course.

Canned or fresh salmon	*Gelatin*
Salt	*Water*
Cayenne	*Mayonnaise*
Lemon juice	*Heavy cream*

Cook 2 cups fresh salmon or, if you use canned salmon, drain and discard any bones from a 1-pound can and mash the meat as smooth as possible with a fork. Add 1 teaspoon salt, a pinch of cayenne, and 2 tablespoons lemon juice to the salmon. Sprinkle 1 package unflavored gelatin over ½ cup cold water. When the gelatin is slightly softened, put it in a saucepan of boiling water until the gelatin dissolves. Add gelatin to salmon, along with 3 tablespoons mayonnaise and ¼ cup heavy cream, whipped beforehand into semi-firm shape. Mix well with the salmon and pour it into a 1-quart mold. Chill in refrigerator until firm. When ready to serve, unmold on a cold platter. Garnish with watercress and deviled eggs. Makes a lovely luncheon dish, especially in warm weather. *Serves 4.*

MACARONI PIE WITH OYSTERS

Arthur favored this dish at dinners at which he served turtle steak. The richness of the turtle was balanced by the relative blandness of the macaroni. We find this a good accompaniment for a roast today or an excellent entrée for a light lunch or supper.

Macaroni	*White wine or vermouth*
Oysters	*Salt and pepper*
Butter	*Cracker crumbs*
Flour	*Almonds*
Oyster liquid	

Boil water and cook ½ pound macaroni according to package directions. Butter a deep casserole that can be brought to the table for serving. Drain 30 oysters and save the liquor. Place a layer of macaroni in the casserole, then a layer of oysters, continuing to alternate layers until both are used up. Make a white sauce using 2 tablespoons butter and 2 tablespoons flour, combined with equal parts of the oyster liquor and white wine. Add salt and pepper to taste. Pour over the casserole. Sprinkle the top with finely ground cracker crumbs and dot with butter. Bake in a medium-hot (350° F.) oven until brown. Sprinkle chopped toasted almonds over the top and serve. *Serves 6.*

TURTLE STEAK À LA CHESTER ARTHUR

At Chester Arthur's sumptuous dinners, this dish was just one of many special-ties of his chef. Today, its richness and unusual quality would elevate it to position of honor as the main course.

Turtle steaks	*Mushrooms*
Flour	*Salt and pepper*
Butter	*Red wine*
Shallots	

Prepare six turtle steaks beforehand by soaking. Keep them in salted water for several hours at least, preferably overnight. Dry them well and dredge thoroughly in flour. Heat a large skillet with ¼ cup butter until butter is melted and bubbly, but not browned. Place the steaks in the skillet. Sauté quickly on both sides, then reduce the heat, cover, and simmer. While steaks are simmering, place ¼ cup butter in another skillet and sauté 2 tablespoons chopped shallots and 1 cup sliced mushrooms in it. When cooked, add to the turtle steaks and continue to simmer. As the steaks become tender, season them with salt and pepper lightly. Add 1 cup red wine, cover and continue to simmer. Steaks are really tender when they can be pierced easily with a fork. Serve on a heated platter, garnished with parsley. *Serves 6.*

MUGWUMP IN A HOLE

This dish hardly sounds elegant enough for an epicure like President Arthur, but what's in a name? Well, there's American history in this one. A mugwump was the derisive name given to Republicans who bolted their party in the 1884 election. The dish is actually a Virginia adaptation of the classic English dish, Toad in a Hole. Whatever you call it, it is a delicious way to use up leftover beef, veal, fowl, or President Arthur's favorite mutton.

Egg	*Flour*
Milk	*Leftover meat or fat beef*
Salt	*Pepper*

Beat lightly 1 egg and add to it 2 cups milk and 1 teaspoon salt. Whip all together. Slowly add 1 cup flour, and beat until light and smooth. Place 1 pound cooked meat (leftovers possibly?) into a buttered 2-quart casserole. Season with salt and pepper. Pour the batter over the top and bake 1 hour, in a moderate (350° F.) oven. Serve the mugwump from his hole, or remove and place on a heated platter, along with cooked vegetables. The hole can be served separately then. We prefer mugwump, hole and all, ourselves. *Serves 6.*

NESSELRODE PUDDING

This dessert, like Charlotte Russe, hit a peak of popularity during Chester Arthur's administration, admittedly a very elegant age. This version is only one of many that were served at the time.

Gelatin	*Macaroons*
Milk	*Rum or brandy*
Sugar	*Vanilla*
Eggs	*Salt*
Raisins	*Maraschino cherries*
Almonds	*Whipped cream*

Soak 2 tablespoons unflavored gelatin in 1 cup cold milk. In a double boiler add ⅔ cup sugar to 2 cups scalded milk. Then add, beating as you add, 5 egg yolks. Stir well and cook for 2 or 3 minutes, until the yolks thicken slightly. Then stir in the soaked gelatin. Stir until dissolved. Add ⅔ cup chopped raisins, 3 tablespoons ground almonds, and ¼ pound broken macaroons. Mix well and re-move pan from the heat. When slightly cool, add 1 tablespoon rum or brandy and 2 teaspoons vanilla. Beat 5 egg whites until very stiff. Add ⅛ teaspoon salt during the beating. Then fold the egg whites into the cooled mixture. Place the mixture in a wet pudding mold. Chill well in the refrigerator. At serving time, unmold the pudding on a fancy plate and garnish with Maraschino cherries. Serve with a side dish of whipped cream. *Serves 12.*

NEWPORT POUND CAKE

Like many of his friends in fashionable Old New York, Chester Arthur was fond of vacationing in Newport, Rhode Island. Newport soon became such a popular resort of the rich and the new-rich that it was immortalized with this elegant version of the old-fashioned pound cake.

Butter	*Salt*
Flour	*Vanilla*
Eggs	*Baking powder*
Powdered Sugar	

Cream ⅞ cup butter, gradually adding 1½ cups flour. Beat 5 egg whites until stiff but not dry. Beat ¾ cup powdered sugar into the egg whites, along with a dash of salt and 1 teaspoon vanilla. Set aside. Beat 5 egg yolks until thick and lemony and add ¾ cup powdered sugar to the yolks gradually. Mix carefully into the butter–flour mixture, then beat well. Fold egg whites into the mixture. Sift 1 teaspoon baking powder over the dough, then beat thoroughly. Bake about 1 hour in a moderate (350° F.) oven in a deep pan, well buttered and floured.

DEVIL'S FOOD CAKE

It is hard to think that there was a time in American life when this "classic" cake was not known. Yet it dates back only to the 1880s, when it suddenly appeared on the tables of Chicago hostesses. When first served at the White House, it caused a mild sensation. A rich velvety devil's food, made from scratch, is *still* capable of causing a sensation, as you will discover with this recipe.

Baking chocolate	*Flour*
Egg yolks	*Salt*
Sour milk	*Soda*
Butter	*Liquid coffee*
Brown sugar	*Vanilla*

Melt 6 squares of baking chocolate over hot water in a double boiler. Add 2 beaten egg yolks, stirring constantly. Slowly stir in 1 cup sour milk. Cook and stir until thickened, then set aside to cool. Meanwhile cream together ½ cup butter and 2 cups sifted brown sugar. Set aside while mixing and sifting 3 cups regular flour (not cake flour), 1 teaspoon salt, and 1½ teaspoons soda. Add the flour mixture to the butter–sugar mixture alternately with 1 cup strong black coffee. Stir well after each addition. Finally add the chocolate mixture and 2 teaspoons vanilla. Beat thoroughly and bake in a well-greased tube pan in a low-medium (325° F.) oven for almost an hour, or until a straw comes out clean.

ROCKS ✓

President Arthur's sister, Mary McElroy, delighted in serving little cakes such as these with afternoon tea at her receptions. Rocks, in spite of their humble name, have been an elegant addition to tea tables in England for centuries.

Butter	*Flour*
Sugar	*Salt*
Eggs	*Ground cloves*
Soda	*Nuts*
Hot water	*Raisins*

Cream 1 cup butter, gradually adding 1½ cups sugar. Cream together until fluffy, then add 3 well-beaten eggs and mix thoroughly. Dissolve 1 teaspoon soda in 1¼ tablespoons hot water and add to the butter–egg mixture. Mix well. Then add 2 cups flour, sifted with ½ teaspoon salt and 1 teaspoon ground cloves. Mix well before adding ½ cup chopped nuts (preferably walnuts), 1 cup raisins, and 1¾ cups additional flour. Mix well and drop by spoonfuls onto a greased baking sheet. Bake in a hot (375° F.) oven about 10 minutes. *Makes approximately 5 dozen.*

✳✳✳

XXII and XXIV

The Pursuit of Privacy

✳✳✳

It would be difficult to find two men more unlike than the outgoing and incoming Presidents of 1885. The only thing they had in common was their aversion to personal publicity, their desire to barricade their private lives from public view.

But even here they differed. Chester Arthur hated publicity concerning his family and managed quite successfully to avoid it. Only one photograph of his little daughter was captured by the press.

But Grover Cleveland, Arthur's successor, was pursued, hounded, and constantly overtaken by newsmen and photographers.

As for culinary tastes, habits, and personal style, they were disparate types. Grover Cleveland's idea of an epicurean feast was corned beef and cabbage. Reports of his culinary excursions must have made Chester Arthur wince, as he polished off a Charlotte Russe at Delmonico's.

Of course politically, Cleveland's place is assured as one of our strongest, most dynamic Presidents, while poor Arthur is all but forgotten, an accident of fate. Which is but further proof that gourmetship is no match for statesmanship, a sad fact we cooks must face bravely.

The election campaign of 1884 had been one of the nastiest, if not the nastiest, in our history. Supporters of James Blaine, Cleveland's Republican opponent, tried to picture Cleveland as a "boorish, beer-swilling" uncouth lout with the manners of a peasant. Washington society shuddered at the thought of what his Presidency would mean socially. Some delicate souls visualized a return to the Jacksonian receptions, with cheese-smeared carpets and vandalized curtains.

They were in for a surprise. It was true that Cleveland, a man of relatively simple tastes, was not fond of large formal social affairs. But he had a strong, dedicated sense of what the Presidency and the White House should represent to the nation. In national affairs, this took the form of putting country above party at a time when this was no popular course of action. Socially, he felt the White House should set an example of good taste and manners.

The new President was forty-eight years old and unmarried. Like other bachelors and widowers before him, he was fortunate in his choice of White House hostess. Rose Cleveland, younger sister of the President, was a teacher and writer who brought charm, dignity, and a cultured outlook to her duties as official hostess. (One might do a treatise sometime on why single Presidents have been so much luckier in their official hostesses than some of the married ones.)

Cleveland's first official dinner must have made the capital's social butterflies sigh with relief. Here was no gauche lout, but a dignified man who could entertain as lavishly and elegantly as any other sophisticate of the period. Not up to Arthur's standard, but still no slouch at providing an elaborate entertainment.

The decorations at that first state dinner—given for his new Cabinet members—says much about the expectation level of "society" of the day. Swans and eagles dominated the decor. Flowers and potted plants were in abundant evidence—palms, roses, azaleas, tulips, hyacinths, orchids, and—of course—that Victorian treasure, the rubber plant. White wax swans, with wings outstretched to protect their snowy eygnets, dominated one end of the enormous table. Besides being rather splendid decorative figurines, they were functional too: they supported molds of jellied *pâté de foie gras.* But lo, as if this were not decoration enough, the other end of the table was dominated by carved eagles, whose sole function was to uphold more *pâté de foie gras* arranged on little horseshoes.

What really made the ladies "ooh" and "ah" that evening were the bouquets of roses and ferns. Each bouquet was tied with a wide satin ribbon of white, on one end of which was painted the colors of the Union. On the other end was a black-and-white etching of the White House and grounds, with the date of the dinner, January 14, 1886, immortalized in gilt. Could there be a lovelier reminder of a memorable evening? One can see each Victorian lady tenderly pressing her souvenir bouquet in her memory book.

President Cleveland had overcome his sister's objections to wine (was this the common view of the nineteenth-century educated woman? One remembers Mrs. Fillmore and Mrs. Hayes) that evening—and all subsequent evenings, one might add. At each place were six wine glasses and a champagne glass.

Throughout his Presidency, Cleveland maintained this eloquent Victorian standard of entertaining at official functions. His private dining habits were something else again. In fact, during the tedium of one long, rich multi-course meal, he was heard to murmur that he would prefer a plate of corned beef and cabbage.

Cleveland had brought from Albany his cook, who had served him faithfully as Governor and knew exactly how to prepare the simple dishes he liked best. Frank Carpenter, journalistic observer of the time, noted aspects of the President's personal dining habits. "At eight he is ready for his breakfast. This is not a large meal, and the woman he brought from Albany with him knows exactly what he likes. She cooks for him oatmeal, beefsteak, eggs or a chop, with coffee to wash it down."

Lunch for the President, according to Carpenter, was virtually a snack. "It rarely consumes more than fifteen minutes." Dinner was "a plain meal, sometimes with wine, and sometimes without."

Commenting on Presidential entertaining, Carpenter further noted that the role of the President as national host was a taxing one. He had to entertain, "and at his parties, which he pays for out of his own pocket, he has to invite people for whom he cares not a straw, people who will eat his terrapin and drink his champagne tonight, then go off and plot to break down his reputation tomorrow. The position of the President of the United States is not an enviable one."

Rose Cleveland was a definite asset to her brother, but he did not require her services for more than a year, for on June 2, 1886, he married his twenty-two-year-old ward, Frances Folsom, the lovely daughter of Cleveland's former law partner in Buffalo.

The wedding was not the complete surprise that President Tyler's had been. Ever since Cleveland became President, there were the usual rumors everytime he was seen talking to any female. When he was noted spending a good deal of time with Frances Folsom and her widowed mother, it was assumed that he was courting Mrs. Folsom. Jokingly but significantly, Cleveland commented: "I don't see why the papers keep marrying me to old ladies all the while—I wonder they don't say I am engaged to marry her daughter." In truth he was, but nobody at that time believed him.

Later, in planning his wedding, the President felt the White House might be the best place for it, so that it could be as quiet as possible. He wrote his sister: "I want my marriage to be a quiet one and am determined that the American Sovereigns shall not interfere with a thing so purely personal to me. And yet I don't want to be churlish or mean or peculiar for the sake of being peculiar. But if the example of the President is worth anything, I want in this matter to be in the direction of sense and proper decency."

The wedding was a quiet one, as Cleveland had wished, but the anxious bridegroom was determined it would be as perfect as possible for Frank, as he called his young bride. He supervised the purchase of new rugs and pictures and ordered special cut glass from Corning and made-to-order Wedgwood dishes.

For the ceremony, Cleveland had the Blue Room turned into a veritable garden. Floral monograms of bride and groom were arranged in banks of pansies and roses, along with the date of the wedding written in flowers. Flowers seemed to climb the walls and burst from corners. Blazing red begonias glowed from the fireplace.

President Cleveland wrote his own invitations—only forty guests were invited. The President's interest in every aspect of the wedding service was intense. He actually had the word *obey* eliminated from the ceremony.

There may have been only forty guests inside the White House for the wedding, but outside the crowds of curious citizens filled the White House grounds, eager for a peek at the new First Lady. Long before the hour of the ceremony—7 P.M.—the lawn was jammed with sightseers.

Quiet as the wedding may have seemed to Grover Cleveland, it was certainly lavish as well. The guests were treated to a wedding supper of terrapin (almost *de rigueur* at Washington's gala affairs), breast of spring chicken, fish in a variety of fancy shapes, cold meats, salads, *pâté de foie gras,* imaginative ice cream molds, bonbons (a Victorian specialty), and fruits. Dominating the table was a full-rigged three-mast floral ship centerpiece of roses, pansies, and pinks. The elegant Hayes china added to the festivity of the table. Guests milled happily; some sat at the table; others preferred to promenade slowly around the room, eating, chatting, and discussing the menu and festive display.

The spread was generous, the atmosphere informal—just to President Cleveland's taste. A four-tier wedding cake had been ordered from New York. It rested in a double circle of roses, with larger cakes on either side of it. As a remembrance, each guest was presented a small piece of cake "to dream on," carefully packaged in a white satin box, with hand-painted flowers and the wedding date on top.

When Secretary of the Navy William C. Whitney toasted the young bride in champagne, she drank Apollinaris, a mineral water, in return. This was a harbinger of days to come.

Shortly thereafter the bridal couple departed for Deer Park in the mountains of Maryland on their honeymoon. In hot pursuit were platoons of reporters, columnists, and peripheral members of the press. Robert McElroy reported the attack on the Clevelands' privacy launched by the press:

"A President on a honeymoon was something of a gold mine to ambitious reporters with eyes on space. No incident of the life at Deer Park lodge could be too trivial for use, and the President and his wife were literally compassed about with reporters. The persecutors erected a whispering post opposite the cottage and, armed with powerful field glasses, settled down to the task of telling the public how a newly-married President of the United States passes his time."

This was only the beginning. The Clevelands' years in the White House were plagued with continuous probing and prying. And of course, the more the Presidential family withdrew, the harder they were pursued. In a way it was only natural. Cleveland was the first President to be married in the White House, and "Frank" Folsom Cleveland was a most attractive First Lady.

For being so young, she was extraordinarily well-composed, and had definite ideas about the management of the social side of the Executive Mansion. Cleveland had thoughtfully hired a housekeeper, so his new bride could be free of the myriad details of running the establishment and could devote more time to the pleasanter aspects of her job as the nation's hostess.

Mrs. Cleveland responded to her new role with enthusiasm. Her friendliness and warmth were so appealing that at public receptions, people would "go round again" so they could shake her hand and see her smile a second time. As the receptions became so enormously popular, such repeat visits weren't possible. The line waiting to be received sometimes stretched from the White House entrance to the Treasury Building. At one of her "afternoons," it was noted, nine thousand people passed through the Blue Room and shook hands with her. She had to have both arms massaged, "as the left set up a sympathetic ache." One wonders if the effervescent Frank was still smiling at this point.

One of her innovations was a second weekly reception, held each Saturday, so working women would have a chance to meet her. Inasmuch as there was no feminine suffrage at this time, no cynic could accuse her of wooing votes for her husband.

Luncheon assumed special importance in Mrs. Cleveland's day. She enjoyed doing her official entertaining at this meal and rather liked doing it formally. Her formal invitations read: *Mrs. Cleveland requests the pleasure of the company of Miss —— at luncheon Wednesday, January 12, at 1:30 o'clock, 1887.* These affairs, in spite of a certain external formality, were usually enlivened by Frank's own ebullient personality and often by little extra touches with floral arrangements or favors. At a luncheon on Washington's Birthday, 1887, she served thirteen courses (only a few more than par for the day), but what caused the comment and aroused the interest of her guests was a novelty she had devised. In each guest's candy stand was a surprise—chewing gum "done up in fancy papers." (Little did she suspect what her clever novelty would lead to in later American life.)

In spite of the thirteen courses, one thing missing from Frances Cleveland's luncheon table was wine. Her own views on the subject were akin to "Lemonade Lucy's," but she never imposed them on her husband, who was actually quite a connoisseur of wines. At state dinners, seven or eight wine glasses were at each plate. But when dinner began, Mrs. Cleveland's glasses were unobtrusively removed. Only her water glass remained.

Cleveland was undoubtedly delighted to have his wife fulfill her hostess duties at luncheons, thus freeing him as much as possible in the evenings. Of course, state affairs were a necessity, but the "spare time" he had, he preferred spending informally with his family. The Presidential schedule was rigorous, allowing little time for diversions.

It was Cleveland's custom to arise early, read his newspapers before breakfast, and after his breakfast immediately begin work. At one o'clock he would break for lunch. On his way to the private dining room, he would pass through the East Room, where a crowd was usually assembled to see him. It was noted that he "wastes no time, but goes along the line like an old-fashioned beau dancing the grand right and left figure in a cotillion, and then goes to luncheon."

After lunch, it was back to his desk until five o'clock. There was usually a respite then until dinner at seven. By eight-thirty he was back at work again, going strong until midnight. Cleveland was, by nature, a hard-working man, but his terms of office were marked by grave national crises, requiring all his energies.

Cleveland was defeated in his try for a second term. But on the eve of the Clevelands' departure from the White House, February 28, 1889, as they made way for the new Presidential family, the Benjamin Harrisons, Mrs. Cleveland had a few words for the White House staff. According to Colonel Crook, the staff members were distressed and in tears, for they had expected another four years of the Cleveland regime with sunny Frances Cleveland in charge. But the twenty-five-year-old First Lady, composed as always, admonished them: "I want you to take good care of all the furniture and ornaments in the house and not let any of them get lost or broken, for I want to find everything just as it is now when we come back again. We are coming back just four years from today."

Mrs. Cleveland was both prophetic and determined. And correct. Four years later the new President of the United States was Grover Cleveland, hardly a stranger to the White House.

◊◊◊

RECIPES

BOEUF CORNE AU CABEAU

While eating elaborate and richly sauced dishes during a formal White House function, President Cleveland got the scent of corned beef and cabbage being prepared for the kitchen staff. He asked if he could trade his dinner for theirs. On another occasion, after having his favorite corned beef, he commented, "It was the best dinner I had had for months . . . this *Boeuf corne au cabeau!*" Here it is now, to the President's taste.

Corned beef	*Potatoes*
Peppercorns	*Onions*
Garlic	*Cabbage*
Carrots	

Place a 4- or 6-pound piece of corned beef in a large kettle in enough cold water to cover. Add 8 peppercorns and ½ clove garlic and bring meat to a boil. Remove the scum, then lower the heat, cover the kettle, and simmer gently for 4 or 5 hours, or until tender. Add boiling water to keep the beef covered while cooking. In the last ½ hour of cooking, add peeled, quartered carrots (3 or 4), potatoes, (3), and onions (2 or 3); then, 15 minutes before the meat is done, add wedges of 1 head of cabbage. If you add the cabbage too far ahead it gets too watersoaked and overcooked. Serve the corned beef on a platter surrounded by the vegetables. Delicious served with horseradish sauce. *Serves 8 to 10.*

To make horseradish sauce: Mix 4 tablespoons horseradish with 1½ table-spoons vinegar, a few grains of cayenne, and ½ teaspoon salt. Mix well and add ½ cup cream, beaten stiff.

"FRANK" CLEVELAND'S BROWN BREAD

During the Kennedy administration, one of the office secretaries ran across a handwritten recipe of Mrs. Cleveland's, long buried in the archive that is the White House. The recipe evidently had not been published before. Written on stationery bearing the seal of the United States, it read:

BROWN BREAD
One bowl Indian meal
One bowl rye flour
One bowl sour milk
One large cup molasses
One teaspoonful soda
One tablespoonful salt

Steam two and a half hours, and bake from twenty minutes to one-half hour, depending upon heat of oven.

F. F. Cleveland

This sounds about as vague as any recipe could be, yet in translating the indefinite *bowl* into the modern 8-ounce measuring cup, Mrs. Cleveland's recipe turns out to be surprisingly accurate. But Mrs. Cleveland's recipe, unlike most, omits any whole-wheat flour. We amend this to 1 cup rye flour or sifted all-purpose white flour, 1 cup cornmeal, and 1 cup whole wheat flour. (It is possible to make it with 1½ cups cornmeal and 1½ cups rye flour.) Further amendments include using 2 teaspoons soda instead of Mrs. Cleveland's 1 and 1 teaspoon salt instead of 1 tablespoon. Sift the dry ingredients, stir in 2 cups soured milk or buttermilk, and ¾ cup molasses. Beat well. Fill greased molds ⅔ full, using 2 1-pound coffee cans or 1 7-inch mold with a hollow center. Place waxed paper over the top and tie securely. Steam the bread 2½ hours (just as Mrs. Cleveland says), uncover, and set mold in a slow oven (about 300° F.) for 15 to 20 minutes.

At serving time: Cut the bread in the old-fashioned way, by drawing a string around the hot loaf, crossing the ends and pulling them to cut off the slices. This technique keeps the bread light and makes neat pieces. Serve piping hot with plenty of butter—and you will understand why freshly made brown bread was always such a treat. *Makes 4 small loaves or 2 large ones.*

VARIATION: BROWN BREAD IN A PRESSURE COOKER

Steam 15 minutes with the petcock open. Then bring the pressure up to 15 lbs. and steam 40 minutes for small loaves, 1 hour for larger ones. Dry the loaves out in the oven, as above.

SNICKERDOODLES

In an era when the American upper classes had developed an appreciation of the epicurean traditions of the Continent, when turtle stews sold like hotcakes at $35 a quart, there was still an appreciation of "native vittles." Cleveland was, himself, as we have noted, fond of simple American fare. Such a basic cooky as this old New England one was a great favorite.

Sugar	*Salt*
Eggs	*Baking powder*
Butter	*Milk*
Vanilla	*Raisins*
Flour	*Cinnamon*

Gradually add 2 cups sugar to 2 well-beaten eggs. Stir in ½ cup soft (not melted) butter and mix well. Add 1 teaspoon vanilla. Sift 4 cups flour with 1 teaspoon salt and 4 teaspoons baking powder. Add to the egg mixture, alternately with 1 cup milk. Beat well after each addition. Stir in 1 cup chopped raisins. Drop the batter by teaspoonfuls on a greased baking sheet about 1 inch apart. Mix 1 teaspoon cinnamon with 1 tablespoon sugar and sprinkle over the dough on the baking sheet. Bake in a medium-hot (350° F.) oven 15 to 20 minutes, or until done. *Makes approximately 3 dozen.*

TEMPERANCE PUNCH

The Cleveland period was noted for much social drinking, as well as a strong reaction to it. The Clevelands themselves embodied both viewpoints in American life. Mrs. Cleveland was fond of serving light, refreshing nonalcoholic punches, such as this famous one, but she never interfered with her husband's taste for wine, beer, or stronger beverages.

Oranges or orangeade mix	*Water*
Lemons or lemonade mix	*Sugar*
Cranberries or cranberry juice	

With today's abundance of frozen and bottled juices, it is possible to make this refreshing drink very easily. You just mix 1 6-oz. can each orange and lemonade mixes with 6 cups water and 2 cups bottled cranberry juice. Pour into a punch bowl with a large chunk of ice in the middle, and garnish with slices of oranges and lemons and whole raw cranberries. But if you *like* to do things the hard way, squeeze the juice of 1 dozen lemons, ½ dozen oranges (about 2 cups, each lemon and orange juice) and mix with 1 pint cranberries that have been heated until the juice is extracted. Mix the juices with about 1 quart water and sugar to taste. Serve garnished with lemon and orange slices. *Makes 20 servings, about 2½ quarts.*

XXIII

The Presidency, Family Style

The kindest word that could describe the four years of Benjamin Harrison's Presidency is *dull*. Politically, of course, there were accomplishments. But socially, his administration lacked style.

The fault, unfortunately, lay with the President himself. Short and slight, he seemed to live in the shadow of his grandfather, old "Tippecanoe." Nor did the press help his self-confidence by constantly comparing him to his famous ancestor. Dignified and reticent, a proper Victorian gentleman, Benjamin Harrison seemed to many a "cold fish."

In contrast, his wife, Caroline Scott Harrison, was a warm, kindly, motherly woman of many interests. At official functions she did her best to counteract the aloof impression her husband often gave.

The Harrison family was a large, affectionate one, and they treated the White House as a comfortable family home. Caroline may well have been the best housekeeper among our First Ladies. Certainly she needed no paid help to perform this function for her. She managed the staff and all the details of family living with tremendous equanimity.

Each morning the family members met in an upstairs room or in the library. The President's son, Russell, was on hand, as was his daughter, Mrs. James R. McKee. Both children's families gathered, and the family prayed together before going down to breakfast. It was their way of beginning each day as a family group.

Mrs. Harrison has often been pictured as a country homebody from Ohio who marched into the White House, rolled up her sleeves, and began methodically housecleaning. The rolled-up sleeves were more figurative than literal. The Harrisons had lived in Washington during his term as Senator, and Caroline was well liked as a gracious, attractive hostess.

Nobody could complain of the Harrison parties. They were perfectly proper. Every detail was attended to with perfection. The food was good, the floral displays in keeping with the opulence of the day, but some little spark was missing. Perhaps the knack that had made Dolley Madison so unique—that innate ability to combine congenial people and bring out the best in them.

Judging by the menu for the evening of January 7, 1890, when the President and his wife entertained in honor of Vice-President Levi Morton and members of the Cabinet, official dinners were on a par with others of the era. Green turtle soup (that perennial Washington favorite) was served, followed by Chesapeake oysters on the half shell, poached salmon, fillet of beef à la jardiniere, and roasted canvasback duck. The dinner was punctuated with assorted ices, molded into the shape of roses and chrysanthemums.

To help achieve this level of entertaining, the President hired a steward, Hugo Ziemann, who had catered for Prince Napoleon and had other impressive credits to recommend him. He had worked for the Hotel Splendide in Paris and at opulent establishments in New York and Chicago. After all, this was an era in which wealthy Americans thought nothing of importing their own European valets and chefs. The elite had come a long way from syllabub. This chef collaborated on the original White House cookbook.

If leading American private citizens had their own special European chefs, it was hardly likely that the President could do less. But journalist Carpenter noted at the time that President Harrison "likes the plain dishes of Dolly Johnson, the colored cook he engaged from Kentucky, better than the complicated French menus of her predecessor, Madame Pelouard. In her way, Dolly Johnson, too, is an artist. With a Virginia girl named Mary to help her, she can produce a State dinner with as succulent meats and as delicate pastries as delight the patrons of Delmonico's."

Carp found the Presidential family charming in its homeliness: "There is nothing fancy about Mrs. Harrison's methods. She has none of the pretense of affectation of Washington hostesses who ape the embassies' foreign customs and cooking."

Certainly the Harrison Christmas dinner was about as American and unpretentious as the family itself. The dinner began with Blue Point oysters on the half shell, followed by consommé à la Royale, chicken in patty shells, and then the pièce de résistance, stuffed roasted turkey, cranberry jelly, Duchess potatoes, and braised celery. Then came terrapin à la Maryland, lettuce salad with French dressing, and assorted desserts: mince pie, American plum pudding, tutti fruitti ice cream. For those still hungry, ladyfingers, Carlsbad wafers, and macaroons were passed, followed by fruit and coffee.

On such family occasions, the staid Benjamin unbent somewhat. We like particularly the image of him at his grandson's fourth birthday party, March 16, 1891. Fifteen highchairs were arranged around the big table. The centerpiece for the toddlers was a plat of ferns, topped by two crossed flags. Each child's plate had by its side a rush basket of bonbons. Part of the birthday feast included "big dishes of beaten biscuits . . . in the form of little chicks with outspread wings." Bouillon—a Harrison family favorite—was also served, along with cakes and ice cream. The President led his grandson and namesake to the corridor, the little guests following eagerly. He then led all the children in the Virginia Reel, dancing merrily along with them.

Such occasions may have been frequent in the White House, but the public knew little about them. The public was aware, however, of the "sprucing up" Mrs. Harrison was giving the White House. The façade remained the same, but inside dramatic, and if we may be forgiven the pun, sweeping changes were being undertaken. Rotting floorboards were removed, five layers at a time in certain areas, and new floors were laid. The kitchens were renovated and modernized; electric lights and bells were installed throughout the house, and the greenhouses were rejuvenated and enlarged.

Caroline Harrison's special interest—and probably real contribution to White House history—was china. She was quite talented at hand-painting china herself and had a real love for fine old china. During the housecleaning and redecorating of the White House, she decided to have a china closet installed. It occurred to her that a collection of the finest pieces from each Presidential administration would serve as a guide to American taste and a fascinating aspect of the social history of the White House.

This may seem an insignificant thought until one remembers that it had been the custom, up to the Harrisons' day, to destroy all the old china of past administrations. Thus Caroline had quite a task rounding up prize pieces of china from the days of Monroe onward.

The Benjamin Harrison administration was short and memory of it fleeting. But it was not without value or effectiveness, proving perhaps that dullness hath its own reward.

◇◇◇

RECIPES

CORN SOUP

The Harrisons were a soup-loving family. This was a special favorite.

Grated corn	*Flour*
Onions	*Butter*
Milk	*Salt and pepper*

Cut enough fresh corn from the cob to make 2 cups. Boil this in boiling salted water very briefly—2 or 3 minutes. Add 2 sliced onions to 1 quart whole milk in a saucepan and bring to a boil. Slowly add the milk, a few spoonfuls at a time, to a roux made from 2 tablespoons flour and 2 tablespoons butter. Stir the mixture until smooth, add salt and pepper to taste. Then add the drained corn kernels. Simmer over a low fire for 10 to 12 minutes, but do not boil. *Serves 4 to 6.*

FISH CHOWDER

This rich, nourishing chowder must have had special appeal to family-oriented, motherly Caroline Harrison. We find it a good hearty broth for Sunday night supper.

Shad or whitefish	*Tomatoes*
Potatoes	*Salt and pepper*
Onion	*Milk*
Bacon	*Crackers*
Water	

Bone a medium-sized shad or whitefish and cut into pieces. Peel and dice 4 potatoes and 1 onion. Cut ¼ pound bacon slices into ½-inch pieces. Fry the onions and bacon until they are light brown. Then place the fish into a large kettle, along with the bacon, onions, and 2 sliced tomatoes. Add salt and pepper to taste. Do not oversalt, as the bacon is salty. Cover with water and allow mixture to simmer 20 to 25 minutes. When the soup is just about ready, boil 1 pint milk and thicken it with broken crackers. Allow to stand 5 minutes, until crackers have dissolved, then add to the chowder. Stir for the first time, boil for 1 minute, and serve hot. *Serves 6.*

AMBER SOUP

It was Mrs. Harrison's homy custom to serve this hot clear soup at her White House teas and receptions. We may use it under different circumstances today, but it is still a splendid soup.

Chicken	*Onion*
Water	*Parsnip*
Ham	*Parsley*
Soup bone	*Cloves*
Bouquet garni	*Egg whites*
Celery	*Caramel*
Carrot	*Salt and pepper*

Put 1 cleaned and washed stewing chicken in 4 quarts water, along with 1 small slice of ham and 1 soup bone. Boil together over a low fire for about 3½ hours. Then add a bouquet garni, 2 stalks celery, 1 carrot, 1 onion, 1 small parsnip, 2 or 3 sprigs parsley, and 3 cloves. Cook another ½ hour, then strain the liquid and chill it in the refrigerator overnight. Shortly before serving time, remove the wedge of grease that has formed on top of the jar and pour the jellied broth in a saucepan (omit the sediment on the bottom). Beat 2 egg whites and add to the jellied mixture. Boil quickly for 1 minute and then pour the soup through a jelly bag. Add 1 tsp. caramel, made by mixing brown sugar with a little water over a low fire until browned, but not burned. Add salt and pepper to taste. *Makes 2 quarts.*

SCALLOPED OYSTERS WITH MACARONI

It would be hard to spend any time in Washington and not be infected with the local disease of oysteritis. The Harrison family was as fond of oysters—in a variety of forms—as any long-time Washington residents. This recipe was a family favorite, culled from the collection of Mary Harrison McKee, the President's daughter. As noted, raw oysters were a Christmas custom at Harrison dinners. (This dish is a blander variation of one favored by Chester Arthur.)

Macaroni	*Butter*
Oysters	*Oyster liquid*
Salt and pepper	*Breadcrumbs (optional)*

Boil 1 pound package macaroni according to package instructions. When it is soft and tender, put 1 layer in a 2-quart greased casserole. Cover with a layer of 12 drained fresh oysters. Save the liquid. Sprinkle with salt and pepper, dot with butter, then cover with another layer of macaroni, then another layer of oysters, and so on, until the casserole is filled. Pour the oyster liquid over the top, dot with butter. Bake in a 350° F. oven until oysters are cooked. Optional: Put buttered breadcrumbs over the top, before baking. *Serves 6 to 8.*

MRS. HARRISON'S SAUSAGE ROLLS

So addicted was Caroline Harrison to good food properly prepared that she actually compiled a cookbook during her time in Washington (one of her many hobbies). The indefatigable Mrs. H. collected favorite recipes of various legislators' wives and bound them together under the title *Statesmen's Dishes and How to Cook Them*. The recipes are interesting for a variety of reasons. Some of the dishes listed are delicious still. But we found it significant that the dishes contributed were not necessarily regional in character. A Representative from Michigan's wife contributed "Veal Fricandeau"; "Apple Pan Dowdy" came from the Delegate from Arizona; an eggplant dish from Pennsylvania, and so on. Good food knew no geographic boundaries in American life by this date. In Mrs. Harrison's own handwriting was a recipe for her special sausage rolls, which today make a lovely hot *hors-d'oeuvre.*

> *Biscuit mix (or biscuit dough from*　　　*Cocktail sausages*
> *scratch if you have time)*

Make a light biscuit dough either from a mix or from scratch. If you make it from scratch, *à la* Caroline Harrison, use milk and let it rise overnight. In the morning roll it thin and cut it into tiny shapes with a biscuit cutter. In the center of each piece place a sausage, or if you make your own sausages as Mrs. H. did, "place a roll of sausage the size of a good-sized hickory nut" and roll it up in the dough. Bake in a hot oven until golden brown, and serve with cocktail picks.

If you want to make a more substantial dish of this, cut the biscuit shapes larger and use slices of the sausage that comes in a fatter roll. Serve as a main course at luncheon, accompanied by mushroom sauce.

DEVILED ALMONDS

This recipe of Mrs. Harrison's makes a delicious, easy-to-prepare tidbit to serve with cocktails. In the Harrisons' day, it was considered a "nibbly" at a tea or reception, and may still be used as such today.

> *Blanched almonds*　　　*Cayenne*
> *Butter*　　　*Salt*

Put ½ pound blanched almonds in a preheated skillet with 2 ounces butter. Sauté the nuts gently until they are light brown. Drain on absorbent paper. Place them in a cake pan, sprinkle cayenne and salt lightly over them, shake the nuts well. Serve hot.

SADDLE OF MUTTON VINTAGE 1890

Mrs. Harrison's cookbook is fascinating as a guide to how different cooking was in her day, the 1880s and 1890s. One recipe, suggesting a saddle of mutton as the *pièce de résistance* for Christmas dinner, reads: "Send for your butcher about November 1st, and order him to take a week in selecting your Christmas mutton. If you take the shoulder too, you can get the whole for 18 cents per pound." Now we know what is meant by "the good old days!"

> *Saddle of mutton*　　　*Water*
> *Vinegar*　　　*Currant jelly*
> *Salt*

Wash the saddle of mutton, wrap it in heavy muslin, and hang it where the temperature can be kept below freezing. Every few days wet the cloth with vinegar to keep the mutton from drying out. After 6 weeks it is just ready for the Christmas dinner. Then wash it in salt and water. Place in a large roasting pan in a slow (250° F.) oven and baste frequently while roasting. Allow 20 minutes to the pound. (We favor a slightly rare mutton.) In serving, use currant jelly as an accompaniment. This old recipe places final responsibility for the dish on the carver instead of the cook, saying, "The delicious flavor depends in part on the carver. He should cut the slices very thin, and parallel with the backbone."

YOUNG ROAST PIG FOR CHRISTMAS

Another recipe for Christmas shows how times had changed by Mrs. Harrison's day from the early days of our Republic, when a roast pig was content with an apple in his mouth. Victorian ornamentation suggested the following:

When ready to a turn, place on the platter on its knees; put on his back a little Chinese doll on a saddle of blue satin, with reins of smilax, and for a bit an ear of popcorn; wire the cue of the doll so it will stand straight out, and you will be astonished at the rate of speed which his pigship is making across the table. Garnish the dish with holly and mistletoe, and if you have a lot of merry children about you will be well paid for your trouble in watching the pleasure which this jaunty little race horse will give them.

PRESIDENT HARRISON'S CHRISTMAS TURKEY

As homespun as the Presidential Christmas dinner was for its day, it still required elaborate preparation. We think these directions for preparing a turkey deserve a footnote of comment. If you raise your own turkeys (doesn't everyone?), you may find this advice inspirational.

> *Turkey*   *Sherry*
> *English walnuts*

The turkey should be cooped up and fed well some time before Christmas. Three days before it is slaughtered it should have an English walnut forced down its throat three times a day, a glass of sherry once a day. The meat will be deliciously tender, and have a fine nutty flavor. [What a lovely way to go!]

CHICKEN SALAD WITH HOMEMADE MAYONNAISE

Changes in food fashion are apparent in the progression of this dish from the days of President Buchanan, when chicken salad was served at the inaugural ball, to today when we consider it good picnic fare. The Harrisons enjoyed it as regular luncheon or dinner fare, as evidenced by this recipe. Rather fancy it was too, when served as Mrs. Harrison preferred it. Naturally, the mayonnaise was homemade.

Chickens	*Red pepper*
Celery	*Eggs*
Olives	*Lemon juice*
Capers	*Lettuce*
Olive oil	*Beets*
Vinegar	*Carrots*
Salt	

Boil 2 large stewing chickens, remove the skin and fat, and dice the meat. Mix with the meat 3 cups diced celery, 3 chopped black olives, and 2 teaspoons capers. Make a dressing of 6 tablespoons olive oil, 2 tablespoons vinegar, 2 teaspoons salt, and a dash of red pepper. Mix well and pour over the chicken. Allow to stand 2 or 3 hours in refrigerator.

To make mayonnaise: Add 1 pint high-quality olive oil to 2 egg yolks. Stir steadily with a silver fork. As the dressing thickens, thin with lemon juice, keeping the consistency like that of rich cream. Add salt and cayenne to taste. At serving time, make a mound of the chicken salad on a platter, pour the mayonnaise over it, and garnish with lettuce, olives, and with beats and carrots cut into fancy forms. *Serves 12.*

EGG YOLK DRESSING FOR CHICKEN SALAD

This variation is easily made with an electric blender.

Egg yolks	*Cayenne*
Hard-boiled eggs	*Lemon juice*
Salt	*Olive oil*

Place 4 egg yolks in blender. Add yolks of 4 hard-boiled eggs, ½ teaspoon salt, ¼ teaspoon cayenne, and 3 tablespoons lemon juice. Blend until smooth. Keep motor running as you gradually add 2 cups olive or corn oil. Blend and then mix with diced chicken and other ingredients.

CRAB SALAD

Benjamin Harrison's daughter, Mrs. John McKee, was fond of this recipe and frequently prepared it for the entire family.

Fresh crabs or crabmeat	*Olive oil*
Egg yolks	*Lemon juice or vinegar*
Salt and pepper	*Lettuce or watercress*

If using fresh crabs, boil 1 dozen for 30 minutes in very salty water, using ½ cup salt to a quart water. Allow to cool and then remove the meat. Mix with mayonnaise, homemade or otherwise, and place the salad on crisp lettuce leaves or on watercress.

SPICY MACARONI

Mrs. Harrison was known for her ingenuity in the kitchen. This spiced-up macaroni is a good example.

Macaroni	*Mustard*
Milk	*Butter*
Red pepper	*Cheddar cheese*

Boil 1 pound macaroni in 2 quarts water with 1 teaspoon salt until tender. Drain and put into a greased casserole with 2 cups milk. Add a dash of red pepper, 1 teaspoon dry mustard, and 2 tablespoons melted butter. Grate Cheddar cheese thickly over the top. Brown casserole in moderately hot (350° F.) oven about 25 minutes. Serve hot. *Makes 6 to 8 servings.*

PUFF OMELET

In her cookbook Mrs. Harrison collected a number of basic recipes that had been "dressed up," among them this heavenly omelet.

Milk	*Salt and pepper*
Cornstarch	*Dill*
Eggs	

Heat 1 cup milk. Add 1 tablespoon cornstarch moistened with a little cold milk. Stir and heat. Remove from fire. When cool, add 4 well-beaten egg yolks. Then add 4 egg whites that have been beaten stiff but not dry. Beat all together. Add salt and pepper to taste. Pour into a buttered baking dish and bake a short while in a hot oven. Fifteen minutes in a moderately hot (375° F.) oven should be sufficient. This is a highly ornamental and delectable breakfast dish. We like it with a pinch of dill added along with the salt and pepper.

CORN SPECIALTIES OF THE HARRISON MENAGE

The Ohio–Indiana-bred Harrison family were all corn addicts, favoring a great number of recipes for serving this useful vegetable. America's corn repertoire had grown considerably from Colonial days.

Canned corn may be used if the kernels are chopped fine.

GREEN-CORN FRITTERS

Sweet corn	*Salt and pepper*
Eggs	*Flour*

Cut through each row of kernels of sweet corn with the point of a sharp knife. With the back of the knife, press out the pulp. Or use canned or frozen corn. Mix 1 pint corn pulp or kernels with 4 well-beaten egg yolks, 2 tablespoons flour, salt and pepper to taste. Mix well. Add the 4 stiffly beaten whites. Drop by spoonfuls on a buttered griddle, so that each spoonful forms a small cake. Brown the cakes on both sides. Serve hot as a side dish with meat or chicken. *Serves 6.*

STEWED CORN

Corn	*Salt*
Milk or cream	*Sugar*

Split the kernels of corn before removing them from the cob. In cutting them off, cut through several times, leaving much to be scraped off, thereby making a fine mass. Bring 1 pint milk or cream to a boil, slowly add 2 cups corn. Bring to a second boil, then cover saucepan and cook 15 minutes, with just a little salt and sugar added. *Serves 6.*

PRESIDENTIAL FIG PUDDING

In a way, this dessert epitomizes Benjamin Harrison's food preferences. It is made of a staple, common food, but it is prepared very well indeed, with imagination exercised in the preparation. Mrs. Harrison was justifiably proud of her concoction and included it in her cookbook.

Soda	*Cinnamon*
Hot water	*Nutmeg*
Milk	*Black molasses*
Eggs	*Suet*
Flour	*Dried figs*

Dissolve 1 teaspoon soda in 1 tablespoon hot water and then mix with 1 cup milk. Set aside momentarily. Beat 2 eggs until frothy, and stir them into the milk. Sift 3¼ cups flour with 1 teaspoon cinnamon and ½ teaspoon nutmeg. Add to the milk–egg mixture. Beat thoroughly. Combine 1 cup molasses with 1 cup chopped suet and 1 pint finely cut figs. Mix well and turn into 2 small or 1 large well-buttered, brown-bread molds. Steam for 5 hours,* covered tightly. Serve warm with hard sauce.

FRESH FIG PIE WITH WHIPPED CREAM

President Harrison was extremely fond of figs, particularly served as desserts. His clever wife was kept busy contriving interesting new ways of serving them. We think you will find this as appealing as he did.

Flour	*Sugar*
Salt	*Eggs*
Butter	*Cornstarch*
Ice water	*Sherry*
Figs	*Lemons*
Water	*Cream*

Make a pie crust of 3½ cups flour, a pinch of salt, 1 cup butter mixed together. Then add ½ cup ice water. Mix lightly and refrigerate for 24 hours. Next day roll the dough, line 2 pie tins, and bake the crusts in a hot (400° F.) oven until lightly browned. Clean 30 fresh figs and cut them into small pieces. Add ½ cup water and 1½ cups sugar to the diced figs and cook over a low fire for 8 minutes. Set aside. Combine 3 beaten egg yolks with 2 tablespoons cornstarch. Add 2 tablespoons sherry, juice of 2 lemons, and a little water. Mix well and add 1 cup cream. Mix thoroughly again. Pour on the fig mixture and cook in a double boiler 5 minutes. Cool slightly. Meanwhile, beat 4 egg whites until stiff. Slowly fold into the fig mixture. Pour the mixture carefully into the pie shells and brown a few minutes (about 12) in hot (400° F.) oven. Top with whipped cream, slightly sweetened with sugar. *Makes 2 large (9 or 10 inch) pies.*

FRUIT PUDDING OF GENERAL SHERIDAN'S WIDOW

One of the ladies whose recipes Mrs. Harrison collected and prized was General Philip Sheridan's widow. Her fruit pudding must have pleased her husband as it did Mrs. Harrison.

* Can be done in a pressure cooker in 1 hour. Follow manufacturers directions for steamed puddings.

Sponge cake	*Gelatin*
Strawberries, raspberries, black-	*Egg yolks*
berries, currants, or pineapple	*Sugar*
—fresh fruit is best	*Cream*
Milk	*Lemon juice*

Line a mold with slices of sponge cake (store variety will do). Put a layer of fresh fruit on top. The fruit may be any of those listed, but is better if fresh. Tear fruit into bits. Place a layer of hot custard over the fruit, followed by a layer of sponge cake, then fruit, then custard again, until the mold is full. Place in refrigerator until thoroughly chilled. Serve turned out of the mold with sugar and cream or whipped cream on top.

To make the custard: bring 1 pint milk to a boil, add 1 envelope i.e., 1 tablespoon unflavored gelatin which has been soaked in a little cold water and then dissolved in ¼ cup hot milk. Beat 4 egg yolks with ¼ cup sugar till light. Gradually add the hot mixture. Finally, off-heat, turn egg yolks into the custard. Continue cooking until thickened about 5 minutes. Remove from heat, stir in ½ cup heavy cream and at the last add juice of 1 lemon, about 3 tablespoons.

PECAN CAKE

Caroline Harrison's daughter inherited her love of cooking and her skills. This recipe of Mary Harrison McKee's makes a deliciously light cake.

Butter	*Milk*
Sugar	*Powdered sugar*
Flour	*Grated pineapple*
Baking powder	*Pecans*
Egg whites	

Cream 1 cup butter with 2 cups sugar. Mix well. Sift 2½ cups flour with 2 teaspoons baking powder. Whip 8 egg whites until foamy but not quite stiff. Add a little bit of the egg-white mixture to the sugar–butter mixture, then add 1 cup of the flour to the mixture, and beat. Add a little—¼ cup—milk, then 1 cup more of the flour. Then add another ¼ cup milk and the rest of the flour. Finally add the rest of the egg whites. Beat and pour into a greased and floured cake pan. Bake in a preheated moderate (350° F.) oven until a toothpick comes out of the cake center clean.

To make frosting: Beat 6 egg whites until stiff adding gradually 12 tablespoons superfine sugar. Add 1 small can drained grated pineapple, along with 2 cups pecans, chopped fine. (The nuts and pineapple should be mixed first, so nuts can be softened by the pineapple.) Beat well. Cover the cake. Place pecan halves over the top of the cake while frosting is still soft.

VICTORIAN GOODIES

The 1890s were the heyday of candy-making. Ladies exchanged bonbon recipes as rapidly as new ones were acquired. Making the candy was half the fun; but of course eating it was no small joy, as the sweets-loving Harrison family could testify. It wasn't just the President's grandson who liked bonbons. Grandfather ate his share. These candy recipes were in Mrs. Harrison's collection.

BIRTHDAY BONBONS

Egg whites	*Seedless dates*
Cold water	*Blanched almonds*
Powdered sugar	*Candied cherries*

Form a stiff dough with 2 egg whites beaten together with an equal quantity of cold water and enough powdered sugar to give body (about 2 pounds powdered sugar will be needed). Set dough aside while preparing the fruit. Fill seedless dates with the dough and cover with it. Cover blanched almonds with it. Form the dough into round or small oblong balls and put a cherry on top (English walnuts may be used too).

SAUCISSONS DE CHOCOLAT

Sweet chocolate	*Blanched almonds*
Honey	*Cloves and cinnamon*

Melt 2 squares (2 ounces) of sweet chocolate in the top of a double boiler. Remove double boiler from heat and add 2 tablespoons honey, or enough to mold the chocolate. Mix 1 cup blanched almonds, cut into pea-size pieces, into the chocolate, along with a dash of powdered cloves and cinnamon. Mold with hands into "sausages" about 5½ inches long, 1 inch thick. Wrap in wax paper and chill. The "sausages" keep for months. To serve, slice them thinly and offer in a pretty bonbon dish.

REGENT PUNCH

The Harrisons lived in an age when punch was all the rage. Official receptions and lawn parties thrived on festive drinks, and Mrs. Harrison, no slouch in the kitchen, had a variety she offered guests. One such was this favorite of the times.

Loaf sugar or rock candy	*Orange juice*
Strong black tea	*Lemon juice*
Brandy	*Ice*
Rum	*Champagne*

Dissolve 1 pound sugar or rock candy in 1 cup strong black hot tea. Allow to cool. Then add ¾ cup brandy, ¾ cup rum, 1 cup orange juice, ¾ cup lemon juice. Add ice. Just before serving, add 1 bottle champagne. Serve in chilled punch bowl with a big block of ice in the center. *Serves 16 to 20.*

SUMMERTIME APPLE TODDY

Apples	*Peach brandy*
Boiling water	*Curaçao*
Jamaica rum	*Sugar*
Brandy	

Bake 12 large apples thoroughly. When very soft (even overdone), put them into a jar and mash them well. Pour 3 quarts boiling water into the jar. Cover and allow to cool. Then add 1 pint Jamaica rum, 3 pints brandy, ½ pint peach brandy or Southern Comfort, and ½ pint Curaçao. Sweeten to taste with sugar. Allow to stand a day or so at least, occasionally mashing the apples further. Strain before serving. To serve, use small chilled glasses filled with ice. The same toddy may be served hot in winter. Simply reheat the day after toddy has been made, then strain and serve in heated mugs. *Makes 48 small servings.*

NOGGS, CIDER AND EGG VARIETIES

For all the Puritan aspects of the late Victorians, they were great social drinkers. Punches and toddys reigned supreme in most hostesses' recipe books. These two Harrison noggs were perenially popular.

1890 CIDER NOGG

Egg yolks	*Cider*
Sugar	*Ginger*

Beat 4 egg yolks to a foamy froth. Add 2 tablespoons sugar and beat again. Slowly add 2 quarts good cider. A dash of ginger may be added if favored. Stir well and serve. *Makes 16 4-ounce servings.*

MARYLAND EGG NOGG

Eggs   *Brandy*
Sugar   *Jamaica rum*
Grated nutmeg   *Milk or cream*

Separate 1 dozen eggs and beat the yolks to a froth with 1 cup sugar. Add 1 grated nutmeg, 1 pint brandy, 1 pint Jamaica rum. Beat altogether thoroughly. Then add 1 gallon milk or cream. Beat egg whites until stiff and they stand in mounds. Place the liquor–milk mixture into a punch bowl and cover with the egg whites, or else pour the mixture into individual cups or glasses, and then scoop out the egg whites and place a layer on top of each cup. *Makes 60 servings.*

XXV

Victorianism with a Vengeance

Presentially speaking, one might call William McKinley our last Victorian. Certainly his *fin de siècle* administration brought Victorianism in all its pomp and ceremony to a crescendo in American social life.

The stage had been set for the McKinleys' triumphant appearance. Each administration since Grant's had been leading up to the climax and finale the McKinley administration provided. The flood of flowers at state banquets, the floral souvenirs at each lady's plate, the emphasis on spectacle, all seemed to become grander and grander as each Presidential family tried to keep up with and even surpass the previous one. But with the splendor and opulence of the McKinley regime reaching its dizzying heights, there was nowhere to go but down.

Before McKinley became President, there was nothing to indicate that he would follow such an elaborate path. As Governor of Ohio he was not known for lavish entertainments. Ida Saxton McKinley, his wife, was a semi-invalid, an epileptic who was subject to frequent seizures, which resulted in brief spells of unconsciousness. It is small wonder the McKinleys did not care for large-scale entertaining.

But when McKinley was nominated for President, the subject of his wife's health became a campaign issue. Would her health permit her to fulfill the functions of the First Lady? Would she be able to sustain the rigorous social schedule that had become *de rigueur* in the White House? Doubts were raised by many.

The doubters reckoned without the indomitable will of Ida McKinley. To quell the doubts of many voters, she staged a sumptuous reception in honor of the McKinleys' silver wedding anniversary. For six hours she stood valiantly at her husband's side, greeting guests. Hundreds of well-wishers and curiosity-seekers wandered through the old McKinley house in Canton, Ohio, the home in which Ida and William had begun their married life together. Flowers were everywhere, and tables were piled high with lobster salad, sweets of all kinds, claret and coffee—*cuisine à la* Canton. Throughout the afternoon an orchestra played appropriate romantic themes.

Fears about Ida McKinley's stamina (or lack of it) were assuaged. Before long, Ida and husband were happily ensconced in the White House, and a long procession of lengthy formal dinners began.

To preserve his wife's fragile health, President McKinley tried to eliminate all unnecessary entertaining. The gala luncheons that had marked the Clevelands' style vanished. Social events at the White House were distilled into large formal dinner parties and enormous evening receptions. McKinley felt the building should be accessible to the public (Cleveland had hugged all the privacy he could get), so the public flocked there as often as possible, even resorting to gate-crashing when necessary.

The dinners must have been something to behold. As more and more countries had diplomatic representation in Washington, the official guest list had grown considerably since the Civil War. In Cleveland's day, the last diplomatic dinner had to be held in the White House corridor to accommodate all the guests. Only Chester Arthur's Tiffany glass screen sheltered the guests from the chilling drafts of the vestibule. The McKinleys continued this dining arrangement. One can imagine how much the ladies, in their light finery, enjoyed those three-hour dinners.

The dining area was so cold when the front door opened and sent blasts of wind into the vestibule that divans were robbed of their cushions to provide warmth for the ladies' feet. The McKinley guest list grew to 100 for dinner. Dinner began at 8 P.M. and seemed, to many of the guests, to extend to infinity. Mark Hanna, the political leader, used to attend the dinners and sit with watch in hand, timing the service when it was slow.

Another guest, John D. Long, considered the White House dinners—and all the Washington galas that followed the Presidential style—"horrible." "Language can not express the reluctance with which I stretch myself out on the altars of these sacrifices," he wrote. "The same food, the same dishes, same waiters, each ejecting the same breath on your right shoulder; the same courses, the same long hours, the same men and women; exactly the same conversation; and the same everything. Nobody wants to give them. Nobody wants to attend them."

Long's view, the long view one is tempted to say, may have been shared by many, but only under their breath, for on the surface people scrambled for invitations to the White House and other noted establishments.

No one enjoyed such dinners more, or so it seemed, than Mrs. McKinley. Yet one wonders how. Heavily dosed with medication, she sat tensely with hands tightly clasped, eyes glazed, smiling vaguely, nodding and bowing. Perhaps medication was the solution to enjoying a McKinley banquet. The President altered protocol by insisting on sitting beside Mrs. McKinley at formal dinners. He wanted to be near her when she was subject to an attack.

The President had suffered through one dinner apart from his wife, but he was, in the words of an observer, "anxious to the point of distraction" about Ida. Later he asked a confidant, "Could it possibly offend anyone for me to have my wife sit beside me?" There is something pathetically touching about the President's query. His concern and love for his wife were among his strongest qualities.

At each public dinner that concern and love were put to the test, and the President invariably received high marks. When a seizure was imminent—and McKinley was tuned in to catch the first vibrations—the President quickly placed his handkerchief or table napkin over Ida's convulsed face. As her body relaxed, indicating she was recovering, he removed the covering. There is something almost surrealistic in the fact that for Ida time stood still. As soon as she recovered, she resumed the conversation she had been in the midst of as the attack struck—in midsentence, as it were—seemingly unaware of the interruption. Considering that the dinner table often extended from the East Room down the corridor as far as the State Dining Room, it is no wonder that Ida's seizures went almost unnoticed by some of the guests.

The McKinley hospitality was certainly generous. Even Long, who found the receptions "more than ordinarily dreary," could not complain of the abundance of the fare. During the first McKinley winter in the White House an all-time record was achieved, never to be challenged: the McKinleys served a dinner consisting of seventy-one courses. The occasion was a banquet in honor of President and Mrs. Sanford B. Dole of the Republic of Hawaii, who could hardly fail to have been impressed.

Seventy-one courses for eighty to a hundred guests: it all seems rather staggering today. The one consolation seems to have been that guests could retire early. The dinners broke up early and informally—"American fashion," as someone noted at the time.

In studying the portraits of President and Mrs. McKinley one becomes aware that gargantuan meals were probably very much to their taste. Portly, almost pyramidic, they thrived on large meals three times a day. Both liked plain food, in substantial quantities. Both breakfasted on army portions of eggs, hot breads, potatoes, steak or chops, fish on occasion, fruit, and coffee. Breakfast, however, was only the beginning. Lunch and dinner followed the same abundant and starchy path.

As other Presidents before him had, McKinley received numerous gifts from well-wishers. Many of these were food, a fact duly appreciated by both members of the family. On one occasion, the President was presented with a prize melon from Georgia that was two and a half feet long and six feet in circumference. This monument was wrapped in an American flag, tied with white ribbon, and presented with great ceremony. Representative Livingston jokingly assured President McKinley that "No office seeker is enclosed within it."

To conserve what strength Ida McKinley had, she took most of her meals in the family quarters, coming to the table only for large formal affairs, where her presence was expected—or at least she felt it was. But when her husband won re-election in 1900, Ida seemed to gather a fresh reserve of strength, for she helped them plan an enormous centennial celebration to mark the day, December 12, 1800, when the John Adams family became the first occupants of the White House. This was practically the only affair that Ida took an active part in planning.

In a way, President McKinley fulfilled many of the functions a First Lady normally fills. While conducting a war abroad and trying to solve economic problems at home, he was also planning state dinners, organizing the floral festoons needed for each official affair, and providing tender nursing care to a half-incapacitated wife.

On September 6, 1901, Ida McKinley's nurse and boon companion was shot while attending the Buffalo Exposition. Eight days later he died. It was feared that the shock would be too much for Ida, that she too would succumb shortly from despair at her loss. But that indomitable will was stronger than anyone suspected. It was six years before the frail Ida McKinley joined her husband.

◇◇◇

R E C I P E S

THE MCKINLEY OMELET

Eggs were a standard on the McKinley breakfast table, usually fried or scrambled, but sometimes "fancied up," as in this omelet. Steaks or chops often accompanied the omelet at a McKinley breakfast.

Eggs	*Cornstarch*
Milk	*Baking powder*
Salt and pepper	*Meat gravy*

Beat 4 egg yolks until light. Add ⅓ cup milk and beat again. Then add salt and pepper to taste, as well as ½ teaspoon cornstarch and ½ teaspoon baking powder.

Mix well. Then fold in 4 egg whites that have been beaten stiff but not dry. Pour the mixture into a greased casserole and bake in a moderately hot (375° F.) oven until slightly brownish on top. Serve on a warm platter with gravy made from turkey, chicken, roast beef, or pork poured over the top. If you use the gravy, this would make a better lunch or dinner omelet. But by today's taste standards, the omelet alone and unadorned is superior breakfast fare. *Serves 2.*

BOILED FISH *A LA* MCKINLEY

While the formal menus were even more elaborate than during preceding administrations, McKinley dinners *en famille* were simple affairs with plain home-cooking. This dish was a family favorite.

Fresh fish	*Hard-boiled eggs*
Onion	*Cold boiled beets*
Cloves	*Oil and vinegar dressing*
Lemon	*Mayonnaise*

Clean and skin any fresh fish you favor. Do not halve it. Prepare a skillet with oiled paper on the bottom. Place the fish on the paper, along with 1 sliced onion and 2 whole cloves. Cover with water and poach gently over medium heat until fish is tender, not many minutes. Remove fish to a platter and pour the juice of 1 lemon over it. Take the whites of 2 hard-boiled eggs and chop very fine. Sieve the yolks. Place a row of whites down the middle of the fish, with a row of sieved yolks along each side of the whites. Next to the yolks on each side place a row of cold boiled beets cut into fancy shapes. Pour an oil and vinegar dressing over the fish and drop a dab of mayonnaise on each beet shape. Garnish the platter with lettuce leaves. A very simple dish can thus be made very attractive through its presentation.

RED FLANNEL HASH

This old New England specialty found favor in Victorian times with Midwesterners like the McKinleys. Good, nourishing, and filling, it was their kind of food. It is believed that to make a good hash, you need a good hasher—an old-fashioned wooden chopping bowl and chopper. The metal ones just aren't the same.

Corned beef	*Salt and pepper*
Cooked beets	*Worcestershire sauce (optional)*
Cooked potatoes	*Light cream*
Onion	*Bacon drippings or salt pork*

Mix 2 cups chopped corned beef with 2 cups chopped cooked beets and 3½ cups chopped cooked potatoes. Chop all ingredients into cubes. Add 1 medium onion, finely chopped, and salt and pepper to taste. A modern innovation is 1½ teaspoons. Worcestershire sauce, which we think adds zing to the recipe. Mix all the ingredients with just enough light cream to hold together. Melt ¼ cup bacon drippings or salt pork in a heavy iron skillet. Spread the hash evenly over the bottom of the skillet. Heat over a low fire, watching carefully. Loosen the edges and shake the skillet from time to time to keep the hash from burning. When a nice brown crust forms on the bottom, turn the hash with a spatula. Serve on a warm platter. *Serves 6.*

MARK HANNA HASH

In Ohio this variation of hash is still popular. Mark Hanna, after all, was a prominent Ohioan at one time. As political leader and Senator from McKinley's home state, he exerted considerable influence on the McKinley administration. This hash, named for him (but not intended to reflect his executive ability), was eaten by the President—with or without relish we couldn't be sure.

Very simple to make, you just make a regular corned beef hash and serve it with a soft-boiled or poached egg on top. There are those among us who are partial to it for breakfast.

HOT LOBSTER SALAD

A perennial favorite in the Victorian era, this dish was prized enough by the McKinleys to be served as the focal point of their silver wedding anniversary celebration. It had been a Benjamin Harrison favorite as well.

Lobsters	*Madeira*
Salt	*Egg yolks*
Red pepper	*Light cream*
Truffles	

Boil 2 large lobsters and split them open. Pick all the meat from the shells and cut it into 1-inch lengths, as much the same size as possible. Put the lobster meat in a saucepan on high heat, adding a dash of salt, ½ teaspoon red pepper, and 2 medium-size truffles cut into small pieces. Cook 5 minutes, stirring often to keep from burning. Add ⅓ cup Madeira and continue cooking until ½ the wine disappears. Beat 3 egg yolks with ½ pint cream until light. Add to the lobster, stir until it thickens. Pour the lobster mixture into a hot bowl and serve piping hot. Good on toast triangles. *Serves 4 to 6.*

PRESIDENTIAL ICEBOX COOKIES

We would call these refrigerator cookies today, but call them what you like, we think you'll like them as much as the Presidential family did.

Butter	*Flour*
Brown sugar	*Baking powder*
Eggs	*Nuts*

Cream 1½ cups soft butter and 2 cups brown sugar. Add 2 well-beaten eggs and mix well. Sift 3 cups flour with 2 teaspoons baking powder and add to the egg–butter mixture. Beat well and then add ½ cup nuts, preferably walnuts. Divide the dough into 2 or 3 pieces. Place each piece on a piece of waxed paper and shape it into a roll. Wrap tightly and chill in refrigerator. When firm, (preferably after 24 hours) slice ⅛ to ¼ inch thick onto a cooky sheet and bake in a hot (375° F.) oven 12 to 15 minutes. *Makes 6 dozen.*

CARDINAL PUNCH

President McKinley and other Victorians considered this as an accompaniment to turkey or chicken. As illustrative of the Changing Times Department, we would serve it today as the finale to a rich, elaborate dinner. It is a pleasant, refreshing variation of Roman punch.

Sugar	*Strong tea*
Water	*Brandy*
Orange juice	*Curaçao*
Lemon juice	

Boil 2 cups sugar in 4 cups water for 10 to 12 minutes. Slowly add ⅔ cup orange juice and ⅓ cup lemon juice. Strain ¼ cup strong tea and add it. Allow mixture to cool and then put it in the freezing unit of your refrigerator until it turns mushy. Remove and add ¼ cup each of brandy and Curaçao. Return to freezer and freeze until firm. Serve in tall chilled coupe glasses. *Makes approximately 2 quarts.*

XXVI

Moose, not Mousse: A New Era Begins

When Theodore Roosevelt moved into the White House in 1901, one of the first things he did after looking around at his new home was to pitch the potted palms out of the reception rooms. Teddy evidently decided that he wanted his jungle authentic, not the hothouse variety.

This small action was symbolic of Teddy Roosevelt's desire to change and simplify what had become a most unwieldy structure, both socially and decoratively.

The Roosevelts were an attractive, ebullient family. In addition to the President and his wife, Edith, there were six children, from baby Quentin to seventeen-year-old Alice. Theodore, Jr., was away at school much of the time, but Archie, Kermit, and Ethel were natural, noisy youngsters who were not in the least in awe of the White House. It was so much "just plain home" to them that when Archie was in bed with measles, the other children smuggled the family pony into the basement and up the elevator to Archie's bedroom. Archie was delighted, but there is no record available indicating what the White House staff thought about the escapade.

As the boys roller-skated along the upstairs corridors and played leapfrog over the satin upholstery of the establishment, their father was at work making the house itself more livable. He enlarged the State Dining Room (high time!) and, under the supervision of the famous architect Stanford White, removed the ornate false timbers from the East Room and curlicues and gingerbread trim from many of the other rooms. By removing the gimcracks, he simplified the basic interior. The house had been described, with all the hodgepodge additions from various eras, as a cross between Neo-Classic and Mississippi River Boat.

There were many ways in which the Roosevelts brought fresh air into the White House after decades of stale style and artificial elegance. Nowhere was this more easily seen than at the table. Years later, the President's daughter, Mrs. Nicholas Longworth, described the Roosevelt family food preferences for "coarse food and plenty of it." She added that "the family really cared very little for exotic foods." An observer at the time noted that Mrs. Roosevelt favored "simple food for her family and herself as heartily as she believed in fresh air and exercise."

Yet at one point a magazine article of the period called President Roosevelt a gourmet. Rough Rider Teddy could not let such a dastardly challenge go by unanswered. He replied: "When anyone desires to make a widespread impression that the President and family sit down to a four or five course breakfast, a six or seven course lunch and a ten course dinner, the President feels that a denial is not inappropriate." (At a time when Teddy was battling the robber barons, it is possible he didn't want his public image tarnished by being called, heaven help us, a gourmet. The pendulum of national taste was swinging back again.)

The Roosevelts were a comfortably affluent family who could eat what they liked. What they liked happened to be simple—not Spartan, as some reports have suggested—but good simplicity in hearty helpings. For breakfast, the President had hard-boiled eggs with rolls and coffee. He varied this occasionally by having a big bowl of hominy with salt and butter. Teddy had set ideas, within the limitations of his food preferences, of just how his food should be prepared. The eggs *must* be hard-boiled, not medium or soft. Rolls must be homemade and served in great quantities. Coffee, too, was consumed in volume. Ted, Jr., recalled that his father's coffee cup was "more in the nature of a bathtub."

If the President lunched alone, he had a bowl of milk, sometimes with crackers, sometimes not. But he was capable of eating quantities of food if the occasion arose. One observer, O. K. Davis, said, "I have seen him eat a whole chicken and drink four large glasses [of milk] at one meal, and chicken and milk were by no means the only things served."

Lunch with the family usually consisted of cold meat (often leftovers), freshly baked bread, cantaloupe in season, and tea. Family dinners were often three-course affairs, but sometimes only two. The food was generously served but unpretentious. The White House received many gifts of game, an unending delight to Teddy. He was also very fond of chicken, as has been implied, and had pronounced ideas on serving it, saying once: "The only way to serve fried chicken is with white gravy soaked into the meat."

Steak was a popular food with the President. In carving it, he insisted on the rule that each portion should include some of the meat from above and some from below the bone of a porterhouse or club steak. His intake of the food he liked was prodigious. Lloyd Griscom recalled that the President stoked up "as though he were a machine."

One guest at the White House table recalled a delicious lunch of bouillon, salt fish, chicken in rice, baked beans and fresh rolls, followed by Bavarian cream, preserves, and cake. President Roosevelt had seconds of beans, and seemed partial to the dessert as well. He had a great sweet tooth and usually used as many as seven lumps of sugar in his coffee (with a bathtub cup, one would expect this).

Hominy was a staple at the Roosevelt table. In addition to being part of break-fast, it was often served as a starch at lunch and dinner, with meat gravy over it. Archie Butt, military aide to the President, recalled a serious discussion at the Roosevelt table as to whether gravy improved the flavor of hominy or not. Roosevelt claimed that his partiality for hominy stemmed from his mother, a Southerner. Like it he did, and even included it on the menu at certain state dinners.

T.R.'s one great gourmet interest was exotic teas. Alice Longworth recalled recently that her father favored especially a smoky tea called Ku-Kwa and served it often in the White House. (Alice must have inherited this interest, for the day of the interview, she served an interesting Earl Grey mixed with a smoky blend.)

Ku-Kwa was a favorite with the Hyde Park branch of the family as well. Cousin Sally (F.D.R.'s mother) used to sit on the knee of the original Ku-Kwa, the Chinese merchant or "go-down," when the family made one of its frequent trips to the Orient.

Teddy Roosevelt also expressed admiration for the famous Caravan tea, which financier J. P. Morgan sent his friends for Christmas. It was unlikely, considering the ferocity of the feud between T.R. and Morgan, that the White House ever received any Caravan from that source.

The President was far less fond of alcohol. At informal dinners with friends, only one wine was served, a far cry from the previous administrations' six and seven glasses. It is possible that alcohol did not agree with T.R., for his wife, writing about the inaugural luncheon of 1901, when Teddy become McKinley's Vice-President, noted:

"He drank two glasses of champagne, thinking it was bad fizzy water, and being very thirsty. Happily, it took no effect whatever, which speaks volumes either for Ted's head or the President's champagne."

Even so, Roosevelt, like other Presidents before and since, incurred the wrath of the temperance groups. Resenting a slur by one such group that he was a drunkard, fiery Ted instituted a libel suit—and won. His daughter, Mrs. Longworth, believes that the stories about her father's drinking habits date back to the golden goblet of Ultima Thule, a story in itself.

The San Francisco Chamber of Commerce presented T.R. with a magnificent champagne coupe more than a foot high, a triumph of the goldsmith's art. It had a long slender stem and could hold more than a pint of liquid. The President adored the gift and insisted on having it at his place at all dinners, family or formal. When he held it in his hands, he said, it made him feel "like the King of Ultima Thule."

It is possible that when he sipped from the enormous cup at state dinners some of the more cynical guests suspected that the goblet was a device for concealing whiskey. In truth, the President could not abide the taste of undiluted alcohol. His golden treasure cup contained his favorite "white wine and Poly water [Appolinarus]."

The keynote of the Roosevelt household was informality, a trait shared with the latter Hyde Park Roosevelts. Lunch was particularly relaxed. At the White House, as well as during the summers at Sagamore Hill, it was common for the President to have two or three last-minute, spontaneously invited luncheon guests. Somehow the kitchen was always geared for such emergencies. (Perhaps it was the other way around: the family alone was the real emergency, so frequent were the extra places at the table.) If the guests were family rather than official friends, the Roosevelt children and their governess participated along with the grown-ups. A friend called the Roosevelts "a transient boarding house."

During the White House years, when the Roosevelts entertained with small dinner parties the dinner hour was seven-thirty, half an hour later for banquets. On such occasions, the children had their dinner separately at eight-thirty.

Special holidays were practically the *raison d'être* of the family, or at least its younger members. Birthdays were jubilantly celebrated occasions. Thanksgiving, of course, was one of the yearly high points. Dinner was on a far grander scale than the usual family meal. One White House Thanksgiving on record cites the following menu: Roast pig with an apple in his mouth, turkey, sweet potatoes served sugared, Southern style (Teddy's mother's influence again), spinach, boiled rice, creamed pea soup, lettuce and alligator pear salad, champagne, apple pies, mince pies, and ice cream molded in the shape of quails, with melted brown sugar poured over each to simulate gravy.

Christmas was *the* day of the year, as in most households. The fun-loving Roosevelts seemed to derive special pleasure from the day. Their first Christmas in the White House was a time of great festivity. Perhaps the contrast with the reserved, retiring McKinleys made the gaiety seem particularly electric. Headlines in the sedate New York *Herald* just before the holiday predicted a JOLLY CHRISTMAS AGAIN FOR WHITE HOUSE. During all the Roosevelt years in the Executive Mansion, the family never let the *Herald* down.

Before seven on Christmas morning, the children were up, dressed, and pounding at their parents' door. On entering, they found that Santa had already come and gone, for there, at the bedroom fireplace, hung their six stockings, full of lumps and bulges.

After emptying the stockings, the children were eager to press on to bigger game, but the President insisted that breakfast came first. Finally the children were allowed to rush into the library and find their major treasures. In all the merriment of the morning, only one thing was missing: a Christmas tree. Nobody knew why the Presidential family lacked one. Some guessed that T.R.'s interest in conservation prohibited it, others felt that he wanted greater simplicity. The following year, however (1902), Archie went against the family tradition and smuggled a tiny tree of his own into the library. So when the children burst through the library doors, they weren't the only ones with surprises awaiting them. Their father was amazed and delighted with Archie's *coup*.

Christmas day was a highly congenial one at the White House during the Roosevelt years. Friends dropped by all morning long to wish the Presidential family a Merry Christmas. The hospitable Roosevelts offered them coffee and delicious sweet biscuits, served hot with melted butter.

Dinner on Christmas day was essentially a family affair. The President carved the turkey for a gathering of relatives and close friends. Later in the evening, other guests appeared and were treated to a promenade concert and a gala holiday dance. For most people, it would have been a long, strenuous day. For the dynamic Roosevelts it was probably about par.

Although the mood was informal at the White House, the President and his wife were capable of rising to the highest heights of formal entertaining when protocol required it. To serve food for the family in the plain, unadorned way the family liked it, Edith Roosevelt brought the regular family Irish cook from Sagamore Hill to Washington. But for official functions, a contract was given to a French caterer to serve state dinners at eight dollars a plate.

There were numerous affairs for visiting dignitaries, and the Roosevelts met the challenge of such entertaining with their usual vigor. Somehow, in spite of the elaborate menus, the floral adornments, and formal atmosphere, official entertaining seemed gayer and more light-hearted than it had for generations. Edith Roosevelt balanced her husband's impetuous ebullience with a gracious equanimity. She gave each gathering, in the words of Archie Butt, "its own character." She circulated among the guests "like a shuttle, keeping everything in harmony."

Perhaps the most talked-of and elaborate party of the entire Roosevelt eight years was the stag dinner given for Prince Henry of Prussia in February 1902. Important members of the State, Navy, and War departments were on hand to toast the Prince. Nautically inclined, he no doubt was pleased with the elaborate decorations, which included electric lights arranged as naval symbols—anchors, stars, ropes—hung all over the East Room (where the banquet was held) from windows, posts, mirrors, and the ceiling. The room was aflutter with flags, literally hundreds of them, American and German.

Although ladies were excluded from this naval launching, Edith Roosevelt took special care to select the menu herself. Ten courses were included, among them

Baltimore terrapin, *filet de Boeuf Hambourgeoise,* canvasback duck, capon, and hominy. The *pièce de résistance* was ice cream molded into fruit shapes and tinted to look real, served in candy sea shells. The German eagle and American coat of arms graced opposite sides of the shells. Atop the ice cream flew sugar flags of both countries. Punch was served in small boats, each flying the flag of the *Meteor,* the American yacht Prince Henry had just purchased. It was a festive occasion, full of pledges of good will from one country to the other. The next day Alice Roosevelt launched the *Meteor* with a good, vigorous Rooseveltian cracking of champagne bottle against her bow.

Alice Roosevelt dominated the newspapers during the years of her father's Presidency, probably more so than any other single member of the family except the President himself. The press dubbed her "Princess Alice" and avidly reported her every smile. She herself was launched early in her father's term—but not, to her regret, with champagne. She made her debut shortly after the family was settled in their new home, and newspapers, always eager to report Presidential domestic news, treated her coming-out party as if it were the Inauguration.

"Princess Alice" was a spirited, lively girl with elegant taste and a style very much her own. She was reportedly chagrined that her debut during the Christmas holidays of 1902 was such a sedate, comparatively simple affair. She bargained for champagne and got nonalcoholic punch, for a cotillion and got a dance.

Her wedding four years later was considered the biggest White House social news since Nellie Grant's wedding decades before. The contrast between the two was enormous, reflecting changing tastes and times. In the East Room an improvised altar had been erected, and the entire room had the air of restrained elegance. Edith Roosevelt's well-bred sense of propriety and good taste was strongly felt. Cabinet members, the diplomatic corps, and battalions of personal friends were on hand for the ceremony and the wedding breakfast that followed.

The breakfast was served about twelve-thirty, with Alice and her groom, Nicholas Longworth, and the bridal party in the small private dining room and the hordes of other guests in the State Dining Room. Breakfast consisted of croquettes, salads, *pâtés,* sandwiches of all types, ice cream hearts, wedding rings and bells, *petits fours,* champagne, claret punch, lemonade, tea, and coffee. Dominating all was the wedding cake, a masterpiece thirty inches high, three feet across.

To bake the cake, the Roosevelts hired a specialist from New York, Madame Blanche Rales, who came to the White House to do the baking. The cake was beautifully decorated in orange blossoms and doves. It weighed 130 pounds— quite a cake it was. Alice, with her customary flair for improvisation, borrowed the sword of a military aide to cut the cake. She had become too impatient with the slower, laborious knife. Even so, neither Alice nor her groom had a taste of the magical concoction. Too many guests were crowding round to wish the bridal couple well.

It was a frenzied but happy day, typical of Rooseveltian gaiety, and typical of the family's White House years. Until the arrival of the Kennedys more than half a century later, probably no Presidential family enjoyed the Executive Mansion as much as the Teddy Roosevelts. The President's own words expressed that feeling more eloquently than anyone else might. In a letter to his son Kermit at school in 1904, before the Presidential election, he wrote:

> Incidentally, I don't think any family has ever enjoyed the White House more than we have. I was thinking about it just this morning when Mother and I took breakfast on the portico and afterwards walked about the lovely grounds and looked at the stately historic old house. It is a wonderful privilege to have been here and to have been given the chance to do this work, and I should regard myself as having a small and mean mind if in the event of defeat I felt soured at not having had more instead of being thankful to have had so much.

Teddy need not have worried. The country had taken the Roosevelts very much to heart. And for another four years the family lived and laughed their way through those hallowed, historic White House halls.

◇◇

R E C I P E S

FAT RASCALS

In Edith Roosevelt's most cherished cookbook, which now rests on a shelf in the parlor of Sagamore Hill, is this recipe for hot biscuits. Served right from the oven, with butter on them, they make a delicious coffee-klatch or teatime snack. We like to serve them as well at breakfast, as a change from coffee cake or rolls. One taste and you will see why Teddy Roosevelt enjoyed breakfast so much—eggs, coffee, and rolls or biscuits like these make mouth-watering eating.

Flour	*Butter*
Salt	*Currants*
Sugar	*Milk*
Baking powder	

Sift 4 cups flour with 1 teaspoon salt, ¼ cup sugar, and 4 teaspoons baking powder. Mix well. Cut in 1½ cups butter. Then stir in 1 pound dried currants. Mix well again and add 1 cup milk, little by little. With each addition, mix with a fork until a soft dough forms. Roll the dough approximately ½ inch thick on a lightly floured board. Use a 2-inch round cutter to shape the biscuits. Bake biscuits on an ungreased cooky sheet until nicely browned. Bake in a hot (450° F.) oven about 12 minutes. When done, remove from oven, split and butter each biscuit, and serve piping hot. *Makes approximately 3 dozen.*

SAGAMORE HILL SAND TARTS

Sweets, especially cookies, were a Roosevelt weakness. The President gobbled cookies such as these sand tarts as fast as they appeared on the plate. This recipe, a particularly cherished one in the family, was found written on the inside cover of one of Edith Roosevelt's many cookbooks. The family offered these cookies to friends who dropped in Christmas morning. Served with hot coffee, they were perfect Christmas welcomers.

Butter	*Vanilla*
Sugar	*Flour*
Eggs	

Cream 1 cup butter until it is as smooth as mayonnaise. Then add 2 cups sugar and cream until light and fluffy. Add 2 eggs, one by one, beating after each addition. Beat in one additional egg yolk and 2 teaspoons vanilla. Stir in 4 cups sifted flour. Mix again well. Roll the dough on a lightly floured board until quite thin. Cut with a 2½-inch cooky cutter. Then beat remaining egg white just enough to stir it up a bit. Brush the egg white on top of the cookies. Sprinkle with a cinnamon-sugar mixture and bake on a greased cooky sheet in a moderate (350° F.) oven for about 8 minutes. *Makes 6 dozen.*

Variation for the holidays: Eliminate the extra egg white and cinnamon–sugar topping. Use fancy Christmas cooky cutters. Bake as you would regular sand tarts. When cool, decorate with powdered sugar and milk icing, colored Christmas colors.

CORN CHOWDER WITH BEAR'S PAW POPCORN

In the town of Newfane, Vermont, there is a very special old inn that doubles as the town jail. The Windham County Hotel and Jail is probably the only place in the country where the best food in town is found at the jail. Mary Margaret McBride likes to tell the story that Teddy Roosevelt, after a visit to the Hotel, claimed that he would have liked to commit a small crime so he could have the pleasure of eating his way through his sentence behind the bars of that charming old inn. The specialty of the establishment is good, solid old-fashioned Vermont cooking for guests and prisoners alike. Their old-time corn chowder appealed to President Roosevelt who liked it with popcorn as a garnish. In Newfane, the popcorn is called Bear's Paw, because the local variety kernel looks (when popped) like the track of a bear in the snow.

Salt pork   *Milk*
Onion   *Corn (fresh, frozen, or canned)*
Potatoes   *Salt and paprika*
Water   *Popcorn*
Soda crackers

Cube 3 slices salt pork and sauté them in a skillet until crisp but not too brown. Add 1 large sliced onion and sauté until golden. Add 3 sliced potatoes and 2 cups water and continue cooking over low heat until potatoes become tender. Place 8 soda crackers in a large bowl. Pour 1 cup milk over them to soak. When the crackers have absorbed the milk, add to the skillet. Also add 2½ cups fresh corn or thawed frozen corn or whole-kernel canned corn, 1 teaspoon salt and ⅛ teaspoon paprika. Simmer the mixture over the same low heat for at least 10 minutes. Serve hot, garnished with popped corn (Bear's Paw or regular variety). *Serves 4.*

CHILLED SENEGALESE SOUP

The Roosevelt family, addicted as its various members were to foreign travel, had a special interest in India and the Far East. Though normally partial to relatively simple foods, they were fond of certain dishes from the East, such as this delicious curried soup.

Chicken stock   *Egg yolks*
Curry powder   *Cream*
Chicken (cooked)   *Salt and pepper*

Put 3½ cups chicken stock into a saucepan and bring it to a boil. Then add ½ teaspoon curry powder and 1½ cups finely chopped cooked chicken meat. Simmer gently. (More curry powder may be added if you like a stronger flavor.) Blend 4 slightly beaten egg yolks with a tablespoon of the hot chicken stock, and slowly add 2 cups warm cream to the yolks. Stir slowly into the simmering chicken and stock. Keep stirring, while the soup thickens, over a very low heat. Do not let the soup come to a boil. Add ½ teaspoon salt and pepper to taste. Remove the soup from the fire, cool, and then put it in the refrigerator until chilled. Serve cold. *Serves 6.*

FIDDLEHEAD FERN SALAD

Although President Roosevelt pooh-poohed the idea that he could possibly be a gourmet, he seems to have had a much more sensitive palate than he liked to admit. One proof of this was his fondness for the subtle, delicate, elusive flavor of fiddlehead ferns, those early spring fronds of bracken fern which are cut like asparagus before the leaves appear. Cooked quickly in slightly salted water, the ferns are delicious served hot with melted butter, a dash of lemon juice, and freshly ground pepper and salt. We think you will find them equally as delicious as Teddy Roosevelt did served as a salad.

Fresh or frozen fiddlehead ferns	*Salt and pepper*
Sweet red pepper or pimento	*Dry mustard*
Light olive or French walnut oil	*Chives or scallions*
Lemon juice	

Allow at least 8 to 10 fern fronds per person. Arrange them neatly on individual salad plates, chilled if possible. Cut thin strips of sweet red pepper or pimento and garnish the fronds. Serve with a cruet or bowl of special salad dressing made as follows: Combine ¾ cup olive oil with ¼ cup lemon juice. Add ½ teaspoon salt, ⅛ teaspoon freshly ground black pepper, ¼ teaspoon dry mustard, and 1 tablespoon chopped chives or scallions. Mix or shake well before serving with the fronds.

TEDDY ROOSEVELT'S EDIBLE LEAVES

Going a-greening in the woods was a favorite pastime in the days of President Roosevelt. The fields and woods were full of wild asparagus (sparrow grass), wild rhubarb, bullrushes, manna, fireweed, wild mustard greens, wild collards, wild chicory (related to Belgian endive), nasturtium, watercress, spice grass, marigolds, and many other delicacies ready for the picking. Gooseneck greens, which grew along the Eastern sea coast, were a special favorite of Teddy Roosevelt. He liked them "boiled in meat stock, drained and served with a rich cream sauce flavored with a tablespoon of prepared mustard." Another green he favored, as do we, was wilted dandelion greens. You'll find a good supply available all summer long.

WILTED DANDELION GREENS

Dandelion greens	*Mustard*
Bacon drippings	*Sugar*
Vinegar	*Garlic clove (optional)*
Salt and pepper	*Breadcrumbs or buttered toast*

Wash a large bunch of dandelion greens (about 3 quarts), taking care to cut off the roots and discard coarse or damaged parts. Drain in a colander. When thoroughly drained, tear the greens into smallish pieces. Set aside. Heat ⅓ cup bacon drippings in a skillet. Add ⅓ cup plain or wine vinegar, salt and freshly ground black pepper to taste, a pinch of dry mustard and sugar, and, if you like, though it is not traditional, add 1 crushed garlic clove. Add the drained greens to the skillet, cover and cook over a low heat until the greens are just wilted—a very few minutes. Serve immediately, sprinkled with lightly browned breadcrumbs or on strips or squares of hot buttered toast. *Serves 6.*

CREAM OF CUCUMBER SALAD

The Roosevelts loved to eat the fruits of their own beloved Sagamore Hill. Game from the nearby woods, fresh fish from the rivers and streams, and freshly picked fruits and vegetables from their vast garden were all cherished by the family; all graced the family table, depending on the season. Cucumbers ripe from the garden found their way to the table in various disguises, such as this salad.

Gelatin	*Pimento*
Hot milk	*Tarragon vinegar*
Cucumber	*Lemon juice*
Heavy cream	*Salt*

Soften 2 teaspoons gelatin in 2 tablespoons cold water. Then add ¼ cup hot milk and stir until gelatin is dissolved. Add 1 peeled and cubed cucumber, 1 cup heavy cream whipped, ½ chopped sweet pimento, 1 teaspoon tarragon vinegar and lemon juice and salt to taste. Mix thoroughly. Pour into a mold and chill for at least 12 hours in refrigerator. At serving time, unmold on lettuce leaves and serve with French dressing. *Serves 4.*

STUFFED CUCUMBERS

Cucumbers	*Mayonnaise*
Tomatoes	*Chili sauce*
Apples	*Worcestershire sauce*
Celery	*Salt and pepper*
Walnuts	

Cut 4 young but large cucumbers into 12 cup-shaped pieces. Scoop out the insides. Skin 3 tomatoes by placing them in boiling water for just a moment. Scoop out their insides as well. Chop 2 apples, ½ pound celery, ½ pound walnuts, and the tomato shells. Mix well and add 2 tablespoons mayonnaise, 1 tablespoon chili sauce, and ½ teaspoon Worcestershire sauce, with salt and pepper to taste. Mix well and stuff the cucumbers with this mixture. Top the cucumber with a dash of mayonnaise (or sour cream, if you prefer). Finely chopped walnuts may be sprinkled on top of the mayonnaise if you like. *Serves 6.*

CREAMED OYSTERS

As people-loving as the Roosevelts were, sometimes they seemed almost gluttons for punishment. For instance, after their own open-house Christmas celebrations in 1903, Mrs. Roosevelt gave a party the very next afternoon for the children of the President's official family. Six hundred sons and daughters of Cabinet members, Senators, and other departmental officials romped and frolicked throughout the White House. All six hundred children were fed supper, and, as was noted, "the President himself dispensed the creamed oysters." (We prefer ours under slightly less frantic circumstances.)

Butter	*Worcestershire sauce, lemon juice,*
Flour	*or sherry*
Oysters	*Buttered toast*
Oyster liquid	*Parsley*
Salt and paprika	

Melt 2 tablespoons butter in a saucepan. Add 2 tablespoons flour and stir until blended. Drain 1 pint oysters and slowly stir 1 cup of the oyster liquid into the saucepan, stirring all the while. (If oyster liquid does not equal 1 cup, add cream to fill.) Then add ⅛ teaspoon paprika and ½ teaspoon salt. Stir until the sauce is smooth and almost at a boil. Then add the oysters and cook until the sauce comes almost to a boil again. Add ½ teaspoon Worcestershire sauce or, if you prefer, 1 teaspoon lemon juice or sherry. Blend and serve at once on hot buttered toast. (If you want to be a bit fancier, serve in patty shells.) Sprinkle with chopped parsley.

Variation: To serve *au gratin,* place the oysters in a buttered baking dish, cover with buttered breadcrumbs or grated Cheddar. Brown lightly under a broiler. *Serves 4.*

PIGS IN BLANKETS

Oysters wrapped in bacon and broiled were a favorite at the White House during Teddy Roosevelt's time.

BROILED SHAD WITH CREAMED ROE

When the Roosevelts went to the White House, they took with them Rose and Mary Sweeney, two sisters from Ireland, who had cooked for them at Sagamore Hill. The Sweeney specialty was seafood, and they were particularly adept at preparing shad and shad roe, as in the following recipe.

Shad	*Cream*
Salt and pepper	*Flour*
Butter	*Egg yolks*
Shad roe	*Breadcrumbs*
Lemon juice	*Lemon slices*
White wine	*Parsley*
Onion	

Have a 4-pound shad boned. Place it on a greased broiler rack, skin side down. Season with salt and freshly ground pepper. Brush with melted butter. Broil at a fair distance from the flame for 15 minutes. Meanwhile place shad roe in a saucepan and cover with boiling water. Add 3½ tablespoons lemon juice or dry white wine and simmer over low heat for 15 minutes. Drain, and remove outer membrane from roe. Mash the roe. Then melt 2 tablespoons butter in a pan and sauté 1½ tablespoons grated onion in the butter. Add the roe, and stir in ½ cup cream and 2½ tablespoons flour. Mix well. When the mixture begins to come to a boil, remove from fire and stir in 2 egg yolks. Add another dash of lemon juice or white wine and mix again. Spread the mixture over the thin part of the shad, as soon as you have removed the fish from the oven. Cover the fish with buttered breadcrumbs and brown it lightly under the broiler. Serve at once garnished with lemon slices and parsley or watercress. *Serves 4.*

SAGAMORE HILL LIVER AND BACON

Alice Roosevelt Longworth confided that both she and her father were partial to liver and bacon—for breakfast. They also shared a fondness for innards (or "offal"), such as the recipe below for kidney stew.

Bacon	*Salt and pepper*
Onion	*Lemon*
Calf's liver	*Lemon juice*
Flour	*Garlic*

Sauté about 8 slices bacon until lightly browned and crisp. Remove from skillet. Sauté 1 sliced onion in skillet. Set onion slices aside. Remove the skin and membrane from 1 pound calf's liver and cut into ½-inch slices. Dredge with flour that has been seasoned with salt and pepper. Sauté liver slices in the bacon drippings over a hot fire for 3 or 4 minutes. Add 1 tablespoon lemon juice to pan. (Pan may be rubbed with 1 clove garlic before cooking the bacon.) If you wish a sauce, remove liver to a hot platter, add 4 tablespoons red wine to skillet and heat. Pour over liver on serving platter. Garnish with bacon slices and with onion slices served on top of the liver. Serve with a side dish of lemon slices or wedges. *Serves 4.*

KIDNEY STEW—BREAKFAST SPECIALTY

Beef kidneys	*Flour*
Vinegar	*Sherry or lemon*
Bay leaf	*Salt*
Bouillon cube	*Paprika*
Butter	*Parsley*

Remove the white tissue from 2 small beef kidneys. Simmer them in enough boiling salted water to cover. Add 1 tablespoon vinegar and cover pan. Cook until tender. Remove kidneys and cool. Meanwhile, remove the fat from the stock and add 1 bay leaf and simmer gently. Add 1 bouillon cube for flavor. Strain the stock and set aside. Slice the cooled kidneys very thin and sauté them in 2 tablespoons melted butter. Stir in 2 tablespoons flour. Add the stock slowly, stirring all the while until smooth. Bring to a boil and then add 2 tablespoons sherry or 1 slice lemon. Season with salt and paprika to taste. Serve kidneys and gravy on toast, with chopped parsley on top. *Serves 4.*

ANNIE THE COOK'S SIMPLE SUGAR WAFERS

Alice Roosevelt Longworth recalls that all the Roosevelt children took after their father in his penchant for sweets. Many of the sweets served, however, were "horrid things like floating island, with strings of egg in it." Alice detested this almost as much as she did junket. But one of the cooks made sugar wafers that were so good that Alice still serves them at tea today. A rich, delicate sugar cooky, this wafer is dropped and spread out thin and crisp, but never hard.

Butter	*Eggs*
Vanilla	*Flour (cake)*
Sugar	

Cream 1 cup butter until light and fluffy. Add 1 teaspoon vanilla. Gradually beat in ⅔ cup sugar and 2 well-beaten eggs. Stir in 1½ cups cake flour. (Regular flour may be used, but the cookies will not be as delicate.) Mix well and drop by teaspoonfuls on a cooky sheet. Spread thin with a knife dipped in cold water. Bake in a hot (375° F.) oven about 8 minutes. *Makes 5 dozen.*

SNOW ICE CREAM

In Washington, D.C., snow is a great event. Even a modest snowfall calls forth a mood of carnival mixed with consternation—sleddings and traffic jams. Alice Roosevelt Longworth recalls that in her days at the White House a snowfall was the occasion for joy undiffused. When the snow actually fell six or more inches (a rare event) the joy among the seven Roosevelt children was almost delirious, for it meant there would be snow ice cream. The requisites were stiff: the weather had to stay cold, for the snow must be well frozen, not too soft or wet. The children then dug into the fresh drifts with spoons and filled buckets as easily as if it were sand at the beach. Snow ice cream was commonly made with only milk, vanilla, and sugar added. But the best snow ice cream—and the kind favored by the young Roosevelts—was made with boiled custard. To keep the snow from melting, the Roosevelts made it outdoors, right on the egg-rolling stretch of White House lawn. The children worked in teams of two, one pouring the custard slowly into the bucket of dry white snow, the other stirring briskly with a spoon, adding as much snow as could be made to disappear into the custard. The snow ice cream rarely ever reached the table—it was usually consumed outdoors, before it could melt.

Milk	*Shelled bitter almonds*
Sugar	*Eggs*

Heat 2 quarts milk, 2 cups sugar, and ½ cup shelled bitter almonds. Bring just to a boil, then cool for five minutes and strain. Beat 8 eggs and pour milk–sugar mixture over the eggs. Beat vigorously. Cool. Fill halfway glasses or chilled mugs with fresh clean snow. Pour custard on top of the snow, mix quickly, and serve at once.

Children's short-cut: Mix 1 cup fresh milk with 1 teaspoon vanilla and 1 teaspoon sugar. Pour over chilled glasses half full of fresh snow.

MILK ICE

For a family of simple tastes such as the Roosevelts, milk ice was a guaranteed pleasant refreshment. No matter how sophisticated your particular palate, we think you'll find it refreshing as well.

Sugar	*Milk*
Lemons	

Mix 2 cups sugar with the strained juice of 3 lemons. Allow to stand at least 6 hours. Then add 1 quart ice-cold milk and freeze immediately. Serve cold. *Serves 6 to 8.*

TEDDY ROOSEVELT'S BAKED INDIAN PUDDING

Whether it was a result of his wife's New England background or his own fascination with Indians, Teddy Roosevelt had a great love for Indian pudding. To him it was not merely a dessert, it was the main event at many a Sunday supper. The secret of this particular recipe is its slow, careful baking. It is at its best when baked in a stone crock (a bean crock fills the bill perfectly). This large recipe— geared to a Roosevelt-size family—makes 2 quarts of pudding. It may be stored for months in the freezer, and leftovers may be heated with a little extra liquid in the oven or in the top of a double boiler.

Yellow cornmeal	*Salt*
Dark molasses	*Baking soda*
Sugar	*Eggs*
Butter or lard	*Milk*

Combine 1 cup yellow cornmeal with ½ cup dark molasses, ¼ cup sugar, ¼ cup butter or lard, ½ teaspoon salt, ¼ teaspoon baking soda, and 2 eggs. Stir this mixture into 3 cups hot milk. Mix well and bake in a well-greased stone crock in a very hot (475° F.) oven until pudding comes to a boil. Leave top uncovered, but add 3 additional cups hot milk and lower oven temperature to 250° F. Cook for 5 to 7 hours. Serve pudding warm with plain cream or sweetened whipped cream. Traditionalists would shudder, but it is also quite tasty topped with vanilla ice cream. *Makes 2 quarts.*

PICKET FENCE PUDDING

This homy-sounding dessert is actually quite rich and partyish.

Chocolate	*Ladyfingers*
Powdered sugar	*Whipped cream*
Hot water	*Vanilla*
Eggs	

Melt 2 squares bitter chocolate in the top of a double boiler. Slowly stir in 2 tablespoons powdered sugar. Add 4 tablespoons hot water and 4 egg yolks. Beat well. Remove from heat and cool. Beat 4 egg whites until very stiff, then fold them carefully into the chocolate mixture. Line a serving dish with 1 dozen ladyfingers and turn the pudding into the dish, on top of the ladyfingers. Fill the dish with whipped cream flavored with vanilla to taste. *Serves 4.*

"PRINCESS" ALICE' JUMBLES

The press was so intrigued with Alice Roosevelt's debut and numerous parties and beaux that she was soon dubbed "Princess Alice." These favorite cookies of hers are worthy of royalty.

Sugar	*Baking powder*
Butter	*Flour*
Eggs	*Milk*

Cream together 2 cups sugar with 1 cup butter until light and fluffy. Add 3 well-beaten eggs, 1 small teaspoon baking powder, ½ cup milk, and just enough flour to form a soft dough. Mix well, then roll very thin on a floured board, cut into rings with a doughnut cutter, and bake in a moderate (350° F.) oven until lightly browned only about 5 minutes. *Makes 4 dozen.*

TEDDY ROOSEVELT'S MILK PUNCH

When Teddy drank out of his Ultima Thule cup, his guests may have thought he was drinking whiskey on the rocks, but in truth he was imbibing a simple and delicious milk punch. William Brown, an exceedingly formal butler who served at White House functions during Teddy's day, revealed that the punch was made exactly as one would make a highball, except that milk substituted for water and soda. To top it off, the President liked a generous spoonful of sugar stirred into the cup, and nutmeg or cinnamon sprinkled on top.

MINT TEA

Mint melted Teddy Roosevelt. He liked it in juleps and was equally fond of it in tea, as this recipe demonstrates.

Water	*Mint leaves*
Sugar	*Lemon juice*
Black tea	

Boil together ½ cup water and ½ cup sugar for approximately 5 minutes. Then add 1 teaspoon black tea and ¼ cup chopped mint leaves, either fresh or dried. Cover and let steep for 10 to 12 minutes. Then strain the mixture and add the liquid to 1 quart boiling water. Add ½ cup lemon juice and bring to a boil again. *Serves 6.*

CATAWBA MAY WINE

When we hear the name Longworth, we think of the man Alice Roosevelt married. But to the public of the Roosevelts' day, Nicholas Longworth was the man who made Catawba famous. Early in the nineteenth century, Longworth popularized this delicious sparkling white wine, produced in Ohio from the American Catawba grapes. Many considered it a sort of superior champagne. (Longworth's great-grandson married "Princess Alice.") Often in May the White House would receive gifts of fresh woodruff. This, combined with strawberries from the garden and the favorite Catawba, made a popular and delightful spring punch, similar to the German *maibowle*.

Dried and/or fresh woodruff	*Catawba or champagne*
Dry white wine	*Cognac (optional)*
Fresh strawberries	

Combine 2 or 3 cups fresh woodruff (both leaves and stem) or 1 cup dried woodruff with 1 bottle dry white table wine. Cover and allow to steep for 3 or 4 hours or overnight. Then strain and pour over a large chunk of ice in a punch bowl. Add 3 more bottles of chilled white wine. Garnish with fresh strawberries.

At serving time, add 1 bottle of well-chilled sparkling Catawba or champagne (or sparkling water). If desired, you may also add 1 or 2 cups cognac. Serve in chilled champagne or wine glasses. Garnish each with a strawberry. *Makes 30 servings (5 quarts).*

A ROOSEVELTIAN JULEP

Although Teddy Roosevelt abolished the greenhouses of the White House soon after he became President, he was so fond of mint he decided to grow it on the White House grounds. He liked to use it in his mint juleps, although a true Southerner would have been aghast at his treatment of the beloved regional drink. T.R. liked his drowned in sugar and smothered with mint, the better to disguise the whiskey flavor, which he disliked. We can sympathize with his point of view, but feel a julep is a julep is a julep—and should be served pure.

Fresh mint leaves	*Crushed ice*
Sugar	*Bourbon whiskey*
Brandy	

Break 3 or 4 fresh mint leaves into a mug or julep cup. Add ¼ teaspoon sugar and 1 tablespoon brandy. Muddle this well with the mint. Put crushed ice into the mug and fill the cup with bourbon and stir vigorously until the mug frosts over. Then it is good and chilled and ready to be served. Decorate with another sprig or two of mint, and serve to appreciative julep fanciers, who will sip slowly and appreciatively, savoring the scent of mint as T.R. did.

COFFEE À *LA* ROOSEVELT

The Maxwell House in Nashville, Tennessee, is best known to Americans as the brand name of a widely distributed coffee. But in times past the Maxwell House was the center of social and diplomatic life in the South. Its most famous chef, M. Antoine of New Orleans, probably served as many Presidents as any other chef in America. Located near Andrew Jackson's beloved Hermitage, the famous inn is known also for its association with another President, Teddy Roosevelt.

One night, after the President, visiting the inn, had eaten "a most excellent dinner," he was enjoying his after-dinner coffee. He heaved a sigh of enormous satisfaction and is reputed to have remarked, as he put his drained coffee cup back on its saucer: "My, that was good to the last drop." This story sounds almost too good to be true, but it has been repeated so often as gospel that we are content to accept it as fact.

Cold water   Finely ground coffee

For each cup of water used, use 1 to 3 tablespoons finely ground coffee. The number of tablespoons will depend on the strength of coffee you prefer. Place the coffee in the strainer part of your percolator. Add either very cold or boiling water. Put the top on the pot and place over the heat (or plug in, if you have an electric pot). When coffee reaches the boiling point, reduce the heat and percolate slowly for about 10 minutes—until the liquid turns amber.

XXVII

T *is for* Taft
(*Also for* Thrift)

When William Howard Taft took over in 1909 as Captain of our Ship of State, it seemed very likely that he would rock the boat, at least figuratively. But then his trim, elegant wife intervened and put him on a diet.

President Taft was a tall man—six feet, two inches—but even that height wasn't quite enough to carry off with aplomb his three hundred thirty-two pounds. To his chagrin, the doctor insisted that he reduce his twelve-ounce breakfast steak to eight ounces. It was a traumatic request for such a hungry man.

Taft would have had to defer to several others when the title of Presidential gourmet was awarded, but there is no doubt he deserved the award as leading gourmand. Some of his "snacks" have become legendary. On a visit to Savannah, he once breakfasted on grapefruit, potted partridge, broiled venison, grilled partridge, waffles with maple syrup and butter, hominy, hot rolls, bacon, and more venison. It helped him get through the morning.

A typical Taft lunch might include bouillon, smelts with tartar sauce, lamb chops, Bermuda potatoes, green peas, and—for dessert—raspberry jelly with whipped cream, salted almonds, bonbons, and coffee. Like his predecessor and mentor, Teddy Roosevelt, Taft was a great coffee consumer.

Dinner some hours later would be, typically, lobster stew, salmon cutlets with peas, roast turkey with potato salad, cold roast tenderloin with vegetable salad, cold tongue and ham, followed by frozen pudding, cake, fruit, and coffee. Not what one might label a frugal repast.

Small wonder then that a special bathtub had to be installed at the White House. When the newspapers printed the story, the President, by then somewhat sensitive about his weight, denied it. But a picture taken at the time of four workmen sitting comfortably in the tub is damning evidence, and a fascinating memento.

The President laughed about his diet, telling his housekeeper: "Things are in a sad state of affairs when a man can't even call his gizzard his own." Nevertheless, the bathtub story embarrassed him. When he visited Provincetown, Massachusetts, in August 1910, to dedicate a Pilgrim monument, he commented: "There are certain stories that I'd like to deny. We have no special bathtubs made for any Executive of any particular size." When the crowd laughed, the President added that he, too, had arrived in a ship named the *Mayflower*. "It did not happen from any particular arrangement, only that the vessel was the most suitable, leaving out the question of bathtubs." With that the crowd roared and burst into applause. It was enough to make one forget all about diets.

In fact, every time the President left the White House he managed conveniently to forget the word *diet*. At home, under the watchful eyes of a well-meaning wife, he might docilely nibble at his eight-ounce breakfast steak, his two oranges, several pieces of toast and butter, all washed down with quantities of coffee with cream and sugar. This meager breakfast sustained him somehow.

But on the road he let himself go. A banquet held in his honor on November 1, 1909, in Jackson, Mississippi, at the Edwards House was called "the greatest feast ever held in Mississippi." The menu was hardly Spartan:

Back Bay Plant Oysters
Clear Green Sea Turtle Soup
Celery   Radishes   Green Olives
Salted Almonds
Filet of Pompano, *à la* Menniere
[brown butter poured over the fish]
Parisienne Potatoes
Cucumbers en Gelée
Filet Mignon of Mutton
Béarnaise Sauce
Tomatoes stuffed with corn
Roast Wild Turkey
Grilled Sweet Potatoes with Rice
Fritters
Lettuce and Artichokes Heart Salad
Cheese Biscuits
Cigars   Fancy Glaces   Bonbons
Cigarettes   Petit Fours   Coffee

Hosts for the dinner were the Governor of Mississippi and the Mayor of Jackson. An appreciative President commented, at the end of the evening: "Boys, I have had the time of my life."

Another "time of his life" was had by Taft at Loblolly Cove. In his day, a rude little camp perched on a knoll of sea-washed rocks at Cape Ann, Massachusetts, was known throughout the East as a place for incomparable shore dinners. Captain Frank Haskell, proprietor, had a special way of steaming clams on rocks and broiling over charcoal and driftwood the lobsters he caught in the cove.

At one time or another, the cream of North Shore society visited Haskell's: Henry Clay Frick and his family came regularly from their summer home at Pride's Crossing; the John Jay Hammonds sailed over from their castle in Gloucester. But Haskell's most distinguished guest was the President of the United States.

William Howard Taft appeared at Haskell's one August afternoon in 1912, with his wife and family and thirty-two guests in tow. Being away from the White House routine, the President really let himself go. After enjoying Haskell's famous lobster dinner, he participated in a clambake, prepared the old New England way, with lots of green corn, sweet potatoes, lobster, fish fillets, and juicy clams, all steamed together in a pile of seaweed out on the rocks.

In an account of that historic visit, written much later in 1943, Ray Corsini, the Marchese de Corsini, noted:

> It was quite a field day. Though the Captain and his father tried to keep the President's visit a secret, word got out and hundreds of people filled the road and surrounding hills, and even stood by in dories and sailboats to watch the Presidential feast. Luckily, Taft was a jolly, affable man and did not mind the crowd of spectators. He ate with his usual hearty appetite and liked the rough natural setting so much that he cancelled an afternoon drive to spend a few more hours at Loblolly Cove.

For years afterward, Captain Haskell showed off the rush-bottomed chair that President Taft had sat in while eating Cape Ann lobsters.

President Taft was as genial and generous a host as he was a guest. Francis Parkinson Keyes reported: "Nothing could have exceeded the elegance and prodigality of the entertaining that went on at the White House during the first part of his term there."

Later, in the post-Presidential years, after Taft became Chief Justice of the Supreme Court, his entertainments took the form of stag dinners. Invitations to such affairs were much sought after. Part of the reason lay in the dishes served— canvasback duck and other delicacies—but also in Taft's elan as host. Praised for his "supreme *savoir faire*," he was a "superlative host."

President Taft enjoyed entertaining. In fact, just eight days after his inauguration in 1909, before the family was really settled in, the first diplomatic tea was given at the White House. Lobster *à la* Newburg, chicken pâtés, salad, rolls, and assorted sandwiches were served, as well as ice cream, cakes, candies, coffee, and punch. It was a spread in the Taft tradition.

Besides footing the bill at teas and ordinary state affairs, the President ordered food to be served at the four state receptions. With approximately two thousand people milling about at each of these, this represented a considerable investment, to say nothing of the logistics involved. Forty or fifty extra servants had to be imported for each affair, at which elaborate buffet suppers were served. The good-hearted, generous President Taft would have it no other way.

Probably the most celebrated Taft entertainment was the Presidential couple's Silver Wedding anniversary. Invitations that stated *1886–1911* were sent to eight thousand persons. (An additional fifteen thousand reputedly stood outside the fence and tried to look in.)

The evening of the event started with much gaiety and dancing. Then, at eleven o'clock, the State Dining Room was opened to one and all for a buffet supper. Those wishing to eat outdoors could watch the illuminated grounds and fountains, sit at tables on the west terrace, and luxuriate in the freshness of the June night air. Great bowls of Rhine-wine punch were visible throughout the dining room, and champagne poured freely.

A gargantuan wedding cake was specially baked by a leading New York caterer and carefully expressed to Washington. A newspaper account gave this awe-inspiring account:

> Its frosting was circled with twenty-five crystal hearts imbedded in scrolls at regular intervals. Out of the top were seen dainty cherubs whom the froth of a frosted sea seems to have cast up against a great cornucopia filled with reproductions of a rare exotic of the gardener's art, with clinging angels clamoring for them. Around the great circle of confectionery, and alternating with the hearts, were twenty-five miniature silken reproductions of Stars and Stripes and the President's flag. At the base were roses, cut from their stems and hung against the towering sides. Fluttering on the edge of the cake were turtle doves in their customary attitude as the poet sees them.

On the informal level, the Tafts entertained constantly. In fact, the cook never began preparing lunch until half an hour before it was scheduled to begin. Experience had taught her that the President would be late and/or would have one or more unscheduled guests with him. Even so, Taft might be as much as an hour late. The breakfast and dinner schedules were less uncertain than luncheon, although one evening, Taft delayed a diplomatic dinner to accommodate the Russian Ambassador. That gentleman had arrived in civilian dress, but, on noting the other guests bursting with braid and decorations, rushed home to don uniform and braid himself.

Considering the uncertain hours and informality of President Taft's approach to entertaining, it is no wonder the Tafts had servant problems. Even the lure and glamour of the White House failed to impress cooks who liked to function on a regular schedule.

The Tafts began their White House years with an entirely new system of household management. Mrs. Taft abandoned the old order, in which a steward managed the daily routine and outside caterers supervised special events, state dinners, and the like. Instead, she hired a housekeeper, Mrs. Elizabeth Jaffray, as she believed only a woman could really handle the job. In Mrs. Taft's words:

> I wanted a woman who could relieve me of the supervision of such details as no man, expert steward though he be, would ever recognize. The White House requires such ordinary attention as given by a good housekeeper to any home, except, perhaps that it has to be more vigilantly watched. Dust accumulates in corners, mirrors get dim with dampness; curtains sag and lose their crispness; floors, their gloss; rugs turn up at the corners, or fray at the ends, and chair cushions get crushed and untidy. . . . Pantry boys get careless; maids forget to be immaculate and the linen is not properly handled.

In addition to the housekeeper, Mrs. Taft employed three cooks. She preferred Irish cooks, and when one left to get married, another soon replaced her. For one reason or another (one left because she didn't like Mrs. Taft's frequent excursions into the kitchen to see what was cooking) the mortality rate of cooks during the Tafts' four-year span was high.

Helen Taft couldn't overcome her habit of peeking into pans and pots. She was a highly organized manager, probably the efficiency expert among our First Ladies. When the Presidential salary was boosted to $75,000 a year and the government for the first time assumed the burden of paying the White House servants (a liability earlier Presidents had to absorb), Mrs. Taft was determined to prove that the salary increase did not mean any increase in the Presidential scale of living.

First of all, she returned to the Andrew Johnson practice of keeping a cow on the White House grounds. Washington was shocked, but the rest of the country was impressed by the wisdom of the First Lady. When Mooly-Wooly, as the staff called the cow, didn't work out, Mrs. Taft, undaunted by the teasing the cow provoked, went ahead and bought another cow, Pauline. Pauline performed admirably, giving the Presidential family milk as fresh as could be had anywhere in the country.

In spite of the Taft propensity for food in volume, the family's monthly food bill was a mere $868. It would probably have been thrice that, but again Helen Taft's efficiency reigned supreme. She ordered all food in wholesale lots—butter by the tub, vegetables by the crate, and potatoes by barrels—and decreed that no out-of-season (hence expensive) food would be served at the Executive Mansion.

The President himself acquired certain economical practices, through osmosis perhaps. Although he ordered a "cellar of fine wines" from Europe and frequently served champagne at important large luncheons, he kept a sharp eye out for the cost. On one occasion, when the principals in a tariff fight that was plaguing him came to dinner, he decided to economize on the wine served. Feeling it "perfect nonsense" to serve vintage wine to men who had no real appreciation of it, he bought only four bottles of the rarest vintage he could find. Then he ordered his staff to serve this to Senator Root, Senator Hale, the Speaker of the House, the Attorney General, and a few select guests who were known to be *bon vivants* and connoisseurs. The other guests were served a more ordinary wine.

Taft himself did not drink, but he did not share other teetotalers' intolerance of the vine. Wine was offered freely to his guests (vintage or *ordinaire,* what matter?), but the President himself was content to sit back and watch others drink. Perhaps he figured that drinking might decrease his appetite, heaven (or Helen) forbid!

◇◇◇

R E C I P E S

ALICE'S SOUR MILK WAFFLES

Alice, the second cook at the White House, was the waffle and griddle-cake specialist. The President was fond of waffles for breakfast—along with his standard steak, of course. The only breakfast dish that President Taft would not eat was eggs—he couldn't abide them. Of course, stirred up in waffles they were perfectly fine—as long as they were not recognizable as eggs.

Eggs	*Baking soda*
Sour milk	*Sugar*
Melted butter	*Salt*
Flour	*Baking powder*

Beat 2 egg yolks until light and lemony, and then add 1¾ cups sour milk. Beat well. Melt 6 tablespoons butter and add to the egg–milk mixture. Beat all well and set aside for a moment. Sift together 2 cups flour, ¼ teaspoon soda, 1 tablespoon sugar, ½ teaspoon salt and 2 teaspoons baking powder. Add to the egg–milk mixture very quickly, with only a few strong strokes. Beat 2 egg whites until stiff but not dry. Fold them into the batter lightly. Cook in preheated waffle iron. Serve hot with butter and syrup or jam. *Makes 6 waffles.* (Not very Taftian a serving.)

TAFT TERRAPIN SOUP

One of President Taft's favorite luncheon dishes was terrapin soup. But a certain ritual was connected with it. When it was served at state dinners, Mrs. Taft hired a special cook to make *it*. The fee was $5. And Mrs. Taft, as part of the ritual, had to go to the kitchen to taste the soup, just to be sure. . . . The President insisted that champagne be the accompaniment at any meal in which terrapin soup was served.

Veal knuckle	*Thyme*
Onions	*Salt and pepper*
Carrots	*Water*
Celery	*Turtle meat*
Tomatoes	*Sherry*
Bay leaf	*Hard-boiled egg*
Marjoram	*Lemon slices*

Brown 4 pounds veal knuckle in just enough fat or shortening to prevent burning. When it is a good crusty brown, add 2 sliced onions, 2 carrots, cut in half, 2 stalks celery, halved, 3 cups tomatoes, preferably fresh, 1 bay leaf, ¼ teaspoon marjoram, ¼ teaspoon thyme, salt and pepper to taste, and 3 quarts water. Simmer over a low fire for approximately 3 hours. At that time, cut the meat from 1 turtle into 1-inch cubes and simmer it gently for 15 minutes in 1 cup sherry. Then strain the broth from the veal mixture and add it to the turtle meat. Mince 1 hard-boiled egg very fine and add to mixture. Simmer a few minutes and serve hot with slices of lemon floating on top. (If you prefer a thicker soup, blend in a little flour mixed with an equal amount of melted butter just before serving.) *Serves 10 to 12.*

BILLI BI

One of the gastronomic enthusiasms of the Taft era—and a great favorite of the President himself—was a cream of mussels soup. Its origins are mysterious. One story claims it was created by Maxim's Restaurant in Paris, around 1905, and named for William B. Leeds, a leading financier of the period. But Louis Vaudable, owner of Maxim's disclaims credit, saying it was created by Ciro's at Deauville for a William Brand. The dish is, however, a specialty of Maxim's, and for years has been popular in Washington's diplomatic circles. Give credit where you think it may be due, but by all means credit William Howard Taft with the sense to enjoy one of the great culinary creations of his age.

Mussels	*Dry white wine*
Shallots or garlic	*Butter*
Small onions	*Bay leaf*
Parsley	*Thyme*
Salt and pepper	*Heavy cream*
Cayenne	*Egg yolk*

Scrub well 2 pounds mussels, removing all exterior dirt and sand. Place in a large kettle, along with 2 shallots, coarsely chopped, or 1 clove garlic crushed through a press. Add 2 small onions cut in quarters, 2 sprigs parsley, salt and freshly ground pepper to taste, a dash of cayenne, 1 cup dry white wine, 2 tablespoons butter, ½ bay leaf, and ½ teaspoon thyme. Cover the kettle and bring to a boil. Simmer for 5 to 10 minutes, or until the mussel shells open. Discard any mussels that fail to open. Strain the liquid through a double thickness of cheesecloth. Remove the mussels from the shells and use them to garnish the soup if you like, or save them for another use. Then bring the liquid to a boil; add 2 cups heavy cream, and bring it to a boil again. Remove from heat at once. Add 1 beaten egg yolk and heat just long enough for the soup to thicken slightly. Do not boil. Soup may be served hot or cold. *Serves 4.*

CLAMBAKE NEW ENGLAND FISHERMAN'S STYLE

Ike Hoover, a member of the White House staff for many years, called President Taft "a good feeder," one who ate everything. Nowhere was this more apparent than at a New England clambake, for the President dearly loved all kinds of seafood.

Seaweed	*Potato chips*
Live lobsters	*Beer*
Clams	

Seaweed is as essential as clams to a successful clambake. (Beach seaweed, by the way, may be gathered and kept in the freezer.) First, dig a large hole in the sand, and then line it with rocks. After placing a few of the largest rocks at the bottom of the hole, build a base fire, then pile the hole with coals and other rocks. When the coals become fiery and the rocks heated, cover them with a layer of seaweed. Top this with a layer of lobsters, followed by another layer of seaweed and a layer of clams. Alternate seaweed and clams until the clams are used up—allowing about 24 for a good-sized bake. Top with a heavy covering of seaweed, and then a large canvas tarpaulin held down with rocks. Usually it takes at least 20 minutes for the clams to cook and the shells to open. Serve the clams with potato chips and beer.

LOBLOLLY BUTTER

When President Taft had his lobster dinner at Loblolly Cove, he enjoyed the Cove's specialty, loblolly butter, as well. Like many another visitor to the Cove, he was intrigued by the name. For years Captain Haskell himself had tried to trace the origin of the word. One dictionary called it a species of pine tree that grew in, of all places, the South. Harvard professors told him it was a type of gruel.

One day a woman visited Haskell's and, after eating three lobsters in a row, exclaimed, "My, this loblolly is delicious." The Captain pounced when he heard the word, and the lady explained that loblolly was the liver. As a girl in Wales she had been brought up to think of it as a great delicacy. (One hates to be a spoilsport about such a pleasant story, but the truth is that Webster's Unabridged Dictionary defines loblolly as an onomatopeic word derived from lob, meaning to boil or bubble, the sound made by porridge as it boils "lob, lob, lob." What the Welsh lady probably said was not loblolly, but tonnally—the classic name for lobster liver.)

Lobster liver and/or coral	*Cayenne*
Butter	*Mace or nutmeg and/or clove*
Cooked lobster meat	

Combine equal parts of well-pounded or finely ground lobster coral (roe) and/or liver with butter and cooked lobster meat. (In Taft's day, a mortar was used for grinding the meat, but you can use a blender or even a beater.) Season with a pinch of cayenne and, if desired, a few grains of mace or nutmeg and a dash of clove. To serve, spread the "butter" on canapes or use as decoration on a lobster mold or a lobster salad.

BAKED HAM

William Howard Taft did not care how elaborate the food was as long as it was attractively served—and served in quantity. Baked ham filled the bill every time.

Ham	*Brown sugar*
Vinegar	*Bay leaf*
Molasses	*Clove*

Put a ham in a large pot, along with ½ pint each of vinegar and molasses. Add enough water to cover. When the ham is slightly tender, remove it from the pot, cut away the skin and excess fat, and place in a baking pan. Place ham in a very hot (500° F.) oven and bake until very tender. Baste frequently with a sauce made from ½ cup vinegar boiled with ½ cup brown sugar, 1 bay leaf, and 1 whole clove. Serve ham with sweet potatoes and a Waldorf salad.

PEACH SALAD WITH CREAM CHEESE

Salads were a special favorite, almost a perennial on the Taft luncheon and dinner tables. This peach salad was held in high esteem.

Peach	*White grapes*
Lettuce	*Cream cheese*

Place ½ canned or fresh peach on a lettuce bed. Fill the cavity with washed white grapes. Make a ball of cream cheese as the topping.

VEGETABLE SALAD

Asparagus tips	*Lettuce*
Cauliflower	*Ripe olives*
Carrots	*Onion*
Cucumber	*Parsley*
Heart of palm	*French dressing or mayonnaise*

Marinate a variety of vegetables: cooked asparagus tips, cooked or raw cauliflower (if raw, slice paper-thin; if cooked, break into flowerets), raw carrots in strips, raw peeled cucumber strips, and canned heart of palm, sliced. When ready to serve, arrange the vegetables attractively, alternating colors, on a salad plate or bowl, with lettuce underneath. Garnish with ripe olives, chopped raw onion, and/or parsley. Serve with French dressing or mayonnaise.

SALMON SALAD

Considering how much President Taft liked salads and how much he enjoyed salmon, this combination was bound to score with him.

Salmon	*Lettuce*
Mayonnaise or French dressing	*Ripe olives*
Cucumber	*Tomatoes*
Celery	*Hard-boiled egg*

Mix canned, cooked, or flaked salmon with mayonnaise—or, if you prefer, with homemade French dressing. Add cucumber, diced fine, and 1 stalk celery, diced fine. Mix well. Place on a bed of lettuce. Garnish with ripe olives, sliced fresh tomatoes, and slices of hard-boiled eggs. Serve cold.

DEVILED ALMONDS

One of Taft's weaknesses was salted almonds. He nibbled on them whenever he had the chance (when his diet-conscious wife was looking the other way). Fixed this way, the almonds made especially tempting nibblies for Taft—or anyone else. We like to serve them with cocktails, although in the Taft era they were more popularly served at teas or receptions.

> *Blanched almonds*   *Cayenne*
> *Butter*   *Salt*

Put ½ pound blanched almonds into a preheated skillet with 2 ounces of butter. Sauté the nuts until they are a light brown. Drain on absorbent paper. Then place the nuts in a cake pan, sprinkle cayenne and salt lightly over them; shake well, so the seasoning is spread evenly around the nuts. Serve hot. One half pound almonds was, as far as President Taft was concerned, too much for one, not enough for two.

BOUNCING BABIES

This old-fashioned farm-style dessert was in the Taft tradition. Bouncing babies are big, fat, light, and golden-rich with eggs.

> *Popover batter*   *Eggs*
> *Powdered sugar*   *Salad oil*

Add 1 tablespoon powdered sugar to regular popover batter made of 1 cup flour, 1 cup milk, ½ teaspoon salt, 2 tablespoons melted butter or salad oil. Mix lightly and add 3 eggs. Beat again. Have 10 large custard cups or small casseroles ready; brush each lightly with salad oil. Fill about ⅓ full with the batter and bake like popovers. Easiest method: Place in cold oven, set at 450° F. Bake 30 minutes. Bring piping hot to the table.

Serve with maple syrup or powdered sugar sprinkled lightly on top or with lemon wedges squeezed over them. Delicious for a hearty Sunday breakfast or as dessert for supper. *Makes 10 or 12.*

DEACON PORTER'S HAT

This spicy dessert, familiar in the Taft family through the President's mother, Louisa Maria Torrey Taft, owes its picturesque name to Deacon Andrew W. Porter. Long a trustee of Mount Holyoke, he was known for his keen interest in all school matters. He supervised the accounts and paid frequent visits to the grounds. His tall stovepipe hat was a familiar sight to all Holyoke students, including Mrs. Taft, during her short stay in 1843–1844. The "hat" of the Deacon became a delicious cylindrical plum pudding, long a mainstay at Mount Holyoke Thanksgiving dinners. (Mrs. Taft was not the only relative of a President familiar with the famous Deacon's hat. Grace Howe McKinley, niece of the President, graduated in the Class of 1899.)

Flour	*Suet*
Baking soda	*Molasses*
Nutmeg	*Milk*
Ginger	*Chopped nuts*
Cloves	*Raisins*
Cinnamon	

Mix and sift together 3 cups flour, 1 teaspoon baking soda, ½ teaspoon nutmeg, 1 teaspoon ginger, ½ teaspoon cloves, and 1 teaspoon cinnamon. Set aside while preparing the rest. Chop or grind 1 cup suet very fine. Mix it with 1 cup molasses and 1 cup milk. Add the sifted ingredients and mix well. Add ½ cup chopped nuts, preferably walnuts, and ½ cup raisins. Mix again and pour into a greased 2-quart mold. To steam the pudding, place the mold on a rack in a large kettle. Pour boiling water into the kettle to half the depth of the mold. Steam on top of the stove for 2 hours. The pudding is best if served warm with chilled Hard Sauce. *Serves 8.*

To make Hard Sauce: Cream soft (not melted) butter and add enough sifted powdered sugar to make firm. Flavor with 1 teaspoon vanilla or cognac. Beat until light and smooth. Place in fancy serving dish, put in refrigerator, and chill until serving time.

FOUR-COLOR CREAM FRUIT PIE

This is a far more delicious and unusual dessert than its rather mundane name implies. President Taft doted on these super-size tarts. The easy accessibility of so many fruits today makes it much easier to prepare now than in the Taft era.

Strawberries	*Powdered sugar*
Bananas	*Vanilla*
Pineapple	*Sherry*
White grapes	*Pastry shell*
Whipped cream	

Wash the fruits: ½ box strawberries, 1½ cups bananas, 1½ cups pineapple, and 1½ cups white grapes. Dice all, keeping each type separate. Whip ¾ quarts cream with 2 tablespoons powdered sugar, 1½ tablespoons vanilla and 2½ tablespoons sherry. Add ½ cup of each of the fruits to the whipped-cream mixture, folding in carefully. Bake 6 individual small pie crusts. When cooled, place a small glass or custard cup in the center of each. Arrange the different types of fruit—one type to each ¼ crust—around the pie crust. Then remove the glass in the center and fill the space with the whipped cream mixture, piled high. *Serves 6.*

DATE PIE

A penchant for rich and tasty desserts such as this may have contributed to the Taft girth. But to look at it another way, perhaps it may have been a sweetening agent, for the President was known as a friendly, jovial man. In Taft's day, you would most likely have sampled this pie at the Hotel Benedick in Washington.

Dates	*Salt*
Milk	*Pastry shell*
Eggs	

Heat 2 cups pitted dates in the top of a double boiler with 1 pint milk, ¼ teaspoon salt. When very soft and mushy, the mixture should be strained through a wire sieve. Separate 2 eggs and beat the yolks into the milk mixture. Place in an unbaked pie shell. Set the pie in the bottom of a hot (450° F.) oven for 10 minutes. Then move it to the middle shelf of the oven and reduce the heat to 350° F. Bake 40 minutes longer, or until done. Meanwhile beat 2 egg whites until stiff gradually adding 4 tablespoons sugar. When pie is cooked, place meringue over the top and return to oven for light browning only 2 or 3 minutes at 500° F.

CHAMPAGNE PUNCH

Although Taft was a teetotaler, his wife enjoyed a cocktail before dinner—an interesting switch for a Presidential family. The President was no prude, however, and delighted in serving fine wines, especially champagne, to his guests. This punch was his standby at receptions. Ike Hoover called it "the pride of the household and the pleasure of the guests."

Champagne	*Lemon*
Sparkling water	*Sugar*

Mix 1 quart champagne with 2 (12 oz.) bottles of sparkling water. Add a little lemon juice and sugar to taste. Serve in a large punch bowl with a cake of ice floating in it. *Makes 14 servings of ½ cup each.*

XXVIII

A Time of Tumult

Just as the Wilson era marked a tumultuous turning-point in America—its involvement in the Great War and its spurning of the League of Nations—so did Woodrow Wilson's years in the White House run the gamut—from gaiety and entertainment in the first few months, through the illness and death of the first Mrs. Wilson, a period of great loneliness for the President, his romance and remarriage, the war, and then the perishable peace he tried—and died—to save.

Indeed, it is doubtful if any other President's years in the White House produced such extremes of personal and national happiness and sorrow, carefreeness and crisis.

Woodrow Wilson was the second President (after John Tyler) to be widowed in the White House and then remarried to a considerably younger woman. Two of his daughters and a niece were married in the White House.

While these personal events of happiness and sorrow were taking place, America was prospering in the short years between the Taft administration and the tragic austerity of the war, and later facing (or not facing) the international responsibilities thrust upon the country by the peace settlement.

So there is no single pattern to entertaining at the White House during Wilson's two terms in office. Virtually no entertaining was done during the war. There was little during the period of Wilson's illness in the latter months of his administration. State dinners having important diplomatic objectives continued to be held, however—a dinner for an important Japanese delegation or a British naval delegation, for example, and a large and spectacular luncheon for Lord Balfour and other members of a British delegation.

Despite its diplomatic importance, the Balfour luncheon menu strikes the mind, as it would strike the palate, as unusually bland; it proceeded through clear soup (not otherwise identified on the menu), fillet of sole with tartar sauce, fillet of beef with mushrooms, breast of chicken, hearts of lettuce, strawberry ice cream, cake, and mineral water.

The Japanese delegation was entertained at a White House dinner only slightly less conventional—leavened by the inclusion of a Virginia ham, a frequent item on menus during the Wilson administration. Virginia ham was a Presidential favorite by taste and by heritage.

The Japanese dinner menu started with muskmelons and the seemingly inevitable clear soup, and went on to roast capon with vegetables and potatoes. Then came the ham, followed by a Waldorf salad, peach ice cream, cake, and coffee. The somberness of the menu would seem in retrospect to have been relieved somewhat by the accompanying claret, champagne, sherry, Scotch whisky, brandy, cigars, and cigarettes. There were seventy-eight at table, with Mrs. Wilson the only woman present. Scarlet and yellow gladioli decorated the table in the State Dining Room.

Still another prosaic, but by contrast somewhat more interesting, menu was that served at the wedding of the Wilsons' daughter Jessie in the White House in November 1913: bouillon, chicken patties, boned capon and peas, Virginia ham, salad, and pastries.

These conventional menus contrast rather strongly with some of the bountiful fare the Wilsons received when they dined out. For example, a dinner given for the Wilsons by the Secretary of the Navy and his wife hints rather strongly that Mrs. Josephus Daniels came from North Carolina. It included chicken gumbo soup, Eastern Carolina shad, roast Carolina turkey, roast Carolina suckling pig, and tipsy cake.

This dessert, Mrs. Daniels reported, was made "with a sponge cake filled with as many blanched almonds as you can make it hold, and over the cake is poured sherry; a heavy boiled custard is placed on that, and the whole is topped with whipped cream." This dessert recipe obviously dates earlier than Secretary Daniels' famous order barring liquor from Navy messrooms—an order followed henceforth in the Daniels' own home, "for we would not serve ourselves what was denied to . . . the men on the ships." One wonders what might have happened if Mrs. Daniels' tipsy cake had appeared on the mess tables of, say, the USS *North Carolina*.

Mrs. Daniels had visited the White House a number of times during the Cleveland administration, and was obviously a woman fascinated all her life by diplomacy and protocol as they were expressed in the social life of Washington.

So she was an astute observer of the White House during the Wilson years. It was Mrs. Daniels, for example, who quickly observed that President Wilson rebelled at a custom that dated back to George Washington—that the President always preceded his wife. "I am glad to recall that [President Wilson] never forgot that his wife outranked him by an older law than that of Washington officialdom," Mrs. Daniels later wrote, "and always accorded her the honor of preceding him." (But Mrs. Daniels added, in a more reflective moment, that "now, in private life, I see some instances where rules of precedence would bless and not harm, and where unhappiness might be avoided by some of the usages in which Washington delights.")

On first arriving at the White House, President and Mrs. Wilson were determined to make the Executive Mansion the home of a family long used to privacy—the sort of house they had left behind in Princeton, N.J., after Wilson had been elected to the highest office in the land. But while the President chafed at the evaporation of his quiet, campuslike home life, his wife and daughters were able to combine the achievement of privacy and the fulfillment of the demands of the White House.

Evening receptions were a chief feature of the early Wilson years. These gatherings began promptly at nine o'clock with the sound of a bugle heralding the entrance of the President and Mrs. Wilson and members of the Cabinet and their wives—all the women carrying large bouquets of flowers from the White House conservatory—in a procession of grandeur down the grand stairway of the White House to the assembled guests below.

These evening receptions lasted three hours—the President, the Cabinet members and their wives receiving for that time in the Blue Room, and the guests being entertained by musical selections provided by the United States Marine Band.

While generally, even today, an invitation to a White House function is a "command performance" in the sense that one may not decline on the basis of a prior engagement, Mrs. Wilson sometimes gave smaller receptions that achieved a lower pitch of protocol, wording invitations to say that the guest, "if he has no previous engagements, will be welcomed" to the reception. In strict social usage, this wording provided the invitee a chance to decline gracefully, but it was not noticed that attendance at receptions was in any sense reduced by this usage.

There were two striking innovations at the very start of the Wilson administration. First, there was no inaugural ball, for the first time in anyone's memory. Second, President Wilson chose to announce the names of his Cabinet members at a buffet luncheon at the White House directly after the inauguration—and, until Wilson introduced them at the luncheon, only the Cabinet members themselves knew their identity.

There was much speculation about the omission of an inaugural ball. But one Cabinet wife reported that "those of us who knew something of the strong, quiet figure in the background, Ellen Axson Wilson, and of the ambitions she had cherished for her husband, understood that to her this was a dream reverently come true, and that she could not bear to have its sacredness tarnished by the fripperies and frivolity, the new dances just then coming in, the selling of invitations, the folly and empty heartaches of a ball."

Mrs. Wilson once described her aim as mistress of the White House: "I would like to show that dinners and other social functions at the White House can be both beautiful and simple."

Mrs. Daniels concluded that Ellen Axson Wilson was successful in this aim. "In the too few months—nineteen—before her illness, the White House irradiated gracious hospitality with gaiety and happiness. . . . The First Lady measured up to the high standards that make the White House the pattern of American social life," Mrs. Daniels wrote later. "I thought also it had the quality that most of us who live south of the Potomac think of as peculiarly southern, though I was to learn that it was American and found in all parts of the republic. Her teas and luncheons and receptions had a quality of their own, and, in her state dinners, she realized her goal—both beautiful and simple."

And Mrs. Daniels was a good judge. She once invited 800 women to a reception at her relatively small Washington home—and 1500 showed up.

Eleanor Wilson became the second Wilson daughter to be married in the White House, when she became the wife of Secretary of the Treasury William Gibbs McAdoo in May 1914. This was said to be the last social event in the White House personally attended by Ellen Axson Wilson. That same summer, she died—on August 6, 1914, just before the war broke out in Europe.

After a period of inconsolable loneliness, President Wilson, on December 18, 1915, married Mrs. Edith Bolling Gant, an attractive Washington widow. The wedding took place in Mrs. Gant's Washington home, not in the White House. The following year, President Wilson was elected to his second term—and a few months later, the United States declared war on Germany. Social life in the White House changed abruptly.

In the comparatively few months that preceded the entry of the United States into the war, Edith Bolling Wilson achieved the reputation, shared only with Mrs. Grover Cleveland (also married to a President while he was in office), of being the White House's most gracious and charming hostess.

Yet President Wilson's disinterest in food posed some White House problems. The White House physician was constantly concerned at the President's lack of weight and robustness and by the fact that Wilson could not relax while he was eating or taking exercise.

An elaborate survey was taken by the White House staff to determine the President's food preferences—which dishes he seemed to enjoy and eat, which he left untouched. Chicken salad was a favorite and was frequently requested by Wilson as a luncheon dish.

And once, when he was to visit friends who lived outside Washington in the Virginia countryside, he wrote ahead—in an untypical burst of gustatorial fervor: "I am very fond of country hams, peach cobblers, butter and buttermilk, fresh eggs, hot biscuits, homemade ice cream and plain white cake." This contrasts oddly with a later report that the President's favorite breakfast consisted solely of two raw eggs in grapejuice—but this may possibly be blamed on the physician's attempts to add to the presidential girth.

At any rate, the White House cuisine during the Wilson years could fairly be described as simple American food, with strong Southern and country overtones, served simply but always correctly and with great dignity and graciousness.

◇◇◇

R E C I P E S

CORNMEAL PANCAKES

Edith Bolling Wilson's fondness for all foods made from corn received an early test with the outbreak of World War I, when Washington—along with the rest of the country—observed wheatless days that grew in number per week as the war wore on. Northerners among the Washington contingent complained about corn-bread, but Southern women raised on corn pone did not complain.

Mrs. Wilson's fondness for corn is nowhere better illustrated than in this company-breakfast triumph.

Cornmeal	*Milk*
Salt	*Melted butter or salad oil*
Syrup or sugar	*Flour*
Egg	*Baking powder*

Place in a bowl 1 cup white or yellow cornmeal, 1 teaspoon salt, 1 tablespoon sugar or syrup. Make a well and slowly pour in 1 cup boiling water, stirring it round and round. Allow to stand for 10 minutes. Beat together 1 egg, ½ cup milk, 2 tablespoons melted butter or salad oil, and add to cornmeal mixture. Sift together ½ cup all-purpose flour and 2 teaspoons baking powder, and stir into batter with a few quick strokes. Bake in a greased frying pan or greased (380° F.) griddle, turning only once.

These should be served with syrup and butter or, in true Virginia style, with chicken or turkey hash. The pancakes may be small or large. For a luncheon dish, make large ones, place a couple of spoonfuls of hash on one side, fold over, sprinkle with grated cheese, and place under broiler to melt cheese. *Makes 12 cakes.*

APPLE MUFFINS

During the early Wilson years, the White House at any given moment usually contained a number of relatives and friends, who came for a day and stayed for four or five. So the informal breakfast came to be a White House institution in these years—and a frequent arrival at the breakfast table were these muffins, expressive in their simplicity of Ellen Axson Wilson's desire for perfection, yet they are unusual, well worth trying.

Eggs	*Salt*
Butter	*Apples*
Sour cream	*Baking powder*

Sift 1½ cups all-purpose flour with ½ teaspoon salt, 2 teaspoons double-action baking powder. Separate 2 eggs. Beat yolks well. Add 2 tablespoons melted butter, ½ cup sour cream. Mix together. Fold in stiffly beaten whites of 2 eggs and at the last minute fold in 2 peeled, diced apples. Spoon into 24 well-buttered muffin tins (2 inches in diameter). Bake in moderately hot oven (375° F.) about 25 minutes. *Makes 2 dozen.*

STRAWBERRY PANCAKES

A marvelous, if somewhat startling, breakfast combination dating from the Wilson years in the White House is this version of pancakes served (believe it or not) with fried eggs, one to a stack, each stack surrounded by bacon and topped with maple syrup. For the modern eater, no matter how hearty, I would suggest leaving the fried eggs for another occasion, for strawberry pancakes with bacon and syrup would seem to be enough to satisfy anyone.

Pancake batter (prepared mix may   Mashed fresh or frozen strawberries
*   be used)*

Make a standard wheatcake recipe or use a prepared pancake mix, preparing enough batter to serve pancakes to four persons. Add to the batter 1 cup crushed strawberries (if fresh, sweeten to taste; if frozen, no additional sugar will be needed). Bake on griddle, being sure they do not brown too much.

These versatile pancakes will serve nicely for a dessert (without the bacon, of course), and may be served with sour cream instead of syrup. *Serves 4.*

SHRIMP MULL

From Ellen Axson Wilson's native Georgia comes an old favorite along the coastal strip, brought to the White House for family suppers—thus contributing still another regional specialty to the permanent White House cuisine.

Butter	*Celery*
Onion	*Tabasco sauce*
Garlic	*Pepper*
Salt	*Lemon juice*
Tomatoes	*Shrimp*
Water	*Cracker crumbs*
Ketchup	*Rice*

Melt 3 tablespoons butter or margarine in large, deep skillet. Add 1 small chopped onion and cook over low heat until onion is transparent but not brown. Crush 1 clove garlic and add along with 1 teaspoon salt, 2 cups tomatoes, 2 cups water, ½ cup tomato ketchup, ½ cup chopped celery, 2 drops Tabasco sauce, and pepper to taste. Cover and simmer for an hour. Add 1 tablespoon lemon juice and 1 pound peeled raw shrimp or a 1-pound package of frozen shrimp. Cook 5 minutes, or until shrimp are pink and done through. Add 2 tablespoons cracker crumbs and heat thoroughly while stirring constantly. Serve over cooked rice (you will need about 2 cups). *Serves 4.*

RUSSIAN SAUCE MAYONNAISE

One of the rituals for visiting dignitaries to Washington, in Wilson's day as now, is the visit to Washington's tomb at Mount Vernon. Nowadays the symbolic visit, on which a wreath is set beside the tomb, is generally made by automobile. But President and Mrs. Wilson usually made the trip aboard the Presidential yacht *Mayflower,* either accompanying the foreign dignitary themselves or delegating the chore to a member of the Cabinet.

The routine of a cruise down the Potomac often included a dinner aboard the yacht. During one such dinner, in 1919, this sumptuous mayonnaise was served. Luxurious though the taste may be, it is quick and easy to prepare.

Egg yolks	*Chili sauce*
Mayonnaise	*Salt*
Anchovies	*Paprika*
White pepper	*Caviar, onions (optional)*

Press 2 hard-boiled egg yolks through a fine strainer; mix with 2 tablespoons mayonnaise. Add 3 finely chopped anchovy fillets, ½ teaspoon ground white pepper, 2 tablespoons chili sauce, ¼ teaspoon salt, and ½ teaspoon paprika. Mix well. If desired, just before serving fold in 2 tablespoons caviar and 1 onion, chopped very fine. *Makes ½ cup.*

GUINEA SQUASH (EGGPLANT)

An old name for eggplant used in Ellen Axson Wilson's native Georgia is "Guinea squash," a name undoubtedly brought from the West Coast of Africa. Slave-traders were known as Guinea-traders, Guinea being the name applied by Europeans to the West African coast.

And Mrs. Wilson brought an old Georgia recipe to the White House that combines history with delicious flavor.

Eggplant   *Pepper*
Breadcrumbs   *Nutmeg*
Salt   *Butter*

Broil eggplant until skin can be removed; cut in slices crosswise, then cut each slice in half. Place a layer of eggplant in the bottom of a small casserole, cover with thin layer of breadcrumbs (you will need about 1½ cups breadcrumbs to a medium-size eggplant, altogether), add scant dash each of salt, pepper, and nutmeg. Dot with butter. Cover with another layer of eggplant slices, more breadcrumbs, seasonings, and butter. Continue until all eggplant is in the casserole and top with breadcrumbs and butter. Pour ½ cup water over top, bake in a 350° F. oven until nicely brown on top. As a variation, onions and thinly sliced apples may be added.

STRAWBERRY ICE CREAM

A constantly requested favorite of President Wilson was strawberry ice cream, combining his favorite form of dessert with one of his favorite fruits. The story is told that President and Mrs. Wilson driving out into the Virginia countryside and stopping, unannounced, at a crossroads tearoom. The Secret Service men accompanying the Presidential party deployed around the tearoom, and two of the guards encountered a man in the back yard of the tearoom engaged in picking large, juicy, ripe strawberries from a patch there. After some haggling, the Secret Service men struck up a deal and bought the panful of fresh berries, borrowed some sugar and a couple of spoons. As the last bite was being devoured, the man reappeared in the strawberry patch, hopping mad. "You've eaten all the ripe berries," he hollered, "and the President and Mrs. Wilson are inside having tea—and guess what they've ordered!"

Light cream   *Almond extract*
Sugar   *Strawberries (fresh or frozen)*
Salt

Bring 1 quart light cream barely to boiling point, stir in 1 cup sugar, ¼ teaspoon salt. Add 2 cups mashed ripe strawberries, fresh or frozen, sweetened if needed. ½ to 1 teaspoon almond or vanilla extract may be added if desired. It brings out the flavor. Freeze. *Serves 6 handsomely.*

RASPBERRY OR STRAWBERRY ICE

For a somewhat lighter version of the Wilson favorite, here are two variations of a fruit ice that can be as easily made in the refrigerator in this day and age as it could be in a hand-cranked freezer some years ago when one could prevail on someone else to turn the crank.

Strawberries or raspberries (fresh or frozen)	*Salt*
	Water
Sugar	*Lemon juice*

Mash 4 cups berries, mix in 2 cups sugar and allow to stand for an hour at room temperature. Force through fine strainer, add a very small amount of salt, 1¾ cups water, and 1 teaspoon lemon juice. Freeze. *Makes 1 quart.*

CHERRY PUDDING

Traditionally, this wonderfully fragrant fruit custard should be made with wild cherries—at least, it always was, in the Wilson White House. But sour pie cherries make an interesting variation and are considerably easier to come by if you are not in the mood for climbing trees.

Eggs	*Sherry*
Flour	*Vanilla*
Cornstarch	*Cherries (wild or tame)*
Sugar	*Cream*

Beat yolks of 2 eggs, fold in 1 tablespoon pastry flour, 1 tablespoon cornstarch, ½ pound sugar, 1 tablespoon sweet sherry, and ½ teaspoon vanilla. Cook until thick in double boiler and add 2 cups fresh, pitted or canned pie cherries, drained. Cool, fold in 2 beaten egg whites, pour into your prettiest casserole or a silver bowl, spread with whipped cream. *Serves 6 to 8.*

GEORGIA KISS PUDDING

A favorite recipe brought to the White House via the President's House at Princeton University is available to us in two versions—both rich and delicious—as garnered in her native Georgia by Ellen Axson Wilson.

KISS PUDDING I

Eggs   *Sugar*
Milk   *Cornstarch*
Butter

Beat 4 egg yolks, add 4 cups milk, 2 tablespoons butter and 1½ cups sugar. Bring to a boil. Add 3 tablespoons cornstarch blended with small amount of water. Stir constantly, cooking until thickened. Pour into a greased casserole, top with meringue made by beating stiffly 2 egg whites and adding 4 tablespoons powdered sugar. Bake in medium (350° F.) oven until meringue is nicely browned. *Serves 6.*

KISS PUDDING II

Proceed exactly as for Kiss Pudding I, except that you do not cook mixture after combining ingredients, add coconut on top of meringue, brown in oven, and then cool thoroughly. There will be a syrup at the bottom of the casserole when it is served. This should be ladled on top of pudding. *Serves 6.*

CREAM CAKES

For more elaborate White House desserts, these meringues (for these are actually what cream cakes, or "kisses," are) were often served with fresh strawberries or raspberries and make a delightful party touch to a summer menu, either for luncheon or dinner.

Egg whites   *Lemon extract*
Powdered sugar

Beat 3 egg whites stiffly with ⅛ teaspoon salt; add 1 cup powdered sugar 1 tablespoon at a time while continuing to beat, until mixture is as thick as a very thick batter. Add ¼ teaspoon lemon extract. Drop by tablespoonfuls onto cooky sheet covered with very lightly greased brown paper. Bake about 45 minutes in very slow (250° F.) oven until surface has hardened—but be careful not to have the cakes turn brown. Remove with spatula, place in pairs, bottom-to-bottom, in colander; return to oven (which has meanwhile been turned off) to dry briefly. *Makes 30 pairs of meringues.*

SUGAR CAKES

More like shortbread or cookies are these simple but delightful cakes that appeared at receptions at the White House before World War I curtailed entertaining.

Butter	*Flour*
Sugar	*Milk*
Eggs	*Salt*

Cream 1 cup butter with 1 cup sugar. Beat 3 whole eggs well, add to butter and sugar mixture. Add 4 cups flour alternately with enough milk—about 4 to 6 tablespoons—to form a stiff dough. Roll out, cut in shapes, bake on cooky sheet in 350° F. oven. *Makes 6 dozen 3-inch cakes.*

XXIX

The Not-Always-So Roaring Twenties

****

With the Roaring Twenties came the arrival of the Ohio Gang in the White House—a political nadir in America, but a welcome hustle and bustle in Washington social life after the austerity of the late Wilson era. Sometimes it seemed as if the Harding-inspired social whirl was bustle for bustle's sake—as if it mattered not what inspired it or what it yielded.

The Harding years in the White House were a mixture of almost frantic entertaining at elegant, even ostentatious, luncheons, dinners, and garden parties, intermingled with such innovations as stag breakfasts and stag dinners where plebeian fare was gulped down with beer.

Florence Kling Harding, on the day of her husband's inauguration, remarked that the Hardings were "just folks" and wanted to be regarded as such. Yet not long afterward Mrs. Harding sent the White House flat silver out to be triple gold-plated—and one member of the White House staff had trouble thereafter remembering to say *goldware* instead of *silverware*.

Ostentatious though it sounds, the goldware created a dramatic effect in the State Dining Room at the White House when it was teamed with the Dolley Madison gold service—a centerpiece made up of a gold-bordered flat mirror in three sections, four tall gold candlesticks (each with fifteen candles), and three colossal gold epergnes—and the Wilson gold-bordered china service.

For all state and formal entertaining, the White House of the Hardings strictly observed the Eighteenth Amendment. Wine was banished from the table even at such elegant state dinners as the series given for delegates to the World Disarmament Conference. But one member of the White House staff afterward recalled vividly the sight of the austere Mrs. Harding—five years her husband's senior, her gray hair meticulously marcelled—mixing drinks for the Hardings' friends in the private apartments of the White House. Prohibition, it seems, was not carried into the Hardings' personal life.

For most formal entertaining, Florence Kling Harding—called "The Duchess" by the President and their close friends—was content to leave matters in the hands of the White House staff and, for larger occasions, outside caterers. Perhaps because her energies were almost entirely directed to the advancement of her husband's political life, The Duchess did not leave any special imprint upon White House social life. Efficiency, entertaining on a large scale, undistinguished cuisine, and a general aura of mediocrity—these in retrospect seem to be the hallmarks of the Harding years in the White House, at a time when even speakeasies in New York served better food.

In later years, when the political excesses of the Harding administration became known, Mrs. Harding's self-applied tag of "just folks" took on a bitter ring. An inspection of White House menus does, however, seem to bear her out—but perhaps only in the culinary respect. If "just folks" could be taken to mean a willingness to accept the average, the phrase could certainly be applied to White House cuisine during the Harding era.

Fortunately, there were exceptions to this rule. But these exceptions are almost invariably found in the dishes the Hardings liked to serve at small, intimate private dinners and stag breakfasts rather than in the cuisine for formal occasions. We have chosen most of our recipes from the exceptions.

◇◇

R E C I P E S

FILLET OF BEEF HARDING

In more formal cooking, particularly under the aegis of the Hardings' Oriental chef, Lee Ping-quan, steward on the *Mayflower,* there recurs a subtle touch that is worth remembering in today's kitchen—the gentle addition of sherry to beef, pork, or veal dishes. This touch is nowhere better displayed than in this sumptuous and elegant dish.

Beef fillet	*Bacon*
Sherry	*Mushrooms*
Lemon juice	*Flour*
Worcestershire sauce	*Butter*
Salt and pepper	*Beef stock*

Place a beef fillet—1 pound for each three persons to be served—in a shallow dish, sprinkle over it ¼ cup dry sherry and ¼ cup lemon juice. Leave at room temperature for half an hour, turning several times. Toward end of marinating period, add several dashes of Worcestershire sauce and season with salt and freshly ground black pepper. Remove fillet from dish, arrange on broiling pan with several slices of bacon placed across fillet and their ends anchored under the fillet. Broil 8 to 10 minutes (it must be rare). Meanwhile, slice 1 lb. mushrooms and brown gently in ¼ stick (2 tablespoons) butter. Blend in 1½ tablespoons flour; add 2 cups beef stock. When it begins to thicken, add 1 wine glass sherry. When fillet is done, slice thinly at an angle. Serve with mushroom sauce on top.

At the White House, the Hardings generally served stuffed sweet potatoes and fresh asparagus with the fillet.

BARBECUED LOIN OF PORK WITH SHERRY

Another White House rceipe from the Harding period makes the same clever use of sherry—this time with pork. This is basically a sophisticated version of a country dish, but it could grace even a formal dinner table—as it did at the White House on numerous occasions.

Loin of pork	*Worcestershire sauce*
Sherry	*Tomato paste*
Brown sugar	*Salt and pepper*

Place a 5- or 6-pound loin of pork in deep dish and marinate in 1 cup dry sherry, ½ cup brown sugar, 2 tablespoons Worcestershire sauce, and 2 teaspoons tomato paste. Place pork on skewer (if your oven has barbecue attachment) or in roasting pan on rack, and cook in slow (300° F.) oven until done (at least 1½ hours), basting frequently with marinade. Meanwhile, start to work on:

FRESH CORN CAKES

Eggs	*Salt*
Flour	*Corn*
Milk	

Beat 2 eggs lightly, add 1 cup flour, ¾ cup milk, and ½ teaspoon salt. Fold in 1 cup corn—either whole-kernel canned or cut fresh off the cob. Adjust, adding a little milk if necessary to make a very heavy batter. Fry in large flat cakes on griddle or in frying pan greased with bacon.

When pork is done, slice and serve a generous chop on a corn cake for each portion, topped with a spoonful of sauce from the pan. *Serves 12 amply and richly.*

CALF'S LIVER AND BACON

Here is still another unexpected appearance of sherry as an ingredient—this time with calf's liver. It must be admitted, though purists will not like it, that very thin slices of beef liver or lamb liver are delicious prepared this way. (For formal occasions, it is best to stay with the old reliable calf's liver.)

Calf's liver	*Bacon*
Sherry	*Cream*
Flour	*Salt, pepper*
Eggs	

Three pounds of calf's liver, sliced as thin as possible, will be needed to serve 8. Marinate liver in ½ cup sherry, dredge each slice in flour, then in two eggs that have been beaten with a little cream. Dredge again gently in flour and sauté in fat for 10 minutes.

Serve with bacon crisped to a turn and, if you want, a prepared tomato sauce. Hashed creamed potatoes are traditional with liver and bacon, in which case omit the tomato sauce.

COLD VEAL LOAF

Here is an interesting and unusual dish from the White House summer buffet table—especially popular for formal luncheons given by Mrs. Harding. By multiplying the proportions, it can be made to serve any number, and should be accompanied by potato salad and a vegetable salad.

Veal cutlet	*Cream*
Eggs	*Butter*
Cracker crumbs	*Salt, pepper*

Simmer 2 pounds veal cutlet for 45 minutes, cool and chop fine. Add 2 eggs, beaten, and 1 cup cracker crumbs. Moisten with 2 tablespoons cream and 1 tablespoon butter. Shape into roll and dip in 1 beaten egg to which 1 tablespoon cream has been added. Cover with more cracker crumbs and bake in 350° F. oven for 30 minutes. Chill thoroughly and slice with very sharp knife. *Serves 4 to 6.*

JELLIED PIGS' FEET

Another dish from the White House cold buffet with an unusual note—yet a dish not too remote from the Ohio country cuisine on which both the President and Mrs. Harding were raised—is this delicious concoction that takes full advantage of the natural gelatine in the bones.

Pigs' feet	*Cinnamon*
Bay leaves	*Cloves*
Vinegar	*Salt, pepper*

Have butcher split 6 pigs' feet (not, of course, the feet from 6 pigs, unless you are planning a very large buffet!). Wash thoroughly, place in pot, cover with cold water, add 3 bay leaves. Bring to a simmer, cook very slowly for about 4 hours, or until pigs' feet are thoroughly tender. Remove pigs' feet, retaining liquid. Wash the pigs' feet and carefully remove all bones (not as difficult as it sounds—they pop right out). Meanwhile, add 4 cups vinegar to the liquid, bring it to a boil with ½ stick cinnamon and eight whole cloves. Reduce liquid by ¼, and pour over pigs' feet in fairly deep dish. Jell and chill thoroughly. Unmold and serve with spiced apples or crabapples. *Makes from 6 to 12 servings depending on your love of pigs' feet.*

CHICKEN POT PIE

Another Midwestern country favorite, and one that could come with aplomb and grace to the most formal dinner table, is this authentic chicken pie brought to the White House by Mrs. Harding. It is lifted to elegance by the addition of ½ pound sliced mushrooms, lightly browned in butter and added to the pie just before the top goes on. This is not traditional, however, and you can be proud of this dish even if you leave out the mushrooms.

Stewing chicken (fowl)	*Butter*
Bay leaf	*Salt, pepper*
Potatoes	*Biscuit dough or pie crust*
Onions	*Egg*

Simmer a large fowl with bay leaf in water to cover until thoroughly tender. Remove meat from bones, separate into fairly large pieces. Retain chicken stock. Boil 8 or 10 small peeled potatoes and 6 or 8 small white onions in the stock until tender. Grease a deep baking dish with butter; combine chicken, potatoes, and onions. Pour in thickened stock—enough barely to cover the other ingredients—season with salt and pepper to taste, and top with biscuit dough or pie crust. Paint top with slightly beaten egg, bake in medium (350° F.) oven until top is nicely browned.

Serve with remainder of stock, slightly thickened, in gravy boat. Resist the temptation to add cream or milk to the sauce. Country folks never do. *Serves 4 to 6.*

KNOCKWURST AND SAUERKRAUT

"Forget that I'm President of the United States," Harding would say as he slipped into his place at the poker table. "I'm Warren Harding, playing poker with friends, and I'm going to beat hell out of them."

Before the poker session began, likely as not Harding had entertained his cronies at a stag dinner at the White House that almost always included the Presidential favorite, knockwurst and sauerkraut. Sometimes frankfurters were served, but knockwurst seems to elevate this dish. Beer is the traditional accompaniment.

Sauerkraut	*Knockwurst or frankfurters*
Apples	*Beer or white wine*
Ground black pepper	*Mustard*
Caraway seeds (optional)	

Wash thoroughly enough fresh or canned sauerkraut to allow about ½ pound for each person to be served. To serve 6 use 3 pounds. Place a third of it in bottom of lightly greased pot that has tight-fitting cover. Top sauerkraut with 1 finely-chopped peeled apple, sprinkle with freshly ground black pepper and, if you like, 1½ teaspoons caraway seeds. Place 6 knockwurst on top of the sauerkraut, then add another third of the sauerkraut, another chopped apple, another 6 knockwurst, more pepper and caraway seeds. Top with final layer of sauerkraut. Pour gently over the top enough beer or dry white wine to allow 1 cup per pound of sauerkraut, i.e., 3 cups. Place pot on heat until liquid starts to steam. Immediately reduce flame to barest simmer; cover tightly, and cook for at least an hour. More cooking will not harm this dish. Add additional wine or beer if it seems to be needed. Serve with array of prepared mustards—including, for the purists, dry powdered mustard mixed with more of the same beer or wine used in cooking.

KNOCKWURST AND SAUERKRAUT II

Another way of preparing President Harding's favorite—not as traditional, but richer and more unusual—is a roasted version using much the same ingredients with the addition of bacon. This version appeals to those who do not like sauerkraut cooked a long time.

Sauerkraut   *Pepper*
Knockwurst or frankfurters   *Caraway seeds (optional)*
Bacon

Arrange 3 pounds sauerkraut in roasting pan (allowing ½ pound per person.) Place 12 knockwurst (or frankfurters) on top, and arrange 12 strips of bacon—on top of that. Add ½ teaspoon cracked peppercorns and, if wanted, 1 teaspoon caraway seeds. Bake in 325° F. oven for 45 minutes. Some of the sauerkraut should be browned on top, and all of it should be a rich, golden hue. Good dish for cold winter evenings. *Serves 6.*

SQUALLS

Part of the incongruity of the Roaring Twenties was that while bathtub gin was taking its place high on the American social scale and good Scotch whisky was being served in the private apartments at the White House, garden-party guests on the south lawn were imbibing (if that is the word) gentle fruit punches, unspiked, and something called "squalls" that might more properly be called fruit squashes.

The garden party became a favorite form of entertaining for Mrs. Harding, and here are two of the squalls that lent an air of sober elegance to the delightful outdoor scene:

For a *fresh green mint and lemon squall,* boil the peels of six lemons in a quart of water for 5 minutes, add stalks of six branches of mint (retaining leaves), simmer gently for 5 more minutes. Strain liquid, add to it 1½ pounds sugar, 2 quarts water, and ½ teaspoon baking soda. Mix together, pour over block of ice. Serve in small glasses or punch cups with a mint leaf floating in each. *Makes 3 quarts, 24 servings.*

For a *pineapple and lemon squall,* boil lemon peels in water as above, strain, and add juice of the same number of lemons. Grind a peeled pineapple in meat grinder, force through sieve, add the pineapple juice and pulp to the lemon liquid, blend in 1½ pounds sugar and ½ teaspoon baking soda. Pour over ice. Serve in small glasses or cups, each garnished with thin lemon slice. *Makes 14 servings.*

BAKED APPLES WITH MERINGUE

Here again is a substantial and rather prosaic country dish to which the White

House, in Harding's day, added a sophisticated touch that makes it suitable for a formal meal—even a White House dinner.

Apples	*Molasses*
Sugar	*Lemon*
Cinnamon	*Egg whites*
Butter	*Powdered sugar*
Water	

Core 6 apples, cut off tops, and arrange snugly in deep baking dish. Fill hole in each apple with sugar, add dash of cinnamon and piece of butter to each. Pour enough water in pan to reach about ½ way up sides of apples. Pour over tops of apples 1 cup sugar, 1 tablespoon molasses and one lemon sliced thin with seeds removed. Bake in 375° F. oven for 30 minutes. Make a meringue according to a standard recipe, using whites of 2 eggs and 4 tablespoons superfine sugar. Divide meringue among tops of apples, then place pan back in oven just long enough to brown the meringue slightly. *Serves 6.*

WAFFLES

One innovation brought to the White House by the Hardings was the use of the breakfast table as a way of entertaining. Mrs. Harding rarely slept late, so the President was on hand for staggering country-style breakfasts that ran the gamut of rich and substantial fare. A typical breakfast eaten by Harding and his friends included grapefruit, hot cereal, scrambled eggs and bacon, wheatcakes with maple syrup, corn muffins, toast, and the proverbial gallons of coffee.

Only when Mrs. Harding herself presided at the breakfast table was there any important change in the menu. Like many another first lady, Mrs. Harding liked waffles and brought her own recipe for them to the White House.

Eggs	*Baking powder*
Melted butter	*Milk*
Flour	*Salt*
Sugar	

Separate 2 eggs, place yolks in large bowl, and beat with 2 tablespoons melted butter. Sift together 1½ cups flour, 2 tablespoons sugar, and 2 teaspoons baking powder. Stir dry ingredients into beaten eggs and butter, alternating with up to 1 cup milk to make a thin batter. Beat egg whites until stiff, fold into batter, bake in waffle iron. *Serves 6*—but if you have very hungry waffle-eaters on your hands, better double the recipe.

BANANA COCKTAIL

As the Hardings' main dishes tended to be on the heavy side, there was frequent need on White House menus of that day for a light first course or a light dessert. And here is a White House favorite from Harding days that serves in either capacity with equal aplomb.

Banana   *Brandy*
Strawberries   *Sherry*
Melon   *Sugar*

Cut banana in half lengthwise. Carefully remove the meat, saving the skin whole, and dice. Also dice several strawberries and a small piece of melon. Add 1 tablespoon each brandy, sherry, and sugar; mix thoroughly and replace in the two halves of the banana skin. Chill quickly, and serve at once.

XXX

Cooling It With Cal

***

The stereotyped image often obscures the real man—and in no case is this more true than that of Calvin Coolidge. True, he was spare, taciturn, acidulous, frugal—typical of the public image of the remote New England farmer. But he was also a man who was at his worst in large groups. And, since the public saw him only when he was making formal appearances, American legend has added "Silent Cal" to its list of characters.

Cal was silent, all right, but it was the kind of silence that comes before the *bon mot.* Many are the stories about his quips—part of the legend, but somehow never told as an example of his warmth, only of his coldness. He would sit silently at a formal dinner table, literally because he had nothing to say in such surroundings. Once a woman sitting on his right said she had made a bet with some friends that she could get the President to say more than two words during dinner. He turned to her and said, "You lose."

The reason for the "dehumanization" of President Coolidge during his years in the White House was that these were years of prosperity for America, however synthetic, that came between the excesses of the Harding administration (of which Coolidge was only titularly a member, as Vice-President) and the depression-borne post-market-crash era of Herbert Hoover.

Although Coolidge's ascendancy to the chief executive's office came on the sudden death of Warren Harding, the public was ready for the absolutely unquestioned honesty of Silent Cal. And the sparse surroundings of Coolidge's oath-taking—he was sworn in at three o'clock in the morning in the parlor of his father's house in Plymouth, Vermont—endeared him immediately to America, which at that moment wanted stability in the White House beyond all else.

Coolidge's idiosyncrasies drove some people mad. He was a nibbler, not an eater, and whether he was in the private Presidential apartments at the White House or in the Executive Office, at his elbow were bowls of nuts and fruits, crackers and jars of preserves. It was often wondered why the President did not attain the proportions of former President (then Chief Justice) William Howard Taft—but the slim Vermonter kept his spare figure all through his White House years, despite the constant nibbling.

Unflattering though Coolidge's personal image may seem in retrospect, it was marvelously counterbalanced by the totally different image of the First Lady, Grace Goodhue Coolidge—and it has been said that never were a Presidential couple more unlike, though both were born and raised in Vermont and shared the Vermonters' love of good, simple food and dislike of unnecessary conversation.

When Coolidge was Governor of Massachusetts, his wife was seldom in the public eye. The Bay State in those days maintained no executive mansion for its governor, so Mrs. Coolidge and their two sons, John and Calvin, Jr., lived on in the Coolidge home in Northampton, while Governor Coolidge spent weekdays in a Boston hotel and caught the day coach for Northampton each Saturday to spend the weekend with his family.

And in Washington, as wife of the Vice-President, Mrs. Coolidge quickly learned that the office her husband held often dipped into comparative insignificance. The public had little opportunity to get to know Grace Coolidge until she became mistress of the White House. Then, however, America quickly discovered that Mrs. Coolidge balanced with tact, cheerfulness, spontaneity, graciousness, and warmth the somewhat dour image summoned up by the President.

To start with, Mrs. Coolidge continued the time-honored custom of White House evening receptions, in which members of the Cabinet and their wives followed the Presidential couple down the grand staircase into the East Room as the Marine Band played "Hail to the Chief." At some of these elaborate receptions, as many as 3500 guests were on hand.

President Coolidge knew and appreciated his wife's contribution to the type of hospitality the nation expected of the White House. "While the President has supervision over all these functions, the most effective way to deal with them is to provide a capable Mistress of the White House," he wrote in his memoirs. "I have often been complimented on the choice which I made nearly 25 years ago."

President Coolidge vastly preferred the family dinner table to formal banquets, yet it seems that it was only in the Coolidge era that the President, his wife, and one or two of their children dined in evening clothes in the State Dining Room—even when there were no guests.

Once the Coolidge's eldest son John returned from a tea dance in Annapolis a scant few moments before the dinner hour. Respectfully he asked his father if, in view of the late hour, he could join his parents for dinner without changing into dinner clothes. "You will remember that you are dining at the table of the President of the United States," said the stern Coolidge, "and you will present yourself promptly and in proper attire." John never forgot the tone of his father's voice.

Despite the air of formality President Coolidge tried to maintain at even small dinners, there was one famous dinner—for President Machado of Cuba—where everything seemed to go wrong. The bow tie of one of the guests fell into his soup. Then the President's military aide, fresh from a visit to the dentist, lost a temporary front tooth. A naval aide lost an epaulette. To top off the string of disasters, the chimney caught fire. At the end of the meal, the guests breathed a sigh of relief that nothing else could go wrong. Only then was it discovered that one of the guests had gone through the seat of his chair, and it took two strong men to extricate him.

President Coolidge had more odd ideas about food than perhaps any other White House resident. For one thing, he insisted upon referring to all meals as *supper* even if they were actually breakfast or luncheon or a formal state dinner. For another, he generally breakfasted (or supped, as it were) on hot cereal prepared in the White House kitchen by combining three parts whole wheat and one part whole rye, cooked in its unground state. And then there was the ceaseless nibbling.

There was the President's preoccupation with thrift and frugality. When he left the White House for retirement at the end of his term (it will be recalled that he had said "I do not choose to run" for a second elected term), he is supposed to have made certain the partly consumed jars of preserves in various parts of the White House were collected and transported to Northampton so he could finish them there.

Under President Harding's administration, Congress had provided that meals at the White House would be paid for by the government if government business was transacted. President Coolidge's sense of thrift was aroused by this, and he fell into the custom of inviting Congressmen to have breakfast with him, promptly at eight in the morning in the small dining room of the White House.

As the Congressmen ate their fruit, buckwheat pancakes, and maple syrup and drank their coffee, Silent Cal lived up to his public image and tersely consumed his homemade hot cereal. Sometimes not a single word was spoken at these official breakfasts—yet Coolidge maintained he did not have to talk to Congressmen to get to know them. Looking them over, he said, was generally sufficient. And the government picked up the tab. Thus Coolidge was able to indulge in two of his favorite occupations—entertaining inexpensively and getting somebody else to pay the bills.

Yet the President realized that this economy could not extend to the more formal dinners and receptions given at the White House under Grace Coolidge's careful, and not at all frugal, supervision. Once he prowled through the White House kitchens before reception, looking over the trays of elaborate pastries and decorated hors-d'oeuvre. The kitchen staff waited anxiously for his reaction to all this munificence—and Silent Cal finally glanced down to the floor where dishes of dog food had been set out for the Coolidge canines. "Mighty fine-looking dog food," he said, and walked out.

When Coolidge was Vice-President, the couple was frequently invited out to dine. Almost invariably they accepted such invitations for, as canny Calvin observed, "Got to eat somewhere."

Sometimes the heavy banquet-type food proved to be more than a Vermonter of simple tastes could stand. "Sometimes I don't know whether I'm having food or soda mints," Coolidge once remarked, "I have to mix the two so often." But later, the President hit upon a way of surviving the heavy food. Unnoticed by the guests, a waiter would slip a plate of roast beef before the Pesident, no matter what entree was being served officially.

The New England atmosphere surrounded the Coolidges, prompting Alice Roosevelt Longworth, to remark that "The first time we went to the White House after the Coolidges were there, the atmosphere was as different as a New England front parlor is from a back room in a speakeasy." Mrs. Longworth perhaps meant no disparagement of the Coolidges' predecessors.

The Coolidges were not in residence at the White House the entire period of their administration. Upon learning there was real danger that the roof might fall in, the Coolidges rented a house on DuPont Circle that had been designed by Stanford White and which seemed adequate, with its thirty rooms, to meet at least some of the demands of Presidential society. It was in this house, for example, that the ill-starred dinner for President Machado took place. And it was here that the Coolidges entertained their most famous guest, Charles A. Lindbergh. Another guest at the same occasion was Dwight Morrow—and the stage was set for the most publicized romance of the times, that of Lindbergh and Dwight Morrow's daughter Anne.

◇◇◇

RECIPES

BREAKFAST GEMS

President Coolidge was at his most critical when it came to breakfast. He would complain about the small size of the griddle cakes that were served with his beloved Vermont maple syrup, and once appeared in the housekeeper's office with a minute griddle cake between his fingers. "Why can't I have big griddle cakes like they have downstairs?" he would ask, referring to the griddle-size variety made for the servants' table. This recipe for breakfast gems met all the presidential specifications and thus appeared frequently at family breakfasts and sometimes at the "official" breakfasts Coolidge gave for small groups of Congressmen.

Flour	*Egg*
Milk	*Salt*
Baking powder	*Sugar*

Put 1⅔ cups flour, 1 cup milk, 3 teaspoons baking powder, 1 unbeaten egg, 1 pinch salt, and 2 teaspoons sugar into bowl all at once. Beat just until lumps disappear. Pour into very hot greased gem pans, bake in very hot (450° F.) oven for 25 minutes. *Makes 24 (2 inch) gems.*

CORNMEAL MUFFINS

Nowhere was the Coolidge fastidiousness more apparent than in the constant struggle and failure to get the kind of cornmeal muffins the Vermont President wanted. He and Mrs. Coolidge were both fond of these country favorites but had trouble getting the White House kitchen to turn them out to perfection. So Mrs. Coolidge sent off to the inn at Northampton for the recipe, adapted it somewhat, and this was the way cornmeal muffins were finally made at the White House during the Coolidge years there.

Eggs	*Sugar*
Milk	*Baking powder*
Cornmeal	*Salt*
Flour	

Beat 2 eggs, add 1 scant cup milk. Blend 2 cups cornmeal, 1 cup flour, 4 tablespoons sugar, 2 tablespoons baking powder, and ¼ teaspoon salt, and mix into egg–milk mixture. Put into well-greased muffin tins and bake in hot (450° F.) oven for 25 or 30 minutes. *Makes 2 dozen 2-inch muffins.*

LICHEE-NUT FRUIT CUP

Often the rather simple cuisine of the White House, as in many other homes, needed amplification through the addition of an elegant first course. None is more elegant or more delicious than this fruit cup with an Oriental touch that was served on a number of occasions on the Presidential yacht *Mayflower* while cruising down the Potomac to Mount Vernon.

Strawberries	*Preserved lichee nuts*
Pineapple	*Sherry*
Oranges	*Brandy*

Dice 1 cup fresh strawberries, 2 slices canned pineapple, and 2 peeled, seeded oranges. Add 1 can preserved lichee nuts, 2 tablespoons sherry, and 2 tablespoons brandy. Blend well; serve in wine glasses. *Serves 4.*

WHOLE APPLE COCKTAIL

Young John Coolidge was first exposed to the hazards of formal dining during the Coolidge family stay at an inn at Northampton. At the end of the meal, John found himself confronted by a cut-glass fingerbowl, containing water with a thin slice of lemon floating on top. John turned to his father and asked what it was for. "To drink," replied the dry-witted Calvin Coolidge. The boy, much to his father's amusement, did just that.

A favorite of the Coolidge boys at the White House was this apple cocktail—but, in their case, it was made without the sherry and whiskey. This makes an especially handsome way to start a meal or, for a simpler menu, it does nicely as a dessert.

Apples	*Sugar*
Strawberries	*Whiskey*
Pineapple	*Sherry*
Maraschino cherries	

Carefully core 4 nice apples, remove pulp and dice it, reserving the shell. Add to the pulp 1 cup fresh strawberries, 4 slices canned pineapple, ½ cup Maraschino cherries—all diced finely—and blend in 4 teaspoons sugar, 4 teaspoons sherry, and 4 teaspoons whiskey. Mix thoroughly, replace in apple shells, cover with top of apples and chill thoroughly. *Serves 4.*

VERMONT COUNTRY PICKLES

Alice Roosevelt Longworth is generally (but incorrectly) credited with first saying that Coolidge looked as if he had been weaned on a pickle. Actually, according to Ishbel Ross, Mrs. Longworth's doctor picked up this description from a patient—but, undeniably the sharp-witted Mrs. Longworth spread the remark liberally around Washington. Coolidge would not have minded, for he was inordinately fond of the pickles of his native Vermont—so this recipe for country-style pickles, easy to make and delicious to eat, is dedicated to Silent Cal.

Cucumbers	Sugar
Onions	Celery seed
Salt	Mustard seed
Vinegar	Salad oil

Slice 2 dozen cucumbers very thin, peeling them or leaving the peel on, as preferred. Add 1 dozen small onions, sliced as thin as possible. Dust with ⅔ cup salt; let stand at room temperature overnight. Wash thoroughly in cold water, drain. Pour 4 cups vinegar, 4 tablespoons sugar, 2 teaspoons celery seed, and ½ cup mustard seed over the cucumbers and onions, blend well. Add 1 cup salad oil (olive oil is better), blend again, pack in sterile jars, seal carefully, and store in a cool place. *Makes about seven pints,* if medium-size cucumbers are used.

PICKLE SOUFFLÉ DRESSING

A piquant salad dressing that made a frequent appearance at the Coolidge luncheon table combines the spicy tartness of mustard and Worcestershire sauce with the airiness and froth of beaten egg whites—a dressing elegant enough to grace the fanciest salad, yet easy and quick to make.

Mayonnaise	Dry mustard
Eggs	Salt
Worcestershire sauce	

Blend 1 tablespoon mayonnaise into 3 beaten egg yolks; add 1 teaspoon Worcestershire sauce, ½ teaspoon dry mustard, and a pinch of salt. Fold in the stiffly beaten whites of 2 eggs. Chill thoroughly. *Makes enough dressing for a salad for 6.*

COOLIDGE PICKLE SAUCE (FOR HAM)

President Coolidge's preoccupation with thrift led him many times into the White House kitchens to see if all was well. Once, before a large dinner, he counted six Virginia hams in the ovens. Why, he asked the housekeeper, were six hams necessary for one dinner? Because, she replied, there would be 60 guests, and this allowed one ham to every ten guests. "That seems like a lot of ham to me," said Coolidge—and, as so often happened, he was right. There was a lot left over and perhaps the leftovers were served with this sauce—an unparalleled sauce that adds a subtle touch of sharpness to the mellowness of any ham but is particularly good with Virginia ham or any smoked country ham.

Vinegar	Cornstarch
Cinnamon	Sweet pickles

Bring 1 cup cider vinegar to a boil, blend in 2 tablespoons powdered cinnamon and 1½ tablespoons cornstarch blended with a little cold water. Add 1 cup finely chopped sweet pickles. Cook gently until thickened, and serve with ham. *Makes 2 cups.*

SAUCES FOR FISH

Except for an occasional stroll in the vicinity of the White House, in Northampton, or in Vermont, President Coolidge was not noted for indulging in any exercise other than fishing. He was an avid angler. On fishing trips, the profusion of trout, pickerel, or pike that appeared in the kitchen challenged those who cooked for the President to come up with sauces. Also, fresh fish were frequently sent to the White House as gifts and were dutifully cooked for the President's own table. Here are two of the better fish sauces devised in the Coolidge years—one an excellent tartar sauce, the other studded with capers.

FISH SAUCE I

Salad oil	Pickles
Egg yolks	Onion
Dry mustard	Olives
Salt	

Add 2 cups salad oil very slowly to 3 beaten egg yolks, beating constantly. Add 1 teaspoon dry mustard and ¾ teaspoon salt. Blend in ½ cup finely chopped sweet pickles, 1 finely chopped medium onion, and 1 cup pimento-stuffed olives, finely chopped.

FISH SAUCE II

Mayonnaise	Capers
Egg yolks	Pimentos
Mustard	Salt
Worcestershire sauce	

Blend 1 tablespoon mayonnaise into 3 well-beaten egg yolks. Add ½ teaspoon dry mustard, ½ teaspoon Worcestershire sauce, 12 capers, chopped fine, and 2 pimentos, chopped fine.

MRS. COOLIDGE'S CHICKEN CHOP SUEY

In spite of her many years association with New England cooking, Grace Coolidge was enamored of Oriental cuisine. The Oriental steward who served on board the Presidential yacht *Mayflower* during the Harding, Coolidge, and Hoover administrations aided and abetted her infatuation. One dinner turned out by this skillful Oriental gentlemen included: homemade candy, almonds, celery, and olives; grapefruit cocktail in baskets, consommé and crackers, hot dinner rolls, fried soft-shell crabs on corncakes, Russian sauce, potato chips; roast capon, cranberry sauce, green peas, buttered beets, mashed potatoes; chicken chop suey with rice, bamboo shoots and tomato salad; cheese and crackers, strawberries and whipped cream, almond cookies, small cakes, coffee.

So that she could cook it for President Coolidge after he retired to Northampton, Mrs. Coolidge begged the chef to give her the chop suey recipe, made in Cantonese fashion and bearing no resemblance to the Chinese-American restaurant variety. He did, and here it is.

Water chestnuts	*Chicken stock*
Celery	*Salt, pepper*
Bamboo shoots	*Soy sauce*
Chinese beans	*Chinese rice wine (or Japanese sake)*
Chinese greens	*Cornstarch*
Chicken	*Rice*
Butter	

Cut into very thin strips 2 cups each water chestnuts, celery, bamboo shoots, Chinese beans, and Chinese greens. Add 2 pounds white meat of chicken, also sliced in very thin strips. Fry in butter in skillet; place in saucepan and pour 2 cups chicken stock over. Cook for a few minutes and season to taste with salt and pepper. Add 2 tablespoons soy sauce, 2 tablespoons rice wine or sake, and 1 tablespoon cornstarch mixed with a little water. Cook briskly for 5 more minutes. Serve with rice. *Serves 12.*

CHICKEN CHOW MEIN

President Coolidge had the usual country feeling that a chicken could not really be good unless it was raised close by the kitchen door. So he had a chicken yard built in back of the White House and kept a small flock of Vermont chickens there. Somehow, chickens from this coop, when prepared for the White House table, had a curiously fragrant and mysterious flavor. Investigation showed that Coolidge's chicken-yard was built right on top of President Teddy Roosevelt's mint bed. This chicken chow mein, another Oriental favorite of Mrs. Coolidge, may of course be made with mint-fed chicken, if you happen to have any. But an ordinary chicken will do nicely. Here again, the recipe is not similar to those found in Chinese restaurants as a rule, but is a true Cantonese dish.

Chicken	*Cornstarch*
Water chestnuts	*Soy sauce*
Celery	*Chinese rice wine or cocktail sherry*
Bean shoots	*Salt, pepper*
Chinese beans	*Chinese noodles*
Onion	

Simmer a 6-pound fowl in water to cover until tender, remove white meat, and continue simmering the rest of the chicken in the stock. Cut water chestnuts, celery, bean shoots, and Chinese beans—2 cups each—and an onion into shreds. Cut dark meat of chicken in shreds and combine with stock and the cut-up vegetables. Add 1 tablespoon cornstarch, 2 tablespoons soy sauce, and 2 tablespoons rice wine; cook until thick, stirring constantly. Serve on heated Chinese noodles and topped with shredded white meat of chicken. *Serves 12.*

CREAMED CHICKEN BALLS

Mrs. Coolidge liked to serve these chicken croquettes-with-a-difference. Pork may be used instead of chicken, and they were traditionally served at the White House with a white sauce (which most chefs insist on calling Béchamel) and shoestring potatoes.

Cooked chicken meat	*Sherry*
Butter	*Chicken broth*
Mushrooms	*Cream*
Celery	*Eggs*
Flour	*Cracker crumbs*

Melt 3 teaspoons butter in saucepan; add 3 cups diced chicken meat, 1 pound diced mushrooms, 3 stalks diced celery. Stir in 3 tablespoons flour, 3 tablespoons sherry, 1 cup chicken broth, and ½ cup cream and cook slowly, stirring constantly. Then cool and form into balls or cakes. Roll in flour, then in beaten egg, then in cracker crumbs, and fry in deep fat at 370° F. until brown. Drain on paper towels. *Makes 18 croquettes.*

PRESIDENT COOLIDGE'S CURRY OF VEAL

The President himself had a favorite Oriental dish—one that, in the years since, has become an American favorite. It was served often during cruises on the

Presidential yacht down the Potomac and at White House lunches, accompanied by an excellent mango chutney.

Veal	*Curry powder*
Egg	*Flour*
Salt, pepper	*Chicken stock or beef stock*
Butter	*Cream*

Chop 1 pound lean veal very fine; add 1 beaten egg and salt and pepper to taste. Roll in small balls and fry in deep fat for a few minutes, until brown. Melt 3 tablespoons butter in skillet, blend in 3 tablespoons curry powder and 2 tablespoons flour and cook until slightly browned. Carefully blend in 4 cups chicken or beef stock, stirring until thickened. Drop veal balls into skillet, stirring carefully to avoid breaking. Just before serving, add ¼ cup cream. Serve on rice. *Serves 4.*

MANGO CHUTNEY

Mangoes	*Raisins*
Baking soda	*Ginger*
Alcohol	*Hot chile peppers*
Sugar	*Cinnamon*
Lemons	

Peel and slice 8 large or 12 small mangoes; sprinkle with 2 tablespoons baking soda and let stand for several hours. Dry the mango slices and cover with 1 pint alcohol, and let stand overnight. Combine 2 pounds sugar and juice of 4 lemons; add to mangoes that have meanwhile been removed from alcohol and drained. Stir in 2 cups white raisins, ½ pound chopped preserved ginger, and 2 hot peppers, chopped fine. Add 1½ teaspoons cinnamon. Simmer gently over low flame for 1½ hours. Put in jars, and steam for 1½ hours more, then seal. *Makes 8 pint jars.*

NOTE: When curry was served at the White House, it was accompanied not only by this mango chutney but also by chopped raw onions, chopped green pepper, chopped hard-boiled eggs, chopped almonds, Bombay duck (a dried fish), chopped bacon, and many other sambals, all served on small dishes so that guests might help themselves to one, several, or all.

DEVILED CRABMEAT

With its proximity to the Chesapeake Bay crab country, the White House has always featured on its table some form of this most delectable seafood. Here is the way the Coolidges liked it best.

Onions	*Wine or sherry*
Celery	*Salt, pepper*
Butter	*Cream*
Flour	*Cracker crumbs*
Crabmeat	*Chile sauce*
Egg	

Chop 3 onions and 2 stalks of celery; brown slightly in 2 tablespoons butter. Blend in 2 tablespoons flour and mix in 1 pound crabmeat. Add 1 beaten egg, ¼ cup white wine or sherry, salt and pepper to taste. Bind with a little cream, place in crab shells or in buttered casserole. In either case, cover with layer of cracker crumbs, dot with butter, and brown in medium (325° F.) oven for 30 minutes. Serve with chile sauce. *Serves 4 to 6.*

QUEEN MARIE'S LOBSTER À LA KING

This should really be called "lobster à la queen" for it was included in the menu of a state dinner given by the Coolidges for Queen Marie of Rumania—a menu that started with caviar, consommé, and the lobster and proceeded to filet of beef with mushrooms, potato balls, green beans, cold turkey in aspic, green salad, ice cream with maple sauce (the Vermont touch!), cakes and coffee. The lobster was a triumph—and one that can be duplicated in any kitchen. It is served in "dented" creampuff shells.

Lobster meat	*Eggs, hard-boiled*
Bacon	*Sherry*
Mushrooms	*Cream*
Green peppers	*Water*
Pimentos	*Salt*
Flour	*Lard*
Butter	

Carefully dice 2 pounds lobster meat, fresh or canned. Dice 3 slices of bacon and fry out in skillet, adding 1 pound diced mushrooms, 5 diced green peppers, and 5 diced pimentos. Then blend in 2 tablespoons flour and 2 tablespoons butter; and add lobster meat. Cook for about 10 minutes. Dice 3 hard-cooked eggs and add. Then blend in ¼ glass dry sherry with 1 cup cream and a little hot water, and add to lobster and vegetable mixture. Keep hot, and do not allow to boil.

Meanwhile, make the puffs with this creampuff mixture: mix 1 cup flour and 1½ cups boiling water, stirring over heat until mixture leaves sides of pan. Add ½ teaspoon salt and beat in 5 eggs, one at a time, beating until light after each egg is added. Drop 1 heaping tablespoon of dough into deep hot lard, cook rapidly at 375° F. until brown. Remove puffs with strainer, make a dent in each one, and serve each puff filled with the lobster à la king. *Makes 12 large puffs.*

SAILORS IN HAMMOCKS

Lobster is one of the truly great contributions to international cuisine, so it is not surprising that the archives of the White House contain a large number of ways to prepare and serve it. Here is a somewhat less formal lobster dish that would be perfect for a Sunday-night supper, as it often was at the White House. The sharp-eyed may recognize its resemblance to Chinese egg rolls.

Lobster meat	*Salt, pepper*
Shrimp	*Flour*
Onions	*Milk*
Celery	*Cream*
Mushrooms	*Cracker crumbs*
Eggs	

Chop together very fine 1 pound lobster meat (fresh or canned), 1 pound shelled raw shrimp, 2 small onions, 2 stalks celery, and ½ pound fresh mushrooms. Add 1 beaten egg and salt and pepper to taste. Meanwhile, make batter with 1½ cups flour, 2 eggs, ½ cup milk, and a little cream. Drop onto griddle like pancakes, but make fairly large ones. Place spoonful of lobster mixture on each pancake, and fold, tucking ends under. Roll each carefully in a little cream, sprinkle with cracker crumbs. Hold together with toothpicks and brown quickly in hot oil or butter. Or set under broiler for a minute or two. *Makes 12 "hammocks."*

PORK APPLE PIE
(a dessert)

Calvin Coolidge, during his White House years, used to say he never ate anything as good as his mother's pork apple pies—a dessert! The pork consists of just a few small pieces of salt pork—but the effect on the pie is indescribably delicious.

Apples	*Flour*
Maple sugar	*Salt*
Cinnamon	*Salt pork*
Nutmeg	*Pie crust*

Core, peel, and slice at least 10 tart apples, and put into deep pieplate without a bottom crust. Sprinkle 1 cup maple sugar (light brown sugar will do, but is not quite as good), ½ teaspoon nutmeg, ½ teaspoon cinnamon, 1 tablespoon flour, and generous pinch of salt over the apples. Dot with about 10 tiny pieces of salt pork. Cover top with pie crust and bake in hot (400° F.) oven for 10 minutes, reducing heat to medium (350° F.) for another half hour. Serve with cream cheese mashed with a little cream. *Makes a 9-inch pie.*

COOLIDGE CUSTARD PIE

There was considerable difficulty in the early days of the Coolidge administration in turning out custard pies that were to the President's taste. Finally, a Massachusetts inn yielded a recipe that filled the bill—so this is the way custard pies were made for the Coolidges from that day on, in two versions.

Sugar	*or*	*Flour*
Flour		*Sugar*
Salt		*Salt*
Eggs		*Eggs*
Milk		*Milk*
Nutmeg		*Vanilla*
		Coconut

For version I, combine ¾ cup sugar, 1 tablespoon flour, pinch of salt, 2 beaten eggs, and 2 cups milk. For version II, combine 2 tablespoons flour, ¾ cup sugar, pinch of salt, 2 well-beaten eggs, 2½ cups milk, and ½ teaspoon vanilla. In both cases, pour into 9 inch unbaked pie shell, bake in hot (450° F.) oven for 10 minutes, reduce heat to moderate, bake another half hour until custard is set. Second version calls for coconut to be sprinkled on top, the first for nutmeg. Either way is delicious!

MRS. COOLIDGE'S LEMON PIE

Here is a wonderful version of lemon pie, so good it would be a shame to top it with meringue. It was a favorite of Mrs. Coolidge's, and the White House cooks made it from her own recipe.

Eggs	*Lemon*
Sugar	*Butter*
Flour	*Salt*

Beat yolks of 2 eggs, stir in 1 cup sugar, and 2 tablespoons flour. Add juice of 1 lemon, 1 tablespoon melted butter, and scant pinch of salt. Fold in stiffly beaten whites of 2 eggs. Line a 9 inch pie tin with very rich pastry, bake in very hot (450° F.) oven for 10 minutes to set the crust, then pour in the filling and bake in slow oven 325° F. for 30 minutes or until the filling is set.

MAPLE WALNUT COOKIES

Grace Coolidge received at tea twice a week in the White House or, while it was being repaired, at the mansion on DuPont Circle. Surprisingly, these teas were virtually open houses, since a notice would be placed in the society columns of the Washington newspapers to the effect that Mrs. Coolidge was giving a tea. In theory, the teas were supposed to be limited to those who had left calling cards at the White House, but evidently no particular check was made on the women who attended. There were always fresh flowers in abundance, along with unusual cakes and cookies—among which this particular kind was a favorite combination of tea-party elegance and the well-known Coolidge preference for maple flavor.

Maple syrup	*Powdered sugar*
Egg whites	*Walnuts*
Sherry	

Boil 2 cups maple syrup for 10 minutes, and pour slowly over 3 stiffly beaten egg whites. Stir until thick over hot water, add 1 tablespoon sherry and ½ cup powdered sugar. Stir in 2 cups finely chopped walnuts. Force through pastry tube onto lightly buttered and floured cooky sheets. Bake in slow (325° F.) oven for 15 minutes. *Makes 5 dozen 1-inch cookies.*

WATERMELON SALAD IN BASKET

Mrs. Coolidge included this fanciful dish as a salad on many a White House menu—but today we would think of it more as a dessert, and a wonderfully elaborate one at that. This makes a refreshing conclusion to a heavy meal and is not at all difficult to make.

Watermelon	*Walnuts*
Honeydew melon	*Lemon juice*
White grapes	*Sherry*
Pineapple	*Whipped cream*
Strawberries	

Cut a large watermelon in half lengthwise; remove inside and dice meat carefully, discarding all seeds. Combine watermelon pulp in bowl with 1 peeled, diced honeydew melon, 1 pound white grapes, 1 can crushed pinapple, and 2 cups fresh strawberries, diced. Add ½ cup walnut meats, cut up in small pieces, juice of 1 lemon, and 1½ tablespoons sherry. Mix all together and replace in watermelon shells. Chill thoroughly. Top with small quantity of whipped cream or sherbet. *Serves 20.*

STRAWBERRY À LA KING PIE

This was reputed to be Mrs. Coolidge's favorite dessert. It has a surprising elegance.

Cream	*Honeydew melon*
Strawberries	*Powdered sugar*
Pineapple	*Rich pie crust*

Whip 1 pint cream, fold in 1 box frozen strawberries or 2 cups fresh berries, 2 slices pineapple diced, ½ cup honeydew melon diced, and 4 tablespoons powdered sugar. Heap into a cooled 9-inch pie shell and chill thoroughly. *Serves 6 to 8.*

APPLE PIE

Mrs. Coolidge had some fine recipes but she herself was not much of a cook—at least during her White House days. The story goes that she decided to make an apple pie herself, using a treasured recipe. It looked exactly the way a good apple pie should look. Her husband ate his piece, waited until everyone else had finished, and said: "Don't you think a road commissioner would be willing to pay something for this pie-crust recipe?"

This is an unusual recipe for apple pie, favored by the Coolidges. It calls for the addition of spices at several levels of the pie instead of all at the top as in most recipes.

Apples	*Cinnamon*
Pie crust	*Butter*
Sugar	*Lemon juice (optional)*
Nutmeg	

Core, peel, and slice 6 or 7 large tart apples; put half of them in an unbaked pie crust lining a 9-inch pan. Sprinkle with ½ cup sugar, ¼ teaspoon nutmeg, and ¼ teaspoon cinnamon and dot with 1 tablespoon butter. Add rest of apples, adding more if needed to make highly rounded pie, and then repeat the nutmeg, cinnamon, sugar, and butter. If apples are sweet rather than tart, add 1 tablespoon lemon juice. Cover with pastry, cut several slits in top to allow steam to escape, bake in a 350° F. oven for 1 hour.

Serve with generous slice of President Coolidge's favorite Vermont Cheddar cheese, or with vanilla ice cream.

XXXI

Clean Sweep— With a Hoover

With the Hoover administration elegance returned to the White House. Despite the fact that Herbert Hoover came from a humble background—the son of a blacksmith, he worked his way through college by manual labor—his feeling was for grandeur and elegance, and this is what the Hoovers represented. President Hoover, even when dining alone, ate in solitary splendor in the State Dining Room. The appearance of the White House changed markedly during the Hoover regime. The Hoovers brought with them and installed in the White House the many art objects they had collected in the Orient, Russia, and Europe. Mrs. Hoover was greatly interested in White House history and she attempted diligently to restore the White House to its past glories.

One of Mrs. Hoover's projects was the restoration of the Monroe Room, a sitting room on the other side of the Oval Room. She had copies made of the priceless furniture the room had contained when used by the elegant James Monroe and his wife. The furniture makers worked from descriptions in old records that Mrs. Hoover unearthed.

The Hoovers abandoned the rigid economy of the Coolidge regime and began entertaining on a scale the White House staff had not seen in years. Guests arrived for breakfasts, luncheons, and dinners and even spent weekends at the Hoover's retreat in the Shenandoah Valley. Mrs. Hoover was perfectly capable of holding two teas at different hours the same afternoon, or even two simultaneous teas in different rooms, moving from one to the other to greet her guests. During their first three years in the White House, the President and Mrs. Hoover were reputed to have dined alone together only three times—each time on their wedding anniversary.

As the Hoovers were both wealthy and hospitable, they set a record in Washington entertaining. It took three secretaries to arrange the guest lists for Mrs. Hoover. Three or four thousand handwritten invitations might go out for a single reception.

To provide variety at evening entertainments, Mrs. Hoover liked to receive guests in different rooms each time and she encouraged the members of the Cabinet to move about among the guests in a democratic manner, rather than sticking to the receiving line.

Sometimes the food ran short, not from insufficient supplies ordered but from a superabundance of unexpected guests, all of whom were always made welcome. On one memorable occasion, picnic hampers which had been packed in advance for a weekend trip were unpacked hurriedly and their contents served to an unexpectedly large crowd.

The watchword had been economy while the Coolidges lived in the White House. Now it was elegance. The best of everything was served—sometimes out of season, often imported. And this policy extended to the servants, who were apt to be cheered, when home ill, by a basket of food and flowers sent with Mrs. Hoover's card. Mrs. Hoover never questioned the amount of food consumed or its cost. Her only requirement was that it be of the best quality, well cooked and well served. But her interest in things culinary was from her desk where she interviewed the housekeeper and the cook. When Eleanor Roosevelt came to the White House to be shown around the new home she would be moving to after the election, Mrs. Hoover, as was customary, took her on a complete tour—until they reached the door to the kitchens. Mrs. Hoover stopped at the threshold, drew herself up, and said that she was sorry. The housekeeper would have to show Mrs. Roosevelt the kitchens: she herself never entered them.

Efficiency became a watchword. Mrs. Hoover, in her desire for perfection and uniformity, decided that all the butlers who served in the dining room should be of the same height. The staff presented a uniform appearance until Mrs. Hoover, breaking her own rule, hired Alonzo Fields who, at six foot four, then towered over the rest of the staff. This was an exception. The household, eager to accede to the wishes of the new First Lady, fell in with her wishes for efficient service. One time when a fresh salmon was sent down from Bangor, Maine, as a gift to President Hoover, the fish was quickly dispatched to the kitchen, its head removed, and recipes dug out for preparing it. When the Maine Congressman who accompanied the gift appeared to have his photograph taken with the fish and the President, the fish had already been decapitated. Quickly someone sewed the head back on, the photograph was taken, and the print was sent back to the constituents in Maine, no one the wiser except the kitchen staff. Maine did not go Democratic for three more years.

The Hoovers usually had breakfast, when the weather was seasonable, under the magnolia tree said to have been planted by President Jackson in memory of his wife Rachel. Otherwise, the Hoovers breakfasted in the China Room on the ground floor, where the Presidential china of different administrations is exhibited. Breakfast was served promptly at eight o'clock. President Hoover liked to discuss national affairs at the breakfast table, and his "Medicine Ball Cabinet" met on the White House lawn before breakfast every morning, rain or shine. For half an hour they tossed a medicine ball back and forth—keeping fit—and then at eight o'clock they breakfasted on fruit, toast, and coffee under the huge old magnolia tree.

The Hoovers were punctual at all meals. Luncheon was at one o'clock and dinner at eight. Both husband and wife were very formal. At dinner the President wore a dinner jacket, and seven courses were standard even if there were not a formal dinner party. Entree, soup, fish, a meat course, salad, dessert, and fruit was the usual dinner. Once in a while President Hoover would become impatient if it seemed to him that the dinner hour was lasting too long. Then he would signal the housekeeper and she would omit a course to hasten things along. President Hoover, himself, was an extremely rapid eater, and the kitchen staff used to make bets as to how long it would take him to speed through a meal. He is reputed to have finished at least one full-course dinner in eight minutes flat. For state dinners he would slow down so his guests would not be left too far behind.

Despite the formality of the household, the Hoovers were not demanding. It has been said by members of their staff that our 31st president was one of the easiest men in the world to please. There is a story, perhaps apocryphal, that the only time President Hoover was heard to raise his voice was once when he went to the window and called out to say how much he had liked something.

◇◇◇

R E C I P E S

RAMOS GIN FIZZ

The real art of making a gin fizz is in the proper shaking. During Prohibition, of course, part of the art was in having some gin stashed away in the cellar, against a thirst. This gin fizz was a favorite drink of Herbert Hoover, and he learned the art of reproducing the drink which had became famous in the Ramos Brothers Bar.

"Don't just shake it up," read the directions. "You need plenty of ice and you should shake until the contents of the fizz become so creamy that you can't hear the ice tinkle against the sides." Aside from an incredible amount of shaking, there is another secret to a proper gin fizz—charged water from a siphon bottle, added at the last. And the drink must be consumed at once or its natural taste is lost. A blender saves exertion, makes a fine gin fizz.

Lemonade concentrate	*Orange flower water*
Egg white	*Cracked ice*
Cream	*Soda water*
Gin	

For each drink, place in the blender 1 teaspoon lemonade concentrate (or 2 tablespoons lemon or lime juice and 1 teaspoon sugar), 1 egg white, 2 teaspoons cream, 1½ jiggers gin, a few drops orange flower water, ½ cup cracked ice. Blend until ice disappears. Pour into chilled 8-ounce glass and add a good squirt of soda water. The fizz should be thick even after the soda is added.

MARY RATTLEY'S MARYLAND CARAMEL TOMATOES

Mary Rattley was the Hoover family cook from the time Herbert Hoover was Secretary of Commerce. Her inventiveness at concocting new specialties won her quite a reputation and of course endeared her to the Hoovers. Among her specialties was a cucumber sauce to be served with fish and crabs. Another was vanilla wafers. Still another was Mrs. Hoover's favorite oyster soufflé. But Mary Rattley seldom parted with her recipes, and those lucky guests who tasted one of her inventions rarely learned how these delectable dishes were made.

One recipe Mary Rattley did part with, however, is this caramel tomato dish. It is extremely good.

Tomatoes	*Salt*
Butter	*Parsley*
Sugar	*Toast rounds*

Cut off the tops of 6 large, firm tomatoes and make a cavity in the top of each. Fill each hole with 1 teaspoon butter and cover the butter with 1 teaspoon sugar. Sprinkle with salt and bake until the tomato is cooked, but not squashed. Stick a sprig of parsley into the top of each tomato and serve on rounds of toast with the tomato juice spooned over the top. *Serves 6.*

ASPARAGUS SOUFFLÉ

Another of Mary Rattley's recipes, with which she was willing to part, is this unusual asparagus soufflé. It makes an ideal luncheon dish and would be a beautiful first course at a formal dinner.

Butter	*Eggs*
Flour	*Salt, pepper*
Cream	*Asparagus tips*

Melt 1 tablespoon butter and stir into it 1½ tablespoons flour. Add gradually, stirring all the while, 1 cup heated cream. Cook this over low heat until smoothly thickened. Add, one at a time, the yolks of 4 eggs, beating as you add them. Remove from heat, add salt and pepper to taste and 1 cup cooked asparagus tips. Fold in 4 egg whites, beaten stiff. Pour this into a buttered soufflé dish, set into a pan of warm water, and bake in a preheated (325° F.) oven for 35 minutes or until it has set. Before removing from oven, brush the top with melted butter. Serve at once. *Serves 4.*

GUMBO À LA CREOLE

President Hoover used to go down to Opelousas, Louisiana, to eat gumbo at a small restaurant he particularly liked. For a President, a recipe is always available. The White House kitchen was soon given the details of this, the President's favorite gumbo. (Our directions have been simplified.)

Onions	*Salt, pepper, cayenne*
Butter	*Bouquet garni*
Flour	*Shrimp*
Fish stock	*Crab*
Tomatoes	*Oysters*
Okra	

Chop fine 4 small onions and cook them in 4 tablespoons butter until well browned. Add 4 tablespoons flour and cook and stir for 5 minutes. Add 2 quarts rich fish stock and 6 quartered tomatoes, ½ pound sliced okra, and salt, pepper, and cayenne to taste. Then add 1 bouquet garni tied in cheesecloth, 2 dozen raw peeled shrimp, 6 hard-shelled crabs (cleaned and prepared), and 2 dozen shucked oysters. Cook over low heat for 2 hours. Serve in soup bowls over a spoonful of rice cooked dry. *Serves 6 (heartily).*

LOBSTER À LA HOOVER

Although an inlander, Hoover was particularly fond of lobster. However, he and his wife were world travelers and had acquired a rather cosmopolitan palate. Of course the Hoovers were not alone in finding lobster a delectable dish—it was a Presidential favorite. This is an unusual way of preparing this seafood.

Lobsters	*Eggs*
Butter	*Sherry*
Flour	*Cream*
Mushrooms	*Water*
Peppers	*Toast points*
Pimentoes	

Boil 5 pounds live lobster (about 1½-pound lobsters are an ideal size for tenderness and succulence) for 20 minutes to ½ hour. Remove from water and cool. Remove the meat from the shells and dice it. Melt 3 tablespoons butter and stir in 2 tablespoons flour. Stir and cook over low heat for 3 minutes. Add 1 pound sliced mushrooms, 4 diced green peppers, 6 diced pimentoes. Mix and cook for 10 minutes. Add 3 diced hard-cooked eggs, 3 tablespoons sherry, 1 cup cream, and 2 tablespoons hot water and the lobster. Stir gently and continue cooking over low heat until it is heated through. Serve on toast points. *Serves 6.*

MARY RATTLEY'S VIRGINIA HAM

This was another of Mary Rattley's famous recipes. President Hoover liked it especially.

Virginia ham or other country ham	*Vinegar*
Water	*Currant jelly*
Brown sugar	*Breadcrumbs*

Wash, scrape, and soak overnight a mild cured ham. Cover with cold water to which has been added 2 cups brown sugar and 2 cups vinegar. Let it come to a boil, then simmer slowly until the skin puckers. Cool it in its own water to keep the juices in the meat. Skin it, rub it all over with currant jelly (Mary Rattley made her own jelly, but this is up to you). Cover the ham with breadcrumbs. Brown in the oven.

EGG TIMBALES

In the Hoover household this was a frequent luncheon dish. The President invariably, so we are told, asked for a second helping.

Rich milk	*Paprika*
Eggs	*Tomato or cheese sauce*
Salt, pepper	*Cooked rice*

Scald 1 cup rich milk and pour it over 3 slightly beaten eggs. Add salt, pepper, and paprika to taste. Pour the mixture into timbale molds or custard cups and place them in a pan of hot water. Bake in a slow (325° F.) oven for 20 minutes. Serve in a ring on a warm platter, bordered with cooked rice and with a bowl of cheese or tomato sauce in the center. *Serves 6.*

PRESIDENTIAL CORNED BEEF HASH

A prominent businessman had occasion to be entertained at the White House a number of times over a period of years. His first visit was a luncheon with President McKinley at which corned beef hash was served. It was not his favorite dish; nevertheless he enjoyed his lunch and the Presidential company. A few years later he lunched with President Theodore Roosevelt and again sat down to corned beef hash. When he was invited to breakfast during the Taft administration, President Taft, who had a robust appetite, munched on a large steak, but offered his guest "something a little lighter"—corned beef hash. Unbelievable as it may seem, when this businessman lunched with President Coolidge, corned beef hash was again the main course. The man began to feel that he was the victim of some practical joke. His last visit to the White House was during the Hoover administration and on that occasion, too, hash made its appearance. Shortly afterward tne story of his five visits and the five menus came out. He didn't start out liking hash according to his wife. But over the years "he got used to it." It is a good hash.

Cooked corned beef	*Onion*
Boiled potatoes	*Celery*
Hot milk	*Green pepper*
Butter	*Salt, pepper*

Mince 2 cups corned beef. Mash 4 medium boiled potatoes and beat in ½ cup hot milk and 2 tablespoons butter. Mix this with the corned beef, add 2 tablespoons each of minced onion, chopped celery, and chopped green pepper. Salt and pepper to taste. Bake 30 minutes in a greased pan until a rich golden brown. *Serves 6.*

AUNT MILLIE'S CARROT PUDDING

"My recollections of Iowa food," wrote Herbert Hoover, "are of the most distinguished order." Iowa food meant his Aunt Millie. Despite world travels, President Hoover always maintained that some of the finest food he ate in his life came from his Aunt Millie's kitchen.

Carrots	*Sugar*
Flour	*Raisins*
Currants	*Nutmeg*
Suet	*Cloves*
Cinnamon	*Salt*

Boil 5 large carrots until tender. Peel and strain through a colander. Add 1 cup flour, ½ cup currants, 1 cup suet chopped fine, 1 teaspoon cinnamon, 4 tablespoons sugar, 1 cup raisins, 1 teaspoon nutmeg, ½ teaspoon cloves, 1 teaspoon salt. Pour into well-greased mold with a tight cover, and steam for 4 hours. This is delicious served with a creamy sauce. *Serves 6.*

INDIAN DRESSING

This delicious salad dressing is a good change from the French dressing one finds so often on tossed salads. This was immensely popular with the Hoovers and their guests.

Hard-cooked egg	*Sugar*
Green pepper	*Paprika*
Pimento	*Pepper*
Beet	*Oil*
Parsley	*Vinegar*
Salt	*Lemon juice*

Chop together 1 hard-cooked egg yolk, ¼ green pepper, ¼ pimento, ½ medium sized beet (cooked), 1 sprig parsley. Season with ¼ teaspoon salt, ¼ teaspoon sugar, a pinch each of paprika and pepper. Slowly add 1 cup oil, ⅛ cup vinegar, juice of ¼ lemon about 2 teaspoons lemon juice. Mix well and pour over mixed greens or a vegetable salad. This must be used at once; it cannot be stored. *Makes 2 cups.*

APRICOT WHIP

Unlike many of his predecessors, President Hoover was not particularly fond of desserts. Lou Hoover preferred light ones, such as fruit whips and sponges. This was one she especially liked. In many respects it is like a simple prune whip.

Canned apricots	*Orange*
Egg whites	*Egg yolks*
Sugar	*Heavy cream*
Lemon juice	*Nuts (optional)*
Almond extract	

Combine 1 cup thick apricot pulp (obtained by whizzing some pitted canned apricots through a blender), 3 egg whites, 4 tablespoons sugar, 2 tablespoons lemon juice, 2 drops almond extract, and the grated rind of 1 orange. Beat with electric mixer or hand beater until the mixture stands in soft peaks. Set aside to chill.

Serve with this sauce: Put juice and the remaining pulp from a quart can of apricots in a double boiler. If necessary, add enough orange juice to make 2 cups liquid. Scald with 2 tablespoons sugar. Cook for 15 minutes. Beat yolks of 3 eggs with 2 tablespoons lemon juice and fold into hot mixture. Cook 5 minutes more, stirring constantly until it thickens. Cool and then chill in refrigerator. Before serving fold in 1 cup whipped cream. Chopped nuts can also be sprinkled on top for a texture contrast. *Serves 6 to 8.*

LITTLE OAT CAKES

This is a simple, not very sweet dessert. It can be used as a tea cake, or simply for munching.

Eggs	*Butter*
Sugar	*Baking powder*
Rolled oats	*Vanilla*

Beat 2 egg yolks until stiff and lemon-colored. Add 1 cup sugar gradually and continue beating. Add 2 cups rolled oats, 1 tablespoon melted butter, 2 teaspoons baking powder, 1 teaspoon vanilla. Then stir vigorously. Finally, fold in 2 stiffly beaten egg whites. Drop by spoonfuls on a well-greased baking sheet and bake at 350° F. for 10 to 12 minutes. *Makes 4 dozen.*

COFFEE SOUFFLÉ

A light dessert that Mrs. Hoover found appropriate after one of the multi-course dinners that graced her table. You may find this coffee soufflé attractive to serve even after a small dinner. Its delicate flavor is most appealing.

Coffee	Sugar
Gelatin	Salt
Milk	Vanilla
Eggs	Heavy cream

Mix 1½ cups strong hot coffee, 1 tablespoon gelatin softened in 2 tablespoons cold water, ⅓ cup scalded milk in top of double boiler. Add 3 egg yolks beaten slightly and ⅓ cup sugar and ¼ teaspoon salt. Cool and stir over simmering water until it thickens. Remove from heat, cool, and add 3 egg whites beaten stiff with ½ teaspoon vanilla. Pour into mold or serving dish and chill. At serving time, cover with mounds of sweetened whipped cream. *Serves 4.*

MANGO ICE CREAM

This is an exotic flavor and an ice cream as delicious as it is out of the ordinary. The Hoovers often served homemade ice cream as a dessert. Sometimes it was served in molds the shape of the White House.

Mangoes	Heavy cream
Pineapple juice	Egg yolks
Sugar	Sherry
Boiling water	Vanilla

Cut in half 6 ripe mangoes and remove the pulp. Combine the pulp with ½ cup pineapple juice. Combine 3 cups sugar with 1 cup boiling water, boil for 1 minute, and then allow to cool. Beat in 1 quart cream, 4 egg yolks, 1 tablespoon sherry, and 1 teaspoon vanilla. Add mango pulp and mix well. Place in ice cream freezer and freeze until firm. *Serves 8.*

BAKED COCONUT KISSES

In later life, after his wife died in 1944, the former President took up quarters in the Waldorf Towers in New York. There he still clung to many of his favorite dishes, although he cut down on the complexity of his meals. He continued to nibble black cherries sent to him from Oregon by the same friend who used to send them to the White House. On occasion he even allowed himself the luxury of griddle cakes or fried cornmeal mush which the cooks from the home kitchen of the Waldorf learned to prepare the way he liked it.

When he allowed himself a sweet, it was often a homemade candy, something to which he was partial. It is amusing to recall that thirty-two out of thirty-five White House menus during his administration began surprisingly with homemade candies. His secretary, Bernice Miller, recalls hearing him talk about the luscious walnut creams and home-sugared almonds that were placed in silver bonbon dishes "one for each couple all around the table." These are half candy, half cooky, completely delicious.

Sugar	*Lemon*
Water	*Coconut*
Egg whites	

Boil 1 pound sugar with 1½ cups water for 10 minutes until syrupy. Beat 4 egg whites until stiff and pour the hot syrup over them gradually. Add the juice of 1 lemon. Drop by spoonfuls on a board, and bake in a moderate (350° F.) oven for 5 minutes. Remove from oven, split in half and remove insides. Replace the insides with freshly grated coconut. Replace in slow (250° F.) oven for 5 minutes to dry out. *Makes 80 kisses.*

✳✳✳

XXXII

The Longest Years

✳✳✳

When the Roosevelts came to Washington, in the depths of the Depression, they brought not only a ray of hope to the economically blighted country. They brought, also, to the White House, the first real family the Executive Mansion had seen since their cousin, T.R.'s, term of office. During the long years that the Roosevelts occupied the Executive Mansion, through the halls and rooms, at the tables, and up and down the stairs echoed the laughter and talk of a big American family, with children and grandchildren.

The Roosevelts enjoyed hearty, typically American food—like creamed chipped beef, bread puddings, and fried cornmeal mush. When they were alone, which wasn't often, that was what they wanted from the White House kitchen. Mrs. Roosevelt and I had many chats about food and she told a good deal about her attitudes toward eating. Her reputation was not built as a cook but as a world traveler, lecturer, and urbane diplomat. But actually she was very well informed about food, and took a great interest in seeing that her family was well fed and the food prepared properly. She was fascinated by the regional cooking of America. A great many dishes which have been prepared in the White House kitchens since 1933 were introduced by Eleanor Roosevelt.

Welsh rabbits (or rarebits) were a family favorite for Sunday-night suppers, and cheeses of all types were always on hand for Roosevelt snacks or desserts. The family liked doughnuts both at breakfast and teatime, a typically American and rather homy choice for a family who could command just about anything from the kitchens.

Roosevelt breakfast time meant oversized coffee cups, and the traditional breakfast coffee was half coffee and half hot milk. Mrs. Roosevelt always poured the coffee and when there were many guests around the breakfast table, as there often were, the staff sometimes placed a small side table beside her piled with the huge cups. She used left- and right-hand pots to facilitate the pouring of the coffee and the hot milk. Although Mrs. Roosevelt was present bright and early (and cheery) to tend the breakfast table, the President took his breakfast on a tray in his room. His choice of coffee was a dark French roast, prepared in the White House kitchens from green coffee beans. A coffee maker was placed on the President's breakfast tray so that he could regulate the brewing to his satisfaction.

Luncheon was not really a family meal for the President. Very often he would lunch at his desk from a tray, with one or two members of his Cabinet or a guest. If he was alone, occasionally a member of the family might join him for a tray lunch. When work was not pressing, he sometimes ate with Mrs. Roosevelt in the sun porch, the garden, or in her sitting room.

Dinner brought the Roosevelt family together—those who were home—to dine in the family dining room in jolly splendor, often with many children and grandchildren at the table. The President was "Pa" and Mrs. Roosevelt was "Ma," and they teased and joked and argued, causing even the sedate staff to grin behind the serving doors. Despite the informality of family dinners, state occasions were marked by the pomp and ceremony that has always been expected of First Families.

In the early years of Roosevelt's administration, engraved invitations bearing the President's seal embossed in gold were sent out by messenger, a custom since George Washington's time, but as the limits of the District of Columbia began to spread to the outlying hills of Maryland and Virginia and official families began to make their homes there, the messenger service became obsolete. Luncheon and dinner invitations were mailed three weeks ahead of the occasion. Protocol demanded that they be acknowledged immediately and in the affirmative (unless illness or absence from the city prevented acceptance). The guest list included many fascinating people. Alexander Woollcott, famous raconteur and wicked wit, came to swap stories with the President, camped in splendor in a guest bedroom, and even invited his own guests for meals. Russian Foreign Minister Molotov was also a White House guest, and brought with him his own black bread, sausages, and a revolver. George the Second of Greece, King Peter of Yugoslavia, and Queen Wilhelmina of Holland were all wartime guests. Madame Chiang Kai-shek curtailed her customary entourage of forty to two nurses, two nieces and a nephew, but still requested her customary fresh silk sheets daily. The Roosevelts were hosts to the first British monarch to visit America, when King George VI and Queen Elizabeth spent a day and night at the White House. They were entertained in a typically American manner with homy American food.

The Roosevelts handled official functions with enormous endurance, warmth, and urbanity. Thousands were entertained at dinners and receptions during their 12½ year administration. Mrs. Roosevelt might be called on to shake hands with 1500 visitors at an afternoon reception, and the same night, in a receiving line with the President, shake another 1500 hands.

At small informal White House dinners, guests removed their wraps and were ushered through the long corridor to the Red Room, where they were introduced to those who had already arrived. After a few minutes Mrs. Roosevelt would appear and greet each guest with her characteristic warmth. "How nice that you are here!" or "I am so glad to see you!" were characteristic comments offered with her customary warm smile.

When dinner was over, Mrs. Roosevelt stood up and the ranking gentlemen would accompany her to the door. The ladies would follow her to the Green Room for coffee and cigarettes. The men remained around the dining room table for coffee, a smoke, and another glass of wine, after which they rejoined the ladies.

Sunday-night suppers at the White House were intimate occasions to which invitations were highly prized. The President sat at one end of the long table and Mrs. Roosevelt scrambled eggs in a chafing dish at the other. On both sides of the table, between the host and hostess, sat artists, sculptors, writers, ambassadors, world travelers, and friends. Supper consisted of Mrs. Roosevelt's scrambled eggs, ham, bacon, or sausage, a salad, a dessert, and coffee.

Eleanor was the soul of kindness and hospitality. All guests were treated with great warmth and courtesy. Not only were breakfast trays, brightened with flowers and cigarettes, sent up to rooms from six in the morning to noon, but on more than one occasion Mrs. R. gave up her own bed and slept on a couch to make a guest welcome. Almost anyone who visited the White House was sent on his way with a picnic lunch, because in wartime it was difficult to get food on trains. Boxes and baskets of sandwiches, fried chicken, stuffed eggs, fruit, cake and thermoses of coffee or milk or lemonade accompanied the many guests who spent the night at the White House.

Mrs. Roosevelt, unlike certain other First Ladies, was not interested in redecorating the White House. But she did redesign the kitchens, equipping them with electric stoves and dishwashers to lighten the work of the staff. Her attitude toward servants was deeply considerate. She disliked making too much work for the cooks with highly elaborate menus. Another reason for this, of course, was that the Roosevelt regime spanned some of the hardest years the country has known: depression, war, and rationing. She undertook to have served at the White House the series of low-priced menus prepared by the Department of Agriculture during the Depression. Her son Jimmie, home from college during one of these austerity periods, asked his mother, "Ma, if I gave you five cents would the Department of Agriculture let me have a glass of milk?" Part of Mrs. Roosevelt's defense effort was to cut down on the servants' food, too. She called the staff to a meeting, sat on the edge of a desk, and explained that "we will have one egg instead of two, one slice of bacon, toast, and coffee for breakfast.

"Mrs. Roosevelt was in many ways an enigma to the staff. She helped guests at the table herself, sometimes causing confusion behind the scenes. She ordered an austerity diet for everyone, and yet when her boys came home hungry from college, complaining "Isn't there anything to eat in this house?" she would order whopping great teas, with the heartiest tea sandwiches the staff had ever seen. The servants were vastly amused by her custom of ordering raw onions to be served: "She entertains all these romantic young couples and then tries to kill the romance!"

Many years later Mrs. Roosevelt talked about the stories of her casual hospitality when she was First Lady. Once she said rather wistfully, "I know I'm known as a poor housekeeper." When her husband became President, she had no realization of the size or complexity of the Presidential menage. "I'm afraid I am a stupid person," she said, admitting that she had simply moved her housekeeper and her own servants from Hyde Park to Washington. "I thought I could keep on doing what I had always done, only on a larger scale."

She always underestimated herself. With her enormous energy and her desire to do her share she was unsparing of herself. She might give a luncheon, two teas, and a dinner in one day and be up at dawn the next to catch a plane to speak in New York or San Francisco. Every Christmas Eve she went out herself with baskets for the poor homes of Washington. At the last minute she would appear, a little out of breath but still game, to preside at the tremendous annual Christmas Eve party. The President lit the Community Tree and broadcast a Christmas message to the country. Then he read Dickens' *Christmas Carol* to the family. At midnight Mrs. Roosevelt and Miss Thompson attended midnight service at St. Thomas' Church. Only twice did Mrs. Roosevelt miss her Christmas party. When Franklin, Jr., was ill in the hospital in Boston she flew up to be with him, and when her daughter Anna was ill in Seattle she flew to her bedside. But even then, she made sure that a festive Christmas was well launched for those at home before she left.

When Prohibition was abolished, the Roosevelts sent for barrels of glassware which had been kept in White House storerooms during the "Dry Years." Rare cut glass and crystal dating back to the Harrison administration appeared, along with wine glasses of every description. Although President Eisenhower was given a great deal of newspaper credit for introducing American wines into the White House, it was actually Mrs. Roosevelt who gave new status to the wines of this country. Immediately after the end of Prohibition and as soon as the wine glasses were unpacked, the Roosevelts began looking about for good wines from New York as well as California. This was a quest beset with difficulties as the vintners were scattered or decimated, and in many cases vineyards had been neglected and the good older wines had all been sold off to private cellars awaiting the repeal of Prohibition.

Nevertheless, Mrs. Roosevelt recalled that "we always served American wines.

Except," she laughed, "to Winston Churchill, who insisted on having his own favorites. He even stipulated the brand, the year, and the shipper."

In no time at all gifts from winemakers poured into the White House. Some was really unsuitable for the table but it did not go to waste. The White House became famous—or infamous—for the purple punch and the yellow punch that were served at musicales. Into these bowls of punch went all the liquid gifts— even Japanese sake.

Although she had been accustomed to wines all her life except during the "Drought," it was noted by Washington columnists that Mrs. Franklin Roosevelt left "the wine in the crystal golden-crusted goblets untasted." She was following a precedent set by many First Ladies.

Arguments about wine have always flowed over the White House, but these have been ripples compared with the tidal waves of fury about serving distilled spirits. In the days of Andrew Jackson a guest created a mighty stir that lasted for months when he complained publicly and bitterly that whiskey had been put into his wine. Henry Clay, who was in one of his more captious moods at that moment, remarked that he had observed this guest's behavior and had suspected as much.

For a good many years during the twentieth century, even when wines and hard liquor were legal, distilled beverages were not served at formal or state dinners or at receptions.

The repeal of Prohibition meant that many Colonial recipes, and some from later administrations, which called for wine in their preparation, could be restored to the White House tables. It meant also that President Roosevelt could revive his favorite interlude in the day—the cocktail hour, when he fed tidbits to Falla and enjoyed a welcome Martini made from gin and Argentine vermouth. He was noted for his Martinis, which he measured meticulously, using from 5 to 7 parts gin to one part vermouth, depending on his mood or his guests. Cocktail hour lasted about twenty minutes or so, and President Roosevelt never made too much or too little. Like all knowledgeable Martini fanciers, he was contemptuous of dividends left in the cocktail shaker. If seconds were wanted, he made them in exactly the same say as the first round and there was never, to quote a constant observer, "even the essence of a drink left in the shaker."

When Churchill was a houseguest, quantities of Scotch would evaporate. Alonzo Fields, longtime White House major domo, recalls that late one night he was summoned to the library to find that President Roosevelt had retired for the night and the Prime Minister was sitting among a rather large display of empty bottles. Fields must have looked rather astonished at the request for more Scotch, because he reports that Churchill said, "Yes, my man, I need a little more to drink. You see, I have a war to fight and I need fortitude for the battle. And there is one more favor I hope you will do for me." "Yes, sir," Fields answered. "Well," Churchill grinned and said, "I hope you will come to my defense if someday someone should claim that I am a teetotaler." Fields has done so, in a book.

◊◊

R E C I P E S

CAVIAR CONTINENTAL

Mr. and Mrs. Roosevelt were not great fanciers of hors-d'oeuvre. For special occasions delicacies like smoked rainbow trout or smoked oysters would appear at cocktail time. Caviar was an exception, because it was often sent as a gift by the Russians, and the President was fond of it. The White House kitchen extended the prized gift by serving it this way.

Eggs	*Onion*
Lettuce	*Lemon juice*
Caviar	

Fill 12 well-buttered individual ring molds with 1 uncooked egg white each. Bake in a 350° F. oven for 10 minutes, or until firm. Remove the molds onto crisp, green lettuce leaves laid on a large platter. Fill the centers with caviar, mixed with grated onion and a little lemon juice. Cook the yolks of the 12 eggs in almost boiling salted water until quite firm. Rub through a sieve and sprinkle over the caviar. This makes a delicious tidbit with cocktails or a rather splendid first course. *Serves 6.*

CHICKEN-LIVER BALLS

One other Roosevelt family favorite with drinks was this unusual version of chopped chicken livers. The basic ingredient goes further by the addition of the pickles and the beets. Traditionists won't like this, but others will find it most piquant.

Chicken livers	*Paprika*
Butter	*Mayonnaise*
Gherkins	*Pickled beets*
Salt, pepper	

Sauté 1 cup chicken livers in browned butter. When they are cooked through, mash them to a paste. Add ½ cup chopped gherkins, and salt, pepper, and paprika to taste. Moisten with sufficient mayonnaise to enable you to form the chicken liver into small balls. Roll these in finely chopped pickled beets (about 2 tablespoons should be sufficient) from which the juice has been drained. *Produces about 12 balls.*

PHILADELPHIA PEPPER POT

The Roosevelt family loved soups. All during their White House years the big steel soup kettles were steaming away in the kitchens and soup was served twice a day. The soups were of many varieties, good planning at a time when food was scarce. A Presidential favorite was this Pepper Pot, a White House tradition since the days of George Washington.

Tripe   *Mixed herbs*
Water   *Red pepper*
Veal joint   *Salt*
Bay leaves   *Cayenne*
Onions   *Flour*
Potatoes   *Beef suet*
Parsley

This recipe takes 2 days to prepare. Scrape 4 pounds tripe and wash in 3 waters. Put into cold water to cover and boil gently for 7 or 8 hours. Cool in its own liquid, then cut into ½-inch squares. The next day, simmer a veal joint, with its meat on it, for 3 hours in 3 quarts cold water. Skim off the scum as it cooks. When it is cooked, cool it and then separate the meat from the bones and dice it. Strain the broth, add 2 bay leaves and 2 onions chopped coarsely and simmer another hour. Strain the soup and add 4 diced potatoes, 2 teaspoons minced parsley, 1 bunch mixed herbs, 1 red pepper cut into dice. Add also the meats, 2 teaspoons salt, ½ teaspoon cayenne, and dumplings which you have made from 2 cups flour, ½ pound beef suet, and salt. Make these dumplings small, about ½ inch in diameter. Drop them into the simmering soup, cover tightly, and cook about 5 minutes longer. Serve at once. *Serves 6.*

CHICKEN SOUP AMANDINE

A bowl of soup and a dish of fruit was often the lunch Mrs. Roosevelt ate before one of her supercharged afternoons. Cream of almond was a favorite. The White House also served it as a first course on formal occasions.

Rich milk   *Bay leaf*
Chicken stock   *Butter*
Almonds   *Flour*
Onion juice   *Heavy cream*
Salt, pepper

Add 1 pint rich milk to 3 cups strong chicken stock. Blanch and grind 1 cup almonds and add half these to the soup with 1 teaspoon onion juice, salt and pepper to taste, and a bay leaf. Blend 1 tablespoon butter with 1 tablespoon flour to a smooth paste and gently stir this into the soup, making sure there are no lumps. Bring to a boil and remove from heat. Serve with a blob of whipped cream on top and sprinkle with the remaining ground almonds. *Serves 10.*

SARA DELANO ROOSEVELT'S FISH CHOWDER

F. D. R. was extremely partial to fish soups. His mother supplied the Roosevelt cook with recipes for her son's favorites. One of them was this excellent fish chowder.

Salt pork	*Milk*
Onions	*Salt, pepper*
Flour	*Whitefish*

Cut 5 thick slices of salt pork into cubes and brown in frying pan. Skim off excess fat and add 4 sliced onions. Fry until onions are clear. Skim out the pork and onions and set aside. Make 1 cup rich white sauce using the fat in the pan. When white sauce is smooth and creamy gradually add 1 quart milk. Return pork and onions to pot, along with a pound or more of raw whitefish boned, ½ teaspoon salt, and ¼ teaspoon pepper. Simmer 15 minutes, or until fish has turned white and flakes easily. *This serves 4 heartily or 6 as a first course.*

MONGOLE SOUP

For some reason, mongole soup was an inaugural-day favorite during the Roosevelt administration. A number of these occasions were rainy as well as cold, and the hordes who showed up for lunch found this a satisfying and warming addition to the standard cold cuts, salads, and rolls. It also made a hearty midnight snack for Roosevelt guests who were often a little peckish in the late hours.

Yellow split peas	*Onion*
Tomato juice	*Salt, pepper*

Soak overnight ½ cup yellow split peas. In the morning, drain the peas and set over low heat with 2 cans tomato juice. Simmer several hours, or until the peas disintegrate. Season with 1 teaspoon grated onion and salt and pepper to taste. *Serves 6.*

OXTAIL SOUP

Another midnight favorite was oxtail soup—which is, of course, such a thick and hearty dish it can easily double as a supper. The broth, if you should make a double quantity, is an excellent base for another evening's dumpling soup.

Oxtails	*Salt*
Water	*Carrots*
Celery	*Tomatoes*
Onions	*Barley*

Combine 4 oxtails, 4 quarts water, 2 stalks celery, sliced, 2 chopped onions, and 1 teaspoon salt. Boil until the meat is tender. Remove oxtails, separate meat from bones, and replace the bits of meat in the soup, along with 2 diced carrots, 1 cup chopped tomatoes (either fresh or canned), and ¼ cup barley. Cook until barley is done and carrots are tender. This can be strained for a broth, but for hearty eating serve it to 6 hungry people unstrained.

GREEN GUMBO

This rich soup is a version of the traditional Gumbo z'herbes of Louisiana, descendant of the Callalous of Dahomey, the "palaver steirs" of Nigeria. It was a great luncheon favorite of President Roosevelt.

Spinach	*Scallions*
Dandelion greens	*Ham bone or fowl carcass*
Turnip tops	*Water*
Beet tops	*Bacon grease*
Celery leaves	*Flour*
Cabbage leaves	*Filé powder*
Watercress	*Salt*
Parsley	*Rice*
Red pepper	

Wash and chop coarsely 1 handful each spinach, dandelion greens, turnip tops, beet tops, and celery leaves. Add to these, coarsely chopped also, 3 outside cabbage leaves, 1 bunch watercress, ½ bunch parsley, 1 pod red pepper, and 1 bunch scallions. Put the vegetables in a large pot with a ham bone or chicken or turkey carcass (no stuffing left in, please), and 2 quarts water. Boil slowly for an hour, strain off liquid and set aside. Heat 1½ tablespoons bacon grease and stir into it 2 tablespoons flour. Stir and brown lightly. Add greens strained from the water. Fry 2 minutes, then gradually add liquor and cook for an hour. Pick meat from ham bone or carcass and add this, along with 1 tablespoon filé powder and 1 teaspoon salt.

When this hearty gumbo was used for lunch at the White House, a tablespoon of rice, cooked separately, was added to each plate. *Serves 6.*

ITALIAN CHICKEN CORDIALE

This dish reminds us of the egg-drop soup served in Chinese restaurants all over the United States, but it hails directly from the "little rays" soup of Italy. It was a Roosevelt family joy.

Chicken broth	*Salt, pepper*
Eggs	*Sherry*
Lemons	

Prepare or obtain 1 quart chicken broth and set to simmer. In a soup tureen beat 4 eggs well. Add juice of 2 lemons and season with salt and pepper to taste. Be sure the egg and lemon mixture is well beaten and frothy when you add, beating vigorously all the while, the boiling broth. Serve at once with 1 teaspoon sherry to each portion. *Serves 4.*

GREEN TURTLE SOUP

Like many American Presidents, Franklin Roosevelt had a predilection for turtle and terrapin. Soon after his inauguration some terrapin were sent to the White House. Mrs. Henrietta Nesbitt, the housekeeper the Roosevelts had brought with them from Hyde Park, was entirely unaccustomed to turtle life "and the huge brutes," as she told it, "would crawl around in the cellar" rather to her alarm. When Mrs. Nesbitt spoiled the first terrapin, President Roosevelt was furious. The next time a terrapin arrived he arranged to have someone in from the Metropolitan Club to prepare it.

Despite the fact that terrapin appeared not infrequently at the White House, Mrs. Roosevelt never liked it. She said that she never forgot the occasion when she sat next to a well-known zoologist who looked at his serving of terrapin carefully and said in a voice of authority, "These are the bones of rats." To terrapin lovers, many of them from the Eastern Shore, this is sacrilege. This turtle soup always created a great fuss in the kitchen of the White House when special cooks came in to prepare it. Nevertheless it was trotted out for a number of appreciative visitors, among them Will Rogers.

Turtles	*Mace*
Pickling spices	*Cream (light)*
Celery	*Butter*
Onions	*Flour*
Carrots	*Salt, pepper*
Green peppers	*Sherry*

Plunge 2 turtles into boiling water to kill. (If you are using snapping turtles, scrub and then scald them.) Boil turtles whole, with ½ pound pickling spices tied in a bag, 2 sticks celery, 2 onions, 3 carrots, 2 green peppers, and a blade of mace, for 40 minutes or until skin turns white on legs and head and it separates and can be slipped off. Cool and remove turtles. Separate the meat from the bones and strain the broth. Mix 2 quarts light cream with ½ cup butter and ½ cup flour to make a white sauce. Add the bits of meat and 2 quarts liquid reduced by boiling for an hour. Season with salt and pepper and add 1 cup sherry. *Serves 16.*

CRAB GUMBO

This is another crab soup the Roosevelts liked, but quite different from the historic crab bisque. This one has a New Orleans flavor and is much thicker. It really would serve beautifully as a Sunday-night-supper dish, which is how the Roosevelt family enjoyed it.

Bacon fat	*Salt*
Green pepper	*Water*
Onion	*Red pepper pod*
Okra	*Crabmeat*
Canned tomatoes	*Cooked rice*

Place 1 tablespoon bacon fat in a skillet and melt it. Add 1 green pepper sliced thin, 1 onion sliced thin, and 8 okra pods sliced as thick as your finger. Sauté these slowly but do not brown them. Add 1 large can tomatoes cut up, including the juice, salt to taste, and stew covered for 15 minutes. Transfer this mixture into a soup kettle and add 1½ quarts water and 1 pod red pepper broken up. Cook for 15 minutes more and add 1 pound crabmeat, cut in large chunks. Simmer for 15 minutes more and serve over a small quantity of boiled rice in individual soup plates. *Serves 8.*

ABALONE STEAKS

Both seafood and game were used extensively in the White House during the years when everyone had to consider meat-ration points. During this time the Roosevelts had a visitor from California who talked incessantly about abalone. Neither the housekeeper, the cook, nor anyone in the Roosevelt family knew anything about that seafood. But the visitor proceeded to expound at luncheon about the way one had to pound the meat first and then sauté it in cracker crumbs and butter. The very next day, by chance and from a completely different source, some abalone arrived from California.

"If it weren't for that girl," said Mrs. Nesbitt, "I never would have known what to do with it. Providence, I call it." This is the recipe.

Abalone steaks	*Butter or olive oil*
Egg	*Lemon*
Cracker meal	*Tartar sauce*

Allow 1 or 2 steaks to a serving, depending on their size. Abalone should be sliced about ½ inch thick. On the West Coast the steaks have usually been "tenderized" when you buy them. Otherwise, pound them with a wooden mallet or rolling pin or sprinkle them with meat tenderizer. Some cooks slash the edges to prevent curling. Dip the slices in beaten egg mixed with a little water. Then dip them in fine cracker crumbs. Pan-fry the steaks in hot melted butter or olive oil for 26 seconds on each side. (Madness? I don't know. Abalone-steak cooks swear the timing is what counts.) Your object is to turn them a pale topaz on one side and then turn them fast and cook them to the same color on the other. And then to the table at once! Delicious. Get out your stop watch for this dish. They should be served with wedges of lemon and a dollop of tartar sauce. Shoestring or waffled potatoes are fine with abalone steaks. It would be foolhardy to attempt home French fries with the sort of timing that's necessary for the abalone.

PRESIDENTIAL HOT DOGS

Much has been made of the fact that the Roosevelts served hot dogs to the King and Queen of England. The hot dogs loomed so large in historic gossip that most people have quite forgotten that the rest of the visit was distinctly lavish. President Roosevelt himself took a great interest in the entertainment of his royal guests and planned the state dinner at which they dined on diamondback terrapin from Maryland and hothouse grapes from Belguim. That was, in fact, the only state dinner during the years of the Roosevelt administration that compared in formality and elegance with the dinners the Hoovers gave regularly.

Back to the hot dogs. It has been far less publicized that Queen Elizabeth returned the compliment and served hot dogs to visiting members of the American Bar Association at a garden party at Buckingham Palace in 1957. Far from scorning the hot dogs, the royal couple enjoyed them greatly.

Mrs. Roosevelt was particularly enthusiastic about this version which we served her. Instead of the usual frankfurter bun, we used brown 'n serve club rolls, which are similar to crusty French bread.

Brown 'n serve club rolls	*Melted butter*
Frankfurters	*Garlic, chervil, or other herbs*

Slice almost off, but not quite, about one third of the top of the rolls and scoop out the underside just enough to accommodate a frankfurter. Brush the inside and outside of each roll with melted butter flavored with garlic, chervil, chopped chives, or your favorite herb. Place the frankfurters in their own little beds and brush them with the butter and herbs too. Replace the tops and heat in a hot (450° F). oven 10 to 12 minutes or until delicately brown. At serving time, arrange on a platter with an array of relishes and coleslaw.

CHAFING DISH SCRAMBLED EGGS

Sunday-night suppers in the Roosevelt household were a tradition. The family and friends would gather around the table for the scrambled eggs that Mrs. Roosevelt herself cooked in a silver chafing dish. Mrs. Hoover never stepped into the kitchens; Mrs. Roosevelt brought the kitchen into the dining room. These scrambled eggs are superior; they call for the use of heavy cream.

Butter   Cream
Eggs   Salt

Melt 1 tablespoon butter in pan. Stir in 6 eggs lightly beaten with 3 tablespoons cream. Add ½ teaspoon salt and cook and stir gently until softly firm. *Serves 3.*

MRS. ROOSEVELT'S KEDGEREE

Mrs. Roosevelt said many times that this was one of her favorite dishes. In the White House it was often made for the family from leftover fish. Cooked crab or lobster, canned salmon, tuna, or bonita may be used.

Cooked flaked fish   Butter
Cooked rice   Salt, pepper
Cream or fish stock   Hard-cooked eggs

Mix 1 cup cooked flaked fish, or crab, lobster or canned fish, with 1 cup cooked rice. Moisten with ¼ cup cream or fish stock and sauté lightly in 2 tablespoons melted butter. Do not press down—the dish must be light and fluffy. Season with ½ teaspoon salt, ¼ teaspoon pepper. Add 2 hard-cooked eggs, cut in quarters, sliced, or chopped. Heat thoroughly.

Serve with an extra grating of freshly ground black pepper or a dash of Worcestershire sauce. A tomato-and-onion salad goes particularly well with kedgeree and was often served with it by the Roosevelts for Sunday-night supper. *Makes 4 servings.*

BROILED WILD DUCK

The war and rationing played havoc with the meat-and-potatoes fancier. To the Roosevelt family, it brought a whole series of dishes composed from gifts of game from admiring hunters. Onto the Roosevelt table came pheasant, grouse, partridge, quail, sandpipers, venison, ptarmigan, caribou, buffalo tongue, even filet of moose. The latter, served with grape jelly and scalloped potatoes, the President declared delicious.

So far as we can judge, Franklin Roosevelt was probably the best carver among all the Presidents. He took great pride in this accomplishment and could operate as effectively on a pheasant or a duck as he could on a turkey, a ham, or a roast beef. His family remembered that the carcass of any bird would be shiny, bare, and bright before he would call for a replacement on the platter. When the family group was large, the Roosevelt boys were often called upon to help with the carving, and there was great amusement in comparing the number of guests the President could serve from one turkey, for example, with the boys' efforts.

Wild duck was a family favorite, and no wonder. They enjoyed it both broiled and roasted, the more usual method of preparation. Here is the Roosevelt recipe:

Wild ducks	*Salt*
Butter	*Black Pepper*

See that the ducks are well cleaned, washed, and dried. Split; salt and pepper well; brush with butter all over. Place low under broiler for 20 to 30 minutes or till done. Turn only once.

ROAST WILD DUCK

Mrs. Roosevelt liked wild duck best when roasted. She often asked for it for her birthday dinner. This is the way the White House kitchen prepared it.

Salt, pepper	*Butter*
Wild ducks	*Water or wine*
Apple stuffing	*Beef cube*

Salt and pepper well-cleaned, washed and dried birds. Stuff with an apple dressing and place in a 500° F. oven for 20 minutes. Baste occasionally with 2 tablespoons butter in 1 cup of water into which a beef cube has been dissolved. (If you prefer, you can use a cup of heated red wine for the basting.) After 20 minutes reduce the heat to 400° F. and continue cooking for 10 minutes more. Start the birds breast down, for the first 10 minutes, then turn them.

SALMI OF WILD DUCK

This is a treat that rarely occurs. Like leftover steak, who has leftover wild duck very often? However, if you should fall heir to more wild duck than you can eat at a sitting, do as the Roosevelt family did and enjoy it as salmi of wild duck.

Butter	*Madeira or port wine*
Minced ham	*Chili powder*
Flour	*Celery salt*
Bouillon cubes	*Stuffed olives*
Meat extract	*Cooked duck*
Water	*Meat sauce*

Melt 2 tablespoons butter; stir in 1 tablespoon minced ham and 2 tablespoons flour. Gradually add 2 bouillon cubes and 2 teaspoons meat extract dissolved in 1 cup boiling water. When the mixture is smooth and has reached the boiling point again, add ¼ cup wine, ½ teaspoon chili powder, ¼ teaspoon celery salt, 10 pimento-stuffed olives, sliced, and 2½ cups coarsely cut-up cooked duck. Heat thoroughly and serve on toast or with plain boiled rice. May also be made with domestic duck, but the flavor will be different. *Serves 3 or 4.*

ROAST LONG ISLAND DUCK

Wild duck is not always available. A delicious dish can be made from Long Island ducklings prepared so that all the fat is rendered from the breast, leaving a crisply delicious dish. This recipe, from the White House, was a particular favorite with "Mrs. R."

Duck	*Salt, pepper*
Wild rice dressing	*Oranges*

Stuff a 4-pound duck with a wild rice dressing after salting and peppering the inside and out. Prick the skin lightly all over to permit the fat to ooze out. Place in a 425° F. oven for 30 minutes, then pour off some of the fat. Pour over the duck the juice and grated rind of 3 oranges and lower the heat to 350° F. Continue to roast for another 1½ hours, basting frequently. *Serves 4.*

BREAD SAUCE

This is the sauce F. D. R. always preferred with pheasant, quail, and woodcock.

Milk	*Onion*
Fresh white breadcrumbs	*Butter*
Salt, pepper	*Sherry*
Cloves	

Boil 2 cups milk and 1 cup breadcrumbs. Season with salt and pepper to taste and add ⅛ teaspoon powdered cloves and ½ small onion, finely chopped or grated. Add 2 tablespoons butter and beat the sauce till smooth. Just before serving, stir in ¼ cup sherry. *Serves 8.*

MARYLAND CHICKEN

Of the domestic fowl used during the Roosevelt administration, chicken outran all the others. The family enjoyed it in many forms, considered it one of the most versatile foods in the world. In addition, of course, chicken required no ration points. For a family dish, the Roosevelts seemed to prefer their chicken oven-fried with Maryland gravy.

Chicken	*Fat*
Flour	*Milk or cream*
Salt, pepper	

Place several cut-up pieces of chicken in a paper bag with flour, salt, and pepper. Shake them until they are well coated. Repeat this until all the chicken has been floured. For 1 chicken use 2 tablespoons flour, 1 teaspoon salt, and ½ teaspoon pepper. Melt bacon fat, butter, a combination of the two, or any cooking oil you prefer in a heavy pan and fry the pieces of chicken until well browned on all sides. Remove the chicken to a covered dish and put into a slow (200° F.) oven to finish. Meanwhile, add the remaining seasoned flour to the original pan and stir until browned. Add enough rich milk or cream to make a gravy. When the chicken in the oven is fork-tender, pour over it the Maryland gravy and serve at once, preferably with plain boiled rice.

MRS. JAMES ROOSEVELT'S CURRIED CHICKEN

This New England version of an exotic Oriental dish comes from F. D. R.'s mother. She donated the recipe to the White House kitchen when her son took residence there.

Onions	*Carrots*
Butter	*Chicken*
Flour	*Water*
Curry powder	*Salt*
Apples	*Pepper*

Fry 2 onions, sliced, in butter until browned. Add 2 teaspoons flour mixed with 2 teaspoons curry powder (more if you like it hot) and blend well. Add ½ grated apple, 1 grated carrot, and 1 chicken cut into serving pieces. Add enough boiling water or broth to cover the chicken. Simmer about 2 hours, or until chicken is tender. Salt and pepper to taste. Serve over plain boiled rice. *Serves 4 or 5.*

ASPIC OF CHICKEN

A delicious summertime favorite is this delicate aspic of chicken. It is not only cool and attractive for hot-weather eating, it has the added advantage of being even better if made the day before.

Fowl	*Bay leaf*
Water	*Cloves*
Celery	*Salt, pepper*
Carrot	*Gelatin*

Boil a 4-pound fowl in salted water to cover, along with a cut-up stalk of celery (including the leaves), 1 sliced carrot, 1 bay leaf, and a few cloves. When chicken is tender remove it from the broth, take meat from the bones and cut it fine. Put the bones back in the pot and continue to boil until broth is reduced to 1 pint. Add salt and pepper to taste. Soak 1 package of gelatin in 4 tablespoons cold water, then stir it into the hot strained broth. Pour this over the cut-up chicken, which has been arranged nicely in a mold. *Serves 8.*

SWEET POTATO PUDDING

According to Mrs. Nesbitt, during the time the Roosevelts lived in the White House, the kitchens experimented with sweet potatoes in every form known to man. They turned out to be a universal favorite, especially with women guests. This recipe was the all-time choice.

Sweet potatoes	*Citron*
Sugar syrup (commercial)	*Raisins*
Brown sugar	*Currants*
Egg	*Cinnamon*
Butter	*Ground cloves*
Milk	*Nutmeg*
Water	*Hard sauce*
Flour	

Grate ⅔ cup sweet potatoes and combine with 1 tablespoon sugar syrup and ⅓ cup brown sugar. Add the beaten yolk of one egg, 1 tablespoon melted butter, ⅔ cup milk, and ⅓ cup water. Dredge with 2 tablespoons flour the following fruits:

3 tablespoons each of citron, raisins, and currants. Mix into the fruit ⅛ teaspoon each of cinnamon, cloves, and nutmeg. Add the fruit mixture to the sweet potatoes and then fold in a beaten egg white. Turn into a buttered baking dish and bake at 350° F. for about 1½ hours. Serve with hard sauce. *Serves 4.*

BLUEBERRY PUDDING

This is a simple dessert Eleanor Roosevelt like to make. What the White House staff thought of serving a glorified bread pudding to the President of the United States we never heard.

White bread	*Butter*
Blueberries	*Heavy cream*
Sugar	

Cut the crusts from 8 slices of good, white bread. Line the bottom and sides of a buttered bowl with the bread. Pour in cooked sweetened blueberries to cover the bottom. Then add more sliced bread, then more blueberries, alternating until the dish is filled. Put in refrigerator for several hours so that the berry juice will soak into the bread. Serve with sweetened whipped cream. *A quart of berries and 8 slices of bread will serve 6.*

DUTCHESS COUNTY COCOA ROLL

In the early days of his political career, Franklin D. Roosevelt was often called, by admirers and detractors as well, "the Squire of Dutchess County." This delicate but rich dessert has been a favorite for years among Dutchess County hostesses. Nan Stone, a Connecticut neighbor, got it from her mother-in-law's cook, who was known for miles around as one of the testiest as well as one of the most accomplished bakers in the area. Surprisingly, the cake contains no flour.

Eggs	*Vanilla*
Sugar	*Cocoa*
Salt	*Heavy cream*

Beat 5 egg yolks until they are light and creamy. Gradually add ¾ cup superfine sugar, a dash of salt, and 1 teaspoon vanilla. Then add 7 tablespoons Dutch cocoa.

Whip 5 egg whites until stiff and rather dry and fold these lightly into the batter.

(Egg yolks, sugar, cocoa, and vanilla can be prepared in a blender. Whir for about 40 seconds, remove from blender, and fold in beaten egg whites).

Line a shallow 10-by-15-inch pan with greased, unglazed paper and spread the batter on it. Bake in a moderate (325° F.) oven for about 20 minutes. Allow to cool in the pan for 5 minutes, then invert the cake onto a moist, warm tea towel, trim off the hard edges, and roll like a jelly roll.

Meanwhile whip until stiff 1 cup heavy cream and flavor with vanilla, coffee essence, or peppermint essence. Unroll the cake, spread it with the cream, reroll it, and chill it for an hour. *Serve in thick slices to 6 or 8.*

THE ROOSEVELT'S INCH FROSTING

This rather dramatic frosting is similar in some respects to an old-fashioned boiled frosting, but is easier to work with. In addition it is unusually light and delicate. The secret lies in the gelatin.

Sugar	*Egg whites*
Water	*Vanilla*
Gelatin	

Mix 1 cup sugar with 1¼ cups hot water and boil until the syrup spins a thread or reaches 243° F. on your candy thermometer.

Meanwhile soak 2 teaspoons (less than 1 package) unflavored gelatin in 3 tablespoons cold water, then stir over boiling water until dissolved. Strain through a fine sieve into the syrup. Beat 2 egg whites very stiff and pour into them the hot syrup, beating all the time. Continue beating until the frosting is very stiff. Flavor with ½ teaspoon vanilla and spread thickly on your cake. Allow the frosting to stand at room temperature for several hours or overnight. Will cover generously top and sides of an 8-inch 2-layer cake.

✳✳✳

XXXIII

"We're From Missouri"

✳✳

When the Trumans took over as the First Family, Mrs. Truman very quickly made herself loved by the entire White House staff. She knew what she wanted, she knew how things should be done, and she knew how to give orders in a pleasant way. President Truman often referred to her as "the boss." Although Mrs. Truman was shy and hid, when she could, from newspaper reporters, she was not mousy. A housekeeper who remarked that "This wasn't the way Mrs. Roosevelt did it" was shortly replaced.

The Truman ways were not the Roosevelt ways. Mrs. Truman took the household bookkeeping in hand and ran it herself. She ruled out breakfast for the daily sleep-out employees, to cut the huge food bills. Every day she sat at her desk and tried to run the White House like a business.

Like the Roosevelts, the Trumans did not care for elaborate food but, unlike their predecessors, they demanded it better-cooked. Mrs. Truman was a very good cook and she expected good cooking on her table. As a matter of fact, she brought with her to the White House Vietta Carr, the family cook from Independence, who would sometimes prepare special back-home dishes the family particularly liked.

The Trumans set a record for mealtime punctuality. Breakfast was served at eight o'clock, luncheon at one, and dinner at seven. Mrs. Truman had breakfast with her husband (the Roosevelts rarely saw each other before dinnertime). The President's breakfast menu remained nearly constant: orange juice, grapefruit, or tomato juice; hot cereal in winter and cold cereal other times; whole-wheat toast and milk—sometimes buttermilk. The staff had to learn to make coffee for the Trumans. After Mrs. Truman had taken some coffee in her spoon to look at the color a few times, the kitchen experimented to produce a coffee that would please her. Alonzo Fields, the major-domo, was sent on a tour of the mess on the Presidential yacht to instruct the cooks in the brewing of coffee to please the Truman taste.

This attention to detail was typical of Bess Truman's attitude toward food. She gained the reputation of serving the best of home-cooked food, even for guests who came to the big White House teas. No thrown-together snacks, as there had sometimes been under the Roosevelts, or cake mixes such as the Eisenhowers later favored. President Truman described himself as a "meat and potatoes man," though he was actually a light eater. But the meat and potatoes were well prepared. At one time when the White House was giving a luncheon for Prime Minister Churchill, Mrs. Truman was away and the President ordered the menu. It was simple American fare: oyster soup, celery hearts, assorted olives, filet mignon with mushrooms, watermelon pickles, asparagus hollandaise, grilled tomatoes, hard rolls, hearts of lettuce salad with Roquefort dressing, strawberry shortcake. Champagne was served to please the palate of the Prime Minister.

As a result of Mrs. Truman's careful housekeeping, only rolls from the White House kitchen were served at the Truman table—not warmed-over baker's rolls. So the Prime Minister enjoyed a real "home-cooked" dinner.

Not until World War II was over did official entertaining return to normal. By that time the diplomatic corps had increased so much that two dinners had to be given to accommodate them in the State Dining Room. On this occasion an amusing protocol was used. Those of the diplomatic corps who were the odd numbers listed in the State Department's little blue book were invited to the first dinner; the even numbers were invited to the second dinner.

Dining informally, President Truman never permitted himself to be fenced in. In good weather meals were served on the south-side porch. Otherwise the three Trumans dined in the family dining room, one of the most beautiful and comfortable rooms in the White House. The room has a vaulted ceiling and over the dining table, which seats sixteen, hangs a crystal chandelier that holds real candles. Candlelight is the only illumination used in this room, which gives it great charm. This room was a favorite of the Roosevelt family, too, for informal occasions.

A typical menu for a state occasion is this one, served to (then) Princess Elizabeth and the Duke of Edinburgh.

Bluepoints on half shell
Crackers

Sherry

Clear soup with marrow balls
Celery hearts and assorted olives
Melba toast

White
wine

Lobster Thermidor
Parsleyed sliced tomatoes and cucumbers
Whole-wheat bread-and-butter sandwiches

Red
wine

Roast Filet of beef with wine essences
Watermelon pickles
Broiled mushrooms
French-fried potato balls
Asparagus hollandaise

Champagne Green salad with artichoke hearts with herb French dressing

Baked Old Missouri ham
Corn Sticks
Vanilla ice cream-melon molds
Brandied Macaroons
Angel Food cake

The Trumans treasured their privacy and resisted attempts to invade it. Written requests for pet recipes went unanswered. Special family "receipts" were guarded in the "Confidential File." While this book was in preparation, one of our "spies" met Margaret Truman at a party. Anxious to be of help, our "agent" asked Miss Truman, by this time Mrs. Clifton Daniels, if now, with the White House years so far in the past, some of the Truman culinary secrets might be divulged in the interests of history. Margaret's reply proved her to be her candid daddy's daughter, "We never publicised our private life while we were in the White House and I'm d——ed if I will now." Spoken like an outspoken Truman!

It was this quality of spunkiness which endeared Harry Truman and his family to their fellow Americans. The Trumans looked like the personification of "just folks," but a slightly tart independence kept them apart—and gave their years in the Executive Mansion a flavor all their own.

◇◇

RECIPES

SENATORS' BEAN SOUP

One of the most famous soups in the United States is the bean soup served in the Senate Restaurant. Harry S. Truman was a Senator long before he was President, and he carried his fondness for this excellent soup from one position to the other. The original recipe for Senate Bean Soup has been endlessly printed and reprinted but here is a delectable version easily and tastily reproduced through the use of shortcuts.

Condensed bean soup (canned)	*Garlic*
Cream of celery soup (canned)	*Parsley*
Water	*Ham*

Heat 2 cans condensed bean soup with 1 can cream of celery soup, 3 cups water, 1 small clove garlic crushed, ¼ cup fresh chopped parsley or 1 heaping tablespoon dried. Simmer 5 minutes. Add a 1-pound chunk cooked ham, cut in quarters. Heat thoroughly. Remove ham and cut into bite sizes. Serve accompanied by celery sticks, carrot sticks, green onions, radishes, with yellow mustard for a dip *Serves 8.*

CHEESE RING

This interesting molded ring may have been a recipe brought from home by Mrs. Truman. It was certainly a favorite on the family table and is unusual enough to intrigue guests at a summer evening buffet.

Plain gelatin	*Cream cheese*
Water	*Yellow American cheese*
Milk	*Heavy cream*
Salt	

Soften 2 packages gelatin in ½ cup cold water. Heat 1 cup milk and stir in gelatin until dissolved. Season with salt and set aside to cool. Mash 2 small packages cream cheese with fork and mix in 1 cup grated American cheese. Add to gelatin mixture and chill until thickened but not fully set. Whip 1 cup cream until stiff and fold it into gelatin and cheese mixture.

When molded this can be used as a base for a fresh fruit salad. *Serves 4 to 6.*

COUNTRY BOILED DRESSING

This is a wonderful old-fashioned dressing for a mixed green salad. It would even make an excellent base for a sandwich mix—say chopped ham.

Vinegar	*English mustard*
Eggs	*Butter*
Sugar	

Scald 1 cup vinegar. Beat 2 eggs thoroughly, gradually adding 1 cup sugar, ½ teaspoon English mustard, and 2 tablespoons butter. Pour hot vinegar over this, beating constantly. Put over low heat and let it thicken, stirring vigorously. Set aside to chill before serving. *Makes 1½ cups.*

MASHED BROWN POTATO BALLS POTOMAC STYLE

This dish can be prepared ahead of time. The final heating can be done shortly before serving time, a great boon to the hostess without a helper in the kitchen.

Potatoes	*Butter*
Salt, pepper	*Cream*
Eggs	*Milk*

Wash, peel, and cut into even-size pieces 4 pounds potatoes. Boil in salted water until tender. Drain thoroughly and shake over low heat until all water is evaporated. Mash them with salt and pepper. Combine 2 egg whites, 2 tablespoons butter, ½ cup cream, and ½ cup milk and beat until thick. Mix these into the mashed potatoes gradually and mix until well blended. Form the potato mixture into 12 balls. Place in a flat pan and coat them with 1 well-beaten egg yolk. Put into 350° F. oven to brown. *Serves 6.*

GREEN CORN PUDDING

Missourians like their corn puddings, especially with a batch of fresh-caught fish, crisply fried. This green corn pudding is delicious with fish, but equally good with many other things.

Green corn	*Milk*
Eggs	*Sugar*
Salt	*Butter*

Cut off the cob kernels from 1 dozen ears corn still in the milky stage. Beat 5 eggs lightly, add salt, 1 quart milk, and sugar to taste and combine with corn.

Butter thoroughly the bottom and sides of a pudding pan and pour in the mixture. Bake at 325° F. for 3 hours. This may be eaten with a sweet sauce. Or, omitting the sugar, it is good as a vegetable side dish. It can even be eaten hot for breakfast with butter—if you are ever up three hours before breakfast.

MOTHER BLANTON'S CORN DODGERS

This is another Old Missouri favorite.

Cornmeal	*Salt*
Sourmilk	*Lard*
Soda	*Hot water*

Sift 1 pint cornmeal. Add ½ cup sour milk, ¼ teaspoon soda, a pinch of salt, and 1 heaping tablespoon lard. Mix with your hands to form a stiff dough, sprinkling in a little hot water as needed. When thoroughly mixed, form into little dodgers and bake on a hot greased iron griddle in a hot (450° F.) oven for 30 minutes.

HOME-STYLE BUTTERMILK BISCUITS

Occasionally the Trumans would bring back from trips home to Missouri some sorghum molasses. It was a family favorite served with cornbread. Margaret Truman was particularly fond of it with these plump old-fashioned buttermilk biscuits, served piping hot.

Flour	*Buttermilk*
Salt	*Soda*
Shortening	

Sift 2 cups flour and ½ teaspoon salt. Add scant ⅓ cup shortening and scant ¾ cup buttermilk with ½ teaspoon soda dissolved in it. Mix well and roll out thick on a floured board, handling lightly. Cut with biscuit cutter and turn over once in melted shortening. Place in baking pan without crowding and bake at 425° F. for 12 minutes. Serve hot. *Makes 12 biscuits.*

CORNMEAL DUMPLINGS WITH TURNIP GREENS

This is a real old country favorite. It didn't appear on the table on state occasions, but it was enjoyed many times at Truman family private suppers.

Turnip greens	*Celery seed*
Salt	*Salt*
Water	*White mustard*
Cornmeal	*Onions*
Sugar	*Shortening*
Pepper	

Wash and pick over 2 pounds fresh turnip greens. Place in heavy pot with tight lid and add salt to taste and ½ cup water. Steam for about 20 minutes. Then add cornmeal dumplings, made as follows:

Sift and measure 2 cups cornmeal. Combine with ½ teaspoon sugar, ¼ teaspoon pepper, ½ teaspoon celery seed, 1 teaspoon salt, 1 teaspoon white mustard. Sprinkle with 3 grated onions. Add 2 tablespoons melted shortening and enough boiling water to make a stiff dough. Mix well and let stand 5 minutes. Shape into small flat pones or cakes and drop on top of turnip greens. Cover pot again and cook for 20 minutes. The dumplings will remain whole and have a delicious flavor.

SOUTHERN-STYLE GREENS

This can be made equally successfully with kale, beet tops, mustard greens, spinach, turnip greens, or collards. The distinctive flavor comes from the salt pork. Needless to say, this dish is rich in minerals and vitamins.

Salt pork	*Greens*
Water	*Salt, pepper*

Wash ½ pound salt pork and score it through fat down to the rind in several crosswise slashes. Place in kettle with ½ inch boiling water and boil about 45 minutes or until tender. Add 2 pounds washed greens. Cover and cook only until crisply, tender and slightly wilted—about 10 minutes for kale, beet tops, mustard greens; 5 minutes for spinach; 15 minutes for mustard greens or collards. Remove salt pork, drain and chop greens. Add salt and pepper to taste. *Serves 6.*

GREENS AND EGGS

This is a good luncheon dish. If you cook enough greens in the manner described in the preceding recipe, you will have the basic ingredients ready for this one.

Onions	*Eggs*
Butter or margarine	*Black pepper*
Salt	*Paprika*
Cooked greens	

Mince 2 small onions and cook gently in 4 tablespoons butter or margarine but do not allow to brown. Salt to taste and add 2 cups cooked chopped greens and mix well. Cover and steam over low flame until greens are heated and are well flavored with onion. Transfer greens to a buttered baking dish. Make four dents with the back of a tablespoon and drop in without breaking 4 raw eggs. Dot each egg with butter or margarine and season with freshly ground black pepper and paprika. Bake at 325° F. until eggs are set. *Serves 4.*

CALLAWAY HAM

When Sir Winston Churchill went to Westminster College in Fulton, Missouri, to deliver an address at President Truman's invitation, he and the President were served typical Midwestern company fare. Almost invariably this means fried chicken and Callaway County baked ham. This occasion was no exception, and although it was no novelty to the President, it *was both* a novelty and a treat for the Prime Minister. Here is the recipe for the ham, a genuine country ham which requires boiling before baking.

Smoked ham	*Ginger*
Mustard	*Whole cloves*
Cinnamon	*Pineapple juice*

Scrub a country ham and place in water to cover overnight to soak. Drain off water and cover with fresh water and simmer about 6 hours. Drain again, cool and skin. Make up a paste of mustard, cinnamon, and ginger and spread thickly over the ham. Using whole cloves, make a diamond pattern on the top and side surfaces of the ham. Place in large roasting pan and bake uncovered at 400° F. for about 30 minutes. Baste every 5 minutes very gently with pineapple juice, but do not disturb the crust. A Callaway County ham may weigh about 25 pounds and serves about 50 people.

PICADILLO À LA CREOLLO

Perhaps no Cuban dish has ever received wider coverage in Washington than the picadillo prepared and served by and to the ladies in Mrs. Truman's Spanish class. It was, to be exact, on April 20, 1946, "when a Spanish-speaking gentleman appeared in the White House kitchen and began giving orders to the apron-clad First Lady and her classmates." Picadillo, or Cuban hash, was prepared under the eye of the instructor, Professor Ramón Ramos, and it was reported in the public press that the distinguished ladies (among them Mrs. Dean Acheson, wife of the then Assistant Secretary of State, Mrs. Lester Pearson, wife of the Canadian

Ambassador Mrs. Leverett Saltonstall, wife of the Senator from Massachusetts) chopped and mixed several varieties of meat and seasoned the dish with spices and garlic, almonds, pimentos, olives, and raisins.

Picadillo à la Creollo is served traditionally not only in Cuba, but all over Latin America, with black beans and white rice, a combination known as Moors and Christians.

Onions	*Green olives*
Green pepper	*Capers*
Garlic	*Almonds*
Olive oil	*Raisins*
Chopped beef	*Sherry*
Chopped pork	*Salt, pepper*
Chopped ham	*Pimento*
Tomatoes, canned or fresh	

Chop 2 medium-sized onions, 1 green pepper, and 2 cloves garlic. Lightly brown in 2 tablespoons olive oil in a heavy skillet until the onions are quite soft but not darkened. Add 1¼ pounds chopped round steak, ½ pound chopped pork, and ¼ pound chopped raw ham (or, if you prefer, 2 pounds beef only). Add 2 cups canned tomatoes (or an equal quantity cut-up fresh tomatoes), about a dozen small green olives (pimento-stuffed), 2 tablespoons capers or chopped almonds (or both) and 2 tablespoons small seedless raisins. Season with salt and pepper and cook slowly, stirring occasionally until meat is well cooked and mixture is rather dry. Just before removing from heat, stir in 4 tablespoons dry sherry.

Serve to 6, garnished with pimento strips and strips of green pepper and accompanied by Moors and Christians. These are served in separate serving dishes, but mixed on the plate. To be absolutely correct, fried bananas should also accompany this dish.

A favorite way of serving picadillo all along the Gulf Coast is as *moyettes,* with the picadillo used as a filling for crusty buns which are deep-fat fried. According to a recipe much treasured by Washington hostesses, you break off one side of the bun near the edge and carefully scoop out the interior. Stuff the picadillo mixture into the hollow. Pin the edges back on the bun with toothpicks. Dip in beaten egg or a mixture of milk and egg as for French toast and pan-fry in butter on each side. Or if you like to use deep fat, drop them into deep fat like doughnuts. Moyettes are usually made fairly small and served two to a person. Delicious with a green salad or a fruit salad.

MOORS, CUBAN STYLE

These are the beans served with picadillo.

Black beans	*Green pepper*
Water	*Garlic*
Ham hock or shoulder	*Olive oil*
Onion	

Cover 1 cup black beans with 3 cups water and boil 2 minutes. Allow to stand overnight. The next day add ½ pound ham hock or a small piece of ham shoulder and simmer covered until beans are tender. This may take about 2 hours. If it seems dry, add more hot water. Brown 1 small onion, chopped, with 1 tablespoon green pepper and 1 clove garlic in 1 tablespoon olive oil. When soft, add to the beans. *This will serve* 6 with a picadillo and some beautifully fluffy white rice, cooked and served separately.

MRS. TRUMAN'S SCALLOPED APPLES

This is a simple dessert the Trumans enjoyed years before they became the First Family. It is a little like Brown Betty, but not as elaborate.

Apples	*Sugar*
Dry breadcrumbs	*Vanilla*
Butter or margarine	*Water*
Salt	*Medium cream*

Pare and slice 5 large well-flavored apples. Fry 5 tablespoons dry breadcrumbs in slightly browned butter or margarine. Put a layer of apples at bottom of buttered baking dish, sprinkle with breadcrumbs, salt, and 1 tablespoon sugar. Repeat until ingredients are used, but be sure to end with breadcrumbs on the top. Mix 1 teaspoon vanilla with 1 tablespoon water and sprinkle over top. Cover and bake at 400° F. for 15 minutes, then reduce heat to 350° F. and continue baking for 45 minutes more. Serve with cream. *Serves 4 to 6.*

DELICIOUS ICE CREAM

This is an excellent basic recipe. It can be flavored with fruits which are in season, or any exotic and fascinating flavor you happen to be addicted to. The Trumans used it in the White House over and over, in different colors and flavors. Chocolate was daughter Margaret's special delight.

Sugar	*Eggs*
Flour	*Heavy cream*
Milk	

Mix 3 cups sugar and 4 tablespoons flour. Carefully stir this into 2 quarts milk and cook in double boiler until thick. Pour part of the hot mixture slowly onto 4 well-beaten eggs, stirring vigorously as you pour. Return to double boiler and cook 1 minute. Cool and add to 2 quarts heavy cream. Flavor as desired and freeze. *Makes 4 quarts.*

MRS. TRUMAN'S OZARK PUDDING

Another favorite from home which Mrs. Truman introduced to the White House kitchen was this Ozark apple pudding, which turns out rather like a cake and has a wonderful flavor if made with good apples or canned apple slices with a good name on the can.

Egg	*Apples*
Sugar	*Almonds or pecans or walnuts*
Flour	*Vanilla*
Baking powder	*Heavy cream*
Salt	*Rum*

Beat 1 egg well. Gradually add ¾ cup sugar, beating constantly until it is light and creamy. Sift together ⅓ cup flour, 1¼ teaspoons baking powder, and ⅛ teaspoon salt. Add this to egg mixture and blend well. Fold in ½ cup chopped apples and ½ cup chopped nuts. Stir in gently 1 teaspoon vanilla. Pour into greased and floured 1-quart baking dish and bake at 325° F. for 30 minutes. Serve with whipped cream sweetened and flavored with 2 tablespoons rum. *Serves 6 or 8.*

THE PRIME MINISTER'S GINGER SNAPS

In her *New England Cookbook,* Eleanor Early tells this story. In 1947, when President Truman was to visit Canada, he sent Stanley Woodward (later U.S. Ambassador to Canada) to Ottawa to arrange details with Prime Minister Mackenzie King. King invited Woodward to Government House and gave him an immense luncheon, the last course of which was homemade ginger snaps. This made an impression on Woodward, who told the Prime Minister that his father loved ginger snaps and would not hire a cook, no matter how competent otherwise, who couldn't produce good ones.

When the luncheon was over and the details of President Truman's visit arranged for, Woodward was about to leave. At that point King handed him a brown paper bag. "Here are some of my ginger snaps," he said. "I want you to take them home to your father and to your President."

Her recipe, which isn't exactly the Prime Minister's, is a fine one—plain as the back of your hand, sweet with molasses and sharp with spice.

Flour	*Lard*
Sugar	*Baking soda*
Salt	*Hot water*
Ginger	*Molasses*
Butter	

Sift 4 cups flour with ½ cup sugar, ½ teaspoon salt, 1 teaspoon ginger. Cut in ½ cup butter and ½ cup lard with two knives or a pastry blender, or crumble it with your fingers, until it resembles coarse cornmeal. Dissolve 1 teaspoon baking soda in 1 tablespoon hot water. Make a well in the center of the flour mixture and pour in the hot water and 1 cup molasses. Mix well. Form into a roll and wrap in aluminum or waxed paper. Chill thoroughly and then slice ½ inch thick. If you do not wish to refrigerate the dough, roll it out to ⅛-inch thickness on a lightly floured board and cut with a cooky cutter. Place cookies on greased baking sheets and bake at 350° F. for 5 to 7 minutes, or until done. *Makes about 5 dozen ginger snaps.*

BESS TRUMAN'S SPECIAL BROWNIES

Lucille Shearwood, an omniscient genius, tells this story of defying detectives and purloining brownies at a White House tea. It was during a national convention of the AWRT (American Women in Radio and Television). "We expected," she says, "to be greeted only by Mrs. Truman and maybe Margaret, but the President turned up too, all bright and shiny . . . it being not too long before election time, and the group somewhat influential!"

The brownies proved to be perhaps the most spectacular feature of the occasion, especially to a friend of Lucille's who had for some years been working on a chocolate account. Since the friend was a little shy, Lucille offered to ask Mrs. Truman for the recipe. Mrs. Truman made her usual reply to all such requests, which was no. The recipe was her own, a very special one brought from Missouri.

Determined but still faltering, the chocolate-oriented lady whispered to Lucille, whose handbag was capacious, "See if you can't filch a couple so that I can try to reconstruct the recipe." Lucille was willing, but just as she was dropping the tissue-wrapped brownies into her purse she looked down at the floor to see a pair of square-toed shoes planted in front of her. "I looked up," she remembers, "and there were two, very cold, quite obviously private eyes glaring at me!" She had been standing beside a table laden with White House silver.

"Brownies, just brownies," she whispered, waving the package under the nose of the detective, who looked disgusted and walked away.

Not too long afterward a recipe for Bess Truman's Missouri brownies appeared in a Washington newspaper. Whether reconstructed or revealed no one seems to know. The brownies, in any case, are excellent—chewy but not tough.

Meanwhile, challenged by this duel of wits, Lucille Shearwood went to work to reconstruct a brownie that would taste, look, and "chew" like the Truman brownies. She spent six Saturday afternoons making ten different versions. This is the one that comes closest. It is plump with nuts, containing about twice as many as you will find in most recipes, very delicate inside, and not in the least bit gummy. Made with cake flour, the brownie has the character of old-fashioned fudge cake. With all-purpose flour, the brownie is sturdier and a few changes must be made in the recipe: only ½ cup flour and only ⅓ cup shortening is used; the butter or margarine should be melted although not allowed to separate.

A final word of wisdom from Lucille, now possibly the brownie queen. Brownies can be ruined in three ways: cooking in too thin a layer; baking in too hot an oven; baking too long.

Cake flour	*Eggs, Sugar*
Baking powder	*Vanilla*
Salt	*Unsweetened chocolate*
Softened butter or margarine	*Walnuts or pecans*

Sift together ¾ cup already sifted cake flour, ½ teaspoon baking powder, ½ teaspoon salt. Place ½ cup softened butter or margarine in large mixing bowl. Gradually add 1 cup sugar, mixing until light and fluffy. Add 2 unbeaten eggs and 1 teaspoon vanilla. Beat until smooth. Blend in 2 squares melted unsweetened chocolate. Stir in the flour mixture and at the last add 1 cup nuts broken into pieces or very coarsely chopped. Bake in a well greased 8-inch square pan at 350° F. for 30 minutes or until cake springs back in the center when touched lightly. Cool in the pan and then cut into 16 2-inch squares.

HARWICH HERMITS

These are the ancestors of brownies. They originated on Cape Cod, made rich with the spices from the Indies which came back on the clipper ships. This recipe is a particularly spicy one. While baking, these hermits fill the kitchen with tantalizing fragrance.

Butter	*Cloves*
Sugar	*Mace*
Eggs	*Nutmeg*
Molasses	*Allspice*
Flour	*Citron*
Salt	*Raisins*
Cream of tartar	*Currants*
Cinnamon	*Nuts*

Cream ½ cup butter and ½ cup sugar until light. Add 2 well-beaten eggs and ½ cup molasses. Beat well. Sift 2 cups flour with ½ teaspoon salt, ⅔ teaspoon cream of tartar, 1 teaspoon cinnamon, ½ teaspoon cloves, and ¼ teaspoon each of mace, nutmeg and allspice. Take from this flour and spice mixture ¼ cup and stir into it 3 tablespoons chopped citron, ¼ cup chopped raisins, ½ cup chopped currants, and ¼ cup chopped walnuts or pecans. When fruit is well coated with flour, which keeps it from sticking, combine all ingredients and mix well. Spread evenly in a well-greased large rectangular pan and bake at 350° F. for about 15 minutes, or until a toothpick comes out clean. Cut into squares while still warm. *Makes 4 dozen.*

PINEAPPLE FAIRY FLUFF

This is a wonderfully cool and refreshing dessert for a hot night. It looks lovely and it has the tang and lightness that summer desserts should have. It has the added advantage of not being very caloric.

Fresh pineapple	*Hot water*
Lemon	*Eggs*
Sugar	*Ladyfingers*

Squeeze half a fresh pineapple and grate the other half. In a double boiler cook the pineapple juice and grated pineapple together with the grated rind and juice of 1 lemon. Add 8 tablespoons sugar and 3 tablespoons hot water and stir constantly until mixture is hot and sugar dissolved. Beat yolks of 5 eggs and stir gently into mixture. Cook a little longer, until the yolks have thickened. Cool and fold in the white of 5 eggs beaten stiff. Chill well and serve in stemmed glasses with ladyfingers. Can also be made with canned shredded pineapple, but the flavor will be quite different. *Serves 6.*

BAKED CHOCOLATE ALASKA

Chocolate dessert was almost a must on the menu during the Truman administration, especially when Margaret was home, because she was so fond of chocolate. One of her favorite desserts was this baked Alaska made with chocolate ice cream and served with chocolate sauce.

Sponge cake	*Meringue*
Chocolate ice cream	*Chocolate sauce*

Bake or buy a sponge cake in the shape of a loaf of bread, not the shape that comes out of a tube pan. Cut off the top and scoop out the inside. Pack the shell with hard chocolate ice cream and replace the top. Put in the freezing compartment of the refrigerator to harden. Just before serving, place on a paper-covered board, cover entirely with a meringue prepared from a standard recipe, and brown quickly in a 450° F. oven. Serve with a good chocolate sauce.

AUNT LIZ' TRANSPARENT PIE

Not only is this an unusual-looking pie, it is also unusual-tasting. Although transparent pie is an old-fashioned favorite, few modern cooks have heard of it, eaten it, or made it. It is well worth trying. The meringue gives the finished pie a particularly festive look.

Butter	*Lemon*
Sugar	*Baked pie shell*
Eggs	*Vanilla*

Cream together until light and fluffy ½ cup butter and 1 cup sugar. Beat until light 4 egg yolks and combine with the sugar mixture. Stir in 1 teaspoon lemon rind and 3 tablespoons lemon juice. Beat until stiff 2 egg whites and fold into the mixture. Pour this into a baked 8-inch pie shell and bake at 325° F. about 30 minutes or until firm. Cool. Take the 2 remaining egg whites and make a meringue with sugar and vanilla according to a standard recipe. Cover the pie with meringue, trailing a knife over it to make light swirls. Return to slow (250° F.) oven for 5 to 10 minutes until meringue is faintly browned.

SENATORS' RUM PIE

Almost as famous as the bean soup served in the Senate dining room is the rum pie—more often served in the form of rum tarts. This became a great favorite of Truman's during the many years he served as a Senator.

Milk	*Dark rum*
Sugar	*Graham cracker crust*
Salt	*Pecans*
Eggs	*Bitter chocolate*
Flour	*Heavy cream*
Cornstarch	*Vanilla*
Butter	

Heat 1½ cups milk in top of double boiler with ¾ cup sugar and a pinch of salt. Beat 5 egg yolks lightly with ½ cup milk and gradually beat in ¼ cup flour and 2 tablespoons cornstarch. Stir the egg-yolk mixture into the milk, which should be hot but not boiling. Cook and stir this until thick and smooth. Be sure it does not boil. Allow to cool slightly and beat in, a little at a time, ½ cup softened butter. Stir in 2 tablespoons dark rum. Pour this into a pie pan lined with graham cracker crust or into muffin tins lined with graham cracker crust and chill.

At serving time decorate the pie or tarts with whipped sweetened cream flavored with vanilla, chopped pecans, and a grating of bitter chocolate. *This recipe makes a 9-inch pie or 12 small tarts.*

President Truman's beloved bourbon (bourbon and branch water was his drink) may be substituted for the rum in this recipe, although there is no record that this was ever done in the Senate dining room. When bourbon is used, black walnuts make a happy substitute for the pecans.

XXXIV

The Nation Likes Ike —and Mamie, Too

When the Eisenhowers moved into the White House in 1953, it was a landmark in more ways than one. Since their marriage in 1916, they had shared more than thirty different homes; they were to share this distinguished one for 8 years—a longer period than any of the others!

It was quite a household Mrs. Eisenhower became mistress of. The backstage areas of the White House had been completely remodeled and were being run by a large and highly efficient staff. Despite a reputation for disinterest in culinary affairs, Mrs. Eisenhower was said to devote more hours to domestic duties than any other recent First Lady. Her day started with conferences with the head usher, who is in charge of the social program, the *maître d'hôtel*, who is in charge of the staff of butlers, and the housekeeper, who oversees the cleaning and maintenance of the large house. From these meetings, Mrs. Eisenhower then went on to answering mail and receiving callers.

As a former Army wife, Mrs. Eisenhower would occasionally bring the staff up to snap with white-glove inspection tours. Although Mrs. Truman had acquired a reputation for economy, Mrs. Eisenhower amazed the staff by ordering that all the leftovers be saved. The help were afraid to throw away even the little dibs and dabs, lest they be called for at any moment.

Mamie Eisenhower broke with tradition in many ways in her entertainment. Fewer meals were served in the White House during the Eisenhower administration than in most others of recent times. The Trumans had held vast receptions for as many as 1500. The Eisenhowers kept their entertaining to a much smaller scale, and the President actually preferred the intimacy of stag dinners.

One notable party, which lingered in the memory of the staff was, typically, a Halloween party given by Mrs. Eisenhower for the wives of the White House staff members. Variously described by guests as a "gasser" and "the most interesting party ever given in the dignified setting of the White House," it included skeletons hanging from the State Dining Room chandeliers and witches on broomsticks riding over the white tablecloth. Forty-nine guests sat at the E-shaped table, scattered with autumn leaves, ears of Indian corn, nuts, and dried gourds.

The Eisenhower administration was notable for entertaining more royalty and heads of state than any other administration. Among the guests during that period were Emperor Haile Selassie of Ethiopia; the Presidents of Panama, Haiti, Turkey, Italy, Ireland; the rulers of Greece, Nepal, and Denmark.

President Eisenhower began his term in office by a knife-and-fork series—breakfasts, lunches, and dinners for the members of Congress. Within four months he had entertained all but four of the Senators and Congressmen. When the get-acquainted phase of his entertaining was over, the President began to give small stag dinners for business leaders, administration officials, publishers, editors, writers, educators, artists, sportsmen, Republican party leaders, old soldier friends. Dinner was usually at seven-thirty, and guests were invited to wear business suits if they liked, although the President wore black tie.

Big news for the reporters was the fact that despite an earlier announcement that alcoholic beverages would be served only when required by protocol for exchanging toasts with foreign dignitaries, in actual fact wines and liqueurs were offered at the first dinner of the season, for the Cabinet. The stir this raised caused the White House announcement that the reporters who were to cover the Supreme Court dinner two weeks later would be welcomed as guests, but not as reporters. The Press took the hint.

The Eisenhowers never acquired the reputation for being gourmets. Mrs. Eisenhower was happy to be with her husband alone at every meal, and many times the President and First Lady took their dinner on trays while watching television. Gossips say the trays contained frozen TV dinners. When the President's health made state dinners too exhausting, elaborate luncheons were substituted as the official entertainment for a visiting head of state and his wife.

The word placid has been used to describe Ike's eight years in office. Culinarily, placid might be changed to bland. In spite of the numerous formal affairs for foreign visitors, the general spirit of Executive House entertaining lacked sparkle. Our 34th President's widely acknowledged personal magnetism was rarely transferred to his menus, meals or galas.

◇◇

R E C I P E S

COLD CURRY SOUP

When the White House entertained Nikita Khrushchev and his wife, the Russian Premier brought his own food taster. Except for this rather unusual soup, the menu featured typically American dishes: roast turkey, cranberry sauce, sweet potatoes, a tossed salad. The soup, however, gave the food taster, and the Premier, something to think about.

Butter	*Curry powder*
Onion	*Milk*
Celery	*Bouillon cubes*
Salt, pepper	*Coconut*
Flour	

Melt ⅓ cup butter in saucepan over low heat. In it sauté ¼ cup minced onion and ¼ cup diced celery. Continue cooking over low heat until transparent. Blend in 1 teaspoon salt, ⅛ teaspoon pepper, ¼ cup flour and 1½ to 4 tablespoons curry powder (depending on strength of the powder and durability of your palate). Add 1 quart milk, stirring constantly. Cook until smooth and thickened. Add 2 chicken-bouillon cubes and stir until blended. Chill thoroughly. Serve in chilled bowls sprinkled with freshly grated coconut. *Serves 6.*

CHICKEN NOODLE SOUP

Soups were a favorite dish of the Eisenhowers. The President himself sometimes cooked them, if he was in the mood. Other times he and his wife enjoyed the excellent soups that emanated from the White House kitchens.

Stewing chicken	*Onions*
Water	*Salt, white pepper*
Carrots	*Noodles*
Celery	*Parsley*

Stew a chicken in cold water to cover, until tender, with 3 sliced carrots, 3 stalks of celery, sliced, 1 sliced onion, 1 teaspoon salt, and ⅛ teaspoon white pepper. Remove chicken and strain the stock. Cook in separate water 1 cup fine noodles. When tender, add these to the soup stock. Take the chicken liver and slice it fine and add it to the soup. Garnish with a sprinkle of freshly chopped parsley. *Serves 6.*

The chicken is used for sandwiches, creamed chicken, etc.

OXTAIL SOUP

A cold-weather favorite of President Eisenhower was this delicious oxtail soup, a truly hearty military dish.

Oxtails	*Leek*
Salt	*Carrots*
Flour	*Garlic*
Butter	*Celery*
Onions	*Turnips*
Beef stock or consommé	*Parsley*

Cut 2 small oxtails in 1-inch pieces and parboil for 5 minutes in salted water. Drain, roll in flour and sauté in 6 tablespoons butter. As they start to brown, add ⅔ cup chopped onions and brown them too. Place the meat and onions in soup kettle with 6 cups beef stock with a bouquet garni of 1 leek, 2 small carrots, 1 clove garlic, 1 quartered onion, and 2 stalks celery tied in a cheesecloth bag. Cover and cook over low flame for 2 hours or until oxtails are tender. Remove bag of vegetables and strain the soup. Pick bits of meat from bones and add to soup. Cut into attractive small pieces ¾ cup celery, ¾ cup carrots, and ¾ cup turnips; boil separately until tender. Add these to the soup and serve sprinkled with parsley. *Serves 4.*

STONE CRAB BISQUE

This is a party dish. There's something about crabmeat in any form that gives a touch of elegance to a meal. This bisque was a favorite recipe of François Rysavy, the French chef who reigned over the White House kitchen for about two years and added a number of glamorous recipes to the repertoire.

Crabs	*Fish seasoning*
Carrot	*Butter*
Onion	*Flour*
Celery	*Cream*
Thyme	*Dry breadcrumbs*
Bay leaf	*Croutons*

Cook in boiling salted water enough stone crabs (or ordinary crabs) to produce 1½ cups crabmeat. In the same water also cook, at the same time, ½ cup chopped carrot, 1 chopped onion, 1 chopped stalk celery, a sprinkle of thyme, 1 bay leaf and ½ teaspoon fish seasoning (obtainable at your fish store). Simmer 25 minutes, remove crabs and pick them, and strain the stock. You should have 4½ cups stock. Make a *roux* of 3 tablespoons butter and 3 tablespoons flour. Add the stock gradually and 2½ cups medium cream, but do not allow the cream to boil. Add one half the crabmeat and whir in blender. When it is creamy, remove from blender, add ⅓ cup dry breadcrumbs and the rest of the crabmeat; stir. Serve with a sprinkle of parsley and croutons sautéed in butter. Canned crabmeat is a timesaver. With canned crabmeat use 4½ cups chicken broth in place of fish stock. *Serves 8.*

CREAM OF ALMOND SOUP

Here's another exquisite soup—sure to make a *succès fou* at a small dinner party.

Butter	*Heavy cream*
Flour	*Salt, pepper*
Canned chicken consommé	*Slivered toasted almonds*
Blanched almonds	

Melt 1 stick butter in frying pan and add 1 rounded tablespoon flour. Stir and cook for 2 or 3 minutes, then gradually add 3 cans undiluted chicken consommé, stirring constantly until smooth. Add 1 cup grated almonds (you can put these into a blender or nut grinder) and cook 10 minutes longer. Season to taste. Add ½ cup cream very gradually and continue cooking until cream has heated but not boiled. Salt and pepper to taste. Put through blender and serve in individual soup bowls. On top place a fluff of whipped cream (unsweetened) and a sprinkle of toasted almonds. *Serves 6.*

CREAM OF CELERY–CLAM SOUP RYSAVY

In his second month in the White House, Chef Rysavy served a soup he had invented in France, which he thought would please the Eisenhowers. It did. Mrs. Eisenhower insisted upon immortalizing its inventor by naming the soup after him. Here it is.

Celery soup	*Chicken consommé*
Bottled clam juice	*Chives*

To one can undiluted celery soup add twice as much clam juice and half a can chicken consommé. Whir in blender until creamy. Heat thoroughly and serve in small cups. Sprinkle with chopped chives. *Serves 6.*

CREAM OF ARTICHOKE SOUP

According to her secretary, who is now living in Fontainebleu outside Paris, Mrs. Anthony Biddle preferred to all others her now-famous artichoke tureen. Madame Victorin writes: "Mrs. Biddle told me it was her favorite piece. And at the time when Ambassador and Mrs. Biddle had to leave Warsaw, which was being bombed, she carried that piece herself all the way to France in a hatbox." Guests who were entertained at the Biddle household recall a delicate and delightful cream of artichoke soup served to them from the artichoke-topped tureen. A charming thought, except that memory has enhanced the picture. Madame Victorin reports that no soup was ever served from the vermeil tureens. They were used for flowers, just as they are now at the White House.

General Eisenhower was a frequent guest at the Biddle home in both London and Paris. Three of the distinguished dishes he particularly enjoyed when dining with the Biddles deserve a place in the annals: Biddle boeuf à la mode, boeuf à la mode en gelée, and this cream of artichoke soup.

Artichoke bottoms	*Salt, pepper*
Butter	*White wine (Lillet or vermouth)*
Shallots (or white onions)	*Chicken broth*
Hazelnuts	*Cream*
Potatoes	

Cook until just tender 6 artichoke bottoms or 1 package frozen artichoke hearts. (If you use the artichoke hearts, purée and strain them through cheesecloth.) Cut up the artichoke bottoms into small pieces and cook gently in 2 tablespoons butter along with 2 finely chopped shallots or 1 small white onion. Place in blender with 1 cup of the water in which artichokes were cooked. Add 2 tablespoons hazelnuts and ¾ cup diced cooked potatoes, 1 teaspoon salt, ¼ teaspoon pepper, 2 tablespoons white wine. Cover and turn motor on high. Remove cover and while motor is still running add 1 cup rich chicken broth, ½ cup cream, and 2 tablespoons butter.

At serving time, heat mixture over simmering water and serve with a garnish of slivered hazelnuts. Soup may also be served ice-cold. The original Escoffier recipe called for hazelnut butter, but adding shelled hazelnuts to the mixture in the blender produces about the same result. *Serves 6.*

FAIRY TOAST

All through the annals of the White House kitchen, from the earliest days, appears an item called Fairy Toast. It has been a soup accompaniment for some Presidents, a teatime snack for others. You'll find it rather like commercial melba toast, but more interesting and of a better texture.

Slice white sandwich bread very thin. Remove crusts. Lay out on board to dry for half an hour. Place on cooky sheet and bake at 400° F. with oven door open until golden brown on top. It isn't necessary to turn these because they are so thin.

SUMMER SUCCOTASH

An old Kansas favorite that President Eisenhower remembered from his early Midwest days, and asked for from the White House kitchen, was succotash. What makes it different from many succotash recipes is the beef in the boiling water.

Corn on the cob	*Cream*
Beef	*Butter*
Lima beans	*Salt, pepper*

Boil 12 ears corns with ¼ pound beef and 1 quart shelled limas. When beans are tender, drain, saving ½ cup of cooking liquor. Cut corn from the ears, mix with beans, and add 1 cup cream, 1 tablespoon butter, salt, pepper, and the reserved cooking liquor. Bring to the boiling point and serve at once.

PRESIDENT EISENHOWER'S OLD-FASHIONED BEEF STEW FOR SIXTY

President Eisenhower left the running of the house to his wife, with one exception. He was very fond of cooking an occasional dish of a homely variety. Beef soup was one of his specialties, and he would leave the soup simmering on the stove in the kitchen for hours, causing much mouth-watering among the kitchen staff. As the President and Mrs. Eisenhower differed on the subject of onions (he loved them, she hated them), this was his chance to indulge one of his favorite tastes. Quantity did not faze the President. His beef stew recipe serves sixty and, although he had help from the staff in preparing the vegetables, he was there in the kitchen in his favored apron, stirring, tasting, seasoning.

Beef cut for stew	*Fresh tomatoes*
Beef stock	*Bouquet garni*
Small Irish potatoes	*Flour*
Small carrots	*Salt, pepper*
White onions	

Stew 20 pounds beef in 3 gallons beef stock until partially tender, about 2½ hours. Season and add 8 pounds peeled potatoes, 6 bunches scraped carrots, 5 pounds peeled onions, 15 quartered tomatoes, and a bouquet garni (bay leaf, parsley, garlic, thyme tied in a cheesecloth bag). When vegetables are tender, strain off 2 gallons of stock and thicken with enough flour to make a medium-thick sauce. Remove cheesecloth bag, add thickened gravy to the meat and vegetables, season to taste with salt and pepper and cook for another half hour.

EISENHOWER BEEF STEW FOR SIX

In case you are not serving sixty, but would like to try the President's excellent beef stew, here is a worthy adaptation that will serve 6. Eisenhower himself used this recipe when the party was small.

Beef for stew	*Carrots*
Butter or other shortening	*White onions*
Canned bouillon	*Tomatoes*
Water	*Salt, pepper*
Bouquet garni	*Flour*
Small Irish potatoes	

Brown 2 pounds beef cubes in 2 tablespoons shortening, then add 2 cans bouillon and 1 can water. Simmer, covered, until meat is nearly tender. Add bouquet garni and 12 potatoes halved, 1 bunch carrots cut in inch lengths, 12 white onions, 2 large tomatoes cut in eighths, and the salt and pepper. Simmer until vegetables are tender. Remove bouquet garni and drain off liquid. Make a *roux*, using 2 tablespoons flour to a cup of liquid. Return gravy to pot and cook over low heat, stirring, until well thickened.

BIDDLE BOEUF À LA MODE

Traditionally the beef should be larded with fat bacon, but since it is difficult to find larding needles or a butcher who will bother—and because we are all so cholesterol- and calorie-conscious—most American housewives dispense with the larding and buy a round of beef for this dish. Either choice or prime should have enough marbling to make it juicy and flavorsome.

Round of beef	*Dry white wine*
Salt, pepper	*Beef stock or bouillon*
Garlic	*Onions*
Cinnamon	*Shallots (or leek)*
Ginger	*Carrots*
Nutmeg	*Thyme*
Salt pork	*Bay leaf*
Calf's foot	*Parsley*
Clove	*Cognac*

Rub a 4-pound round of beef with salt, pepper, and little crushed garlic, and the merest suggestion of cinnamon, ginger, nutmeg, and clove. Pour on a small amount of cognac and allow beef to marinate for 2 hours, turning occasionally. Cut ½ pound salt pork into cubes and render in heavy kettle over brisk flame. Add a calf's foot cut in pieces (including bones) and the beef. Sear meat well on all sides; remove and keep warm. Add to the cooking fat 1 cup dry white wine and 1 quart beef stock or bouillon. Bring to boil, reduce heat, and add 18 small white onions, 2 shallots or 1 sliced leek, 1 pound carrots sliced thick (or small whole or halved baby carrots). Season with sprig of thyme, a bay leaf, and some parsley, plus a clove of garlic impaled on a toothpick for easy removal. Put back beef and calf's-foot pieces and simmer about 5 hours.

When meat is meltingly tender, remove garlic, skim off fat, and bone the calf's foot. Correct the seasoning, and bring to a boil. At serving time, serve all together, with a sprinkle of parsley on the beef. *Serves 8.*

BOEUF À LA MODE EN GELÉE

Although boeuf à la mode is frequently served hot, as in the preceding recipe, it is in its glory when served cold, either molded or from a terrine. The method of operation is the same as for the boeuf à la mode served hot, but when it is cooked, it should be cooled out of its liquid, and all fat removed. Then the meat is sliced into serving pieces and attractively arranged in layers on top of the carrots and onions. A shallow terrine makes a good serving dish. If possible, fix the vegetables in a design; pour the juices carefully so as not to disarrange the design. Put into refrigerator to jell. A wreath or nosegay of fresh herbs makes an attractive decoration.

QUICK BOEUF EN GELÉE

A startlingly easy and simple version of this classic dish can be achieved by using any good pot roast or slices of leftover roast beef. You can even use sliced roast beef from the delicatessen.

Lay 6 good slices of well-seasoned pot roast or 6 thick slices of roast beef, trimmed of fat, in a shallow serving dish. Arrange in overlapping layers and cover with an aspic made by combining 2 cans condensed consommé with 1 can water. Soften 2 tablespoons gelatin in ½ cup water. Then dissolve it in 1 cup boiling water. Add this to the consommé and stir. Garnish the top of the dish with cooked baby carrots and cooked small white onions, allowing about 3 carrots and 2 onions per portion. Cover well with liquid and put into refrigerator to jell.

QUAIL HASH

The Eisenhowers did not always share the same tastes for food. The President loved garlic and onions. Mrs. Eisenhower couldn't bear their odor or taste and was heard to remark more than once, "I smell onions in my house." For this reason, probably, this excellent quail hash has neither ingredient, but I suggest you include them both—they add a certain zest.

Quail	*Garlic*
Chicken stock	*Flour*
Butter	*Salt, pepper*
Onion	

Put 2 quail in a saucepan with ½ cup chicken stock and cover. Steam for 10 minutes, then add another ½ cup stock and simmer until tender. Remove quail from liquid and dice. Gently sauté in 1 tablespoon butter 2 tablespoons finely minced onion and ½ clove minced garlic. When soft but not browned, add 1 tablespoon flour and make a *roux,* using remaining stock for liquid. Replace quail in pan, pour the gravy over it, and heat 10 minutes longer. *Serves 2 or 3.*

FRESH MINT SAUCE

Mrs. Eisenhower, with her penchant for mint, always preferred mint sauce rather than gravy with her lamb. This is so good it is worth raising a mint bed.

Fresh mint	*Apple-mint jelly*

Take a large bunch of freshly gathered mint; wash, dry, and chop, discarding all the stems. Place the chopped mint in a pan with 1 cup apple-mint jelly and simmer over low heat about 10 minutes. Serve warm with roast leg or crown of lamb.

DANISH TOMATOES

This is a dish Mrs. Eisenhower enjoyed preparing. It is simple but rather unusual and would be an excellent side dish in summer when large beefsteak tomatoes are abundant.

Tomatoes	*Brown sugar*
Salt, pepper	*Vinegar*

Slice 4 large ripe tomatoes thickly. Place a layer of slices on the bottom of a flat serving dish. Sprinkle with salt and pepper and 1 tablespoon of brown sugar.

Place a second layer of slices on top and repeat the seasoning. Pour over all a sprinkling of good wine vinegar. Set aside in refrigerator for flavors to ripen. *Serves 4.*

MRS. EISENHOWER'S GINGERBREAD WITH APPLESAUCE

Gingerbread has always been a White House favorite. Dolley Madison made it and used powdered sugar. Mrs. Eisenhower liked it especially with the applesauce topping described here. A welcome change from the usual whipped cream or ice cream.

Butter	*Cloves*
Lard	*Ginger*
Sugar	*Cinnamon*
Egg	*Hot water*
Molasses	*Tart apples*
Flour	*Lemon*
Soda	*Red coloring*
Salt	

Cream ¼ cup butter, ¼ cup lard, and ½ cup sugar. Add 1 beaten egg and 1 cup dark molasses. Combine 2½ cups flour, 1½ teaspoons soda, ½ teaspoon salt, ½ teaspoon cloves, 1 teaspoon ginger, 1 teaspoon cinnamon. Add these to the butter mixture and stir. Then add 1 cup hot water and beat with electric beater or in a mixer for several minutes. Pour into buttered pan and bake at 325° F. for ½ hour.

To make the applesauce: Peel 8 tart apples and cut into small pieces. Add juice of 1 lemon, cover, and simmer until apples are soft. Be careful not to let them burn; they have no water added. When apples are tender, put them through a sieve and add 2 drops red food coloring. Serve as a topping on the gingerbread.

This is a very tart applesauce. If you would like it a bit sweeter, add sugar to taste while apples are cooking.

Serves 8.

RUM FRUIT SAVARIN

This dessert was served during the Eisenhower regime at more stag dinners, company dinners, and formal occasions of state than any other dessert. The recipe *serves about 30;* but it freezes well, so it is worthwhile to make it in this quantity and freeze the rest for another time.

Yeast	*Water*
Milk	*Orange rind*
Flour	*Rum*
Sugar	*Heavy cream*
Salt	*Instant vanilla pudding*
Eggs	*Fruit*
Butter	

Put a cake of yeast in ½ cup lukewarm milk. Meanwhile combine in a mixing bowl 4 cups flour, 1 tablespoon sugar, and ½ teaspoon salt. When the yeast rises to the top of the milk, add it to the dry ingredients with 8 whole eggs, beaten. Beat this mixture in an electric mixer at low speed for 10 minutes.

Add ½ pound melted butter by pouring on top of the dough. Cover and let rise a little. Beat a second time, this time beating in the butter. Let mixer run at low speed for 2 minutes.

Pour the batter into 3 generously buttered and floured ring molds. (Use molds with curved bottoms, such as are used for aspics.)

Bake at 400° F. for 15 minutes, then at 350° F. for 10 minutes more, or until the savarin ring holds its shape when touched.

When cool, remove from pans and baste with boiling syrup made by combining 2 cups sugar, 3 cups water, and the rind of 1 orange, coarsely chopped. Boil 15 minutes and add ½ cup strong rum. Remove from stove at once and baste the savarin rings with the hot syrup until they are soft and puff out. Let them cool slowly.

At this point, you can freeze 2 of the rings, and fill the other to serve 8. (This filling is sufficient for one ring.) Mix 1 cup milk with 1 package instant vanilla pudding. Add ¼ cup good rum. Just as the pudding begins to set, fold in almost 1 pint cream whipped stiff, reserving a little for decoration. Do your folding with a light hand. Finally, fold into the cream and pudding mixture 2 cups drained fruit. (You can use strawberries, or canned fruit mixed with fresh berries.) Put the savarin ring on a serving platter, curved side up. Fill the center with the fruit mixture and ornament the top of the ring with the reserved whipped cream and a few berries or pieces of fruit.

The flavor of the rum mellows if you fix the ring the day before serving. Add the fruit and pudding filling just before serving.

LIME SHERBET MELON MOLD

Mrs. Eisenhower loved the flavor of mint, as did Theodore Roosevelt, although she did not follow his example of raising it on the White House grounds. Two recipes that use mint were concocted for Mrs. Eisenhower by François Rysavy during his two-year stint in the White House kitchen. One was this melon mold; the other was the minted peach meringue, the recipe for which follows.

Lime sherbet   *Strawberries*
Mint

Fill a melon mold with lime sherbet the day before you are going to use it. Put it in the freezer until serving time. Unmold it, by dipping it quickly into a container of hot water, and place it on a serving dish. Surround it generously with mint leaves and whole ripe strawberries arranged like little hearts among the clusters of green. *Serves 8.*

MINTED MERINGUE PEACHES

Peaches   *Egg whites*
Mint jelly   *Sugar*
Mint extract

Put peach halves (canned or fresh, peeled) into the bottom of a saucepan. Pour over them a hot mixture of 1 glass melted apple-mint jelly and several drops of mint extract. If the peaches are fresh, cook slowly about 10 minutes or until flavor and color penetrate the peaches and they are tender. Strain, lay in a baking pan, and fill the center of each peach with a meringue made of egg whites and sugar (from a standard meringue recipe). Bake at 200° F. until meringues are dry, about 10 minutes.

PRESIDENTIAL PRUNE WHIP

One of President Eisenhower's favorite desserts was prune whip—a favorite shared by other Presidents, too, including Franklin D. Roosevelt. This is the recipe used in the White House during Ike's years there.

Prunes   *Egg whites*
Lemon juice   *Sugar*
Water   *Vanilla*
Unflavored gelatin   *Heavy cream*

Cook 1 generous cup dried prunes according to directions on package. Pit and strain them and run through the blender while hot with 2 teaspoons lemon juice and ½ envelope gelatin dissolved in ¼ cup water and melted over hot water. When the mixture is smooth remove it from the blender. Add to it 4 egg whites beaten stiff with ⅔ cup sugar and 1 teaspoon vanilla. The mixture can be molded in a mold or bowl. President Eisenhower liked it with cream poured on it. It is also good unmolded and decorated with whipped cream. *Serves 6.*

RUM CUSTARD FOR PRUNE WHIP

An interesting accompaniment to prune whip is this delicate and easy-to-prepare custard sauce.

Instant vanilla pudding	*Rum*
Milk	*Heavy cream*

Prepare 1 package of instant vanilla pudding according to directions on the package, but use only 1 cup milk instead of 2. Add to this mixture when it begins to thicken 2 tablespoons rum and 1 cup heavy cream beaten stiff. Merely fold the cream in lightly. If you mix it too much it will cause the pudding to become too liquid. *Makes 2 cups.*

MRS. EISENHOWER'S STRAWBERRY SHORTCAKE

When Mrs. Eisenhower served strawberry shortcake, the President always had another dessert. Nevertheless when Mrs. Eisenhower's mother, Mrs. John Doud, was a White House guest, strawberry shortcake usually appeared at least once on the menu.

Flour	*Milk*
Salt	*Butter*
Shortening	*Strawberries*
Baking powder	*Heavy cream*
Sugar	

Make a dough, as for regular biscuits, from 1 cup flour, ½ teaspoon salt, 2 tablespoons shortening, 2 teaspoons baking powder, 1 tablespoon sugar, and ⅓ cup very cold milk. Roll 1 inch thick on floured board and cut with large biscuit cutter into 4 biscuits. Bake according to usual directions for biscuits but wait to put these into the oven until you have started dinner so that they will be hot when you eat them. When biscuits are baked, split and butter them and serve with sliced sweetened strawberries in the middle and on top. Mrs. Eisenhower liked hers served with heavy cream in a pitcher, but you may prefer sweetened whipped cream. Both are salubrious. *Serves 4.*

WHITE HOUSE NUT BREAD

This recipe for nut bread was developed by Chef Rysavy. It produces a nice, dry loaf that is not too rich, since the nuts provide the shortening and no other is added.

Egg yolks	*Baking powder*
Lemon peel	*Salt*
Milk	*English walnuts*
Sugar	*Pecans*
Flour	

Combine 2 egg yolks, ½ teaspoon finely grated lemon peel, and 1 cup milk with ⅔ cup sugar. Add to this 2 cups flour, 2 teaspoons baking powder, and 1 teaspoon salt. Beat with an electric beater or in a mixer for 7 minutes at medium speed. Add ⅔ cup coarsely chopped English walnuts and ⅓ cup chopped pecans and beat for an additional 3 minutes. Pour into a well-greased loaf pan and let sit for ½ hour. Then bake at 350° F. for about 50 minutes, or until a toothpick will come out clean.

MILLION-DOLLAR FUDGE

This is a recipe Mrs. Eisenhower brought with her to the White House. She had been making it for years, and the President himself named it. There are some who say it came originally from a giveaway booklet. (And others who insist it should have stayed there!) If you love fudge—it's lovely.

Evaporated milk	*Semi-sweet chocolate bits*
Sugar	*Sweet chocolate*
Butter	*Marshmallow whip*
Salt	*Walnuts*

Mix 13½-ounce can evaporated milk, 4½ cups sugar, 2 tablespoons butter and a sprinkle of salt in a saucepan and bring to a boil. Stir and boil for 7 minutes. Then pour the boiling mixture over the remaining ingredients, which you have combined in a large bowl: 12 ounces chocolate bits, 12 ounces sweet chocolate broken into pieces, an 8-ounce jar marshmallow whip, and 2½ cups chopped walnuts. Beat until fudge is creamy, then pour into a buttered pan to cool.

MRS. EISENHOWER'S DEEP DISH APPLE PIE

Just like every red-blooded American, President Eisenhower was fond of apple pie, particularly this deep dish pie made from a favorite recipe of his wife. It is delicious.

Tart apples	Cinnamon
Sugar	Butter
Lemon juice	Pie crust
Nutmeg	Heavy cream

Pare and slice thin a dozen tart apples. Season with ⅔ cup sugar and 2½ tablespoons lemon juice, ½ teaspoon nutmeg, ½ teaspoon cinnamon. Melt ½ stick butter and mix into the apples. Pour into a deep 8-inch Pyrex dish, cover with a regular pie crust rolled a bit thicker than usual, and bake at 350° F. for 45 minutes. The Eisenhowers liked this pie served warm with a pitcher of thick cream on the side. *Serves 6.*

BROWN BETTY

When the Eisenhowers entertained King Baudouin of Belgium the dessert served was called Betty Brune de Pommes. It drew an amusing comment from the Washington *Daily News* the next day. The paper observed that "You don't need a French-English dictionary to recognize . . . plain, old, respectable, uninspired Brown Betty. We don't know what kind of dessert the White House cooked up for Winston Churchill, but that was the time for Brown Betty." The British, it observed, are noted for undistinguished desserts. "Brown Betty would put them in ecstasy. But for the King of the Belgians, a people with a civilized palate, no, no, no!" Nevertheless, Brown Betty stole the show.

Coarse moist breadcrumbs	Cloves
Melted butter	Salt
Apples	Lemon rind
Brown sugar	Lemon juice
Cinnamon	Raisins
Nutmeg	Walnuts

Combine 2 cups breadcrumbs with ½ cup melted butter. Line a baking dish with ⅓ of the crumbs. Peel and slice enough apples to make 2½ cups. Place half the apples in the dish. Combine ¾ cup brown sugar, 1 teaspoon cinnamon, ¼ teaspoon nutmeg, ¼ teaspoon cloves, ½ teaspoon salt, and 1 teaspoon grated lemon rind. Cover apples with ½ the sugar mixture. Sprinkle with 1 tablespoon lemon juice and 2 tablespoons water. Cover them with ⅓ the crumb mixture, ¼ cup raisins which have been soaked in hot water half an hour, the remaining apples, and the remaining sugar mixture. Sprinkle this with 1 cup coarsely chopped walnuts and 1 tablespoon lemon juice. Place on top the remaining ⅓ crumb mixture. Cover the dish and bake at 350° F. for about 40 minutes, or until apples are nearly tender. Remove cover and increase heat to 400° F. to permit the pudding to brown for 15 minutes. Serve hot, and pay no mind to the *Washington Daily News! Serves 6.*

PUMPKIN CHIFFON PIE

This is a little different from the usual hearty, after-the-Thanksgiving-dinner dessert. The gelatin makes the difference. It is a favorite of Mrs. Eisenhower.

Eggs	*Cinnamon*
Brown sugar	*Unflavored gelatin*
Cooked pumpkin	*Cold water*
Milk	*Granulated sugar*
Salt	*Heavy cream*
Nutmeg	

Combine 3 beaten egg yolks with ¾ cup brown sugar, 1½ cups pumpkin, ½ cup milk, pinch of salt, ½ teaspoon nutmeg, and 1 teaspoon cinnamon. Cook in double boiler until thick, stirring constantly. Soak 1 envelope unflavored gelatin in ¼ cup cold water and then stir into hot mixture until well dissolved. Set aside to cool. When cool, put into the refrigerator until partly set. Beat 3 egg whites until stiff, gradually add ¼ cup granulated sugar, and beat until it makes soft peaks. Fold into partly set gelatin mixture. Pour into baked pie shell and chill until firm. Garnish with whipped cream. *Serves 6 or 8.*

ENGLISH RICE PUDDING

Ike preferred his rice pudding cooked the British way, which takes longer than making it from cooked leftover rice. However, it is worth the extra trouble for the sake of the delicate flavor.

Rice	*Raisins*
Milk	*Salt*
Lemon rind	*Nutmeg*
Egg yolks	*Powdered sugar*
Sugar	

Cook over low heat ½ cup rice mixed into 3 cups milk, with 1 teaspoon finely grated lemon rind. When rice is tender, combine with 3 beaten egg yolks, ½ cup sugar, and ½ cup raisins and a pinch of salt. Pour this into a buttered baking dish and sprinkle the top lightly with nutmeg. Bake at 300° F. for 35 minutes. Just before removing from oven, cover the top heavily with powdered sugar and place it under the broiler to caramelize, but be careful not to burn it. Serve with a pitcher of heavy cream. *Serves 4.*

APPLE CARAMEL

The pitcher of heavy cream passed with dessert is almost an Eisenhower trademark. This is another dessert that isn't too frightening to calorie-watchers until they come to that inevitable pitcher of cream.

Sugar	*Vanilla*
Butter	*Heavy cream*
Apples	

Melt 5 tablespoons sugar in an iron skillet over a very low flame. Continue to cook until sugar is light brown. Add ½ stick butter and blend it into the caramelized sugar. Add 5 apples, peeled and cut into wedges. Cover and simmer until apples are soft, adding ½ teaspoon vanilla at the last. Serve warm with cream. *Serves 4.*

XXXV

Food on the New Frontier

At the time of John F. Kennedy's election, Betty Beale, an outstanding White House columnist, wrote an open letter to the First Lady listing what Washington officials and local residents hoped to see accomplished in the White House. The letter was published in November 1960 and drew an immediate and warm handwritten response from Mrs. Kennedy.

"You will see," she said to her one-time journalistic colleague. "Within a year I bet I will have done most of the things you suggested."

At the end of that year, the changes and accomplishments were many. They included giving stimulus, encouragement, and prestige to the arts, varying the guest lists so that the magnificent state dinners at the White House included many famous Americans, among them such cultural leaders as Robert Frost, Carl Sandburg, Leonard Bernstein, Marian Anderson, George Balanchine, Lawrence Langner, Aaron Copland, and Samuel Barber.

Mrs. Kennedy was singularly successful "in making the White House a show-place for the best in food and fashions," another of Betty Beale's suggestions. It was generally conceded in Washington that the best restaurant in town was 1600 Pennsylvania Avenue. Mrs. Kennedy's tastes, and those of her chef, were classic and French. Like Thomas Jefferson, whom she and her husband both greatly admired, she was criticized for what has been called a gastronomic subservience to foreign cuisine. The three-course dinner served by the Kennedys to Nobel Prize winners in April 1962 followed their pattern—a pared-down classicism.

Puligny	La Couronne de l'Élu Victoria
Montrachet	
Combetter	Filet de boeuf Wellington
1er Cru	Pommes Chipp
1959	
Château Mouton-	
Rothschild	
1955	Fonds d'artichauts Favorite
	Endive Meunière
Piper Heidsieck	Bombe Caribienne
1955	Petits-fours assortis

(One note in this menu, of course, sends the traditional gourmet into a spin. Potato chips were served with the filet of beef Wellington, and listed as *Pommes Chipp*.)

At the first reception held by the Kennedys, society reporters had an intimation of the innovations that were to follow. At the buffet, in addition to the usual and ever-present little sandwiches and cakes were hors d'oeuvre: fresh shrimp, celery and cauliflower with a tangy mustard dip, tiny hot cheese balls, and cocktail canapés. And cocktails were served at an official party in the Executive Mansion for the first time in the memory of those present. The First Lady was dispensing the same hospitality she did in her own home. Jacqueline Kennedy spent considerable time looking for a sideboard that disappeared in the days of Lemonade Lucy, Mrs. Rutherford B. Hayes. The sideboard may have disappeared when Mrs. Hayes, a dedicated teetotaler, removed from the White House all the appurtenances of drinking. The Kennedy's, themselves, who could never be called "drinkers" restored to respectability and brought back into full sight the bar and hard liquor at the White House.

After repeal, beginning with the Franklin D. Roosevelts, straight drinks and mixed drinks have been served at White House parties, but the bar was always almost shame-facedly hidden. The Kennedys eliminated the hypocrisy—and the furore was far less vocal than might have been expected. Objections in the press were scattered and only a few bone-dry Midwestern critics went on record protesting the innovation. Actually, even the Temperance people could not be too vexed, for John Kennedy himself was almost a teetotaler.

At a dinner for the President of Peru, Señora de Prado was asked her impressions of the meal. She said that it had been complete perfection. Was there anything different from what she might have expected? There wasn't. And yet this menu marked a great change in the history of dining at the White House. This was possibly the first state dinner at which only four courses were served. Even in the regime of Mrs. Franklin D. Roosevelt, whose motto was simplicity, five courses were served—a major revolution after the Hoovers, who always had a seven-course dinner even when they were alone.

But Mrs. Kennedy felt that five courses are too much for the average dinner today—too much food and too much time required to serve and to eat it. She preferred to shorten the meal and keep the guests awake for the after-dinner conversation or music or Shakespeare in the East Room. The four-course menu for the Prados began with a salmon mousse garnished with a tomato-and-cucumber salad. It was followed by Tournedos Héloise, thick slices of filet mignon with pâté de fois gras, truffles, artichokes, and mushrooms. There were roasted potatoes, green beans with almonds, a tray of assorted cheeses and crackers. This was followed by St. Honoré Cake.

Privately and publicly, Mrs. Kennedy stressed her desire that the White House should reflect the best of American life and American taste. Few knew, however, that the President himself also took a great interest in the decoration and entertaining in the White House.

Before each dinner party, President Kennedy popped into the kitchen to taste the wine. Usually, White House dinners under the Kennedy regime included both a red and a white wine as well as a champagne. For diplomatic reasons the Kennedys seldom disclosed the names of their favorite wines, nor did they customarily identify the wines in the menus. They did serve both domestic and imported wines.

When the young Presidential family needed a chef for the White House they turned to the owners of La Caravelle Restaurant in New York. Joseph Kennedy, father of the President, was a great booster of this elegant establishment. When the President was a Senator he dined there often, with Mrs. Kennedy, especially during the 1960 campaign. The owners of La Caravelle, Fred Decré and Robert Meyzen, turned to their chef, the famous Roger Fessaguet, to find a good chef for the White House. He suggested René Verdon, who had worked at the Essex House and the Carlyle Hotel, and invited him into the Caravelle kitchens to work and learn about the type of food the Kennedys liked.

The Kennedys also invited the Caravelle owners to come down on an inspection tour of the White House kitchens to make suggestions to improve the cooking facilities.

M. Verdon, the new chef, brought with him an expert in the art of the classic buffet—Julius Spessot, a young man who spent a number of years as a specialist behind the scenes on the Italian liners. He excelled in decorating, particularly in the creation of spun sugar flowers, ice carving, and elegant aspics. He was responsible for the ice statues four and five feet high that decorated the table at buffet luncheons and supper parties.

Mrs. Kennedy was well aware of the fact that practically every President and his wife have faced some sort of attack on their dinners and their services. The men who came from the old frontier often found the White House cuisine too elaborate. But she realized it was important for each family to set its own style. The word style with a capital S soon came to symbolize the Kennedy administration.

No administration in recent history made so many and such thoughtful changes. For example, instead of a reception line in the Blue Room behind closed doors where each guest got a thirty-second peek at the President and his wife, the Kennedys practically banished reception lines. Members of Congress were ecstatic when "they discovered that at a white-tie reception in their honor they did not have to stand in line at all. The President and his wife moved among all their guests in every room and behaved like normal hosts at a normal, formal party."

Mrs. Kennedy revolutionized flower arrangements, not only on the tables but all through the White House, filling antique tureens, cachepóts, pitchers, and bowls with bouquets that looked as if they had been lifted off the canvases of French painters. These arrangements aroused some comment from newspaper columnists, who wondered what Mrs. Margaret Thompson Biddle would have thought of the fabled gold soup tureens she bequeathed to the Executive Mansion being used for flowers. (This is amusing because from what we have been able to learn from Mrs. Biddle's family and secretary, the tureens were practically never used in her household for anything else.)

When the arrangements at state tables were high, they were set into slender vases so that it was easy to see under and around them. Mrs. Kennedy restored the customary seating of hosts and sat opposite her husband even at the state dinner table.

After dinner men and women were no longer herded into separate rooms. The Kennedys moved among their guests as informally as any couple might do.

But perhaps the most startling innovation was the revoking of the old dictum that the President must make the first move to break up the party. Even Mrs. Roosevelt, who disliked this particular manifestation of protocol, was unable to alter it. But the Kennedys did. At one White House dinner the two of them stood, one on either side of the foyer, while the guests went up to thank them for a lovely dinner, just as you might at anybody's dinner party.

An insouciant comment by columnist Art Buchwald summarizes a good deal about the social patterns of the Kennedys:

> Washington is the most social-conscious city in the world and your status in the nation's capital depended on whether you had been invited for cocktails or dinner and by whom.
>
> In previous administrations you received points if you were asked to the home of a senator or a Supreme Court justice or even a cabinet minister. Since the

Eisenhowers rarely entertained, the point spread was on a much lower level and the scoring was very complicated. But all this has changed. . . .

If you are invited to a private dinner at the White House and asked to stay for the evening you get six points. If you're asked to come in after dinner for dancing, three points, but you get an extra point if it turns into a twist party.

If the President dances with your wife or if you dance with Mrs. Kennedy you automatically get twenty points.

The only way you can get more points than this is if your child is invited to a birthday party for Caroline. You get twenty-five points for this and an extra five points if your kid is also in Caroline's dancing class.

Whenever there was a lull in the official social calendar, the Kennedys invited a few couples in for a quiet dinner. Frequent guests included the Franklin D. Roosevelt, Jr.'s, columnist Joseph Alsop and his wife, the President's brother (then Attorney-General) Robert Kennedy and his wife Ethel, Mr. and Mrs. Charles Bartlett, Lemoyne Billings and Charles Spaulding. President Kennedy always insisted on a good cigar after a good dinner. The conversation was lively, but in view of the tiring Presidential schedule, the guests were usually gone before ten-thirty.

The Kennedy years were gay and exuberant while they lasted. One sensed, through interviews and quips and the wry comments that he made, that J.F.K. reveled in his job, in the historic house in which he and his young family lived, and the general ambience of the Presidency. His barely contained pleasure reminds the historically-minded of Teddy Roosevelt's similar happiness in the White House.

In fact, not since Roosevelt's day did the house ring with the voices and pranks of such young children. Little Caroline tottering into a press conference on her mother's high heels or riding her pony Macaroni on the White House grounds, and her baby brother John-John waving goodbye to their father as he took off by helicopter from the lawn, were just a few of the photographic images that endeared the children and their parents to their countrymen.

As the public in T.R.'s day devoured all news about the Roosevelts, and especially young Alice, so did a latter-day public gobble every possible tidbit about the leader of the New Frontier and his beautiful and chic young wife.

In a conversation with Theodore H. White, the journalist, shortly after her husband's death, Jacqueline Kennedy referred to a song from the musical "Camelot," which had been a favorite of Jack's. The lines he particularly liked were: "Don't let it be forgot, that once there was a spot, for one brief shining moment that was known as Camelot."

◇◇

RECIPES

MRS. KENNEDY'S CHOPPED EGG CANAPÉS

At teatime, or with sherry or cocktails before dinner, Mrs. Kennedy preferred the simplest kind of canapés. Her favorite was made of chopped hard-cooked eggs, "boiled not too long so that they don't become dry and mealy, chopped not too fine to avoid making them mushy."

Hard-cooked eggs	*Garlic*
Mayonnaise (homemade)	*Black pepper*
Salt	

Chop the eggs coarsely and moisten them with mayonnaise. Season with salt and a little garlic juice (or garlic powder). At serving time, a scant spoonful of the egg mixture is placed on rounds of crisp melba toast. Sprinkle the tops with a bit of freshly ground coarse pepper.

RADZIWILL SAUCE

One of the frequent houseguests at the White House was the Princess Radziwill, Mrs. Kennedy's younger sister Lee, married to Prince Stanislas Radziwill of Poland. No culinary report of the Kennedys could be complete without reference to the classic and traditional Radziwill Sauce, which is listed in many gourmet cookbooks. It is a slightly sweet and spicy mayonnaise that is delicious with hot or cold smoked meats like tongue or ham. Particularly delightful with cold game.

Mayonnaise	*Salt*
Freshly grated horseradish	*Tabasco sauce*
Guava jelly	*Heavy cream*
Prepared mustard	*Sherry*
Tarragon vinegar	

Beat ½ cup mayonnaise with 2 tablespoons horseradish. Add 2 tablespoons softened guava jelly, 1 teaspoon mustard, 1 tablespoon vinegar, a little salt, and a couple of drops of Tabasco. Stir thoroughly. Then fold in ½ cup heavy cream beaten stiff. At the last minute, stir in 1 tablespoon dry sherry.

KENNEDY'S CINNAMON TOAST

No story of the Kennedys' likes and dislikes would be complete without a mention of the President's fondness for milk. This is not to imply, however, that milk was the only beverage J.F.K. favored. Possibly as a result of his upbringing in England, where his father was the Ambassador to the Court of St. James, President Kennedy was partial to tea, which was served to him each day at four. Upstairs in the private quarters of the White House the Kennedys had a family kitchen and a butler's pantry installed. All the cabinets had marble tops and there was a special broiler for the President's steaks and lobster. From this pantry emerged the four o'clock tea and the President's favorite cinnamon toast. When the news of his predilection for this became common, cinnamon toast eating took a spurt in Washington. Mrs. Kennedy often served it at her own teas.

Thomas Jefferson is credited with having introduced the first waffles and the first waffle iron, to the White House. But Kennedy deserves credit for returning waffles to high Presidential favor. Whenever there was a suitable occasion, he liked to have waffles served with New England maple syrup. His fondness for maple extended even to a variation of cinnamon toast—New England cinnamon toast made with maple sugar. Another household favorite that Mrs. Kennedy served at her teas was a marmalade toast, made on small rounds of buttered toast mounded with orange marmalade—preferably the type made with long strips of rind. She had, in fact, a collection of marmalades of different flavors, made of oranges from Seville, of limes, lemons, and also of ginger.

This cinnamon toast recipe was especially favored.

Homemade white bread	*Light or dark brown sugar*
Cinnamon (or packaged cinnamon sugar)	*Butter*

Cut slices of bread in half, making two rectangles or two triangles. Toast one side in the oven. Spread the other side with softened butter and sprinkle thickly with white or brown sugar mixed with cinnamon (1 teaspoon cinnamon to ½ cup sugar). Set under the broiler again until topping begins to bubble. Serve at once.

ICED TOMATO SOUP

At a spring luncheon at the White House of which the main course was an *entrecote* with a watercress garnish, the first course was a delicious and unusual cold soup:

Ripe tomatoes	*Flour*
Onion	*Chicken bouillon cubes*
Cold water	*Boiling water*
Salt and pepper	*Heavy cream*
Tomato paste	

Combine 6 large ripe tomatoes, coarsely chopped, with one onion chopped. Add

¼ cup cold water, salt and pepper, and cook over moderate heat for 5 minutes. Combine 2 tablespoons tomato paste with 2 tablespoons flour. Dissolve 2 bouillon cubes in 2 cups boiling water and stir this into the tomato-paste mixture. Add the combination to the hot tomato–onion mixture and simmer gently for 3 minutes. Rub through a fine sieve or whir in blender and chill several hours. Before serving stir in 1 cup heavy cream. Season to taste with dash of salt and pepper and garnish each serving with a thin slice of tomato. *Serves 6.*

HYANNISPORT FISH CHOWDER

The entire Kennedy clan favor this hearty fish soup—for a change not a New England clam chowder, but a New England *fish* chowder.

Haddock	*Celery*
Boiling water	*Bay leaf*
Salt pork	*Salt, pepper*
Onions	*Milk*
Potatoes	*Butter or margarine*

Cook 2 pounds haddock in 2 cups boiling water over low heat for 15 minutes. Drain and measure broth; add enough water to make 3 cups. Remove bones and skin from fish; flake fish coarsely. Cook 2 ounces diced salt pork in a heavy skillet over moderate heat until golden brown and crisp. Remove pork pieces. Add 2 onions, sliced, to the fat and cook and stir until golden brown. Add fish, 4 large potatoes diced, 1 cup chopped celery, 1 crushed bay leaf, 1 teaspoon salt, a dash of pepper, and the 3 cups of fish broth. Cover and simmer gently for 30 minutes. Add 1 quart milk and 2 tablespoons butter or margarine. Simmer over very low heat 5 minutes longer. Serve chowder in warm bowls and sprinkle with crisp pork cubes. *Serves 6.*

BOULA BOULA SOUP

Although President and Mrs. Eisenhower initiated the tradition of serving an international menu in the White House on UN Day, October 21, it was Mrs. Kennedy's menus for that day that stirred the greatest amount of interest. One UN dinner menu represented four countries in its four courses. It began with Boula Boula soup from the United States, went on to a minced lamb curry from India, a mimosa salad from England, and an apple charlotte from France. The soup recipe is Mrs. Kennedy's own, one she enjoyed serving for years at her Georgetown house.

Green peas (fresh or frozen)	*Sherry*
Sugar	*Sweet butter*
Tarragon	*White pepper and salt*
Canned green turtle soup	*Whipped cream*

Cook 2 cups shelled peas or frozen with ½ teaspoon sugar and a touch of tarragon until tender. Put through a fine sieve or into an electric blender to make a purée. Mix with 2 cups turtle soup and ½ cup sherry (Mrs. Kennedy used one full cup, but I think it's too much). Add 2 tablespoons sweet butter, a little white pepper, and salt to taste. Heat but do not boil.

At serving time, ladle the hot soup into individual heatproof cups and top each with a spoonful of unsweetened whipped cream. Place under the broiler until the top is delicately brown. Serve at once. *Serves 6.*

An interesting variation is the addition of a little grated Parmesan cheese sprinkled on top of the whipped cream.

MIMOSA SALAD

The mimosa salad from England served at the UN dinner, has colors reminiscent of the golden flowering mimosa trees. In English country houses, not only salad but eggs are served à la Mimosa, which means garnished with mayonnaise and hard-cooked egg yolks.

Salad greens	*Salt, pepper*
Garlic	*Mayonnaise*
Hard-boiled eggs	*Sour cream, yogurt, or lemon juice*

Place sufficient crisp greens to serve 6 in a bowl lightly rubbed with garlic. Cut the whites of 2 or 3 hard-cooked eggs into fine dice and mix with the greens. Season with salt and pepper and toss with mayonnaise that has been thinned with a little sour cream, yogurt, or lemon juice. Crumble the egg yolks evenly with a silver fork and sprinkle over the salad. Eggs should not be cooked too long or they become dry and tasteless. If desired, oil and vinegar may be substituted for the thinned mayonnaise.

MUSHROOMS WITH HERBS

An unusual and piquant way to prepare mushrooms is this White House favorite.

Mushrooms	*Salt, pepper*
Olive oil	*Tarragon vinegar*
Onion	*Tarragon*
Chives	*Thyme, Garlic*
Parsley	*Butter or margarine*

Wipe and slice 1 pound of mushrooms. Combine with ¼ cup olive oil, 1 tablespoon each grated onion, chopped chives, and chopped parsley. Add 1 clove garlic, minced, ¾ teaspoon salt, a dash of pepper, 3 tablespoons tarragon vinegar, and a sprinkling of tarragon and thyme. Let stand 2 hours. Melt 4 tablespoons butter or margarine in a skillet, add mushrooms and marinade, and cook over medium heat 10 minutes, stirring frequently. *Serves 6.*

HOT CHEESE CORNBREAD

This cornbread is an interesting variation on an old favorite.

Yellow cornmeal	*Sharp American cheese*
All-purpose flour	*Egg*
Sugar	*Milk*
Salt	*Soft shortening*
Baking powder (not double-acting)	

Sift together 1 cup yellow cornmeal, 1 cup sifted flour, ¼ cup sugar, ½ teaspoon salt, and 4 teaspoons baking powder. Add 1½ cups shredded cheese, 1 egg beaten, 1 cup milk, and ¼ cup shortening. Beat with rotary beater until smooth, about a minute. Don't overbeat. Pour into greased 8-inch square pan and bake 30 minutes in preheated 375° F. oven. Serve hot. *Serves 8.*

CASSEROLE MARIE-BLANCHE

Despite its rather chic name, this unusual noodle casserole is a homy dish—and delicious!

Noodles	*Chives*
Creamed-style cottage cheese	*Salt, pepper*
Commercial sour cream	*Butter or margarine*

Combine 1 pound noodles, cooked, drained and buttered, with 1 cup creamed cottage cheese, 1 cup sour cream, ⅓ cup chopped chives, and a generous sprinkle of salt and pepper. Pour into buttered 2-quart casserole and bake at 350° F. for 30 minutes, until noodles begin to brown. *Serves 6.*

INDIVIDUAL CHEESE SOUFFLÉS

This Kennedy favorite makes a delicious lunch or supper main dish or an elegant first course for a dinner party when there's help in the kitchen and you have dependable guests.

Butter or margarine	*Eggs*
Flour	*Salt, white pepper*
Milk	*Onion juice*
Sharp American cheese	

Preheat oven to 350° F. Melt ¼ pound butter or margarine, but do not brown it. Blend in ¼ cup flour, and gradually stir in 1 cup heated milk. Cook and stir constantly until smooth and thickened. Add ½ cup shredded cheese and cook over low heat until cheese melts. Cool 5 minutes and stir in 3 well-beaten egg yolks. Add ½ teaspoon salt, ¼ teaspoon white pepper, and 1 teaspoon onion juice. Cook and stir 1 minute. Cool mixture 5 minutes longer, then fold in 3 stiffly beaten egg whites. Pour into 4 ungreased individual casseroles. Place these in a baking pan half-filled with hot water. Bake until center is firm—about 45 minutes. Serve at once. *Serves 4.*

POTATOES SUZETTE

This is a delicious variation on an old favorite, stuffed potatoes. Can be prepared ahead of time and held for the final baking.

Large baking potatoes	*Egg yolk*
Butter or margarine	*Salt, pepper*
Heavy cream	*Parmesan cheese*

Bake 3 large potatoes until fork-tender, about an hour. Cut in half lengthwise, and scoop out the pulp without breaking shells. Mash thoroughly and beat in 2 tablespoons butter or margarine, 3 tablespoons heavy cream, and 1 well-beaten egg yolk. Beat mixture vigorously until fluffy. Season with salt and pepper and replace in shells. Sprinkle with 1 tablespoon Parmesan cheese and bake 15 minutes at 400° F., until tops are golden. *Serves 6.*

BAKED SEAFOOD CASSEROLE

The Kennedys were fond of fish. One delightful way they enjoyed it was in this seafood casserole, which may be prepared ahead of time and popped into the oven when the time is right.

Crabmeat (fresh cooked, canned,	*Celery*
or frozen)	*Salt*
Shrimp	*Worcestershire sauce*
Mayonnaise	*Potato chips*
Green pepper	*Paprika*
Onion	

Combine 1 pound crabmeat, 1 pound cooked, shelled, and deveined shrimp, 1 cup mayonnaise, ½ cup chopped green pepper, ¼ cup minced onion, 1½ cups finely chopped celery, ½ teaspoon salt, 1 tablespoon Worcestershire sauce. Pour into buttered casserole. Top with 2 cups crushed potato chips and sprinkle with 1 teaspoon paprika. Bake at 400° F. for 20 to 25 minutes, longer if mixture has been waiting in the refrigerator. *Serves 8.*

SALMON MOUSSE WITH CUCUMBERS

A delicate dish for summer, this salmon mousse was another of Mrs. Kennedy's specialties.

Canned red salmon	*Green pepper*
Water	*Heavy cream*
Gelatin	*Cucumber*
Salt	*Mayonnaise*
Onion juice	*Green food coloring*
Celery	

Drain 1 large can good-quality salmon; add water to liquid to total 1½ cups. (Or use 2 cups cooked salmon and 1½ cups fish stock or chicken broth.) Sprinkle 1 tablespoon (1 envelope) unflavored gelatin over ½ cup of this liquid. When gelatin has softened, stir it into the remaining cup of liquid which has been heated; add ½ teaspoon salt, and stir over low heat until gelatin is dissolved. Remove from heat and add 1 tablespoon onion juice. Chill to consistency of unbeaten egg white. Flake fish and combine with ¼ cup finely chopped celery and 2 tablespoons chopped green pepper. Fold fish mixture into chilled gelatin. Gently fold in 1 cup heavy cream, whipped. Turn into 1-quart mold and chill in refrigerator until firm. When set, unmold onto serving plate and garnish with 1 large cucumber, very thinly sliced, and 1 cup mayonnaise, tinted pale green with food coloring. *Serves 6.*

WESTPORT POINT SWORDFISH

About an hour's drive from the Kennedy's summer house at Hyannis is Westport Point, considered by many the swordfish capital of the world. The secret of the quality of the swordfish is the chill of the waters plus the uncompromising attitude of the people who insist that swordfish must not be kept overnight. To be good, they feel, the swordfish must be "leaping fresh."

At Lees Wharf, at Westport Point, every day including Sundays and holidays, from the end of June through Labor Day weekend, you can select a swordfish steak according to the local mores: Neither the customer nor the seller is supposed to say anything. The thickness of the steak is indicated by a finger placed against the huge slab of fish. A proper Lees Wharf swordfish is about as wide as a small tree, about 13 or 14 inches across, and at its center (the most desirable section) about 7 inches high.

Since swordfish is very delicate, it is broiled only on one side, never turned. It's a good idea to cook it in the same ovenproof dish in which you serve it.

Fresh swordfish steak	*Lemon*
Salt, pepper	*Worcestershire sauce and cream*
Butter	*(optional)*

Slice the black skin from 2 pounds of swordfish sliced 1½ inches thick. Sprinkle with salt and freshly ground black pepper. Dot generously with butter. Place on a preheated broiling pan or ovenproof platter and broil about 2 inches from the heat. Cook 10 minutes on one side only; do not turn. Test for doneness by inserting a fork in the thickest part of the fish. The meat should be moist but not glassy-looking. If it doesn't seem done you can broil a little longer or finish it by turning on the oven and baking it for a few minutes. Be careful not to overcook; the top of the fish should be golden brown with no blackish edges.

Serve with lemon wedges and, if you want to be traditional, pour over the fish 2 tablespoons heavy cream mixed with a dash of Worcestershire sauce. Most people who take the Worcestershire sauce and cream omit the lemon. A proper accompaniment would be parsley potatoes, sliced beefsteak tomatoes marinated in French dressing, and fresh corn on the cob. *Serves 4 or 5.*

TROUT IN WHITE WINE

Chef René Verdon made his White House debut with a luncheon given by President Kennedy for Prime Minister Macmillan of Britain and sixteen other guests. "The verdict," according to newspaper reports, "was that there was nothing like French cooking to promote good Anglo-American relations." It was a perfect luncheon for early spring: trout cooked in chablis and served with Mayonnaise Vincent, roast filet of beef au jus garnished with artichoke bottoms Beaucaire (filled with a fondue of tomatoes simmered in butter), giant asparagus with Sauce Maltaise, and for dessert a Vacherin, or meringue shell filled with chocolate ice cream covered with fresh raspberries. The trout is prepared in the following manner:

Trout	*Onion, Bouquet garni*
Salt, pepper	*Gelatin*
Chablis or a California Pinot	*Lemon*
Chardonnay	*Watercress*

To serve 4, you will need 4 to 5 pounds of fish. In France the trout are usually prepared with the head on, but you can do as you like. Clean the trout and rub with salt and pepper inside and out. Cover completely with a court bouillon made by heating together 3 cups white wine, ½ teaspoon salt, a sprinkling of pepper, 1 medium onion chopped, and a bouquet garni (2 or 3 sprigs parsley, ½ bay leaf, and a pinch of thyme). Cover and cook slowly but do not allow to boil. When the fish flakes off easily at the touch of a fork, remove carefully from the court bouillon and reduce the liquid to half, by boiling uncovered. Soak 2 tablespoons gelatin in ½ cup water for 5 minutes and then stir it into hot court bouillon until dissolved. Allow to cool in the refrigerator until syrupy.

Remove the skin from one side of the trout only and arrange the fish on a long platter. Glaze with the cooled court bouillon and chill in refrigerator until needed. Decorate with thinly sliced lemon and bouquets of fresh watercress.

MAYONNAISE VINCENT

The excellent sauce served with the trout above is a type of green mayonnaise flavored with herbs, made verdant with watercress and spinach, and studded with capers or pickled nasturtium buds.

Spinach	*Capers*
Watercress	*Chives*
Lemon juice	*Chervil or dill*
Mayonnaise	

Rub ¼ cup fresh spinach leaves and ¼ cup fresh watercress leaves (but not the stems) through a fine sieve or place in blender along with 2 tablespoons lemon juice. Fold puréed greens and lemon juice into 2 cups mayonnaise, add 1 tablespoon coarsely chopped capers, 1 tablespoon chopped chives, and 1 tablespoon chopped chervil or dill. Chill at least 2 hours. This is equally delicious with cold trout or salmon. *Makes enough for 4 to 6.*

MALTAISE SAUCE

While we're on the subject of sauces, here is another of the excellent ones that appeared on the Kennedy's dining table. It's a variant of Hollandaise and was originally made with the juice of blood oranges, which gave a rosy color. Now we approximate the color with a couple of drops of red food coloring. This sauce is superb with white asparagus.

Hollandaise sauce (bought or homemade)	*concentrate*
	Orange rind
Orange juice or frozen orange	*Red food coloring*

Make 2 cups Hollandaise according to the usual recipe or buy it in a jar. When it is just ready to serve, stir in 3 tablespoons orange juice or 1 tablespoon frozen orange concentrate, thawed. Add ½ teaspoon finely grated orange rind and a couple of drops of red food coloring, blend well. *Makes 2 cups.*

STEVENSON'S SHRIMP AND ARTICHOKE

Historically only one defeated Presidential candidate had been linked to a culinary specialty. That was Tilden. A cake named for him is still popular in the South. His unique distinction must now be shared by Adlai Stevenson, whose shrimp and artichoke casserole was served to President Kennedy and UN Secretary-General U Thant at Mr. Stevenson's apartment in the Waldorf Towers.

The recipe was published in the newspapers after the luncheon and in the words of Mrs. Viola Reardy, his housekeeper, "created such a to-do, you can't believe it." Dainty and soft-spoken, Mrs. Reardy was with the Stevenson family for many years. She preferred to cook in the large kitchen at Libertyville, Illinois, but she brought with her to New York not only the Stevenson family recipes but a good deal of the savor of the Illinois countryside.

President Kennedy found this dish delicious and you will too.

Butter	*Cooked shrimp*
Flour	*Mushrooms*
Milk	*Sherry wine*
Heavy cream	*Worcestershire sauce*
Salt and pepper	*Parmesan cheese*
Artichoke hearts	*Paprika (optional)*

Melt 4½ tablespoons butter and blend in 4½ tablespoons flour. Cook over low heat, stirring constantly. Add ¾ cup warm milk and then ¾ cup heavy cream very gradually, stirring all the time, with a wire whisk, until thick and smooth. Season to taste with salt and freshly ground black pepper.

Drain one No. 2 can artichoke hearts or cook one package frozen artichoke hearts according to directions. Arrange artichokes over the bottom of buttered baking dish.

Cook 1 pound fresh shrimp. Remove shells and devein. Arrange on top of artichokes. Slice ¼ pound mushrooms and sauté in 2 tablespoons butter for 6 minutes. Spoon mushrooms over shrimp and artichokes. Flavor the cream sauce with ¼ cup (or less) dry sherry and 1 tablespoon Worcestershire sauce. Pour this over shrimp, mushrooms, and artichokes. Sprinkle with 4 tablespoons freshly grated Parmesan cheese and a little paprika if desired. Bake 20 to 30 minutes at 375° F. and serve from its own baking dish. *Serves 4.*

MRS. REARDY'S CASSEROLE, QUICKENED

An equally delicious version, much quicker to make and not quite so rich, may be concocted from quick-frozen shrimp and a can of mushrooms. The method is quite simple.

Condensed mushroom soup	*Frozen cooked shrimp*
Sherry	*Canned sliced mushrooms*
Worcestershire sauce	*Parmesan cheese*
Frozen artichoke hearts	*Paprika (optional)*

To a can of condensed mushroom soup, add ¼ cup sherry and 1 tablespoon Worcestershire sauce. (No other seasoning is necessary.) Arrange 1 package frozen artichoke hearts, cooked, at bottom of buttered baking dish; scatter 1 package cooked frozen shrimp over them and add a 4-ounce tin broiled-in-butter sliced mushrooms with their juice. Cover with the mushroom soup–sherry–Worcestershire mixture. Sprinkle with 4 tablespoons grated Parmesan cheese and a little paprika if desired. Bake at 375° F., about 20 minutes or until bubbling hot and lightly browned. *Serves 4.*

Either version of this dish is delicious served with rice (either wild or tame) and a green vegetable like leaf spinach.

ASPARAGUS VINAIGRETTE

Jacqueline Kennedy was fond of serving ordinary vegetables prepared in out-of-the-ordinary fashion. A perfect example is this simple but rather different way of serving asparagus.

Olive oil	*Vinegar*
Parsley	*Salt, pepper*
Chives	*Asparagus*

Combine 3 tablespoons olive oil, 4 tablespoons chopped parsley, 2 tablespoons chopped chives, 2 tablespoons vinegar, 1 teaspoon salt, ⅛ teaspoon pepper. Beat with rotary beater until well blended. Serve over 1½ pounds cooked and chilled fresh or frozen asparagus. *Serves 6.*

ENTRECÔTE

The Kennedy dining table gained some of its reputation for exquisite French cooking because of the marvelous beef dishes that appeared there. For example, Mrs. Kennedy served an entrecote (also called a rib steak) pan-sautéed in its own fat, seasoned with salt and pepper, and with a sauce of melted butter, chopped parsley, and lemon juice. A garnish of watercress is the final touch.

TOURNEDOS HÉLOÏSE

The tournedos Héloïse that appeared often on the White House menu were individual filet mignons, browned in butter in a heavy skillet, served atop an artichoke bottom, and garnished with pâté de foie gras and a truffle slice. A ring of these filets can be arranged on a heated platter the center of the dish filled with creamed mushrooms. Usually the tournedos were served with Madeira sauce, which is a brown gravy, or Sauce Espagnol with Madeira added. Some people like the tiny bits and pieces scraped from the pan to be left in the sauce, but classic tradition insists they be strained out, and this was done at the White House.

CONTREFILET RÔTI, SAUCE BORDELAISE

Another White House favorite was termed a Contrefilet Roti with Sauce Bordelaise. To duplicate this dish as it was served have your butcher cut a so-called shell steak about 3 inches thick. The meat is roasted in a 350° F. oven 10 to 15 minutes per pound. Sometimes the meat is wrapped in fat, which should be removed during the last 10 minutes of roasting. It should be served rare. What gives this contrefilet its ultimate distinction is the Sauce Bordelaise.

SAUCE BORDELAISE

Sauté in butter celery, carrots, onions, shallots, bay leaves, thyme, parsley, pepper, cubed beef, and a few pieces of pork skin. Remove the excess fat, if any; sprinkle with flour and set for about 15 minutes in a hot oven about 400° F. Then add brown stock and red Bordeaux wine (twice as much stock as wine) and cook slowly on top the stove for about 3 hours, stirring occasionally. Pass through a fine sieve and add a few bits of butter. The resulting sauce should be thick and dark and rich.

If this is too time-consuming, try an Easy Bordelaise, quickly made by adding 1 crushed shallot and ½ cup claret to 1 (10½ oz.) can beef gravy. Simmer 15 minutes. Stir in bit by bit 2 tablespoons butter. Serve with a poker face.

FILET DE BOEUF WITH SAUTEED VEGETABLES

Still another use of filet mignon is in a dish the White House called filet de boeuf with sautéed vegetables. To produce a delicious dish for 4, broil 4 6-ounce filets 4 to 5 minutes on each side. Sauté 2 cups potato balls (made with a melon scoop) in butter for 10 minutes. Add ¼ pound sliced mushrooms, and sauté with the potatoes 5 minutes longer. Add to these salt, pepper, and ¼ cup sherry. Simmer 2 minutes longer, then arrange over the broiled filets.

POULET CHASSEUR

During their first summer in the White House, President and Mrs. Kennedy gave a party at George Washington's country house, Mount Vernon, in honor of the President of Pakistan, Mohammed Ayub Khun. About 140 guests were transported down the Potomac in four yachts. On arrival, they were greeted by American mint juleps and French cuisine. Music was provided by the National Symphony Orchestra, the Lester Lanin Trio (who played for all the White House parties), and the Air Force Strolling Strings, who prompted the comment "the Red Coats are coming, with instruments yet."

Dinner was served in a tent pavilion rigged for the occasion by Tiffany's of New York, who also took care of the special lighting.

The menu was a problem in logistics, according to Letitia Baldridge, Mrs. Kennedy's social secretary. René Verdon, the White House French chef, discussed at length with Mrs. Kennedy the pros and cons of various main dishes. In the end they selected a Poulet Chasseur for which he developed a special sauce which would mellow and deepen in flavor during the trek from the White House kitchens to Mount Vernon.

The guests and the press were ecstatic in praise of the Mount Vernon hegira. The idea had occurred to Mrs. Kennedy during official visits to Europe that spring. She had been so delighted by the entertainments offered the Presidential party at the Versailles Gardens outside Paris and at the Chambrun Palace in Vienna that she wanted to arrange something similar.

Despite a backwash of criticism from some who questioned the cost of the entertainment and others who wondered why Mrs. Kennedy with all her interest in the American past should have served a French dish at historic Mount Vernon, the public in general was enthralled by the novelty of the main course. We like the fact that it travels so well. Here is the recipe, scaled down to serve 6.

Chicken	*White wine*
Lemon	*Brown sauce*
Salt, pepper	*Tomato sauce*
Butter	*Cognac*
Mushrooms	*Parsley*
Shallots (or onion)	*Tarragon*
Garlic	

Disjoint 2 tender young chickens, rub the skins with lemon and season with salt and pepper. Melt ¼ pound butter in a large skillet and when the butter is hot and bubbly, but not brown, add the chicken pieces a few at a time and brown them quickly on both sides. This should take about 10 to 12 minutes. Since white meat cooks more quickly than dark meat, it's a good idea to remove the white-meat pieces first. Place the sautéed chicken in a heatproof casserole that could come to the table and cover with Chasseur Sauce. Cover the pan and continue cooking about ½ hour either over low heat or in a moderate (350° F.) oven.

Chasseur sauce is made by slicing ½ pound mushrooms and cooking them in 4 tablespoons butter for 2 or 3 minutes, or until tender. Add ½ teaspoon salt, ⅛ teaspoon pepper, and cook a little longer until mushrooms are lightly browned. Add 2 finely chopped shallots or 1 small finely chopped onion, 1 clove garlic, and 1 cup dry white wine, and cook until reduced to about half its original quantity. Add 1 cup good light brown sauce (canned beef gravy will do), 1 tablespoon tomato sauce, 1 tablespoon cognac, and 1 teaspoon each chopped parsley and fresh tarragon (or ½ teaspoon of the dry herbs). Pour this over chicken and finish cooking as above. At serving time, sprinkle with more parsley and serve with crusty French bread or rolls—these are a must. The wine should be a well-chilled white wine. *Serves 6.*

NOTE: A 4-ounce can sliced mushrooms may be used. Drain and add liquid to the chicken.

POULARDE MAISON BLANCHE

The first lesson Chef Verdon had when studying the likes and dislikes of the Kennedys in the kitchen of La Caravelle Restaurant prior to departing for the White House as chef was the preparation of chicken in champagne sauce, a great favorite with J.F.K. and a dish which still appears from time to time on the Caravelle menu as Poularde Maison Blanche. Here it is, altered ever so slightly for the home cook.

Chicken necks and gizzards (or	*Butter*
Chicken bones)	*Flour*
Water	*Mushrooms*
Leeks	*Lemon*
Celery	*Heavy cream*
Carrots	*Champagne*
Onion	*Shallots*
Cloves	*Parsley*
Thyme	*Chickens*
Bay leaves	*Rice*
Garlic	*Raisins*
Peppercorns	

To start with, make a chicken broth by boiling together 4 chicken necks and 4 gizzards or 1 pound of chicken bones in 4 quarts of water. When it comes to a boil, decant it into another container and wash out the pot. Then start again with 2 leeks, 3 branches of celery, 3 carrots, 1 onion studded with 4 cloves, 1 pinch of thyme, 3 bay leaves, 3 unpeeled garlic cloves, and a few peppercorns. Simmer for 1 hour, skimming off fat occasionally, then strain. You should have a little more than 2 quarts of broth.

Melt 4 ounces butter and stir in ½ cup flour. Cook over low heat, stirring continuously, for 5 minutes. Add slowly 4 cups chicken broth, stirring vigorously with wire whisk. Cook this gently for 30 minutes. The result is a chicken velouté.

Clean and boil 32 small mushroom caps in salted water with a little lemon juice and 1 tablespoon butter for 5 minutes or longer, and drain and set aside.

Melt 2 tablespoons butter, add 1 teaspoon chopped onion, and cook a few minutes. Add 2 cups washed rice and ½ cup white raisins. Mix. Add 4 cups hot chicken broth, salt to taste, and bring to a boil. Cover with a circle of buttered brown or waxed paper the size of the pan, cover, and bake at 350° F. for 18 minutes. Remove to a cold container and mix in a little butter with a fork.

Roast 2 chickens (about 2½ pounds each) in a 350° F. oven 25 to 30 minutes. Remove from oven and add 6 shallots, 6 mushroom stems, and 4 parsley stems. Return to oven and finish roasting (about ½ hour). When done remove the chickens and skim the fat. Add 1 cup champagne and reduce liquid by about ⅔. Add the chicken velouté and 1 pint heavy cream. Cook 20 minutes over low heat, strain, and add 1 tablespoon butter. Sauce must be light-colored.

Arrange bed of rice on platter. Top with chickens and the mushrooms. Pour champagne sauce over all.

POULARDE MAISON BLANCHE SIMPLIFIED

To achieve nearly the same results with a great deal less work, bake cut-up chicken pieces in a 350° F. oven about 30 minutes. Remove from oven and add shallots, mushroom stems, and parsley as above and return to the oven to finish baking. Meanwhile soak white raisins for ½ hour and then cook them in canned chicken broth for 5 minutes. Prepare instant rice according to directions, using broth with raisins for your liquid.

Prepare a sauce of canned chicken gravy and heavy cream—half as much cream as gravy. When chicken is cooked, remove from the pan and set it on a bed of rice. Add 1 cup champagne to the pan in which the chicken was cooked and reduce the liquid by about ⅔. Add the chicken gravy and cook 20 minutes over low heat. Strain and add 1 tablespoon butter in little dabs. Sprinkle chicken with contents of large can sliced mushrooms (drained) and pour over this the champagne sauce.

OMELETTE RENAISSANCE

Another delicious—and this time an easy—way to serve chicken, is this chicken-filled omelette of which Mrs. Kennedy is still fond. Here you may use a chicken velouté sauce as above or canned chicken gravy.

Eggs	*Mushrooms*
Parsley	*Butter*
Chives	*Chicken velouté*
Salt, pepper	*Hollandaise sauce*
Diced chicken (cooked)	*Whipped cream*
Tomatoes	

Beat 8 eggs mixed with a pinch of chopped parsley and a pinch of chopped chives. Season with salt and pepper. Cook as an omelette and, when folding, fill with a mixture of 1 cup diced cooked chicken, 2 fresh tomatoes, stewed, 4 mushrooms diced and sautéed in butter. Cover with a combination of 1 cup chicken velouté mixed with 2 tablespoons Hollandaise sauce and 2 tablespoons whipped cream. Glaze under broiler about ½ minute. *Serves 4.*

CHICKEN HASH À LA REINE

Another chicken favorite was the chicken hash the Kennedys often had when staying at their favorite hotel in New York, the Carlyle. In some respects it is like the recipe above, since it uses a chicken velouté (or canned chicken gravy) and Hollandaise.

Chicken	*Sherry*
Onion	*Heavy cream*
Carrot	*Chicken velouté (or canned chicken*
Celery	*gravy)*
Salt, Butter	*Hollandaise sauce*

Boil a 2-pound spring chicken for 30 minutes with 1 onion, 1 carrot, 2 stalks celery, and salt. Cool and cut the chicken into small dice. (Or use 2 cups diced canned chicken.) Put chicken in saucepan with 3 ounces butter; let it get warm and add 2 tablespoons sherry. Keep on low heat until completely reduced. Pour in ½ pint heavy cream and heat but do not boil. Add 2 tablespoons velouté sauce or canned chicken gravy and 2 tablespoons Hollandaise sauce. Stir well and serve. Excellent served with rice, its usual accompaniment. *Serves 6.*

MRS. TAWES'S MARYLAND CRAB CAKES

Such a hullabaloo was engendered! In January 1963 Senator Jay Glen Beall, Republican of Maryland, made a gastronomic attack on the Democratic administration. He charged that under its aegis the Maryland crab cakes at the Senate Restaurant were an insult to his state. A few days after this public declaration, Senator Beall arose in the Senate and announced that he had received support from a Democrat—the wife of Maryland Governor J. Millard Tawes. He waved the letter from Avalynne Tawes aloft in a second condemnation of what he called "spurious Maryland crab cakes." It is not known whether the Senate dining room has changed its recipe as a result, but here is the authentic version, according to Maryland crab-cake fanciers.

Fresh crabmeat (Canned crabmeat is often used, but nobody ever admits it.)	*Mayonnaise*
	Flour
	Breadcrumbs } *or cracker crumbs*
Salt	*Deep fat*
White pepper	*Horseradish mustard (or dry*
Eggs	*mustard)*
Mustard	

Place a pound of crabmeat in a mixing bowl. Add ½ teaspoon salt, ½ teaspoon white pepper, 2 beaten eggs, 1 teaspoon mustard, 2 tablespoons mayonnaise. Mix well but lightly. Divide into 4 cakes and shape. Dip into flour, then into beaten egg, then into breadcrumbs, or simply dip in cracker crumbs. Fry in deep hot fat at least ¾ inch deep at 370° F., browning on both sides. Drain on paper towels and serve very hot. *Serves 4.*

BOMBE GLACÉE MANDARIN

This bombe is a wonderful ending to a meal in which a chicken dish is the main course. Mrs. Kennedy served it often—a fairly light but handsome dessert and appropriate for any season.

Vanilla ice cream
Sponge cake or ladyfingers
Grand Marnier
Orange or tangerine sherbet

Fresh oranges
Fresh tangerines or canned Man-
darin oranges

Spread ice cream inside a mold to a thickness of about ¾ inch. Spread one layer of diced sponge cake or ladyfingers over the ice cream. Moisten cake lightly with Grand Marnier. Fill rest of mold with sherbet. Put in freezer and leave until very firm. At serving time, unmold upside down and decorate with slices of chilled fruit.

TUILES

Lacy rolled cookies have long been a White House favorite. When the Kennedys and their French chef René Verdon arrived at 1600 Pennsylvania Avenue the cookies continued to be served, but under a new name—Tuiles. Whatever you call them, they are delicious, delicate sweets.

Butter
Sugar
Eggs

Cake flour
Almond extract
Blanched almonds, finely chopped

Cream together in a bowl 1 cup butter and 1¾ cups fine sugar. Add 5 eggs, one by one, and then 2⅔ cups sifted cake flour. Stir well and add 2 teaspoons almond extract. Pipe this mixture onto a baking tin in rounds with the aid of a pastry bag. The cookies spread, so leave plenty of room, about 3 inches between them. Bake at 350° F. about 10 to 12 minutes. While still warm, bend each one over a rolling pin so they are given the shape of curved tiles (tuiles). *Makes about 6 dozen.*

HOT FRUIT COMPOTE FOR 100

Mrs. Kennedy is reported to have served this dessert to a rather large gathering —and with great success—but there's no verification for this. Even though the pedigree of this recipe is in doubt, its value is not. Should you ever need to serve a light and unusual dessert to a hundred guests, this is ideal.

Canned apricots
Peaches
Canned pineapple chunks
Pitted Bing cherries
Oranges

Lemons
Light brown sugar
Nutmeg
Sour cream

Combine 16 cups canned apricots cut in large pieces, 16 cups sliced peaches, 16 cups pineapple chunks, 32 cups Bing cherries. Drain the fruits and save the juices. Grate rind of 16 oranges and 16 lemons into 8 cups light brown sugar. Then peel oranges and lemons and cut into very thin slices.

In a baking pan put layers of the fruit, sugar-and-rind mixture, and a sprinkling of nutmeg. Continue until all fruit is used. Pour mixed juice over fruit until it comes halfway up the pan. Bake at 350° F. for about ½ hour, or until fruit is very hot. Serve in individual compote dishes or sherbet cups with a dab of sour cream on each.

HOT FRUIT COMPOTE FOR 8 TO 10

The ingredients are the same as for the recipe above. But scale down the proportions: Use 1½ cups apricots, peaches, pineapple, 3 cups pitted cherries, 2 oranges, 2 lemons, and 1½ cups light brown sugar. The procedure is the same. The results . . . equally delicious!

NEW FRONTIER CHOCOLATE MOUSSE

One of the White House parties that may go down in history was the dinner given the night Colonel John Glenn made his triple orbit around the world. Officially the guests of honor were Vice-President Johnson, House Speaker McCormick, and Chief Justice Warren, but it was agreed by all present that the most fervent toasts were to the astronaut.

The menu was outstandingly elegant. Only four courses, according to New Frontier traditions, but somewhat richer and more elaborate than usual for chef René Verdon. There was seafood Île de France, roast duck à l'orange, wild rice, a green salad served with a veal filet in aspic, and this chocolate mousse.

Confectioner's sugar	*Sugar*
Unsweetened cooking chocolate	*Vanilla*
Milk	*Salt*
Unflavored gelatin	*Heavy cream*
Water	

Combine ½ cup confectioner's sugar with 2 one ounce squares unsweetened chocolate, melted. Gradually add 1 cup heated milk and simmer over low heat, stirring constantly, until mixture almost reaches boiling point and chocolate is well dissolved. Remove from heat and stir in ¾ cup granulated sugar, ¼ teaspoon salt, a teaspoon vanilla, and 1 envelope gelatin softened in 3 tablespoons cold water. Continue to stir until gelatin is completely dissolved. Chill until slightly thickened. Beat with rotary beater until light and fluffy. Fold in 2 cups heavy cream, whipped. Pour into a 2-quart serving dish or individual dishes and chill thoroughly. *Serves 6 or 8.*

BOMBE GLACÉE COPPELIA

At a state dinner for the President of the Sudan, which was followed by Shakespeare in the East Room, the dessert on the menu shared honors with the Shakespearean players in the nation's newspapers. It was a Bombe Glacé Coppelia—coffee ice cream in a mold around a center of praline ice cream, garnished with marrons (candied chestnuts), and served with a marron sauce.

Hundreds of letters flooded the White House asking for the bombe recipe.

Coffee ice cream
Vanilla ice cream
Pecan pralines or butter, sugar,
salt, pecans

Marrons glacés
Sugar, water, butter,
rum/or vanilla
Heavy cream

Chill a 1-quart melon mold and rinse in very cold water. Line the mold with coffee ice cream about ¾ inch thick. In the center place a neatly shaped ball of praline ice cream, and fill remaining space with more coffee ice cream. Praline ice cream can be made by adding a cup of finely crushed pralines to 1 quart vanilla ice cream. Pralines can be bought or made by rubbing a heavy frying pan lightly with butter, adding ½ cup sugar and stirring over moderate heat until the sugar melts. Then add more sugar, half a cup at a time, stirring constantly, until the result is a clear brown syrup. Add a few grains salt and as much chopped pecans as you have syrup. Pour into lightly buttered pan, cool, and break up with rolling pin. Sift or not, as you please. If you are rushed, use bought peanut brittle to make your praline powder, but it won't be exactly the same.

The mold, filled to overflowing with the two ice creams, should be covered with its own lid or two thicknesses of aluminum foil pressed down tight and tied.

Place mold in freezer and leave until thoroughly frozen. Unmold on a chilled plate. Decorate with marrons glacé and ribbons of whipped cream, if desired.

Pass the marron sauce separately. It is made by cutting up half a dozen marrons glacés into small bits (using the chopped marrons that come in jars) and combining with a syrup made of a cup granulated sugar and a cup water cooked together until it spins a thread or registers 230° F. on a candy thermometer. Stir in little by little 4 tablespoons butter and when that is melted, 3 or 4 tablespoons rum or 1 teaspoon vanilla. Pass warm or cold to spoon over bombe. *Serves 6.*

MACAROON SOUFFLÉ

A private nonofficial dinner dance given for the Stephen Smiths, JFK's sister and brother-in-law, in February 1962 let loose a storm of publicity when it became known that both John and Jackie had danced the twist, until four-thirty in the morning. The menu as well as the guest list and entertainment were widely publicized. For dessert a macaroon soufflé was served and it elicited high praise from at least one knowledgeable guest—the French Ambassador.

Eggs	*Macaroons (almond)*
Sugar	*Heavy cream*
Unflavored gelatin	*Chocolate sauce*
Rum	

Combine in a bowl 4 eggs, 3 egg yolks, and ½ cup sugar. Beat with electric beater until very thick and pale in color. Or you can put the bowl over hot water and beat vigorously with a rotary beater. Soften 2 tablespoons gelatin in ¼ cup rum and dissolve it over hot water. Add the gelatin and rum mixture to the beaten eggs, along with 1 cup crushed macaroons. Mix well. Fold in 1 stiffly beaten cup cream.

Brush a 6-inch band of wax paper or aluminum foil with salad oil or sweet butter and tie like a collar around the soufflé dish. (An 8-inch soufflé dish is best for this recipe.) Fill the dish with the mixture and chill until set.

At serving time, carefully remove paper and decorate with finely crushed macaroons and swirls of whipped cream. Serve with a thin rum-flavored chocolate sauce with or without ½ cup whipped heavy cream folded into it. *Serves 8.*

An interesting variation is the substitution of 1 cup sweetened chestnut purée for the crushed macaroons.

BABA AUX FRAISES

A wonderful and rather elaborate dessert for strawberry time is Mrs. Kennedy's favorite baba aux fraises.

Dry yeast	*Salt*
Water	*Eggs*
All-purpose flour	*Currants*
Sugar	*Rum*
Butter or margarine	*Strawberries*

Sprinkle 1 package dry yeast over ½ cup lukewarm water and stir until dissolved. Add ½ cup flour and 1 tablespoon sugar. Beat until smooth. Cover and let rise in warm place about 45 minutes or until double in size. Beat ¼ cup sugar into ½ cup softened butter until fluffy, adding sugar gradually. Add ½ teaspoon salt, 3 well-beaten eggs, 1½ cups flour, 3 tablespoons currants, and the yeast mixture. Beat for 5 minutes. Pour mixture into well-greased 3-quart ring mold. Cover and let rise in warm place about an hour, or until double in bulk. Bake at 350° F., 40 minutes. Cool 5 minutes and invert cake onto serving dish.

Combine 1 cup sugar and 1 cup water in saucepan and boil 5 minutes over moderate heat. Cool and stir in ¼ cup rum. Spoon this sauce over cake. Slice most of 1 quart strawberries and sweeten with ⅓ cup sugar. Place sliced strawberries in center of cake and garnish with perfect whole berries. *Serves 8.*

APRIL DÉSIRE

The correct, formal name for this dessert is a Vacherin. It is a large crown of meringue, generally made up of several small meringue shells mounted one on top of the other on a sweet-pastry base, forming a kind of bowl decorated with meringue piped through a pastry bag. The center is filled with ice cream.

This Vacherin, or April Desire, was the dessert served to Prime Minister Macmillan at the luncheon that marked Chef René Verdon's White House debut.

To make a simplified version of April Desire—and achieve a really beautiful party dessert "without really trying"—you can utilize meringue shells from the bakery.

Chocolate ice cream	*Candied violets*
Meringue shells	*Candied mint leaves (optional)*
Fresh raspberries	*Sugar*
Heavy cream	

Fill a ring mold with 2 quarts chocolate ice cream and freeze until firm. Turn out, upside down, onto a chilled platter. Press around the sides a dozen or more small meringue shells (or macaroons). Use enough to make a kind of fence around the ice cream. Cover the top of the ice cream with raspberries and fill the center of the ring with sweetened whipped cream. Decorate with candied violets and mint leaves. *This serves 12 and causes gasps of pleasure.*

XXXVI

The White Ranch-House

We have seen throughout these chapters how each President has set his own style. Often it has differed radically from that of his immediate predecessor, almost as though the President is determined to show, "See, I am my own self, not a shadow."

Nowhere has this been so strikingly demonstrated as in the contrast between the Kennedy and Johnson administrations. In spite of the powerful shadow of a much-admired martyred President, it did not take Lyndon Baines Johnson long to impress his own identity on the nation's consciousness.

Critics imply that the much-touted Texas simplicity of LBJ is deceptive, that in fact he is a more complex individual than he or his press representatives would have us believe. Be that as it might when it comes to politicking, in matters culinary there is little doubt that simplicity rules the Johnson roost—or ranch.

While certain Presidential aides seem to regard queries about the President's food preferences as much off-limits as the goings-on at Los Alamos or troop movements in Vietnam, we have managed to ferret out a good many Presidential "secrets."

For one thing, spies tell us that President Johnson is a nibbler. At receptions and cocktail parties, he has been known to stand before a bowl of deep-fried shrimp and demolish them practically single-handed. One suspects that such compulsive nibbling has echoes of the regime of William Howard Taft. Like Taft,

LBJ must oblige his wife and doctors by dieting. Since his serious heart attack in 1955 (56?), it has been imperative for him to regulate his weight.

One suspects, however, that at receptions and public affairs, where his well-intentioned wife cannot enforce her watch, the President allows himself to indulge a bit in foods he enjoys. There is another side to the nibbling coin, however. On the frantic schedule the President must maintain, his meals are often irregularly scheduled, and sometimes the reception tidbits take the place of dinner altogether. There seems to be a complusiveness to the President's eating habits, reminiscent of a small boy's exposure to a cooky jar. Stopping becomes very difficult. Witness the opening of the baseball series one spring. We have no official confirmation or denial of the number of hot dogs the President is supposed to have consumed, but eyewitness observers have testified that Mr. Johnson ate at least one dog per inning. Now, even if the game didn't go into extra innings, that's a lot of wieners! From the meat-industry point of view, the Johnson performance has probably done more for hot dogs than anything since the day the Roosevelts served the lowly (but lovely) beasties to the King and Queen of England. What the medical profession thinks of such indulgence we won't venture to say.

Of course it is no secret in Washington that with the Johnsons steak, of all foods, reigns supreme. It is served for breakfast, for lunch, and for state dinners (though certainly not all in the same day). The President once said: "All my life I have drawn sustenance from the rivers and from the hills of my native state." He may not have been referring to food, but in all his years in Washington he has shown a marked preference for the foods that abound in his native Texas, and none more so than a good hearty Texas filet of beef.

In fact, at the Presidential inaugural luncheon, Texas heart of filet mignon was served. Afterward Democratic John McCormick, Speaker of the House of Representatives, was asked about the lunch. With partisan fervor he pronounced it "delicious," adding that the Texas filet was "wonderful." Equally partisan, Republican Charles Halleck, Minority Leader of the House, avowed "I prefer New York sirloin." Partisanship, amusingly, dominated comments on the dessert as well. McCormick said that it, a Bavarian Cream listed on the menu as "President's Delight," was delicious. Halleck dismissed it as "a kind of glorified custard pudding."

Inauguration day proved a big steak day for the President. Like a child who is allowed all his favorite foods on his birthday, the President, whether by choice or chance, actually did manage to have steak twice on that big day in his life. No, not at breakfast. That meal was a light one, served on trays in the Presidential bedroom. But the dinner before the big inaugural ball was a private one, in which bouillon, *sirloin,* spinach, potatoes, mixed green salad, and Baked Alaska were served.

Johnsonian hospitality was amply demonstrated during the pre-inaugural-week festivities. Twenty-two guests, friends and relatives from "down home" Texas way, were invited to stay at the White House for the week. Mrs. Johnson, in addition to being a charming and gracious hostess, is a well-organized housekeeper; it was not difficult for her to plan for the extra guests and avoid confusion. Because of the varied schedules and quick timing involved, meals were served in the guests' bedrooms (using the historic Benjamin Harrison china) on trays or buffet-style downstairs. The guests were delighted at the service and extra attention during such a busy time, but the staff doubtless sighed with relief at the post-inaugural return to normalcy.

A typical Lady Bird Johnson touch was the huge supply of deer-meat sausage on hand to make fellow Texans feel at home in the Presidential house.

The President's food preferences seem to veer toward simple classics, well-prepared by the family cook of twenty-odd years, Mrs. Zephyr Wright. Old friends of the Johnson family insist that Mrs. Wright is one of the country's great cooks, able to shift from corn pone to a chocolate soufflé without batting an eye. (Both dishes are LBJ favorites, incidentally, though since he has had to become calorie-conscious in recent years, Mrs. Wright's menus have emphasized simpler foods.) Friends consider it their great good fortune "to come over for a little pot luck," as Lady Bird puts it. Mrs. Wright's idea of pot luck is anybody else's Sunday-best dinner.

As a native Southerner from Texas herself, Mrs. Wright is in a position to know the Johnson tastes exactly. Rich foods once dominated the menu, but now low-calorie dishes have taken precedence. The President is known to be very much the boss in his own house, and nowhere is this more evident that at the table. Mrs. Wright cooks what the President wants, or should have, instead of trying to appeal to all members of the family. Fortunately, through chance or conditioning, the feminine side of the family generally like Father's choice.

When it comes to his diet, the President jokingly says that Mrs. Wright is boss, though he doesn't always accept her dictums without a certain amount of grumbling. One night, presumably after certain complaints that his favorite foods were being denied him, LBJ found this note from Zephyr under his dinner plate:

Mr. President, you have been my boss for a number of years and you always tell me you want to lose weight, and yet you never do very much to help yourself. Now I am going to be your boss for a change. Eat what I put in front of you, and don't ask for any more and don't complain.

The next night, the Johnsons were giving a diplomatic reception. In a conversation with Senator William Fulbright, who sometime earlier in a lecture had expressed the fear that "we are succumbing to the arrogance of power," the President denied Fulbright's assertion:

"A man can hardly have an arrogance of power when he gets a note from his cook, talking up to him like this," and he pulled Zephyr's note from his pocket and read it aloud. "If and when I feel arrogance of power, Zephyr will take it out of me."

When a huge Texas steak isn't on the table, Southern fried chicken often is, along with spoonbread, popovers, or other home-baked hot rolls. Mrs. Wright makes brownies frequently, but the President's very favorite dessert is an old-fashioned homemade ice cream, made with cooked custard and fruit, churned by hand or in an electric freezer. Like her husband, Lady Bird favors simple dishes, and is partial to deer bacon, pickled okra, turkey dressing, and spareribs.

All the Johnsons are great milk consumers. After the blessing at the beginning of each meal, Mrs. Johnson usually asks "Sweet milk or buttermilk?" and pours from the appropriate pitcher. It is almost a ritual. LBJ himself is a buttermilk addict, but for weight reason limits himself reluctantly to one glass per day. When the Johnson daughters were living at home, Mrs. Wright would keep a good supply of low-calorie soft drinks on hand. Difficult as weight watching is for LBJ himself, he insists on it for his wife and daughters, preferring to see the female side of the family svelte and slim.

Maintaining such svelteness is not easy—to judge by a report by Lee Winfrey, one of the press entourage who accompanied Mrs. Johnson on one of her many trips around the country. It seems that in St. Petersburg, Florida, a chef with a more highly developed imagination than cultivated palate concocted a "Lady Bird Delite" as a tribute to the First Lady.

Lee Winfrey described the creation: "Brown [chef Harry W. Brown] started with a cream puff in the shape of a swan. He topped this with peanut butter ice cream, which he claims to have invented. Over this he squirted whipped cream and sprinkled confectioner's sugar. This glob he set floating in a pool of papaya sauce." The appearance of this spectacle left many of the guests numbed. But Lady Bird, known for her indomitable spirit, tackled the "creation" and ate every bite.

" 'By God,' said a local politician among the guests. 'That woman's got my vote. Anybody who could eat that thing without flinching could be elected President herself.' "

We cite this as an example of the culinary astonishments committed for the entertainment of the Presidential family. And being in the public eye, they must do their best to cope. No one could deny that Mrs. Johnson deserves an *A* for coping.

A Presidential wife must cope in other ways too, for mealtime, especially with President Johnson, is always uncertain. His schedule is highly unorthodox. He arises early, breakfasts lightly, and works strenuously for several hours. He then takes a nap and works through until two or two-thirty, when he breaks for lunch, often a working lunch with staff or Cabinet members. Another nap follows, and then a long work session followed by a late supper. Lady Bird usually waits to eat with him, no matter how late it may be. It is often ten or eleven o'clock.

Christmas 1963 required all Mrs. Johnson's resourcefulness to cope with her husband's irregular habits and spontaneous decisions. Just as the elaborate dinner was to be served at the Johnson ranch in Johnson City, Texas, the President decided to give the reporters who had accompanied him to his home a detailed tour of the premises.

As the turkey, all steaming from the oven and decked out on its platter on the table, became cooler and cooler, Mrs. Johnson and the staff became warmer and warmer. The tour lasted almost an hour, during which time everything on the table had to be returned to the kitchen and reheated. A day in the life of the President, a spur-of-the-moment hospitable President!

Hospitality is a basic in the Johnson vocabulary. And it functions at its best in the casual, congenial surroundings of the President's home terrain. When West German Chancellor Erhard paid his official visit to Washington, he was whisked to Johnson City for two days of Texas-type welcome. A Fort Worth caterer, Walter Jitton, prepared—as he has often done in the past—a beef barbeque for LBJ and his honored guest. So popular is the Jitton barbeque style with the Johnsons that he even staged a "cue" in Washington for a gala for Lynda Bird during LBJ's Vice-Presidency. The Jitton barbeque, as the Johnsons prefer it, combines beef briskets and ribs with either a tomato puréed sauce or a vinegary dip. As accompaniment, coleslaw and potato salad are served, with apple turnovers for dessert. It is simple, hearty fare, served in hearty country fashion.

As the Johnson personal style of entertaining differs from that of his New England predecessor, so does the official style. Certain Kennedy innovations remain: the shortened menu, consisting of four courses—fish or soup, entrée, salad and cheeses, and dessert. And at state dinners the deadly long, formal horseshoe table which the Kennedys abolished is still out. Traditionally, the President sat flanked by Cabinet members and their wives at dinner after dinner after dinner. (Such considerations as the affability and geniality of a man's wife could well have affected one's choice of Secretary of State. After all, she would be one's constant dinner companion for four or eight long years.) The Kennedy system of seating guests was to substitute small round tables for ten for that tedious horseshoe. Thus, as Elizabeth Carpenter, Mrs. Johnson's Press Secretary, says, "the lions could be scattered around," and the Cabinet officers interspersed amongst them, to help the President by acting as assistant hosts. American wines are now served routinely at all state functions.

Like the Kennedys, the Johnsons remain after the dinner and entertainment to mingle with the guests, making them feel comfortable. That they succeed is evidenced by White House bread-and-butter mail. Thank-you notes stress the guests' feeling that "the White House seemed like a real home." It hasn't always.

Our own observations, during the gala for Italian Prime Minister Aldo Moro, were that Mrs. Johnson is particularly adept at making her guests feel relaxed. A naturally warm, spontaneously friendly person, she exudes pleasure and a sense of enthusiasm. Shortly before midnight the crowd thinned somewhat and the President and his wife quietly and unobtrusively disappeared, leaving those with stamina to spare to continue dancing in the foyer (a Johnson innovation) to the music of the Marine Band.

At state dinners, René Verdon (of New Frontier fame) continued for a while to cater for the Great Society. He was fond of naming dishes in honor of the distinguished foreign visitor of the evening. As a result, fancy-sounding Coppelia U Thant, served in honor of the Secretary General of the United Nations, turned out to be a regular coffee *bombe*. Pompano Moro, which must have impressed the Prime Minister as a concoction created just for him, was in fact a standard fish dish in the Verdon repertoire.

Verdon's departure from the Johnson staff caused a mild *brouhaha* in the press. Diplomatically, he insisted the reasons were personal, but, temperamentally, he couldn't resist hinting that a French chef found it demeaning to become a specialist in barbeque, fried chicken, and spoon bread. Nettled at being asked to prepare cold puree of chick peas, calling them "already bad hot," he bridled at fixing "curiosities" from standard American cookbooks.

"I am going to ask my pastry chef, who has been making Yule logs for 40 years, to look in a cookbook?" Verdon was incredulous. Unmentioned, but obviously of some importance, was René's displeasure at being subordinate to a woman nutritionist. Some months earlier, Lady Bird had hired Mrs. Mary Kaltman, former director of foods at the Driskill Hotel in Austin, Texas, to coordinate all White House menus.

All Johnsons maintained a dignified silence at Verdon's departure, but they managed to have the last word even so. LBJ's press secretary, William Moyers, commented tartly—and publicly—"His [Verdon's] reputation as a chef far exceeds the pleasures he delivers to the table." Moyers, as a fellow Texan, may be forgiven a few culinary prejudices of his own.

Although no less distinguished than René Verdon in his profession, the chef whom the Johnsons chose as his replacement, Henry Haller, was an impressive contrast in many ways. He is probably the handsomest chef who ever officiated at the White House and probably the least temperamental. Brisk, businesslike but at the same time warm, friendly and exceptionally articulate, generous with recipes and "secrets."

Mrs. Johnson has introduced a new element to official entertaining. When the guests arrive at 8 P.M. for an official dinner, they are received by the President and his wife in the East Room. If the guest is a foreign Head of State, this is the moment when the exchange of gifts takes place. The Johnsons present their gift to their distinguished visitors—and Mrs. Johnson's innovation is immediately evident. Instead of formal, rather impersonal presents, such as the Steuben glass given so often in the past, Mrs. Johnson has gone to considerable effort to choose a memento with some personal meaning to the visitor.

For example, President de Valera of Ireland was given a framed etching of his New York birth certificate and christening certificate. The Prime Minister of Israel was presented a silver spoon, made by a Jewish silversmith who had been a contemporary of Paul Revere. Prime Minister Saito of Japan received an antique post-office box, to commemorate the many years of his career spent in the postal service.

Such examples of thoughtfulness are typical of Mrs. Johnson's approach to her role as First Lady. It is said that the Johnson receiving lines are much slower than most—because the interested Mrs. J. spends more time actually chatting with her guests than did many of her predecessors.

This Presidential family seems to adapt a different style to each different location. The official entertaining in the White House calls forth a quieter, more formal President. Upstairs, in the family quarters of the Executive Mansion, where Zephyr Wright rules the culinary roost, and where working dinners are more the rule than the exception, the President is more animated, more himself.

But it is when he gets back to his Texas roots that the real Southwesterner emerges, and the President shows signs of being totally relaxed. One spring, on a typical walk with reporters around the White House grounds, he confessed that the White House was not a home, and that he would like to arrange his schedule to spend more—possible up to 25 per cent—of his working time in Texas, where he would feel freer to work, think, and plan.

Like many another President who felt hemmed in by the Executive Mansion, President Johnson said: "It's not the kind of place you would pick to live in; it's a place you go to after work." Even so, the President has shown a strong sense of appreciation of the history-laden house in which he currently lives. The piques of the moment will undoubtedly pass. Certainly Lyndon Johnson, in a very short time, put his own special brand on the historic "place" on Pennsylvania Avenue.

◊◊

RECIPES

POMPANO MORO

There was no unanimity on the quality of the dinner for Italian Prime Minister Moro. First-time visitors to the White House tend, at state dinners, to find the whole experience so awe-inspiring that they hardly notice the food. Repeaters are less easily overwhelmed and often more critical of details. In this instance, comments by guests ranged from "superb" to "poor." Reconstructing the sauce for the fish, we feel this course at least was a delight. We think you will find this basic sauce useful in serving many types of fish.

Pompano (or sole, flounder, perch)   Red or green pepper
Water   Butter
White vermouth   Tomatoes (fresh)
Peppercorns   Pepper
Carrot   Saffron
Onion   Cream
Salt

Cut 3 pounds filet of pompano into small serving pieces. In a shallow, flame-proof baking dish heat on top of the stove: 1 cup water, 1 cup white vermouth, 6 peppercorns, 1 raw carrot sliced thin, 3 thin slices of onion, and 1 teaspoon salt. Boil 5 minutes. Remove from heat and arrange fish in the pan. If there is not enough liquid to cover the fish completely, add a little more hot water. Cover the pan and bake in a moderately hot (375° F.) oven about 15 minutes, or until the fish flakes easily when a fork touches it. While the fish is baking, prepare the sauce: Sauté 1 tablespoon finely chopped onion and 1 tablespoon finely chopped red or green pepper (red gives a nice color) in 3 tablespoons butter until onion is soft and yellow. Add 1½ cups peeled, seeded, and diced tomatoes, ½ teaspoon salt, ¼ teaspoon pepper, and ½ teaspoon saffron soaked for 2 or 3 minutes in 2 tablespoons boiling hot water. Cook gently about 8 minutes. Then stir in ½ cup cream. Heat but do not boil. At serving time, drain the fish and serve the sauce as a border. *Serves 6 as a first course.*

BARBEQUE SPARERIBS À *LA* LADY BIRD

Mrs. Johnson once said, "There is no nice way to eat ribs." This doesn't stop her, however, from indulging in one of her favorite dishes. Judging from a wirephoto of her nibbling a rib, she manages to handle this messy dish as gracefully as anyone can.

Spareribs   Brown sugar
Salt and pepper   Butter
Canned tomatoes   Ketchup
Onion   Vinegar
Garlic   Dry mustard
Worcestershire sauce   Cayenne

Cut the spareribs from 4 racks into manageable sections for eating with the fingers. Preheat the oven to 350° F. and place the ribs on a rack in a largish roasting pan. Sprinkle with salt and pepper and bake for approximately 30 minutes, turning from time to time. Then brush the barbeque sauce over the ribs and continue baking at 400° F. Turn often and brush with lots of sauce. Bake about ½ hour longer.

To make the sauce: Cook 1 large can tomatoes, well broken up, with 1 large chopped onion, 2 small cloves chopped garlic, ½ cup Worcestershire sauce, 1½ tablespoons brown sugar, and 1 tablespoon butter. Bring to a boil, then add ½ cup ketchup, ½ cup vinegar, ¼ teaspoon mustard, a pinch of cayenne, ¼ teaspoon pepper, and 1 teaspoon salt. Mix well, lower heat, and simmer gently for at least ½ hour. Baste the ribs with this, providing a nice glaze in the cooking. *Serves 6 to 8.*

TEXAS FRIED CHICKEN

Between the 1964 election and the January inauguration of 1965, the Johnsons were overwhelmed with company, official and unofficial, as well as meetings and official involvements. Twenty-two lunch and dinner guests were almost a daily occurrence. Lady Bird in all that time had, as she put it, only "one golden day" of leisure and escape. The family was in Texas at the time. She used it lazily, as she deserved to, by taking daughter Lynda Bird for a drive to the Lost Maples, a lone grove of maple trees, rare in that part of the country. They took a box lunch and wandered happily alone. Spies have not been able to find out the contents of that celebrated lunch, but knowing the family fondness for fried chicken, hot or cold (we recommend it either way), it might well have been that Southern specialty.

Chicken	*Bread or cracker crumbs, ground*
Salt and pepper	*fine*
Flour	*Butter or lard*
Egg	*Chicken stock*
Milk	

Clean well and cut into manageable pieces a 3-pound roasting chicken. Mix salt and pepper with a little flour and sprinkle the mixture over the chicken pieces. Dip the chicken into a mixture of 1 egg and ¼ cup milk beaten together. Then dip the chicken into finely ground cracker crumbs or breadcrumbs and place in a skillet in which ¼ cup lard (or butter or bacon fat) has heated to a high degree. Brown all the pieces of chicken. Add ¼ cup boiling chicken stock or water. Cover the pan and place it in a low (300° F.) oven and cook until tender, about ½ hour. If you prefer a thicker sauce, add a little flour to thicken the drippings. Season to taste. Serve hot or cold. *Serves 4.*

LBJ'S PEDERNALES RIVER CHILI

Considering the border Texas shares with Mexico, it is small wonder that Mexican food has long been a favorite of Texans, who have been brought up on the famous chilis and tamales of their Southern neighbors. President Johnson is especially devoted to a good chili, such as this one.

Ground chuck	*Cumin seed*
Onions	*Canned tomatoes*
Garlic	*Hot water*
Salt	*Chili powder*
Oregano	

Lightly brown 4 pounds coarsely ground beef chuck in a large skillet with 2 small chopped onions and 2 or 3 cloves crushed garlic. As soon as the meat turns color, add 2 teaspoons salt, 1 teaspoon ground oregano, 1 teaspoon cumin seed, 2 1-pound can tomatoes (broken up), and 2 tablespoons chili powder. Pour 2 cups hot water over all and mix all together thoroughly. Simmer over low heat for about 1 hour. Skim fat as it develops. May be served hot at once or stored in the refrigerator and reheated. *Aficionados* think sufficient time should be allowed for flavor blending, and therefore the cooked chili should "settle" several days before reheating and serving. *Makes 2½ to 3 quarts.*

RANCH TURKEY AND LADY BIRD'S CORNBREAD DRESSING

Once you have tasted this delicious stuffing, you will, we hope, agree with us that it makes the usual long Christmas or Thanksgiving dinner wait well worth it. The Johnsons traditionally serve whipped sweet potatoes, cranberry salad, giblet gravy, and hot rolls as well.

Turkey	*Celery*
Cornbread	*Onions*
Bread	*Butter*
Turkey stock	*Sage*
Eggs	*Salt and pepper*

Clean and prepare your turkey as you normally would. Then stuff it with the following dressing, lace up, butter the outside, and place on a roasting pan. Cover with aluminum foil and roast in a medium-hot (400° F.) oven for 20 minutes. Then reduce the heat to 350° F. and continue baking until tender. Remove foil ½ hour before serving to allow top to brown.

To make dressing: Bake 1 medium-sized pan cornbread. Crumble it up in a large bowl and mix with 4 slices toasted bread, also crumbled. Pour turkey stock over the bread, using enough to keep bread moist and not stiff and dry. Add 6 well-beaten eggs, 1 stalk of chopped celery, 3 large onions chopped, ¼ cup melted butter, a dash of sage, and salt and pepper to taste. Mix all together. Stuff turkey, putting extra dressing into a square baking pan. Bake along with turkey. *Serves 8.*

LADY BIRD'S LIMA BEAN SPÉCIALITÉ

During World War II, the wife of then Congressman Lyndon Johnson kept a vegetable garden in the backyard of their Washington home. In it she grew tomatoes, English peas, black-eyed peas, and other vegetables she loved. We can't vouch for the fact that she grew lima beans there, but we do know for certain that this lima bean dish is a family favorite, frequently served, and the object of much praise by guests. It is a delicious and somewhat fancy addition to a steak dinner.

Baby lima beans	*Milk*
Butter	*Grated cheese*
Mushrooms	*Salt and pepper*
Flour	*Chili powder*

Cook 2 packages frozen baby lima beans in salted water (or use fresh limas if you prefer, allowing enough time to cook them tender). Drain and set aside. Melt 3 tablespoons butter in a saucepan and add ½ pound fresh or 1 4-ounce can drained sliced mushrooms. Cook approximately 5 minutes, then sprinkle mushrooms with 4 tablespoons flour. Slowly add 2 cups milk and stir and cook until the sauce thickens and is smooth. Remove from heat and stir in ¼ cup grated cheese (sharp cheddar is especially good). Add ½ teaspoon salt, ¼ teaspoon pepper, and ½ teaspoon chili powder. Mix well. Add the cooked, drained limas gently, to keep them from mushing. Reheat and serve piping hot. *Serves 6.*

LADY BIRD'S SPINACH SOUFFLÉ

The White House has announced that this recipe is a favorite of the First Lady. We can understand why spinach was served at the Presidential inaugural dinner.

Butter	*Eggs*
Flour	*Spinach*
Milk	*Grated cheese*
Salt and pepper	*Onions*

Make a thick white sauce of 2 tablespoons each of butter and flour, slowly blended with 1 cup milk (rich milk or light cream preferred). Add ½ teaspoon salt and ⅛ teaspoon pepper. Mix well. Slowly stir into the sauce 3 egg yolks beaten until thick and lemony. Add 1 cup chopped cooked spinach and ½ cup grated cheese. Sauté ¼ cup chopped onions in just a little butter and add to the mixture.

Beat 3 egg whites until stiff and fold carefully into the spinach mixture. Turn into a greased casserole. Place the casserole in a pan of hot water and bake in a preheated (350° F.) oven 45 to 50 minutes. Serve immediately when done. This makes a superb accompaniment for a simple main dish, such as steak or roast. *Serves 4 to 6.*

ASPARAGUS BARI

This delicious treatment of asparagus was named in honor of Italian Prime Minister Aldo Moro's home town in Puglia, a region of Italy on the Adriatic. It was served at the President's state dinner for the Prime Minister.

Asparagus   *Cream*
Hollandaise

Lightly cook fresh spring asparagus and serve with the following sauce: Combine equal parts Hollandaise sauce and heavy cream whipped until stiff. Heat in the top of a double boiler over hot water. Do not allow sauce to come near boiling point.

WESTERN SALAD

The Presidential family is fond of salads, but usually "when eating on their own time," without guests, they prefer their salad served with a low-calorie dressing. Even during LBJ's late Senate days, when he lunched in the Senate Dining Room, one of his staff would bring in his special low-cal dressing. At official affairs, however, calorie worries evaporate, and an elaborate salad somewhat similar to a Caesar salad, is served.

Salad oil	*Salt and pepper*
Garlic clove	*Grated Parmesan cheese*
Bread cubes	*Blue cheese*
Salad greens	*Lemon juice*
Worcestershire sauce	*Egg yolks*

Prepare and set aside, mixed, ¼ cup salad oil and ½ garlic clove. Toast enough bread to make 2 cups cubed. Fill a large salad bowl with 6 to 8 cups washed and dried salad greens, fresh and crisp. Add 1½ teaspoon Worcestershire sauce, 4 tablespoons salad oil, 1½ teaspoons salt, ½ teaspoon freshly ground pepper, and 3 tablespoons grated Parmesan cheese. Mix well. Crumble 3 tablespoons blue cheese over the greens, add ¼ cup lemon juice, and coat leaves with 2 raw egg yolks. Mix lightly but well. Toss until all leaves are covered and mixed. Then dip the croutons in the garlic oil and add them to the salad. Toss again and serve *immediately. Serves 6 to 8.*

ZEPHYR'S OLD-FASHIONED FRUIT ICE CREAM

In 1955 the Women's National Press Club published a most helpful and interesting book titled *Who Says We Can't Cook!*. Recipes from many of Washington's notables are included. Prominent among them is this favorite recipe of Senator Lyndon B. Johnson, along with the following note about the Senator's cook: "Zephyr, the Texas cook of Senator and Mrs. Lyndon Johnson, is one of their proudest assets. Not only can she whip up dinner for a dozen on an hour's notice, but she can serve it complete with 'cornbread for the Speaker' [Speaker Sam Rayburn of the House of Representatives was a fellow Texan and long-time friend of the LBJs]. . . . Zephyr is showered with compliments at every turn. The Senator puts his best political foot forward to keep her happy. All guests join in the campaign. Speaker Rayburn pays his respects in the kitchen after each meal. . . ."

Sugar	*Milk*
Eggs	*Vanilla*
Cream	*Fruit*

Beat together 1 cup sugar and 3 eggs. Add 1 quart cream and 1 pint milk. Cook over a low fire until mixture boils. Let it cool. Then add 1 tablespoon vanilla and ½ gallon favorite fruit (peaches, strawberries, or whatever you choose) that has been mashed with enough sugar to sweeten. Chill for a while, then freeze in an electric or hand-turned freezer. *Serves 20.*

ZEPHYR'S VANILLA ICE CREAM

Eggs	*Cream*
Sugar	*Vanilla*
Milk	

Beat 5 eggs with 1½ to 2 cups sugar. Add 1 quart each of milk and cream. Add 2 tablespoons vanilla. Chill and freeze as above.

LBJ'S DOUBLE DIVINITY FUDGE

When a President has a sweet tooth, there is one fine way to appease it—with this special sweet much favored by our thirty-sixth President.

Sugar	*Vanilla*
Water	*Salt*
Light corn syrup	*Egg whites*

Combine ½ cup sugar with ⅓ cup water and cook in a saucepan at 240° F. or until a tiny bit of syrup forms a soft ball when dropped in cold water. Then, in a separate pan, cook 1½ cups sugar, ⅓ cup water and corn syrup at 254° F. until it forms a hard ball in cold water. Cool the first syrup a little. Then slowly add it to two egg whites, ¼ teaspoon salt beating constantly 1 or 2 minutes, or until the syrup mixture loses its glazed look. Add the other syrup the same way. Then add 1 teaspoon vanilla and pour the mixture into a well-greased pan. When cold, cut into squares. The candy is supposed to be softer and creamier than regular divinity. *Makes 35 to 40 pieces.*

THE AMBASSADOR'S SURPRISE OR ADLAI STEVENSON'S BIRTHDAY CAKE

On February 5, 1965, the then United Nations Ambassador, Adlai Stevenson, arrived at the White House for a consultation with the President. At the end of the conference, Mrs. Johnson appeared in the room—laden with a "Happy Birthday Adlai" surprise birthday cake, decked out in pink lettering with only one candle to commemorate the Ambassador's 65 years. It was a sponge cake filled with a candied-fruit-spangled white icing. News services across the country ran a photograph of Mrs. Johnson happily licking the frosting from her fingers. The cake was baked by René Verdon and the White House second chef, Ferdinand Louvad. We offer our own version of the Ambassador's Surprise.

Egg yolks	*Baking powder*
Hot water	*Salt*
Sugar	*Heavy cream, whipped*
Almond extract	*Candied fruit, diced*
Cake flour	

Preheat oven to 325° F. Beat 10 egg yolks in large bowl, gradually adding ½ cup hot water; beat until almost double in volume. Continue beating gradually add 1 cup sugar. Add 1 teaspoon almond extract. Sift together 1⅔ cups cake flour, ½ teaspoon baking powder, ½ teaspoon salt. Fold in the sifted ingredients, one-fourth at a time, with a rubber spatula or wire whisk. Line bottoms of two deep 9-inch cake pans with waxed paper. (Or use a 10-inch tube pan.) Pour batter into pans; bake 30 to 40 minutes or until golden brown. Invert pans to cool.

To frost: Whip 1 pint heavy cream until stiff. Combine 1 cup whipped cream with ½ cup diced candied fruit. Spread between layers. Cover top, sides with remaining whipped cream. Sprinkle remaining candied fruit on top. Refrigerate until ready to serve. *Serves 10.*

PICCATA DE VEAU LUGANESE

Although Chef Haller favors classic French cuisine, this delicious veal dish is from his native Switzerland.

Eggs	*Corn oil*
Milk	*Butter*
Parmesan cheese, grated	*Shallots*
Parsley	*Garlic, finely chopped*
Flour	*Tomatoes*
Salt	
White pepper	
Veal	

Beat together 3 eggs, ¼ cup milk, 3 tablespoons grated Parmesan cheese, and 1 tablespoon chopped parsley. Combine ¾ cup flour with 1 teaspoon salt and ½ teaspoon white pepper in a separate bowl. Dip 12 thin slices raw veal (preferably boneless loin), one at a time, into the flour mixture and then into the egg batter. Fry in ½ cup corn oil and ¼ cup butter or margarine until golden brown on both sides. Remove from pan and keep warm. Sauté 1 tablespoon finely chopped shallots and 1 clove garlic, finely chopped, in the same oil and butter until golden. Add 6 medium tomatoes, peeled, seeded, and coarsely chopped. (Be sure not to add any of the liquid that might have come out from the tomatoes while you chopped them.) Cook for 3 to 4 minutes.

Place veal slices on a bed of saffron rice (see below). Garnish with tomato mixture. *Serves 6.*

P. S. from P. C.: You may use 1 (1 pound, 13 ounces) can of peeled Italian tomatoes, but be sure to drain well and pat dry on paper towels.

SAFFRON RICE, TEXAS STYLE

Few people realize that Texas is one of the great rice-raising lands of the world representing the ultimate in the cultivation of this most ancient grain. Using American techniques it takes 4 man-hours to plant and harvest an acre of rice as compared to 400 man-hours in the Orient. Not only Texas rice but also our recipes are being shipped to the far corners of the world.

Onion	*Chicken bouillon cube*
Garlic	*Salt*
Butter	*Saffron*
Oil	*Bay leaf*
Rice	

In a large skillet, sauté 1 medium onion, chopped, and 1 clove garlic, chopped, in 2 tablespoons butter or margarine and 2 tablespoons oil, till golden brown. Add 1½ cups long grain rice and mix. Remove from heat. In a separate pan, bring to a boil 3¾ cups water, 1 chicken bouillon cube, 1 teaspoon salt, ⅛ teaspoon powdered saffron and 1 bay leaf. Add rice mixture, stirring well. Bring to a boil again. Reduce heat, cover tightly and simmer for 20 minutes or until all the liquid is absorbed. Keep covered until ready to serve. *Serves 6.*

POTAGE ST. JACQUES

This soup is said to have been "invented" for the Johnsons during the regime of Chef Haller who likes it so well that he serves it to his own family on his rare days off.

This delicate, creamy scallop soup derives its name from the legend that all shellfish are sacred to Saint James. It may be served hot or cold. If served hot, warm up soup before adding cream, but do *not* boil.

Bay Scallops	*Thyme*
Chablis wine	*Olive oil*
Onion	*Flour*
Celery	*Heavy cream*
Peppercorns	*Monosodium glutamate*
Salt	*Parsley*

In a large saucepan, combine 1½ pounds bay scallops, 2 cups Chablis wine, 1 medium onion, chopped (about ½ cup), ½ cup chopped celery, 2 teaspoons whole peppercorns, and ½ teaspoon each salt and powdered thyme. Bring to a boil, reduce heat and simmer 10 minutes. In a separate saucepan, combine 2 tablespoons each olive oil and flour with a wire whip. Strain the scallop broth. Add to oil mixture. Stir well. Bring to a boil, then simmer for 10 minutes, stirring frequently. Dice strained scallops very finely. If the tiny, sweet bay scallops are not available (they are scarce and seasonal), use sea scallops cut into quarters. Take broth off the heat. Add diced scallops. Allow to cool and chill thoroughly. Add 2 cups heavy cream and ½ teaspoon monosodium glutamate, to taste.

Garnish with 2 tablespoons chopped parsley. *Serves 6.*

PRESIDENTIAL ZUCCHINI

Any firm squash or even young cucumbers may be prepared in this fashion.

Zucchini	*Salt*
Onion	*Pepper*
Butter	

Cut 2 pounds zucchini into ¼-inch slices lengthwise and then cut slices into 1-inch pieces. Place zucchini in a large saucepan with ½ cup finely chopped onion, 2 tablespoons butter or margarine, 1½ teaspoons salt and ½ teaspoon pepper. Stir to mix well. Cover pan and cook over medium heat, stirring occasionally with a fork, 8 to 10 minutes or until zucchini is just tender. *Serves 6.*

CHEF HALLER'S LEMON SOUFFLÉ

This recipe represents a drastic departure from tradition for it is baked not in the classic soufflé dish but a shallow oval casserole. Why? Because it has more crust and everybody loves the crust.

(Practical note: More people have shallow casseroles, too.)

Butter	*Salt*
Flour	*Eggs*
Milk	*Grated lemon rind*
Sugar	

Grease and place a 3-inch foil collar around a 2-quart oval soufflé dish. Sprinkle dish lightly with sugar and set aside.

In a large saucepan, melt ⅓ cup butter or margarine. Add ½ cup flour and stir to form a smooth paste. Gradually stir in 1½ cups scalded milk, cook 2 to 3 minutes or until mixture is thickened and smooth. Add ⅓ cup sugar and ¼ teaspoon salt and mix again. Remove from heat and stir in 8 egg yolks, adding one at a time, mixing well after each addition. Stir in 2 tablespoons grated lemon rind. Beat 8 egg whites until foamy. Stir in 2 tablespoons sugar and continue beating until stiff, but not dry. Gently fold egg white into flour-egg batter. Spoon mixture into prepared soufflé dish. Bake in a preheated (375° F.) oven 45 minutes or until golden brown and puffy. Serve immediately with sauce Anglaise au Kirsch otherwise known as Elegant Soft Custard. *Serves 6.*

ELEGANT SOFT CUSTARD

The classic name is Sauce Anglaise au Kirsch. It is one of Chef Haller's private joys. If kirsch is not available, a light rum or even a brandy may be used.

Egg yolks   *Kirsch*
Sugar   *Vanilla extract*
Milk

In top of double boiler, combine 5 egg yolks and ⅓ cup sugar. Stir in 2 cups scalded milk. Mix well with wire whip. Place over hot water in bottom of double boiler and cook, stirring, 15 minutes or until sauce thickens enough to coat spoon. Add 2 tablespoons kirsch and 1 teaspoon vanilla extract and stir again. Serve with Lemon Soufflé (see preceding recipe). *Makes 3 cups.*

INDEX